Predictable and Avoidable

This book is dedicated to my beloved wife, Daniela,
to my adorable twin sons, Alessandro and Federico,
and to my parents for their unconditional love, trust, and inspiring values.

Predictable and Avoidable

Repairing Economic Dislocation
and Preventing the Recurrence of Crisis

IVO PEZZUTO

GOWER

Published by
Gower Publishing Limited
Wey Court East
Union Road
Farnham
Surrey
GU9 7PT
England

Gower Publishing Company
110 Cherry Street
Suite 3-1
Burlington
VT 05401-3818
USA

www.gowerpublishing.com

Ivo Pezzuto has asserted his right under the Copyright, Designs and Patents Act, 1988, to be identified as the author of this work.

Gower Applied Business Research
Our programme provides leaders, practitioners, scholars and researchers with thought provoking, cutting edge books that combine conceptual insights, interdisciplinary rigour and practical relevance in key areas of business and management.

British Library Cataloguing in Publication Data
A catalogue record for this book is available from the British Library.

The Library of Congress has cataloged the printed edition as follows:
Pezzuto, Ivo.
  Predictable and avoidable : repairing economic dislocation and preventing the recurrence of crisis / by Ivo Pezzuto.
     pages cm
  Includes bibliographical references and index.
  ISBN 978-1-4094-5445-8 (hardback) -- ISBN 978-1-4094-5446-5 (ebook) -- ISBN 978-1-4094-7358-9 (epub) 1. Financial crises. 2. Finance--Government policy. 3. Financial risk management. 4. Economic policy. 5. Global Financial Crisis, 2008-2009. I. Title.

  HB3722.P49 2013
  339.5--dc23

                                                                        2013018246

ISBN: 978-1-4094-5445-8 (hardback)
ISBN: 978-1-4094-5446-5 (PDF – ebook)
ISBN: 978-1-4094-7358-9 (PDF – epub)

Disclaimer
The opinions expressed in this book are solely those of the author (Ivo Pezzuto) and represent his personal view only. Any information presented, and any opinions given, do not represent in any form the views of any of his academic affiliations. The research work undertaken for this book has been entirely self-funded by the author.

Printed in the United Kingdom by Henry Ling Limited, at the Dorset Press, Dorchester, DT1 1HD

Contents

List of Figures and Tables

Figures

Tables

About the Author

Dr Ivo Pezzuto is a professor of business administration and a management consultant. He holds a BS degree in business administration from NYU Stern School of Business (USA), an MBA degree from SDA Bocconi School of Management (Italy), and a DBA degree from SMC University (Switzerland) on corporate governance. He teaches courses at undergraduate, graduate, and doctoral levels and specializes in corporate education and executive seminars. He is professor of business administration at SMC University in Zurich; Fondazione ISTUD Business School in Baveno; Università Cattolica del Sacro Cuore of Milan; and guest lecturer at MIP School of Management of Politecnico di Milano. Prior to his academic career he was Senior Manager in Accenture, Head of Product Development and Portfolio Management for American Express Europe, and more recently Vice President (Credit Cards Division – Europe) for Diners Club. He has authored many journal articles and contributed to a number of books.

Acknowledgements

I would like thank and acknowledge those organizations and individuals who have been instrumental in the preparation and completion of this work. In particular, the publisher Gower Publishing, and also the participants in the *Global Thought Leaders Survey* who have significantly enriched the quality and depth of this book with their precious ideas, advises, contributions, and insightful perspectives.

Listed below are the 22 distinguished and highly qualified scholars, industry experts, and analysts, who have provided, in the first half of 2012 interviews for this book. At the time of the interviews their professional appointments were the following:

Antonio Argandoña, Professor of Economics and holder of the "la Caixa" Chair of Corporate Social Responsibility and Corporate Governance at IESE Business School in Barcelona.

Alfonso Asaro, Director of Financial Services Analytical Applications Europe at Oracle Corporation and Expert of Enterprise Risk Management Programs, Austria.

Elio Borgonovi, Full Professor of Economics and Management of Public Administration at Bocconi University, Senior Professor of SDA Bocconi (Public Management and Policy Department) and Former Dean of SDA Bocconi from 1997 to 2002.

Antonio Castagna, Financial Modelling Expert at Iason Ltd.

Fabiano Colombini, Full Professor of Economics of Financial Institutions and Markets at the Faculty of Economics of Università di Pisa.

Aswath Damodaran, Kerschner Family Chair in Finance Education at NYU Leonard N. Stern School of Business.

Gregorio De Felice, Head of Research and Chief Economist, Intesa Sanpaolo Bank.

Victor Di Giorgio, Vice President and Technology Country Head Italy at Citi. Western Europe Corporate O&T Cultural Change Ambassador at Citi.

Darrell Duffie, Dean Witter Distinguished Professor of Finance at the Graduate School of Business, Stanford University.

Charles Goodhart, Emeritus Professor at the London School of Economics and Director of the Financial Regulation Research Programme and former member of the Bank of England's Monetary Policy Committee (1997–2000).

Etienne Koehler, Associate Professor of Financial Mathematics at La Sorbonne University of Paris and Expert of Credit Risk Analytics.

Alexander N. Kostyuk, Professor of Corporate Governance and Finance and Director of the International Center for Banking and Corporate Governance, Ukrainian Academy of Banking of the National Bank of Ukraine; Professor of Corporate Governance and Finance at the Hanken School of Economics (Finland); Editor-in-Chief, *Corporate Ownership and Control* journal; Editor-in-Chief, *Corporate Board: Role, Duties and Composition* journal; Editor-in-Chief, *Risk Governance and Control: Financial Markets and Institutions* journal; Editor-in-Chief, *Journal of Governance and Regulation*.

George Koukis, Founder and President and Founder of Temenos Inc.

William W. Lang, Senior Vice President and Lending Officer Supervision, Regulation and Credit at the Federal Reserve Bank of Philadelphia and Fellow of the Wharton Financial Institutions Center.

Fabio Mercurio, Head of Quant Business Managers at Bloomberg LP, New York and Director of the Research Committee of Iason Ltd.

Massimo Meterangelo, Head of Group Wide Portfolio Consolidation at Unicredit Group.

Wolfgang Munchau, President of Eurointelligence ASBL and Associate Editor of the *Financial Times*.

Fabrizio Pezzani, Full Professor of Business Administration, Accounting and Control and Director of the Bachelor Degree in Management of Public Administration and International Institutions (CLAPI) Bocconi University, and Senior Faculty member of the SDA Bocconi Graduate School of Management, Department of Policy Analysis and Public Management.

Richard Posner, Senior Lecturer in Law at University of Chicago Law School and Judge of the US Court of Appeals for the Seventh Circuit.

Gabriele Sabato, Head of Portfolio Management – Retail Credit Risk at Ulster Bank (Royal Bank of Scotland) Ireland, PhD in Banking and Finance, and Credit Risk Management.

Giulio Sapelli, Full Professor of Economic History at the Università degli Studi di Milano, board member of Unicredit Banca-Impresa and President of Audit and Control Committee, scientific advisor of OECD for non-profit sector.

Giacomo Vaciago, Full Professor and Director of the Institute of Economics and Finance at Catholic University of Milan.

I would like also to express in particular my deep gratitude to the following globally recognized and distinguished people and institutions for their precious contributions and research work: Senior Research Economist *Yuliya Demyanyk* of the US *Federal Reserve Bank of Cleveland*; *William W. Lang*, Senior Vice President and Lending Officer Supervision, Regulation and Credit at the *Federal Reserve Bank of Philadelphia* and Fellow of the *Wharton Financial Institutions Center, the Federal Reserve Bank of San Francisco*, and *the Board of Governors of the Federal Reserve System*; *Giovanni Dell'Ariccia*, Advisor in the Research Department of the *International Monetary Fund (IMF)*, the *Basel Committee on Banking Supervision of the Bank for International Settlements, NERA Economic Consulting, John B. Taylor*, Professor of Stanford University, *The Corporate Governance and Leadership Research Center for Leadership Development and Research*, and *the Rock Center for Corporate Governance at Stanford University and the Stanford Graduate School of Business; Otto Van Hemert*, Professor of *New York University* – Department of Finance; *Eric Janszen* of *iTulip Inc.*; *Oxford University Press*; *Arvind K. Jain*, Professor of Concordia University; *Tom Robinson*, Senior Manager Licensing, Rights and Information Services of *AICPA*; *John H. Nugent*, Interim Chair and Associate Professor, School of Management of Texas Woman's University.

List of Abbreviation

ABCP	Asset-backed Commercial Paper
ABS	Asset-backed Securities
ABX	Asset-Backed Securities Index
AIG	American International Group
AIRB	Advanced Internal Rating Based
ALM	Asset and Liability Management
AML	Anti-money Laundering
AMR	Adjustable Mortgage Rate
ARM	Adjustable Rate Mortgage
ASRF	Asymptotic Single Risk Factor
ATM	Automated Teller Machine
ATR	Ability to Repay
AUM	Assets under Management
AVC	Asset Value Correlation
BAPCPA	The Bankruptcy Abuse Prevention and Consumer Protection Act
BBA	British Bankers' Association
BIS	Bank for International Settlements
BSC	Balanced Scorecard
CAPM	Capital Asset Pricing Model
CCP	Central Counterparties
CDO	Collateralized Debt Obligation
CDS	Credit Default Swaps
CEO	Chief Executive Officer
CEPR	Center for Economic and Policy Research
CFaR	Cash Flow at Risk
CFO	Chief Finance Officer
CFPB	Consumer Financial Protection Bureau
CFTC	Commodity Futures Trading Commission
CIPE	Center for International Private Enterprise
CLO	Collateralized Loan Obligation
CLTV	Combined Loan-to-Value
COSO	Committee of Sponsoring Organizations
CPA	Certified Public Accounts
CPI	Consumer Price Index
CPSS	Committee on Payment and Settlements Systems
CRA	Community Reinvestment Act
CRA	Credit Rating Agencies
CRAOB	Credit Rating Agency Oversight Board
CRO	Chief Risk Officer

CSR	Corporate Social Responsibility
CVA	Credit Valuation Adjustment
DCO	Dedicated Clearing Organization
DFAST	Dodd–Frank Act Stress Test
DSGE	Dynamic Stochastic General Equilibrium
DTI	Debt-to-income Ratio
EaR	Earnings at Risk
EBA	European Banking Authority
ECB	European Central Bank
EDP	Excessive Deficit Procedure
EMIR	European Market Infrastructure Regulation
EPS	Earnings Per Share
ERM	Enterprise Risk Management
ESM	European Stability Mechanism
ESO	Executive Stock Options
EU	European Union
EVA	Economic Value Added
FCIC	Financial Crisis Inquiry Commission
FDIC	Federal Deposit Insurance Corporation
FEN	Financial Economics Network
FHA	Federal Housing Administration
FHFA	Federal Housing Finance Agency
FICO	Fair Issac and Company
FIRB	Foundation Internal Rating Based
FOR	Financial Obligation Ratio
FRM	Fixed–rate Mortgage (Loans)
FSA	Financial Services Authority
FSB	Financial Stability Board
FSOC	Financial Stability Oversight Council
GDP	Gross Domestic Product
GMaR	Gross Margin at Risk
GSE	Government-sponsored Enterprises
HFT	High Frequency Trading
HOEPA	Home Ownership and Equity Protection Act
HQLA	High-quality Liquid Assets
HUD	Housing and Urban Development
IAASB	International Auditing and Assurance Standards Board
IASB	International Accounting Standards Board
IC	Internal Controls
ICGN	International Corporate Governance Network
ICT	Information Communication Technology
IFRS	International Financial Reporting Standards
IMF	International Monetary Fund
IOSCO	International Organization of Securities Commissions
IRB	Internal Ratings-based
IRR	Internal Rate of Return
IRSA	Interest Rate Swap Agreement

IWG	Investors Working Group
KPI	Key Performance Indicator
KRI	Key Risk Indicator
LCFI	Large Complex Financial Institutions
LCR	Liquidity Coverage Ratio
LIBOR	London Interbank Offered Rate
LTCM	Long-term Capital Management
LTRO	Long-term Refinancing Operations
LTV	Loan-to-Value
MBO	Management-by-objectives
MBS	Mortgage-backed securities
MES	Marginal Expected Shortfall
MoU	Memorandum of Understanding
MSA	Metropolitan Statistic Area
NINA	No Income/No Assets
NPV	Net Present Value
NRSRO	Nationally Recognized Statistical Rating Organization
NSFR	Net Stable Funding Ratio
OBSE	Off-balance-sheet entities
OECD	Organisation for Economic Cooperation and Development
OIG	Office of Inspector General
OIS	Overnight Indexed Swap
OLA	Orderly Liquidation Authority
OLS	Ordinary Least Squares (regression)
OMT	Outright Monetary Transactions
OTC	Over-the-Counter
OTD	Originate-to-Distribute
OTH	Originate-to-Hold
PCAOB	Public Company Accounting Oversight Board
PCE	Personal Consumption Expenditures
PDCF	Primary Dealer Credit Facility
PPP	Purchasing Power Parity
QM	Qualified Mortgage
QRM	Qualified Residential Mortgages
QSPE	Qualified Special Purpose Entities
RAPM	Risk-adjusted Performance Management
RMBS	Residential Mortgage-backed Securities
RoE	Return on Equity
ROI	Return on Investment
RWA	Risk-weighted Assets
S&P	Standard and Poor's
SAS	Statements on Auditing Standards
SDR	Swaps Data Repositories
SEC	Securities and Exchange Commission
SEF	Swap Execution Facilities
SFO	Serious Fraud Office
SIFI	Systemically Important Financial Institution

SIV	Structured Investment Vehicle
SOX	Sarbanes Oxley Act (Not SOA)
SPE	Special Purpose Entities
SPV	Special Purpose Vehicle
SSM	Single Supervisory Mechanism
SSRN	Social Science Research Network
TAF	Term Auction Facility
TALF	Term Asset-Backed Securities Loan Facility
TARP	Troubled Asset Relief Program
TILA	Truth in Lending Act
UL	Unexpected Loss
US	United States
USPAP	Uniform Standard of Professional Appraisal Practice
WACC	Weighted Average Cost of Capital
WTO	World Trade Organization

CHAPTER 1

Introduction

The dramatic events that generated the US subprime meltdown in 2008, and the following liquidity conflagration, as well as the systemic financial and economic crises which have reverberated throughout the global markets, have led to Wall Street's biggest crisis since the Great Depression. In the last quarter of 2008, the US banking system and those of other major economies were on the brink of collapse and systemic failure.

Central banks and governments in the US and in other countries have, since 2008, orchestrated strong actions and an unprecedented set of policies aimed at restoring some degree of trust, stability, and liquidity in the financial markets through an unusual level of liquidity injection, aggressive monetary policies, massive bail-outs, banks' and de facto corporate nationalizations, rescue plans, and other governmental interventions and fiscal policies. The point of these initiatives, of course, was to avoid the potential implosion of the overall banking and financial markets and the likely consequent long-term global economic recession and probable depression. Some prominent authors, such as Nobel Laureate in Economics, Paul Krugman, argues that the crisis we are currently experiencing is not just a prolonged and deep recession but rather a true depression. In fact, he states that what we are experiencing these days is essentially the same kind of situation that John Maynard Keynes described in the 1930s: "A chronic condition of subnormal activity for a considerable period without any marked tendency either towards recovery or towards complete collapse" (Krugman, 2012, p. x).

Instead, according to Luigi Zingales, the US has finally recovered from the 2008 financial crisis, reaching the pre-crisis gross domestic product (GDP) growth rate. This slow economic recovery trend, according to Zingales, is quite typical of severe financial crises. Thus, according to him, the current major threat to the US economy growth is represented by two other major crises. One is the Eurozone crisis and the other is the difficult-to-sustain welfare system in most Western economies. The welfare crisis might be solved in the years to come but it will require radical structural reforms (that is, to the welfare system), greater labor market mobility in Europe, and some painful social costs for the citizens as a result of the loss of entitlements and adjustments in entry salaries. In Europe, the Eurozone crisis may be resolved in the years to come, according to Zingales, but it will require the strengthening of solidarity mechanisms on a pan-European scale (Zingales, 2012).

Regardless of the fact that one might have a preference for Krugman, Zingales, or other scholars' perspectives of the current economic situation and scenario analysis, one thing is quite clear to many observers. Both in the US and in Europe, five years since the start of the financial crisis, only limited effective reforms to prevent new future crises and to fix the distortions that led to the 2007–2009 financial crisis have been introduced.

If political and economic leaders had opted for a no bail-out policy in 2008, the potentially devastating impact of a crisis of this magnitude would have been unimaginable, particularly given our current highly complex and interconnected global economy. Certainly, the bail-outs, rescue plans, and the unprecedented fiscal and monetary policies undertaken since the beginning of the crisis have placed a significant burden on current and future generations in terms of high social costs for taxpayers, higher unemployment rates, higher bankruptcy rates, higher levels of volatility in the markets, and higher governments' sovereign debt levels and solvency risks.

According to Rutgers Professor Cliff Zukin and Michael Greenstone, who was Chief Economist at the White House Council of Economic Advisers in 2009 and 2010, a shift to a downwardly mobile society may be lasting. This terrible recession is threatening to unravel the American dream for Generation Y professionals, making it very difficult, if not impossible, for them to do better than their previous generation (Blair-Smith, 2012).

Today there is a general consensus among political leaders, industry experts, academic scholars, investors, and ordinary people that the governments' and central banks' massive, unprecedented, non-conventional interventions to rescue the global banks were indeed quite prudent and timely decisions. At the peak of the crisis in 2008, under the pressure of a potentially systemic risk implosion, there was probably little more that policy makers could have done to immediately and effectively mitigate that emergency situation. The potential domino effect of the default of a number of so-called too-big-to-fail global banks forced governments and central banks to use any possible means to restore a degree of trust, stability, and liquidity in the financial markets. Some may argue, however, that the timing, cost, allocation, and impact of the policy decisions and interventions that were taken might not have been optimal. Nevertheless, in those troubled days the pressure was so great, the markets were panicking, and the fear of replicating the tragedy of 1929 was overwhelming, thus there was a need for an immediate intervention to shore up banks and other financial institutions from the subprime meltdown, and the perceived liquidity and solvency crisis. There is no doubt, however, that given the dramatic and extremely risky situation, policy makers have demonstrated a good degree of flexibility, pragmatism, and unconventional wisdom, in addressing the most immediate and difficult phase of the crisis. Some argue, supported by sound evidences, however, that since the Bear Stearns crisis, a high level of uncertainty surrounding the US Government's rescue plans for financial institutions have significantly increased risk spreads thus worsening the dramatic situation (Taylor, 2009, pp. 25–26).

Regarding the bank reforms in the US, EU, and in other markets, the timeliness and effectiveness of the new proposed reforms might be a bit more questionable since, once the crisis had passed its worst stage, the coordinated emergency approach reached by the political and economic leaders of the G8/G20 countries in the peak critical days of the crisis turned into a new one with a stronger focus on the national and local economic and political interests. I recall that in that new phase (2009) I reported in an interview to the Brazilian news agency, *Agência Estado*, the following statement: "Banking and Finance these days are global whereas politics is still mainly local" (Pezzuto, 2009a).

Starting from the most dramatic days of the financial crisis in the last quarter of 2008, a massive number of books, articles, and publications have been written on this topic, offering to the general reader and to researchers a rich, detailed, and highly specialized and diversified perspective on the topic. I have also contributed to shed light on what I believe are the real causes and possible consequences of the financial crisis since October 2008, through the publication of a number of papers, articles, and a book chapter by the title "Miraculous Financial Engineering or Legacy Assets" (Pezzuto, 2010a, pp. 119–123), published in Robert W. Kolb's 2010 book titled *Lessons from the Financial Crisis: Causes, Consequences, and Our Economic Future*. Robert W. Kolb is Professor of Finance and

Frank W. Considine Chair of Applied Ethics School of Business Loyola University Chicago. In my first paper on the topic dated October 7, 2008 I reported analyses and claims that were, by and large, confirmed three years later by the Final Report of the US Financial Crisis Inquiry Commission (FCIC) issued in January 2011. In that paper I also raised attention to the potential risk of a sovereign debt crisis in the Eurozone, and in particular in those countries (peripheral economies) with slower GDP growth rates, high level of sovereign debt and/or budget deficits, structural economic problems, and current account imbalances. The underlying assumption being that these weaker economies (as a result of slow or negative GDP growth and high debt) would certainly have a harder time coping with banks' bail-outs, local economic shocks, and prolonged interventions of automatic stabilizers than other more solid nations, following the global economic slowdown in the international trade and consumptions, the credit crunch, the progressive deleveraging process of financial firms, and the worsening imbalances (surplus versus deficits countries) among Eurozone nations. These mature economies also lost significant competitive advantages in global trade versus the more dynamic emerging markets, in particular when the globalization phenomenon reached a turning point in the year 2000 with the progressive decline of barriers to the free flow of goods, services, and capital (China entered the World Trade Organization – WTO – in December 2001) (Pezzuto, 2008; Hill, 2012). The lack of a real European labor market with effective mobility, of a European Central Bank (ECB) with a lender of last resort mandate, of symmetric economic shocks, and of a fiscal mechanism of solidarity among the Eurozone economies made it difficult for political and economic leaders to handle the impact of the 2007–2009 financial crisis and its aftermath (Zingales, 2012; Pezzuto, 2012).

In spite of the large amount of existing publications on the topic of the financial crisis, the majority of them seem to focus mainly on the causes of the crisis or on the responsibility (who was to blame) and only indirectly and more recently (mainly since 2009) on whether it was preventable and avoidable. Some have reported, soon after the most acute phase of the crisis in 2008 – 2009, that it was just the result of unpredictable and uncontrollable property prices and mortgage lending bubbles, bad luck, system instability, imbalances, or the so-called "black swans" (tail-risk or extremely low probability events). These assumptions, although partially true, are now largely questioned by the most prominent and influential scholars, regulators, and industry experts such as, Richard Posner, Phil Angelides, Brooksley Born, Robert J. Shiller, Luis Gaircano, Dean Baker, Simon Johnson, Nouriel Roubini, Paul Krugman, Luigi Zingales, Peter Schiff, Raghuram Rajan, Nassim Nicholas Taleb, Anat Admati, Frank Partnoy, Robert W. Kolb, Jeffrey Friedman, Amar Bhidé, Steven Gjerstad and Vernon L. Smith, Joseph E. Stiglitz, John B. Taylor, Perter J. Wallinson, Viral V. Acharya and Matthew Richardson, Juliusz Jablecki and Mateusz Machaj, Lawrence J. White, Yulia Demyanyk, Otto Van Hemert, William W. Lang, Peter J. Wallinson, Daron Acemoglu, David Colander, Michael Goldberg, Armin Haas, Mike Stathis, Katarina Juselius, Alan Kirman, Thomas Lux, and Brigette Sloth. These authors have clearly addressed and thoroughly explained that the global financial crisis was not just a normal business cycle downturn, a normal asset bubble, the result of bad luck, or just an unpredictable black swan (Friedman et al. 2011). It was, instead, as clearly stated also in the final report of the FCIC, "the result of human action and inaction, not of Mother Nature or computer models gone haywire" (FCIC, 2011, p. xvii).

The reader today will find easily available an overabundance of publications on the topic. Some of the most scholarly ones are indeed very insightful and intriguing and their precious contributions have been a hallmark for the preparation of this work. They generally provide the following assumptions as root causes of the financial crisis: the responsibility of bank executives' excessive risk-taking and short-term compensation goals (greed); inadequate or missing regulations in the financial industry; the faulty monetary policy of the Federal Reserve Bank; the governments' inadequate response to the crisis or its intrusion in the banking and financial markets; others also blame bad luck, the so-called black swans, faulty risk models, the rating agencies, or the irresponsible and illiterate mortgage borrowers. Perhaps the true story will never be fully disclosed to the general public, given its complexity, although reading some of the most fascinating, fact-based, and educated available analyses, it is probably possible to get closer to the big picture of what really happened.

This book aims to provide a series of fact-based evidences on the topic from the most prominent scholarly publications that, combined with a comprehensive perspective of the interconnected events related to the crisis and the precious contributions of a restricted number of interviews I have undertaken in 2012 with selected thought leaders and industry experts, will allow the reader to realize that the 2007–2009 financial crisis was predictable and avoidable. Of course, I am not the first author to state this hypothesis (although I first wrote of it in 2008) nor certainly the most distinguished one, but I hope that my little contribution might add some additional value to the study of this topic. The book also intends to explain what I believe are the combined triggering factors that have contributed to create such a devastating event. Finally, it aims to explore some possible enhancement in regulatory, corporate governance, and corporate cultural changes hoping to prevent other similar crises in future.

A few authors report that this crisis could probably have been managed sooner and better; that it could have been significantly mitigated, and perhaps even avoided, if authorities had played a more proactive and effectively coordinated role in reducing financial firms' excessive risk-taking in the shadow banking market and the astonishing expansion of the property and lending bubbles. As is well known today, a number of brilliant scholars and industry experts actually reported early warnings on the topic even before 2007 in their articles, papers, presentations, and interviews, but unfortunately they did not receive adequate attention or support from political leaders, policy makers, and regulators.

According to Gerald Epstein and Jessica Carrick-Hagenbarth's working paper of the UMASS Political Economy Research Institute (2010), titled "Financial Economists, Financial Interests, and Dark Corners of the Meltdown: It's Time to Set Ethical Standards for the Economic Profession," conflicts of interest might have prevented a number of economists from timely and effectively reporting to policy makers and regulators early warning messages on the potential financial meltdown or on new and effective financial reforms to stabilize the global financial markets and economy. They revealed that there are potential conflicts of interest among academic economists who have contracts with the institutions in question in writing about the financial crisis and financial reform for a general audience. Focusing on the Squam Lake Working Group on Financial Regulation (2010) and the Pew Economic Policy Group's Financial Reform Project (2010), they found that a majority of the economists involved had affiliations with private financial institutions, yet few of them disclosed those affiliations even in academic publications, preferring to identify themselves by their university affiliations (Epstein, Carrick-Hagenbarth, 2010, p. 28).

Everybody knows that financial institutions, as well as multinational corporations, have always given very generous grants to universities, business schools, and financed scholarships, fellowships, professorships, research projects, and advisory services. Thus, although their financial support represents an essential contribution for innovation and development in the field of banking and finance, in particular extreme circumstances it may also represent a potential constraint to independent research. The 2007–2009 crisis might have been one of these situations, at least immediately after the crisis occurred. But today there is such an excess of information available from online and offline sources, whistleblowers, prosecutors, and financial service authorities that it is practically impossible to protect undisclosed information for a long time. And in fact, after a while, the true story of what caused the global financial crisis begins to be in the public domain.

Powerful banking lobbies have spent billions of dollars since the beginning of the global financial crisis in an attempt to mitigate, through their activities, stricter financial reforms, regulatory oversight, and reputational damages, or to comply with the new rules and to settle law suits and fraud cases.

Nepotism and cronyism (cartels, lobbies, and sects of all kind), with their asymmetric power, indifference for inequality, and arrogant oligarchy, are the enemies of free-market economy, and ultimately, of a true capitalist democracy.

Since 2008, the financial crisis has quickly spread all kinds of risks on a global scale as a result of the globalization of markets and the high interconnectedness of institutions and stakeholders, but at the same time it also owes to the globalization of information sharing (internet, social networks, online publications, and so on) the identification of its complex root causes, in spite of any potential attempt of the organizations involved in the crisis to limit their disclosure.

In addition to the generous financial contributions of banks and financial institutions to universities and research centers, the financial sector is also a significant contributor to political campaigns, through its powerful and rich lobbying activity; it also has an influence in the placement (that is, primary dealers) and trading of sovereign bonds. Furthermore, financial institutions directly or indirectly control or influence most companies' decisions and strategies, and even households, through lending, funding, and investment advice (that is, consumer, retail, commercial, and corporate banking, investment banking, venture capital, private equity funds, hedge funds, asset management firms, and so on).

Thus, it is possible, as some authors say, that a number of financial economists might have preferred not to report to policy makers and regulators early warning messages on the incumbent financial meltdown simply because (1) they were not interested in the topic (that is, crises are not "cool"); or (2) because their economic ideologies, expectations on asset prices, and risk model assumptions (that is, scenario analyses and stress testing) were inherently faulty and inaccurate. Furthermore, regarding the use of wrong risk models, financial economists most likely have used models for predicting the probability of defaults based on unfit historical data sets which did not correctly reflect the boom-bust scenario of the period 2003–2006. Many of them apparently also did not pay enough attention to the explosive growth of the uncontrolled and poorly capitalized shadow banking system and on the impact of the systemic risk (banking panic) this complex, opaque, and highly leveraged sector could have on the overall financial industry stability. Finally, (3) even assuming that financial economists might not have had direct conflicts of interest with financial institutions, they might have perceived anyway a psychological pressure and threat going against the mainstream ideologies and theories of the leading international academic community (a contrarian view). So this psychological conditioning might have discouraged them from expressing a truly independent and unbiased opinion on the topic. They just did not want to jeopardize their academic reputation, prestige, and career opportunities (that is, to become a black sheep).

In summary, the power and influence of the financial sector as a whole on politics, on the real economy, and on society has always been significant but in the last decades this influence has rapidly escalated to what we now call the "too-big-to-fail" phenomenon. Even some multinational corporations have, in recent years, reached a similar excessive power and dominance in politics, leading in some cases to dramatic corporate governance failures, fraud scandals, and perverse conflicts of interest between the corporate world and politics. This concept has also been confirmed by Luigi Zingales in his book *A Capitalism for the People: Recapturing the Lost Genius of American Prosperity* (Zingales, 2012).

Probably, after the publication of the final report of the FCIC in 2011 (issued by the US Government) and the widespread distribution of related literature on the topic of the financial crisis (online and offline), today there is a general consensus about some of the root causes of the financial crisis, confirming the assumptions stated by few initially (before 2007), that this was not a crisis of economics but rather a crisis of excessive power and influence of some financial industry players over politics, regulators, policy makers, and oversight authorities that has led to moral hazard, conflicts of interests, perverse short-term financial incentives, poorly regulated financial activities, and market distortions.

I tend to believe that this was mainly a crisis of "common-sense" and excessive dominance of the corporate world, and in particular of the banking and financial services industry, over politics, regulators, and oversight authorities, since there were too many warning signs prior to 2007 not to see it coming or, quoting the words of Her Majesty the Queen Elizabeth II at a speech to the London School of Economics in November, 2008, "How come nobody could foresee it?" The answer came from Professor Luis Garicano, to whom the Queen directed her question when she visited the LSE. He replied: "I think the main answer is that people were doing what they were paid to do, and behaved according to their incentives, but in many cases they were being paid to do the wrong things from society's perspective" (Stewart, 2009, July 26).

In my paper written in the most critical phase of the crisis (October 7, 2008), soon after Lehman Brothers filed for Chapter 11 bankruptcy protection (September 15, 2008), I stated that the crisis probably had nothing to do with a failure of economic ideologies (that is, Free-Market Capitalism/Libertarianism or Keynesianism) but that it was instead related to a failure of regulation, oversight, perverse short-term financial incentives and mainly to a misconduct of numerous players in the banking and financial services industry. From my point of view, capitalism and democracy are the *best inventions* of mankind (as long as they go hand in hand together). The events that led to the financial crisis indicate that probably, over the years, one of these two elements had lost some sparkle, and I don't think it was the first one. As Luigi Zingales has explained, "Business has become too politically influential. For a system to be well balanced you must have a good democratic balance to the power of business and that paradoxically is true for business itself." And he added: "What's needed is a rebalancing of the system, shifting the pendulum back from a state that has become unduly pro-business to one that is pro-market" (NUS Think Business Staff, 2012; Brittan, S., 2012).

The 2007–2009 global financial crisis was the result of a natural behavior (in Darwinian terms) of a large number of people driven by either self-interest (astonishing short-term financial incentives triggered also by booming lending and housing markets) or more simply by their bosses' orders. According to Adam Smith's *invisible hand* doctrine, self-interest is actually good, but in this case, unfortunately, it occurred in an environment of generalized lax or bad regulation, poor or no oversight, and lack of accountability at all levels.

There was extreme systemic risk-taking, perverse financial incentives, powerful and influential corporatism, and most of all, strong interference of the financial industry lobby in politics and industry regulations and probably some degree of collusion between the two. Over the decades, these behaviors have built up the conditions and distortions in the economy, triggered also by important changes in the macroeconomic environment, that have led to the global financial crisis (Pezzuto, 2008).

My opinion on this crisis is probably close to the one of Richard Posner in the sense that we both consider capitalism good as long as its animal spirit can be controlled and contained within a proper regulatory framework and with proper oversight in order to maximize all stakeholders' interests and to avoid its implosion. A solid and pure capitalism requires the existence of a healthy and well-balanced democracy. Thus, with this conclusion, my view of capitalism and democracy seems to be quite close also to Luigi Zingales's perspective on the matter. Well, I am probably starting to feel like a Chicago boy. Of course, I am just joking! I am not a world-renowned economist, but just a seasoned professor and consultant of international business and strategic management/business policy with probably good analytical and systemic thinking capabilities. I have been, however, near Chicago (St. Charles) three or four times, many years ago, to participate in very exciting executive development programs. Having been educated in the US (NYU Stern School of Business), I am indeed a full supporter of free-market economy, open competition, and of a well-functioning and meritocratic capitalist system, but as long as there are simple, fair, and effective rules for all in the marketplace (that is, a democracy) and not the business dominance on politics, regulators, and all other institutions (cartels, lobbies, nepotistic practices, corruption, collusions, conflicts of interests, and other forms of closely knit groups to keep outsiders at bay – or as explained by Luigi Zingales, a crony capitalism, in other words a capitalist system in which success depends more on whom you know in the business world or in politics than what you know).

Individualism, as anticipated by Adam Smith back in 1776, can be a real booster of economic growth and development in the interest of all in society. However, individualism and a free market based on effective regulation and oversight is one thing, free-riding and self-interest without rules, just like in the case of unregulated financial capitalism is quite another. As we have learned from this recent global financial crisis, this kind of individualism or, more precisely, industry dominance over other democratic institutions (that is, politics) may lead to perverse, opportunistic, deceiving, and in some cases, even fraudulent behaviors that can bring the global economy to the brink of collapse. What we have experienced with the 2007–2009 financial crisis is what some people call the drift of capitalism. Personally, I am not in favor of the industry dominance (and in particular of the banking industry) over other democratic institutions, just like I am not in favor of excessive and bureaucratic regulation, or of the Governments' dominance over business with perverse interferences in the free market economy that may cause distortions. Most of all, I am certainly not in favor of the combined industry, regulatory, and governments' dominance over main street through, for example, the well-known "sliding doors" practices that allow banking lobbies to directly occupy key leadership positions in politics, associations, and regulatory authorities and vice versa. To be more specific, I am not in favor of an elite clan (clubby system) that engages in crony capitalistic practices to increase its own political and economic power at the expense of others (that is, higher concentration of power and profits in the hands of the "clan" while socializing costs in the downturns).

The corporate world, and in particular global financial capitalism, have to discover and embrace a new philosophy, the one that marketing guru, Philip Kotler calls Marketing 3.0 or values-driven marketing and organizations (Kotler et al., 2010). Thus, individualism in itself is certainly not a *sin* but rather a necessary, positive, and healthy driver of personal development, self-actualization, and a precious contribution to economic growth. A potential threat to free-market economy, fair competition, and true capitalism can be, instead, a generalized culture of short-term oriented reckless pursuit of selfish interests (that is, short-term bonus-oriented culture) not balanced with "sound" values, norms, and regulatory oversight. In this type of culture, characterized by an excess of collective self-interest, nepotism, and cronyism, aggregated groups of individuals are more likely to engage in collusive behaviors that may damage other peoples' interests, and support leaders (both political and economic) that better fulfill their short-term oriented aspirations, regardless of the fact that these ambitions may not be based on merit, may lack basic fundamental values, or may be triggered by fraudulent intentions. Thus, the drift of capitalism comes when a large number of powerful and influential individuals and institutions, driven by strongly interconnected lobbyist interests, short-termism, and contemptuous arrogance (mutually supporting one another as an exclusive circle of power and trust) engage for many years in nepotism and cronyism to preserve the wealth, dominance, and secrecy of their privileged clan.

As reported by Richard A. Posner (2009), not many economists apparently warned regulators and policy makers about the crisis or saw the perverse relationship between executive compensation, risky lending, excessive leverage, and the riskiness of mortgage-backed securities (MBS), or collateralized debt obligations (CDO) and credit default swaps (CDS). They also did not anticipate the affect that a 20 percent or more drop in housing prices would have on bank solvency (Posner, 2009, p. 257).

Furthermore, Richard A. Posner (2009) reported that many finance professors, although quite familiar with the developments of the crisis, probably preferred not to openly criticize the banking and finance industry or to suggest tighter regulation to avoid becoming a black sheep and losing lucrative consulting projects. Thus this conflict of interest might have caused some economists and financial analysts to refrain from providing useful contributions to policy makers, the media, and regulators in order to anticipate the risk of this dramatic meltdown (Posner, 2009, pp. 258–259).

We do not know for sure whether some economists and other scholars had conflicts of interest that discouraged them from providing a completely unbiased opinion on the financial crisis in 2007 or 2008, but certainly, in more recent years, a sizeable literature has flourished with many new interesting analyses and hypotheses on this topic and sometimes with even very weird and unrealistic conspiracy theories.

The "above-the-line" communication on the topic undertaken by the mass media at the beginning of the subprime crisis (2007–2008) has been, by and large, not particularly informative on what really fueled the crisis – the root causes. Rather, they have mainly reported the events themselves and their possible consequences on the financial markets and economy, giving greater attention to the actions and policy decisions undertaken by the political leaders and central banks. As some authors also stated, politically captured newspapers have been reluctant to investigate the topic and to unveil to the public the real causes of the crisis (notable exceptions and examples of excellent journalistic independence are *Bloomberg*, *Financial Times*, *Huffington Post*, and *The New York Times*). In some cases, the mass media have reported generic information to the general public such as, "it is everybody's fault" or "there is enough blame to go around." Many journalists and analysts reported statements such as, "People took loans they shouldn't have borrowed, lenders took advantage of consumers, investment bankers did not do their due diligence, rating agencies did not properly rate debt securities," and so on.

With statements such as these, although partially true, it is easier to come to the conclusion that since it is everybody's fault, no one can be blamed for the complex crisis; thus the property price bubbles and mortgage lending bubbles are identified as the main causes of the crisis, and, as some bankers even said after the subprime meltdown: "Bubbles just happen in the business world every few years. It is a sort of cycle in the industry. It is nobody's fault!" Fortunately, today, thanks also to the brilliant contribution of the FCIC (FCIC, 2011) and others, this thesis is too trivial to be believed.

This book aims to provide an overview of the main lessons learned from a crisis of this magnitude, thanks to the powerful insights and research findings on the topic reported by leading scholars. The book also aims to explain key concepts related to the crisis and its aftermath with an holistic perspective, balancing the use of simple words with more technical terminology, in order to allow general educated readers to get an understanding of the full picture but also allowing researchers, scholars, and professionals to appreciate some of the more technical aspects.

In a previous paragraph I have mentioned that I call this dramatic crisis a crisis of "common-sense." To be more specific I would like to clarify that probably even the mortgage borrowers are not entirely free of responsibility for their irrational (or overoptimistic) behavior. There is no doubt, however, that many of the mortgage borrowers, and especially the subprime borrowers, have been easily influenced by the unexpected and miraculous market conditions of the early 2000s (constantly growing property values and prices coupled with low interest rates on mortgage loans but also high political pressures forcing the Federal Home Loan Bank, Freddie Mac, and Fannie Mae to promote "liar's loans," and a generalized overleveraged situation). In fact, such subprime loans required limited or only formal due diligence to be performed on the data of the loan application (income, assets: known as NINA loans – "no income no assets," and so on). Both lenders and borrowers in those days might have had unrealistic expectations on the sustainability in the long run of this market, or perhaps even a less responsible speculative approach to their decisions for greed or other reasons.

On whatever side one might analyze this crisis, there is no doubt that many early warning signs and support analyses were available from the beginning of the housing and lending bubbles that might have allowed policy makers, regulators, and political leaders to prevent the escalation from the subprime mortgage lending crisis to the perceived systemic solvency threat for the major global financial institutions. Certainly, since 2005 or 2006 many red flags were already available to policy makers and regulators in order to spot the housing market boom bust scenario and its possible aftermath and to allow for immediate emergency actions and the introduction of radical policy reforms in the industry.

As Sir John Templeton was once quoted as saying, "Anytime they tell you this time it is different (in this case no due diligence needed), run away don't walk away, fundamentals always win!"

It is true that a number of probably underqualified and riskier borrowers did have the benefit, for a while, of purchasing their homes prior to the crisis and the foreclosures. As everybody knows, however, customer profiling, borrowers' creditworthiness assessment, underwriting criteria, credit policies, and mortgage portfolio risk monitoring are "core activities" of lenders, credit originators, and risk managers and not the job of borrowers. Perhaps some borrowers might be blamed for excessive and irresponsible risk-taking given their poor financial situation (moral hazard) or poor financial literacy, but at the end of the day, since they are not professional lenders, their weaknesses or "sins" can be more easily forgiven.

Much of the analyses and observations reported in this book are based on my literature review on the topic and on my own lending and risk management expertise which I have gained working for over 15 years in the banking and financial services industry in Europe (that is, former Chief Risk Officer (CRO) of a global bank in the credit cards division).

Before writing this book, I wrote Chapter 16 of Robert W. Kolb's book (2010) and a paper on this topic, as early as October 7, 2008, titled "Miraculous Financial Engineering or Toxic Finance? The Genesis of the US Subprime Mortgage Loan Crisis and its Consequences on the Global Financial Markets and Real Economy" (Pezzuto, 2008), which has also been listed since 2009 on the Social Science Research Network's (SSRN) Top Ten download list for the Financial Economics Network (FEN) Subject Matter eJournals including: *Regulation of Financial Institutions* eJournal; *Financial Economics Network, History of Finance*; *CGECHDM: Effects on Corporate Governance in Financial and Economic Crises*; *CGN Subject Matter* eJournal, *Corporate Governance and Finance, Corporate Governance Network, Corporate Governance: Economic Consequences, History, Development, and Methodology*; *Governance, Incentives, and Compensation* eJournal; *Banking and Insurance* eJournal; *Corporate Governance and Finance* eJournal; *Corporate Law: Law and Finance* eJournal, *Financial Crises* eJournal; *Risk Management and Analysis in Financial Institutions* eJournal; *Socially Responsible Investment* eJournal and *Sustainability and Economics* eJournal; *Corporate, Securities and Finance Law* eJournal; *Econometric Modeling: International Financial Markets – Volatility and Financial Crises* eJournal; *Derivatives* eJournal and *Econometric Modeling: International Financial Markets* eJournal; *Risk Management* eJournal; *SRPN: Sustainable Capitalism*; *Macroeconomics* eJournal; *SRPN Subject Matter* eJournal; *SRPN: Social Enterprise (Topic) and Sustainability Research and Policy Network*; *SRPN: Social Enterprise* (Topic) (SSRN, 2009–2013). It has also been listed since 2009 in the All Time Hits on SSRN's Top Ten download list for *Investment and Social Responsibility* eJournal and on the *Corporate Governance: Economic Consequences, History, Development, and Methodology* eJournal. I also presented that paper at the International Conference on International Competition in Banking: Theory and Practice organized by the Ukrainian Academy of Banking of the National Bank of Ukraine in Sumy on May 24–25, 2012. Following my participation in this conference, the same 2008 paper was then published in the May/June 2012 issue of the *Journal of Governance and Regulation* edited by Virtusinterpress. The same paper was also reported in 2013 in the list of the Top Ten Papers on Risk Management on the GARP (Global Association of Risk Professionals) website's research section. In that paper I also predicted in October 2008 the risk of a potential EU sovereign debt crisis as a consequence of the 2007–2009 financial crisis. Unfortunately my prediction became reality after about two years.

Based on the large amount of research work I have undertaken since 2008, this book aims to explore how some key players in the industry, driven by multiple triggering factors, have taken too much risk, bypassing for a number of years all kinds of compliance, corporate governance, risk management, internal auditing, due diligence, and supervisory controls, in order to generate such a dramatic meltdown. Also, it aims to address why most of the industry analysts, news agencies, independent auditors, scholars, regulators, and policy makers have apparently failed to timely identify, report, and prevent such a potentially systemic financial Armageddon.

This book combines the most prominent scholarly contributions on the 2007–2009 financial crisis with first-hand interviews that I have undertaken with highly reputable global thought leaders, scholars, practitioners, and industry experts in order to benefit from their additional original and insightful perspectives on the matter. I selected these contributors on the basis of their know-how, expertise, and explicit intention to provide an independent and unbiased analysis of the topic. The opinion of the majority of them seems to converge on some key aspects of the crisis while the differences in their perspectives add unique personal insights on the topic and may suggest interesting areas of further research and investigation.

In order to have a more enriched and diversified perspective, the selection of the thought leaders and industry experts has been based on their expertise on the topics of the research study, on the differences in their professional background and profiles (that is, scholars, practitioners, and industry analysts), on their interest in the research project/interview, and on their declared willingness to provide an unbiased and truly independent opinion on the interview questions.

The scope of this book is to integrate fact-based analyses based on an extensive literature review, with my own personal experience on the topic and the contributions of 22 global, knowledgeable thought leaders selected on the basis of their expertise and complementary perspectives (that is, academic, industry, and subject matter expertise).

The participants in the interviews are internationally recognized thought leaders and subject matter experts of the following organizations: University of Chicago, Stanford University, NYU Stern, IESE Business School, Bocconi University, Catholic University Milan, *Financial Times*, Bloomberg, London School of Economics, Federal Reserve Bank, Intesa Sanpaolo Bank, Unicredit, Citibank, Sorbonne University, Ulster Bank/Royal Bank of Scotland, Eurointelligence, and other leading institutions.

Thought Leaders and Industry Experts Selection Criteria

The following selection criteria have been used by the author to identify the academic and industry expert participants to this study from among many potential candidates.

CRITERIA FOR SELECTING ACADEMIC THOUGHT LEADERS/SCHOLARS:

- Prominent publications on risk management, or finance, or corporate governance, or corporate social responsibility, and the 2007–2009 financial crisis.
- Seasoned academic career as full professor and/or department chair.
- Top ranking and/or award winning professorship (voted "Professor of the Year") in their universities.
- Willingness to openly express their opinion on the topics of the research, independence of mind and spirit, without the security of an anonymous interview.
- Extensive industry advisory exposure and conferences lecturing.

CRITERIA FOR SELECTING INDUSTRY EXPERTS/THOUGHT LEADERS:

- Seasoned "hands-on" expertise in the field of finance, trading, investment banking, or risk management, or board-level corporate governance of financial institutions.
- Senior executive (leadership) status or internationally recognized financial and economic analyst with leading global organizations.
- Willingness to openly express their opinion on the topics of the research, independence of mind and spirit, without the security of an anonymous interview.
- Speakers at international conferences on the topic of risk management, finance, corporate governance, or corporate social responsibility, corporate cultural change, and the 2007–2009 financial crisis.
- Author or co-author of publications on the topics or contributor.

The Main Questions I Seek to Answer in this Book

1. What are the combined factors that have contributed to generate the 2007–2009 financial crisis?
2. Was the financial crisis predictable and/or avoidable?
3. What changes would be necessary in terms of financial reforms, corporate governance models, managerial cultures, and internal controls and enterprise risk management (ERM) framework to prevent other systemic crises in the future?

This Book Also Aims to Assess the Following Assumptions

1. The 2007–2009 Credit Crisis was predictable and proactively controllable given the available data, good "old" common sense, best practices, and solid credit and risk management practices, education, expertise, and an industry-wide perspective.
2. The 2007–2009 Credit Crisis was a major systemic failure of banks' risk management units and corporate governance, credit rating agencies, investment firms, and banking and financial markets' oversight bodies, and regulatory authorities.
3. Time and resources available to policy makers and regulators have not always been used in the most effective way to solve the problems generated by the financial crisis and in some cases (Dodd–Frank Act in the home lending arena and the repeal of the Glass–Steagall Act) may well have precipitated and prolonged the crisis.
4. Greed and conflict of interest of many stakeholders have significantly contributed to generate the crisis and to avoid, after the bail-out, the introduction of adequate structural reforms for the industry.
5. Unregulated shadow banking practices and complex innovative over-the-counter (OTC) financial engineering transactions still continue to threaten the global financial markets for new potential risky arbitrages, bubbles, and crises.
6. New corporate governance frameworks, new effective reforms, and new sets of values and accountability principles need to be introduced in the financial industry in order to drastically turn the raiders' culture that has led the dramatic crisis into a new socially responsible and sustainable culture in the financial markets.

Finally, the book also aims to identify the key lessons learned from this drift of capitalism with the hope of exploring new ideas, guidelines, and proposals that might help repair economic dislocation and prevent the recurrence in the future of other crises through simple, straight-forward, and fair regulations that might rebalance the system; as Luigi Zingales says, "shifting the pendulum back to a state that is pro-market rather than just pro-business." Pope Emeritus Benedict XVI's 2013 new year address to worshippers has condemned "unregulated capitalism" for contributing to world tension triggered by growing instances of inequality between rich and poor. He stated that among the root causes of these tensions and equalities are "the prevalence of a selfish and individualistic mindset which also finds expression in an unregulated financial capitalism," as well as "various forms of terrorism and crime" (BBC News Euro, 2013).

With the following words, another prominent scholar summarized, way before the 2007–2009 financial crisis, the risks associated with unregulated capitalism:

> People of the same trade seldom meet together, even for merriment and diversion, but the conversation ends in a conspiracy against the public, or in some contrivance to raise prices. It is impossible indeed to prevent such meetings, by any law which either could be executed, or would be consistent with liberty and justice. But though the law cannot hinder people of the same trade from sometimes assembling together, it ought to do nothing to facilitate such assemblies, much less to render them necessary. (Smith, 1776)

2 *The Factors that have Led to the Global Financial Crisis*

An Overview of the Main Triggering Factors that Led to the Crisis

In years to come, many people will probably remember the 2007–2009 global financial crisis as the worst economic damage that America and Europe has suffered since the Great Depression. The hope and aim of this book is to raise people's attention and understanding of the causes and consequences generated by this unprecedented crisis, providing them an independent, straightforward, unbiased, and logical description of the events that have led to the subprime meltdown and its triggering factors. Creating a better understanding and a greater awareness of this topic might hopefully lead political leaders, policy makers, scholars, and regulators to promote new, better, and more appropriate financial reforms, cultural and organizational values changes, new governance frameworks, and new policy standards and practices, in order to hopefully prevent similar or even worse disasters in the future.

There is no doubt that in today's globalized world and highly integrated and interconnected financial markets, profits and losses of capital, money, equity, debt, real estate, derivatives, commodities, liquidity, and foreign exchange markets move very quickly across the continents. Technological innovation and the consequent speed of communication devices across the globe, with online and real-time reports and decision support systems (that is, high-speed trading), advanced information communication technology (ICT) architectures, and computer based-solutions, have certainly simplified but also amplified the benefits and threats associated with global financial investing and trading, since the advanced interrelationships and integration of such systems also leads to a higher level of complexity (Pezzuto, 2008).

As also indicated in the conclusions of the report issued by the Financial Crisis Inquiry Commission (FCIC, 2011, xv–xxviii), today there seems to be almost a universal agreement among political leaders, industry experts, academic scholars, investors, and ordinary people, that a number of complex, interrelated, and concurrent enabling factors have contributed (although with different impact) to build, over the years, the unsustainable conditions that have led to the housing market, subprime, liquidity, confidence, financial, and economic crises of this past decade. Among these factors, notable ones are certainly the following:

- very low interest rates (Fed Funds) from 2000 onwards encouraged by low inflation rates;
- lax and predatory lending standards;
- excess of liquidity in the markets seeking high yields;
- underestimation of bank and market liquidity risk;
- counterparty risk;
- underpricing of risk;
- regulatory arbritrage;
- the lack of an integrated company-wide risk management governance;
- increased promotion of methods helping to hide tail-risks (Taleb, 2010);
- serious underestimation of systemic risks by financial firms. In many cases they have also artificially-masked fat tail risks (Nocera, 2009);
- credit rating agencies' failure to timely and correctly rate debt securities (inflated ratings) and mispricing of risk;
- massive downgrades of structured finance products by the credit rating agencies since 2007 that contributed to generate panic in the financial markets (Lang, 2012);
- the perversely designed capital adequacy rules (in particular for off-balance-sheet entities – OBSE) (Friedman et al., 2011, p. 226);
- mark-to-market accounting and resulting procyclicality;
- lack of real reforms to reduce long-term structural imbalances in combination with fiscal stimuli (Lang, 2012);
- the combination of overleveraged financial institutions (Shin, 2009, pp. 101–119), and US families living beyond their means (overleveraged borrowers), with savings rates close to zero percent;
- massive adverse selection of unqualified and financially illiterate subprime borrowers;
- dramatic failure of corporate governance and risk management;
- non-traditional mortgages and the mortgage lending bubble;
- irrational exuberance about the expectations of rising housing market prices that generated the housing bubble;
- securitization and the pitfalls of originate-to-distribute (OTD) lending model of bank credit syndication of loans and proprietary trading;
- non-transparent maturity transformation;
- mortgage-backed securities (MBS) placed in undercapitalized off-balance-sheet Conduits;
- overconfidence in complex, opaque, and unregulated financial engineering innovation (for example, credit default swaps (CDS), collateralized debt obligation (CDOs), MBS, residential mortgage-backed securities (RMBS), collateralized loan obligation (CLO) aimed to maximize short-term profitability and in the sophisticated risk models;
- the excessive growth of the opaque and highly leveraged shadow banking sector designed to circumvent existing regulations;
- reckless use of OBSE to generate "window-dressing" financial reports for investors;
- large quantities of mortgage-related assets and derivatives concentrated in the hands of a set of important and highly leveraged financial institutions;
- lack of transparency and systemic breaches in accountability and ethics at all levels (greed, corruption, conflicts of interest, and fraud);
- an excessive use of leverage by financial firms, taking on too much risk, with too little capital, and depending too much on short-term funding;

- global imbalances (surplus countries versus deficit countries such as the US) and carry trade;
- perverse remuneration incentives for mortgage brokers, appraisers, lenders, securitizers, rating agencies, investment bankers, speculators, and ultimate investors;
- a laissez-faire policy with reduced regulatory oversight, controls on shadow banking, over-the-counter (OTC) derivatives markets, and information asymmetries;
- bad regulation of the financial industry and the passage from the Gramm–Leach–Bliley Act to the repeal of the Glass–Steagall Act in 1999;
- excessive free-market ideology of regulators which have led them to believe that in a highly competitive environment markets are self-correcting;
- excessive interference with the lending practices of the Federal Housing Administration (FHA), Fannie Mae, and Freddie Mac by certain US Congressional Legislators (Nugent, 2011);
- speculative attitude of many players in the industry who have been "gambling with uncertainty" and making very dangerous bets;
- some adverse markets conditions, externalities, and badly estimated probabilities of extreme tail events (black swan), correlations across asset portfolios, and across risk exposures;
- underestimation of the systemic risks related to the firms' interconnectedness;
- investors' loss of confidence in some key financial firms, their fear of systemic contagion, and their panic reaction (wholesale banking panic) in the fall 2008 when the financial markets were on the brink of collapse threatening the value of their investments (Pezzuto, 2008; Stiglitz, 2010, pp. 1–3; Baily et al., 2010, pp. 79–84);
- buildup of underlying macroeconomic distortions for a few years before the crisis occurred (Demyanyk and Hasan, 2009, p.9);
- the high propensity to save in China (Warnock and Warnock, 2006, pp. 50–63);
- energy input fluctuations (supply–demand constraint issues) (Nugent, 2011);
- focus in the US on two wars versus on the economy (Nugent, 2011);
- a flawed set of prudential rules.

The subprime crisis lends support to John Keynes's ideas that the market may be irrational. He learned that markets can act perversely in the short term. Of this, he later famously commented: "The market can stay irrational longer than you can stay solvent" (Maynardkeynes.org, 2011).

Kirman (2010) says that many macroeconomists found themselves unprepared when the financial crisis occurred since there was a general consensus that the fundamental mechanisms of macroeconomics were known and well understood through the use of models such as the Dynamic Stochastic General Equilibrium (DSGE) model which is an applied general equilibrium model (Kirman, 2010, p. 500). As Kirman and others stated (2011): "The implicit view behind standard equilibrium models is that markets and economies are inherently stable and only temporarily get off track" (Friedman et al., 2011, p. 263).

Kirman (2010) also reminds us that two leading figures, Robert Lucas (2003) and Ben Bernanke (2004) underestimated the risks that led to the 2007–2009 financial crises. Lucas, in his 2003 presidential address to the American Economic Association said: "The central problem of depression-prevention has been solved," and Bernanke (2004), Chairman of the Federal Reserve Board, celebrated the "Great Moderation" in economic performance over the previous two decades (Bernanke, 2004) and dismissed the public criticism of Krugman (2009), Shiller (2003b; 2006), and Stiglitz (2003) (Kirman, 2010, p. 501). According to Kirman (2010):

> *One possible view is that the recent near-collapse of the world's banking system corresponds with the collective result of individual banks optimizing in isolation, but unconsciously coordinating on a disastrous solution. The individuals or banks were making the decisions unlikely aware that their increasingly interdependent positions were generating a threat to the stability of the whole system, since they insured their positions with others. (Kirman, 2010, p. 501)*

But such insurance was with CDS, which it turns out was not insurance and had no reserves or collateral requirements. There was no central mind to perceive or tally the ever interrelated systemic risks (Nugent, 2011). The system was, indeed, as Friedrich August von Hayek (1949) argued "organizing itself." However, this self-organization, contrary to a standard and largely ideological view, was not stabilizing – rather it was winding out of control. It worked well for a while until the system froze (that is, confidence, liquidity crises) as a result of a series of related occurrences, and without the actors in the system having the collective view of their individual actions (Kirman, 2010, p. 503).

Sornette (2003) makes the point that:

> *A crisis such as the stock market crash is not the result of a short-term exogenous event, but rather involves a long-term endogenous buildup, with exogenous events acting merely as triggers. (Kirman, 2010, p. 504)*

This echoes Minsky's (1982) reflection on the "disruptive internal processes" in the economy (Sornette, 2003; Minsky, 1982; Schumpeter, 1942) (Kirman, 2010, p. 504).

Kirman (2010), mentioning my chapter (Chapter 16) in Robert W. Kolb's book *Lessons From the Financial Crisis: Causes, Consequences, and Our Economic Future* (Kolb, 2010) points out that given the evidences of the financial crisis, either economists see each of the triggering factors in terms of an exogenous shift, and then consider that their unfortunate coincidence led to market collapse and a radical shift away from equilibrium, or as he prefers to argue, that these are common and co-evolving features of the components of a system which was itself evolving (Kirman, 2010, p. 529).

Interestingly enough, New York University (NYU) Stern School Professor Viral V. Acharya (2011) in the book *Regulating Wall Street: The Dodd–Frank and the New Architecture of Global Finance* mentions "Friedrich Hayek's classic 'The Road to Serfdom', a warning against the dangers of excessive state control. Hayek's book was the number one best seller on Amazon in 2011." He also stated that "at the same time the foundation of much modern economics and capitalism – Adam Smith's 'The Wealth of Nations' – languished around an Amazon rank of 10,000" (Acharya et al., 2011, p. 1).

Acharya et al. (2011) indicate that in the year (2004) when the perfect storm began to develop, "Global banks were seeking massive capital flows into the United States and the United Kingdom by engaging in short-term borrowing, increasingly through uninsured deposits and interbank liabilities, financed at historically low interest rates." By doing so, Acharya argues that they began to manufacture huge quantities of tail-risk, "which would fail only if there was a secular collapse in the housing markets" (Acharya et al., 2011, p. 4).

It appears each financial institution was focusing only on its own institutional risk and "ignored the risk of an entire financial system manufacturing a tail-risk, and they even encouraged – through lower-risk weights – the manufacturing of AAA-rated mortgage-backed tranches" which really only appeared to be AAA-rated (veneer but no substance – garbage in one end with Triple A out the other). So apparently no one saw what was happening on a systemic level, and no one cared enough to find out since everyone was making unearned profits and "taking a highly undercapitalized one-way bet on the housing market" (Acharya et al., 2011, p. 4). All of course while taking home huge bonuses.

> While these financial institutions seemed individually safe, collectively they were vulnerable, and in fact, the housing market crashed in 2007, the tail-risk materialized, and the large, complex financial institutions (LCFIs) crashed, too, like a house of cards. (Acharya et al., 2011, pp. 4–5)

So it appears the 2007–2009 financial crisis is just the coincidental result of an extreme (fat-tailed) risk that led to market collapse – or not? Or not only? The hypothesis framed by Acharya et al. (2011) seems realistic and fascinating but what about the many warning signs reported in the years preceding the crisis by a few prominent but also disregarded economists and industry experts such as Krugman (2009), Shiller (2003b; 2006), Stiglitz (2003), and others? Were there actually no evident early warnings of this crisis? Didn't the leading global experts in finance, leading investment and consulting firms, regulators, Wall Street analysts, global banks' management, and rating agency professionals see anything coming that would have signaled a potential crisis in the making with some basic macroeconomic and scenario analysis and a bit of "good old common sense?"

This book will help shed light on these well-founded doubts and explore (whatever may have been the causes of the financial meltdown) possible solutions to prevent the next financial crisis. If regulators and policy makers do not address the real causes of the crisis, it is likely that the next crisis will be just around the corner and will find our financial system, once again, unprepared and unable to face the new devastating bail-out task. It is critical, however, also to have a forward-thinking approach in developing the new financial regulation in the international markets in order to avoid that the new rules might solve the triggering factors of the last crisis but not the triggering root causes of the new one.

Some even argue that the Fed and other regulatory and oversight authorities have been guided in the years preceding the financial crisis by the excessive reliance on the "unfettered markets" ideology and theories of US economist Milton Friedman (Stern, 2008). In the same vein, the Fed's Chairman Bernanke stated (2010), "I grasp the mantle of Milton Friedman. I think we are doing everything Milton Friedman would have us do" (Nelson, 2011, p. 29). In 2010, Stephen Green, HSBC Chairman, declared that, "American free market economics guru Milton Friedman was wrong to assert that companies should focus on shareholder value above all other considerations" (pure market economic theory). He also said:

> Western capitalism has to progress beyond a simple statement that the only social responsibility of business is to make a profit. Businesses have to earn a satisfactory return on their risk capital, he acknowledged, but he added that they also need to form lasting and sustainable relationships with other stakeholders, such as employees, customers and the communities where they serve. (Cave, 2010)

Even Allen Sinai, Chief Global Economist for Decision Economics Inc., a consulting group, said: "What Milton Friedman said was that government should not interfere," and, "It didn't work" (Goodman, 2008). However, some have probably confused the idea that the hypothesis (Efficient Market Hypothesis) that in the long-run markets are stable does not necessarily mean that they are supposed to be stable even in the short run under exceptional circumstances such as irrational exuberance and extreme tail-risk events, driven by macroeconomics changes.

My view (2008) on the matter is that the financial crisis was not the result of the failure of the free-market economy; but rather of the perverse interference of bad regulation, politics, and powerful banking lobbies over the last decades in the markets (also as a result of the too-big-to fail phenomenon) which have not allowed the market to operate correctly (that is, industry deregulation, unregulated shadow banking, poor regulatory oversight, perverse financial incentives, conflicts of interest, and blind ideology) (Pezzuto, 2008). Certainly, I share the view of Luigi Zingales that crony capitalism has played a major role in the making of the 2007–2009 financial crisis (Zingales, 2012).

In order to properly address the root causes of the global financial crisis and to understand how this dramatic event occurred it is necessary to start with the analyses of the facts and to progress in the quest, connecting the dots, until the full picture becomes clear.

The Property and Lending Bubbles in the US and the Role of the Monetary Policy in the Financial Crisis

As reported by Baily et al. (2010) and illustrated in Figure 2.1, a housing bubble began in the mid-1990s in the US, inflated by a constant increase in home prices and the expectation that future prices would continue to increase for many more years (Baily et al., 2010, p.79).

Steven Gjerstad and Vernon Smith (2009) suggest that the upward trend in the housing market prices probably began in 1997 with the elimination of taxes on capital gains of up to a half million dollars for residences (Taxpayer Relief Act) and was powerfully encouraged by the "homeownership" policy pursued by both President Clinton and President Bush administrations, and the aggressive monetary policy of the Fed since 2001 (Gjerstad and Smith, 2009, pp. 275–277).

During the period 1997–2006 there was a 124 percent increase in house values which today we recognize as the housing market bubble that triggered, along with other factors, the 2007–2009 financial crisis.

In the early years of the new millennium, when the US Federal Reserve sharply lowered interest rates to a Fed Funds rate (the rate at which banks borrow money from each other overnight) of approximately 1 percent (2003) from 6.24 percent (2000), a credit euphoria overwhelmed both lenders and borrowers, fueled the credit bubble, and further inflated the real estate bubble (Pezzuto, 2008).

The US Federal Reserve lowered the Fed Funds rate through a policy of quantitative easing to spur the economy and to limit the damage of the stock market decline resulting from the 2000 dot-com crisis, the September 11, 2001 terrorist attacks, and the subsequent costs of the Iraq and Afghanistan wars.

INDEX VALUE: JANUARY 2000 = 100

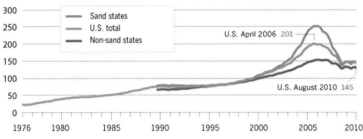

NOTE: Sand states are Arizona, California, Florida, and Nevada.
SOURCE: CoreLogic and U.S. Census Bureau: 2007 American Community Survey, FCIC calculations

Figure 2.1   US Home Prices

Source: Stanford University Rock Center for Corporate Governance.

Fed Funds were reduced to their lowest level since 1962. As Steven Gjerstad and Vernon Smith put it: "2001–2004 saw the longest sustained expansionary monetary policy of the past 54 years" (Gjerstad and Smith, 2009, p. 277). Fed Funds in 2002 actually reached negative real interest rates for longer maturities until 2004 (Friedman et al., 2011, p. 216).

The combination of a massive liquidity injection in the economy and more favorable tax relief laws and fiscal policies determined a phase of *irrational exuberance* (or irrational expectations on the constantly rising housing market prices) that sustained a rapid economic growth in the US driven by the housing market and lending bubbles. These bubbles were ultimately fueled by the ever-increasing households' debt.

The rapid increase of housing market prices, high families' debts, and low interest rates of mortgages ended up concentrating the aggressive monetary policy's benefits and the borrowers' incomes and savings in the real estate (old economy) and in the financial sector, rather than distributing them to improve the innovation and sustainability of multiple sectors of the economy in order to strengthen the country's global competitiveness.

John B. Taylor (2009) presented at the annual Jackson Hole conference in August 2007 evidences highlighting that a loose fitting monetary policy of the Federal Reserve from 2000 to 2006 caused Fed Funds to fall well below what historical experience would suggest the policy should be (Figure 2.2). The analysis he presented proved that the monetary policy was too "loose fitting" – what he named the "Taylor rule." This rule indicates the interest rates one gets by plugging actual inflation and gross domestic product (GDP) into a policy rule. Taylor also stated that, according to him, this policy deviation from the rule was the result of government interventions in order to avoid potential risk of deflation (Taylor, 2009, pp. 2–4).

John B. Taylor (2009) during that presentation provided empirical evidences (regression techniques) that the unusually low interest rates policy was a triggering factor of the housing boom and bust. He also pointed out that the *loose fitting US monetary policy* would create monetary instability, moving away from the period of Great Moderation that worked well in earlier decades to keep both overall economy stable and the inflation rate low (Taylor, 2009, p. 6).

As John B. Taylor (2009) has stated, the excessive risk-taking of the subprime mortgages' rapid growth combined with adjustable rates, lax underwriting criteria, and extra easy monetary policy on interest rates (to please the government programs designed to promote home ownership) are all powerful triggering factors of the financial crisis

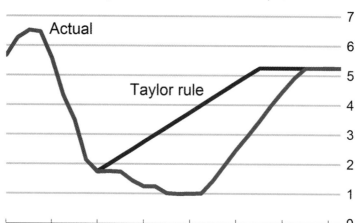

Figure 2.2   Loose Fitting

Source: Original figure and permission to reproduce it granted by John B. Taylor.

(Taylor, 2009, p. 10). But this is not enough since other elements have to be accounted for in this devastating meltdown which will be explained shortly in this book (that is, short-term funding strategies of investment banks and hedge funds, high leverage ratios, originate-to-distribute (OTD) securitization model) (Pezzuto, 2008; 2010a, pp. 120–123).

A general perception of low and decreasing risks in the US macroeconomic environment, driven by rising asset prices, a surge in credit growth, rising risk tolerance, and a very high liquidity, has contributed to generate a strong sense of confidence and optimism for all borrowers (Baily et al., 2010, p. 79).

It seemed to be the realization of the so-called American Dream. Anyone could just become wealthy almost overnight using the properties purchased with mortgage loans as collateral for new and more profitable investments, with apparently no or limited risk. Lenders began to encourage less creditworthy and qualified individuals to take as much credit as they could, to continuously finance and refinance their homes, and to treat their houses as Automated Teller Machines (ATMs) (borrowing against their value) with the objective of maximizing their fees (Stiglitz, 2010, pp. 77–80).

Steven Gjerstad and Vernon Smith (2009) report that mortgage-loan originations, in conjunction with mortgage securitization and tax-free capital gains, increased the housing market to an astonishing level. The mortgage-loan originations increased from $1.05 trillion in 2000 to $3.95 trillion in 2003 (Gjerstad and Smith, 2009, p. 277).

Luc Laeven and Fabian Valencia (2012) of the International Monetary Fund (IMF) explained in their paper titled "Resolution of Banking Crises: The Good, the Bad, and the Ugly" the following findings: "Banking crises are often preceded by prolonged periods of high credit growth and are often associated with large imbalances in the balance sheets of the private sector, such as maturity mismatches or exchange rate risk, that ultimately translate into credit risk for the banking sector" (Laeven and Valencia, 2012).

Furthermore, Ouarda Merrouche and Erlend Nier (2010) of the IMF also confirmed the hypothesis, stating that, according to their study, "Three factors may have contributed to the buildup of financial imbalances: (i) *rising global imbalances* (capital flows), (ii) *monetary policy that might have been too loose*, (iii) *inadequate supervision and regulation*" (Merrouche and Nier, 2010).

The Role of the Securitization Process in the Financial Crisis

The transformation of the residential mortgage market in the US from an originate-to-hold model (OTH) to an OTD model significantly changed the incentives of all the participants in the mortgage origination process (Kolb, 2010b, p. 209). Furthermore, different to typical mortgage products which are part of the banking book, the OTD securitization model has transferred most of the mortgage loans to the trading book, thus with less incentives to undertake rigorous screening and monitoring of these portfolios' quality and origination processes (Pezzuto, 2008; Colombini and Calabrò, 2011, p. 93).

The OTD securitization model allowed banks to sell their fast-growing portfolios of *non-recourse subprime mortgages loans* to investors, through the use of off-balance-sheet investment vehicles (that is, structured investment vehicles – SIVs – or special purpose vehicles – SPVs) traded in the shadow banking market, thus also passing on to these investors the related credit risk. This OTD process, obviously, generated a moral hazard incentive to lenders and mortgage originators since it encouraged a reduced commitment to proper borrowers' creditworthiness screening.

The fast growth of the OTD model has introduced a number of new players into the process with their own incentives, which turned out to be perverse and proved to represent a key contributor to the subprime crisis (Kolb, 2010b, p. 209).

In this new mortgage model (OTD), borrowers had new, greater motivation to seek as much debt as possible, through mortgage financing, since the great incentives for them were represented by cash-out refinancing. This is a type of mortgage on an existing home that allows the homeowner to replace an old mortgage with a new one of a higher balance which allows the borrower to receive cash from the new loan to use for any purpose. In a period of steadily rising home prices, this innovation strongly encouraged homeowners to take a series of new loans on the same home with higher balances in order to receive cash with each refinancing (Kolb, 2010b, p. 211).

This process of repeated cash-out financings has been associated with the concept of using one's home as a piggy bank or, as Joseph E. Stiglitz referred to it in his book *Freefall. America, Free Markets, and the Sinking of the World Economy*, "... treating their houses as ATMs" (Stiglitz, 2010, 78). A similar expression is also reported in Nouriel Roubini's book *Crisis Economics* (Roubini, 2010, p. 18).

This spirit of overconfidence was evidently supported by low interest rates, optimistic expectations, credit and liquidity abundance, and an encouraging trend of home prices expected to constantly appreciate. The same euphoria also affected lenders and investors, since based on the projections of their time-series analysis models, an impressive growth of their portfolios was apparently achievable without a proportional increase in risks.

The Massive Expansion of Innovative Financial Engineering Products and Exotic Mortgage Lending Products

The lower level of risk perception has led to an institutionalization of diminishing risk averseness. The "ownership society" policy announced by President George W. Bush was meant to significantly increase asset accumulation for African–Americans and Latinos through the privatization of Social Security and the encouragement of home ownership via no downpayment Federal Housing Administration (FHA) loans (Stiglitz, 2010, pp. 10–11; Utt, 2010, p. 134).

Based on this policy the two government-sponsored enterprises (GSE) – The Federal National Mortgage Association (typically referred to as Fannie Mae) and the Federal Home Loan Mortgage Association (typically referred as Freddie Mac), which are private corporations with government mandates to provide liquidity to the housing market – were pushed to follow the private market trend toward risky loans to lower-income borrowers or to borrowers purchasing houses in lower-income communities with little if any due diligence being performed (Swan, 2010, p. 51; Utt, 2010, p. 134).

As a consequence of this new orientation, by 2006 almost 50 percent of the US residential mortgage lending was subprime, Alt A, and second loans. A subprime mortgage is typically identified as a mortgage provided to a credit-impaired borrower with a Fair Isaac and Company (FICO) score below 660 and/or with detrimental data such as recent payments with 30-day or 60-day delinquencies, depending on the recency of the delinquency; judgments, foreclosures, repossessions, charge-offs within the previous two years; bankruptcies within the previous five years; relatively high default probability (FICO score below 660 or similar measures); and the limited ability to cover living expenses after debts. The Alt A loans fall into a gray area between prime and subprime mortgages (Utt, 2010, pp. 133–134).

In more recent years, lenders began to believe that charging higher fees and commissions for these subprime mortgages would make it possible to offset the higher risks associated with the characteristics of the product and the profile of the target customer (Utt, 2010, p. 133) – especially if backed by CDOs (a perceived form of insurance).

This approach might work well as long as there are no prolonged adverse economic conditions in the markets or other systemic risks affecting the entire economy, such as the simultaneous reduction of property prices in various areas of the country, with the consequent impact on the value of the mortgage loans' collateral, and a sharp increase in interest rates, or the devastating effect of a massive adverse selection of underqualified and high-risk subprime borrowers with no or limited credit checks in the banks' origination process.

Here is an example of what I call the crisis of "common-sense." Any savvy and experienced lender and risk manager knows that there is no effective protection against a voluntary systemic adverse selection of risky borrowers (subprime) in conjunction with lax credit screening, limited or no downpayment, overestimated (or non-existent) collateral, and in particular during an unprecedented lending and housing market boom–bust scenario. No matter how much risk distribution (diversification) financial institutions set up through securitization, assets-backed securities and other structured products' sales (that is, CDOs,) on a global scale, or what kind of pseudo-credit insurance products they use, such as CDSs, if the entire market simultaneously adopts the same adverse selection massive growth strategy, and if they are highly interconnected to one another and they operate with undercapitalized, overleveraged, and poorly regulated off-balance-sheet vehicles, and they rely significantly on maturity mismatching for funding, then there is no need of disruptive externalities or black swans to blow up the whole thing, since the system is building inside the seeds of its own self-destruction. In summary, it is just a time bomb.

As the perceived risk of the subprime lending products progressively diminished during the years preceding the financial crisis, and the value of the houses (collateral) constantly increased, lenders began to tailor non-traditional and more flexible products and payment terms to rapidly increase their profitable portfolios of these loans. The same flexible offer was then also offered to the Alt A market (mortgages typically issued to borrowers with good credit history who are self-employed, but lack income or asset verification), as well as jumbo loans, and all other lending product categories, both secured and unsecured. As a consequence of the collapse in credit standards and increase in risk appetites, the home ownership rate reached 69.1 percent by the first quarter of 2005, up from 65 percent in the previous ten years, the highest level in American history (Utt, 2010, p. 134). "The housing bubble resulted in many homeowners refinancing their homes at lower interest rates, or financing consumer spending by taking out second mortgages secured by the price appreciation" (Keith and Mueller, 2009).

In this environment of increasing liberalized standards, consumer spending became, even more than before, the main engine of US economic growth, as indicated by the household debt-to-income ratio (US household liabilities as a share of disposable income), which at the peak of the crisis in 2007 stood at 138 percent, growing from 101 percent in 2000. This increase was as large as the increase over the previous 25 years (Baily et al., 2009, p. 1), while the savings rate declined from approximately 12 percent in 1982 to less than 1 percent in 2005 (Utt, 2010, p. 135). In the US, the annual personal consumption grew in the period 2000 to 2007 from $6.9 trillion to $9.9 trillion (44 percent) and faster than the GDP growth rate or household income. In this period, consumption continued to represent the main fuel of the US economy, accounting for 77 percent of the real US GDP. Americans were evidently living way beyond their means (Baily et al., 2009, pp. 1–3).

Johnson and Kwak (2010a) report that, in 2005, one million subprime mortgage loans were used to purchase houses and 1.2 million subprime mortgage loans were used for refinancing. Combined they represent a 20-fold increase over 1993 (Johnson and Kwak, 2010a, p. 128).

Johnson and Kwak (2010a) argue that lenders were no longer interested in the borrowers' ability to pay back their loans since, as long as the prices of the houses (collateral) continued to rise, debt was not perceived as a real potential risk. Furthermore, the OTD securitization model, the off-balance-sheet investment vehicles (SPVs), and the CDS were supposed to assure a stealth-level risk protection against any potential default, and in particular, of the unexpected loss (UL). Thus, the massive use of off-balance-sheet investment vehicles and the OTD securitization process might have been used either for credit risk transfer or window dressing techniques on related potential credit losses and securities write-downs. In this business model, the lenders made high profits (fees) for originating loans, the higher the interest, the higher the fees. Refinancing also allowed lenders to earn even more fees when interest rates increased and borrowers were unable to make their payments. In the worst case scenario, lenders expected not to face any losses since mortgage loans' risk was typically taken by CDO investors (non-recourse mortgage loans) (Johnson and Kwak, 2010a, p. 128).

Taking a look at a bigger picture provides additional clues on the origin of the credit bubble and the subsequent financial crisis. In the mid-2000s, the housing value and leverage in the US were strongly increasing, while the fiscal and current account deficits were high and rising. This macroeconomic scenario was leading to an unsustainable situation (Obstfeld and Rogoff, 2009, pp. 1–2).

Those days, the combined factors of having the most reliable, low perceived risk and a dynamic financial market in the US, and deregulated global financial markets with fragmented and inefficient regulatory oversight and global imbalances, has contributed a great deal to the global financial meltdown (Obstfeld and Rogoff, 2009, p. 2).

As a consequence of the aggressive and loose US monetary policy implemented after the year 2000, with a drastic reduction of interest rates from 6.5 percent in the year 2000 to 1 percent in the year 2003, massive foreign capital inflows reached the US from fast-growing economies in Asia (with huge reserves of dollars), oil exporters, and other surplus countries with very low interest rates in order to take advantage of the higher yield of the US securities and of the perceived underpriced risk (easy foreign borrowings used to fund the US deficit) (Obstfeld and Rogoff, 2009, pp. 14–15). Amar Bhidé (Friedman et al., 2011, p. 69) also indicates that misaligned exchange rates sustained large global financial imbalances.

Thus while fast-growing economies were exporting goods to the US and other mature economies and/or economies with current account deficits, the US and other economies with deficits used the emerging economies' surpluses to fund their deficit and to grow their GDP, consumption, and housing investments. Apparently this was a "win–win situation" (Obstfeld and Rogoff, 2009, p. 3).

In those days, the Chairman of the Federal Reserve, Alan Greenspan, supported the idea that the drop in rates would have the effect of leading to a surge in home sales and refinancings. He had encouraged Americans in 2004 to switch to Adjustable Rate Mortgages (ARMs) to take advantage of the excellent market conditions determined by very low interest rates, high liquidity, and constantly rising home prices (Kirchhoff and Hagenbaugh, 2004).

Combining the Fed Chairman's guidelines with the repeal in 1999 of the Glass–Steagall Act, and a number of other factors previously mentioned, it becomes quite clear how the credit and property bubble was generated.

A few months after his recommendation, Greenspan began raising interest rates and in a two-year period these monetary interventions brought the Fed Funds rate to 5.25 percent. Meanwhile in 2005, the New Bankruptcy Law or The Bankruptcy Abuse Prevention and Consumer Protection Act of 2005 (BAPCPA) was passed by Congress and signed into law by President George W. Bush, aiming to make it more difficult for some consumers to file for bankruptcy (Martenson, 2007).

With the introduction of the New Bankruptcy Law, bankers expected to be more protected in case of borrowers' defaults, since given the historical low-risk trend, the constantly rising value of the houses, the homes repossession (collateral), and the sale of the foreclosed properties would probably generate higher values than the mortgage loans' outstanding balance (Martenson, 2007).

Given the market conditions in the years leading up to the crisis, predatory and fraudulent lending practices began, and mortgage lenders dramatically increased mortgage debt with a willful disregard for a borrower's ability to pay (FCIC, 2011, p. xxiii).

Excessive irresponsible lending was booming with an incredible variety of new types of mortgages, such as the "no-doc" mortgages, the 100 percent non-recourse mortgages (with no downpayment), ARMs with teaser rates, Option ARMs, "liar loans" (applicants were not required to prove their income or assets, thus borrowers were encouraged to overstate their income and assets), mortgages with zero percent interest for the first year, NINA or NINJA loans (loans made to people with no income, no job, no assets), interest-only loans with negative amortization (Stiglitz, 2010, pp. 85–89), "pay option mortgages where borrowers could choose to pay less than the monthly interest on the loan, causing the principle balance to go up instead of down" (Johnson and Kwak, 2010a, pp. 126–128), or the so-called 2/28 and 3/27 "hybrid ARMs" (Jarsulic, 2010, p. 10).

With constant mortgage refinancings and these types of unconventional and risky loans, issued with lax underwriting standards, low or no documentation, low income and downpayments, and high loan-to-value (LTV) ratios, the collateral would not be adequate to protect the lenders, or to say it better, investors (given the CDOs sales) from default unless housing prices continued to rise (Johnson and Kwak, 2010a, pp. 126–127).

Furthermore, as reported by Marc Jarsulic (2010), despite no improvements in the market areas' economic conditions, in the period 2001–2006 subprime mortgage loans' denial rates declined, demonstrating with clear evidence that lending standards deteriorated during this period (Jarsulic, 2010, p. 10).

According to the FCIC (2011), "nearly one-quarter of all mortgages made in the first half of 2005 were interest-only loans and in the same year 68 percent of the Option ARM loans originated by Countrywide and Washington Mutual had low-or-no-documentation requirements" (FCIC, 2011, p. xxiii).

After the repeal in 1999 of the Glass–Steagall Act, which had separated commercial and investment banking and their activities, banks started to make extremely risky loans and to engage in excessive risk-taking practices that generated extremely large fees (Johnson and Kwak, 2010a, pp. 126–133).

This has led to the awareness of the well-known too-big-to fail doctrine, meaning that in case of potential bankruptcy, the government would have to rescue them to avoid an unbearable systemic risk in the economy. Based on this new paradigm, banks had become bigger and bigger, just as did their subprime mortgage origination practices. As the financial crisis peaked in 2007–2008, this too-big-to-fail assumption actually proved to be all too real, as many leading global banks and financial institutions had to be bailed out to avoid a systemic global financial and economic meltdown, an unimaginable global recession, or perhaps, a global depression (Stiglitz, 2010, pp. 36–37).

In 2006, the last year of the housing boom, the US subprime mortgage market had reached a rate of 23.5 percent of the total mortgage lending market (Figure 2.3), and most of the subprime loans were securitized (Inside Mortgage Finance, 2008). Even the foreclosures and the delinquency rates of the subprime mortgages (Figure 2.4) sharply increased as a consequence of: (1) poor underwriting and risk management criteria; (2) lax and predatory lending standards; (3) overleveraged subprime borrowers; (4) excessive recourse to refinancing; (5) "no-doc" mortgages; (6) decreasing property values (collateral); (7) rapid shadow banking expansion; and (8) short-term funding strategies of investment firms. The adjustable rate subprime mortgages originated in 2006 reached in 2009 the astonishing delinquency rate of approximately 40 percent.

*In 2006, $600 billion of subprime loans were originated, most of which were securi-
tized. That year, subprime lending accounted for 23.5% of all mortgage originations.*

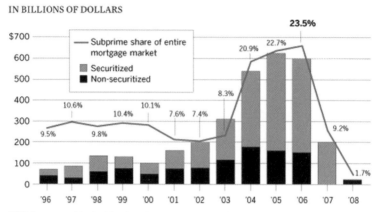

Figure 2.3   Subprime Mortgage Originations

Source: Stanford University Rock Center for Corporate Governance.

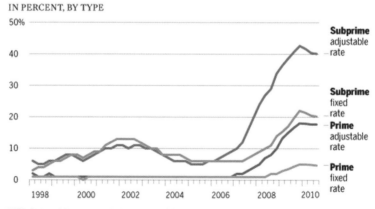

Figure 2.4   Mortgage Delinquencies by Loan Type

Source: Stanford University Rock Center for Corporate Governance.

As the housing market prices' boom ended, after a decade of rapid growth, the whole economy was negatively affected by an average drop in price value of approximately 30 percent in the period 2006 to 2009. Since in the US the housing market represented approximately 30 percent of the total GDP in 2007, it is quite evident that a systemic and generalized drop in the housing market value on a national scale would badly hit consumer spending and saving rates, thus leading to the recession. It is also important to consider the very high average household-debt-to-income ratio, the lax underwriting criteria, and the significant increase in adjustable mortgage rates in the period 2004 to 2006. The consequence was that in a couple of years the real GDP in the US drastically decreased and the unemployment rate soared from 4.5 percent to 9.5 percent (Blanchard et al., 2011, p. 507).

A significant root cause of the financial crisis and a major trigger of the subsequent economic crisis on a global scale has been the combination of short-term funding and high leverage ratios of investment banks and hedge funds. When the housing and lending bubbles finally burst, mortgage loans' delinquency and foreclosure rates suddenly soared on a national level generating a paralysis in the credit markets and the collapse of liquidity for MBS due to the drastic write-downs. Since many financial firms, and in particular the investment banks, hedge funds, and the GSE, had very high leverage ratios and relied on short-term funding, they had insufficient capital to absorb major losses and were trapped into a liquidity crisis. The combination of limited capital availability, short-term funding, and the lack of confidence among financial institutions related to their undisclosed potential losses on mortgage loans and MBS (counterparty risk), generated a severe liquidity shortage, since many institutions reduced their exposures in the interbank markets. The withdrawal caused interbank rates and spreads, along with CDS spreads, to increase. A frozen interbank market triggered panic selling of all kind of securities on the markets in a desperate aim to scramble some liquidity. As a consequence of these triggering factors the stock market crashed causing a drastic contraction of investments and consumptions and thus spreading the financial crisis to the real economy (economic crisis).

Thus the subprime mortgage loans crisis triggered a liquidity, confidence (counterparty risk), and credit crunch crisis that, amplified by high leverage ratios, short-term funding, and poor transparency on the financial institutions' real value of losses (shadow banking), generated the panic on the markets that caused the financial crisis. The financial crisis then spread on a global scale, determining the global financial crisis and economic crisis, through massive reduction in international trade (imports and exports) and financial firms' deleveraging initiatives. From July 2008 to February 2009 US imports declined by 46 percent. Since the US is the largest importing nation (13 percent of total global imports) in the world, the consequence was a globalized slowdown (contagion) of the world economy with direct impact on foreign countries' exports, manufacturing, jobs, consumptions, and so on (Pezzuto, 2008; 2010a; Blanchard et al., 2011, p. 507).

Originally, the purpose of the two GSE – Fannie Mae and Freddie Mac – was to add liquidity to the home mortgage market and to facilitate home sales. They purchased mortgage loans and MBS on the secondary market and they insured them in order to allow banks to offer more mortgage loans at lower prices, since the risks associated with potential defaults were shifted to the GSE. These entities were offering loans and mortgage loan guarantees, and also created a market for MBS as a way of appearing to collateralize home mortgages and spreading risks through diversification. The process consisted of pooling the mortgages purchased and selling them as MBS to investors on the open market. The guarantees and pooling of mortgages (diversification of the portfolios) were aimed at reducing the risks of the MBS (Congleton, 2010, pp. 23–25).

As reported by Johnson and Kwak, the GSE relaxed their underwriting standards in order to maximize their profits and to penetrate a larger share of the sizeable subprime mortgage loans market (Johnson and Kwak, 2010a, p. 127). Friedman (2011) reports that Fannie Mae introduced a 3 percent-down mortgage in 1997, when traditionally the non-FHA mortgages were required to have a 20 percent downpayment with a LTV of 80 percent (Friedman et al., 2011, p. 4).

Since 2001, the Federal Reserve policy of low interest rates (Fed Funds) fueled the housing and securitization boom since low interest rates induced existing homeowners to refinance their mortgages, thus providing more raw material for the securitization pipeline (Pezzuto, 2008; Johnson and Kwak, 2010a, p. 146).

When the GSE became privatized, they no longer had the formal backing of the US Government, but investors continued to believe that the Government would back up the GSE in the case of a crisis, which turned out to be true in September 2008, when the Government was forced to place Fannie Mae and Freddie Mac under the conservatorship of the Federal Housing Finance Agency (FHFA) in order to save them from collapsing (Congleton, 2010, pp. 23–24).

The GSE (Fannie Mae and Freddie Mac) grew significantly a few years before the 2008 subprime meltdown, and became major players in the mortgage finance markets. Together they issued more than 70 percent of MBS in 2000 and 60 percent of MBS in 2002. These entities purchased or guaranteed 84 percent of new mortgages (Congleton, 2010, pp. 25–26). Friedman (2011) also reports that in 2000 the Department of Housing and Urban Development (HUD) increased the target for low-income mortgage lending borrowers to 50 percent and that about 40 percent of all subprime loans were guaranteed by the GSE (Friedman et al., 2011, p. 5).

Fannie and Freddie remained major players in the mortgage market even when they were on the brink of collapse into bankruptcy in 2007 and 2008. They decided to aggressively grow into the riskier mortgage market since they were very confident in their sophisticated risk management models, in a possible Government intervention in case of crisis, but because of the higher fees that were charged for these riskier mortgages (Friedman and Friedman, 2010, pp. 34–35). In 2007 they were also the financial institutions with the highest leverage ratios (Blanchard et al., 2011, p. 512).

The GSE were not allowed to purchase and hold very risky mortgages, aside from the so-called *conforming loans*. In the period 2004–2006, however, they grew rapidly in the senior (AAA-rated) tranches of MBS backed by subprime debt instead of the conforming loans (Johnson, 2010). That is, subprime loans went into the pipe at one end and came out the other end rated AAA.

As explained by Johnson and Kwak (2010a), the GSE' purchases of MBS were a mechanism that allowed the US Government to create pressure on Fannie and Freddie in order to increase lending to low-income communities. The GSE were forced to buy and securitize subprime mortgage loans, relaxing their underwriting criteria, reducing documentation requirements and lowering credit standards. Even the funding (Figure 2.5) of the mortgages has changed over the decades. Johnson and Kwak state that the Government pressure on Fannie and Freddie contributed to the housing bubble by

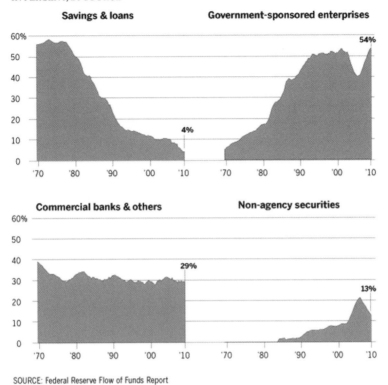

The sources of funds for mortgages changed over the decades.

IN PERCENT, BY SOURCE

SOURCE: Federal Reserve Flow of Funds Report

Figure 2.5 Funding for Mortgages

Source: Stanford University Rock Center for Corporate Governance.

increasing the amount of money flowing into the securitization pipeline (Johnson and Kwak, 2010a, p. 146). Friedman (2011) also indicates that an implicit federal guarantee allowed the GSE to borrow money more cheaply than private competitors (Friedman et al., 2011, p. 4).

Juliusz Jablecki and Mateusz Machaj (2011) report that the maturity mismatching applied by the financial firms, with short-term funding and purchase of long-term assets (MBS), of course, was not an unusual practice in the industry, whereas a significant increase in risk and an additional triggering factor of the crisis was also represented by the use of maturity mismatching in conjunction with OBSE such as a SIV. The increased risk for the SIVs was represented by the lack of depositors' insurance of a conventional bank in case of a bank run or crisis. In the years leading to the crisis the SIVs have indeed financed the purchase of MBS with short-term liabilities such as the asset-backed commercial papers (ABCPs).

The combination of the SIVs' high leverage rates and the mark-to-market valuation of the MBS generated a liquidity freeze in the interbank market, and the SIV sector to disappear when the lending and housing markets actually collapsed (Friedman et al., 2011, pp. 213–224).

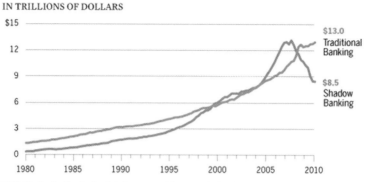

The funding available through the shadow banking system grew sharply in the 2000s, exceeding the traditional banking system in the years before the crisis.

NOTE: Shadow banking funding includes commercial paper and other short-term borrowing (bankers acceptances), repo, net securities loaned, liabilities of asset-backed securities issuers, and money market mutual fund assets.

SOURCE: Federal Reserve Flow of Funds Report

Figure 2.6   Traditional and Shadow Banking System

Source: Stanford University Rock Center for Corporate Governance.

Juliusz Jablecki and Mateusz Machaj (2011) also reported that analyzing two measures, the average CDS price for banks' debt and the spread between the three-month London Interbank Offered Rate (Libor) and repo rates, they have noticed that a liquidity squeeze occurred in 2007 in the interbank market prior to the increase in the average prices of bank-debt CDSs (default risk indicator). Thus, this analysis seems to show that banks initially stopped lending to each other, not for counterpart risk but rather because they faced liquidity problems to support the OBSE (SIVs) they had taken back onto their ledgers when they suffered a significant decline in fair value (Friedman et al., 2011, pp. 223–226).

The two GSE were at the same time dominant players in the home mortgage market and highly leveraged entities with thin capital ratios. Given such condition of limited capital, any significant decline in the value of the underlying assets would easily threaten their solvency (Barth et al. 2010, p. 100).

As previously mentioned, the US housing bubble rapidly grew when the US Federal Reserve began to lower interest rates (Fed Funds) to approximately 1 percent in the years following 2000 to spur the economy after the 2000 dot.com crisis/bust, the September 11, 2001 terrorist attack in New York, and the subsequent costs of the Iraq and Afghanistan wars (Pezzuto, 2010a, p. 100).

The aggressive monetary policy of the Federal Reserve, the rising home prices, the unrealistic expectations about future house prices, combined with the US Government's *ownership society* mission, the general perception of diminishing perceived risk and volatility, and the massive inflow of funds from emerging market economies (due to the global imbalances), all contributed to fuel the lending bubble.

Furthermore, in the years leading up to the crisis, the high consumption and low savings rates in the US were encouraged by lenders who have applied relaxed and unconventional credit conditions in their origination processes. The housing market began to grow at a very fast pace, fueled by very aggressive, convenient, and low-rate mortgage financing, which created a further stimulus for more home demand and pushed up home prices. Millions of homeowners took advantage of low mortgage rates to refinance their mortgages several times, thus dramatically increasing their level of leverage and their LTV ratios (Pezzuto, 2010a, p. 120).

The US bubble rapidly escalated in those years and housing prices peaked in 2006 (Figure 2.1). The overconfidence in rising home prices led to excessive borrowings based on unrealistic expectations on future home prices and to negative savings rates, as homeowners began to depend, more and more, on their home's price appreciation to fund their retirements (Pezzuto, 2008; 2010a, p. 120).

Faulty financial engineering innovations, derivatives, and securitizations also provided a significant contribution to the financial crisis. The subprime mortgage crisis would have remained a severe but probably more contained crisis limited to the banking industry alone if the mortgages had not been securitized and systematically sold to other financial institutions (OTD model) at inflated credit ratings (AAA), such as hedge funds, pension funds, and investment and commercial banks, with all of this activity occurring in highly unregulated (OTC markets), overleveraged, and undercapitalized shadow banking markets. Financial institutions just became too interconnected while taking unprecedented levels of risk with high leverage, opaque OTC trading of derivatives, and short-term funding (Pezzuto 2008; 2010a, pp. 121–122).

Between 1998 and 2005 the number of subprime loans that were securitized, according to First American Loan Performance, increased by 600 percent (Johnson and Kwak, 2010a, p. 132).

Lenders in the years preceding the subprime meltdown have seriously contributed to the financial crisis creating a very complex OTD lending model of bank credit, which has spread the risk of non-recourse mortgage loans out of the conventional banking industry perimeter to a much larger target of stakeholders (for example, investors, pension funds, insurance companies, and so on), and has generated strong incentives for bankers, hedge funds, and speculators to grow their subprime mortgage portfolios as much as possible and as fast as possible to take advantage of highly profitable fees (Berndt and Gupta, 2010, pp. 267–268).

The widespread use of badly controlled financial engineering innovations (for example, derivatives, securitizations, CDS, CDO, CDO-squared, MBS, RMBS, CLO) have greatly amplified the impact of the subprime lending bubble and of its risks as a result of the highly interrelated global reach of banking and financial markets. As previously stated, fueled by securitization, lenders have transformed bank credit into an OTD model, by which banks can originate loans, earn their fees, and then distribute the mortgage loans and their risks (non-recourse mortgage loans) to third-party investors. This distribution of loans occurred in a largely opaque trading environment since there was no centralized exchange or clearinghouse in which such transactions were recorded (Berndt and Gupta, 2010, pp. 271–272.)

As explained by David Mengle, Head of Research at the International Swaps and Derivatives Association, "A credit derivative is an agreement designed explicitly to shift credit risk between the parties; its value is derived from the credit performance of one or more corporations, sovereign entities, or debt obligations" (Mengle, 2007). The vast majority of credit derivatives take the form of the CDS (Mengle, 2007, p. 1). "The premium for a credit default swap is commonly known as a CDS spread and is quoted as an annual percentage in basis points of the notional amount" (Mengle, 2007, p. 13). "The spread is essentially the internal rate of return that equates the expected premium flows over the life of the swap to the expected loss if a default occurs at various dates" (Mengle, 2007, p. 4). "The protection buyer effectively takes on a short position in the credit risk of the reference entity, which thereby relieves the buyer of exposure to default. The protection seller, in contrast, takes on a long position in the credit risk of the reference entity, which is essentially the same as the default risk taken on when lending directly to the reference entity." A CDS on MBS, for example, provides protection against credit events on securitized home equity lines of credit (Mengle, 2007, p. 3). A naked CDS is a synthetic CDS since the buyer does not own the underlying debt.

CDOs are like MBS but instead of being built out of just mortgages are built of MBS and other asset-backed securities (ABS) (for example, credit cards loans, auto loans, and student loans) (Johnson and Kwak, 2010a, pp. 123–124).

CDOs provide a way for financial intermediaries to remove assets from their books and thereby reduce their regulatory capital requirements, while continuing to earn fees for originating and servicing the mortgages. Synthetic CDOs are typically used for hedging default risks that are on the balance sheets of investment banks (Buckberg, E., Dunbar, F.C., Egan, M., Schopflocher, T., Sen, A., Vogel, C., 2010, p. 14).

Synthetic CDOs are leveraged bets, meaning they may result in a potentially large payout without requiring that a large amount of funds (collateral) be set aside. Furthermore, these bets are made in the shadow banking environment (OTC). Differently from the CDOs, the synthetic CDOs do not require a vehicle to buy a pool of MBS as collateral to protect against borrowers' potential default on their credit exposures (or a specified "credit event") but just the use of a sort of insurance (CDS) on securities that already exist in the market. As reported by Johnson and Kwak (2010a), synthetic CDOs allow a bank to create CDOs based on the housing market without the trouble of buying new MBS as collateral (Johnson and Kwak, 2010a, p. 125).

Even Joe Nocera reported in the *New York Times* that prior to the creation of CDS and synthetic CDOs, there could only be as much exposure as there were mortgage bonds in existence. At the peak of the housing market bubble there were well over $1 trillion in subprime and Alt A mortgages that were securitized. For this reason, according to Nocera, Wall Street, with the introduction of synthetic CDOs, no longer needed to originate new subprime loans since subprime originators were starting to run out of higher-risk borrowers, and it was possible to continue to make an infinite number of bets on the bonds that already existed (Nocera, 2010).

The FCIC also stated in its final report (2011) that the synthetic CDOs contained no actual tranches of MBS and did not finance a single home purchase, instead in the place of real mortgage assets they contained CDS (FCIC, 2011, p. 142).

In a synthetic CDO, the issuing special purpose vehicle (SPV) enters into a number of CDS contracts where it sells protection on a reference portfolio. The premiums paid by the counterparties (buyers of protection) in these CDS provide a stream of cash flows to investors in the synthetic CDO. If credit events occur, the contingent payments reduce the cash flow to synthetic CDO investors. If large enough, credit events may result in calls on investors in the "unfunded class" of the synthetic CDO to put up cash to fund the contingent payments. (Buckberg, E., Dunbar, F.C., Egan, M., Schopflocher, T., Sen, A., Vogel, C., 2010, p.14)

Synthetic CDOs reference a portfolio of securities and are themselves securitized into notes in various tranches, with progressively higher levels of risk. The seller of the synthetic CDOs takes the "long" position, betting that the referenced securities will perform. The buyers of the synthetic CDOs takes the "short" position, betting that the referenced securities will default. The buyer receives a large payout by the seller if the referenced securities default (Nocera, 2010).

Joe Nocera indicates that with the rise of synthetic CDOs, financial firms used CDS to short subprime mortgage bonds, thus turning an already bad situation into a worse one. A similar interpretation of the events has been reported also in Lewis's book *The Big Short* in which an handful of savvy financial gurus pushed Wall Street hard to give them a way to short the market (Nocera, 2010). Hybrid CDOs are a combination of traditional and synthetic CDOs.

CDOs-squared are built combining CDOs in order to generate higher yields and supposedly lower risks (Johnson and Kwak, 2010, p. 124). It should be noted here in the aftermath of the crises that these instruments and underlying assets (CDO-squared) are almost impossible to untangle in order to determine ownership rights (Nugent, 2011).

It is also worth mentioning that the massive use of the securitization and credit derivatives in conjunction with high concentration of assets-backed securities having similar underlying assets has significantly amplified the risks of poor credit screening and monitoring of mortgage-loan originations thus generating a multiplier effect on the products' losses and ABS write-downs (Greenlaw et al., 2008).

The "myopic" perspective of many banks in the years leading up to the financial crisis allowed them to reduce as much as possible the credit risk exposure of the risky subprime mortgage loans, through the use of the securitization (credit risk transfer) and credit derivatives, but did not allow them to fully understand that they were also investors in the very complex, risky, innovative and correlated MBS, due to asymmetric information and the lack of a systemic and holistic perspective of the industry. Since every firm was probably maximizing its own risk–reward business model in isolation they lost sight of the highly correlated and interconnected similar strategies of their competitors. In other words, they probably believed they could beat the competition and be ahead of the game (Pezzuto, 2008; Franke and Krahnen, 2005; Krahnen and Wilde, 2008).

Continually rising housing prices seemed to eliminate the risks of default. Low risk perception on the markets lowered the price of CDS on MBS, thus making it easier to create CDOs and synthetic CDOs (Johnson and Kwak, 2010a, p. 124).

Investment bankers became very eager to boost growth of high interest rate subprime mortgage loans since they were crucial to creating high-yield CDOs (Johnson and Kwak, 2010a, pp. 124–126).

In 2005 a consortium of Wall Street banks created standard contracts for credit derivatives based on subprime mortgages in order to make it easier to create synthetic subprime CDOs (Johnson and Kwak, 2010a, p. 132).

These developments all confirmed the prediction of economist Hyman Minsky who had warned that speculative finance would eventually turn into Ponzi finance (Johnson and Kwak, 2010a, p. 132).

Securitization is a process in which mortgage loans are pooled and act as collateral to back the issuance of other securities. The process allows securitizers to transform a future stream of revenues into an asset base that can be used for further lending. With the sale of these structured ABS in the unregulated over-the-counter markets, banks transfer the rights to the mortgage payments, along with the related credit risk, to the investors of the securities. Thus, through securitization and sale of the structured ABS, MBS, CDOs,

CDOs-squared, and synthetic CDOs, mortgage originators and banks have transferred the high-risk subprime mortgage debt as collateral of investment grade securities to pension funds, hedge funds, investment banks portfolio, and so on, spreading the contagious risk all over the world (Pezzuto, 2008).

The purpose of the securitization process was to convert illiquid assets into liquid securities, to improve risk sharing, and to reduce banks' cost of capital (Weighted Average Cost of Capital – WACC) from the well-known Capital Asset Pricing Model (CAPM) methodology. With an AAA-rate or other investment grade securities (CDOs), funding certainly became much more convenient, even if the underlying asset of the CDOs is a risky mix of subprime mortgage loans. With the transformation from the OTH model to the OTD model, banks and mortgage originators shifted the default risk of mortgage lending to investors in exchange for high fees earned in rapid order (Pezzuto, 2008). "By creating distance between a loan's originator and the bearer of the loan's default risk, perceived securitization reduced the lenders' incentives (moral hazard) to carefully screen and monitor borrowers' risk and increased information asymmetry between the two parties" (Keys et al., 2010, p. 217).

According to Bruce I. Jacobs, co-founder and principal of Jacobs Equity Management, the extension of credit was driven by "lack of due diligence on the part of mortgage brokers, lenders, and investors; a lack of oversight by banks and credit rating agencies," and a lack of regulation and enforcement by government agencies (Jacobs, 2010, p. 225).

A huge and explosive amount of structured finance products based on subprime mortgage loans and financial engineering instruments such as RMBS, CDOs, CDOs-squared, SIVs, and CDSs were created in exchange for high fees – thus shifting the risk of mortgage lending defaults from one party to another, until many lost sight of the real risk of the underlying loans. "Mortgage-related securities were packaged, repackaged, and sold to investors all over the world" (Jacobs, 2010, p. 225; Pezzuto, 2008).

Juliusz Jablecki and Mateusz Machaj (2011) report that the total amount outstanding of privately issued MBS (with no GSE guarantees) increased five-fold between 2000 and 2007 (Friedman et al., 2011, p. 219).

Mortgage lenders pooled, repacked, and sold the risky subprime mortgage loans through off-balance-sheet SPVs established by mortgage originators or by banks in the financial markets. SPVs pooled residential mortgages to create RMBS, thus removing the loans and their risk exposures from the lenders' balance sheet. With less risk on their balance sheets, the lenders were subject to thin capital requirements and therefore had more capital for issuing more loans (Jacobs, 2010, p. 226; Pezzuto, 2008). The high fees earned by quickly amalgamating, packaging, securitizing, and reselling such paper, as a measure of the thin capitalization, yielded stellar earnings per share for the institutions and big bonuses for the bankers involved (Nugent, 2011).

"CDOs rely on a structured securitization, which takes the payments on the underlying mortgages and redirects them, along with any associated losses" (Jacobs, 2010, p. 226), to tranches of increasing seniority (equity/first loss, mezzanine next, then senior, and finally super-senior). "At the more senior level of debt (senior tranche) offers to investors the lowest yield, and it is the least risky because it has a higher credit rating and it is protected from losses by the tranches below it. Any losses are absorbed first by the bottom tranche (equity tranche)" (Pezzuto, 2008; Gibson, 2004, p. 1). Jacobs (2010) also added:

If losses totally erode that tranche, further losses are directed to the next-higher tranche, and so, the equity tranche is the riskiest, but if the underlying assets perform well, it can offer very high returns. The mezzanine tranche falls between the equity and the senior tranches in terms of both risk and return. (Jacobs, 2010, p. 226)

"Subordination shifts risk within the RMBS' structure and allows the transformation of subprime mortgages into AAA-rated senior tranches (investment grade) and BBB-rated mezzanine tranches, with a generally small, unrated equity tranche bearing the major risk" (Jacobs, 2010, p. 226). Potential buyers of RMBS include packagers of CDOs. These CDOs represent a pool of underlying assets, such as RMBS, which are carved into tranches of different risk-and-return profiles (Pezzuto, 2008).

RMBS and CDOs can be protected through the purchase of CDS sold by insurers, banks, and hedge funds. In case of default of the RMBS or CDO the risk remains with the CDS seller in exchange for a negotiated premium. CDSs are largely unregulated derivatives. Thus the risk is not eliminated but only shifted from one party to the next one. However, with CDS there is no mandated, regulated capital reserve requirement as with regulated insurance. The securitization and the OTD process should have protected lenders and other participants in the process to reduce the risk of the fast-growing non-recourse subprime mortgages loan portfolios through diversification, and the massive use of CDSs (imaginary insurance). In fact, had CDSs had a capital reserve requirement, like a real insurance (capital reserve base), it would have mitigated some of the risk. In reality the risk-reducing benefits of diversification are limited when the underlying risks are not specific but instead systemic, such as the risk of default resulting from housing price declines, borrowers' loss of jobs, and massive adverse selection with limited or no credit screening (Jacobs, 2010, pp. 226–228; Pezzuto, 2008).

It is typically the securitizer who issues a variety of securities, or tranches. These tranches of securities are based on the cash flows from one pool of mortgages. In general, "The various tranches of securities are ordered in terms of priority of payments, as previously indicated depending on the seniority (equity/first loss, mezzanine, senior, super-senior), with the claims of the most senior tranches of securities being paid in full before the next tranche receives any payment" (Kolb, 2010, p. 213).

"This gives rise to a waterfall of cash spilling down into the empty bucket held out by the senior tranche" (Kolb, 2010, p. 213). "When the bucket of the most senior tranche is completely filled"/honored (Kolb, 2010, p. 213), "the excess cash spills to the next most senior tranche, and so on, until either the cash flows are exhausted or until even the bucket of the most junior tranche is filled"/honored (Kolb, 2010, p. 213).

Cash-based CDOs are fully funded, meaning that investors pay in advance for their bonds. The money is used, in turn, to purchase the securities that back the structure. Synthetic CDOs can have funded and unfunded classes (Buckberg, E., Dunbar, F.C., Egan, M., Schopflocher, T., Sen, A., Vogel, C., 2010, p.15).

Michael S. Gibson in his paper (2004) "Understanding the Risk of Synthetic CDOs" reported the following analysis:

Synthetic CDO tranches can also be either "funded" or "unfunded." If a tranche is funded, the CDO investor pays the notional amount of the tranche at the beginning of the deal and any defaults cause a write-down of principal. Throughout the deal, the investors are entitled to cash flows (LIBOR plus a spread that reflects the riskiness of the tranche) subject to availability.

The investor's funds are put into a collateral account and invested in low-risk securities (government or AAA-rated debt). (Gibson, 2004, p. 3) Assuming no (or limited) credit events, they will continue to receive payments of principal and interest (as derived from premiums from the buyers of protection). (Buckberg, E., Dunbar, F.C., Egan, M., Schopflocher, T., Sen, A., Vogel, C., 2010, p.15)

"Unfunded" tranches (typically the super-senior tranches) are similar to swaps. No money changes hands at the beginning of the deal. The investor receives a spread and pays when defaults in the reference portfolio affect the investor's tranche (after any subordinate tranches have been eaten away by previous defaults). Because unfunded tranches rely on the investor's future ability and willingness to pay into CDO, they create counterparty credit risk that must be managed (Gibson, 2004, p. 3).

The FCIC also explains in its final report (2011) that the funded "long" investors is the one that pays cash to purchase actual securities issued by the CDO; unfunded "long" investors are instead those who enter into a swap with the CDO making money if the reference securities perform. The "short" investors buys the CDS on the reference securities, making money if the securities fail (FCIC, 2011, p. 142).

Thus, while funded investors receive interest if the reference securities perform, they can lose all their investment if the reference securities default. Unfunded investors, which are highest in the payment waterfall (cash flow waterfall and credit tranching), receive premium-like payments from the CDO as long as the reference securities perform but would have to pay if the reference securities deteriorate beyond a certain point and if the CDO does not have sufficient funds to pay the short investors. The short investors buys the CDS from the CDO and pays the premiums (FCIC, 2011, p. 142).

Michael S. Gibson (2004) reports in the conclusion of his 2004 paper the following statements:

Synthetic CDOs are popular vehicles for transferring the credit risk of a portfolio of assets ... CDO tranches and other innovative credit products, such as single-tranche CDOs and first-to-default basket swaps, are sensitive to the correlation of defaults among the credits in the reference portfolio ... Investors in mezzanine CDO tranches are taking on leveraged exposures to the underlying credit risk of the reference portfolio. A tranche's credit rating does not convey all aspects of the tranche's risk. If investors disclose the notional amounts of their portfolio, broken down by credit rating, the leveraged nature of a mezzanine tranche's risk exposure would not be obvious. (Gibson, 2004, pp. 25–26)

In the standard process the securitizer performs due diligence on the loans to ensure that they are as described and worth the price being demanded. But evidently, based on what happened in the financial crisis, the due diligence quite frequently has not been done rigorously as financial incentives, conflicts of interest, and short-term profitability goals have probably altered the due diligence activities (Kolb, 2010, pp. 213–214). In fact, there is evidence that Goldman Sachs was working with clients to short such instruments in the market in the belief they would go down in value while at the same time it was selling such instruments to its other clients (Nugent, 2011).

With this process mortgage originators and banks have actually transformed risky subprime mortgages into AAA-rated or other investment grade securities (with the assistance of the credit rating agencies) and sold them to pension funds and other institutions, also receiving the seal of approval of the respective rating agencies (even though their mortgage loans risk models were based on historical data of low volatility periods, tighter underwriting criteria, limited product innovation, and lower concentration in the industry of subprime borrowers), earning unprecedented fees, and leading the entire financial system to misjudge and misprice the risk of these *miraculous* or probably more properly called *toxic assets* (Stiglitz, 2010, p. 7; Pezzuto, 2008).

Negligence and/or irresponsible behavior of the rating agencies might have caused them to underestimate the systemic risk of such practices, but apparently it did not matter, since they were doing their job of maximizing their sales and profits. Thus, the rapid increase in delinquency rates, the unfit historical data of their statistical models, the booming house prices and declining LTV ratio of mortgages, and many other parameters were not taken into account by the rating agencies while assessing subprime mortgages risk (Pezzuto, 2008; 2010a; Friedman, 2011, pp. 11–13).

As clearly explained by John B. Taylor (2009) and myself (2008), the crisis that led to the devastating global financial crisis was not just the result of a short-term liquidity shortage, of lack of risk management skills and tools, but rather the crisis of trust and confidence among banks and in the banks' own assets as subprime borrowers were no longer able to pay back any type of debt when the whole "house of cards" and its damaged collateral finally collapsed (Taylor, 2009; Pezzuto, 2008).

The rating agencies played a critical role in the subprime crisis, granting generous ratings for the high-risk subprime mortgage loans for lucrative incentives and relying mainly on FICO scores, with limited attention to other indicators (that is, macroeconomic and industry-wide systemic risk perspective). The entire securities market relies almost entirely (90 percent of the credit rating business) on ratings provided by three organizations such as Standard and Poor's, Moody's, and Fitch, that also work as consultant and advisor for their bank clients (Pezzuto, 2008).

Evidence of this assumption is indicated in the FCIC final report (2011). In the report the FCIC indicates that 83 percent of mortgage securities rated AAA by Moody's in 2006 were then downgraded by the same rating agency in the same year (FCIC, 2011, p. xxv). This sudden downgrading process also contributed to generated panic in the market (Lang, 2012, personal communication).

Furthermore, it is quite interesting to note that on September 6, 2008 when Fannie Mae and Freddy Mac requested a $200 billion rescue plan, they were still rated AAA.

The same occurred with Lehman Brothers, since a few hours after its bankruptcy announcement on September 14, 2008, it was still rated as an investment grade organization (Pezzuto, 2008).

Furthermore, a number of risk managers also underestimated (or were encouraged to overlook) the buildup of risk due to complicated cross-correlations between different asset classes (tranches) and the complexity of the structured products (that is, CDOs) in their portfolios. They have also improperly monitored their derivatives not taking into account the market-to-market value (fair-value accounting practice) of these assets, their liquidity, and thus making confusion between the banking book and trading book. They also relied significantly on the rating agencies' assessment of MBS which had inflated ratings, thus those assets were mispriced (*The Economist*, 2008).

Overleveraged Financial Institutions in the Shadow Banking Sector

In the years preceding the financial crisis, the explosive growth of subprime mortgage lending in conjunction with the exponential growth of securitizations and complex derivatives and financial engineering products (derivatives), traded in an opaque under-regulated (OTC) and undercapitalized manner, and in limitedly controlled shadow banking markets, created perverse and flawed incentives and conflicts of interest for all participants (borrowers, mortgage brokers, mortgage originator, mortgage appraiser, risk managers, securitizers, rating agencies, investors) in the OTD model of mortgage production (Kolb, 2010, pp. 214–215).

The term "shadow banking system" was used by Friedrich August von Hayek (1935) to refer to the credit growth by unregulated institutions. In the book *Prices and Production*, Hayek pointed out that the "shadow banking system" was "other forms of media of exchange which occasionally or permanently do the service of money" (Tian, 2010, p. 3).

In 2008, the failure of the financial markets indicated the imperfection of the credit risk models since asset prices can dramatically deviate from their fundamentals during liquidity, confidence, and solvency crises, even though they do not reflect the asset's losses (Tian, 2010, pp. 3–4; Gorton, 2009). Gorton described the credit risk models' failure as "Slapped in the Face by the Invisible Hand" (Gorton, 2009, pp. 42–43).

Tian (2009), mentioning in his paper "Shadow Banking System, Derivatives, and Liquidity Risks" the state-of-the-art credit risk management techniques I have reported in my paper written on October 7, 2008, indicates that the flawed risk models cannot fully explain the risks that led to the financial crisis. His analysis seems to confirm, instead, that a combination of other triggering factors have caused the financial meltdown such as the financial firms' failure to proactively recognize systemic risks related to their interdependent positions, their moral hazard (failure in risk management and corporate governance as a result of the too-big-to-fail doctrine), the massive expansion of the so-called shadow banking sector, and the panic reaction generated by the liquidity and confidence crises (Pezzuto, 2008; Tian, 2010, p. 4; Kirman, 2010, pp. 502–505).

Some of the state-of-the art credit risk management techniques at the time of the 2007–2009 financial crisis are reported in my paper (2008) and include:

> *Timely and systematic use of early warning indicators (KPIs) sourced from credit scoring systems (application and behavioral scoring from FICO, NextGen, VantageScore, and the CE Score), bureau scores (from credit bureaus like Equifax, Experian, and TransUnion), portfolio aging and vintage analyses, delinquency/roll rates/flow rates analyses (transition matrices), prediction of Loss Given Defaults, internal ratings-based approaches, external rating agencies' models, classified accounts for corporate exposures, Basel II models, CreditMetrics, Credit Portfolio View, CreditRisk+, Merton OPM/KMV Moody's, Reduced Form KPMG/Kamkura, VaR, Algorithmics models, and so on. (Pezzuto, 2008)*

Figures 2.7 to 2.9 describe the OTD process and some financial engineering products involved in the 2007–2009 financial crisis.

Financial institutions packaged subprime, Alt-A and other mortgages into securities. As long as the housing market continued to boom, these securities would perform. But when the economy faltered and the mortgages defaulted, lower-rated tranches were left worthless.

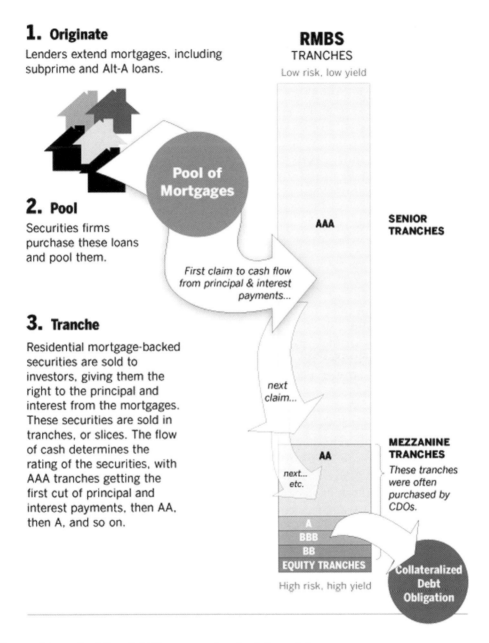

1. Originate

Lenders extend mortgages, including subprime and Alt-A loans.

2. Pool

Securities firms purchase these loans and pool them.

3. Tranche

Residential mortgage-backed securities are sold to investors, giving them the right to the principal and interest from the mortgages. These securities are sold in tranches, or slices. The flow of cash determines the rating of the securities, with AAA tranches getting the first cut of principal and interest payments, then AA, then A, and so on.

RMBS
TRANCHES
Low risk, low yield

AAA

First claim to cash flow from principal & interest payments...

next claim...

AA

next... etc.

A
BBB
BB
EQUITY TRANCHES
High risk, high yield

SENIOR TRANCHES

MEZZANINE TRANCHES
These tranches were often purchased by CDOs.

Collateralized Debt Obligation

Figure 2.7   Residential Mortgage-backed Securities

Source: Stanford University Rock Center for Corporate Governance.

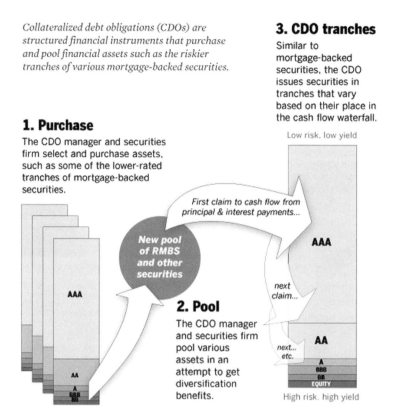

Figure 2.8   Collateralized Debt Obligations

Source: Stanford University Rock Center for Corporate Governance.

As indicated by Peter L. Swan in "The Global Crisis and Its Origins", banks could profit by making loans that they knew would never be repaid so long as they could either sell them to bigger fools or implicitly hide them from public view by selling them to themselves through SPVs (Swan, 2010, p. 51). These vehicles are typically set up by banks and other financial institutions to benefit from off-balance-sheet financing practices.

This same concept was also reported by Joseph E. Stiglitz in his book *Freefall. America, Free Markets, and the Sinking of the World Economy* (Stiglitz, 2010, p. 14), and by myself in my 2008 SMC University Paper titled, "Miraculous Financial Engineering or Toxic Finance? The Genesis of the US Subprime Mortgage Loans Crisis and its Consequences on the Global Financial Markets and Real Economy" (Pezzuto, 2008).

As a consequence of the rapid growth of the banks, hedge funds, and investment banks' assets due to the housing and credit bubbles, many of the firms in the industry began to pay very generous compensation packages to their senior executives. These payments were much higher than in other industries and served as a re-enforcement for the behavior that led to these practices in the first instance.

As reported by the FCIC (2011), "the compensation system has been strongly influenced by an environment of cheap money, intense competition, light regulation, and overleveraged investment banks, which rewarded the investment bankers' short-term profit orientation" (FCIC, 2011, p. xix).

Synthetic CDOs, such as Goldman Sachs's Abacus 2004-1 deal, were complex paper transactions involving credit default swaps.

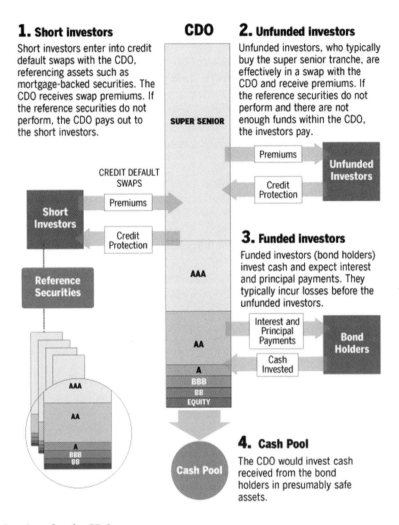

1. Short investors

Short investors enter into credit default swaps with the CDO, referencing assets such as mortgage-backed securities. The CDO receives swap premiums. If the reference securities do not perform, the CDO pays out to the short investors.

CDO

2. Unfunded investors

Unfunded investors, who typically buy the super senior tranche, are effectively in a swap with the CDO and receive premiums. If the reference securities do not perform and there are not enough funds within the CDO, the investors pay.

3. Funded investors

Funded investors (bond holders) invest cash and expect interest and principal payments. They typically incur losses before the unfunded investors.

4. Cash Pool

The CDO would invest cash received from the bond holders in presumably safe assets.

Figure 2.9   Synthetic CDO

Source: Stanford University Rock Center for Corporate Governance.

The high level of leverage of many financial institutions was often "hidden in derivative positions in off-balance sheet entities, thus the lack of transparency and window-dressing techniques of the financial reports" have been used to present to the investing public a different picture of the real level and quality (risk) of debt of these institutions. The kings of debt as indicated by the FCIC (2011) were Fannie Mae and Freddie Mac (FCIC, 2011, p. xx).

The Rapid Expansion of Perverse Remuneration Incentives in the Financial Sector

In 2007, at the peak of the financial crisis, while their organizations were on the brink of collapse due to the huge exposure to toxic subprime mortgage loans, senior executives of leading global banks and other financial institutions were rewarding themselves with unprecedented compensation packages (Figure 2.10). John Thain, CEO of Merrill Lynch, received $84 million; Lloyd Blackfein, CEO at Goldman Sachs, received $68.5 million; John Mack of Morgan Stanley received $41 million; Richard Fuld, CEO of Lehman Brothers, and James Dimon, CEO of JPMorgan Chase and Co., received about $34 million and $28 million, respectively. During 2004–2008, as a result of its high leverage ratio, Lehman's CEO received more than $269 million in salary and bonuses (FCIC, 2011, p. 63).

In 2007, Wall Street paid workers in New York roughly $33 billion in year-end bonuses alone and the total compensation for the major US banks and securities firms was estimated at $137 billion. The dangers of the new pay structure created incentives for it to continue in the same pattern. As former Citigroup CEO Sandy Weill told the FCIC:

> I think if you look at the results of what happened on Wall Street, well, this one's doing it, so how can I not do it, if I don't do it, then the people are going to leave my place and go somewhere else. Managing risk became less of an important function in a broad base of companies I would guess. (FCIC, 2011, pp. 63–64)

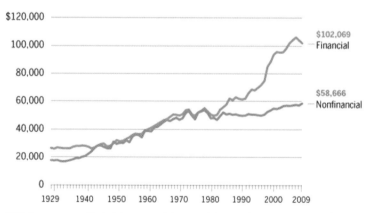

Compensation in the financial sector outstripped pay elsewhere, a pattern not seen since the years before the Great Depression.

ANNUAL AVERAGE, IN 2009 DOLLARS

NOTE: Average compensation includes wages, salaries, commissions, tips, bonuses, and payments for government insurance and pension programs. Nonfinancial sector is all domestic employees except those in finance and insurance.

SOURCES: Bureau of Economic Analysis, Bureau of Labor Statistics, CPI-Urban, FCIC calculations

Figure 2.10 Compensation in Financial and Non-financial Sectors

Source: Stanford University Rock Center for Corporate Governance.

Jarsulic (2010) reports that in 2006 the ten largest originators in terms of market share (HSBC, 8.8 percent, New Century Financial, 8.6 percent, Countrywide, 6.8 percent, CitiGroup, 6.3 percent, WMC Mortgage, 5.5 percent, Freemont, 5.4 percent, Ameriquest Mortgage, 4.9 percent, Option One, 4.8 percent, Wells Fargo, 4.7 percent, and First Franklin, 4.6 percent) made more than 60 percent of the subprime loans and most of the profits/executive compensation over the latter years (Jarsulic, 2010, p. 23).

These same organizations were, by and large, the same major institutions that directly or indirectly controlled the highly concentrated market of subprime MBS. Thus they were both major mortgage originators (60 percent of total market) and also the major issuers of subprime MBS (63.3 percent of the total market) (Jarsulic, 2010, pp. 23–24).

The tendency of corporate management in the period preceding the financial crisis was to cling to the bubble and hope for the best while trying to maximize short-term profits. As Richard A. Posner indicated:

For them, every day they were in business was like a lottery since they were making a lot of money. They also knew that when the bubble would eventually burst they would be well off since they had negotiated a very generous severance package (golden parachute) with their board of directors. Furthermore, even the limited liability of their companies was for them a positive factor too, since neither the executives heavily invested in their companies' stock, nor any other shareholder would be personally liable for the company's losses should it go broke. (Posner, 2009, pp. 93–94)

Stiglitz (2010) added:

America's financial markets have failed to perform their essential societal functions of managing risk, allocating capital, and mobilizing savings, while keeping transaction costs low. (Stiglitz, 2010, p. 7)

Johnson and Kwak (2010a) report that the public was furious in 2009 when American International Group (AIG) was rescued by commitments of up to $180 billion in taxpayers' money since AIG executives and traders had been granted $165 million in bonuses after the company had nearly gone bankrupt in September 2008 (Johnson and Kwak, 2010a, p. 3).

As Johnson and Kwak (2010a) wrote: "… by 1998, it was part of the worldview of the Washington elite that what was good for Wall Street was good for America" (Johnson and Kwak, 2010a, p. 10). They go even further on this concept, stating:

… the Wall Street banks are the new American oligarchy; a group that gains power because of its economic power, and then uses that power for its own benefit. Runaway profits and bonuses in the financial sector were transmitted into political power through campaign contributions and the attraction of the revolving door. (Johnson and Kwak, 2010a, p. 6)

The Beginning of the End of the "Miraculous" Financial Engineering Era

In this complex context, as the housing lending market ramped up, mortgage quality fell drastically because of poor credit origination standards, ineffective risk assessment, and massive adverse selection of unqualified applicants and extreme compensation for inappropriate acts. In the 2000s approximately 80 percent of US mortgages issued to subprime borrowers were Adjustable-Rate Mortgages (ARM). In June 2004, as the Federal Reserve began to increase short-term interest rates and the index for many ARM, delinquency, and default mortgage rates soared, interest rates rose up to 5.25 percent in 2006 from approximately 1 percent in 2003 (Pezzuto, 2010a, p. 121).

This event has had a significant impact on the subprime borrowers' delinquency and default rates since a significant number of subprime mortgages had LTV ratios of up to 100 percent and thus they were particularly sensitive to housing prices (Buckberg et al. 2010, p.11).

When US house prices began to decline in norminal terms at a rate of 18 percent during the bust period (Cohen et al., 2012), ARM began to set at higher rates, and refinancing became more difficult.

The housing bubble started to deflate, causing poor households across the US to struggle to keep up with their payments. The decreases in home prices resulted in many owners finding themselves in a position of negative equity (under water). The dramatic rise in mortgage delinquencies and foreclosures in the US triggered borrowers' defaults, bankruptcies, and repossessions, yet the pace of lending did not slow (Pezzuto, 2010a, p. 121).

In 2006 and 2007 the sudden and apparently unexpected deterioration of the subprime mortgage loan portfolios, the rapid increase in mortgage delinquency rates and foreclosures, and the consequent RMBS, CDOs and CDS crises generated in the financial markets a sense of panic among investors about the solvency of their securities and their underlying assets (subprime mortgage loans) (Pezzuto, 2008).

In the middle of October 2008, the lack of reassurance to investors and wholesale bankers, who were scrambling for liquidity, brought the financial system to the brink of collapse. The signs of the dramatic credit and liquidity crisis were quite evident in those days when the CDS and the Interbank rates (such as, Libor, Euribor, overnight rates, and so on) reached very high rates, and these rates remained very high for a while, "regardless of the massive central banks' cash injections, interest rates reductions, and government bail-out deal agreements, protections from bankruptcies, commercial markets' coverage, and bank nationalizations" (Pezzuto, 2008).

"With the collapse of the first banks and hedge funds in 2007, the rising number of foreclosures helped speed up the decline in housing prices as the number of subprime mortgage defaults began to increase" (Pezzuto, 2008).

"As many CDO products and other derivatives were held on a mark-to-market basis (a fair value accounting rule that puts a current market price on any financial instrument held and traded), the paralysis in the credit markets and the collapse of liquidity in these products led to dramatic write-downs in 2007 (sudden rise of collateral haircuts taken on many classes of structured securities)" (Pezzuto, 2008, 2010a, pp. 119–123; Gorton, 2009, p. 33).

Several billions of dollars of CDOs, RMBS, ABS, CDSs and other derivatives were mainly traded in opaque (asymmetric information), unregulated, undercapitalized OTC markets, with reduced regulatory oversight. This situation led banks, hedge funds, and investment firms to become suspicious of: (1) one another's undisclosed credit losses (related to the defaults of the subprime mortgage loans used as collateral to the CDOs and other securities and to the solvency of counterparties); (2) the huge amount of off-balance-sheet debt (SPVs); and (3) the limited capital requirements of the financial institutions involved in these OTC operations. Hence, such institutions preferred to reduce their exposures in the interbank and shadow banking markets, thus creating a liquidity crisis in the securitization, money, and capital markets (Pezzuto, 2010a, pp. 119–123).

This withdrawal caused interbank interest rates and spreads, along with credit CDS spreads to increase. Furthermore, as the securitization market froze, investors and wholesale bankers experienced panic and started selling all kinds of distressed securities (stock and bonds) to scramble and realize some liquidity. This frenzy was exacerbated by the need to meet margin calls because of declining underlying values (Nugent, 2011). Thus panic sales spread from subprime assets to completely unrelated asset classes (Gorton, 2009, p. 31). Funding problems thus led to the vicious circle of fire sales (fire sales externalities and debt overhang problem) and depressed prices. A liquidity shortage and tightened credit conditions for consumers and businesses quickly ensued (Pezzuto, 2010a, pp. 119–123; Kashyap, 2010, pp. 10–11).

Fostel and Geneakoplos (2008) argue that many banks were not prepared to declare a loss in the principal associated with a loan since then they would have been obliged to write their assets down and thus advertise their potential insolvency. This increased the uncertainty in the interbank market. But, inevitably it became apparent that some banks and insurance companies were indeed, insolvent (Fostel and Geneakoplos, 2008, pp. 1211–1244).

The degree of uncertainty in the financial markets triggered by the banks' write-downs and the fear of potential undisclosed losses (due to the financial firms' moral hazard), the high leverage ratios, and the freeze in the interbank markets, with consequent liquidity problems, all contributed to the contagion of the crisis, from a relatively small segment of the market to the others. Thus, panic selling led to the crash of the stock markets, the credit crunch (due to reduction in regulatory capital caused by the market-to-market accounting rule – Financial Accounting Standards Board 115 or FASB 115) and the confidence crisis led to the deleveraging of financial institutions, the recessionary trends in the real economy, and the collapse of the securitizations and ABS activities.

The combination of highly interconnected financial institutions, and complex, innovative, and exotic financial products traded in opaque (OTD) markets, with the risk transferred to investors unable to correctly assess the real value of their assets, triggered a panic reaction (irrational behavior) in the final stage of the boom–bust pattern that generated the meltdown since institutions were unprepared for such event, not having incorporated such assumptions in their risk management models. Furthermore, as reported by Friedman (2011), the world's commercial banks had in their portfolios approximately half of all investments in private-label MBS, and more than $852 billion in agency MBS (GSE' MBS) thus, when the value of these securities collapsed these commercial banks generated a massive credit crunch on the "real economy" (Friedman et al., 2011, p. 21).

Banks, hedge funds, and investment firms were also victims of this crisis, since they (as institutional investors) have purchased a large number of these toxic assets. Many of them have made massive purchases of securitized subprime mortgage loans (as CDOs and other derivatives) from overleveraged off-balance entities such as SPVs, SIVs – a special-purpose entity that raises money by issuing commercial paper and invests it in long-term high-yielding assets), and Conduit, with reduced capital requirements and regulatory oversight. SIVs enabled banks to take on more risks in structured securities with the same amount of capital since they are technically not part of the bank. Their assets (off-balance-sheet) are not counted for determining capital requirements (Johnson and Kwak, 2010a, pp. 129–132).

According to Jarsulic (2010), in 2007 there were an estimated $1.4 trillion in Conduit securities and about $400 billion in SIV securities outstanding. This means that the combined Conduit and SIV sector in 2007 was about 20 percent of the size of the entire US commercial banking sector (Jarsulic, 2010, pp. 63–64).

The leverage that for a number of years was a positive multiplier of their profits suddenly became a negative multiplier, generating an exponential driver of losses. The collapse of the securitization market and the attempts of the banks to rescue the SIVs, SPVs, and Conduits caused them to accrue major losses. The difficulties at Conduits and SIVs had a dramatic effect on the size of the ABCP market. Investors under pressure and panic, scared by the lack of transparency of the balance sheet activities of major institutions, operating in the shadow banking environment, in an attempt to seek liquidity, were selling all kinds of securities they possessed, and in particular asset-backed commercial papers – thus the stock market plummeted. By then the CDS market had also been hit by severe losses as investors sought cover for the potential default risks of the CDOs and other derivatives that used subprime mortgage loans as collateral. The major players in the CDS industry are banks, hedge funds and insurance companies (Jarsulic, 2010, pp. 55–65).

As explained by Yale and NBER Economist Gary Gorton (2009), a systemic event, (banking panic) triggered the financial crisis in August 2007. As described in Gorton's own words: "Unlike the historical banking panics of the 19th and early 20th centuries, the current banking panic is a wholesale panic, not a retail panic ... The current panic involved financial firms 'running' on other financial firms by not renewing sale and repurchase agreements (repo) or increasing the repo margin ('haircut'), forcing massive deleveraging, and resulting in the banking system being insolvent." At the heart of the crisis, according to Gorton, there was the shadow banking system, with its complexity and lack of transparency. Gorton recommends the introduction of new regulation to make the shadow banking system less vulnerable to panic (Gorton, 2009, abstract).

Apparently the size, opacity, complexity, and interconnectedness of the shadow banking system and its short-term funding (repo), and the high leveraged business model, determined a sort of explosive mix in conjunction with the housing market and lending boom-bust scenario. In spite of the advanced financial, risk, and liquidity management models and best practices used by leading financial firms, big industry players got caught off guard to anticipate early warnings of a systemic risk.

The financial crisis, according to John B. Taylor (2009), reached an acute phase on August 9 and 10, 2007 when the money markets' interest rose dramatically as signaled by the sudden jump of the Libor–OIS spread (Figure 2.11). John B. Taylor and John Williams called this event "A Black Swan in the Money Markets" (Taylor, 2009, pp. 13–14).

There was another severe impact of the contagion resulting from the credit crisis to the financial markets and the commercial banks around the world, as the ABCP market began to shrink (Figure 2.12), and commercial banks became less willing to lend to each other. This unwillingness is clearly reflected in the TED spread. The TED spread is a measure of credit risk for interbank lending. The TED spread was originally calculated as the difference

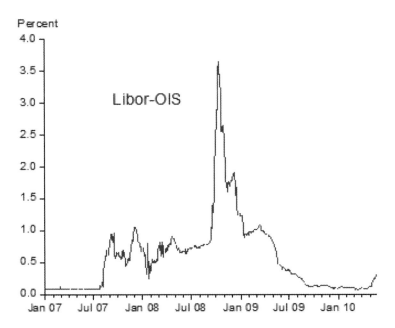

Figure 2.11 The Libor–OIS Spread

Source: Original figure and permission to reproduce it granted by John B. Taylor.

At the onset of the crisis in summer 2007, asset-backed commercial paper outstanding dropped as concerns about asset quality quickly spread. By the end of 2007, the amount outstanding had dropped nearly $400 billion.

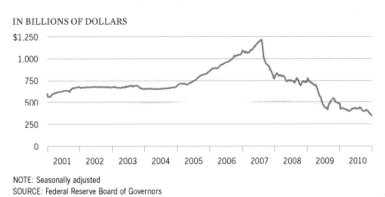

NOTE: Seasonally adjusted
SOURCE: Federal Reserve Board of Governors

Figure 2.12 Asset-backed Commercial Paper Outstanding

Source: Stanford University Rock Center for Corporate Governance.

between interest rates on three-month T-bills and three-month Eurodollar contracts with identical expiration months. The acronym is derived from the word "Treasuries" and the ticker symbol for Eurodollars, which is ED. Today, the TED spread is calculated as the difference between interest rates on three-month T-bills and three-month Libor. A higher spread indicates that banks perceive each other as riskier counterparts. The value of the TED spread during the subprime mortgage crisis leapt dramatically reaching a value ranging between 150–200 basis points, with a peak in excess of 300 basis points in September 2008, from a value in 2006 ranging between 25 to 60 basis points (Jarsulic, 2010, pp. 65–66; Investing Answers, 2011).

Financial institutions preferred to replace traditional insurance contracts with such instruments (CDS), which are traded in shadow banking markets, since they provide credit default risk coverage but also additional significant benefits such as less costly reserves, limited regulatory oversight, and lower transparency and disclosure obligations. By naming such instruments something different from insurance contracts, they thought they would simultaneously achieve the objective of obtaining credit default risk insurance while also escaping tighter regulatory requirements on reserves and transparency. This financial engineering architecture, unfortunately, did not work since in their risk models these institutions did not properly contemplate the likely occurrence of a systemic lending boom–bust scenario, the probability of falling house prices, the risk of reckless subprime underwriting practices with poor credit screening and no borrowers' documentation, or they simply did not care about the possible consequences driven by obsessive greed, short-term goals, and by the certainty that the government would eventually bail them out in case of crisis as a guarantor of last resort.

There had also been, in the years of the credit bubble, speculation, orchestrated by investment banks and hedge funds, who had been heavily involved in short-selling and other operations to generate profit at the expense of unaware investors and pension/retirement funds.

The losses were amplified by the exponential growth in the financial firms' trading activities of unregulated derivatives, short-term repo lending (Figure 2.13), and limited oversight in the shadow banking markets.

It is very likely that borrowers took out mortgages that they never had the capacity or intention to pay. Equally the credit policy and credit approval/underwriting processes which represents the core business practices and competence of lenders were not prudently applied either.

As a consequence of this critical situation, when the financial meltdown caused the financial market to be on the brink of collapse and the economy plunged into deep recession, central banks had to inject massive quantities of cash into money markets and reduced interest rates in an attempt to shore up banks in order to restore confidence within the financial system (conventional monetary policy). When reducing interest rates alone was no longer sufficient to stabilize the financial system and to stimulate economic recovery, central banks adopted even more aggressive and unconventional policies such as massive series of quantitative easing. Quantitative easing increases the money supply by flooding financial institutions with capital, through the purchase of financial institutions' assets, in an effort to promote increased lending and liquidity. Governments implemented bail-out agreements, issued protections from bankruptcies, and organized recapitalizations and bank nationalizations to rescue banks from disastrous bankruptcies to avoid an even worse economic recession. Governments also

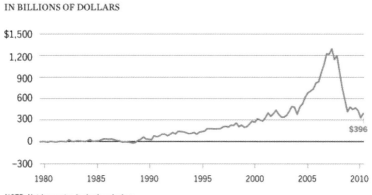

Broker-dealers' use of repo borrowing rose sharply before the crisis.

IN BILLIONS OF DOLLARS

NOTE: Net borrowing by broker-dealers.
SOURCE: Federal Reserve Flow of Funds Report

Figure 2.13 Repo Borrowing

Source: Stanford University Rock Center for Corporate Governance.

supported the recovery from the crisis through aggressive fiscal policies targeted to sustain consumer spending and consumer and business investments. These policies included increasing government budget spending and investments, and automatic stabilizers designed to increase unemployment and welfare benefits and adjusting tax rates. The inevitable consequence of all these fiscal policies, including also the bail-out of banks, has been the huge increase of sovereign debts in many countries affected by the global financial crisis, such as those that have replicated the US housing and mortgage lending bubble–bust scenarios and those countries that before the crisis had low GDP growth rates, very high sovereign debts, current account imbalances, low productivity rates, inefficient and bureaucratic public sectors, unsustainable welfare systems, high levels of bribery and corruption, high tax evasion, and high cost of the political establishment (Pezzuto, 2008).

In the US, among the emergency measures of the central bank introduced at the beginning of the crisis to improve banks' access to Fed's borrowings, there was the Term Auction Facility (TAF). This new facility introduced in December 2007 allowed banks to avoid going to the discount window and to bid directly for funds from the Fed. However, the goal of this intervention, despite an initial benefit to reduce the spread in the money markets, did not prove to work since the spread rose again since it was not addressing the right issues (counterparty risk) (Taylor, 2009, pp. 17–18).

Since the previous measure did not seem to produce the expected result, in April 2008 the Fed undertook a sharp reduction of the Federal Funds rate to 2 percent, thus allowing the re-setting of the adjustable mortgage rates. Since the credit crunch worsened, along with the related perception of counterparty risk, a number of massive rescue plans have been introduced to avoid the risk of a potential depression. These interventions include: the Troubled Asset Relief Program (TARP), guarantees by the Federal Deposit Insurance Corporation (FDIC), and the Federal Reserve support for the commercial papers (Taylor, 2009, pp. 23–24).

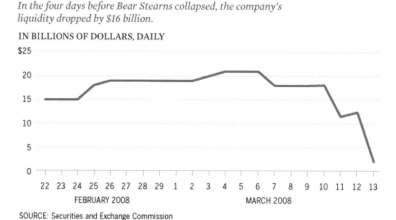

In the four days before Bear Stearns collapsed, the company's liquidity dropped by $16 billion.

IN BILLIONS OF DOLLARS, DAILY

SOURCE: Securities and Exchange Commission

Figure 2.14 Bear Stearns Liquidity

Source: Stanford University Rock Center for Corporate Governance.

According to John B. Taylor (2009) the problem of uncertainty about the procedures and criteria (lack of clarity of policy makers' decisions) for government intervention to prevent the meltdown of the financial institutions, which was perceived since the time of the Bear Stearns intervention (Figure 2.14), has actually driven up interbank spreads and CDS spreads, worsening the confidence in the financial markets (Taylor, 2009, pp. 25–26).

On October 3, 2008, the Government launched The Troubled Asset Relief Program rescue package commonly referred to as TARP, proposed by Henry Paulson, US Secretary of the Treasury to help banks and other companies strongly affected by the crisis with potential systemic risk (the program was intended to purchase assets and equity from financial institutions to strengthen the financial sector). Major beneficiaries of TARP funds ($700 billion bail-out) include: Citigroup, Bank of America, AIG, JPMorgan Chase and Co., Wells Fargo, GMAC Financial Services, Goldman Sachs, Morgan Stanley, and others).

"In 2010, 157 banks were closed or taken over by the Federal Deposit Insurance Corporation (FDIC) surpassing" the number affected in 2009 and the previous years. 2010 represents the year with the "highest number of bank failures since 1992" (FDIC, 2011; Dough Roller, 2011). Some banks probably took advantage of the insurance protection provided by the FDIC to make riskier loans since they shifted the risk of default from the banks to the FDIC (Posner, 2009, pp. 43–44).

Since the beginning of the financial crisis a large number of banks, mortgage originators, hedge funds, and other financial institutions went bankrupt or filed for bankruptcy protection such as: "Douglass National Bank, Hume Bank, First Integrity Bank, IndyMac, Silver State Bank, Lehman Brothers, Washington Mutual, and others" (FDIC, 2011; Dough Roller, 2011).

Lehman Brothers filed for Chapter 11 bankruptcy protection on September 15, 2008 mainly due to the eroding confidence in the valuation of its assets by the repo counterparties who decided to drain their liquidity supply (for example, Citigroup, JPMorgan Chase and Co.) thus leaving the investment bank insolvent (US Bankruptcy Court Southern District of New York – Examiner's report, 2010, pp. 2–14).

Lehman was an investment bank with annual revenues of nearly $60 billion, earnings in excess of $4 billion for its fiscal year ending November 30, 2007 and a per share stock value of $62.19 on January 2, 2008. Less than eight months later, on September 12, 2008, Lehman's stock closed at $3.65, a decline of nearly 95 percent from its January 2008 value (US Bankruptcy Court Southern District of New York – Examiner's report, 2010, p. 2).

Prior to its demise, Lehman managed, with a very aggressive, high-risk, high leverage business model, approximately $700 billion of assets and corresponding liabilities of approximately $25 billion. Assets were predominantly long term while the liabilities were largely short term. Lehman funded itself through the short-term repo markets. It borrowed tens of hundreds of billion dollars each day. Its survival depended exclusively on the confidence of its repo counterparties. When this confidence ended, Lehman's fate was sealed unless the US Government would provide a bail-out, but this did not happen (US Bankruptcy Court Southern District of New York – Examiner's report, 2010, pp. 3–14).

Early warning signs of Lehman's subprime unit's demise were quite evident in August 2007 when the firm decided to shut down BNC Mortgage LLC, its subprime-lending unit, and laid off 1,200 employees in 23 locations, and took a $25 million after-tax charge and a $27 million reduction in goodwill. In the second fiscal quarter of 2008 the MBS crisis triggered a panic in the financial markets which caused Lehman losses of $2.8 billion and forced the firm to sell off $6 billion in assets (Onaran, 2007; Kulikowski, 2007; Anderson and Dash, 2008).

Some other prestigious banks and financial institutions in the US and in Europe suffered severe losses and had to be rescued by their governments. It seems a bit awkward and difficult to believe that some of the best risk managers and savvy financial analysts of the world have suddenly "missed the boat" and apparently ignored the buildup signs of a potential systemic risk that caused dramatic bankruptcies (that is, Douglass National Bank, Hume Bank, First Integrity Bank, IndyMac, Silver State Bank, Lehman Brothers, Washington Mutual, and others), bank runs, or severe losses to many prestigious banks and investment firms, mutual/private/hedge equity funds and insurance companies which then had to be saved through recapitalizations, nationalizations, debt/equity swaps, or by the acquisitions/takeovers of competitors or investors (that is, Bear Stearns, Countrywide, Merrill Lynch, Hbos, AIG, Northern Rock, Fannie Mae and Freddie Mac, Fortis, Bradford and Bingley, Morgan Stanley, Dexia, and others) (FDIC, 2011; Dough Roller, 2011; Pezzuto, 2008).

The struggling lender Dexia, a Franco–Belgian bank, for example, has been rescued three times since 2008 to avoid its default and has received nearly €15 billion in state support (bail-outs) in four years (Wilson, 2012).

In the US the financial meltdown became so dramatic during the summer of 2008 that it provided an effective additional spur to the election of Barack Obama as President of the US (Pezzuto, 2010a, pp. 119–123).

The FCIC in January 2011 issued a final report on the causes of the financial and economic crisis in the US in which it states:

> ... the reason why more than twenty six million Americans are out of work, cannot find full-time jobs, or have given up looking for work; about four million families have lost their homes to foreclosures, and another four and a half million have slipped into the foreclosure process or are have serious difficulties to make their mortgage payments; and nearly $11 trillion in household wealth has vanished, with retirement accounts and life savings swept away, and

many business have gone bankrupt or face serious economic troubles, is due to the fact that the captains of finance and public stewards of the financial system ignored warnings and failed to question, understand, and manage evolving risks within a system essential to the well-being of the American public. (FCIC, 2011, pp. xv–xvii)

The FCIC (FCIC, 2011, pp. xvii–xxviii) in its final report also emphasizes the following points:

- *we conclude that this financial crisis was avoidable;*
- *we conclude dramatic failures of corporate governance and risk management at many systematically important financial institutions were a key cause of this crisis;*
- *we conclude a combination of excessive borrowing, risky investments, and lack of transparency put the financial system on a collision course with crisis;*
- *we conclude the government was ill prepared for this crisis, and its inconsistent response added to the uncertainty and panic in the financial markets;*
- *we conclude there was a systematic breakdown in accountability and ethics;*
- *we conclude collapsing mortgage-lending standards and the mortgage securitization pipeline lit and spread the flame of contagion and crisis;*
- *we conclude OTC derivatives contributed significantly to this crisis;*
- *we conclude the failure of credit rating agencies were essential cogs in the wheel of financial destruction.*

Empirical evidences show that the highly leveraged synthetic CDOs and CDO-squared exposures to the housing market in the years leading up to the financial crisis have significantly magnified the severity of losses suffered by investors when the US housing market experienced a downturn. The models on which CDOs were based proved tragically wrong. The MBS turned out to be highly correlated in their performances across the country since the borrowers of the subprime and Alt A mortgages were heavily concentrated in a few regions (FCIC, 2001, pp. 129–134). Thus, even rating agencies faced significant challenges estimating the probability of default for the MBS purchased by the CDOs and synthetic CDOs and their correlation – in other words the likelihood that those securities would default at the same time. The FCIC final report seems to indicate that the credit rating agencies probably did not use proper models to assess the MBS probability of defaults and their corrections and did not properly account for the originators' poor underwriting criteria, fraud practices, innovative and "exotic" products, riskier borrowers' profiles and concentration, and bad collateral appraisals during the housing market bubble (FCIC, 2001, p. 146; Pezzuto, 2008; 2010a).

CDOs are designed to facilitate diversification, thus a diversified portfolio of debt assets should have less risk than its constituent assets, however, a high correlation of default risk among the collateral assets can significantly reduce the impact of a well-diversified portfolio risk strategy. In fact, for example, many CDOs-squared contain tranches of other CDOs as part of their portfolios (Buckberg et al., 2010, p.13).

The final report of the FCIC (2011) also indicates that at the peak of the crisis approximately 80 percent of the CDO tranches were rated triple-A despite the fact that they generally comprised the lower-rated tranches of MBS (FCIC, 2001, p. 127).

Between 2003 and 2007, house prices in the US rose 27 percent nationally and $4 trillion in MBS were created. In the same period, nearly $700 billion in CDOs were issued that included MBS as collateral (FCIC, 2001, p. 129).

As explained by Barth et al. of the Milken Institute (2009), the excessive leverage of many financial firms certainly contributed to the financial crisis since it reduced the loss absorption capacity of financial institutions when the panic of potential banks' insolvencies emerged on the market. Looking at the leverage ratios of different types of financial firms, calculated as total assets/common equity on June 2008 data, it becomes quite clear that in the years preceding the financial crisis, financial firms were overleveraged. Below are some examples of leverage ratios sourced from data of the FDIC, Office of Federal Housing Enterprise Oversight, National Credit Union Administration, Bloomberg, Google Finance, and Milken Institute (2008) (Barth et al., 2009, pp. 17–18):

Freddie Mac	*67.9:1*
Fannie Mae	*21.5:1*
Federal Home Loan Banks	*23.7:1*
Brokers/hedge funds	*31.6:1*
Savings institutions	*9.4:1*
Commercial banks	*9.8:1*
Credit unions	*9.1:1*

(Barth et al., 2009, p. 18)

Thus, there has been a dramatic decline in the capital-asset ratio and the long-term increase in the leverage of commercial banks. Fannie Mae and Freddie Mac became the dominant players in the home mortgage market, holding or guaranteeing more than $5.5 trillion in home mortgages. They were enormously highly leveraged. With thin capital ratios, they have suffered substantial losses when housing prices began to decline. In the third quarter of 2008, both institutions were reporting insolvency on a fair value basis. "The subprime-backed securities alone accounted for 71 percent of the core capital of Fannie Mae, and 116 percent of the core capital of Freddie Mac" (Barth et al., 2009, p.19).

As explained by Frank Partnoy and Jesse Eisinger (2013), "The financial crisis had many causes – too much borrowing, foolish investments, misguided regulation – but at its core, the panic resulted from a lack of transparency." After Lehman Brothers collapsed in 2008 no one could understand, as a result of the lack of disclosure, a particular bank's risk or which bank could be the next one to suddenly implode (Partnoy and Eisinger, 2013).

The two authors also state that despite the great resources and effort dedicated to the new financial regulation to restore trust and confidence in the American financial system, "banks today are bigger and more opaque than ever, and they continue to behave In many of the same ways they did before the crash" (Partnoy and Eisinger, 2013).

They also report that, due to the numerous financial scandals, accusations of illegal, and clandestine bank activities, and manipulations and collusions, there are still serious doubts whether the big banks are safe and trustworthy and all these incidents have pushed public confidence in the industry ever lower (Partnoy and Eisinger, 2013).

"According to Gallup, back in the late 1970s, three out of five Americans said they trusted big banks 'a great deal' or 'quite a lot.'" During the following decades, that trust eroded. Since the financial crisis of 2008, it has collapsed. In June 2012, fewer than one in four respondents told Gallup they had faith in big banks – a record low. And in October, Luis Aguilar, a commissioner at the Securities and Exchange Commission, cited separate data showing that "79 percent of investors have no trust in the financial system" (Partnoy and Eisinger, 2013).

As Partnoy and Eisinger explain, a real threat for the whole industry is a crisis of trust among investors. "It is far less obvious than a sudden panic, but over time, its damage compounds. It is not a tsunami; it is dry rot. It creeps in, noticed occasionally and then forgotten. Soon it is a daily fact of life. Even as the economy begins to come back, the trust crisis saps the recovery's strength. Banks can't attract capital. They lose customers, who fear being tricked and cheated. Their executives are, by turns, traumatized and enervated. Lacking confidence in themselves as they grapple with the toxic legacies of their previous excesses and mistakes, they don't lend as much as they should. Without trust in banks, the economy wheezes and stutters" (Partnoy and Eisinger, 2013).

In the following paragraphs, some examples of the major financial scandals that have involved leading financial institutions since the 2007–2009 financial crisis are reported.

Some key players (financial institutions) of the financial crisis have been charged with fraud allegations and fined or have reached agreements on disputes on faulty mortgage loans.

US bank Goldman Sachs agreed to a US$550 dollar fine to settle government fraud charges, as reported by the Securities and Exchange Commission (SEC). The company has been faced with allegations of defrauding investors and "admitted it made a 'mistake' and gave 'incomplete' information to clients. The SEC has accused Goldman of allowing a prominent hedge fund – Paulson and Co. Inc. – to put together a package of subprime mortgages that were sold to clients, but which Paulson has been also betting against" (*The Telegraph*, 2010).

Moreover, Goldman pushed AIG, which has received US Government rescue funds, to cover in full the default swaps Goldman bought from AIG while other AIG customers took huge shavings on their holdings of AIG swaps. In addition to this, Goldman filed to convert to bank status, thus giving it access to the Fed window where it could borrow at virtually no interest. It resumed leveraging while the US Government provided "free" funds many times over in order to earn extreme returns (*The Telegraph*, 2010).

"Bank of America has reached a $3 billion agreement with Freddie Mac and Fannie Mae to resolve a faulty mortgage loan dispute involving Countrywide Financial Corp." The scope of the agreement was to settle an issue of bad mortgages sold by Countrywide to Fannie Mae and Freddie Mac related to the housing crisis of 2008 (Smith, 2011).

In June 2011, Rushe reported that:

> *JP Morgan Chase has agreed to pay $153.6 million to resolve US civil fraud charges that it misled investors in a mortgage-related security created for Magnetar, an Illinois hedge fund that was betting against the deal. The Securities and Exchange Commission alleged that JP Morgan was negligent in failing to tell investors that Magnetar helped select mortgages included in the collateralized debt obligation, known as Squared, and placed a substantial bet to profit from its decline. JP Morgan settled without admitting or denying wrongdoing, and also agreed to reimburse investors in a different CDO, known as Tahoma. (Rushe, 2011a)*

Both banks, Goldman Sachs and JPMorgan Chase and Co., agreed to pay to resolve US civil fraud charges related to misleading investors in a mortgage-related security, but neither of them admitted nor denied wrongdoing (Scannell, 2011a) – and no one went to jail (Nugent, 2011).

As reported by Kara Scannell (2011b) on October 20, 2011 Citigroup agreed to pay $285 million to resolve a SEC probe alleging the bank misled investors in 2007 mortgage-related securities (CDOs). The SEC alleged that Citi was negligent in failing to tell investors in a $1 billion CDO – known as Class V Funding III – that the bank had helped to select $500 million of mortgage assets that went into the security, and was also betting against it. Insurer Ambac, BNP Paribas, and hedge funds and other investors in the deal suffered losses, while according to the SEC, Citi made $160 million in fees and profits through its bets against the security (Scannell, 2011b).

On November 2011, however, "a US judge rejected the Securities and Exchange Commission's $285 million settlement with Citigroup to resolve allegations that the bank misled buyers of a mortgage-related security, and signalled he would no longer approve such deals without admissions of wrongdoing" (Scannell, 2011c).

On September 3, 2011 Tom Braithwaite, Kara Scannell, and Dan McCrum of the *Financial Times* reported that a US regulator, the FHFA, filed suits in the New York State Supreme Court accusing 17 international financial groups (such as, Bank of America, Goldman Sachs, Morgan Stanley, JPMorgan Chase and Co., Citigroup, Nomura, Credit Suisse, Deutsche Bank, HSBC, Société Generale, General Electric, Ally Financial, and First Horizon) "of making 'materially false' statements about the quality of mortgages that were bundled into securities and sold" (almost $200 billion of MBS), before plunging in value in the financial crisis. The FHFA with the law suits demanded compensation for billions of dollars of losses (Braithwaite et al., 2011).

In 2009, "the Dalai Lama, Tibet's exiled spiritual leader, blamed a lack of spirituality among people today for the global financial crisis." When he was asked about the real cause of the economic crisis he replied, "Too much speculation and ultimately greed," adding, "the potential to help is: reduce greed and (increase) self-discipline. Economic crisis is something urgent so it will be helpful to reduce some other conflict (that is going on) in the name of faith and nationality" (Singh, 2008).

A similar tone is seen in the third encyclical of Pope Emeritus Benedict XVI, "*Caritas in Veritate*" (Latin for "Charity in Truth") in which he placed emphasis on the need for the actions of all economic actors to be driven by ethics as well as by profit motives (Singh, 2008).

In October 2011, "the Vatican called for radical reform of the world's financial systems, including the creation of a global political authority to manage the economy. The Pontifical Council for Justice and Peace called for a new world economic order based on ethics" and the achievement of a universal common good. "It follows Pope Emeritus Benedict XVI's economic encyclical that denounced a profit-at-all-costs mentality as responsible for the global financial meltdown" (Simpson, 2011).

On November 1, 2011 Rowan Williams, the then Archbishop of Canterbury, openly endorsed "the *Vickers Commission* that requires routine banking business to be clearly separated from speculative transactions. A second plea is to recapitalize banks with public money, but banks should be obliged in return to help reinvigorate the real economy." Finally, he strongly supported the proposal of a Financial Transaction Tax – a "Tobin Tax" or, popularly, a "Robin Hood Tax" in the form in which it has been talked about most recently, stating that "this perspective cannot be written off as a naive anti-capitalist approach since it has won the backing of significant industry experts such as George Soros, Bill Gates and many others." It is gaining traction among European nations, with a strong statement in support even from Wolfgang Schäuble, the German Finance Minister" (Williams, 2011).

Chief Rabbi Jonathan Sacks, who has been Chief Rabbi of the United Hebrew Congregations of the Commonwealth since September 1991, knighted by the Queen in 2005 and made a Life Peer, taking his seat in the House of Lords in 2009, reported in an interview to Huffington Post (Brandeis Raushenbush, 2011) on the causes of the global financial crisis and on the crisis in the leadership of financial institutions that, "What went wrong in both Britain and America is that the external constraints, the financial regulation authorities, are not enough and we know that they are not enough." He also added:

> Of course, the guys who are making the money are making more than they guys who are regulating. So I would predict that the cleverer guys are the ones who work out the ways of avoiding the regulations rather than the ones who are implementing them. And that's actually what happened and why external constraints never work. You need the voice of God within the human heart (moral constraint). Because unless you're going to stop yourself, nobody is going to stop you – until it's too late. (Brandeis Raushenbush, 2011)

In the beginning of November 2011, Morgan Stanley revealed it was being targeted over alleged mortgage mis-selling by the same law firm that brokered an $8.5 billion settlement with Bank of America. In December 2011, Morgan Stanley took a $1.8 billion charge in settlement with insurance company MBIA Inc. over mortgage-backed investments (Nasiripour, 2011c).

In November 2011, Deutsche Bank and Citi agreed to pay the US National Credit Union Administration a combined $165 million fine to settle allegations the banks misled five failed credit unions over their purchase of mortgage bonds (Nasiripour, 2011a).

In December 2011, the *Financial Times* reported that the State of Massachusetts sued the five biggest mortgage companies in the US, accusing them of "corrupting" the state's "land records through pervasive use of fraudulent documentation in seizing borrowers' homes" (Nasiripour, 2011b).

Martha Coakley, Massachusetts Attorney-General, reported that "five banks (Bank of America, JPMorgan Chase and Co., Wells Fargo, Citigroup, and Ally Financial) failed to perform the various legal steps needed to properly foreclose on a mortgage has adversely impacted titles to hundreds, if not thousands, of properties" (Nasiripour, 2011b).

The Massachusetts Attorney-General alleged that the banks illegally foreclosed on borrowers' mortgages because they were not the actual holders of those mortgages, among other accusations. This was due to their failure to properly review, assign, and transfer critical paperwork, she said, adding that the banks "had no legal right to conduct the foreclosure" (Nasiripour, 2011b).

In December 2011, the *Financial Times* reported that, "Six former top executives at Fannie Mae and Freddie Mac have been charged with securities fraud in a civil case brought by the US Securities and Exchange Commission for allegedly misleading investors," becoming some of the most senior financial executives yet to be accused of wrongdoing in the financial crisis. The executives were accused of understating Fannie and Freddie's holdings of high-risk home loans which have led to a government bail-out that could cost US taxpayers $193 billion until the end of 2014. "Fannie Mae and Freddie Mac executives told the world that their subprime exposure was substantially smaller than it really was," said Robert Khuzami, SEC Enforcement Director. He said these "material misstatements" misled the market "during a time of acute investor interest in financial institutions' exposure to subprime loans" (Nasiripour and Scannell, 2011).

These things occur because managers are only too happy to use corporate funds to pay for personal wrongdoings so long as they do not have to personally pay back ill-gotten bonuses, fines, or go to jail (Nugent, 2011).

In December 2011, the *Financial Times* reported that Bank of America will pay $335 million to resolve US allegations that its Countrywide unit discriminated against African–American and Hispanic borrowers. In fact, from 2004 to 2008, the bank allegedly overcharged more than 200,000 minority borrowers for home loans compared with similar white borrowers, according to the US Department of Justice (Nasiripour, 2011d).

In January 2012, Credit Suisse has started to offer a product to circumvent the short-selling ban imposed in several Eurozone countries to avoid spreading the contagion of the confidence, sovereign debt, and balance of payments crisis (Jones, 2012).

Still in January 2012, President Obama announced the intention to join forces with New York Attorney-General Eric Schneiderman, the US Department of Justice, the SEC, and various federal prosecutors, in order to investigate alleged frauds involving home loans and MBS that led to the global financial crisis (Nasiripour, 2012).

In March 2012, the US Justice Department reported that it was conducting a criminal investigation into a number of banks, including Bank of America, Citigroup, HSBC, JPMorgan Chase and Co., and Credit Suisse of alleged Libor manipulation. The London Interbank Offered Rate, or Libor, is a measure of the cost of borrowing between banks. The scope of this investigation was to determine whether banks were colluding to manipulate these rates in order to appear stronger and more creditworthy during the financial crisis by submitting lower numbers or adjusting trading positions tied to Libor in order to profit from their advanced knowledge of its movements (O'Toole, 2012).

In April 2012, Federal Reserve Chairman Ben Bernanke, speaking at a conference in New York stated that, "Subprime mortgages were as a 'trigger' of the crisis, but 'vulnerabilities' – like a lack of oversight and regulations – were also largely to blame for amplifying the financial shocks" (Censky, 2012).

In 2011, a wave of protest around the world suddenly erupted amoung people hurt by the aftermath of the global financial crisis and determined to express their frustration against the rise of social and economic inequality, greed, corruption, and the dominance of financial sector on governments. This leaderless movement, which includes people of all races, gender, social class, and political orientation, began to spread around the world under the name "Occupy," the most popular of which is certainly "Occupy Wall Street." The movement slogan became "We are the 99 percent" of the population who will not tolerate the greed and corruption of the remaining 1 percent. The protest raised the issue of wealth distribution in the US between the wealthiest 1 percent and the rest of the population.

In 2012, not only the less privileged 99 percent of the population, but also the more wealthy ones (Tea Party) began to express their frustration of the aftermath of the global financial crisis (that is, higher unemployment rates, lower economic growth, more uncertainty and volatility in the markets, and more inequality in wealth distribution). In fact, a number of shareholders began to raise their voice as a result of their frustration about the lack of transparency in the executive compensation schemes and the unsatisfactory profit performances, share values, and capital gains of a number of large and leading financial institutions and the massive executive compensation packages.

The upsurge in investor activism expressed in non-binding votes on pay has indeed affected big banks in 2012 such as UBS, Citigroup, Barclays, Aviva, and Credit Suisse. Investors and shareholders seem to be highly frustrated that executives are generously rewarded for their failures (Schäfer, 2012a).

In April 2012, Ted Kaufman, a former US Senator from Delaware, reported in an article on the topic of shareholders' rights the following statement: "After years of not having to worry much about what their shareholders thought, the Citigroup vote was a wake up call for every corporate board of directors" (Kaufman, 2012).

Another serious evidence of poor oversight on risk management in major financial institutions in the post-crisis era (2012) occurred when JPMorgan Chase and Co. disclosed a $2 billion trading loss (on synthetic credit securities/bets on CDS) on May 10, 2012. As reported by Bloomberg, the committee responsible for overseeing risks at the financial institution did not include enough qualified professionals with seasoned expertise as financial risk managers (Kopecki and Moore, 2012). The JPMorgan Chase and Co. trader in London, Bruno Iksil, whose bets were so big, was nicknamed "the London Whale" and "Voldemort," after the Harry Potter villain (Silver-Greenberg and Eavis, 2012). According to Jamie Dimon the handling of derivatives bet that cost the company more than $6.2 billion in 2012 was due to the fact that some top executives at the largest US bank "acted like children," they just "felt they could take advantage of it personally, they were willing to hurt the company by maneuvering" (Campbell, Kopecki, 2013).

In June 2012, Barclays' management admitted "misconduct" over a period of five years and three continents, in its submission of data to the bank panels that set Libor and Euribor (European interbank rates), following a probe that was launched by the US Commodity Futures Trading Commission (CFTC). "The bank also admitted to lowballing its Libor rate submissions to paint a false picture of its financial health to the market after the collapse of Northern Rock in the UK and Lehman Brothers in the US." As a consequence of their misconduct (attempting to manipulate the Libor) the bank agreed to pay $450 million to end Libor probe (Masters et al., 2012).

Barclays ex-CEO, Bob Diamond, testified to a UK Parliamentary Committee that he was unaware that a group of his company's traders were responsible for the manipulation of the lending rates in the period 2005 to 2007 for personal gain and that other banks, including those that used emergency government funds, were also involved in the same Libor-rigging scandal, also called Liborgate (Goff and Burgis, 2012).

After the Libor scandal the UK Financial Services Authority (FSA) plans to create an independent and formally regulated administrator to oversee the rate-setting process. In addition, according to the FSA, banks have to appoint an executive, approved by the watchdog, in charge of the daily submission of the estimates that contribute to the rate-setting process. Another proposal of the FSA consists of making Libor manipulations a crime and in expanding the participation to the large number of banks to discourage attempts to manipulate Libor. There are, however, according to Suresh Sundaresan, Professor at Columbia Business School, still potential weaknesses in the new proposal since the verification will only be credible if it is based on banks' actual standard funding transactions. He also mentioned that it is still not clear how the whole process will work during a credit crunch phase (Masters, 2012; Touryalai, 2012).

Martin Taylor, the former Chief Executive of Barclays from 1994 to 1997, said the bank's actions amounted to "systematic dishonesty" and that the bank must rebuild its reputation following the Libor scandal (Cooper, 2012).

Even the reputable magazine the *Economist*, in its July 2012 issue, published an article on the Libor Affair titled, "Banksters. How Britain's Rate-Fixing Scandal Might Spread – and What to Do About It." (*Economist*, 2012).

Furthermore, it seems that bankers supplied false information for the setting of a Libor as early as 2007 (Masters and Jenkins, 2012).

In the summer of 2012, Eric Schneiderman, New York Attorney-General, sent subpoenas to Deutsche Bank, Citigroup, JPMorgan Chase and Co., Royal Bank of Scotland, Barclays, HSBC, and UBS related to the alleged Libor-rigging probe, thus making the Libor scandal global. The rate affects trillions of dollars worth of outstanding loans and securities. Among the financial scandals revealed since the 2008–2009 financial crisis, the Libor rigging certainly represents one of the most serious ones. As reported by the New York prosecutor, it is a fraud that reveals "deceitful practices contrary to the plain rules of common honesty" (Nasiripour and Alloway, 2012; Pezzuto, 2012).

Mervyn King, Governor of the Bank of England, regarding the banks' scandals stated the following: "It goes to the culture and the structure of banks – the excessive compensation, the shoddy treatment of customers, the deceitful manipulation of a key interest rate, and today news of yet another mis-selling scandal." By the latter scandal he was referring to Barclays, HSBC, Lloyds Banking Group, and Royal Bank of Scotland which, according to the FSA, mis-sold 28,000 complex financial products (interest rate swap arrangements – IRSAs) to small business customers as protection (hedge) against a rise in interest rates without ensuring they fully grasped the potential downside risks (Elliott, 2012).

It was reported in *The Huffington Post* that the former Countrywide Financial Corp, run by Chief Executive Angelo Mozilo, whose subprime loans contributed to the US financial crisis, "made hundreds of discount loans (as known as VIP Loan Program or Friends of Angelo) to buy influence with members of Congress, congressional staff, top government officials and executives of troubled mortgage giant Fannie Mae" (Margasak, 2012).

Fannie was responsible for purchasing a large volume of Countrywide's subprime mortgages. When Countrywide Financial Corp went bankrupt it was taken over by Bank of America (January, 2008). In 2010 Mozilo agreed to pay a settlement of $67.5 million for the charges that he and two other former Countrywide executives misled investors (Margasak, 2012).

When the House Financial Services Committee and Senate Banking Committee were considering legislation to reform Fannie and Freddie, approximately 70 lobbyists were assigned by Fannie Mae to the Financial Services Committee to make sure that no rules would stop these companies' practices. In September 2008, Fannie and Freddie came under Government control because of their staggering losses. "As of Dec. 31, 2011, the Treasury Department had committed over $183 billion to support the two companies" (Margasak, 2012).

Furthermore, following the Spanish banking crisis of 2012 (as part of the Eurozone crisis) which forced Spain to seek billions of euros in a European rescue plan, the Spanish High Court opened a fraud probe into Bankia executives allegedly responsible for falsifying Bankia's accounts and misleading investors before the €23.5 billion state rescue (Johnson, 2012).

In July 2012 Bloomberg reported a remarkable statement made by Ex-Citigroup CEO Sanford "Sandy" Weill, who built financial conglomerate Citigroup into a massive US commercial and investment bank. In a CNBC interview Weil said, "What we should probably do is go and split up investment banking from banking." Weill helped engineer the 1998 merger of Travelers Group Inc. and Citicorp, a deal that required repeal of the Glass–Steagall Act (Griffin and Harper, 2012).

In the summer and fall of 2012 other shocking financial scandals, which have been reported almost on a weekly basis, have hit the banking industry hard, adding more embarrassment to an industry already negatively affected by a long series of discrediting reputational damages since 2008.

Some of these scandals include the following:

The New York state's Department for Financial Services allegations that Standard Chartered violated Iranian sanctions to the tune of $250 billion which has been quickly solved with the bank's agreement to pay $340 million fine to settle the claims it had strongly denied (Goff and Alloway, 2012).

The US Fed's probe into Royal Bank of Scotland for possible breaches of Iran sanctions (Schäfer and Nasiripour, 2012).

HSBC has been accused by a US Senate Committee of operating a money-laundering Conduit for "drug kingpins and rogue nations," and in particular to have accepted more than $15 billion in bulk cash transactions from subsidiaries in Mexico, Russia, and other countries at high risk of money laundering between mid-2006 and mid-2009 and failing to conduct proper checks (Pratley, 2012).

In August 2012, Citigroup agreed to pay $590 million to settle a shareholder lawsuit accusing the bank of failing to disclose fully its exposure to toxic mortgage products in the run-up to the financial crisis (Braithwaite and Scannell, 2012).

In August 2012, the *Financial Times* reported that the UK's Serious Fraud Office (SFO) was investigating Barclays, under wide-ranging anti-corruption legislation, over payments made to Qatari bank (Qatar Holding LLC) at the height of financial crisis. In fact, Barclays turned to the Qatar Investment Authority in 2008 fearing it would be the next bank to fall following the UK Government's rescues of Northern Rock, RBS, and Lloyds Banking Group, and thus would fall under the UK Treasury control and restrictions on executive compensations. Later that year (2008), Barclays also raised another £7.1 billion from Qatar, Abu Dhabi, and other shareholders. Barclays disclosed that year that £300 million had been paid in fees and commissions as part of the deal, including £66 million to Qatar Holding "for having arranged certain of the subscriptions in the capital raising" (Binham, 2012; Salmon and Duncan, 2012).

In August 2012, Bloomberg reported that the FDIC, in three separate complaints, sued several financial institutions for having overstated the quality of loans underlying MBS ($5.4 billion worth of certificates) they sold to the failed Guaranty Bank in Austin, Texas. The first complaint seeks at least $900 million in damages from Goldman Sachs, Ally Financial's Residential Funding Securities LLC, and from units of Deutsche Bank AG and JPMorgan Chase and Co. A second complaint seeks damages of more than $677 million in damages from JPMorgan Securities LLC, Bank of America's Merrill Lynch Pierce Fenner and Smith Inc. securities unit and a brokerage unit of Royal Bank of Scotland Group Plc. The third complaint seeks almost $560 million in damages from Bank of America, its Countrywide Securities unit and other defendants (Harris, 2012).

Phil Angelides, former State Treasurer of California and the Chairman of the FCIC, analyzing the shocking sequence of scandals affecting the banking industry stated the following: "Money laundering. Price fixing. Bid rigging. Securities fraud. Talking about the mob? No, unfortunately. Wall Street" (Angelides, 2012).

According to Angelides, it seems amazing what is on the news these days: "JPMorgan Chase trading, GE Capital, JPMorgan Chase, UBS, Wells Fargo and Bank of America tied to a bid-rigging scheme to bilk cities and towns out of interest earnings. ING Direct, HSBC and Standard Chartered Bank facing charges of money laundering. Barclays caught manipulating a key interest rate" (Angelides, 2012).

He also added, "Evidence gathered by the Financial Crisis Inquiry Commission clearly demonstrated that the financial crisis was avoidable and due, in no small part, to recklessness and ethical breaches on Wall Street. Yet, it's clear that the unrepentant and the unreformed are still all too present within our banking system" (Angelides, 2012).

In October 2012, the US Department of Justice was reported to have sued Bank of America for more than $1 billion alleging that Countrywide, the California-based mortgage lender that Bank of America bought in 2008, committed civil fraud, selling thousands of defective home loans to Government-backed mortgage companies Fannie Mae and Freddie Mac. More specifically, the fraud suit alleges that Countrywide implemented a process called the hustle and high speed swim lane to deal with loans rapidly without checking their quality. The law suit claims that the financial institutions have removed bonuses linked to the quality of loans and paid them solely on volume. Apparently a number of executives warned of the severe misconduct but they were prohibited from circulating the poor underwriting review findings outside the mortgage group (Braithwaite, 2012b).

In October 2012, Reuters reported that the US Department of Justice filed a fraud lawsuit against Bank of America, accusing it of causing taxpayers more than $1 billion of losses by selling thousands of toxic mortgage loans to Fannie Mae and Freddie Mac. US federal agencies have brought against Wall Street over the financial crisis, including the FHFA's 18 lawsuits over Fannie Mae and Freddie Mac. According to a complaint filed in Manhattan Federal Court, in 2007 Countrywide invented, and Bank of America continued, a scheme known as the "Hustle" to speed up the processing of residential home loans. Operating under the motto "Loans Move Forward, Never Backward," mortgage executives tried to eliminate "toll gates" designed to ensure that loans were sound and not tainted by fraud, the Government said. These lawsuits covered losses on the sales of roughly $200 billion of securities, including more than $57 billion linked to Bank of America, Countrywide, and Merrill. Furthermore, back in February 2012, Bank of America agreed to a $1 billion settlement of False Claims Act allegations over home loans submitted for insurance by the FHA while Citigroup Inc. settled its case for $158.3 million and Flagstar Bancorp Inc. settled for $132.8 million. Deutsche Bank AG settled in May for $202.3 million. Reuters reported that cases were still pending against Wells Fargo and Co and Allied Home Mortgage Corp. (Stempel, 2012).

In November 2012, the FSA fined UBS £29.7 million for failing to prevent unauthorized trading which caused losses of $2.3 billion. The fine followed the conviction of UBS trader Kweku Adoboli, who was found guilty of two counts of fraud by abuse of position and sentenced to seven years in prison. The fine against UBS was set at 15 percent of the revenue of its Global Synthetic Equities trading division conducted from the London branch of UBS (Holt, 2012).

In December 2012, the *Financial Times* reported that JPMorgan Chase and Co. was nearing a settlement with the UK Government in which the US bank and its employees could pay close to £500 million in back taxes that were avoided through the use of an offshore trust for bonus payments (Jenkins, 2012).

Still in the same month of December 2012, the *Financial Times* reported that UBS agreed to pay a record $1.5 billion to US, UK, and Swiss regulators to settle allegations of "pervasive" and "epic" efforts to manipulate interbank lending rates as two of its former traders faced the first criminal charges in the worldwide Libor scandal. The Swiss bank's Japanese subsidiary pleaded guilty to criminal wire fraud as the group acknowledged that dozens of employees had attempted to manipulate the Libor and similar interbank lending rates between 2005 and 2010 (Scannell et al., 2012). The UBS settlement was the second in the investigation of global interest rate benchmarks after Barclays plc agreed to pay £290 million in June 2012 but, according to Bloomberg, the Libor settlements signal more to come (Brush and Mattingly, 2012).

In the fall 2012, British bank Standard Chartered, being charged by US regulators over allegations that it breached anti-money laundering sanctions against Iran for over $250 billion worth of transactions, agreed a $340 million settlement with the New York Department of Financial Services. The settlement came a day before a scheduled hearing in which Standard Chartered was expected to defend its license, allowing it to do business in New York (Touryalai, 2012a).

In December 2012, HSBC Holdings plc agreed to pay a record $1.92 billion in fines to US authorities for allowing itself to be used to launder a river of drug money flowing out of Mexico and other banking lapses. In the same month, the *Financial Times* reported that three former Deutsche Bank staff alleged that the investment bank masked $12 billion of losses during the financial crisis, which helped the bank avoid being bailed out by the Government. According to a spokeswoman at Deutsche Bank, "The allegations of financial mis-statements have been the subject of a careful and thorough investigation and they are wholly unfounded" (Croucher, 2012).

In January 2013, the *Wall Street Journal* reported that regulators have been investigating allegations that more than a dozen banks, including Deutsche Bank, Europe's largest bank by assets, made at least €500 million ($654 million) in profit in 2008 with billions of euros in bets related to the Libor and other global benchmark rates. Furthermore, at that time Deutsche Bank was not including the interest rate bets in the main measurement of trading risks, known as value-at-risk, or VAR (Eagleham, 2013).

Another shameful event for global financial capitalism was reported in December 2012 by Bloomberg. The story says that Deutsche Bank AG, JPMorgan Chase and Co., UBS AG, and Depfa Bank plc were convicted by a Milan judge (Italy) for their role in overseeing fraud by their bankers in the sale of derivatives to the city of Milan (Martinuzzi, 2012).

In January 2013, Bloomberg reported another financial scandal. Deutsche Bank AG designed a derivative ($2 billion) for the Italian bank, Banca Monte dei Paschi di Siena SpA, in December 2008 (at the height of the financial crisis) in order to mask losses at the world's oldest bank (founded in 1472) before it sought a taxpayer bail-out of 3.9 billion euros in 2012. Instead of booking a loss on its equity position Banca Monte dei Paschi di Siena SpA decided to replace the swap. The accounting firm that audited Monte Paschi in 2009 and 2008 is KPMG. Former Monte Paschi Chairman Giuseppe Mussari resigned as ABI (Italian Banking Association) President after this event (Martinuzzi and Dunbar, 2013).

In the same month the *Financial Times* reported that US banks agreed to pay out more than $20 billion in two settlements to resolve claims arising from the mortgage crisis. Bank of America agreed to pay $11.6 billion to Fannie Mae to resolve a protracted legal battle over bad loans. In a separate settlement, ten mortgage lenders, (Bank of America, for many mortgages originated by Countrywide, Citibank, Aurora, JPMorgan Chase and Co., MetLife Bank, PNC, Sovereign, SunTrust, US Bank, and Wells Fargo) agreed to pay more than $8.5 billion to settle regulators' allegations that they were guilty of widespread abuse of the foreclosure system that allowed banks to seize homes from defaulting borrowers (Braithwaite and Nasiripour, 2013).

In January 2013, the Head of Investment Banking at Switzerland's UBS, Andrea Orcel, admitted to the British Parliamentary Commission on Banking Standards, which was preparing a report on how banks' governance and ethics need to change in the wake of the financial crisis and a succession of scandals, that UBS's failure was due to poor governance, badly designed pay structures, and acquisitive growth. Mr Rohner also advocated seeking a new moral path, changing bank remuneration models, to give far more weight to group performance (based on economic profit instead of revenue or pre-tax profit generation); setting up an "ethics and culture hotline" for staff to report deviant behavior; and changing attitude to internal controls (that is, risk managers and compliance staff) from annoyance to adviser. The rapid growth and complexity of the business, according to him, caused a failure in the integration of the different cultures that came with acquisitive expansion (Jenkins and Masters, 2013).

In mid-January 2013, Reuters reported that Goldman Sachs Group Inc. and Morgan Stanley agreed to pay a total of $557 million in cash and other assistance to troubled borrowers to end a case-by-case review of past foreclosures required by US regulators.

This agreement is similar to an $8.5 billion deal agreed between the Fed, the Office of the Comptroller of the Currency, and ten other bank servicers on January 7, 2013 (Viswanatha, 2013).

Royal Bank of Scotland has agreed to pay $610 million (£390 million) to settle the US and UK charges for manipulating Libor (Binham, 2013).

Britan's FSA reported in January 2013, that in addition to the mis-selling of payment protection insurance, high street banks could be forced to pay huge compensation to small businesses for mis-selling interest rate swaps since 2001. In fact, the FSA study reports that more than 90 percent of sales did not comply with at least one or more regulatory requirements (Inman, 2013).

In February 5, 2013, breaking news reported that the US Justice Department had accused Standard and Poor's of defrauding investors. Eric Holder, US Attorney-General, announced the charges stating that in the years preceding the financial crisis the credit rating agency deliberately inflated the ratings of mortgage-related securities (that is, CDOs) in order to earn higher fees and market shares. The US Justice Department requested compensation for the $5 billion fraud claiming also that, from 2004 until 2007, Standard and Poor's had "adjusted and delayed" updates to its rating criteria and models and ignored warnings of its own analysts about the highly likely US housing market boom–bust scenario (Scannell and Nasiripour, 2013).

In an article published by *The Huffington Post* (Gordon, 2013), Marcy Gordon reported that the big banks are also getting tax breaks on the foreclosure abuse deal, since the Internal Revenue Service regards the lenders' compensation to homeowners as a cost incurred in the course of doing business. Result: It's fully tax-deductible. Thus the author of the article clarifies that the banks can deduct those costs against federal taxes as long as they are compensating private individuals to remedy a wrong. By contrast, a fine or other financial penalty is not tax-deductible. The foreclosure abuse deal was agreed to compensate hundreds of thousands of people whose homes were seized improperly, a result of abuses such as "robo-signing." That is when banks automatically approved foreclosures without properly reviewing documents (Gordon, 2013).

In April 2013, investigators from Germany's central bank, Bundesbank, reported having launched a probe on Deutsche Bank based on allegations that the bank has misvalued complex credit derivatives (that is, avoided recording mark-to-market losses on leveraged super-senior trades) during the financial crisis in order to hide up to $12 billion in losses to avoid a government bailout (Braithwaite et al., 2013).

Conclusion

From this overview, based on some of the most relevant publications on the topic of the 2007–2009 financial crisis, overall it seems to be confirmed that irresponsible lending, predatory lending, speculation, short-term profit incentives, and fraudulent practices of many players in the global financial services industry, among other things, have triggered this unprecedented crisis.

As the FCIC stated in the conclusion of its final report: "… the tragedy is that many in Washington and Wall Street have ignored or discounted the warning signs of the crisis" (FCIC, 2011, p. xvii).

The FCIC also reported in their final report the following conclusion (FCIC, 2011, p. xvii):

> … financial institutions made, bought, and sold mortgage securities that they never examined, did not care to examine, or knew to be defective; firms depended on tens of billions of dollars of borrowings that had to be renewed each and every day night (overnight), secured by subprime mortgage securities; and major firms and investors blindly relied on credit rating agencies as their arbiters of risk.

As the FCIC Chairman, Phil Angelides, said during the presentation of the Commission's final report on Thursday January 25, 2011: "The greatest tragedy would be to accept the refrain that no one could have seen this coming and thus nothing could have been done about it. If we accept this notion, it will happen again" (Randall, 2011).

To conclude this general overview of the events that have led to the financial crisis it is probably worthwhile to report Johnson and Kwak's (Johnson and Kwak, 2010a, pp. 10–11) words that state:

> The choices the federal government made in rescuing the banking sector in 2008 and 2009 also have significant implications for American society and the global economy today. Not only did the government choose to rescue the financial system – a decision few would question – but it chose to do so by extending a blank check to the largest, most powerful banks in their moment of greatest need. The government chose not to impose conditions that could reform the industry, or even to replace the management of large failed banks. It chose to stick with the bankers it had.

A final point of attention should be raised by the fact that according to Keith Fitz-Gerald, Chief Investment Strategist, Money Morning, four US banks hold a staggering 95.9 percent of US derivatives and that he believes this represents "the $600 trillion time bomb that's set to explode" (Figure 2.15). Keith Fitz-Gerald in his article indicates the

IN TRILLIONS OF DOLLARS, SEMIANNUAL

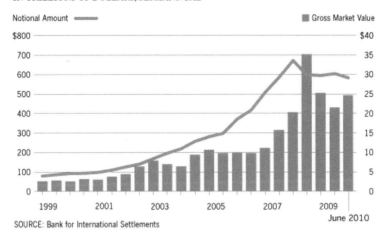

SOURCE: Bank for International Settlements

**Figure 2.15 Notional Amount and Gross Market Value of OTC Derivatives
Outstanding**

Source: Stanford University Rock Center for Corporate Governance.

data of a recent report from the Office of the Comptroller of the Currency. These four
banks are: JPMorgan Chase and Co., Citigroup Inc., Bank of America, and Goldman Sachs
Group Inc. (Fitz-Gerald, 2011).

The world's GDP in 2011 was only about $65 trillion, or roughly 10.83 percent of the
worldwide value of the global derivatives market, according to the *Economist*. So there is
literally not enough money on the planet to backstop the banks trading these things if they
run into trouble (Fitz-Gerald, 2011). Even if the total amount of global derivatives is not
calculated as an aggregate but as the netting the positions it still represents an impressive
and highly concentrated marketplace which, as demonstrated by the JPMorgan Chase and
Co. $2 billion loss reported in 2012, still poses a number of serious doubts on the resilience
of the leading financial firms' risk management practices (Kopecki and Moore, 2012).

Furthermore, in June 2012 the interest rate swaps on the overall European sovereign
debt were roughly 25 times the amount of the sovereign debt of the same economic
region. It is also interesting to consider that at the end of 2012, after the various bail-outs,
nationalizations, and recession trends, most of the Eurozone countries and even the US
have sovereign debts above the *Rogoff and Reinhart's controversial threshold* of 90 percent.
This means, in other words, that in case of new systemic crises, and asymmetric shocks,
unless the Debt-to-GDP ratios are significantly reduced through effective structural reforms
and steady economic growth, and through systemic crises' resolution mechanisms, there
will be only very limited resources available for new rescue plans.

It is worthwhile to conclude this chapter reporting Richard Posner's words (Friedman,
2011, p. 281):

> *The financial crisis would have been averted, or at least would have been much less grave,
> despite the very low interest rates (first cause), had it not been for the second cause – inadequate
> banking regulation: a compound of deregulation, lax regulation, regulatory inattention, and
> regulatory ineptitude.*

He also added that the decision not to save Lehman Brothers from bankruptcy in 2008 was a dramatic mistake since it triggered a series of panic reactions (confidence crisis) that drained capital and liquidity from the market, increased the credit crunch, and spilled the crisis from the financial sector over to other sectors of the economy (Friedman, 2011, pp. 281–282).

In summary, this chapter provides clear evidence of the major triggering factors that have, over the years, set the stage for the 2007–2009 financial crisis and its aftermath. Not all root causes, however, played a major role in the making of the crisis since the perverse sequence that linked the various crises from 2008 (that is, liquidity, confidence, counterpart, credit, deleveraging, economic, Eurozone sovereign debt, banking, political, social) was probably strongly influenced by a few major triggering factors such as poor regulators' oversight activity, unclear rescue plans, poor financial firms' disclosure on risks, faulty corporate governance in financial firms, explosive growth of shadow banking, and a growing crony capitalistic system in the leading so-called "free market" economies.

Probably, the excessive power and influence of the financial sector as a whole over the last decades, on politics led to a perverse sense of overconfidence and impunity in the industry. As philosopher, theologian, and bishop, St Augustine of Hippo (about 354–430 A.D.) wrote: "It was pride (i.e. arrogance) that changed angels into devils; it is humility that makes men as angels" (Brown, 2000).

3 *The Financial Crisis Was Predictable and Avoidable*

The Alleged Inability to Predict and Avoid the Crisis

The first chapter provided a number of evidences that seem to confirm the assumption that a set of combined factors have led to the crises of 2007–2009; and that these factors were identifiable and represented patterns of predictability. Further, these findings were also highlighted in the final report of the Financial Crisis Inquiry Commission (FCIC, 2011) which also supports the same conclusion.

In this chapter the focus is on a more in-depth analysis of some triggering factors that caused the financial crisis, based on a holistic and comprehensive overview of the available data in literature, in order to prove to the reader that the financial crisis was certainly predictable and avoidable, at least at a later stage of the property market and lending bubbles (2005). It will result quite evident, in fact, with the support of basic data and figures available at the time of the housing and lending bubbles, that key industry players and regulators were absolutely aware (through clear early warning signs) of the fact that the subprime mortgage market was going through a classic lending boom–bust scenario.

It will also result quite evident with the available industry data, some credit and risk management expertise, an industry-wide perspective, and some "common sense," that a number of scholars and practitioners were able to recognize the excessive risk-taking strategies of many financial firms, their highly interconnected activities, and the high probability of an incumbent financial crisis. Thus, the reader will realize that a large number of analysts, scholars, organizations, and industry experts were probably aware of the risk of a potential implosion of the financial system, except that many of them could probably not determine (or may not have felt that it was their responsibility to do it) when it would actually occur or what would be the exact magnitude of its aftermath.

Although it seems to be the dominant view that political leaders, central bank leaders, industry leaders, regulators, economists, credit rating agencies, and journalists were caught off guard by the financial crisis and its consequences, the evidences reported in this book prove just the opposite. What is difficult to determine is whether these people were actually caught off guard or whether they just refused to recognize what was really happening due to their ideological beliefs or other purposes (that is, conflicts of interest).

Some authors think that the financial crisis was fueled by lenders' overconfidence in their state-of-the-art risk models, resilience of self-correcting markets, and unrealistic expectations of all stakeholders on constantly rising housing market prices. These understandings, although on a first blush may seem reasonable, do not seem to reflect the full spectrum of findings of this book or that of the 2011 FCIC final report.

To begin with, it is very important to recall, once again, the main conclusion of the US FCIC that states: "The captains of finance and the public stewards of our financial system ignored warnings and failed to question, understand, and manage evolving risks" (FCIC, 2011, p. xvii).

David Colander et al. (Friedman et al., 2011, pp. 262–266) explain that the financial crisis was a failure of the economic profession for a number of reasons. Among these they identify: (1) limited development of economic models on systemic crises; (2) the general idea, based on the standard equilibrium models, that "markets and economies are inherently stable and only temporarily get off track (limited external shocks);" (3) an ethical breakdown due to the fact that economists did not consider their responsibility to warn the public of the limitations (systemic externalities/risk factors) of their models. This brings us to the problem that the economic profession still does not have an ethical code; (4) the fault assumption that all uncertainty can be eliminated through the use of complex and highly advanced derivative instruments. Unfortunately, however, since the simulation-based pricing tools for such structured products (Collaterized Debt Obligations – CDO, Credit Default Swaps – CDS) relied mainly on historical data (from periods of low volatility) they have led to arbitrary assumptions about the correlation between risks and default probabilities; (5) the individual perspective of financial firms' asset-pricing and risk management tools, which caused them to ignore other participants' behavior and strategies thus leading them to have synchronous behavior and built-in contagion.

The final report of the FCIC, also states (FCIC, 2011, p. xvii):

There was an explosion in risky subprime lending and securitization, an unsustainable rise in housing prices, widespread reports of egregious and predatory lending practices, dramatic increases in household mortgage debt, and exponential growth in financial firms' trading activities, unregulated derivatives, and short-term repo lending markets, among many other red flags. Yet there was pervasive permissiveness; little meaningful action was taken to quell the threats in a timely manner.

Joseph E. Stiglitz (2010, p. 1) in his book *Freefall. America, Free Markets, and The Sinking of the World Economy*, says:

A deregulated market awash in liquidity and low interest rates, a global real estate bubble, and skyrocketing subprime lending were a toxic combination. Add in the US fiscal and trade deficit and the corresponding accumulation in China of huge reserves of dollars – an unbalanced global economy – and it was clear that things were horribly awry.

Stiglitz (2010, p. 11) also clearly indicates in his book that the crisis was generated by:

... flawed incentives (for bankers and many other players in the financial markets), a flawed system of corporate governance, inadequate enforcement of competition laws, imperfect information, and inadequate understanding of risk on the part of the investors.

An interesting contribution to shed some light on this matter is also represented by the interview offered in March 2011 by Mervyn King, Governor of the Bank of England, to the British newspaper the *Telegraph*. In that interview he reported that banks pay huge bonuses to their management "because they live in a 'too big to fail' world, in which the state will bail them out on the downside" (Moore, 2011).

According to Mervyn King's view, "Casino-type banking caused the crisis of 2007–2009" (Johnson, 2011b).

Mervyn King also mentioned the following in the interview:

> *Financial services don't like the word "casino." But instruments were created and traded only within the financial community. It was a zero sum game. No one knew which ones were the winners when the crisis hit. Everyone became a suspect. Hence, no one would provide liquidity to any of those institutions. (Moore, 2011)*

Based on the opinion of Mervyn King, it seems quite evident the "moral hazard" of many key players in the industry, who knew what was happening in the real estate and financial markets, but just preferred to progress recklessly in their zero sum game delirium in order to be on the top of the game, to make the most profit, and to beat the competition (Moore, 2011).

Thus this contribution seems to confirm that greed and moral hazard have been a trigger of this vicious zero sum game. They have allowed all agents involved in the industry to systematically and recklessly ignore all early warning signs and to transfer the devastating default risk onto other players or highly vulnerable and uninformed investors all over the world, due to the complexity of the traded financial instruments and the typical asymmetric information in the shadow banking environment (Moore, 2011).

Mervyn King also added in the same interview: "We allowed a system (banking) to build up which contained the seeds of its own destruction" (Moore, 2011).

In their paper "Did Securitization Lead to Lax Screening? Evidence from Subprime Loans," Keys et al. (2010) investigated "the relationship between securitization and screening in the context of subprime mortgage loans," using a sample of more than one million home purchase loans during the period from 2001 to 2006. The empirical findings of this study show that "there was a causal relationship between securitization and lax lending standards/screening" (Keys et al., 2010, pp. 219–222).

Furthermore, their research also indicated that the lenders' behaviors in the subprime market were seriously affected by the ease of securitization and the lack of transparency and disclosure in the originate-to-distribute model (OTD), which created incentives for lenders and other players to take advantage of the asymmetric information between themselves and investors in order to reduce the screening on borrowers' risk and the related costs (Keys et al., 2010, pp. 222–223).

According to the same authors, mortgage originators and banks relied for their underwriting process almost entirely on Fair Isaac and Company (FICO) scores ("hard" information), with limited or no attention at all to the collecting and screening of relevant and critical "soft" information (for example, job verification, income, asset verification, and so on) on the borrowers, which significantly reduced their ability to assess risk and to properly reflect in their risk models the real level of borrowers' risk and their lending policies and strategies (Keys et al., 2010, p. 223).

Even Sabry and Okongwu (2009) of the NERA Economic Consulting organization in their article "How Did We Get Here? The Story of the Credit Crisis," report that relatively lax underwriting and less documentation have contributed, among other factors, to the deterioration of mortgage quality, and ultimately to the crisis. They indicate in their article that, "according to the survey conducted by the Office of the Comptroller of the Currency (OCC), credit underwriting standards were eased during the years 2004 to 2006" (Sabry and Okongwu, 2009, p. 6).

The survey reported a significant increase in the percentage of lenders that have adopted eased retail credit underwriting standards, which rose from 3 percent in 2002 to 28 percent in 2006. The OCC surveyed the examiners of the largest 78 national banks. The same increasing trend was revealed in the survey also regarding the percentage of loans with full documentation, which declined from 64 percent in 2003 to approximately 50 percent in 2007 (Sabry and Okongwu, 2009, pp. 6–7).

Erik F. Gerding (2010) raises the issue that:

> The widespread use of computer-based risk models in the financial industry during the last two decades enabled the marketing of increasingly complex financial products to consumers. (Gerding, 2010, p. 293)

He has stated:

> ... by linking consumer lending to capital markets, these models fueled explosive growth in mortgage and other consumer loans ... thus leading to a situation in which regulators outsourced vast responsibility for regulating risk in consumer finance and financial markets to privately owned industry models, reassured by the ability of risk models to help financial institutions measure and manage risk. (Gerding, 2010, pp. 293–299)

Thus for Gerding (2010), "Lenders and mortgage brokers employed sophisticated data mining and scoring/rating models to target riskier borrowers, confident of their state-of-the-art models." Many of the new "exotic" mortgages have been engineered to convert low fixed rates to higher adjustable rates that the higher credit-risk borrowers would be able to pay, in the worst case scenario, either through refinancing or through the sale of the mortgaged property, as long as the housing market would continue to grow (Gerding, 2010, p. 295).

Gerding also indicates in his article "The Outsourcing of Financial Regulation to Risk Models" (Gerding, 2010, p. 295), that:

> The Federal Bank regulators, including Federal Reserve chairman, Alan Greenspan, expressed reluctance to regulate these practices, citing a belief that the models used by lenders both effectively assessed risk and enabled many high-credit-risk borrowers to afford their first homes.

Lending to a massive number of subprime borrowers, however, is not the same as lending to typical prime customers, or Alt A borrowers. Subprime borrowers, as previously indicated, are in general higher-risk profiles (higher credit default probability). "They are individuals with a weak credit history and are heavily in debt" (Hojnacki and Shick, 2008, p. 25). Moreover, via the liar loan concept, what was placed on paper was accepted as fact with no further due diligence being performed.

"The subprime borrowers' classifications vary among lenders, however, bank regulators typically define them by the following characteristics" (Bender, 2007, p. 4):

- "Two or more 30-day delinquencies in the past 12 months."
- "One or more 60-day delinquencies in the past 24 months."
- "Bankruptcy in the previous 5 years."
- "A high probability of default as measured by FICO credit score," typically with score below 620 and losses in double digits.
- "A debt service-to-income ratio of 50 percent or more."
- Higher mortgage rates than prime borrowers or Alt A borrowers.

Or as Sabry and Okongwu (2009, p. 3) indicate:

- high loan-to-value (LTV) ratio of 80 percent or more;
- less documentation.

Or as Jarsulic (2010, p. 10) indicates:

- mortgage loans originated by lenders specializing in high-cost loans;
- 2/28 or 3/27 "hybrid" mortgages.

Or as Hughlett indicates (Hojnack and Shick, 2008, p. 26):

- the subprime market can be also "segmented by quality, and has grades from A (highest Quality) to D (lowest quality)."

For the approval of these types of mortgage loans, "lenders lowered their standards for creditworthiness, capacity, or collateral, or all three at the same time" (Johnson and Kwak, 2010a, pp. 126–128).

According to Calem et al. (2006), subprime borrowers are typically people living "in neighborhoods with high concentrations of minorities and weaker economic conditions" (Chomsisengphet and Pennington-Cross, 2006, pp. 31–32).

A clear indicator of the higher risk of the subprime mortgage loans portfolio compared to prime mortgage loans was reported a few years before the peak of the final crisis by the Mortgage Bankers Association of America (MBAA). They indicated in their National Delinquency Survey in 2002 that the subprime loan delinquency rate in the third quarter of 2002 was five and a half times higher than that of the prime mortgage loans (14.28 versus 2.54 percent). The subprime loans' foreclosure rate in the same period was even worse; "more than 10 times that for prime loans (2.08 versus 0.20 percent)" (Chomsisengphet and Pennington-Cross, 2006, p. 32).

According to Calem et al.: "The subprime market has introduced many different pricing tiers and product types, which have helped to move the mortgage market closer to price rationing or risk-based pricing" (Chomsisengphet and Pennington-Cross, 2006, p. 32).

They indicate that the risk-based pricing methodology is typically based on the following factors: "Delinquency payments, foreclosures, bankruptcies, debt ratios, credit scores, and Loan-to-Value (LTV) ratios" (Chomsisengphet and Pennington-Cross, 2006, p. 36).

Still according to the same authors, subprime loans differ significantly from the prime loans since they have high upfront costs and continuing costs. Upfront costs include the following fees: "Application fees, appraisal fees, and other fees associated with originating a mortgage" (Chomsisengphet and Pennington-Cross, 2006, p. 32). The continuing costs include the following costs: "Mortgage insurance payments, principle and interest payments, late fees and fines for delinquency payments, and fees levied by a locality (such as property taxes and special assessments)" (Chomsisengphet and Pennington-Cross, 2006, p. 32). The borrower is also allowed to lower the interest rates by paying extra fees. This "practice is called paying points" (Chomsisengphet and Pennington-Cross, 2006, p. 48). In other words, subprime borrowers are a gold mine if their risk is properly managed by lenders and mortgage originators.

Furthermore, it is important to remember that many subprime borrowers were not individuals who owned and occupied their properties, but rather people who held them for investment or speculation purposes. Thus, in the period 2006–2007, with interest rates increasing and house pricing starting to fall (the end of the real estate and credit bubbles), many of the subprime borrowers with Adjustable Rate Mortgages (ARMs), aware of the fact that they had little, no, or even negative equity in their properties, and faced with severe delinquency and foreclosure rates, preferred to simply walk away rather than struggle to make the payments on their mortgage loans. "The borrower has a financial incentive to default on the mortgage loan when the loan amount is larger than the value of the house" and when he/she does not occupy the property (Hojnacki and Shick, 2008, p. 32; Chomsisengphet and Pennington-Cross, 2006, pp. 48–50).

In general, lenders target subprime borrowers to earn all the above mentioned higher interest rates and fees/penalties. As many authors have already stated, subprime, in itself, is not bad, as it may help borrowers who are denied access to other sources of funds to get the money they need to purchase assets and to rebuild their credit ratings. The problems arise when the bankers, mortgage originators, and mortgage brokers are targeting a massive number of subprime borrowers, with poor or insufficient credit screening and with high profitability incentives to take more risks than they should (OTD model), due also to negligent regulatory controls.

This is exactly what happened in the years preceding the 2007–2009 financial crisis. It is always important to remember that, in spite of the sophisticated risk management and financial engineering tools orchestrated by the Wall Street wizards before the financial crisis, the aftermath of the crisis clearly indicates that there was no effective systemic risk mitigation technique available on the market when key players of the industry simultaneously, systematically, and deliberately ignored basic fundamental rules of finance and lending, "good old" common sense, ethical and professional standards, and early warning indicators. Not so much for the severely increased delinquencies and foreclosures rates but rather for the viral diffusion in the industry of mutual distrust among financial institutions and between investors and financial institutions, due to the difficulty in determining the real dimension of the problem (that is, betting on complex derivatives, short-term funding and liquidity issues, mispricing of assets, high leverage ratios, poor due diligence, poor transparency, underpriced CDS, unreliable credit ratings, and so on).

Daron Acemoglu (Friedman et al., 2011, pp. 253–254), addressing the concept of the capitalist economy, recognized that many, driven by ideological notions, have mistakenly equated free markets and self-regulated organizations with unregulated markets in which profit-seeking individuals and institutions (even with reputation capital) have taken risks from which they have earned a lot while others have had major losses. He also mentioned the following important statement: "Few among us will argue today that market monitoring is sufficient against opportunistic behavior" and that "the financial industry which contributes millions of dollars to the campaigns of senators and congressmen, do not have an acute influence on financial regulation" (Friedman et al., 2011, pp. 254–259).

My opinion on the origins of the financial crisis is quite aligned to the one of Daron Acemoglu (Friedman et al., 2011, pp. 260–261; Pezzuto, 2008) in the sense that we both state that the 2007–2009 crisis was not the failure of the capitalist system and of the free economy, but rather the failure of unregulated (financial) markets and unregulated risk management. I also share Luigi Zingales's view that crony capitalism has had a major impact on the 2007–2009 financial crisis (Zingales, 2012).

Early Warnings Reported by Leading Economists and Scholars in the Years Preceding the Crisis

Joseph E. Stiglitz (2010) said that a number of experts and globally recognized scholars, some of whom are Nobel laureates, anticipated the risk of the US economic crash and its aftermath a few years before the crisis. Among these Keynesian scholars he identified himself of Columbia University, economist Nouriel Roubini of NYU, "Princeton's economist Paul Krugman, financier George Soros, Morgan Stanley's Stephan Roach, housing expert Robert Shiller of Yale University, and Clinton's former Council of Economic Advisers/National Economic Council staffer, Robert Wescott." They all reported warnings of what was about to happen to the housing and financial markets but, unfortunately, these red flags were underestimated or disregarded by regulatory and supervisory authorities (Stiglitz, 2010, pp. 18–20). The Bush administration also tried to rein in Freddie, Fannie, and the Federal Housing Administration (FHA) as early as 2001, but was shot down by Dodd/Frank et al.

Table 3.1 aims to report and list some, although probably not all, industry experts and economists (called before the crisis "Cassandras") who have provided substantial and indisputable evidences of their prediction and communication of the early warnings of an incumbent financial crisis to regulatory and supervisory authorities before the end of 2007 but that were mostly ignored.

About the chance that the financial crisis could have been predicted, James Kwak (2010) argues that the mantra of a parade of the financial sector luminaries who appeared before the FCIC was: "no one saw this coming" or "it was the result of a complicated series of unfortunate mistakes, a giant accident" (Kwak, 2010).

Besides the fact that the FCIC (2011) has clearly stated, after three years of investigation, in its final report that the financial crisis was not just an "accident" or as Tim Geithner metaphorically called it "a "hundred-year flood," or in other words a natural disaster, James Kwak adds in his article (Kwak, 2010):

I find this incredibly frustrating. First of all, plenty of people saw the crisis coming. In late 2009, people like Nouriel Roubini and Peter Schiff were all over the airwaves for having predicted the crisis. Since then, there have been multiple books written about people who not only predicted the crisis but bet on it, making hundreds of millions or billions of dollars for themselves.

Table 3.1   Analysts Who Predicted the 2007–2009 Financial Crisis

Who Predicted?	What Was Predicted?	When Was Prediction Made?
Dean Baker, Co-Director of the Center for Economic and Policy Research (CEPR).	In his report "The Run-Up in Home Prices: Is it Real or Is It Another Bubble?" he predicted the start of the bubble in the housing market and the risk that the collapse of this bubble could lead to recession.	Paper published in 2002 (Baker, 2002).
Robert J. Shiller, Yale University Economist. Since 1980 he has been a research associate of the National Bureau of Economic Research (NBER). In 2005 he was Vice President of the American Economic Association in 2005, and in the period 2006–2007 President of the Eastern Economic Association.	Shiller co-authored a 2003 Brookings paper, "Is There a Bubble in the Housing Market?" Shiller subsequently further clarified his opinion in the second edition of *Irrational Exuberance* (2005), stating that "further rises in the stock and housing markets could lead to even more drastic declines in consumer and business confidence, and possibly to a worldwide recession." Writing in the *Wall Street Journal* in August 2006, Shiller raised attention to the problem stating: "there is significant risk of a very bad period, with slow sales, slim commissions, falling prices, rising default and foreclosures, serious trouble in financial markets, and a possible recession sooner than most of us expected" (Malaysia Finance blog, 2010).	His papers/books: "Is There a Bubble in the Housing Market?" (2003); *The New Financial Order: Risk in the 21st Century* (2003); *Irrational Exuberance* (2005); *The Subprime Solution: How Today's Global Financial Crisis Happened, and What to Do about It* (2008).
Nouriel Roubini, "Dr Doom," American Professor of Economics at New York University's Stern School of Business and Chairman of Roubini Global Economics.	He saw the real estate bubble and predicted the crisis. he wrote an article titled "Why Central Banks Should Burst Bubbles."	The Spring 2006 issue of *International Finance* (Roubini, 2006).
Peter Schiff, President of Euro Pacific Capital.	In various interviews, he said that the US economy was not strong and that the housing market would eventually crash causing high unemployment.	December 16, 2006 Fox News Debate (Schiff, 2006), (Schiff and Downes, 2007).

Who Predicted?	What Was Predicted?	When Was Prediction Made?
Raghuram Rajan, Professor of Finance at the Booth School of Business, University of Chicago and former Chief Economist at the International Monetary Fund from 2003 to 2007.	In the paper called "Has Financial Development Made the World Riskier?" presented at the Federal Reserve conference in Jackson Hole he asked: "If firms today implicitly are selling various kinds of default insurance to goose up returns, what happens if catastrophe strikes?"	2005 Federal Reserve conference in Jackson Hole (Rajan, 2005).
Nassim Nicholas Taleb, a Lebanese American philosopher, essayist, and practitioner of mathematical finance and scientific adviser at Universa Investments.	He wrote the book *The Black Swan: The Impact of the Highly Improbable*, an original and audacious analysis of the ways in which humans try to make sense of unexpected events. In this book he criticized the risk management methods used by the finance industry and warned about financial crises.	Random House; first edition April 17, 2007 (Taleb, 2007).
Mike Stathis, Chief Investment Strategist of AVA Investment Analytics.	He anticipated the financial crisis in the following publications: (1) *America's Financial Apocalypse: How to Profit from the Next Great Depression*; (2) *Cashing in on the Real Estate Bubble*; and *America's Financial Apocalypse: How to Profit from the Next Great Depression*, Condensed Edition.	2006 (Stathis, 2006) 2007 (Stathis, 2007) 2008 (Stathis, 2008).
Brooksley Born, the Head of the Commodity Futures Trading Commission (CFTC). From 2009 to February 2011 she served as a commissioner on the FCIC.	She wrote a concept paper in 1998 warning about the dangerous lack of regulation in the over-the-counter (OTC) derivatives market and its potential systemic threat to the global economy.	1998 Concept Paper.

Source: Ivo Pezzuto

Then James Kwak (2010) adds in the same article the following statement:

> Simon Johnson and I just wrote a book (13 Bankers) arguing that the crisis was no accident: it was the result of the financial sector's ability to use its political power to engineer a favorable regulatory environment for itself. In the period preceding the crisis nothing was being priced efficiently. The CDO debt was being priced according to the rating agencies' models, which weren't even looking at sufficiently detailed data. And the credit default swaps were underpriced because they allowed banks to create new synthetic CDOs, which were another source of profits. Here's the first lesson: the idea that markets result in efficient prices was, in this case, hogwash. (Kwak, 2010)

Even (now ex-) Barclay's CEO, Bob Diamond, stated in speech on November 2011 that banks need to learn the lessons of past failures to "become better citizens" (Goff and Smith, 2011).

According to Lang and Jagtiani (2010), the "high mortgage defaults in 2006 and 2007 do not provide a sufficient explanation for why the housing and credit bubbles' shock led to a financial crisis that created doubts over the solvency of a number of major financial institutions" (Lang and Jagtiani, 2010, pp. 124–125).

Other famous academic economists who wrote about the impending crisis before the end of 2007 were Paul Krugman (summer 2007) and Martin Feldstein.

According to these authors, given the "information available at the time and the application of fundamental principles of modern risk management, the large and complex financial institutions" would have been able to protect themselves from the crisis (Lang and Jagtiani, 2010, p. 125).

Lang and Jagtiani (2010) argue in their paper "The Mortgage and Financial Crises: The Role of Credit Risk Management and Corporate Governance," that there are two explanations for the failure of risk management. These are:

> First, given government policies of too-big-to-fail (TBTF) – large firms did not have appropriate incentives to worry about "tail-risk" – the risk of large losses from low-probability events. Second, issues related to corporate governance and principal-agent conflicts have inhibited the function of a firm's internal control and risk management. (Lang and Jagtiani, 2010, p. 125)

The systemically risky banks probably relied excessively on the opaque off-balance-sheet vehicles (special purpose vehicles (SPVs), structured investment vehicles (SIVs), Conduits), on the non-recourse mortgage-backed securities (MBS) sales (distributing the risk to others), and on their advanced risk mitigation techniques (CDS), seriously underestimating in their models and strategies (or they thought it was the regulator's job to do systemic oversight) the probability of a liquidity freeze and of a simultaneous systemic meltdown of all asset classes of their structured products as a result of the lending and housing bubbles bursting (lending and housing market bubbles). Thus the too-big-to-fail phenomenon might have influenced the largest bankers' decision process, but probably, according to the authors, it was not the major driver of the excessive risk-taking.

Lang and Jagtiani (2010) also reported that one of the most serious reasons that led to the financial crisis was the combination of mispricing of the risks of complex securities and the excessive concentration in subprime mortgage-related structured products (Lang and Jagtiani, 2010, p. 125).

The following red flags and early warning signs support the assumption that key players in the industry were aware of the increasing riskiness of the housing and credit bubbles and of the imminent lending boom–bust scenario a few years before the crisis, but they probably had high incentives to ignore them (Stiglitz, 2010, p. 18). Some of these red flags are directly correlated with the roots of the crisis, combined with other factors; while others are more indirectly related to the crisis or to the boom–bust scenario that led to the crisis. Either way, these red flags clearly show how things were quite predictable for industry experts, oversight authorities, and regulators.

A Regulatory Environment that Favored a Wide Expansion of Subprime Lending

Since the 1980s the US Government has put "legislative pressures on banks to facilitate home-ownership by easing mortgage lending requirements," introducing "deductibility of mortgage interest payments and interest on home equity loans, along with real estate taxes, from taxable income and the repeal in 1997 of capital gains tax on most resales of residential property" (Posner, 2009, p. 112).

The "Depository Institutions Deregulation and Monetary Control Act (DIDMCA) of 1980 effectively abolished usury rate ceilings on the first-lien mortgages and thus paved the way for the higher cost subprime mortgages" (Chomsisengphet and Pennington-Cross, 2006, p. 38).

With the subsequent introduction of "the Alternative Mortgage Transaction Parity Act (AMTPA) in 1982, it became legally permitted to use variable interest rates and balloon payments," as well as to charge higher rates and fees to borrowers (Chomsisengphet and Pennington-Cross, 2006, p. 38).

The Tax Reform of 1986, which stimulated the growth of subprime mortgages by prohibiting the deduction of interest on consumer loans for income tax purposes, "has allowed interest expense deductions on consumer loans for a primary residence mortgage as well as one additional home. This tax reform thus encouraged homeowners to make home equity withdrawals (for example, through 'cash-out' refinancing of a mortgage)," as an alternative to the traditional consumer loan, and to choose high-cost mortgage debt instead of traditional consumer debt since it was cheaper. As a consequence of this reform, slightly over one-half of the subprime loan originations have been for cash-out refinancing (Chomsisengphet and Pennington-Cross, 2006, p. 38).

The 1991 Federal Deposit Insurance Corporate Improvement Act (FDICIA) required "prompt corrective action" to prevent weak banks from costing the bank insurance fund money, and to adopt a least cost resolution strategy for banks that did fail. Unfortunately, though, the law made an exception to the least cost resolution requirement in case of systemic risk. This meant that the rule did not apply to banks that got too big to threaten the stability of financial markets (Jarsulic, 2010, pp. 122–123).

Jeffrey Friedman (2011) stated that an amendment to the 1998 Basel Accords, the Recourse Rule, was adopted in 2001 by the Federal Reserve, Federal Deposit Insurance Corporation (FDIC), the OCC, and the Office of Thrift Supervision, which allowed the US banks to gain capital relief for private label mortgage-backed security (PLMBS) on their balance sheets through the creation of SIVs and other off-balance-sheet entities. Thus, according to Friedman, the Recourse Rule and the introduction of the Basel II Framework has encouraged banks to conserve regulatory capital and to free up capital to fund new assets, increasing their exposure to MBS (with high ratings) and government bonds (funded by "debt"). This practice has also encouraged banks to increase their "leverage," meaning the ratio of borrowed funds to capital (Friedman et al., 2011, pp. 26–29).

Jeffrey Friedman (2011) reports that the 1995 revised regulation governing the enforcement of the Community Reinvestment Act (CRA) required that all FDIC-insured mortgage-lending banks to make an active effort to lend to underprivileged borrowers (minorities and poor communities) (Friedman et al., 2011, p. 3).

The "New Bankruptcy Law" or The Bankruptcy Abuse Prevention and Consumer Protection Act of 2005 (BAPCPA) was designed to make it more difficult for some consumers to file for bankruptcy (Martenson, 2007).

The repeal in 1999 of the Glass–Steagall Act, which had separated investment and commercial banks and their activities, and the role of the capital markets, fostered the role of the banks in the development of the subprime mortgage market and has led to:

- the too-big-to-fail banks' phenomenon (implicit government's bail-out guarantee for the largest and systemically risky banks in case of bankruptcy). The smaller institutions probably just adopted a "me too" follower strategy due to their asymmetric information;
- the exponential growth of a largely unsupervised securitization process based on the OTD model;
- great incentives for excessive risk-taking and gambling with derivatives;
- the rapid expansion of the independent mortgage brokers operating in lightly regulated markets;
- a huge secondary market, led by Fannie Mae and Freddie Mac; and
- the creative invention of "off-balance-sheet," undercapitalized, and overleveraged financial vehicles which have severely contributed to the spreading of risk, the increase of operational complexity, and the reduction of transparency and disclosure for many unwary investors (Gramlich, 2007, pp. 50–65).

Financial Firms in Trouble that were mostly Ignored by Regulators, Oversight Authorities, and Other Stakeholders

In 1998, a highly leveraged hedge fund, Long-Term Capital Management (LTCM) faltered, as a result of heavy trading in derivatives, and was taken over by its creditors (Posner, 2009, p. 126).

Toward the end of 2006, some signs of distress in the mortgage market appeared when UBS decided to shut down its hedge funds in 2007 due to losses related to subprime lending products (Kolb, 2011, p. 89).

"In February 2007, HSBC Bank reported a loss of $1.8 billion on its mortgage portfolio, but the markets hardly noticed" (Tully, 2007).

In a press release of February 2007, Freddie Mac announced its intention to cease buying subprime mortgage loans that had a high probability of excessive payment shock and which would likely result in possible foreclosures (Kolb, 2011, p. 301).

On March 13, 2007 the Mortgage Bankers Association reported late or missed payments related to 4.95 percent of all mortgages and 13.4 percent of subprime loans (Kolb, 2011, p. 301).

In April 2007, a monoline mortgage finance company, heavily exposed to subprime lending, New Century Financial, filed for Chapter 11 bankruptcy (Lang and Jagtiani, 2010, p. 7).

"On June 1, 2007 Standard and Poor's and Moody's Investor Services downgraded over 100 bonds backed by second-lien subprime mortgages" (Kolb, 2011, p. 301).

"On June 12, 2007 Moody's downgraded ratings for $5 billion MBS" (Kolb, 2011, p. 301).

On July 11, 2007 Standard and Poor's placed on credit watch 612 securities backed by subprime residential mortgage loans (Kolb, 2011, p. 302), and in conjunction with Moody's, announced a collective downgrade of the credit ratings for 1,043 tranches of residential mortgage-backed securities (RMBS) backed by subprime mortgages as a result of the deteriorating performance of subprime loans (Jarsulic, 2010, pp. 39–40).

"On July 24, 2007 Countrywide Financial Corporation warned of difficult conditions" (Kolb, 2011, p. 302).

On July 31, 2007, Bear Stearns began to disclose some liquidity problems on its funds (Bear Stearns High Grade Structured Credit Strategies Fund and Bear Stearns High Grade Structured Credit Strategies Enhanced Leverage Fund). These funds were coming under pressure after reporting, in April 2007, a 23 percent lower value for the year on the enhanced fund as a consequence of the withdrawal of investors' funds. On June 7, 2007, "Bear Stearns revealed that it spent $32 billion to bail-out two of its hedge funds exposed to the subprime market (the largest bail-out of a fund by a bank in almost a decade)" and sent a letter to investors saying it was suspending redemptions because the investment manager believed that the company would not have sufficient liquid assets to pay investors (Kolb, 2011, p. 302).

Bear Stearns came under Securities and Exchange Commission (SEC) supervision in 2005 and the supervisory authority reported the following findings:

> *The firm's risk managers lacked expertise in mortgage-backed securities, models designed to measure mortgage risk were not reviewed formally, there was persistent understaffing, and a lack of independence from traders. The models that were used to evaluate mortgage-related risk did not incorporate fundamental mortgage credit risk factors, including house price appreciation, consumer credit scores, and delinquency rates patterns. In addition, the SEC Office of Inspector General (SECOIG) found evidence that the overall risk management at Bear was often nothing more than window dressing, with little influence on actual trading decisions. It was not until the end of 2007 that Bear incorporated house price appreciation into its mortgage risk models, but by then it was too late. (Jarsulic, 2010, p. 108)*

On August 9, 2007, "French bank BNP Paribas, suspended three large investment funds citing problems with the US subprime mortgage" lending market and the related securities (RMBs/CDOs). BNP Paribas disclosed that "it could not value the assets in the fund because the market had disappeared." This even caused a sharp collapse in the financial markets and a freeze of the short-term credit markets (Lang and Jagtiani, 2010, p. 131).

On September 14, 2007, Northern Rock, the UK's fifth largest mortgage lender, experienced a classic bank run with depositors lined up outside its branches desperately seeking to withdraw their funds (Kolb, 2011, p. 302).

From January 2005 to January 2007, Merrill Lynch acquired 12 major mortgage-related companies, of which First Franklin was the largest one specializing in subprime loans. It started to experience problems of profitability with its MBS portfolio in 2007 related to the subprime loans.

In October 2007, Merrill announced a write-down of $8.4 billion to acknowledge the declining value of its mortgage-related securities (Kolb, 2011, p. 302).

On October 11, 2007, Moody's downgraded more than 2,000 subprime MBS with an original value of $33.4 billion (Saunders and Allen, 2010, p. 32).

On October 15, 2007, Citigroup, a global lending bank, announced unrecognized losses of $6.4 billion and an additional $11 billion of losses on November 4; Chuck Prince contemporaneously resigned as Citi's CEO and was replaced by Robert Rubin (Kolb, 2011, p. 302) (ex-US Secretary of Treasury and ex-member of the board, and Vice Chairman of Goldman Sachs) (NNDB, 2012).

"On November 7, 2007, Morgan Stanley announces a $3.7 billion write-down. On December 13, 2007, Citigroup brings $49 billion in distressed assets onto its balance sheet" (Kolb, 2011, p. 302).

The Housing Market Bubble was Identified by Industry Experts as well as the Boom–Bust Scenario

According to Dean Baker (2002), Co-Director of the Center for Economic and Policy Research (CEPR), the housing bubble which started in August 2002, the credit bubble, and the lax underwriting criteria are all correlated to one another and were each related to the financial crisis. He reported that the housing bubble began in the late 1990s. He stated that in the period 1953–1995 housing prices mirrored the inflation rate, after 1995 housing prices increased at a rate well above the inflation differential (Baker, 2002, pp. 4–6).

In a research paper written in 2002 and titled "The Run-Up in House Prices: is it Real or Is it Another Bubble?" Dean Baker reported:

> This paper shows that there is no obvious explanation for a sudden increase in the relative demand for housing which could explain the price rise. There is also no obvious explanation for the increase in home purchase prices relative to rental prices. In the absence of any other credible theory, the only plausible explanation for the sudden surge in home prices is the existence of a housing bubble. (Baker, 2002, p. 17)

He also added in his paper of 2002:

> Since 1995 home sales prices have increased nearly 30 percent more than the overall rate of inflation. The average ratio of equity to home values is already near record lows. This ratio will plunge precipitously if the housing bubble collapses. The end of the housing bubble could also lead to serious financial disruptions, since many families are already heavily indebted. (Baker, 2002, p. 18)

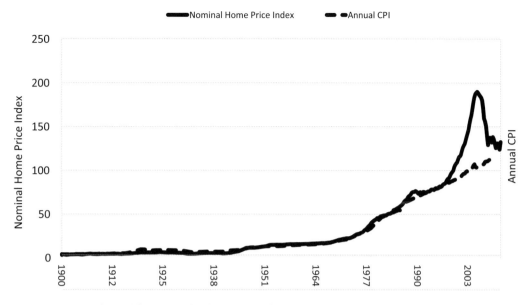

Source: Robert J. Shiller, *Irrational Exuberance*, 2nd. Edition, Princeton University Press, 2005, 2009.

Figure 3.1   Nominal Home Price Index versus Annual CPI

Source: Figure created by Eric Janszen, Founder and President of iTulip, Inc. http://www.twitter.com/itulip based on Robert Shiller's historical annual data from "Irrational Exuberance" 2nd edition, Princeton University Press, 2005–2009, and on the quarterly reported annual CPI data from the Bureau of Labor Statistics.

Robert Shiller (2005) confirmed these findings (as reported in Figure 3.1), as a historical anomaly, indicating that the real price of houses (that is after adjusting nominal prices for inflation) had not changed from approximately 1890 to 1995. Since 1998, however, home prices climbed 6 percent per year. The Home Price line reported the *"Case-Shiller Price Index* is based on data collected on repeat sales of single family homes." This index was developed by "economists Karl Case, Robert Shiller, and Allan Weiss. The index is normalized to have a value of 100 in the first quarter of 2000" (Shiller, 2005, pp. 13–41). In the US, changes in home prices are not directly accounted in the Consumer Price Index (CPI) and price equivalent rentals are used to estimate the housing portion of the CPI for homeowner-occupied units. Since rental prices have had a less rapid increase in the period of the housing market boom the home price increases were not easily visible in the CPI but, of course, as indicated in Figure 3.1, the unusual pattern of housing price increases was easily and clearly visible using a time-series analysis of the National Case-Shiller *Nominal Home Price Index* compared to the CPI for the same time period.

According to Marc Jarsulic (2010), nominal house price appreciation began to accelerate at the end of 2002. Year-on-year growth rates between 1997 and 2002 ranged between 3.37 and 9.38 percent, whereas in 2003 the pace of home price appreciation picked up dramatically, rising to a maximum of 15.68 percent in the 2005 Q1 period, temporarily disguising the effect of bad underwriting standards, consumer expectations, and their personal consumption expenditures (PCE) (Jarsulic, 2010, p. 13).

Figure 3.1 shows that there were clear signs since 2002 that a housing bubble was commencing, and this information was available to everyone, including retail and commercial bankers, mortgage originators, mortgage brokers, securitizers, investment bankers, ordinary investors, and speculators (Shiller, 2005, pp. 13–24).

Combining the evidence presented in this chart with the low cost of credit, the rising housing price trends reported in Figure 3.7, and the unprecedented growth of subprime mortgage loan market and securitizations, it can be easily observed that both a housing and a credit bubble were predictable outcomes in the early 2000s (Sabry and Okongwu, 2009, p. 29).

Economist Nouriel Roubini (2006), in an interview reported the following statements:

> When supply increases, prices fall. That's been the trend for 110 years, since 1890. But since 1997, real home prices have increased by about 90 percent. There is no economic fundamental – construction costs, real income, migration, interest rates, demographics – that can explain this. It means there was a speculative bubble. And now that bubble is bursting. (Robledo, 2006)

A significant and unusual increase of house prices also occurred in Europe during the same years and in particular in the UK, Ireland, and Spain (Blanchard et al., 2011, p. 507).

Nouriel Roubini "in a meeting of the International Monetary Fund (IMF) on September 7, 2006 earned his nickname Dr Doom, as he told the audience that a generational crisis was coming." He stated:

> A once-in-lifetime housing burst would lay waste to the US economy as oil prices would soar, consumer shopping would stop, and the country would go into deep recession. The collapse of the mortgage market would trigger a global meltdown, as trillion of dollars of mortgage-backed securities would be unraveling. The shockwaves would destroy banks and other big financial institutions such as Fannie Mae and Freddie Mac, America's largest home loan lenders. (Rushe, 2008)

The moderator of the meeting commented: "I think perhaps we will need a stiff drink after that," while the members of the audience were laughing (Rushe, 2008).

According to Richard A. Posner (2009), Ben Bernanke, the current Chairman of the Federal Reserve, said in the fall 2005 that the rise in housing prices was not a bubble but rather it was the result, at least primarily, of changes in the fundamental economic forces affecting the housing industry. This statement was made just when the bubble was about to burst and when he was Chairman of the President's Council of Economic Advisers (Posner, 2009, p. 90).

He added, "These price increases reflect largely strong economic fundamentals" (Posner, 2009, p. 119). Marc Jarsulic (2010) added that the end of the housing market bubble was caused by the significant excess supply of single family houses, by the growing inventories of vacant and unsold houses, and by the little home equity non-prime borrowers had when their loans were originated. He also reported that homeowners' vacancy rates during the housing market bubble reflects the same trend as data on unsold inventories of new and existing houses. Furthermore, based on a paper issued by the IMF, it is demonstrated through a regression analysis that the inventory-to-sales ratio has a significant negative impact on house price changes (Jarsulic, 2010, pp. 32–51).

In May 2007, Ben Bernanke declared that mortgage defaults in the subprime market would not have "a serious broader spillover to banks or thrift institutions" (Posner, 2009, p. 132). Chairman Bernanke was not alone in this assessment. Kiff and Mills (2007) wrote:

> Notwithstanding the bankruptcy of numerous mortgage companies, historically high delinquencies and foreclosures, and a significant tightening in subprime lending standards, the impact thus far on core US financial institutions has been limited ... the results suggest that new origination and funding technology appear to have made the financial system more stable at the expense of undermining the effectiveness of consumer protection regulation. (Kiff and Mills, 2007, p. 3)

Ian Welsh of *The Huffington Post* (2009) reported in his article entitled "The Financial Crisis is Not a Black Swan Event" that the crisis was certainly generated by multiple factors, but it was not random, or as Nassim Nicholas Taleb would have named it, a "black swan event." It was instead predictable and predicted (Welsh, 2009). In his articles, he added the following statements:

> We could all read the charts showing a bubble in housing prices and sales. We could all see that derivatives were also in a bubble. We knew that leverage was out of control, ballooning to 30 percent or in many cases even higher numbers. We knew that with financial deregulation firms had started being involved in multiple types of businesses, putting retail banks at risk from their insurance or brokerage or investment banking arms. We all knew that the US savings rate had hit unsustainable lows and that the trade deficit was too high. We knew that the carry trade was introducing tons of hot money to the system (borrowing for nothing in Japan and using that money for leveraged plays elsewhere). And, perhaps most importantly, we should have known that executives in the financial sector paying themselves huge bonuses were concentrating on short term gains and did not care about long term viability of their companies or even care about the honesty of what they were doing, because hey, by the time it all fell apart, they'd be rich, rich, rich and never need to work again. (Welsh, 2009)

Demyanyk and Van Hemert (2011) reported in their paper "Understanding the Subprime Mortgage Crisis" the following words:

> The results of our research provide evidence that the rise and fall of the subprime mortgage market follows a classic lending boom–bust scenario, in which unsustainable growth leads to the collapse of the market ... there was a deterioration of lending standards and a decrease in the subprime-prime mortgage rate spread during the 2001–2007 period ... and the continual deterioration of loan quality could have been detected long before the crisis by means of a simple statistical exercise. We detected an increased likelihood of delinquency in low- and middle-income areas ... Furthermore, the empirical finding seems to suggest that the housing goals of the Community Reinvestment Act and/or Government Sponsored Enterprises – those intended to increase lending in low- and middle-income areas, might have created a negative by-product that is associated with higher loan delinquencies. (Demyanyk and Van Hemert, 2011, pp. 1852–1853)

Demyanyk and Van Hemert (2011) also reported in the introduction section of their paper the following words:

> *There has been a significant and systematic decline in the implicit credit standards of mortgage originators and lenders during the explosive growth of the subprime market in 2001–2006 which have determined a dramatic deterioration in the credit quality of originated mortgages. The deterioration is not directly clear from observed characteristics like the FICO credit score, but rather detected with a statistical technique that adjusts subprime loan performance for differences in borrower characteristics, loan characteristics, and macroeconomic conditions. Using loan-level data, we analyze the quality of subprime mortgage loans by adjusting their performance for differences in borrower characteristics, loan characteristics, and macroeconomic conditions. We find that the quality of loans deteriorated monotonically for six consecutive years before the crisis … and that the poor performance of the loans was not confined to a particular segment of the subprime mortgage market … In addition to the monotonic deterioration of loan quality, over the time, the average combined loan-to-value (LTV) ratio increased, the fraction of low documentation loans increased, and the subprime-prime rate spread decreased … Approximately 55 percent of the subprime mortgage loans were originated to extract cash, by refinancing an existing mortgage loan into a larger new mortgage loan. (Demyanyk and Van Hemert, 2011, pp. 1854–1856)*

The low house price appreciation of "vintages" (mortgage loans booked in 2006 and 2007) seems to have substantially contributed to the crisis. Problems could have been detected (and I add, prevented) long before the crisis, since the lending boom–bust scenario was quite evident before 2006.

> *We (meaning Demyanyk and Van Hemert) have used the proportional odds model to estimate the adjusted delinquency rates and we found out that High-LTV borrowers in 2006 and 2007 were riskier than those in 2001 in terms of probability of delinquency, and that securitizers were aware of the increasing riskiness of high-LTV borrowers since they adjusted mortgage rates accordingly. (Figure 3.2) (Demyanyk and Van Hemert, 2011, pp. 1849–1851, p. 1875)*

The Demyanyk and Van Hemert study (2011) is based on the First American CoreLogic LoanPerformance database as of June 2008 which includes loan-level data on 85 percent of all securitized subprime mortgages (more than half of the US subprime mortgage market). The subprime loans considered in the study are those underlying subprime securities, and in particular a sample of first-lien loans originated between 2001 and 2007, excluding the less risky Alt A mortgage loans. The adjusted delinquency rate is obtained by adjusting the actual rate for year-by-year variation in many variables such as FICO scores, LTV ratios, debt-to-income ratios, missing debt-to-income ratio dummies, cash-out refinancing dummies, owner-occupation dummies, documentation levels, percentage of loans with prepayment penalties, mortgage rates, margins, composition of mortgage contract types, origination amounts, metropolitan statistical area (MSA) house price appreciation since origination, change in state unemployment rate since origination, and neighborhood median income (Demyanyk and Van Hemert, 2011, p. 1849, p.1853).

  Goodman et al. (2012) report that credit availability was too loose during the years preceding the financial crisis. Many borrowers were able to buy homes with very low downpayments and with minimal documentation of income and assets. In fact, according to them, documentation standards were quite relaxed with well over 60 percent of origination being less than full-doc loans. Loan terms were also relaxed with 40 percent of the market in interest-only loans and 60 percent in ARMs. Furthermore, the combined

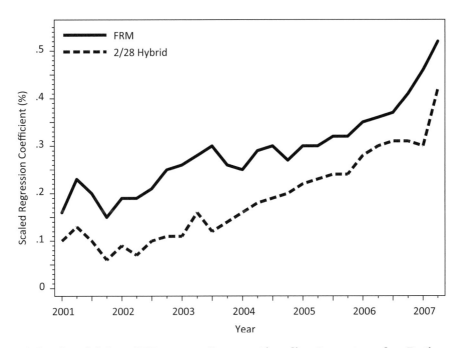

Figure 3.2   Sensitivity of Mortgage Rate to First-lien Loan-to-value Ratio

Source: Yuliya Demyanyk and Otto Van Hemert. *Understanding the Subprime Mortgage Crisis* Rev. Financ. Stud. (2011) 24(6): 1848–1880. By permission of Oxford University Press on behalf of The Society of Financial Studies.

loan-to-value (CLTV) at origination crept up, with 50 percent of loans with a CLTV rate below 80 percent at origination. According to them, these measures do not reflect the fraud that went into both appraisals and misrepresentation of borrower characteristics (that is, income, occupancy status, and so on) (Goodman et al., 2012. pp. 1–2).

With exponential housing market growth, an unprecedented house price appreciation, very low interest rates, massive underserved borrowers (subprime) eager to use mortgage loans to finance home purchases, bankers seeing huge fees for providing subprime loans, credit rating agencies earning huge fees for awarding AAA status to subprime securitizations, and numerous investors eager to earn relatively high yields promised by US subprime mortgage securities, it did not take much effort to have the Wall Street gurus and bankers design new and creative mortgages and financial engineering products to make record profits (Stiglitz, 2010, pp. 6–9; Pezzuto, 2008).

A wave of non-traditional mortgage loans and financial engineering products flourished in the years leading up to the housing and credit bubbles, creating additional stimuli to the rapid growth of both the lending and real estate markets (Jaffe, 2008, pp. 3–4; Stiglitz, 2010, pp. 85–89).

In the worst case scenario, these key players in the industry probably thought that they could still count on a number of key risk mitigation factors to avoid a potential default/bankruptcy. These factors were:

- the use of the OTD securitization allowed lenders to transfer a significant part of the borrowers' risk of credit default to someone else (for example, uninformed investors), through the sales of securities backed by non-recourse subprime mortgage loans, thus lax underwriting standards and poor risk management were not perceived as a major risk for the lenders/mortgage originators (Stiglitz, 2010 pp. 90–94; Pezzuto, 2008);
- the use of the securitization allowed lenders to mitigate risk through the sale (distribution) of different risk tranches of securities-backed by mortgages to a target of highly diversified group of global investors with different risk appetites (Sabry and Okongwy, 2009, pp. 15–17);
- the massive recourse CDS provided a sort of insurance against the risk of borrowers' defaults (Sabry and Okongwy, 2009, pp. 19–21);
- the high value collateral of the mortgage loans, represented by the increasing house prices and the irrational optimism of lenders about the possibility that these prices could keep on rising indefinitely, and was expected to be a sort of lifeline against any potential default threat (Kolb, 2010, pp. 211–213);
- the subprime mortgage rates (tier pricing, risk-based pricing, and ARMs) would be able to cover for the higher risk of the growing subprime lending market and the rising interests rates (Chomsisengphet and Pennington-Cross, 2006, pp. 48–55);
- the combined effect of low mortgage loan rates and high and increasing house prices would allow a certain security for lenders since, in case of borrowers' credit distress, the refinancing of the mortgage loans or sale of the houses would significantly reduce the risk of default (Chomsisengphet and Pennington-Cross, 2006, pp. 48–55);
- the overconfidence/irrational expectations of lenders and investment funds that house price declines would not occur simultaneously in the entire country, affecting all lending products at the same time (systemic risk). A low correlation hypothesis was probably estimated amongst the lenders and other financial institutions (Sabry and Okongwu, 2009, pp. 16–17);
- the reassuring or complacent seal of approval of the credit rating agencies in the assessment of MBS risk also increased the security and confidence of many stakeholders involved in the industry (Stiglitz, 2010, p. 7);
- the significant involvement of the government-sponsored enterprises (GSE) (Fannie Mae and Freddie Mac) in the subprime and MBS markets probably encouraged many investors to believe that these institutions still had a sort of backing of the US Government (Stiglitz, 2010, p. 11).

As a last resort in case of default, if all the above mitigation factors did not work, the major lenders and financial institutions probably felt confident that the Government would eventually bail them out in order to avoid a systemic or "domino effect" failure of the entire financial system and a possible prolonged economic recession or depression. This hypothesis is well-known and called by many knowledgeable authors, such as Stiglitz, Johnson and Kwak, and others, as the too-big-to-fail advantage of largest financial institutions (Stiglitz, 2010, pp. 82–83; Johnson and Kwak, 2010a, p. 12).

According to Richard A. Posner (2009), the housing and credit bubbles were a response to "what seemed to be a new era in finance, the result of the widespread securitization of debt and a global capital surplus that was expected to keep interest rates low indefinitely" (Posner, 2009, pp. 75–77).

It is also important to mention that even though the average FICO credit score did not get worse in the years leading up to the financial crisis, but it actually increased, savvy credit managers, risk and governance managers, and audit and risk review specialists should have been able to identify quite easily a number of evident underwriting process failures, the massive increase of higher risk borrowers' profiles (subprime) in their portfolios, and the unfit "exotic" lending products for this specific target market segment. Through the use of rigorous underwriting criteria, seasoned lending experience, advanced portfolio risk simulation and monitoring models, and portfolio stress testing techniques, they should have been able to identify and prevent these failures. For example, the massive increase in fraudulent mortgage loans applications with corrupted or manipulated data (that is, personal data of the mortgage loan applicants, out of patter profiles, inconsistencies between borrower profiles and loans characteristics, or by geo-demographic characteristics and loan characteristics during the housing market bubble and lending bubble, and so on) could have been significantly reduced with the existing state-of-the-art anti-fraud detection models and the expert supervision of banks' anti-fraud unit and internal controls managers.

The Deterioration of Mortgage Loans Could Have Been Mitigated with Appropriate Timely Monetary and Fiscal Policies and Reforms in the Financial Markets

As reported in Chapter 2 of this book (Figure 2.3), since the beginning of 2004 an impressive growth of subprime mortgage loan originations occurred, by 2006 reaching a rate of 23.5 percent of the total mortgage lending market. "The consequent rise in loan default rates suggests that this increase in subprime loan origination was related to a decline in loan quality," as indicated in Figure 2.4 (Hojnacki and Shick, 2008, pp. 29–31).

Lang and Jagtiani (2010) also reported that the boom in housing prices and in the supply of mortgage loans in the period 2000–2006 was combined with a dramatic decline in underwriting standards affecting in particular subprime loans. "The median combined loan-to-value (CLTV) ratio for subprime loans rose under 90 percent to 100 percent in 2006. Similarly, the share of subprime loans with piggy-back mortgages (simultaneous second mortgages) and low documentation increased substantially over this period" (Lang and Jagtiani, 2010, pp. 126–128).

The growth rate of the private-label RMBS market in the period 2003–2007 was staggering. It reached approximately 56 percent in 2006 from about 20 percent before 2003. There was also a massive growth in non-conforming loans that fueled the tremendous increase of the private-label securitization market and of the CDO issuances (Lang and Jagtiani, 2010, pp. 128–129).

Mian and Sufi (2008) reported in their study that "an expansion in the supply of mortgage loans to high latent demand zip codes" (subprime borrowers) in the period from 2001 to 2005 was due to the relative decline in "denial rates and interest rates and to the relative increases in mortgage lending and house prices," despite the fact that these zip codes had sharp decline of relative (and in some cases absolute) income growth in these neighborhoods (Mian and Sufi, 2008, pp. 1–7).

Mian and Sufi (2008) also identified "a sharp relative increase in mortgage debt-to-income ratios from 2001 to 2005," while the spread between prime and subprime mortgages instead declined to historically low rates from 2001 to 2005. The growth in securitization was much higher than the growth in the high latent demand zip codes. This additional evidence suggested even to these authors "a possible role of securitization in credit expansion" (Mian and Sufi, 2008, pp. 19–21).

Mian and Sufi (2008) also demonstrated "that the supply-driven expansion in lending to high latent demand zip codes" (subprime borrowers) was rapidly followed by a striking increase in default rates. According to Mian and Sufi (2008), the period "2001 to 2005 is the only period in recent US history in which house prices have risen in zip codes with relatively negative income growth." They concluded their research by stating that lenders generated massive increases in mortgage sales to subprime borrowers with the purpose of pushing securitization and consequently the sale of MBS to investors (Mian and Sufi, 2008, pp. 3–4).

Even Gabriel and Rosenthal (2007) reported that the great expansion of a secondary mortgage loan market was generated by a significant increase of mortgage lending to the subprime market (high-risk areas) (Gabriel and Rosenthal, 2007, pp. 26–28).

In addition to Mian and Sufi (2008), even Demyanyk and Van Hemert (2011) reported (Figure 3.3) that the spread between prime and subprime mortgages decreased in the years preceding the crisis. This was an early warning sign of a risky situation since, in general, the interest rates on subprime mortgages are higher than on prime mortgages (subprime mark-up) to compensate the lender for the risk premium associated with subprime loans. Instead the research evidence of Demyanyk and Van Hemert indicates that subprime–prime rate spread (which is the difference between the average subprime and price rates) has been declining significantly over time, with the largest decline between 2001 and 2004, which coincides with the most rapid growth in loans origination, while the riskiness of the subprime mortgage loans was increasing. This decline was not due to general risk aversion, since compared with the BBB and AAA corporate bond yield spreads, "the actual subprime-prime rate spread declined much more and more steadily" (Mian and Sufi, 2008, p. 13; Demyanyk and Van Hemert, 2011, p. 1873).

In order to simplify the analysis on the subprime–prime rate spread, Demyanyk and Van Hemert's paper focused on fixed-rate mortgages, since the price of hybrid mortgages complicates the comparison, being determined by a combination of "initial teaser rate and the margin over the index rate" (Demyanyk and Van Hemert, 2011, p. 1873).

In the following figure (Figure 3.4), the same authors show also, with the use of a cross-sectional ordinary least squares (OLS) regression analysis of loan-level data from 2001 through 2006, and after adjusting for differences in observed loan, borrower characteristics, and house price changes, an evident deterioration over the period of loan quality and a steady subprime–prime spread decline between 2001 and 2007, and on a per-unit-of-risk basis analysis, that subprime–prime spread decreased even more than the level of the spread. In other words, as the quality of the subprime mortgage loans dramatically deteriorated, the subprime mark-up also declined over time, and thus the situation was not sustainable. In fact, the market crashed in 2007 (Demyanyk and Van Hemert, 2011, pp. 1873–1875).

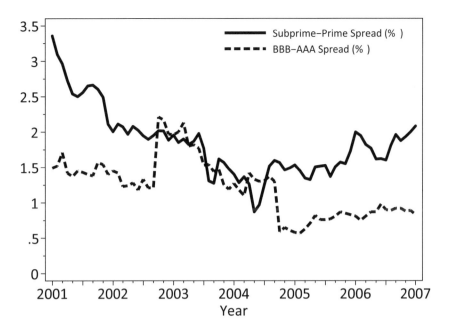

Figure 3.3   FRM Rate Spread and Corporate Bond Yield Spread

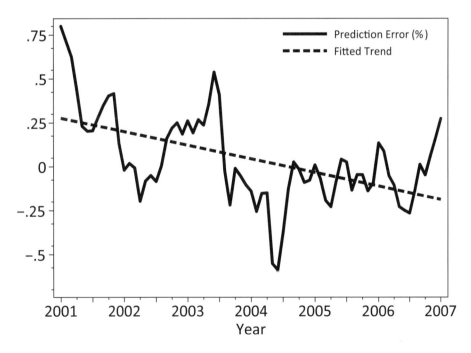

Figure 3.4   Prediction Error in the Subprime–Prime Rate Spread

Source for Figures 3.3 and 3.4: Yuliya Demyanyk and Otto Van Hemert. *Understanding the Subprime Mortgage Crisis* Rev. Financ. Stud. (2011) 24(6): 1848–1880. By permission of Oxford University Press on behalf of The Society of Financial Studies.

The prediction error in the subprime–prime rate spread has been determined in a regression of the spread rate and some loan and borrower characteristics such as: (1) FICO credit score; (2) a dummy variable that equates one if full documentation was provided; (3) a dummy variable that equates one if prepayment penalty is present; (4) origination amount; (5) value of debt-to-income ratio; (6) a dummy variable that equates one if debt-to-income was not provided; (7) a dummy variable that equates one if loan is a refinance; (8) a dummy variable that equates one if a borrower is an investor; (9) LTV ratio based on first lien; and (10) LTV ratio based on second, and third, and so on, liens if applicable (Demyanyk and Van Hemert, 2011, p. 1874).

As stated earlier, experienced credit and risk managers know that there is limited effective protection against a massive adverse selection of subprime borrowers originated with poor credit screening, lax risk controls, and limited documentation and verifications (for example, income, employment, excessive LTV ratio, poor appraisal of the collateral, and so on), inadequate supervisory and regulatory oversight, and under adverse market conditions, major macroeconomic changes, and inadequate assumptions on mortgage loans, probability of defaults and asset correlation of mortgage-backed securities (Pezzuto, 2008).

In terms of observable borrower characteristics a credit originator might not have noticed the early warning signs of the lending boom–bust scenario, focusing only on the FICO score, since such score on average actually increased over those years (Demyanyk and Van Hemert, 2011, p. 1855). Thus a narrow-focused perspective of the portfolio risk of single business lines and the lack of a firm-wide risk perspective and industry-wide benchmarks might have limited to a certain extent the ability of risk managers to identify the triggering factors of a potential systemic risk, even though, COSO ERM framework and its best practices were quite familiar to risk experts in the early 2000s.

Furthermore, given the proliferation of many new and non-conventional mortgage products, the manipulation of subprime borrower's data, and the fact that scoring models were created using data from earlier periods of rising home prices, the only use of the FICO score to assess borrowers' credit risk might have been somehow misleading as an early warning indicator (Lawrence and Solomon, 2002, pp. 43–70; Stiglitz, 2010, pp. 85–94; Sabry and Okongwu, 2009, pp. 5–10; Hinton and Cohen-Cole, 2011, pp. 1–8).

Predatory lenders, mortgage originators, and mortgage brokers have in some cases orchestrated and manipulated a borrower's data (for example, employment, income, home value appraisal, and so on) to increase the approval rate and the loan amounts of subprime mortgages in order to earn higher fees and commissions (Stiglitz, 2010, pp. 85–89).

Even though the loan and borrowers' characteristics have changed significantly in the years leading up to the crisis, a rigorous and timely analysis of the underwriting data might have revealed to expert credit originators and risk managers during 2001–2002 some critical early warning signs of the deterioration of the credit quality of the subprime mortgage loans. The lenders were heavily targeting high credit risk borrowers.

Mortgage lenders might have identified, through rigorous credit screening, evident signs of changing characteristics of the borrowers' profiles and the systematic overrides from standard credit policies and traditional lending practices. Some of these evidences include:

- poor documentation;
- excessive reliance on FICO scores;
- limited or missing additional "soft" information for loan approval;
- overstated and inflated incomes and collateral value appraisals;
- inconsistency between increasing average scores and riskier borrowers' profiles (higher concentration of risky subprime borrowers);
- low relative risk-based pricing for subprime mortgage loans compared to prime mortgage loans;
- excessive borrowers' recourse to refinancing schemes; and
- high debt-to-income ratios and combined LTV ratios (Demyanyk and Van Hemert, 2007, pp. 1–5).

In other words, good old common sense, some macroeconomic data, and some underwriting experience might have generated some suspicion in the mind of any seasoned loan officer or credit risk manager that something was not right. As Joseph E. Stiglitz put it: "Too much money was being made by too many people for warnings to be heard by anyone" (Stiglitz, 2010, p. 18).

Marc Jarsulic (2010), reported that after the failure of IndyMac, the Treasury's Office of Inspector General (OIG) conducted a loss review that revealed that IndyMac's business model was designed to produce as many loans as possible with poor or no adequate underwriting criteria (for example, borrowers' qualifications, income, assets, employment, and property appraisals – no compliance with the Uniform Standard of Professional Appraisal Practice (USPAP)) and to sell them in the secondary market (Jarsulic, 2010, pp. 97–99).

Jarsulic (2010) also reported the statement made by New Century's former Chief Credit Officer who noted in 2004 that the company had no standard for loan quality. This gentleman indicated that the board of directors and senior management told the examiners that their predominant standard for loan quality was whether the loans originated could be sold or securitized in the secondary market (Jarsulic, 2010, pp. 100–101).

Regarding the mortgage GSE (Fannie Mae and Freddie Mac), according to Jarsulic (2010), there had been evident signs of an imminent disaster since the early days of the housing market bubble and lending bubble. Freddie Mac's Chief Risk Officer (CRO), David Andrukonis, was fired in 2004 after writing a message to the CEO, Richard Syron, in which he warned Freddie Mac management to immediately withdraw from the No Income/No Asset (NINA) market, declaring it inconsistent with the company's mission and potential reputation risk. He also stated that his recommendation was based on an adverse selection of the target borrowers and on the evidence that the first-year delinquency rates on these mortgages were ranging from 8 to 13 percent with a high concentration of Hispanic borrowers (which supported his hypothesis of predatory lending) (Jarsulic, 2010, pp. 106–107).

Demyanyk and Van Hemert (2011) reported in their paper, based on the analysis of subprime ("risky" and "exotic") mortgage loans (using the First American CoreLogic LoanPerformance database from 2008), that between 2001 and 2006 the number of originated loans quadrupled, while the average loan size almost doubled, and the share of loans with full documentation fell considerably over the same period (Demyanyk and Van Hemert, 2011, pp. 1853–1855). Strangely enough, however, in spite of the explosive growth of subprime mortgage loans with "light" credit screening (full documentation fell from 77 percent in 2001 to 67 percent in 2007) the average FICO credit score increased 20 points between 2001 and 2005. The combined LTV ratio instead slightly increased due to the increased popularity of second-lien and third-lien loans (Demyanyk and Van Hemert, 2011, p. 1855).

If the credit screening, underwriting models, and control processes were robust and reliable and the mortgage lenders' credit policies and underwriting criteria were just as sound, a profitable growth of the subprime borrowers' segment was certainly achievable, through a more selective credit origination process, with proper collateral appraisals, documentation checks (soft and hard), risk-based pricing, and so on. Instead, empirical evidence and available data seem to indicate that moral hazard probably prevailed in the years preceding the financial crisis (Stiglitz, 2010, pp. 85–89; Johnson and Kwak, 2010a, pp. 176–177).

Key players understood the unprecedented money making opportunity derived by the OTD securitization model and sale in the financial markets of non-recourse mortgage loans backed by "imaginary" insurance, unrealistic expectations on housing market price appreciation, and wrongly priced and over appraised collateral. Once they sold these toxic assets to others, the borrowers' default risk was (in large part) no longer their problem, but instead the massive acquisition of new subprime borrowers was just a source of additional profitability for them. Mortgage originators and banks thus had a strong incentive to stop their standard risk management practices, and became pure risk takers and "gamblers" – with other people's money! Some banks and investment funds dumped the risk of these toxic mortgage loans to uninformed investors (lack of disclosure and transparency) and in some cases even speculated against their clients through short selling and betting on the probability of default of some of the mortgage lending institutions or hedge funds heavily exposed to toxic assets (they were betting against their customers based on detailed knowledge), after having recommended to pension funds and other institutions that they invest in these "safe" securities (Pezzuto, 2008; Stiglitz, 2010, pp. 6–7; Johnson and Kwak, 2010a, pp. 165–179).

Given that, in some cases, probably, the mortgage broker, mortgage appraisers, mortgage originators, banks, securitizers, investment funds, auditors, due diligence analysts, and credit rating agencies might have set this up together in a sort of premeditated plan, it is difficult to determine whether in such circumstances the subprime mortgage defaults can be considered only the result of individual greed and moral hazard or the result of excessive and reckless collective gambling and even fraudulent behaviors (Pezzuto, 2008; Stiglitz, 2010, pp. 6–7; Johnson and Kwak, 2010, pp. 165–179).

As reported earlier in this chapter, Keys et al. (2010) in their paper "Did Securitization Lead to Lax Screening? Evidence From Subprime Loans," have come to the conclusion that there is a causal link between ease of securitization and screening and thus; this relationship explains one of the key drivers of the financial crisis. According to these authors, and based on the evidence of their empirical research on a sample of more than one million home purchase loans during the period from 2001 to 2006, lenders' behavior changed in the subprime market during the years leading to the crisis, thus contributing to the crisis. The ease of securitization generated the failure of the so-called OTD securitization process of non-recourse subprime mortgage loans characterized by limited disclosure to the investors (Keys et al., 2010, pp. 222–223).

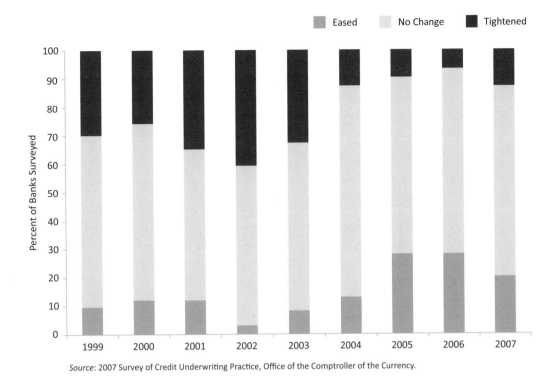

Source: 2007 Survey of Credit Underwriting Practice, Office of the Comptroller of the Currency.

Figure 3.5   Changes in Retail Credit Underwriting Standards Annual Data from 1999 through 2007

Source: (NERA Economic Consulting, 2009, p. 6.) "How Did We Get Here? The Story of the Credit Crisis." Reprinted with permission from NERA Economic Consulting.

In other words, Keys et al. (2010) "demonstrated that portfolios that were more likely to be securitized had higher default rates than portfolios with similar risk profiles (FICO scores) but with a smaller probability of being securitized" (Lang and Jagtiani, 2010, pp. 134–135).

Similarly, Dell'Ariccia et al. (2008) found evidence that increasing recourse to loan sale and asset securitization changed lender behavior and lending standards (Lang and Jagtiani, 2010, pp. 134–135).

Evidences reported by Sabry and Okongwu of the NERA Economic Consulting enterprise (2009, pp. 5–6) seem to confirm the hypothesis that relatively lax underwriting standards and less complete documentation have contributed, among other factors, to the portfolio deterioration of mortgage quality and ultimately to the credit crisis. In their article "How Did We Get Here? The Story of the Credit Crisis" they indicated that according to "the survey conducted by the Office of the Comptroller of the Currency (OCC), credit underwriting standards were eased during the years 2004 to 2006." The share of subprime mortgages backing private-label asset-backed securities (ABS) with full documentation has significantly declined from 2002 and 2006 (Figure 3.5), and the percentage of banks reporting eased credit underwriting standards in the same period has significantly increased (the survey was based on the 78 largest banks) (Sabry and Okongwu, 2009, pp. 6–18).

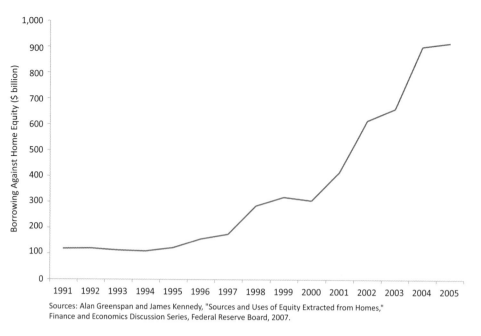

Sources: Alan Greenspan and James Kennedy, "Sources and Uses of Equity Extracted from Homes,"
Finance and Economics Discussion Series, Federal Reserve Board, 2007.

Figure 3.6   Gross Equity Extraction Increased Significantly Since 2000, Annual Data from 1991 through 2005

Source: (NERA Economic Consulting, 2009, p. 8.) "How Did We Get Here? The Story of the Credit Crisis." Reprinted with permission from NERA Economic Consulting.

Another evidence of red flags is provided by Demyanyk and Van Hemert (2007). Looking at the data of the "loan-level database containing information on about half of all US subprime mortgages originated between 2001 and 2006," they identified that "during the explosive growth of the subprime market in period 2001–2006, the quality of loans dramatically deteriorated and the underwriting criteria loosened." They have also stated in their paper the following concepts:

> The seeds for the crisis were sown long before 2007 ... we have found evidence that securitizers were aware of the increasing riskiness of high-LTV borrowers and adjusted mortgage rates ... but a high house price appreciation in 2003–2005 masked the true riskiness of subprime mortgages. (Demyanyk and Van Hemert, 2011, pp. 1851–1852)

There were also other elements that, if timely and accurately monitored during the period 2002–2006, might have represented valuable early warning indicators and potential red flags to prevent or to mitigate the systemic risk of the crisis.

One of these elements has been reported by Sabry and Okongwu (2009) and is shown in Figure 3.6. In the period 2000 to 2005 the homeowners' debt burden increased to levels unseen before. "Homeowners have been borrowing against equity in their homes at unprecedented rates" (Sabry and Okongwu, 2009, p. 8).

Another quite evident red flag of a possible lending boom–bust scenario (Figure 3.7 and Figure 3.8), is represented by the opposing trend in rising housing prices, well over

Source: OFHEO and Freddie Mac

Figure 3.7   Low Cost of Credit and Rising Housing Prices, Monthly Data from January 1992 through March 2008

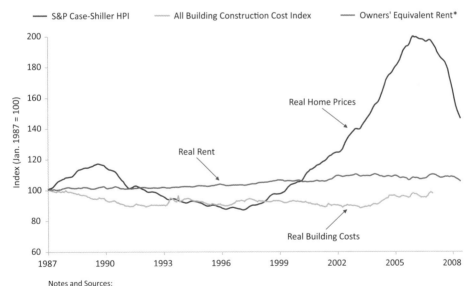

Notes and Sources:
Data are from Federal Reserve Bank of St. Louis, Bloomberg, LP, Standard & Poor's, Bureau of Labor Statistics. Monthly data were first adjusted by CPI and then rescaled to Jan. 1987=100.

* Owners' Equivalent Rent "measures the change in the implicit rent a homeowner would pay to rent, or would earn from renting, his or her home in a competitive market" (see: http://www.bls.gov/cpi/cpifact6.htm).

Figure 3.8   Real Home Prices versus Real Rent and Real Building Costs Monthly Data from January 1987 through June 2008

Source for Figures 3.7 and 3.8: (NERA Economic Consulting, 2009, p. 12.) "How Did We Get Here? The Story of the Credit Crisis." Reprinted with permission from NERA Economic Consulting.

inflation and rental prices, and the low cost of credit during the period 2000–2005 (Sabry and Okongwu, 2009, pp. 9–12).

Another red flag of the credit bubble is represented by the significant increase between 2001 and 2006 of riskier types of non-traditional mortgage products (reported in Figure 3.9), such as interest-only loans, negative amortization loans, and the corresponding decline of the traditional loans (fully amortizing loans) (Sabry and Okongwu, 2009, p. 10).

Still another red flag of the credit bubble was the impressive increase, since 2002, of the Household Debt Service Ratio, reported in Figure 3.10, also defined as "the ratio of debt payments to disposable personal income" (Sabry and Okongwu, 2009, pp. 13–14).

Demyanyk and Van Hemert (2011) reported in the concluding remarks of their paper that the problems in the subprime mortgage market were apparent at least by the end of 2005, stating that the deterioration of the subprime market was already clear based on the worsening of loan quality for five consecutive years. When housing prices stopped climbing and the previous rapid appreciation of housing market was no longer hiding the true explosive risk of the subprime mortgages, the big trouble became apparent and the market crashed (Demyanyk andVan Hemert, 2011, p. 1876).

Evidently, when in June 2004 Greenspan began raising interest rates and in a subsequent two-year period these monetary interventions brought the Fed Funds rate to 5.25 percent (2006) from 1 percent, given the high percentage of AMR subprime mortgage loans, it was perfectly predictable that a worsening of the delinquency and foreclosure rates for the overleveraged subprime borrowers would follow (Pezzuto, 2008; Stiglitz, 2010, pp. 1–3). The perfect storm!

The rapid growth rate of mortgage loans and the deterioration of loan quality, associated with declining house prices, have, since 2006, generated a dramatic increase in delinquency rates and foreclosure rates. The negative correlation between home price declines and *delinquency rates* and *foreclosure rates* increases is quite evident in Figure 3.11, considering also the significant impact of the interest rates' increase from 1 percent of 2003 to 5.25 percent of 2006. The initial trend of this negative correlation has been quite evident since 2006, also following the housing market prices fall, and in particular if compared with trend in the graphs of Figure 3.12 and Figure 3.13 and the early warning signs of the 2006 vintage delinquent rates and foreclosures rates that will be explained later in this chapter.

Some industry statistics clearly reported indisputable early warning signs of the subprime mortgage loans' portfolio deterioration.

For example, the growing risk of subprime MBS can be seen in the increasing delinquency rates of borrowers. The *60+ day delinquency rate* measures the percentage of payments due which is 60 or more days late. This analysis is particularly meaningful when it is based on a historical series which allows one to better understand the past, present, and future trends. This type of analysis is very well understood and widely used in the industry by all practitioners (risk managers, rating agencies, economists, financial and investment analysts, regulatory and supervisory authorities) and is called "vintage analysis." This analysis, which reports the delinquency rates *(60+ days past due)* by months after origination for different years of origination, is a very powerful and reliable early warning indicator of the future probability of risk of a lending portfolio.

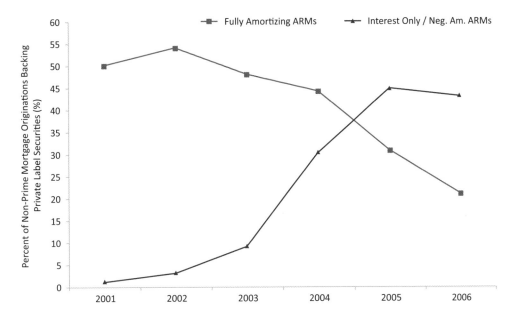

Source: OFHEO, "Housing, Subprime, and GSE Reform: Where Are We Headed?" 18 July 2007

Figure 3.9   Share of Interest-only/Negative Amortization Mortgages have Increased in Non-prime Originations Backing Private-label Securities, Annual data from 2001 through 2006

Source: (NERA Economic Consulting, 2009, p. 10.) "How Did We Get Here? The Story of the Credit Crisis." Reprinted with permission from NERA Economic Consulting.

Source: Federal Reserve

Figure 3.10   Household Debt Service Ratio Quarterly Data from 1Q-1985 through 2Q-2008

Source: (Sabry, F., Okongwu, C., 2009, p. 14.) "How Did We Get Here? The Story of the Credit Crisis." Reprinted with permission from NERA Economic Consulting.

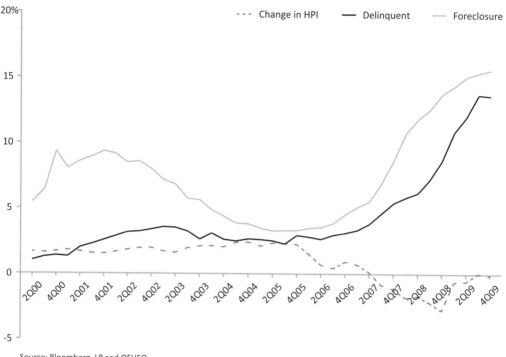

Source: Bloomberg, LP and OFHEO.

Figure 3.11 Quarterly Percentage Change in National Housing Price Index and Share of Subprime Mortgages 90+ Days Delinquent, or in Foreclosure

Source: Buckberg, E., et al. (2010, p. 3) *"Subprime and Synthetic CDOs. Structure, Risk, and Valuation"* Reprinted with permission from NERA Economic Consulting.

Figure 3.14 shows how this rate has evolved for the mortgages originated in the period 2003–2007. It is easy to observe the progressive worsening of the delinquency rates of the more recent years of origination, and in particular, the severe worsening of the vintages for 2006 and 2007 which, just a few months after origination, indicated a level of risk which was much higher than those of all the previous years (vintages). This is also a powerful early warning sign of the progressive quality deterioration of the subprime mortgage loans since 2003 and also a red flag that the very bad and risky delinquency rates of the latest vintages (2006 and 2007) might have generated a panic effect on the MBS market in association with declining housing market prices. As reported in Figure 3.14, the percentage of delinquent subprime mortgages' borrowers 12 months after the origination has increased from 3 percent of the 2003 vintage to above 20 percent of the 2007 vintage. This shows very clearly the progressive deterioration of the subprime mortgage loans over the years of the housing and lending bubbles.

In their study, Demyanyk and Van Hemert (2011) have also reported the actual delinquency and foreclosure rates of the subprime mortgage loans market in the period 2001–2007. From these graphs (Figures 3.15, 3.16, and 3.17) it is possible to notice deterioration of actual delinquency rates over time, and that the 2006 and 2007 vintages

All data at the MSA level. Source: First American Loan Performance and OFHEO.

Figure 3.12 Change in House Prices and the Subprime Delinquency Rate

All data at the MSA level. Source: First American Loan Performance and OFHEO.

Figure 3.13 Change in House-price Deceleration and Changes in Subprime Delinquency Rates

Credit/Disclaimer for Figures 3.12 and 3.13: Reprinted from "House Prices and Subprime Mortgage Delinquencies," FRBSF Economic Letter 2007–14 (June 8) by Mark Doms, Frederick Furlong, and John Krainer. Opinions expressed in this article do not necessarily reflect the views of the management of the Federal Reserve Bank of San Francisco, or of the Board of Governors of the Federal Reserve System.

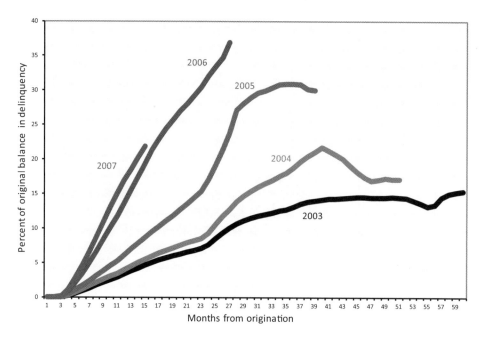

Figure 3.14 Delinquency Rates of Subprime Mortgages by Months After Origination for Different Origination Years

Source: Figure created by Prof. Arvind K. Jain based on the data of International Monetary Fund figure 1.8 taken from the Global Financial Stability Report 2008.

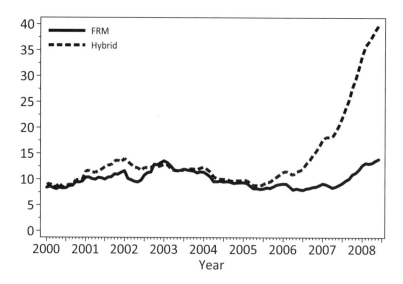

Figure 3.15 Actual Delinquency Rates (%) of Outstanding Mortgages

Source: Yuliya Demyanyk and Otto Van Hemert. *Understanding the Subprime Mortgage Crisis* Rev. Financ. Stud. (2011) 24(6): 1848–1880. By permission of Oxford University Press on behalf of The Society of Financial Studies.

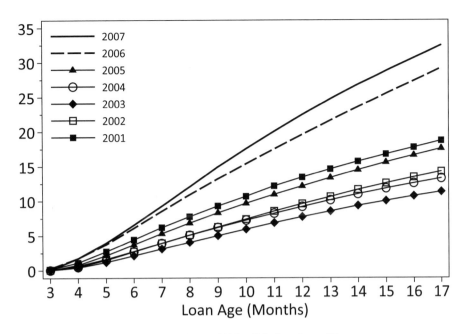

Figure 3.16 Actual Delinquency Rate (%) of Subprime Mortgages

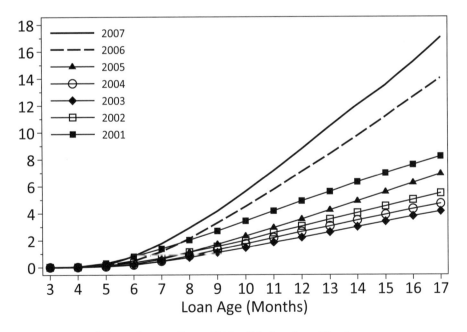

Figure 3.17 Actual Foreclosure Rate (%) of Subprime Mortgages

Source for Figures 3.16 and 3.17: Yuliya Demyanyk and Otto Van Hemert. *Understanding the Subprime Mortgage Crisis* Rev. Financ. Stud. (2011) 24(6): 1848–1880. By permission of Oxford University Press on behalf of The Society of Financial Studies.

show an unusual higher delinquency rate and foreclosure rate than loans originated in earlier years at the same ages. The bad performance of the vintage data for "2006 and 2007 is not limited to a particular segment of the subprime mortgage market." All subprime loans for example, "fixed rates, ARMs and hybrid mortgage loans, cash-out refinancing, low-or-no-documentation mortgage loans, and full-documentation mortgage loans showed substantial higher delinquency and foreclosure rates." Furthermore, although 2001 appears to be one of the worst vintage years in terms of actual delinquency rates due to high interest rates, low average FICO credit score, and low house price appreciation (a "perfect storm"), it is instead the best vintage year in terms of adjusted delinquency rates after adjusting for the unfavorable circumstances (Demyanyk and Van Hemert, 2011, pp. 1850; 1858–1859).

Marc Jarsulic (2010) reports that, based on data from the Mortgage Bankers Association and the Bureau of Labor Statistics (sample period 1999Q1–2008Q4), the regression analysis shows that state-level foreclosure rates are negatively and significantly correlated with house prices increases, and positively and significantly correlated with changes in employment. Furthermore, data also indicates that both price appreciation and changes in employment have a smaller quantitative effect on prime borrowers, whereas instead they have a great impact on the increase of foreclosures rates for subprime loans. With these borrowers having negative equity in their houses, they had an incentive to default, since otherwise they would have overpaid for their homes (Jarsulic, 2010, pp. 41–43).

According to Demyanyk and Van Hemert (2011) calculating adjusted delinquency rates and foreclosure rates with the support of a logit regression model and data from 2001 to 2005, it was possible since 2005 (Figures 3.18, 3.19, 3.20, and 3.21) to clearly see the early warning signs of the subprime mortgage loans' quality deterioration from the vintage corrected delinquency analysis, after adjusting the data for unusual borrower and loan characteristics, and economic circumstances (Demyanyk and Van Hemert, 2011, p. 1866).

Furthermore, the combination of lax credit screening criteria and of loans with higher LTV ratios contributed significantly to the dramatic deterioration of delinquency over time (Demyanyk and Van Hemert, 2011, pp. 1852–1872).

This evidence might have also been identified by credit rating agencies, credit scoring models providers, and other industry analysts simply by combining the data available to them on the financial firms (industry-wide perspective) with some basic macroeconomic data.

According to Marc Jarsulic (2010), the rise in house prices also contributed to overall household indebtedness. The increase in the debt-to-income ratio is reflected in the increased burden of mortgage debt service. The Federal Reserve has calculated an average homeowner financial obligation ratio (FOR), which is calculated as the sum of mortgage payments, homeowner insurance payments, and property tax payments, and divided by the disposable personal income (Jarsulic, 2010, pp. 14–16).

Jarsulic (2010) reports that the value of the FOR has increased significantly since 2000, from 9.07 percent for 2000Q1 to 11.55 percent for 2008 due to mortgage debt payments, whereas the FOR of renters has declined over the same period of time (Jarsulic, 2010, p. 16).

Kristopher S. Gerardi (2009) "attributes most of the dramatic rise in foreclosures in 2006 and 2007 in Massachusetts to the decline in house prices that began in the summer of 2005." According to Gerardi et al., "Subprime mortgages are more sensitive

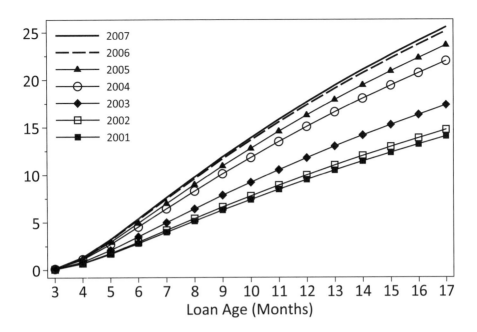

Figure 3.18 Adjusted Delinquency Rate (%) of Subprime Mortgages

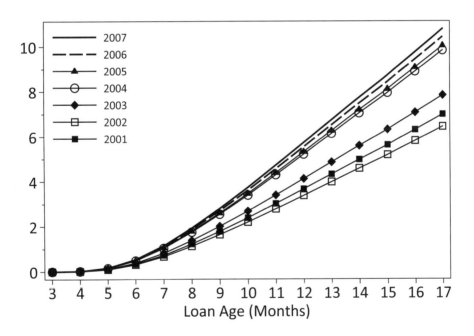

Figure 3.19 Adjusted Foreclosure Rate (%) of Subprime Mortgages

Source for Figures 3.18 and 3.19: Yuliya Demyanyk and Otto Van Hemert. *Understanding the Subprime Mortgage Crisis* Rev. Financ. Stud. (2011) 24(6): 1848–1880. By permission of Oxford University Press on behalf of The Society of Financial Studies.

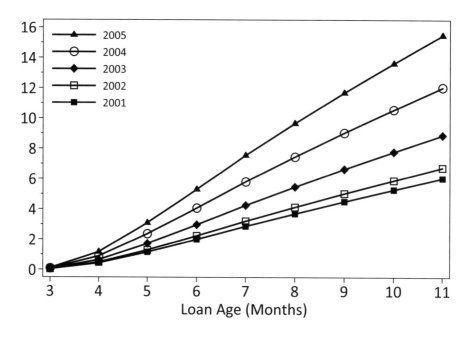

Figure 3.20 Adjusted Delinquency Rate (%); end of 2005

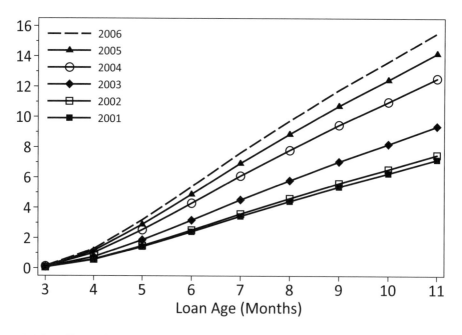

Figure 3.21 Adjusted Delinquency Rate (%); end of 2006

Source for Figures 3.20 and 3.21: Yuliya Demyanyk and Otto Van Hemert. *Understanding the Subprime Mortgage Crisis* Rev. Financ. Stud. (2011) 24(6): 1848–1880. By permission of Oxford University Press on behalf of The Society of Financial Studies.

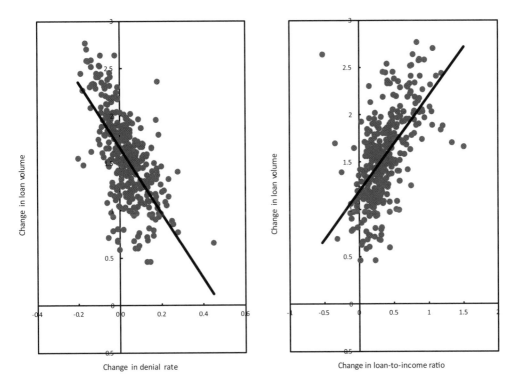

Figure 3.22 Lending Standards and Subprime Credit Boom

Source: Dell'Ariccia, Igan, Laeven (2007) (p. 37) of the International Monetary Fund (IMF). By permission of the authors.

to changes in house prices and to the initial LTV ratio at origination, and far more likely to end up in foreclosure than prime mortgages" (Gerardi, K.S., Shapiro, A.H., Willen, P.S. (2009) pp. 1–3).

Some other authors (Dell'Ariccia et al., 2008) also confirmed that the LTV ratios for mortgages increased significantly in the years preceding the crisis, as reported in Figure 3.22 (Dell'Ariccia, G., Igan, D., Laeven, L., 2008, pp. 5–37).

In particular, IMF economists Giovanni Dell'Ariccia, Deniz Igan, and Luc Lauven (2008), in their working paper, "Credit Booms and Lending Standards: Evidence From the Subprime Mortgage Market" report the following forceful words: "The current subprime mortgage crisis is linked to a decline in lending standards associated with the rapid expansion of this market."

In their study they "show that lending standards declined more in areas that experienced larger credit booms and price increases" (Dell'Ariccia, G., Igan, D., Laeven, L., 2008, pp. 5–37).

The delinquency rate by year or month of origination (vintage analysis) can be a very powerful and very predictable early warning indicator of the current and mainly projected quality and risk of a consumer lending portfolio, for both secured and unsecured lending products. In particular, risk managers often use as an early warning indicator the vintage delinquency rate of the mortgages observed four months after origination in order to estimate the projected future trend of the delinquency rate curve for the following months/

years (Lawrence and Solomon, 2002, pp. 113–132; Siddiqi, 2005, pp. 161–177; Löeffler and Posch, 2011, pp. 55–108; de Servigny and Renault, 2004, pp. 213–248; Pezzuto, 2008).

Vintage delinquency rates analysis, in general, predicts the lifetime risk of a consumer lending portfolio using the early stage (months) delinquency rates. In other words, the early delinquency rate of a mortgage loan portfolio observed just a few months after origination (four to six months), can allow one to predict quite accurately the risk of the entire lifetime of a mortgage loan for a certain year of origination (vintage), assuming that the risk control and collection strategies of the mortgage originator/bank do not change in that timeframe (Lawrence and Solomon, 2002 pp. 113–132; Pezzuto, 2008).

Thus, for example, if a mortgage portfolio has, a few months after origination, a delinquency rate significantly higher than the one expected/planned, and much higher than the historical ones, it is very likely that this new mortgage loan vintage will generate a much higher credit risk in the following 12 months, or beyond, compared with previous vintages. Thus, a very high and unexpected early delinquency rate (for example, four to six months after origination date) may represent, at a very early stage of the credit risk management process, a powerful early warning signal of the true potential risk of a new mortgage loan vintage (Lawrence and Solomon, 2002, pp. 113–132; Pezzuto, 2008).

The combination of this early warning indicator in conjunction with other key indicators such as: (1) average FICO credit score (if meaningful); (2) score distribution analysis and population stability analysis; (3) concurrent and lagged delinquency rates and roll rates (or net flow rates); (4) vintage delinquency rates by score bands; (5) stress tests; (6) chi-square tests on risk model stability; (7) score/ratings' transition matrix; (8) borrower's profile and if he/she is a house-occupier; (9) prepayment rates and penalties; (10) average CLTV ratio (if loans have second, third liens, and so on); (11) value of collateral and if it is second lien; (12) debt-to-income ratio; (13) early payment defaults and foreclosures; (14) mortgage rates; (15) ARM or hybrid mortgage loans margins (spread); (16) loans sourcing channel; (17) full or partial documentation provided; (18) type of loan (for example, ARM, fixed-rate mortgages, hybrid or refinancing – cash-out or no cash-out refinancing scheme); (19) change in home prices since origination; and (20) rating transition matrices; all might provide a very effective and powerful insight to estimate, at a very early stage of the mortgage portfolio lifetime, its projected level of risk and probability of default (Lawrence and Solomon, 2002, pp. 113–132; Pezzuto, 2008).

Even if the lending products are very new, creative and quite "exotic" and the borrowers' population "through-the-door" is significantly different from the traditional target market (or development sample of the scoring model), and still, even if scoring models are not perfectly fit to reflect the new population "through-the door," due to new product features and lax underwriting criteria, the vintage delinquency rate models, adjusted to take into account for loan, borrower, and economic cycle circumstances, risk managers should be able to spot at an early stage some unexpected and out-of-pattern trend of the mortgage loans' portfolio risk. In other words, these are quite evident red flags of a potential crisis (Lawrence and Solomon, 2002, pp. 113–132; Pezzuto, 2008).

Poor credit screening criteria and unfit or unreliable credit scoring models might probably override the mortgage lenders' underwriting and securitization process, but they certainly should not pass unnoticed in the vintage delinquency and foreclosure rates if the bank integrates these analyses with all the other analyses mentioned above in a well-designed and rigorous end-to-end lending and risk management process (Lawrence and Solomon, 2002, pp. 113–132; Pezzuto, 2008).

Despite the dramatic growth of the subprime mortgage loan market and the worsening delinquency and foreclosure rates in the period 2000–2006, the percentage of subprime mortgage loans out of the total mortgage loans in 2006 was probably not too high to make analysts afraid of potential systemic defaults in the industry. Subprime borrowers, as indicated by any credit scoring model, however, in general have a "bad rate" or "good/bad odds" ratio which are dramatically higher than prime borrowers, thus this means that it takes several good accounts to cover the losses of one bad account (defaulting borrower), especially in conjunction with mispricing of risk, declining housing market prices, and inadequate collateral appraisal.

A lending portfolio strategy based on tools being consistently applied and correctly managed (for example, rigorous underwriting criteria, proper appraisal of the value of the collateral, adequate percentage of downpayment for mortgage loans, tier pricing based on borrower's risk profile, limited percentage of override to credit policy criteria, originate-to-hold (OTH) securitization model, and accurate and tight portfolio risk monitoring) can prove to be very beneficial for the bank or mortgage lender in mitigating risk.

When instead a massive growth of lending activity to subprime borrowers is encouraged on a national scale in conjunction with: (1) poor underwriting standards; (2) low or no downpayment, or collateral; (3) no documentation; (4) no income verification; (5) creative new lending and derivatives products; (6) no OTH securitization process; (7) highly volatile housing market conditions; (8) a housing bubble, with unrealistic housing market expectations; (9) poor corporate governance and regulatory oversight; and (10) large deregulation of financial markets; the industry implosion should be quite obvious to anyone who cared to look. It means combining a massive adverse selection of high-risk borrowers with massive deregulation, overleveraged borrowers and investment banks/shadow banking, with risky short-term funding strategies, and in the middle of adverse market conditions (for example, declining house prices, increasing interest rates, and high subprime portfolios' concentrations) which almost always result in financial disaster. It is, however, true that a number of risk models used by providers of credit scores before the financial crisis did not account for numerous macroeconomic factors.

A study undertaken by Liebowitz (2009) on the causes of mortgage foreclosures (data based on the second half of 2008), signals that negative equity was the primary trigger of the problem, followed by an increase in unemployment, subprime FICO score (less than 620), downpayment of less than 3 percent, and upward mortgage rate resets (Liebowitz, 2009).

Lang and Jagtiani (2010) have indicated in their paper, "The Mortgage and Financial Crises: The Role of Credit Risk Management and Corporate Governance," a critical early warning sign that was seriously underestimated by the financial industry in 2007. They report in their work the following evidences:

After a period of unprecedented growth from 2000 to 2006, according to Lang and Jagtiani (2010), by the summer of 2007 housing prices had fallen by about 3.5 percent from their peak, using the Case–Shiller house price index. Was this event outside the stress scenarios used by risk managers? The evidence suggests not. The firms estimated a 5 percent probability that there would be an annual national house price decline of 5 percent for three consecutive years. The evidence suggests that firms analyzing tail-risk would incorporate events at least as bad as the house price declines as of August 2007 (Lang and Jagtiani, 2010, p. 133).

> *Of course, it is possible that irrational exuberance or poor risk models led firms to underestimate the relationship between house price declines and mortgage defaults and, to underestimate the tail-risk from a 3.5 percent house price decline (Lang and Jagtiani, 2010, p. 133).*

As Sauders and Allen (2010) argue, "Any model is as good as its assumptions." Financial engineers estimated that geographical diversification would protect mortgage portfolios from credit losses since in the past this assumption proved to be true. Based on what happened, instead, it seems apparently that the models failed to account for the national decline in house prices. Despite the warning signs reported by highly credible economists such as Robert Shiller, Dean Baker, and Nouriel Roubini, a nationwide housing price decline was considered an extreme tail-event and therefore not a plausible scenario (Saunders and Allen, 2010, p. 31).

Apparently the assumptions used in the models, such as the VAR model used to measure unexpected losses (UL), did not allow correct estimation of the probability of extreme tail-events, the correlation across assets and across risk exposures, such as the correlation across real estate markets (Saunders and Allen, 2010, p. 31). Furthermore, not only might the assumptions of the models not have correctly estimated correlations effects in the housing market but also they probably did not correctly factor in the impact of the risk of a potential banking panic due to the lack of transparency in the shadow banking system and the extremely risky off-balance-sheet operations undertaken by many industry players (that is, OTD securitizations, complex structured products, short-term funding based on repos, thin capital, high leverage ratios, and reckless bets like the "The Big Short") (Pezzuto, 2008; Lewis, 2010).

So apparently the financial crisis could be just the unfortunate result of sloppy and poor risk management, triggered by bad assumptions in the models and a black swan or unexpected extreme tail-event, or just systemic bad luck.

In reality, Löeffler (2008) shed light on this bleak hypothesis by showing in his study titled "Caught In The Housing Crash: Model Failure or Management Failure?" that if banks had used a simple autoregressive model of housing prices (using the OFHEO index, which dates back to 1975), they would have been able to forecast housing price declines that were even worse than those that actually occurred, suggesting that risk measurement tools, if applied correctly, collectively, and consistently, would have alerted banks to the risk of falling housing prices (Löeffler, 2008, pp. 11–12).

Thus, Saunders and Allen (2010) propose another interpretation of the events. They state that most likely financial firms no longer had an incentive to screen and monitor credit risk exposures due to the OTD securitization model which removed risk from their balance sheets and spread them to outside investors. Risk management was no longer a priority for them (Saunders and Allen, 2010, pp. 21–22).

Gorton (2008) notes that securitization was not the cause of the 2007–2009 financial crisis since, according to this author, it was due mainly to the panic reaction of investors who relied exclusively on limited and opaque disclosures of information they received from banks and investment firms on the risk of their securities (Saunders and Allen, 2010, pp. 31–32).

Saunders and Allen (2010) suggest that the 2007–2009 financial crisis was not the result of a single but severe crisis, but rather "it comprises three separate but related phases. The first phase is represented by the national housing market bubble burst" in late 2006 through early 2007, which generated a drastic increase in the "delinquencies and foreclosures in residential mortgages; the second phase was a global liquidity crisis in which overnight interbank markets froze; the third phase in September 2008, initiated by the failure of Lehman Brothers," was the most serious and dangerous one (Saunders and Allen, 2010, pp. 25–43).

According to Saunders and Allen (2010), the first phase of the crisis (credit bubble–bust scenario) was triggered by:

- OTD securitization of non-standard mortgage assets ("packaging and selling loans via off-balance-sheet vehicles") and bad risk assumptions (failed scenario analyses on extreme tail-events).
- Syndication of loans (the bank or lead arranger/lead bank that originates the loan sells or "syndicates" part of the loan to outside investors, thus retaining only a small percentage of the loan and transferring the majority of the risk to others). The loan syndication market increased significantly in 2004 and continued to grow until the year 2006. However, a clear sign of the incumbent credit crisis was evident in the initial three quarters of 2007 when the syndicated bank loan volume sharply declined by 20.53 percent.
- Proprietary trading (hedge funds, private equity funds, venture funds) and investment in non-traditional assets. This typically refers to off-balance-sheet vehicles and subsidiaries (often outside of the SEC regulation and regulatory oversight) engaging in "investment strategies that might be viewed as being too risky if conducted on their balance sheets." Furthermore, investors began to lose confidence in the credit ratings of the rating agencies (Saunders and Allen, 2010, pp. 5–33).

An Unprecedented Growth of the Subprime Mortgage Loan Securitization Market and of the Mortgage-backed Securities

Chomsisengphet and Pennington-Cross (2006) report in their paper "The Evolution of the Subprime Mortgage Market" that a sharp increase occurred in the securitization of subprime loans in the period 1995–2008. They mention that the subprime loan securitization rate had grown from less than 30 percent in 1995 to over 80 percent in 2006. Combining this evidence with the massive expansion of the OTD subprime mortgage loan securitizations and the more lax screening criteria in the period 2001–2007, it is quite clear that the lending boom–bust scenario was likely predictable a few years before the crisis (Chomsisengphet and Pennington-Cross, 2006, pp. 31–36).

Saunders and Allen (2010) also reported that the market for securitized assets, and in particular of the RMBS, experienced explosive growth in the period from 1995 to 2006. They state that at the end of 2006, "the RMBS market exceeded the size of global money markets." Furthermore, they also report that in the three-year period 2004–2006, the growth rate of "CDO issuance was 656 percent in the US market and more than 5,700 percent in the European market." There was also a huge increase in loan syndications, and proprietary trading and investing. "Many hedge funds invested in asset-backed securitization vehicles originated by banks" and in particular in "asset-backed commercial paper, collateralized loan obligations (CLOs), and CDOs. They reported that at the start of the financial crisis, it was estimated that there were over 9,000 hedge funds in existence with over $1 trillion in assets" (Saunders and Allen, 2010, pp. 5–15).

In the years leading up to the crisis, as stated before, there was a low perceived risk in the financial markets which helped fuel a higher risk appetite for many players in the industry. In hindsight, this view may have been akin to an ostrich sticking its head in the sand so it does not have to face apparent risks (Nugent, 2011). In particular, starting from the early 2000s there was in the US market plenty of liquidity, low perceived volatility, risk premiums, and investor returns, and a higher recourse to leverage by investors facilitated by low borrowing to enhance yield. Additionally, the stock market 18 months before the crisis (2006) was very strong (Dow up 19 percent in 2006), and short-term rates were rising, while long-term rates and global savings glut remained steady (Lea, 2008, p. 4).

As indicated in Chapter 2, the securitization market and in general the "shadow banking system, consisting of non-depository banks and other financial entities (for example, investment banks, hedge funds, and money market funds) grew significantly since the year 2000 and played a critical role in lending businesses the money necessary to operate" (SOMO, 2011).

In 2008, the US shadow banking system was approximately the same size as the US traditional depository banking system. The size and rapidly increasing trend of the securitizations of mortgage loans, and in particular the subprime segment of the market in the years preceding the crisis, presented very evident early warning signs of serious risk, given the well-known lack of transparency, asymmetric information, limited regulation, and highly leveraged characteristics of the shadow banking system, in addition to the typical poor credit risk profile of the average subprime borrowers.

The securitization and the over-the counter (OTC) derivatives market boomed in the US starting from the year 2000 to reach the peak in 2008 with a notional outstanding amount more than seven times higher than the one in the year 2000. Among the derivatives, the most frequently traded asset on the OTC exchange were MBS repackaged into new securities – CDOs, synthetic CDOs (or virtual CDO), CDOs-squared, and ABS which amplified the leverage (FCIC, 2011, pp. 45–50).

The repeal of the Glass–Steagall Act contributed to the increase of risk and leverage in the financial markets and ultimately to the financial crisis. In fact, the relatively low equity–asset ratios of banks, which were quite adequate when the Glass–Steagall Act was in force, became increasingly dangerous with the deregulation in 1999 (for example, repeal of the Glass–Steagall Act) (Johnson and Kwak, 2009, p. 36). After Glass–Steagall, commercial banks taking customer deposits were no longer constrained to only take prudent risks, but rather could enter the highly leveraged "go–go" fee-based world of investment banking (Nugent, 2011).

The massive increase of the derivatives market was an early warning sign since, in addition to expanding the highly volatile and unregulated shadow banking system with a high level of leverage, it was also hiding the advantage sought by many financial institutions to reduce the amount of the capital requirement to be held for their trading activities, through hedging with derivatives. Thus, the rapid growth in derivatives permitted financial institutions to lower their VaR calculations and consequently their capital requirements (FCIC, 2011, p. 49).

According to Acharya and Schnabl (2009), some of the investment vehicles were not used to transfer credit risk to other counterparties (investors), but "were often used ... as a form of capital arbitrage that allowed financial firms to take on exposures to tail-risks that were systemic in nature with low regulatory capital requirements" (Lang and Jagtiani, 2010, p. 134).

As reported by Richard A. Posner (2009):

> *One beauty of swaps was that they reduced the amount of collateral a lender needed in order to protect itself from the consequences of the borrower's default. Instead of insisting on collateral as protection against the consequences of default, the lender could pay the premium on credit-default swaps. (Posner, 2009, p. 57)*

He also indicated:

> *Swaps were thought to (and often did) reduce a lender's risk, allowing greater leverage and therefore higher returns with no apparent increase in risk. And swaps themselves became securitized so that institutions all over the world became insurers of mortgage-backed securities. (Posner, 2009, p. 57)*

The combination of excessive leverage and risk-taking, with limited capital requirements and massive OTC trading (shadow banking) of non-recourse subprime MBS with a credit boom–bust scenario, was clearly an unsustainable and explosive mix. The CDS, for example, are OTC-traded derivatives that grew explosively from 2000 to 2008, and resemble an insurance contract, but differ from these contracts as (1) they are unregulated (not insurance); (2) provide no collateral requirements; (3) allow one to speculate on the default of a loan the purchaser does not own (naked CDS); and (4) require much less reserves in case of loss (FCIC, 2011, pp. 45–50).

In recent years "the global market for custom derivatives has grown to over $70 trillion in face value and over $2.5 trillion in market value from almost nothing a decade ago." Much of this derivatives trading is lightly regulated, such as in the case of OTC derivatives (Johnson and Kwak, 2010a, p. 8).

In the US even the Basel II rules were not adopted at the time of the credit boom and bust in the Advanced Internal Rating-Based (AIRB) Approach (the more sophisticated approach). Rather the standard and foundational approaches with a lower risk-focused approach was followed, thus the securitization and derivatives risk assessments were mainly based on the banks' existing risk management models for capital requirements (FCIC, 2011, p. 171).

Furthermore, as reported by the FCIC (2011), securitizers and banks devoted only limited resources to due diligence activities and the SEC had practically no oversight on securities. The SEC just verified that "adequate" disclosure was provided to investors to make their investment decisions (FCIC, 2011, p. 169).

The FCIC reported that as early as 2004 regulators began to notice rising risks in the mortgage market, and they recognized that the new exotic products and the borrowers were "non-conventional," but they did not interfere significantly in the financial sector to mitigate the risk of a potential crisis, rather they allowed financial institutions to pose excessive faith in their internal risk models and self-discipline (FCIC, 2011, p. 171).

The FCIC also reports that John Snow, then US Treasury Secretary, had urgently brought to the attention of the regulators in late 2004 and early 2005 the need to address the issue of the lax lending practice proliferation. The Secretary was ignored (FCIC, 2011, p. 172).

Between 2003 and 2007, all "five major US investment banks (Goldman Sachs, Morgan Stanley, Merrill Lynch, Lehman Brothers, and Bear Stearns)" increased their overall leverage. These banks took on larger and riskier positions that increased their expected profits while increasing their overall risk. "Bear Stearns's leverage reached a ratio of thirty-three to one, meaning that if its assets fell by 3 percent the bank would be insolvent." It was the first to fall in 2008 when rumors that it might be insolvent caused its short-term funding to dry up in a matter of days (Johnson and Kwak, 2010a, p. 140).

In exchange for being allowed to increase their leverage, the investment banks gave the SEC new powers to monitor their operations through the Consolidated Supervised Entity program. However, the SEC declined to take effective action under this program. A 2008 investigation by the SEC inspection general found that:

> *The SEC's Division of Trading and Markets became aware of numerous potential red flags prior to Bear Stearns' collapse, regarding its concentration of mortgage securities, high leverage, shortcomings of risk management in mortgage-backed securities and lack of compliance with the spirit of certain Basel II standards, but did not take actions to limit these risk factors. (Johnson and Kwak, 2010a, p. 140)*

It is also worthwhile mentioning what has been reported by Dewatripont et al. (2010) and myself (Pezzuto, 2008) regarding the breakdown of the Basel Prudential Regime. Investment banks and the so-called shadow banking sector were mainly outside of the Basel regime at the time of the crisis (Dewatripont et al., 2010, pp. 86–87; Pezzuto, 2008).

Gorton (2008) "points out that it is virtually impossible for an investor in a CDO tranche" (with underlying RMBS assets) "to determine its subprime exposure in the CDO portfolio without looking through each of the bonds in the CDO portfolio and other CDOs tranches within the portfolio (asymmetric information). Thus the complexity and heterogeneity of CDOs," according to this author, seem "to have led to opacity in security valuation." This point of view only seems to confirm the hypothesis of moral hazard related to the OTD securitization model, the perverse short-term incentives of many managers in the industry, their overconfidence about constant rising housing prices, reliable risk management models, and the too-big-to-fail government policy (Gorton, 2008, pp. 60–62).

No one can reasonably imagine that thousands of the most highly skilled and qualified finance professionals in the world might have lost their mind simultaneously across the country, in many different organizations, with different missions, visions, organizational values and cultures, corporate and, credit and portfolio strategies, corporate governance and risk management systems, and all of a sudden decided to deliberately or accidently fall in the trap of a highly opaque, overleveraged, undercapitalized, deregulated financial market, in the middle of housing and credit bubbles, with no clues about asset values, mispricing MBS, and relying exclusively on FICO scores, recent historical data, complacent rating agencies, CDS, complex and obscure CDOs and OTD securitizations processes to save their organizations, their jobs and careers, and the overall economy from a systemic and devastating collapse.

At the end of the day, it does not take a genius to imagine that boosting for years a massive adverse selection of subprime borrowers with huge debts, and low home equity value, with poor or no controls, risk management, corporate governance or regulatory and oversight controls during a housing bubble, would eventually lead to a dramatic collapse when the bubble burst or other adverse economic conditions set in (higher interest rates, decreasing house prices, increasing unemployment rate, and so on). To imagine such an event it did not take sophisticated models to analyze complex CDOs but just "good old common sense," or an educated guess, or wishful thinking.

Banks used securitization to remove mortgage assets from their balance sheets creating off-balance-sheet subsidiaries, such as SPVs, also known as special purpose entities (SPEs), or SIVs. "The SPV pools the loans together and creates new securities backed by the cash flow from the underlying asset pool" (Saunders and Allen, 2010, pp. 5–6).

"The underlying loans in the asset pool belong to the ultimate investors in the asset-backed securities" and thus the cash flows are allocated to the investors based on their tranches of the asset pool (Saunders and Allen, 2010, p. 6).

SIVs have been created as structured operating companies (shadow banking) that invest in high-risk/high expected return assets "rather than directly selling the ABS to investors (as do SPVs). They hold the loans purchased from the banks on their own balance sheets until maturity, and sell bonds or commercial paper to investors in order to raise the cash in order to purchase the banks' assets. The loan assets held by the SIVs back the debt instruments issued by the SIVs to investors. Thus, in essence the SIV itself becomes an ABS – SIVs' commercial paper liabilities are considered asset-backed commercial paper (ABCP)" (Saunders and Allen, 2010, pp. 7–8). Saunders and Allen (2010) also stated:

> Whereas SPVs only earn fees for the creation of the asset-backed securities, the SIVs also earn an expected spread between high-yielding assets and low-cost commercial paper, as long as the yield curve is upward-sloping and credit defaults on the portfolio are low … Up until the crisis these SIVs seemed to be offering very favorable return/risk trade-offs. (Saunders and Allen, 2009, p. 10)

Since SIVs typically use commercial paper and interbank loans (for example, repos) to finance their asset portfolios (they cannot issues deposits), the SIVs are exposed to a higher liquidity risk than traditional banks and also rely on "short-term sources of funding such as commercial paper and repos" (Saunders and Allen, 2010, pp. 10–11). Thus, Saunders and Allen (2010) stated:

> Consequently, if the value of the portfolio declines due to deterioration of credit conditions, the SIVs might be forced to sell long-term, illiquid assets in order to meet the short-term debt obligations. (Saunders and Allen, 2010, p. 11)

… and this is exactly what caused the contagion mechanism by which "subprime market crisis was transmitted to other markets and institutions during the crisis" (Saunders and Allen, 2010, p. 11).

An Unusual and Rapid Growth of the Financial Sector Since 1980s With Many Non-traditional Brokers and Lending Incumbents

Deregulation of the banking and financial markets started in President Clinton's administration, under the pressure of the Wall Street establishment and key people like Robert Rubin, Alain Greenspan, and Lawrence Summers (Posner, 2009, p. 135).

Robert Rubin, during Clinton's administration, was the US Secretary of Treasury but he also had 26 years of prior experience at Goldman Sachs where he served also as board member and Vice-Chairman from 1990–1992. During the financial crisis he held the responsibility of Chairman of Citigroup, the bank that received the largest amount of Troubled Asset Relief Program (TARP) bail-out funds. But "on January 9, 2009, Citigroup announced that he had resigned as a senior adviser and would not seek re-election as a board of director member. Press reports noted that Rubin had drawn criticism for his role in the bank's recent problems that drove it to seek federal assistance. He received more than $100 million in cash and stock during his eight years at Citigroup" (*The New York Times*, 2010). Even Henry Paulson, the Secretary of Treasury of President George W. Bush, was a Goldman Sachs alumnus and former chairman. All "very cozy pal" of Wall Street (Nielsen, 2010, pp. 323–324).

Economist Lawrence Summers, at the time of President Clinton's administration, was Deputy Secretary of the Treasury (1999–2001).

Lawrence Summers was Director of the White House's National Economic Council for President Barack Obama until 2010. Prior to this role he was the 27th President of Harvard University from 2001–2006, the Chief Economist of the World Bank from 1991 to 1993, but also the nephew of two Nobel laureates, Paul Samuelson and Kenneth Arrow (Lizza, 2009; Plotz, 2001).

Being convinced of the ideology of free markets and self-correcting mechanisms, but also very close to Wall Street bankers, in a speech to the Congress as Deputy Secretary of the Treasury on the topic of highly leveraged funds and heavy trading in derivatives (after the fall of Long-Term Capital Management – LTCM), Summers said: "The parties of these kinds of contracts are largely sophisticated financial institutions that would appear to be eminently capable of protecting themselves from fraud and *counterparty insolvencies*" (Posner, 2009, p. 127).

Larry Summers started deregulating the derivatives contracts in 1998, when the CFTC issued a Concept Release based on the inputs of practitioners, regulators, and academics with the objective to maintain an adequate regulatory oversight without negatively affecting the OTC derivatives market to grow and the overall US financial firms to remain competitive in the global financial marketplace (Lizza, 2009).

On July 30, 1998, then-Deputy Secretary of the Treasury, Summers testified before Congress stating that large and sophisticated financial institutions are involved in OTC derivatives contracts, therefore risks would be significantly mitigated by the fact that these organizations are perfectly capable of protecting themselves from fraud and counterparty insolvencies (Lizza, 2009).

Summers, like Greenspan and Rubin, who also opposed the Concept Release, was not able to prove any potential misuse of the OTC derivatives contracts by financial institutions. Summers insisted instead on his opinion with the following statement: "To date there has been no clear evidence of a need for additional regulation of the institutional OTC derivatives market, and we would submit that proponents of such regulation must bear the burden of demonstrating that need" (Friedman, 2010, pp. 125–126).

In spite of the disagreement Summers, Greenspan, and Rubin had on the risks associated with the shadow banking market, the dramatic subsequent events of the 2007–2009 financial crisis have proven that they have evidently misjudged the dangers posed by derivatives OTC contracts (Lizza, 2009).

In 1999, Larry Summers endorsed the Gramm–Leach–Bliley Act which led to the repeal of the 1933 Glass–Steagall Act (the separation between investment and commercial banking). He celebrated this event saying, "With this bill, the American financial system takes a major step forward towards the 21st Century" (*The New York Times*, 1999).

The lack of regulation that allowed financial firms to sell hundreds of billions of dollars in CDS on MBS was a direct result of efforts by the Treasury, the Federal Reserve, and the SEC to deregulate the derivatives markets. On the day the CFTC issued a Concept Release, Treasury Secretary Robert Rubin, Greenspan, and SEC Chairman Arthur Levitt, issued a joint statement denouncing the CFTC's move: "We are very concerned about reports that the CFTC's action may increase the legal uncertainty concerning certain types of OTC derivatives" (FCIC, 2011, p. 47).

"Greenspan on October 23, 2008 has confessed in his *mea culpa* to Congress saying that he was 'shocked in disbelief' by the sheer velocity and propagation of the demolition of the edifice of finance capitalism" (Clairmont, 2008).

Friedman et al. (2011) in his book titled *What Caused the Finacial Crisis* reported that:

> *Summers – who spearheaded opposition to the regulatory review of the derivative markets proposed by the CFTC and was the apparent architect of the derivatives-market deregulation – nonetheless said, in an interview with George Stephanopoulos on March 15, 2009, that "There are a lot of terrible things that have happened in the last eighteen months, but what's happened at A.I.G. ... the way it was not regulated, the way no one was watching ... is outrageous." (Friedman et al., 2011, p. 312)*

At the 2005 Federal Reserve conference in Jackson Hole, Raghuram Rajan presented a paper called "Has Financial Development Made the World Riskier?" (2005) in which he raised a number of potential issues and warnings about the financial developments of the past 30 years (Rajan, 2005, pp. 313–364).

Rajan raised concerns about skewed incentives of managers and questionable behaviors among traders, investment bankers, and hedge fund operators who are always expected to outperform the market. Rajan also questioned the way financial firms "goose up returns" by taking risky positions that yield a "positive carry." These reckless behaviors have led Joseph J. Cassano to the top of American International Group (AIG) but also to the perverse underlying conditions that led the firm to the brink of collapse (Lewis, 2009).

In the years leading up to the housing market bubble, the CDS contracts that AIG Financial Products sold provided a stream of premium payments to the company with no expense stream. The massive use of these financial engineering strategies reflect what Rajan calls "goosing up returns" with latent risk. In his paper Rajan posed an important warning: "If firms today implicitly are selling various kinds of default insurance to goose up returns, what happens if catastrophe strikes?" (Rajan, 2005, pp. 313–364).

Justin Lahart, reported in the *Wall Street Journal* in January 2009 former Treasury Secretary Lawrence Summers's response to Rajan's paper at the Jackson Hole conference. "Lawrence Summers, famous among economists for his blistering attacks, told the audience he found 'the basic, slightly lead-eyed premise of [Professor Rajan's] paper to be misguided.' Since in Rajan's work he argued the interbank market could freeze up, and one could well have a full-blown financial crisis, as a consequence of banks potential loss of confidence in one another" (Lahart, 2009).

Steven Gjerstad and Nobel laureate Vernon L. Smith in their 2009 paper titled "Monetary Policy, Credit Extension, and Housing Bubbles: 2008 and 1929" explain in detail: (1) that the derivatives have contributed to the flow of mortgage funds that supported the housing bubble; (2) Brooksley Born's legitimate concerns raised about the dangers of these contracts; (3) Larry Summers's contribution to their deregulation; and (4) how these contracts contributed to the collapse of the financial system in 2007 and 2008 (Gjerstad and Smith, 2009, pp. 270–295).

On April 18, 2010, in an interview on ABC's "This Week" program, Clinton said: "Summers Gave `Wrong' Derivatives Advice" (Zumbrun, 2010).

According to Raghuram Rajan (2011), probably the most likely reason why economists failed to foresee the crisis was ideology. As he reported in his article by the title "Why Did Economists Not Foresee the Crisis?," "We were too wedded to the idea that markets are efficient, market participants are rational, and high prices are justified by economic fundamentals" (Rajan, 2011).

He also adds: "The dominant 'efficient market theory' says only that markets reflect what is publicly known. The theory does not say that markets cannot plummet if the news is bad, or if investors become risk-averse" (Rajan, 2011).

"Free from the threat of regulation, OTC derivatives grew to over $680 trillion in face value and over $20 trillion in market value by 2008. CDS to over $50 trillion in face value and over $3 trillion in market value, contributing to the inflation of the housing bubble" (Johnson and Kwak, 2010a, p. 10).

In 2006, Tim Geithner (then New York Fed President) said that the current wave of financial innovation was a substantial improvement in the financial strength and resilience of the financial system in the US (Johnson and Kwak, 2010a, p. 106).

Even in April 2009, after the financial crisis occurred with its aftermath, Ben Bernanke said: "Financial innovation has improved access to credit, reduced costs, and increased choice. We should not attempt to impose restrictions on credit products and services so onerous that they prevent the development of new products and services in the future" (Johnson and Kwak, 2010a, p. 107).

Regarding Bernanke's 2009 statement, it is probably worthwhile to remember that Warren Buffet in the Berkshire Hathaway 2002 annual report labeled derivatives "financial weapons of mass destruction" (Johnson and Kwak, 2010a, p. 107).

The FCIC indicates in their final report that since the 1980s the financial sector has developed faster than the rest of the US economy. In particular the investment banking arm of some of the most important banks have developed from 2000 to 2007 at a very high rate. The annual rate of growth has been 21 percent for Goldman Sachs, 17 percent for Lehman Brothers, 14 percent for Bank of America, 12 percent for Citigroup, 11 percent for Fannie Mae, and 10 percent for Freddie Mac (FCIC, 2011, pp. 64–65).

Investment banks had much higher leverage ratios than commercial and retail banks due to the fact that they had lower capital requirements. They relied mainly on their internal risk models to determine their capital requirements. The FCIC indicates, for example, that leverage increased significantly for many investments banks in those years. For example in the period 2000 to 2008 the leverage of Goldman Sachs had an increase of approximately 53 percent, whereas the one of Morgan Stanley and Lehman Brothers increased respectively in the same period approximately 67 percent. The FCIC also reported that many investment banks: "… artificially lowered leverage ratios by selling assets just before the reporting period and subsequently buying them back just after" (FCIC, 2011, p. 65).

In those years a significant portion of these institutions' revenues and profits increases were generated by trading, speculative, and investment activities such as, securitizations and derivatives (FCIC, 2011. p. 66).

"Between 1978 and 2007, debt held by financial companies grew from $3 trillion to over $36 trillion, more than doubling from 130 percent to 270 percent of US GDP" (FCIC, 2011, p. 66).

Regarding the mortgage lending industry, the progressive globalization and deregulation of the financial markets, the aggressive monetary policy since 2001, the booming securitization market, and the rising house prices have attracted in the years preceding the crisis a large number of non-traditional and independent players (for example, mortgage brokers and lenders) eager to earn the high fees of the subprime mortgage market and to gain a share of the sizeable minority communities (Hojnacki and Shick, 2008, pp. 28–31). In 2006, 63.3 percent of all subprime loans were initiated through mortgage brokers, while for the mortgage market in total, the broker share was 29.5 percent (Jarsulic, 2010, p. 21).

Even IMF economists Giovanni Dell'Ariccia, Deniz Igan, and Luc Lauven (2008) report that a large number of new lenders entered the subprime market in the years preceding the crisis triggering declines in lending standards. They have also stated that there is clear evidence "the lending standards declined more in areas with higher mortgage securitization rates." Thus, lax credit standards (for example, "decline in loan denial rate and significant increase in loan-to-income ratios"), a massive entrance in the market of incumbent lenders, and the asymmetric information between subprime mortgage originators and investors due to the OTD securitization process, according to these authors, explains the relationship between credit boom and financial instability. They have also stated that, consistently with recent theories, their findings demonstrate that banks and "lenders behave more aggressively during boom times than during tranquil times." Other elements of the aggregate boom–bust credit cycle were also evident as early warning signs, according to them, such as financial innovation (securitization), changes in market structure and disintermediation (many new and non-conventional borrowers/lenders/investors), "fast rising house prices, and ample aggregate liquidity." Evidence indicates that all these elements are related to a decline in the lending standards. They also came to the conclusion that "lax monetary policy may exacerbate the effects of booms on lending standard" (Dell'Ariccia, G., Igan, D., Laeven, L., 2008, p. 3).

Dell'Ariccia et al. (2008) also stated in their paper, based on "data from over 50 million individual loan applications combined with information on local and national economic variables," the following analyses:

> Over the last decade, the subprime market has expanded rapidly evolving from a small niche segment to a major portion of the US mortgage market. This trend suggests that this was accompanied by a decline in credit standards and excessive risk taking by lenders, and possibly by outright fraud. (Dell'Ariccia, G., Igan, D., Laeven, L., 2008, p. 3)

Iacoviello and Minetti (2005) indicated that changes occurred also in the composition of investors, from well-informed domestic financial institutions to uninformed foreign investors (Iacoviello and Minetti, 2008, p. 2268).

The mess of the asymmetric information, lack of transparency, and unfair practices of many financial institutions did not stop with the end of the housing and lending bubble in 2010. The press revealed a significant number of questionable foreclosure practices in the US on mortgages that were issued during the financial crisis.

Several banks have been under investigation in 2010 for "filing false documents in courts to obtain illegal foreclosures, breaking into homes and changing the locks while the residents are still legally living there, and even foreclosing on homes which have no mortgages" (International Business Times Staff Reporter, 2010).

Analyst, Tom Eley (2010), reported the following statements in global research:

The scandal speaks both to the dimensions of the social crisis and the criminality of the big banks. The immediate cause of the mortgage lenders' rampant cheating on foreclosure paperwork is the tidal-wave of families ruined by the economic crisis – a crisis itself set into motion by the banks' predatory lending practices. The goal was to get people out of their homes as efficiently and ruthlessly as possible, skating over legal requirements relating to documentation. (International Business Times Staff Reporter, 2010)

The Proliferation of Many New and Rather "Exotic" Mortgages that has Led to a Massive Adverse Selection Strategy in the Industry

The market was flooded with new and "exotic" mortgage loans aimed to maximize affordability (loan size). Some examples are:

*   the majority of the subprime loans (80 percent) were ARMs;
*   longer-term mortgage loans (40 + years) were offered;
*   hybrid ARMs with low fixed teaser rates for an initial two to three years then resetting to index plus margin;
*   most popular subprime loans were: 2/28, 3/27 (70 percent of 2005/2006 vintages);
*   piggy-backed or second-lien mortgages;
*   high margin for non-prime borrowers;
*   interest-only loans;
*   pay option ARMs; and
*   liar loans (Hojnacki and Shick, 2008, pp. 26–31; Lea, 2008, p. 18).

Financial Sector Compensation Soared to Unprecedented Levels and Unusually Well Over Non-financial Sectors

Since 2000, as indicated in Figure 2.10 (Chapter 2), financial sector compensation has increased 80 percent more than in other sectors, and this phenomenon has never occurred in the US since the Great Depression. Total compensation for major US banks and investment firms in 2007 was estimated at $137 billion, driven by the massive use of stock options, which motivated financial firms to take on more risk and leverage. Due to the large number of OTC shadow banking operations, the high increase of securitizations and the related asymmetric information, the leverage proliferation, and the compensation packages designed to pursue short-term profitability, the predictability and aftermath of a potential crisis was easily perceivable by any analyst looking at this unusual and dangerous trend (FCIC, 2011, pp. 61–63).

According to Marc Jarsulic (2010), "Many subprime lenders offered mortgage brokers a 'yield-spread premium' – a bonus for selling a mortgage with an interest rate higher than the rate for which the borrower could qualify." These higher-priced loans accounted for more than 50 percent of the overall lending activity in 2004 (Jarsulic, 2010, p. 22).

Regarding the link between compensation in the financial industry and the OTD securitization process during the credit boom, "FDIC Chairman, Sheila Bair, told the FCIC that mortgage brokers received standard compensation based on the volume of loans originated and not on the quality of these loans." She concluded, "The crisis has shown that most financial institutions' compensation systems were not properly linked to risk management" (FCIC, 2011, p. 64). The systems in place were very much driven by short-term profitability goals (bonus payments) with no regards to any long-term risk.

Even SEC Chairman Mary Schapiro provided to the FCIC a similar opinion. She stated that: "Many major financial institutions created asymmetric compensation packages that paid employees enormous sums for short-term success, even if these same decisions result in significant long-term losses or failure for investors and taxpayers" (FCIC, 2011, p. 64).

Rating Agencies' Revenues from Financial Instruments Quadrupled between 2000 and 2007

Another quite impressive indirect early warning sign of the credit boom–bust scenario is the incredible increase of the revenues of the rating agencies in the period 2000–2007. These revenues more than quadrupled. According to the findings of the FCIC, based on an analysis of the rating process of Moody's Investors Service, the largest and oldest of the three rating agencies (Standard and Poor's, Moody's and Fitch), there were many conflicts of interest and perverse financial incentives between the rating agencies and the banks/mortgage originators and investment firms (FCIC, 2011, p. 118).

According to Friedman J., et al. (2011), since 1975, the SEC has conferred to the leading three rating agencies (Moody's, Standard and Poor's, and Fitch) a de facto oligopoly status, since only these companies were considered qualified to fulfill the numerous regulatory mandates for investment-grade ratings (Friedman, J., et al. 2011, p. 13).

The analysis of Moody's rating process revealed to the FCIC that they had rated MBS using unfit models (development samples), since they were based on data sets of periods of relatively strong credit performance. They did not properly weight in their models (conflict of interest) the effective deterioration of declining underwriting criteria in the industry, especially for subprime mortgage loans, and the dramatic decline in home prices (FCIC, 2011, p. 118).

"Moody's did not even develop a model specifically to take into account the layered risks of subprime securities until late 2006, after it had already rated nearly 19,000 subprime securities" (FCIC, 2011, p. 118).

Moody's considered in their scenario simulation a number of factors such as, LTV ratio, borrower credit scores, originator quality, and loan terms along with other information but, based on their stress tests and simulation, and despite the unprecedented rise in housing prices, they never contemplated the existence of a housing bubble (FCIC, 2011, pp. 120–121).

Jarsulic (2010) states that rating agencies played an important role in the financial crisis. Their ratings affected the decisions of many purchasers of securities. Money market funds, restricted by law to purchasing investment grade securities, were allowed to buy highly rated structured securities with non-prime exposures; pension funds, which are often required to purchase investment grade securities, also purchased the same non-prime exposures. Even banks had incentives to hold highly rated senior tranches on their balance sheets, since under the banking regulations, with securities of higher ratings, they can have reduced capital charges (Jarsulic, 2010, p. 117).

The FCIC has concluded that Moody's did not sufficiently consider the deterioration of the securitized mortgage loan quality, but it did not matter since as their standard disclaimer reads: "The ratings ... are, and must be construed solely as, statements of opinion and not statements of fact or recommendations to purchase, sell, or hold any securities" (FCIC, 201, pp. 120–121) – Caveat Emptor – let the buyer beware (Nugent, 2011).

A former Standard and Poor's Managing Director, Richard Guglida, reported in an interview to Bloomberg on September 25, 2008, that in the years of the credit boom, there was a market-share war between the world's two largest rating agencies that pushed them to repeatedly ease their standards to pursue "profits from structured investment pools sold by their clients" (Smith, 2008).

In a Bloomberg report, Elliot Blair Smith indicates in his article of September 25, 2008, that: "S&P and Moody's earned as much as three times more for grading the most complex unregulated investment pools known as CDOs, as they did from corporate bonds" (Smith, 2008).

"When homeowners defaulted, the rating agencies downgraded more than three-quarters of the AAA-rated CDO bonds issued in the last two years" (Smith, 2008). Smith also indicates in the article that "SEC's July 8, 2008 report on the role of the credit rating companies in the subprime crisis raises questions about the accuracy of grades on structured-finance products and the integrity of the ratings process as a whole" (Smith, 2008).

A McClatchy investigation found that even as the housing market was about to crumble, Moody's was forcing out executives who questioned the agency's high ratings of structured products and keeping in its compliance department people who supported their "generous" rating policy (Johnson and Kwak, 2010a, p. 139).

Economist Joseph Stiglitz (2008) says on this matter:

> Wall Street underwrote $3.2 trillion of loans to homebuyers with bad credit and undocumented incomes from 2002 to 2007. Investment banks packaged much of that debt into investment pools that won AAA ratings, the gold standard, from New York-based Moody's and S&P. Flawed grades on securities that later turned to junk now lie at the root of the worst financial crisis since the Great Depression. (Stiglitz, 2010, p. 79)

The Imminent and Predictable End (in 2005) of the "Gold Rush" Years (Boom–Bust Scenario) and its Aftermath on the US House Prices

This sustained upward shift of the interest rates in the years 2005–2006 and high debt burden of borrowers has triggered the real estate market to collapse (declining home values), "destabilized neighborhoods, numerous vacant and abandoned properties, and the absence of mechanisms providing entry into and exit out of the distressed mortgage market, thus resulting into a sharp increase of the mortgage loans' delinquencies and foreclosures." It was the end of the property and lending bubble driven by low interest rates, relatively stable employment rates, and a constantly appreciating US house market. The impact of rising interest rates on ARM subprime loan delinquency rates is evident in Figure 2.4 and the relation between house prices, delinquency rates and foreclosures is also just as evident in Figure 3.11 and Figure 3.12 (Hojnacki and Shick, 2008, pp. 30–33).

No Apparent Correlation between Collateralized Debt Obligation Spreads and Mortgage-backed Securities Performances Before 2007

MBS were systematically repacked into new securities – CDOs, synthetic CDOs, and CDOs-squared, thus an early warning sign could have been represented by the apparent lack of correlation between the exponential growth of risky subprime MBS with rapidly rising delinquency rates and the relatively stable or declining CDO spreads before 2007.

As reported by Juliusz Jablecki and Mateusz Machaj (2011), however, starting from early 2007 there were evident signs of (higher-risk) rising costs of insuring RMBS which reflected increasing doubts in the financial markets about the quality of subprime mortgages (underlying asset of the RMBS derivatives) (Friedman et al., 2011, p. 220).

Even the Asset-backed Securities Index (ABX) was a valuable indicator in 2007 that things were turning bad.

Nouriel Roubini (2010) reported the following:

> Over the course of 2007, the ABX Index went into a free fall, as bottom-of the barrel tranches lost upwards of 80 percent of their value. Even the safest AAA tranches lost 10 percent by July 2007 … The fall in the ABX Index revealed that something was going horribly awry especially if compared to the rising costs of insuring mortgage-backed securities. (Roubini, 2010a, p. 90)

"The ABX Index was created in response to demand for a tradable instrument that represents the market for subprime RMBS." The ABX Index, which is used to measure stress in the market for subprime securities, is a series of CDS based on 20 bonds that consist of subprime mortgages. "To help make the index representative of the universe of deals, the index includes no more than four deals from the same loan originator and no more than six deals from the same master servicer" (Lang and Jagtiani, 2010, p. 131).

Gorton and Metrick (2009) explained that starting in early 2007, "the ABX.HE indices showed a steady deterioration of subprime fundamentals and that subprime-related asset classes and firms also deteriorate along with the ABX," but not other asset classes. In other words, the LIBOR–OIS spreads have not been rising with the deterioration of the ABX. Thus they conclude that the subprime crisis was severe but per se did not cause the panic on the financial markets (Gorton and Metrick, 2009; Gorton, 2009).

The panic occurred only later in August 2007 and after Lehman Brothers demise with a jump of the LIBOR–OIS in conjunction with the deterioration of the ABX.HE index and haircuts that combined with the asymmetric information about the locations and sizes

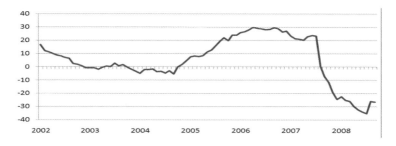

Figure 3.23 % Change in Asset-backed Commercial Paper Outstanding: 2002–2008

Source: William W. Lang and Julapa A Jagtiani, "The Mortgage and Financial Crises: The Role of Credit Risk Management and Corporate Governance", *Atlantic Economic Journal* (2010) 38: 295–316.

of financial firms' exposures to subprime, generated doubts about repo collateral and bank solvency, ultimately triggering fire sales and the financial meltdown (Gorton and Metrick, 2009; Gorton, 2009). In fact, Gorton (2008) stated that:

> As in 2007 the ABX prices plummeted, this event combined with the asymmetric information about the location of risk led to a loss of confidence on the part of banks in the ability of their counterparts to honor contractual obligations … The entire financial system was engulfed when the ability to engage in repurchase agreements essentially disappeared. Collateral calls and unwillingness to engage in repo transactions caused a scramble for cash. (Gorton, 2008, pp. 3–4)

Even Pagano and Volpin (2009) mention in their paper titled "Credit Ratings and Policy Options" that the ratings inflation that has significantly underestimated the risk of structured debt securities prior to the 2007–2009 financial crisis has led to a massive mispricing of risk whose correction later generated the crisis (Pagano and Volpin, 2009, p. 1).

In addition, Figure 3.23 shows the market for short-term ABCP plummeted and private-label RMBS completely dried up in 2008 (Lang and Jagtiani, 2010, p. 131).

As reported by Lang and Jagtiani (2010), "These markets were critical for the continued financing of the highly leveraged positions at many large financial institutions." The funding of long-term mortgage loans relied significantly (as in the case of Lehman Brothers) on the ability to access daily to short-term ABCP. As the market lost confidence in larger financial institutions as a result of their doubtful and allegedly undisclosed/unquantifiable exposure to the mortgage market (lack of transparency), thus in the counterparties' creditworthiness, "many key players in the industry were hit by a severe liquidity squeeze that threatened their survival" (Lang and Jagtiani, 2010, pp. 131–132).

Another indicator of interest to monitor as early warning signs is represented by the spread between the London Interbank Offered Rate (Libor) rate (interbank rates) and the overnight rates.

No Apparent Correlation between the Subprime Mortgage Loans Delinquency Rates and the Relatively Stable Bank Credit Default Swap (CDS) Rates/Spreads before 2007

Another missed red flag consists of the apparent lack of correlation between the rapid growth of subprime mortgage loan delinquency rates and the relatively stable bank CDS rates/spreads before 2007.

The ABCP spread (proxying for ABCP funding liquidity), the Libor-overnight index swap (OIS) spread (capturing bank funding liquidity), and the CDS spread as a measure of bank default risk, all sharply increased only at the onset of the subprime crisis and not in previous years when risks were sharply rising (Frank et al., 2008, pp. 7–17).

As reported by Steven Gjerstad and Vernon Smith (2009) the market for CDS on RMBS, which were the primary form of insurance on these securities, practically evaporated in the summer of 2007. This was another very clear red flag of the severity of the crisis. Furthermore, the CDS market grew from $631.5 billion in notional value in the first half of 2001 to over $62.1 trillion in notional value in the second half of 2007 in the shadow banking market and this astonishing growth apparently did not represent an early warning sign for regulators, oversight authorities and policy makers (Gjerstad and Smith, 2009, p. 285).

All the fact-based evidence, data, graphs, and analyses provided in this chapter, combined with the genesis of the final crisis explained in the initial two chapters, provide a solid and rigorous set of empirical elements suitable to support the hypothesis, further confirmed by other authors, that the 2007–2009 financial crisis was not only predictable and controllable but also actually predicted and warned of by a number of prominent scholars and industry experts with the support of rigorous argumentations. Unfortunately these predictions and warnings were systematically ignored or seriously underestimated.

Conclusion

It is not easy to associate a single root cause with the dramatic events of the financial crisis. It is clearly evident to the reader, after a review of these three chapters, that the factors that contributed to the financial meltdown were: (1) multiple, (2) complex, and (3) strongly interrelated. Additionally, adverse market conditions, externalities, and badly estimated probabilities of extreme tail-events (black swan) each played a role in the crisis of 2007–2009.

The list of triggers of the crisis, reported in Chapter 2, clearly explain the combination of elements that have seriously contributed to the severest financial and economic crisis since the Great Depression of 1929.

However using Lang and Jagtiani (2010) findings, given the modern financial risk management principles and best practices, it is difficult to explain why the financial firms did not avoid disaster starting from August 2007 by simply applying basic principles of financial risk management and not ignoring the numerous early warning signs that many authors communicated and that are listed in this chapter (Lang and Jagtiani, 2010, pp. 142–143).

After all, as was indicated, in many financial organizations modern credit and financial risk management is a standard practice under "normal" market conditions, when executives have "rational" behaviors, realistic expectations about future asset prices/values, and "standard" incentives (Lang and Jagtiani, 2010, pp. 142–143; Pezzuto, 2010a, pp. 119–123).

Saunders and Allen (2010) suggest that the years preceeding the financial crisis were characterized by a dramatic increase in systemic risk of the financial system. The main causes of which were:

- the shift in the banking model from the OTH to the OTD;
- the shift to an underwriting model in which banks originated loans to quickly sell them to the market, in the attempt to avoid self-risks. Among the models used to distribute the risk to others, banks have used various forms such as securitization and loan syndication;
- since the underwriters of ABS were not exposed to the ongoing credit, liquidity, and interest rate risks of traditional banking, they had little incentive to screen and monitor the activities of borrowers. The result was a drastic deterioration in credit quality and a dramatic increase in consumer and corporate leverage, which were not detected by regulators (Saunders and Allen, 2010, pp. 3–15).

Lang and Jagtiani (2010), argue that "the evidence suggests that mortgage models would have clearly indicated very high levels of default under their stress scenarios models" but that financial firms did not recognize or acknowledge these risks due to perverse financial firms' incentives (for example, managers' principal-agent problem, and too-big-to-fail policy/moral hazard behavior), lack of transparency, failures in underwriting and portfolio risk management, and corporate governance (internal controls, monitoring, oversight), high investment firms leverage, high concentration of complex RMBS and CDOs in their portfolios, and limited capital (Lang and Jagtiani, 2010, pp. 138–143).

They reported that modern credit and financial risk management of the financial firms were perfectly suited to assure proper risk management processes as described below:

- risk management models for the estimation of UL as well as accurate forecasting of expected losses;
- risk management models for portfolio risk monitoring, taking into account correlations among assets, and implying concerns for concentrated exposures to common risk factors; and
- risk management models for measuring tail-risk for assessment of capital requirements (Lang and Jagtiani, 2010, pp. 138–143).

Thus, given the above-mentioned assumptions, Lang and Jagtiani (2010) argue that only the following four factors can explain origin of the crisis:

1. irrational exuberance (but the risks of the housing and credit bubbles were visible and proactively warned by many people);
2. the OTD business model (which encouraged the moral hazard of the many agents in the securitization process);

3. overreliance on statistical risk models (but any risk manager knows that their reliability is seriously undermined with No Income, No Jobs or Assets (NINJA) subprime loans); and

4. overreliance on agency ratings (whose conflict of interests with banks and other financial institutions has been openly declared by a number of former top executives of the leading credit rating agencies) (Lang and Jagtiani, 2010, pp. 133–138).

My impression is that the moral hazard that led to the financial crisis was triggered by the goal of many institutions to take advantage of the low funding costs, the housing market and lending bubbles, the highly deregulated financial markets (shadow banking sector), and the poor transparency and information disclosure of the OTD securitization process to maximize short-term profitability for the firms and executive compensation (Pezzuto, 2008).

It seems that the Wall Street "finance gurus" have orchestrated a very convenient way of funding their business model with AAA ratings (low probability of default = low cost of debt capital (weighted average cost of capital – WACC) from the well-known capital asset pricing model (CAPM) methodology) (Sharpe, 1964), thanks to the generous risk assessment of the leading credit rating agencies (Pezzuto, 2008).

Combining the relative good profitability (returns) earned by investment firms on the MBS and CDOs' sales (mispriced securities) with the convenient low cost of funding of these "investment grade" securities, their very short-term nature, the high leverage, and the lighter capital requirements of the external vehicles (SPVs), it becomes quite evident that many players were involved in reckless moral hazard. The gambling was so huge, rich, and bold that only untouchable players could conceive it.

Certainly many of the leading banks and investment firms were, before the subprime mortgage loans crisis, using as a standard practice net present value (NPV) models (to run their businesses models and planning and control processes, adopting a "business case" approach), thus evidently they were fully aware of their: (1) cost of capital; (2) capital structure; (3) NPV and internal rate of returns (IRR); (4) cost of equity; (5) cost of debt; (6) beta coefficients; (7) risk premiums; (8) Altman's Modified Discriminant Function Algorithm (Z Score), and/or Chaos' Discriminant Model and other advanced financial models to monitor their portfolios and the related risk (Pezzuto, 2008; Nugent, 2009a).

Any bad assumptions and early warning signs in business financial and risk management modeling should have been reported, somehow, to management during the years leading up to the crisis allowing senior management and board members to take immediate corrective actions to mitigate firm-wide and systemic risks, but apparently it did not happen or at least it did not stop the excessive risk-taking of many players in the industry. Let's hope that at least in the future it will. In the following table (3.2) is reported a summary of the main causes of the crisis, the consequences, and actionable risk mitigation plans that could have been immediately undertaken by policy makers and regulators to reduce its devastating impact.

Table 3.2   Summary of Causes of the Financial Crisis and Actionable Risk Mitigation Plans

Causes	Effects	Actionable Risk Mitigation Plans
Shift in the banking/ securitization model from the OTH to the OTD in conjunction with the use of non-recourse mortgage loans.	The OTD model and non-recourse mortgage loans encouraged moral hazard for many agents in the securitization process.	Triggered by the early warning signs of the housing market and lending market bubbles, policy makers and regulators should have reduced the risk of moral hazard related to the mortgage loans non-recourse clause, thus holding originators at least partially accountable of the risk of their portfolios, (and of the capital adequacy of these portfolios even if they were placed in off-balance-sheet vehicles). After the securitization and sale on the financial markets of the MBS, regulators should have made more rigorous oversight on banks and should have required tighter underwriting standards, more mortgage loans downpayments, a less risky LTV ratio, and changes in the monetary policy on interest rates to reduce the risk of the bubble. In 2005 or 2006 policy makers and regulator should have introduced the elimination of non-recourse clause for securitized mortgage portfolios or should have introduced the "skin in the game" approach.
	The new model favored banks' and financial firms' lack of accountability, transparency, disclosure, and failure in corporate governance, audit and internal control systems.	Regulators should also have set a new law requiring banks' and mortgage originators' CROs to be accountable for any deliberate malpractice and irresponsible behavior leading to systemic risks. CROs and compliance officers had to be made fully accountable for risks just like CFOs are accountable for the financial statements reporting. Furthermore, in terms of corporate governance reforms, CROs should have been assigned a matrix reporting line to the board of directors in order to give CROs an equal visibility and accountability as other members of the senior management team. Criminal charges should have been introduced for CROs and compliance officers who neglect to report to corporate governance fraudulent behaviors and systems risks.
	With the new banking model financial firms no longer had an incentive to screen and monitor credit risk exposures due to the OTD securitization which removed risk from their balance sheets and spread them to outside investors.	The elimination of the mortgage loans non-recourse clause and the introduction of a reform that makes CROs accountable for risks with a direct matrix reporting line to the board of directors could have been powerful policies to avoid some of the aftermath of the financial crisis.

Causes	Effects	Actionable Risk Mitigation Plans
	Triggered by the ongoing house price bubble and the OTD model, there was an explosion in increasingly risky non-prime lending. Banks, mortgage originators, and predatory lenders have introduced in the market new, questionable, and unconventional mortgage loans (for example, NINJA loans) that have significantly increased borrowers' debt, loosened underwriting criteria, and reduced borrowers' home equity, thus creating a very dangerous building block of the financial crisis, through the origination and risk transfer (OTD securitization) of toxic MBS to investors.	Regulators should have used early warning signs since 2002 of the housing market and credit bubbles reported by Baker, Shiller, the Fed, and other sources, in order to introduce more rigorous controls on mortgage originators, banks, securitizers, rating agencies, and other key agents in the subprime lending industry in order to mitigate potential systemic risks. They should have also compared risk models of different institutions to determine whether they were using excessive homogeneous practices and assumptions. They should have also required more prudential stress tests, and scenario analyses based also on liquidity risks, portfolio asset correlations, portfolio concentrations, exposures correlations, and other systemic risk analyses.
"Irrational exuberance" that has led to both the housing and credit bubbles.	Irrationality in the expectations of the real estate and the financial markets kept the housing market prices rising, thus constantly increasing the value of the mortgage loans collateral (houses), while expectations on mortgage rates remained favorably low for the years to come, with no expectation of a potential negative equity risk for mortgage loans' borrowers.	The irrational exuberance of the markets should have been managed by regulators and policy makers with more prudential, pragmatic, and fact-based approaches relying more seriously on numerous authors' evidences reporting the existence of bubbles. Regulators and financial markets and oversight authorities should have taken more seriously the warnings of the housing bubble reported by Baker since 2002 and then Shiller. They could have introduced reforms to reduce risk of overleveraged subprime borrowers, require more home equity, lower LTV ratios, higher downpayments and credit scores for subprime borrowers. They should have imposed more transparency on the mortgage loans' securitization process and on the shadow banking industry, more controls on the leverage ratios of investment banks and hedge funds, more controls on their short-term funding strategies and long-term investment strategies. They should have imposed higher capital requirements for financial institutions heavily exposed to risky subprime mortgages loans, MBS, and other derivatives linked to the subprime mortgage lending market.

Causes	Effects	Actionable Risk Mitigation Plans
		Government could have reviewed the fiscal policies/tax benefit related to home ownership/home equity financing or refinancing. Regulatory authorities should have required tighter controls for both banks, investment firms, and off-balance-sheet vehicles, to reflect the higher risks of economic bubbles and a more prudential forecasting of the parameters and the stress tests of financial institutions in order to account also for unexpected and extreme tail-risk events and all kinds of systemic risks and their aggregated effects (for example, higher volatility, housing bubble-burst scenarios, portfolios asset correlations, broader backward and forward-looking scenarios analysis, early warning indicators of systemic risks such as asset liquidity risks, funding liquidity risks, asset correlation risks, exposures correlation risks, counterparty risks, credit risks, market risks, operational risks, moral hazard risks, testing qualitative and quantitative analyses, varied assumptions, and tested correlations, concentrations of positions, reverse stress tests).
	In spite of Baker's and Shiller's publications, there has been negligence by many key players in the industry to recognize the existence of a housing market bubble and the risk of a potential boom–bust scenario.	
	A speculative and fraudulent behavior of many players in the industry led them to gamble with uncertainty in the financial markets and to make very dangerous bets.	
	Even low income borrowers and those with impaired credit histories (subprime) were aggressively and unscrupulously encouraged by predatory lenders and greedy brokers to seek as much credit as possible to purchase as many houses as possible, since with very low mortgage rates, rising value of the collateral (houses), and the possibility to refinance their houses, any potential risk of the borrowers' default could be mitigated even with high levels of borrowers' debt and limited or no savings.	

Causes	Effects	Actionable Risk Mitigation Plans
Overreliance of the financial firms on the resilience of what they considered to be sophisticated risk management models to keep risks under control, which were mainly outsourced to external vendors (FICO and others) and to rating agencies, and based on historical data, of years of favorable market conditions, of low and decreasing risks, of conventional lending products, of standard underwriting criteria, and of OTH securitization processes, thus not accounting for the house and lending bubbles, the creative and exotic new innovations introduced in the lending and financial market since the year 2000.	Banks and financial institutions posed too much trust on their (outsourced) risk management tools and best practices, and on the low and decreasing losses of the historical data set, without accounting in their models, stress tests, and scenario analyses models for the impact of the housing and credit bubbles, the growth of questionable new unconventional mortgage products, massive inflows of capital from abroad, high leverage, low saving rates, the explosive OTD securitization, and a massive investment and trading of complex, and poorly regulated/controlled financial engineering instruments traded in shadow banking markets which had toxic subprime mortgage loans as collateral. Even when the early warning signs of higher delinquency and foreclosures rates sparked in the market in 2005 and 2006 and investment firms/ funds began to disclose severe signs of financial distress situations and liquidity problems in 2007, little attention was posed on these critical indicators by regulators.	Regulators should have realized that risk models cannot effectively substitute savvy and experienced risk managers' job, lending policies, corporate governance, and regulations, although they are certainly cheaper. Models should have supported managers' decisions and should not have been used as a single guide to financial firms' policies and regulations, especially since they were not fully back-tested and audited. There is no substitute to sound risk management experience and good old "common sense." Policy makers and regulators should have used the reports, graphs, and other analyses available on the market on the early warning signs of rising risk (rapidly changing borrowers' profiles, realistic assumptions on delinquency and foreclosures rates, vintage analyses, adequate stress tests and scenario analyses, and many other models and reports indicated in Chapter 2 of this book) to impose to financial firms more prudential underwriting processes, risk management processes, audit processes, and procedures.

Causes	Effects	Actionable Risk Mitigation Plans
	The rapid rise in house prices masked the weaknesses of non-prime lending, giving the illusion that even if borrowers had financial problems, they could always refinance or sell their houses (collateral) to pay back their excessive debts.	Given the particular market situation (housing and credit bubbles and a massive subprime adverse selection with unconventional mortgage loans) regulators should have required financial institutions to apply more rigorous and prudent assumptions in their stress testing and scenario planning models (VaR) and in their capital requirements to absorb potentially higher UL.
Aggressive monetary policy of the Fed starting from 2001 to offset dot.com, 9/11, and Iraqi and Afghani war crises, which led to very low interest rates (Fed Funds).	The low interest rates policy of the Fed (Fed Funds), initiated since 2001, has further contributed to boost the housing market bubble and the lending bubble. Significant risks began to rise as massive adverse selection of high-risk borrowers (subprime and Alt A) rapidly increased in the lending industry and mortgage rates began to soar to 5.25 percent in 2006 from 1 percent in 2001. Free-markets' ideology of regulators and policy makers played a significant role in the financial crisis. Preconceptions, shaped by past experience, has reduced reactions to novel challenges in the illusion that competitive markets are always self-correcting.	Regulators and the government should have analyzed Shiller's data to identify the explosion of a housing market prices' bubble, well above inflation and house rentals trends, and should have introduced policies to reduce this gap with monetary and fiscal policies.
Rapid expansion of unconventional mortgage products to be targeted to risky borrowers profiles, without using tested risk ad hoc models for the new exotic instruments and the highly leveraged risky borrowers, originated with limited documentation and verifications.	The lending market has launched unconventional mortgage loans, with option payments, adjustable mortgage rates, limited home equity, low downpayments, low LTV ratios, high DTI ratios, reduced denial rates of subprime applications (without improved economic conditions within the market areas), refinancing schemes, low documentation, and minimum or no savings, without adequate credit screening criteria, thus creating another significant building block for a systemic crisis.	Mortgage products' innovation should have been more closely monitored by regulators instead of leaving the whole supervisory responsibility to the banking industry (ideology of self-correction markets) and to the external vendors of the risk models (FICO, and others) or to the credit rating agencies which proved to be ineffective in identifying the rising systemic risks, or at least had no incentives to spot problems in the process.

Regulators should not have introduced limits to the lending and financial products' innovation but to the gaps in the regulatory rules and policies that have allowed these innovations and moral hazard to become an explosive mix, once the risk has been shifted with the OTD securitization model from the originators to the investors. |

Causes	Effects	Actionable Risk Mitigation Plans
Massive adverse selection of high-risk borrowers (subprime and Alt A) originated without proper underwriting and risk management policies and tools, in other words with a "reckless disregard."	Mortgage brokers, banks, and mortgage originators have targeted a rapid growth of the mortgage loans portfolios to maximize their profitability with limited accountability on credit screening the borrowers since in many cases the risk of their non-recourse loans was transferred to outside investors through the OTD securitization process as collateral of MBS and other securities (CDO, CLO, ABS, RMBS). The lending industry in the period 2003–2006 suddenly turned from what was a niche segment of the market (the non-prime mortgage loans) into a significant portion of the total market. Banks and mortgage originators booked an unsustainable systemic and correlated risk on a national level in their portfolios, with the expectation not to bear the burden of this explosive risk through the immediate securitization and sale of their assets. Large quantities of mortgage-related assets and derivatives concentrated in the hands of a set of large important and highly leveraged financial institutions.	
Global imbalances and deregulation of the financial markets that has favored the rise in systemic risk without the introduction of adequate policies to avoid it.	Since the 1980s the US Government has put legislative pressures on banks to facilitate home-ownership by easing mortgage lending requirements, introducing deductibility of mortgage interest payments and interest on home equity loans, along with real estate taxes, from taxable income and the repeal in 1997 of capital gains tax on most resales of residential property.	The US Government at the beginning of the financial crisis (2007–2008) should have immediately introduced the following regulatory changes: • Make it mandatory for all mortgage loans originators and banks involved with securitizations processes to keep the so-called "Skin in the Game" rule. • To make it mandatory for financial derivatives transactions to be traded in clearinghouses (that is, OTC transactions) and to require all off-balance-sheet transactions assets to have tighter capital and liquidity requirements and limits on leverage, in addition to more severe audit and regulatory oversight, and a clause that obliges Conduit or SIV sponsors to bring them on-balance-sheet in the event of crisis.

Causes	Effects	Actionable Risk Mitigation Plans
	After the repeal of the Glass–Steagall Act, which had separated commercial and investment banking, banks started to make extremely risky loans and to engage in excessive risk-taking practices that generated extremely large fees. This has led to perception in the markets of the "too-big-to-fail" assumption, meaning that in case of potential bankruptcy, the government would have rescued them to avoid an unbearable systemic risk in the economy.	• Individual criminal charges for all employees involved in fraudulent, money laundering, market-rigging, market abuse, or systemic risk activities. • Claw-backs for all employees involved in wrongdoings and no golden parachutes for management. • Industry ban from all global banking and financial services firms associations in case of criminal charges with SIFIS. • Mandatory change management/corporate governance changes for firms charged with systemic risks or market abuse practices.
	The signs of the housing market and credit bubble with the boom–bust scenario were powerful early warning indicators to suggest to regulators to immediately reintroduce a sort of Glass–Steagall Act (Dodd/Frank Act) in the financial markets, since in the years 2007?–2007 the globalized banking and financial markets were too complex and interrelated and the risks of systemic global crises and recessions were very high.	The mistake with the Repeal of the Glass–Steagall Act of the Deregulations in 1999 was that it should have been accompanied with new reforms in terms of capital adequacy and liquidity requirements, more transparency, and information disclosure that would take into account the significant changes occurring in the post-deregulation market conditions (for example, the risks of shadow banking, proprietary trading, securitizations, short selling, arbitrages, speculations, and so on). When the financial crisis erupted, a larger short-run fiscal stimulus should have been combined with some real reforms to reduce long-term structural imbalances (Lang, 2012).

Causes	Effects	Actionable Risk Mitigation Plans
	The Depository Institutions Deregulation and Monetary Control Act (DIDMCA) of 1980 which effectively abolished usury ceilings on the first-lien mortgages and thus paved the way for the higher-cost subprime mortgages.	Deregulations should have been accompanied with new reforms in terms of capital adequacy, transparency, leverage ratios, funding strategies, asset correlations, and information disclosure that would take into account the significant changes occurring in the post-deregulation market conditions.
	With the subsequent introduction of the Alternative Mortgage Transaction Parity Act (AMTPA) in 1982, it legally permitted the use of variable interest rates and balloon payments, as well as to charge higher rates and fees to borrowers.	
	The Tax Reform of 1986, which stimulated the growth of subprime mortgages by prohibiting the deduction of interest on consumer loans for income tax purposes, it has encouraged homeowners to make home equity withdrawals (for example, through "cash-out" refinancing of a mortgage).	
	The "New Bankruptcy Law" or The Bankruptcy Abuse Prevention and Consumer Protection Act of 2005 (BAPCPA) was designed to make it more difficult for some consumers to file bankruptcy.	
	With the "ownership society" policy, President George W. Bush aimed to significantly increase asset accumulation for African–Americans and Latinos through the privatization of Social Security and the encouragement of home ownership via no downpayment FHA Loans. Based on this policy the two GSE Fannie Mae and Freddie Mac were pushed to follow the private market trend toward risky loans to lower-income borrowers or to borrowers purchasing houses in lower-income communities.	
	The financial markets have been highly deregulated since the repeal in 1999 of the Glass–Steagall Act and this condition has allowed shadow banking, the off-balance-sheet vehicles, and OTS trading to flourish in the years following 2000 with limited or no oversight of the regulators, adequate capital requirements, or prudential or mandatory policies for the financial firms operating in the shadow banking system on funding strategies and levels of leverage.	

Causes	Effects	Actionable Risk Mitigation Plans
Rapid growth of new financial firms in the industry (many of which are private labels) eager to grab a piece of the apparently highly profitable credit bubble and of the unprecedented growth of the shadow banking industry and of the CDOs, MBS and derivatives markets related to the mortgage lending products. Many of these markets were highly deregulated, opaque, and poorly controlled by supervisory authorities.	Deregulation and rapid growth in the mortgage lending and securitization markets significantly lowered quality standards and controls leading to a rapid deterioration of the mortgage lending portfolios and to the value of the mortgage loans used as collateral of the MBS traded in opaque and uncontrolled OTC markets.	Regulators should have immediately introduced the following new reforms in the financial markets: 1) all financial instruments should have been traded only in regulated markets – no more OTC; 2) contracts should have been standardized and settled through clearinghouses, rather than in the OTC markets; 3) regulators should have required banks and financial institutions to implement more effective internal controls and audits; 4) the Basel II regulatory framework should have been reworked to avoid pro-cyclical effects and to reduce the impact of systemic risks related to liquidity problems, extreme tail-events, and off-balance-sheet activities; 5) regulators should have reviewed the mark-to-market accounting rules to account also for crisis situations related, in particular, to the boom–bust scenarios; 6) regulators of leading countries (G20) should have coordinated and harmonized immediate global polices and reforms for the banking and financial markets in order to avoid arbitrage opportunities for speculators or to give large financial institutions the freedom to pick and choose where to base their operations in order to benefit from "light" regulation and no controls. When the housing bubble eventually burst in 2006, an immediate debt support negotiation – for instance – would have reduced the amount and the impact of foreclosures and the overall costs for taxpayers (Asaro, 2012). It would have also been wise to rewrite the mortgage servicing agreement so as to better encourage the restructuring of mortgages yet to default (Duffie, 2012; Geanakoplos et al., 2012).

Causes	Effects	Actionable Risk Mitigation Plans
Greed, poor transparency, corporate social responsibility (CSR), and accountability of mortgage brokers, lenders, banks, and other financial firms' risk management, internal controls, corporate governance triggered by short-term financial incentives, and the too-big-to-fail Government's assumption.	Perverse financial incentives generated uncontrollable greed, arrogance, short-termism, managers' principal-agent problem, conflict of interests among agents in the process, and the too-big-to-fail assumption. Reckless use of off-balance-sheet entities to generate "window-dressing" financial reports for investors.	Regulators should have immediately introduced reforms in the financial markets to assure stability, transparency, and to limit the risks of misleading or fraudulent practices to investors.
	Lack of transparency and systemic breaches in accountability and ethics at all levels (greed, corruption, conflict of interests, and fraud).	Regulators should have immediately introduced reforms in the financial markets to assure stability, transparency, and to limit the risks of misleading or fraudulent practices to investors.
Credit rating agencies' failure to correctly rate debt securities (inflated ratings) and their conflict of interests.	The rating agencies contributed significantly to the financial crisis, along with other external risk models vendors, as a result of their inability to correctly rate debt securities backed by subprime mortgage loans and their probable involvement in conflict of interests with their clients. Credit rating agencies' statistical models were inadequate and based on short performance histories of development samples and not based on the latest "creative" product innovations (hybrid ARMs, and so on) or specific products prior to 2007 for the new fast-growing target borrowers (subprime). They did not audit the data they received by RMBS arrangers, thus there was no independent evaluation of the information they received.	Regulators should have introduced an immediate reform of the credit rating industry requiring that credit rating agencies be held accountable for the reliability of their ratings in order to assure a truly independent and unbiased risk assessment of their clients' portfolios and to avoid any potential conflict of interests. Regulators should have introduced a rule, to reduce potential conflicts of interest, that would not allow rating agencies' analysts to be hired for a period of five years by corporate clients they have rated. The same rule should have been applied to analysts working for regulators, financial oversight agencies, or financial investigative bodies (Fed, SEC, or the FCIC).

Causes	Effects	Actionable Risk Mitigation Plans
	This generated significant conflicts of interest with their clients since they were paid for rating the securities but they were also paid for their consulting services helping to structure the CDO deals that they would rate. The SEC reported the market to be very concentrated (12 investment firms arranged 80 percent of the subprime RMBS in dollar terms and 11 firms accounted for 80 percent of the CDO deals – all subject to rating).	
Short-term funding strategies of financial firms involved in the crisis (for example, hedge funds).	The excessive reliance on short-term funding strategies of many hedge funds and investment banks and on their long-term investment strategy concentration on the mortgage lending industry and securities backed by non-prime mortgage loans has been one of the main causes of the financial crisis. Probably the single, most severe event that triggered investors' panic and loss of confidence was in particular the failure of Lehman Brothers which was driven by a liquidity crisis and confidence crisis, related to the short-term funding strategy of this company and its excessive risk appetite.	It is remarkable to notice that the Government, the Fed, the SEC, and other regulators and supervisory authorities have seriously underestimated for a number of years the systemic risks related to the shadow banking system, their thin capital policy, the massive recourse to derivatives, other ABS, CDS, and CDOs to reduce capital requirements for off-balance-sheet vehicles and hedge funds. They should have monitored closely and timely money markets, repo markets, capital markets, and the liquidity while checking on the solvency and real asset valuation of the derivative markets (CDOs, RMBS, MBS, CDS, and so on) in order to impose more strict funding matching policies for investment banks and funds.
Global imbalances (surplus countries versus deficit countries such as the USA) and carry trade.	As indicated by Obstfeld and Rogoff (2009) it was quite clear that the macroeconomic scenario was leading to an unsustainable situation. Low perceived risk and a dynamic financial market in the US, deregulated global financial markets with fragmented and inefficient regulatory oversight, and global imbalances, have contributed a great deal to the global financial meltdown.	Government and regulators should have defined policies that would encourage the inflows of funds from foreign countries while assuring at the same time more transparency on local financial markets, thus regulating the shadow banking system which even today remains still mainly unregulated and controlled.

Causes	Effects	Actionable Risk Mitigation Plans
Failure of the system of financial governance to adequately regulate the exercise of power in finance. Late rescue plans of regulators and policy makers and poor regulatory oversight and neglected timely reaction to early warnings due to discreet consent with the financial community's unscrupulous interests and the powerful banking lobby pressures. Failure of the Federal Reserve, OCC, and the OTS (Office of Thrift Supervision) to use their statutory power and regulations. Large investment banks, formally supervised by the SEC, were lightly regulated and without effective oversight, and there were totally unregulated CDS, CDOs' markets.	A laissez-faire policy with reduced regulatory oversight, controls on shadow banking, OTC derivatives markets, and information asymmetries that granted to the big players in the industry the confirmation of the too-big-to-fail advantage. Bank regulation encouraged the creation of opaque structured products which reduced the capital buffer that protect financial institutions against losses in the underlying assets. For example, a bank holding a subordinated AAA-rated RMBS or CDO tranche is required to have capital equal to 1.6 percent of its value, whereas the whole residential loans have a 4 percent capital requirement.	There were many early warning signs of the housing market and credit bubbles and of the boom–burt scenario soon to occur, but regulators and policy makers seem to have preferred to neglect them, either for excessive free-market ideology or, probably, for a discreet consent toward Wall Street moral hazard and lack of responsibility, what Simon Johnson and James Kwak (2009) call the sliding doors system between Wall Street and Washington. Government, regulators, and supervisory authorities should have immediately suspended dividends distributions, senior managers' bonuses, incentives, or other variable compensations schemes distribution, they should have also reformed the shadow banking industry and required higher capital requirements to those institutions highly exposed to the financial crisis that received Government protection and bail out rescue plans. Shadow banking markets had to be immediately regulated and controlled.

Given the Home Ownership and Equity Protection Act (HOEPA) and the Truth in Lending Act (TILA), the Federal Reserve had a broad authority to create mortgage-related regulations to reduce risk by prohibiting asset-backed lending that ignored the borrowers' ability to repay, requiring income and asset verification, prohibiting prepayment penalties, requiring creditors to establish escrow accounts for property taxes and homeowners' insurances, prohibiting lenders and mortgage brokers from coercing real estate appraisers to misstate houses' values (Jarsulic, 2010). |

Causes	Effects	Actionable Risk Mitigation Plans
		A new reform should have required the permanent presence of a regulatory oversight examiner in the few too-big-to-fail banks and financial institutions, and for the large banks and financial institutions to systematically monitor systemic risks and the integrated risk and anti-fraud management frameworks. Also to participate in all the committees (compensation, International Financial Reporting Standards (IFRS)/audit, Committee of Sponsoring Organizations (COSO) internal controls, Statement on Auditing Standards No. 99: Consideration of Fraud in a Financial Statement Audit (SAS N°99), the Sarbannes Oxley Act (SOX), corporate governance, risk management and business risk review, Basel II/Basel III, scenario analysis/environmental analysis/ vulnerabilities, stress testing, credit policies, financial, compliance, and so on) (Nugent, 2009b). Regulators should have also promptly banned naked short-selling to reduce the impact of financial speculation and discourage the incentive for investment bankers and hedge funds to engage in conflict of interests and insider trading practices.
Inadequate internal controls and compensation.	Mortgage originators, banks and investment firms' internal controls were not very effective in preventing widespread gambling in the years preceding the financial crisis. There has been serious information asymmetries, not to say collusion, between risk managers, securitizers, arrangers, rating agencies, audit and due diligence teams and traders involved in deals. Compensation packages of risk managers were often linked to the institution business activity.	As proposed at the G20 meeting in London (April 2, 2009) by the Financial Stability, the following reforms on compensation could have been implemented earlier during the lending bubble to avoid the perverse incentives that triggered the financial crisis. Risk-based profitability objectives should have been assigned to financial firms' executives and traders, deferred bonuses payments, and claw-backs. • to set longer-term managerial incentives in order to reduce risk-taking (for example, incentives pay made in the form of restricted stock); • adjustment of compensation to risk (including all kinds of risks);

Causes	Effects	Actionable Risk Mitigation Plans
		• compensation oversight by banking supervision should assure a more independent control over the institutions' compensation policies for both the banking and the current shadow banking industry which should be turned into fully regulated, controlled, and transparent entities; • compensation oversight should monitor and regulate any kind of financial benefit not limited only to bonuses and stock options, in order to avoid "clever" initiatives aimed at circumventing the regulation (for example, retirement packages, and so on) or "off-shore rewards" or more creative indirect solutions such as purchasing services from companies co-owned or related by the financial institution's management (Dewatripont et al., 2010).
		Regarding internal controls, audit and risk management the solution should have been to increase accountability of auditors, risk management, internal reviewers, creating a matrix reporting line of the CRO, CFO, and of Director of Internal Control to the CEO and to the Board of Directors with legal accountability of their conduct and the introduction of the corporate and systemic risk crime charges. These reforms and policies had to increase fairness, transparency, accountability and responsibility and to avoid the principal–agent issue and the conflict of interest between manager–shareholder conflict and between manager and other agents in the lending and investment process. A first-class proactive integrated and holistic approach to ERM should have been introduced in the financial firms to mitigate all kind of risks (Nugent, 2009b).

Causes	Effects	Actionable Risk Mitigation Plans
Investors' loss of confidence in some key financial firms, their fear of systemic contagion, and their panic reaction in the fall of 2008, when the financial markets were on the brink of collapse, which threatened the value of their investments.	One of the most important building blocks that have triggered the financial crisis is certainly the loss of confidence of the investors who have invested in securities backed by subprime and other mortgage loans. The lack of transparency in the shadow banking market, the complexity and opacity of the derivatives and of other financial engineering instruments (CDOs, CDS, CLOs, RMBS), and the difficulty in assessing the actual value (mark-to-market value) of their investments, generated a sudden, unexpected and contagious panic reaction in many investors, who just began to sell any perceived risky security they owned in a desperate attempt to shift their investment portfolio toward risk-free assets and to try to recover, as much as possible, some liquidity in their portfolios. This contagious reaction has played a central role in the devaluation of many securities driven by the investors' perception that many institutions were really on the brink of collapse or hiding disproportionate credit losses or liquidity problems.	Once again the mitigation of this problem could have been the immediate introduction of financial reforms that would require banks, investment funds, and other financial institutions to apply a full disclosure of the value of their assets, liabilities, and equities both, on and off-balance-sheet. "Reliable" and "realist" stress tests and scenario analyses should have been implemented to reassure investors about the solidity and solvency of the institutions involved in the financial crisis, instead of granting only governments' rescue plans, TARP programs, bail-outs, and unlimited guarantees (basically a "blank check") to hedge funds, investment banks, and other financial institutions that were not even eligible (non-banking status) to access protection programs, which evidently made many investors, analysts, and observers even more worried about the potential hidden risks of these institutions. Government, the SEC, and Fed should have also encouraged a management and corporate governance change in the so-called TBTF banks and financial institutions that significantly contributed to the financial crisis. They should have introduced a rule that imposes separation of chairman of the board and CEO and the presence of only independent and qualified directors on the board including also the expert CROs.

Source: Pezzuto.

4 *The Need for Improved Risk Governance*

The Post-meltdown Necessary Changes

Combining all the analyses, evidence, and indisputable scholarly data reported so far, it should be quite clear that this dramatic crisis, originating with the US subprime mortgage loans, is the result of many complex and interrelated causes that were predictable and to a certain extent controllable, at least from 2005.

Due to the very nature of the current financial markets and the impact of externalities in a globalized business environment, this severe crisis has evolved over the years internationally from a liquidity, confidence (wholesale banking panic which arose from counterparty solvency fears), and credit crisis (credit crunch) to a financial, economic, and more recently (2011–2013) even political and social crisis (due to deep recession, high sovereign debt/ budget deficits, imbalances and structural differences among the countries, and the tail-risk of a potential default, spillover effect, and break-up of the Eurozone). It still remains difficult, however, to predict what other forms this crisis may take in the future if not properly and timely managed. One of the main differences in the handling of the financial crisis in the US versus the Eurozone in the past five years (2008–2013) is that in the US, despite the initial confusion in policy making, the crisis was managed much more effectively thanks to the following factors: (1) the centralized governance of a single central bank with a lender of last resort mandate, a wider range of monetary policy instruments (aggressive conventional and non-conventional measures), and a less fragmented financial system; (2) the political assertiveness of a single Government (massive bail-outs and bold fiscal stimuli); (3) a more effective reindustrialization policy; (4) the wise decision to immediately clean-up troubled financial institutions' balance sheets and to recapitalize them in order to strengthen the financial system stability, to mitigate the impact of the credit crunch on the real economy, and to help the economic recovery; (5) the Federal Deposit Insurance Corporation's Temporary Liquidity Guarantee Program; (6) the traditional American pragmatism; (7) a single currency, culture (despite the diverse political perspectives), and national identity, and (8) a dynamic and flexible labor market structure. Thus, the US is where this devastating event actually originated but it is also the place where the impact of this unprecedented crisis has been probably better managed thanks to the lessons learned from the Great Depression of 1929. It is true, however, that it is probably still too early to determine what the impact of the accommodative monetary policy undertaken by the Fed in the last five years (2009–2013) will be. Nevertheless, after all, the US still remains the most accomplished, advanced, and admired democracy in the world. One good example is represented by the State of California that made a true turnaround in 2012 (although the recovery was hardly uniform in the state) after a period of five years of brutal economic decline. This turnaround is evidenced by job growth, economic stability, a resurgent housing market and rising spirits in a state that was among the worst hit by the recession. After years of spending cuts and annual state budget deficits, California is expected to post a $1 billion surplus in 2014. The recipe of such success seems to be associated to spending cuts, the Fed's very aggressive monetary policy with extremely low interest rates (close to zero percent), a flexible and dynamic labor market, and the traditional entrepreneurial and innovative spirit of Californian firms (Nagourney, 2012).

In the Eurozone, instead, at least immediately after the peak of the 2008 crisis, the recessionary trends, current accounts imbalances, bank crises, sovereign debt crises, and high budget deficits have amplified the single countries' structural differences and the national political interests and priorities thus complicating and delaying the resolution process. Most of all, however, since the Eurozone countries share a single currency (the euro) but not yet a banking, political, and fiscal union (and centralized treasury), or a central bank with a mandate of lender of last resort, this incomplete framework has certainly not helped to rapidly solve the eurozone crisis.

Unfortunately, instead, the lack of centralized and unified governance made it very difficult after the financial shock of 2007–2009 to handle a crisis of such proportion, although in 2013 many economists consider the financial crisis over in Europe, but not yet the economic crisis, due to the persisting recessionary trends, austerity programs, high level of unemployment, and high sovereign debts (the average Eurozone debt in 2013 is exceeding 90 percent of gross domestic product – GDP). The crisis in the Eurozone pushed political leaders to set up a series of financial support measures for sovereign states such as the European Financial Stability Facility (EFSF) and European Stability Mechanism (ESM) and to overcome the limit of a monetary union without a fiscal union by ratifying, in March 2012, a fiscal coordination mechanism (the European Fiscal Compact). Since sovereign debt is an important part of banks' assets, the financial crisis has generated a vicious circle between sovereign debt risk and banks' risk in the peripheral Eurozone countries. In 2010 Greek government revised its deficit from a prediction of 3.7 percent in early 2009 and estimated to be 13.6 percent. This shocking news generated a panic in the markets and the fear of a bank run. Rumors spread solvency fears on Greece and its potential exit from the Eurozone ("Grexit"), thus it became very difficult for banks (wholesale banking panic) of all the peripheral European countries (fear of potential contagion) to access funding in the capital markets. After all, the painful memory of Lehman's collapse and the panic effect it triggered in the markets was still very present in people's minds. Furthermore, in early 2010, it was revealed that shortly before or after being admitted in the euro, Greece and other euro-zone countries received the assistance of Goldman Sachs, JPMorgan Chase and other banks that developed complex financial products (derivatives) in order to enable these countries to stagger the payments owed for their huge debts over a longer period (that is to mask debt), thus helping them to meet Europe's deficit rules.

Differently from the US, where traditional commercial banking represents only a portion of the sources of funds for companies (that is, working capital and long-term assets financing), in the peripheral European countries, instead, commercial lending has always been highly concentrated in the traditional banking sector which experienced severe liquidity problems (difficult access to the wholesale financial markets) and numerous down-ratings from credit rating agencies. Thus, after the 2007–2009 financial crisis, the credit crunch and a progressing deleveraging process of these financial institutions has evidently worsened the access of many companies to funding sources at competitive rates (and in particular for small and medium-sized enterprises – SMEs) in countries primarily served by the traditional retail and commercial banks. In the US, and other more advanced financial markets, companies have had the benefit of a broader range of funding opportunities from banks but also from more dynamic and innovative capital markets (that is, debt and equity capital markets, hybrid financing, investment banks, venture capital firms, private equity firms, money market funds, asset management firms, credit funds, business angels, hedge funds, and near-banking financial institutions).

There is no doubt that the Eurozone crisis has a part of its roots in the 2007–2009 financial crisis. The analyses provided so far in this book also demonstrate that, in spite of what is often stated by the media and some influential analysts, the 2007–2009 financial crisis was not only the result of a so-called "black swan" or an extreme tail-event, but rather and more likely a prolonged process of build-up over the years (or decades) of excessive risk in the financial services industry as a result of major and unprecedented failures in corporate governance, regulatory oversight, internal audit, and risk management. These epic failures, however, were triggered by perverse incentives, self-interest, cronyism, excessive leverage, mindless deregulation or no regulation at all (shadow banking system), and a general laissez-faire economic regime and moral hazard. So after all, according to my analyses, the original financial crisis triggered by the subprime mortgage loans was not so much a tail-risk event but rather a much more predictable and avoidable one than many claim it to be.

If the euro and the Eurozone still exist in 2013 is probably thanks to people like Mario Draghi, the President of the European Central Bank (ECB) and former Vice Chairman of Goldman Sachs International, who has orchestrated an impressive series of conventional and unconventional monetary policies (two long-term refinancing operations – LTRO – and the Outright Monetary Transactions – OMT – program) to save Europe from a systemic crisis in 2012 and probably from a global recession or depression, He was indeed recognized and rewarded by the *Financial Times* in 2012 as the FT Person of the Year. In fact, when Europe's single currency was disintegrating he came out with a remarkable leadership statement: "Within our mandate, the ECB is ready to do whatever it takes to preserve the euro … And believe me, it will be enough." Draghi's influential statement has strengthened financial markets' confidence in the ECB independence and ability to assure an effective monetary policy governance in the Eurozone (Barber and Steen, 2012).

The ECB declaration to offer the OMT program has significantly discouraged speculation on the peripheral European sovereigns and helped improve the regular flow of liquidity and affordable funding in the Eurozone in 2012–2013 or as Draghi said: to address "severe distortions" in government bond markets based on "unfounded fears." According to Draghi, the ECB had to offer the Outright Monetary Transactions since the ECB monetary policy transmission mechanism was no longer working (BBC News Europe, 2012; Flanders, 2012).

Draghi stated in 2012 that the euro is "irreversible" and promised a potentially unlimited purchase of the Eurozone bonds. Financial markets have well understood the uncompromising commitment of the European Central Bank (ECB) to cut the borrowing costs of debt-burdened Eurozone members in order to ease the Eurozone's debt crisis. Draghi also mentioned that the OMT would only be carried out in conjunction with European Financial Stability Facility (EFSF) or European Stability Mechanism (ESM) programs, and only triggered after a formal request of the countries for a bail-out. Some analysts like Peter Westaway, Chief Economist for Europe at asset manager Vanguard, however, while celebrating the ECB policy decision on the OMT, raised in 2012 concerns on the sustainability of such policies. Peter Westaway, in fact, stated: "There is a long-term question of whether this will be enough to meet the long-term financing needs of Italy, and that probably remains" (BBC News Europe, 2012, Flanders, 2012). Evidently, as explained by Draghi in many circumstances, the ECB interventions are very important to restore the effective monetary policy governance in the Eurozone but the ECB alone cannot solve all the Eurozone' economic problems (it would not be consistent also with its current mandate). With these remarks Draghi meant that the single country's governments and the European Commission have to do their part too in order to foster economic recovery and development in the region through a set of coordinated and integrated measures.

In early 2013, however, there have been signs of interest rate divergences among the Eurozone countries which raised some concerns that these rates could go back to the level they were before the ECB's decision to offer the OMT program. Furthermore, Europe's repo market, which represents the main source of short-term funding for banks, shrank by 12 percent in 2012 which signals an increasing level of distrust among banks.

Furthermore, at the beginning of 2013, the Goldman Sachs' interest rate divergence indicator – which measures cross-border variations in interest rates charged by Eurozone banks on a variety of business loans – has increased, showing that while the measures introduced by the ECB have helped prevent a catastrophic tail-risk of Eurozone break-up (that is, OMT program availability) apparently they failed to ease the credit crunch in much of the region's southern periphery where immediate growth prospects are bleak due to the persistence of the recession (Atkins, 2013a).

Even the 2012 figures from Eurobarometer, the EU's polling organization, analyzed by the European Council on Foreign Relations (ECFR), a think tank, show a vertiginous decline in trust in the EU in countries such as Spain, Germany, and Italy and a soaring Euroskepticism that might feed populist anti-EU politics. It seems that even the stronger Northern European economies have been affected by the recession, bail-outs, wrenching budget and spending cuts. Euroskepticism might also frustrate European leaders' efforts to halt recession and rising unemployment rates, and ensure the effective implementation of structural reforms (Traynor, 2013).

Given the uncertain economic outlook of the Eurozone at the time of writing (April 2013), with some weaker peripheral countries still plagued by demanding structural reforms (tough spending reviews and austerity policies, high unemployment rates and low participation rates, low rate of innovation, prolonged recessionary trends, and current account imbalances), it is quite likely that if things do not get better soon, these countries will be forced to request more time, flexibility, and support to comply with the EU Fiscal Compact, the Stability and Growth Pact known as the Six-pack, and the so-called Two-pack. In this period (April 2013) the peripheral European countries face a tough and challenging dilemma. Either they decide to radically restructure their economic model (enhancing internationalization, reindustrialization, productivity, innovation, the value proposition, and so on) or they will inevitably head in the long run for a potential Eurozone exit. So the new rule of this competitive game in the Eurozone could be summarized by the expression "structural change and sustained rates of economic growth or exit" not forgetting, however, the fiscal consolidation imperative.

In 2013 there is still a high level of uncertainty in the global economy which makes the long-term scenario quite complex to be predicted. Some of the highly interconnected factors that contribute to this scenario are:

(1) the encouraging economic data in the US and the opportunity to start the "exit strategy"; (2) the recent ultra-aggressive fiscal and monetary policies of Japan; (3) the uncertainty about a change of pace of the so-called emerging markets and the threat of China's credit bubble and its huge "shadow banking" sector; (4) the impact of new

innovations and developments in the natural resources and energy industry; (5) structural economic issues related to the ageing of population and the sustainability of the welfare systems in the western economies; (6) the high level of uncertainty generated by the Eurozone countries' anemic growth; (7) the need for a better global harmonization of the financial regulation; and (8) and the political instability in the Middle-East.

Europe as a whole still remains a relatively slow GDP growth area due also to the financial crisis, but mostly, to the fact that a number of economies have lost over the years (or decades in some cases) important competitive advantages. Given the globalized business environment, the increasing power shift towards the so-called emerging markets (in the last 20 years approximately 1 billion people entered the labor market in the emerging economies), and the new competences and resources required to compete on a global scale (high productivity, advanced supply-chains, global networks and so on), a number of EU countries now need to rethink their economic and social/welfare model in order to regain competitiveness.

Among the reasons why the financial crisis was handled better in the US than in the Eurozone there is (1) the rapid decision of policy makers, during the emergency phase of the crisis, to bail-out systemically risky banks and other organizations on the brink of collapse; (2) the attribution of bank status to other financial institutions (with no bank status) to allow them to access the Fed's discount window; and (3) the decision to recapitalize banks and other financial institutions. This way it was possible to strengthen the resilience of the financial service industry, to reduce to a certain extent systemic risk, and the impact of credit crunch and deleveraging on the real economy. Since 2010 such emergency decisions (bail-out) have been progressively substituted by the introduction of the new financial regulation (that is, Dodd–Frank Act, etc.) which aims, among other things, to avoid in the future additional bailouts costs for taxpayers through the use of a bank crisis resolution mechanism.

Influential economists such as Paul Krugman and Nouriel Roubini, business and political leaders (such as, José Manuel Barroso, the European Commission President), and even IMF leaders have argued in early 2013 that the Eurozone periphery still needs austerity (fiscal consolidation), but less than currently, and most importantly they argue that it needs policy oriented toward growth and not just budget cutting, big stimulus in the northern countries to adjust imbalances with the southern countries, and to fight alarming levels of long-term unemployment rates and a prolonged recession. In particular, Nouriel Roubini states that given a situation in the Eurozone of "deleveraging, deepening recession, limited inflation, massive loss of external competitiveness, and the large external deficits that markets are now unwilling to finance," there is a need for a growth strategy and not more austerity (that is, "higher taxes and lower government spending and transfer payments that reduce disposable income and aggregate demand") in order to improve trade balances through a much weaker euro, to reduce the credit crunch, to support monetary easing measures, and structural reforms (Roubini, 2012). Furthermore, Roubini, in an interview on February 22, 2013 with *The Daily Ticker*, also predicted the risk of an asset bubble bigger than the one of 2003–2006. Roubini's rationale is that the Federal Reserve is going to be even more reluctant to pull back in this accommodating monetary policy now (slow exit strategy) than in 2003–2006, given the fact that national and global economic growth is still weak and that inflation is low and below target. In the prior cycle, instead, according to Roubini, the Federal Reserve executed a steady stream of 25 basis point rate hikes in the period 2004–2006 (Task, 2013).

Starting from the analysis of what probably could be considered the most relevant causes of the 2007–2009 financial crisis it is worthwhile exploring some of the major reasons for these failures.

Furthermore, it is also important to assess in this chapter the newly introduced reforms affecting corporate governance and financial regulation, and to consider some additional changes that could be introduced to further strengthen these arrangements in the future to prevent other crises.

As stated by Grant Kirkpatrick (2009), internal control, audit, and risk management failures were caused in many cases by corporate governance failures and not only by inadequate computer models alone. One sentence that alone probably best summarizes this concept is the one stated by Chuck Prince, former CEO of Citibank, about the overleveraged loan market in 2007. Prince said: "While the music is playing, you have to dance" (meaning that the focus was on maintaining their short-term market share) (Kirkpatrick, 2009, pp. 4–5).

Before addressing in more detail some significant evidences of corporate governance failures related to the 2007–2009 financial crisis and a set of new ideas for its improvement in the financial markets, it might be useful to summarize the Organisation for Economic Cooperation and Development (OECD) Principles of Corporate Governance released in April 2004, which are widely accepted as the standard reference point for both OECD and non-OECD countries (OECD, 2004, pp. 9–14).

The OECD Principles of Corporate Governance are intended to assist OECD and non-OECD countries and governments in the development and improvement of good corporate governance practices in their legal, institutional, corporate, and regulatory systems. "The Principles focus on publicly traded companies, both financial and non-financial," although they might be applied also to non-traded privately held companies and state-owned enterprises (OECD, 2004, p. 11).

As reported by OECD (2004), "Corporate governance involves a set of relationships between a company's management, its board, its shareholders and other stakeholders" (OECD, 2004, p. 11).

The following are the 2004 OECD Principles of Corporate Governance:

1. Ensuring the basis for an effective corporate governance framework.
2. The rights of shareholders and key ownership functions.
3. The equitable treatment of shareholders.
4. The role of stakeholders in corporate governance.
5. Disclosure and transparency.
6. The responsibility of the board (OECD, 2004, pp. 17–25).

John D. Sullivan (2009), Executive Director of the Center for International Private Enterprise (CIPE) also adds that, in order for an effective relationship to be maintained between providers of capital and company management, a high degree of trust must exist between the two groups to overcome conflicts of interest, moral hazard, and agency problems. He identifies four key corporate governance requirements that need to be in place for such scope which are:

1. transparency;
2. accountability;
3. fairness;
4. responsibility (Sullivan, 2009, pp. 9–10).

The 2004 OECD Principles of Corporate Governance included some critical topics related to the responsibility, transparency, fairness, and accountability of boards to make "sound" decisions about the strategy and risk appetite of companies and to respond quickly to environmental changes with the support of efficient reporting systems (OECD, 2004, pp. 11–14).

Companies' corporate governance has to assure that risk appetite and corporate objectives are always compatible with their incentive system (remuneration), risk management, and internal control systems (Kirkpatrick, 2009, pp. 14–15).

Corporate Governance and the Failure of the Executive Remuneration System

Significant evidence shows that CEO remuneration and incentive systems have played a critical role in generating the financial crisis. The extremely generous top executive incentive schemes of many financial institutions, combined with the excessive short-term orientation of management, and high levels of firms' leverage, have led to an unsustainable situation in which CEO remuneration did not closely follow the companies' performance but, as Grant Kirkpatrick (2009) puts it, created instead a perverse "rewards for failure" mechanism (Kirkpatrick, 2009, p. 12).

In spite of what Principle VI.D.4 of the OECD (2004) recommends ("aligning key executive and board remuneration with the longer term interests of the company and its shareholders"), the dramatic events of the financial crisis confirm the failure of the application of this principle since banks and investment funds' CEOs have received unusually high rewards in 2007, and in the following years, while their organizations were heading toward bankruptcies, unlimited liquidity supply from Fed, or governments' rescue plans (bail-out) (Kirkpatrick, 2009, p. 13).

An Associated Press study of Standard and Poor's 500 companies revealed that the median pay for CEOs in 2007 was about $8.4 million. (Greely and Greene, 2008)

This trend of CEO remuneration has not come down even when the economy was experiencing the financial crisis. This bad practice proves that the principle was not correctly applied and that the relationship between key executives and board members' remuneration and firms' performance has been often disregarded relative to good corporate governance, or at least not based on measurable standards and with a long-term perspective. The natural consequence of such bad practices in the years leading up to the financial crisis has been an inevitable encouragement of excessive risk-taking to maximize CEOs' personal rewards and severance packages (Kirkpatrick, 2009, pp. 12–16).

According to the OECD (2009), some of the top executives of the major financial institutions received very generous parting payments during the financial crisis. Some examples are the following: Mudd of Fannie Mae ($9.3 million), Syron of Freddie Mac

($14.1 million), Prince of Citibank ($100 million), O'Neal of Merrill Lynch ($161 million), Cayne of Bear Stearns (undisclosed amount) (Kirkpatrick, 2009, p. 14).

As mentioned by film director Michael Moore (2009) in his documentary movie "Capitalism: A Love Story" and by Luigi Zingales (2010; 2012) in his paper "A Market-Based Regulatory Policy To Avoid Financial Crises," the perverse incentives of board members and CEOs, granted probably with the complacent support of some politicians and regulators, have led over the years to highly deregulated financial markets, cronyism, excessive firms' leverage, "casino-style" risk-taking, hazardous financial practices; the too-big-to-fail doctrine, and conflicts of interest, which caused a dramatic systemic failure of corporate governance and put capitalism on the brink of collapse (Moore, 2009, motion picture; Zingales, 2010, pp. 535–538).

The "sins" of corruption and moral hazard have been triggered by some ruthless CEOs, executives, traders, regulators, and politicians who have decided to turn their game of "socializing losses and privatizing profits" into a cynical reality at the expense of shareholders, taxpayers, and the economy as a whole (Moore, 2009, motion picture; Zingales, 2010, p. 535; Kolb, 2011, p. 240).

Limiting the risk of contagion and the multiplier effects of deleveraging was indeed the purpose why after the Great Depression of 1929 the Glass–Steagall Act was introduced to separate different types of financial institutions (Baskin and Miranti, 1997, p. 204; Posner, 2009, p. 15). Deregulating the financial markets in the last decades and non-regulating the highly leveraged shadow banking markets, where complex financial engineering products are often traded on the over-the-counter (OTC) without controls or any connection to the real value of the underlying debt instruments in non-regulated and transparent exchanges, created unprecedented incentives for top executives to generate huge remunerations for themselves (Pezzuto, 2008; Posner, 2009, pp. 174–175).

Given the devastating aftermath of the financial crisis, even the Financial Stability Forum (2008) expressed some concerns on the proper match between the compensation and other incentives of banks and financial firms' top executives and the long-run performance of their institutions. The crisis has demonstrated that there has been no proper balance between risk appetite and risk controls (Financial Stability Forum, 2008, p. 8).

A report by the Institute of International Finance (IIF) (2008) indicates that proper executive compensation is a serious issue and closely related to a firm's long-term profitability and sustainability. In this study they indicate that compensation schemes have to take into account not just companies' revenues but also their cost of capital. All firms' and executives' performances (and compensation) should always be measured and rewarded on risk-adjusted indicators (IIF, 2008, pp. 49–51).

For example a UBS report (2008) indicated that "bonuses were measured against gross revenue after personal costs with no formal account taken of the quality or sustainability of those earnings. Senior management instead received a greater proportion of deferred equity" (UBS, 2008, pp. 41–42).

The Financial Stability Forum study (2008) also indicates an alarming lack of risk adjustment in the CEOs' remuneration which creates concern since the lack of risk adjustment de-links the incentives of employees from the shareholders (agency problem) and leads the firms to overpay their executives versus their contribution to long-term value creation (that is, *Economic Value Added (EVA)*, Stern Stewart Model, Chicago) (Stern et al., 2001, pp. 15–23; Financial Stability Forum, 2008, p. 8; Financial Stability Board, 2010, pp. 8–20; OECD, 2009, p. 17).

Furthermore, "paying out large bonuses based largely on non-risk adjusted performance" resulted in a de-capitalization of the financial institution since many banks failed to consider the true cost of capital, took too much leverage, and invested aggressively in low margin spread trades (Archarya and Franks, 2009, pp. 1–2). High leverage indeed plays an important role in boosting short-term, yearly compensation to very high levels (Nielsen, 2010, pp. 319–321).

Michael Jensen (2002), one of the founders of modern financial *Shareholder Value Theory*, indicates that "the problem of 'value destroying activities' is related to dysfunctional, short-term shareholder value maximization instead of 'long-run value'". He also added that "short-term profit maximization is a sure way to destroy value" (Jensen, 2002, pp. 239–247).

Warren Buffet said in 2004, well before the financial crisis, that, "In judging whether Corporate America is serious about reforming itself, CEO pay remains the acid test. Today the results aren't encouraging" (OECD, 2009, p. 14).

Also, former Securities and Exchange Commission (SEC) Chairman, William Donaldson, prior to the crisis, stated that, "One of the great, as yet unsolved problems in the country today is executive compensation and how it is determined" (OECD, 2009, p. 14).

Even a few years before the financial crisis, CEO compensation and severance packages raised public attention and criticism and were not always perceived as being related to actual performance as in the cases of Pfizer and Home Depot (severance packages of around $200 million) (OECD, 2009, p. 14).

Other significant examples on this issue during the financial crisis include: (1) the $4.5 billion paid out in bonuses by Merrill Lynch in December 2008 before the merger with Bank of America; and (2) the $980,000 per year pension plan negotiated by the "former CEO of Royal Bank of Scotland (RBS) as part of his departure package due at once even though he was only 50 years old." What makes this evidence even less acceptable is the fact that "during the financial crisis the government had to take a strong capital position in order to prevent the possibility of RBS bankruptcy" (OECD, 2009, p. 18).

Compensation in high-leverage finance can be indeed disproportionally very high. In 2009, for example, Goldman Sachs paid out $16 billion in bonuses but in 2008 the same company received about $10 billion in payments from American International Group (AIG). The latter one received similar massive amounts from the Federal Reserve (Nielsen, 2010, p. 321).

Richard R. Nielsen also reported the following:

Federal payments represented 100-cents-on-the-dollar compensation for Goldman's losses on AIG credit default swaps … In addition, since the Federal bailout, Goldman Sachs and other banks have been able to borrow money from the Federal Reserve at near zero interest rate and then made billions of dollars in profits by trading with those funds. Furthermore, Goldman Sachs has been able to sell bonds guaranteed by the Federal Deposit Insurance Corporation (FDIC), which has enabled Goldman Sachs to raise billions of dollars at below market rates of interest. (Nielsen, 2010, pp. 308–321)

All together, the size of the bonuses financial services firms paid is similar to the size of the aid received from the federal government and Federal Reserve. (Nielsen, 2010, p. 321)

George Soros stated that much of the profits made by financial institutions such as Goldman Sachs are "hidden gifts" from the government and taxpayers and:

> *Those earnings are not the achievement of risk takers ... These are gifts, hidden gifts, from the government so I don't think that those monies should be used to pay bonuses. There's a resentment which I think is justified ... With the too-big-to-fail concept comes a need to regulate the payments that employees receive. (Freeland, 2009; Nielsen, 2010, pp. 319–321)*

"Pay for performance" has always been a key concept for shareholders but many times companies have not used proper metrics to link executive compensation to performance criteria. Many banks' top executives who have had a major role in the financial crisis had quite large equity positions in their companies, however, they have also received very large compensation and short-term bonuses (in particular traders) and very rich severance packages which have significantly offset any losses of their equity holdings. Their compensation structure led to excessive risk-taking strategies for their banks and financial firms since the executives faced only restricted losses (OECD, 2009, pp. 16–17).

The very favorable remuneration that many CEOs have received (as fixed salary, non-equity incentives, equity incentives, retirements benefits and options) are likely linked in many circumstances to the *Theory of Optimal Contracting* explained by Bebchuk and Fried (Bebchuk and Fried, 2004a, pp. 1–10; Kolb; 2011, pp. 247–248), based on which principals (shareholders) negotiate a contract with agents (management) in a competitive labor market in order "to align the actions of management with the interest of shareholders" (OECD, 2009, p. 19).

However, according to Bebchuk and Fried (2004), "CEOs have a great deal of bargaining power and therefore they are able to bargain for less 'independent' boards as well as more favorable compensation policies" (OECD, 2009, p. 19). Adams et al. report on the basis of their empirical work that "as CEOs become more powerful, they use this power to reduce the volatility of their compensation." The bargaining power approach, the imperfect information, the asymmetrical information between management and the board, and "the endogenous nature of board oversight are useful in explaining compensation and risk-taking behavior at financial companies" (OECD, 2009, p. 19).

Based on the *Standard Agency Theory*, executive compensation and, in particular, equity-based pay, are in general thought to be excellent reward mechanisms to align executive goals with those of the shareholders (Holmstrom, 1979, pp. 74–91; Grossman and Hart, 1983, pp. 7–45; Murphy, 1999, pp. 53–54). In the last decades, following the OECD 2004 Corporate Governance Good Practice Guidelines, companies have significantly increased the use of equity-based, stock option, and variable compensation in an attempt "to align executive and board remuneration to the long-term interest of the company and its shareholders" (Bebchuk and Fried, 2004a, pp. 159–174) This orientation has encouraged short-term incentives structures, especially for traders and commercial professionals.

Some authors are not in favor of the 2009/2010 executive compensation reform since they declared that many CEOs invested substantially in their firms and that they did not reduce their equity holdings in anticipation of the crisis (Fahlenbrach and Stulz, 2010, pp. 25–26; Core and Guay, 2010, pp. 28–30).

There are a number of scholars who argue, however, that executive compensation, severance packages, and total cash payoff practices were extremely generous compared to the losses their equity-based pay suffered during the financial crisis (Rajan, 2008).

According to the *Rent Extraction Theory*, executive compensation can be abused by a powerful CEO as a way to extract private benefits at the expense of his shareholders. And this problem becomes increasingly worse as the CEO's power over the board increases (Adams and Ferreira, 2007, pp. 217–250; Bebchuck et al., 2002, pp. 753–808; Morse et al., 2009, pp. 1779–1821).

Bebchuk et al. (2010) reported that at least for the two failed giants – Bear Stearns and Lehman Brothers – top executives were able to extract large amounts of compensation even when their firms were collapsing. CEO compensation structure has changed significantly during the financial crisis. According to a study conducted by the consulting firm, Mercer, on 61 banks and other financial services firms, the majority of them have increased basic executive salary and simultaneously decreased bonuses. Many of the large institutions had to do this since they received billions of dollars in bail-out funds by the US Federal Government. This is the case for Citigroup. In June 2009 this bank was reported to have increased salaries by as much as 50 percent to offset the bonus cut after it had accepted $45 billion in bail-out funds (Bebchuk et al., 2010, pp. 5–27).

The Government has exercised a significant intervention on compensation policies of firms that received *Troubled Asset Relief Program (TARP) funds* and other assistance. One of the Government intrusions concerned the appointment of a "pay czar" to oversee and revise executive pay plans at these firms (Kolb, 2011, pp. 239–249). This is also the reason why most of the financial institutions that received such funds, and in 2008 were practically insolvent, rushed to repay the funds to the Government in a relatively short period of time in order to get rid of the so-called "pay czar." This also raises some doubts on where these institutions found all the huge funds in a relatively short period of time, since they were almost bankrupt just a year or so before.

Only good and sound corporate governance and a well-balanced productive tension between CEO and experienced non-executive directors in the board can assure a proper balance between risk appetite, aggressive growth, and short-term profitability goals (Ard and Berg, 2010).

A review of the board activity of six distressed investment banks revealed the following common characteristics:

- The position of CEO and Chairman were combined (this practice is very common among large, publicly listed financial institutions) (Ard and Berg, 2010; Nestor Advisors, 2009, pp. 4–20). This issue should be addressed by the Section 972 of The Wall Street Reform and Consumer Protection Act of 2010 (better known as "The Dodd–Frank Act") (Bainbridge, 2010).
- There may have been too few executives on the board (which allows more concentration of power in the CEO/chairman) and very few with technical experience and independence of mind (Ard and Berg, 2010; Nestor Advisors, 2009, pp. 4–20).
- Boards were less independent than they appeared. Despite the official data (more than 74 of board members of companies listed on the New York Stock Exchange are supposed to be independent) from a more thorough analysis it results that in many cases there is an asymmetrical power exercised by the CEO/chairman, lack of independence of mind and spirit, and therefore lack of productive tension. In many

cases the CEO/chairman gathered around themselves independent non-executive board members that were not so "independent," having been in place for a long time and appointed after the CEO/chairman was appointed (imbalance of authority) (Ard and Berg, 2010; Nestor Advisors, 2009, pp. 4–20).

The Investors' Working Group's (IWG), an independent blue ribbon panel of industry and market experts created by CFA Institute and the Council of Institutional Investors to study ways to improve corporate governance as a key element of financial regulatory reforms, in their July 2009 report, wrote the following findings:

> *The global financial crisis represents a massive failure of oversight. Vigorous regulation alone cannot address all of the abuses that paved the way to financial disaster. Shareowner-driven market discipline is also critical. Too many CEOs pursued excessively risky strategies or investments that bankrupted their companies or weakened them financially for years to come. Boards were often complacent, failing to challenge or rein in reckless senior executives who threw caution to the wind. And too many boards approved executive compensation plans that rewarded excessive risk-taking. Consideration of the above findings led the IWG to propose a number of specific recommendations which include: In uncontested elections, directors should be elected by a majority of votes cast. Shareowners should have the right to place director nominees on the company's proxy. Boards of directors should determine whether the chair and CEO roles should be separated or whether some other method, such as lead director, should be used to provide independent board oversight or leadership when required. Boards of directors should be encouraged to separate the roles of chair and CEO or explain why they have adopted another method to assure independent leadership of the board. Exchanges should adopt listing standards that require compensation advisers to corporate boards to be independent of management. Companies should give shareowners an annual advisory vote on executive compensation. Federal clawback provisions on unearned executive pay should be strengthened. (Investors' Working Group, 2009, pp. 22–23)*

Bebchuk and Fried (2010) propose some guidelines on how to improve the link between executive pay and long-term performance in their paper titled "Paying for Long-term Performance." Focusing on equity-based awards, which is the primary component of executive pay, they recommend the following principles:

Principle 1: Executives should not be free to unload restricted stock and options as soon as they vest, except to the extent necessary to cover any taxes arising from vesting.

Principle 2: Executives' ability to unwind their equity incentives should not be tied to retirement.

Principle 3: After allowing for any cashing out necessary to pay any taxes arising from vesting, equity-based awards should be subject to grant-based limitations on unwinding that allow them to be unwound only gradually, beginning some time after vesting.

Principle 4: All equity-based awards should be subject to aggregate limitations on unwinding so that, in each year (including a specified number of years after retirement), an executive may unwind no more than a specified percentage of her equity incentives that is not subject to grant-based limitations on unwinding at the beginning of the year.

Principle 5: The timing of equity awards to executives should not be discretionary. Rather, such grants should be made only on prespecified dates.

Principle 6: To reduce the potential for gaming, the terms and amount of post-hiring equity awards should not be based on the grant-date stock price.

Principle 7: To the extent that executives have discretion over the timing of sales of equity incentives not subject to unwinding limitations, executives should announce sales in advance. Alternatively, the unloading of executives' equity incentives should be effected according to a prespecified schedule put in place when the equity is originally granted.

Principle 8: Executives should be prohibited from engaging in any hedging, derivative, or other transaction with an equivalent economic effect that could reduce or limit the extent to which declines in the company's stock price would lower the executive's payoffs or otherwise materially dilute the performance incentives created by the company's equity-based compensation arrangements. These authors conclude (Principle 8) by stating it is important to stress the adoption of effective prohibitions on hedging and derivative transactions that can undo and undermine the beneficial incentive effects of long-term equity-based plans (Bebchuk and Fried, 2010).

The following are the Proposed Principles of Conduct for Compensation Policies (2008) which the IIF presented in Washington in their final report of the IIF Committee on Market Best Practices: Principles of Conduct and Best Practice recommendations (IIF, 2008, pp. 49–51).

1. Compensation incentives should be based on performance and should be aligned with shareholder interests and long-term, firm-wide profitability, taking into account overall risk and cost of capital.
2. Compensation incentives should not induce risk-taking in excess of the firms' risk appetite.
3. Payout of compensation incentives should be based on risk-adjusted and cost of capital-adjusted profit and phased, where possible, to coincide with the risk time horizon of such profit.
4. Incentive compensation should have a component reflecting the impact of business unit's returns on the overall value of related business groups and the organization as a whole.
5. Incentive compensation should have a component reflecting the firm's overall results and achievement of risk management and other goals.
6. Severance pay should take into account realized performance for shareholders over time.
7. The approach, principles, and objectives of compensation incentives should be transparent to stakeholders.

In the US, corporate governance reforms affecting executive compensation were introduced in 2010 with the Dodd–Frank Wall Street Reform and Consumer Protection Act signed into law by President Barack Obama on July 21, 2010.

The new corporate governance rules, introduced with the Dodd–Frank Act on executive pay, focused on regulating and overcoming some of the existing weaknesses of the firms' executive compensation practices. The main improvements introduced referred to:

- **Pay and performance disclosure requirements:**

    - aims to create a stronger relationship between historical executive compensation; and financial performance of the company (Uppal, 2011);
    - aims to create more consistency between median annual compensation of all employees and the annual compensation of the CEO (Uppal, 2011);
    - aims to provide disclosure of whether employees can hedge the value of equity securities (Uppal, 2011).

Regarding disclosure and board members' independence, however, Raghuram G. Rajan (2010) reports that "board members are generally poorly informed when they are truly independent and excessively cozy with management when they are not." He reports for example that Lehman's board consisted of very respectable independent directors. At the time it filed for bankruptcy, however, "9 of the 10 members were retired, and 4 were over the age of 75, one was a theater producer, another was a former Navy admiral. Only two directors had experience in the financial service industry" and the risk committee met only twice a year (Rajan, 2010, p. 165).

As reported by Robert Kolb (2011) the issue is that in many instances it is difficult to link compensation to actual performance since the metrics and indicators of performance can be faked and not always focused on long-term goals and value creation strategies (Kolb, 2011, pp. 239–248).

- **Say on Pay** (Section 951 – "Dodd–Frank Act" requires periodic shareholder advisory votes on executive compensation) (Bainbridge, 2010):

    - gives shareholders the right to a non-binding vote on executive pay and golden parachutes (Uppal, 2011);
    - at least once every three years a public corporation is required to submit executive compensation to a nonbinding "*say on pay*" shareholder vote and all members of the compensation committee must be independent (Monks and Minow, 2011, pp. 150–151).

In April 2012 an encouraging sign of shareholders' activism and enhanced direct involvement in corporate governance resulted when more than 50 percent of shareholders rejected, with a "say-on-pay" vote, Citigroup's executive pay scheme due to the bank's failure to tie rewards to long-term performance targets including also an assessment of risk. After six months, Vikram Pandit was ousted as Chief Executive. "Anne Simpson, head of corporate governance for the California Public Employees' Retirement System (Calpers) said that the vote 'shows that Dodd–Frank is working'." The subsequent year

(2013), under the new CEO, Mike Corbat, Citigroup quelled a shareholder revolt on executive pay having introduced improvements to the bonus scheme, which was widely criticized as having soft targets. The new scheme introduced the following features: "objective performance targets and post-termination holding requirements, allowing for stock to be clawed back if executives are later found to have committed serious errors" (Braithwaite et al., 2013; McCrum and Braithwaite, 2012).

- **Claw-back (Sarbanes–Oxley (SOX) Section 304).**

Regarding this latter item it is worthwhile mentioning the opinion reported by reputable scholars on the matter. Raghuram G. Rajan (2010) indicates that simply giving management an equity stake does not seem to solve the agency problem since CEOs realize they have enormous gains if the risk-taking pays offs and that they have limited liability if it does not. In his book *Fault Lines* and in Luigi Zingales's paper "A Market-based Regulatory Policy to Avoid Financial Crises" these topics are explained (Rajan, 2010, pp. 164–165; Zingales, 2010, pp. 553–540). Even Monks and Minow (2011) in their corporate governance book report that claw-backs provisions could be very useful tools to recapture bonuses and incentive payments later found to be unearned (Monks and Minow, 2011, p. 151).

Even "the Squam Lake Working Group (non-partisan group convened by Professor Ken French of Dartmouth College after the recent crisis to propose reforms) has suggested not only holding back some portion of top management bonuses and reducing them if there are future losses" (like claw-backs) but also to write-down these holdbacks "if the firm has to be bailed out in any way." This way the holdbacks would serve as junior equity and would encourage management to take precautions to avoid bail-outs (Rajan, 2010, p. 165).

Claw-backs require that "public companies set policies to take back executive compensation if it was based on inaccurate financial statements that do not comply with accounting standards" (Uppal, 2011).

Under SOX Section 304, in the event a corporation is obliged to restate its financial statements due to "misconduct," the CEO and CFO must return to the corporation any bonus, incentive, or equity-based compensation they received during the 12 months following the original issuance of the restated financials, along with any profits they realized from the sale of corporate stock during that period. Dodd–Frank significantly expands this provision – Section 954 of Dodd–Frank adds a new Section 10D to the Securities Exchange Act of 1934. The Dodd–Frank Claw-back Rule requires each firm to recover excess pay, but differently from SOX, it requires claw-backs even without regard to whether misconduct has occurred. Furthermore, with the Dodd–Frank Act, the look-back period is three years, rather than 12 months. Section 954 applies to current and former executive officers, not just the CEO and CFO. Apparently, however, it does not apply to proprietary traders in case they do not have an executive officers' status or perform a policy-making function (Bainbridge, 2010; Fried and Shilon, 2011a). The provisions of Section 954 of Dodd–Frank (claw-back policy) will become mandatory for all issuers whose securities are listed on the US national securities exchange, including the New York Stock Exchange and the Nasdaq. Section 954 is enforced by the issuer and not the SEC (Davis et al., 2011; Bainbridge, 2010; Fried and Shilon, 2011a).

The claw-back policy applies to incentives-based compensation (including stock options awarded as compensation) but the calculation of the amount of the claw-back does not seem to be very straightforward (that is, the case of equity-based award) (Davis et al., 2011).

- **Enhanced compensation oversight for the financial industry** (Uppal, 2011).

Unfortunately, the DoddFrank Act does not explicitly require a critical recommendation raised by the IIF on executive pay which requires that executive compensation is linked not only to long-term and firm-wide performance but also to overall risk and cost of capital.

The introduction of the Dodd–Frank Act can be considered a starting point in the process of improving the regulation of executive compensation but it is not yet an optimal solution, since risk and cost of capital should be considered as a critical component of the banking industry reform. Even the transparency and relevance of the metrics selected to measure performance and the disclosure of all the different forms of executive compensation should be improved in order to have a full picture of the real value of the full compensation packages and proper criteria to measure actual performance and contribution to long-term shareholders' value creation.

Also as a consequence of the public outrage at perceived excessive executive pay, the US institutions that received TARP funds have been subjected by the Government to remuneration constraints. Some governments have imposed caps on remuneration as part of the rescue plans and support arrangements; however, the *Managerial Power Theory* indicates that CEO compensation (including incentive pay) is in many industries often abused by powerful executives at the expense of their shareholders.

According to Bebchuk et al. (2002) the *Managerial Power Approach* reports that executive compensation has two underlying building blocks: outrage costs and constraints and camouflage. The first refers to the reputational harm to the firm caused by self-serving executives and the loss of support from shareholders. The second refers to the practice of hidden rent extraction which indicates that executives tend to prefer compensation arrangements that enable them to extract funds from the shareholders in a way that these compensation agreements can be camouflaged as optimal contracting (Bebchuk et al., 2002, pp. 753–794).

Robert Kolb (2011) reports that, in spite of the fact that executive compensation is among the most studied problems in corporate governance, it is still very difficult to determine the real value of executive remuneration. CEOs and other top-level executives in the firms receive many different forms of compensation such as salaries, bonuses, incentives payments, deferred compensation plans, stock options, generous pension and retirement plans, and the direct provision of goods. Some of the compensation components can be less visible and more difficult to value, like in the case of *Executive Stock Options (ESO)* since the value of the stocks, restricted stocks, and stock options awarded are not always easy to assess (Kolb, 2011, pp. 246–250).

According to the *Incentive Alignment Theory* or the *Optimal Contracting Approach*, the granting of ESO should be a proper method to overcome the risks of the agency problem (divergence between the interests of the agent and those of the principal). The idea is that restricted shares in the firm and granting ESO should reduce the agency problem, however, according to Robert Kolb (2011), often, as stated in the managerial power approach, CEOs and other top executives exercise their powerful influence over their own pay packages (directly or indirectly) illegitimately transferring wealth from shareholders to executives (Kolb, 2011, pp. 247–248).

An OECD paper on corporate governance and the financial crisis (2009) reported that evidence shows that "managers had too much influence over the level and conditions for performance-based remuneration with boards unable or incapable of exercising objective independent judgment" (OECD, 2009, pp. 14–30).

The same paper also indicates that the "use of company stock price as a single measure of executives' performance does not always allow to effectively benchmark a firm's specific performance against an industry or market average." Furthermore, the OECD reports that remuneration schemes are often overly complicated and obscure and "they tend to be asymmetric with limited downside risk, thereby encouraging excessive risk taking." There needs to be strong improvement to the transparency of remuneration schemes as well as the quantification of the total cost of the programs and the adequate performance measurement criteria that reward executives once the performance has been realized. These criteria should be established through an explicit governance process and remuneration policies and should be subject to annual review approved by shareholders, compliant with the Principles of Sound Compensation Practices issued by the Financial Stability Forum (OECD, 2009, pp. 14–30).

Remuneration criteria should be flexible enough to create a better alignment between corporate governance objectives and market conditions but not too "flexible" from fixed to variable remuneration components of the executives to please only their personal interests during adverse market conditions and financial crises.

A compensation survey developed in 2009 by the IIF and the firm Olivier Wyman, clearly indicates the need to align risk management and compensation so that another crisis of this magnitude can be avoided. With the scope to identify the degree of alignment of the financial firms to IFF compensation principles, an industry self-assessment survey has been undertaken. Based on the findings of this study only 11 percent of the responders reported full alignment to the following compensation principle: "Payout of compensation incentives should be based on risk-adjusted and capital-adjusted profits and phased, where possible, to coincide with the risk time horizon of such profit" (Wheelhouse Advisors, 2009; IIF and Oliver Wyman Compensation Surveys, 2009).

Furthermore, Kevin J. Murphy and Tatiana Sandino (2009), in their paper "Executive Pay and 'Independent' Compensation Consultants," report, that based on their study on potential conflicts of interest faced by compensation consultants that lead to higher observed levels of CEO pay, they found significant evidence in both the US and Canada that CEO pay is higher in firms where the consultants provide other services and where the consultants (US) work exclusively for the board or compensation committee. In fact, many large companies rely on executive compensation consultants to make recommendations on appropriate pay levels, to design and implement short-term and long-term incentive arrangements, and to provide survey and competitive-benchmarking information on industry and market pay practices (Murphy and Sandino, 2009).

In summary, while the SOX Act aims to empower independent directors and in particular independent audit committees to overcome the management lack of accountability that led to the Enron and WorldCom crises, the Dodd–Frank Act aims to empower shareholders to overcome boards' poor corporate governance and lack of accountability (Uppal, 2011).

The objective of the Dodd–Frank Act is to give shareholders a say on pay and proxy access and to hold executives accountable for their behaviors, discouraging the use of perverse incentive schemes and relying also on the SEC reviews to compare industry-wide compensation practices and to increase disclosure and transparency in the banking and financial markets (Kolb 2011, pp. 239–259). In fact, Dodd–Frank § 971 affirms that the SEC has authority to adopt a proxy access rule (Bainbridge, 2010).

The recent financial crises and the financial scandals of recent years (Enron, WorldCom, Tyco, Lehman, Bernard Madoff, Parmalat, Barings Bank, BCCI, BRE-X, Jérôme Kerviel of Société Générale, Kweku Adoboli of UBS, and others) show that the agency problem still remains one of the most critical issues in today's capitalist society and will not easily be solved just by imposing more stringent and invasive regulatory oversights or coercive power. This may have some positive effects in the short term but not in the long term for the sustainability of our society.

In 2006 the International Corporate Governance Network (ICGN, 2006) issued the ICGN Remuneration Guidelines, among which are included the following recommendations:

- The remuneration committee of the board should take ownership of devising, drafting, and implementing the remuneration program.
- The committee should be sufficiently independent to fulfill its role in administering a remuneration program in the best long-term interests of the shareholders.
- The committee should maintain appropriate contact with shareholders.
- There should be an appropriate balance between short-term and long-term incentives and should be strongly linked to the company's performance.
- There should be goals for total remuneration as well as each major component.
- Each component of the remuneration program should be disclosed, justified, and
- explained.
- The report should be detailed enough to allow shareholders to evaluate the minimum and maximum value of remuneration packages on total remuneration under different performance scenarios (ICGN, 2006, pp. 5–13).

In December 2011, the UK Deputy Prime Minister, Nick Clegg, promised a rigorous clampdown on "abhorrent" levels of executive pay (Kirkup, 2011).

Mr Clegg said: "Just as we have been quite tough on unsustainable and unaffordable things in the public sector, we now need to get tough on irresponsible behavior of top remuneration of executives in the private sector" (Kirkup, 2011).

Mr Clegg told BBC One's Andrew Marr Show: "I do not mean that the Government starts going round setting pay rates in the private sector" (Kirkup, 2011).

"I believe people should be well paid if they succeed. What I abhor are people who get paid bucket loads of cash in difficult times for failing" (Kirkup, 2011).

Mr Clegg said he wanted to "break open this closed shop of remuneration committees which seems to be too often an old boy's network ... I scratch your back you scratch my back" (Kirkup, 2011).

Starting in April 2012, a historical and unprecedented event shook Wall Street's financial institutions. Leading global banks' shareholders voted against the massive compensation packages that had been granted to the top executives. Despite the dramatic economic consequences of the financial crisis that led to recessions and high unemployment in multiple countries, compensation on Wall Street has remained relatively high over the years. This has led to this protest. In fact, under the Dodd–Frank financial overhaul law, major US companies are required to allow shareholders to have a "say on pay" vote at least every three years. The votes are not binding but they have certainly sent a clear and powerful message of discontent to the financial firms' management that the banks' owners are unhappy. So it looks like shareholders are starting to get more directly involved, accountable, visible, and empowered by the principles of the new regulation to try to overcome the traditional principal–agent problem represented by the poor oversight over massive executive compensation and unsatisfactory business performances (Associated Press, 2012).

The attempt of the Federal Reserve in May 2012 to prevent concentration risk and dangerous domino collapses among financial institutions, through the proposed regulation of restricting the amount of aggregated net credit exposure (credit-exposure limits) that banks can have to a single counterparty to 25 percent of their regulatory capital, has encountered a fierce attack from leading banks such as Goldman Sachs and Morgan Stanley. In fact this policy is mandated by the Dodd–Frank financial reforms passed into law in 2010. The Fed is proposing to apply an even stricter rule adding a 10 percent limit on the amount of exposure that financial groups with more than $500 billion in assets can have to one another. In spite of the officials' skeptical impressions of the predicted negative impact, the large banks claim that these rules will hurt the real economy in the US, resulting in a market liquidity drop, higher funding costs for corporate debt issuers, crimped growth and lost jobs (Braithwaite, 2012a).

Bebchuk et al. (2012) in their 2010 paper titled "Golden Parachutes and the Wealth of Shareholders," revised in 2012, indicate that the Dodd–Frank Act mandated a shareholder vote on any future adoption of a golden parachute by public firms. They found out, however, "that golden parachutes are associated with higher expected acquisition premia, and that this association is at least partly due to the effect of golden parachutes on executive incentives." They also found out that "firms that adopt a golden parachute experience a reduction in their *industry-adjusted Tobin's Q*, as well as negative abnormal stock returns both during the inter-volume period of adoption and subsequently" (Bebchuk et al., 2012).

Even Steven N. Kaplan (2012) confirms in his paper "Executive Compensation and Corporate Governance in the US: Perceptions, Facts and Challenges," that in particular, top hedge fund managers (operating in the so-called shadow banking industry) are a highly paid group. The average income of hedge fund managers peaked at over $1 billion in 2007 and was as low as $134 million in 2002. These incomes are much higher than the averages for S&P 500 CEOs (Kaplan, 2012).

Fried and Shilon (2011b) argue that although Dodd–Frank's claw-back requirement will substantially improve claw-back arrangements at public firms, it does have a number of limitations. They recommend that boards should consider one or more of the following steps in order to minimize excess pay arising from sales of stock by executives:

1. To reduce executives' ability to reap large profits from prices temporarily inflated by erroneous earnings or other metrics, equity payoffs should not depend on a single day's stock price. Instead, the payoff should be based on the average stock price over a significant period of time, perhaps six months or a year.

2. To reduce executives' ability to profit from selling on inside information, it is required that their intended sales be disclosed in advance. Disclosures of large or unusual sales would intensify scrutiny of the firm's accounting results and prospects, lowering the stock price and executives' trading profits when such scrutiny leads investors to believe that the stock is overpriced.
3. To eliminate (not just lessen) executives' ability to trade on inside information and substantially reduce their incentive to manipulate the stock price, adopt a "hands-off" arrangement under which restricted stock and stock options are cashed out according to a fixed, gradual, and preannounced schedule set when the equity is granted (Fried and Shilon, 2011b).

To conclude, the Dodd–Frank financial overhaul law, which allows shareholders to have a "say on pay" and other rules, certainly represents an improvement in corporate governance with regards to executive compensation and oversight and pay for performance. However, more still needs to be done in terms of transparency and disclosure on executive pay and in aligning compensation incentives with shareholder interests and long-term, firm-wide profitability and value creation, also taking into account overall risk and cost of capital in a regulated financial environment (no to allow the use of shadow banking and off-balance-sheet vehicles to reduce capital requirements or to hide excessive risk-taking strategies, or to design window dressing techniques).

Luckily, regarding the topic of executive compensation it seems that recently a wave of cultural change is affecting the financial world. Triggered by some of the most influential corporate governance activists (activist investors), who have been shocked by the numerous scandals in the financial industry (London Interbank Offered Rate – Libor, and so on) since the start of the global financial crisis, a number of executives have been forced to give up their generous bonuses and to face drastically reduced compensations (Schäfer, 2012b).

New Regulations on Risk Management after the Financial Crisis

Another key component of firms' corporate governance is risk management (Kirkpatrick, 2009, pp. 5–8). The OECD (2009) indicates in their report that the corporate governance aspects of risk management have failed at a number of banks in the years leading to the financial crisis. In fact they state that there has been a "widespread failure of risk management since it was not managed on an enterprise basis but rather by product or division." Furthermore, the OECD report unveils that risk managers were often not directly involved in the management meetings since they were not considered an essential part of the companies' strategy. In many circumstances, "risk managers lacked status to enforce policy and red flags," in other words, they were not considered members of the firms' top management (OECD, 2009, p. 31).

The OECD report (2009) also emphasizes that this situation was made worse by the fact that in a number of cases board members were absolutely ignorant about risk management despite the fact that financial firms are regularly faced with many categories of risks, often highly correlated with one another, such as strategic risk, market risk, reputational risk, compliance risk, concentration risk, operational risk, fraud risk, credit risks, and others (OECD, 2009, p. 31).

In the banking sector there are some specific risks, as demonstrated during the financial crisis, that are of great importance for regulators. One of these risks is the liquidity risk, which is strongly driven by short-term borrowing and long-term lending (*maturity transformation*). During the financial crisis the combination of excessive leverage, excessive risk-taking with "exotic" subprime loans (and the undisclosed losses), and the high recourse to maturity transformation have led to the confidence crisis that triggered the failure of important organizations such as Lehman Brothers and Bears Stearns.

Although the 2004 revision of the OECD Principles of Corporate Governance identified risk management as an oversight duty of the board, as events have demonstrated with the widespread failure of risk management during the financial crisis, the principle recommendations were mostly ignored (OECD, 2009, pp. 32–34).

Principle VI.D.1. of the OECD Principles of Corporate Governance recommends the following:

> *The board should fulfill certain key functions including reviewing and guiding corporate strategy, major plans of action, risk policy ... while VI.D.7. defines a key function to include such as: ensuring the integrity of the corporation's accounting and reporting systems ... and ensuring that appropriate systems of control are in place, in particular systems of risk management, financial, and operational control. The annotations to principle VI.D.1. note that risk policy (sometimes termed risk appetite) is closely related to strategy and will involve specifying the types of and degree of risk that a company is willing to accept in pursuit of its goals. It is thus a crucial guideline for management that must manage risks to meet the company's desired risk profile. Furthermore, Principle VI.D.2. lists a function of the board to be monitoring the effectiveness of the company's management practices and making changes as needed. The annotations to Principle VI.D.7. report that ensuring the integrity of the essential reporting and monitoring systems will require the board to set and enforce clear lines of responsibility and accountability throughout the organization. The board will also need to ensure that there is appropriate oversight by senior management. Principle V.A.6. calls for disclosure of material information on foreseeable risk factors and the annotations go on to remark that disclosure about the system for monitoring and managing risk is increasingly regarded as good practice. (OECD, 2009, pp. 32–33)*

> *The most common source of reference with regards to risk management is COSO. COSO is derived from the Committee of Sponsoring Organizations of the Treadway Commission. (OECD, 2009, p. 35)*

The Committee of Sponsoring Organizations (COSO) has issued three major works on risk management:

- Internal Control – Integrated Framework (1992) (OECD, 2009, p. 35).
- Enterprise Risk Management – Integrated Framework (2004) (OECD, 2009, p. 35; Nugent, 2009a).
- Risk Assessment in Practice (2012) (Curtis and Carey, 2012).

The first framework, Internal Control – Integrated Framework, describes internal control as part of a process consisting of five main components:

- a control environment;
- risk identification;
- control activities;
- information and communication;
- monitoring (OECD, 2009, p.35).

Each part of this model has been designed to support the following three key corporate objectives:

- efficiency and effectiveness of operations (the continuity of the business);
- reliable, timely, and accurate financial reporting;
- compliance with laws and regulations (OECD, 2009, pp. 35–36).

The combination of the five components of the Internal Control – Integrated Framework with the above-mentioned three key corporate objectives (operations, financial reporting, and compliance), and a segmentation of the five components of the Framework by organizational units and activities, can be shown graphically as the COSO "CUBE."

The *COSO Enterprise Risk Management (ERM) Framework* (2004) instead is represented with three additional components to the front face of the cube. These components are: objective setting, event identification, and risk response (OECD, 2009, p 36; Nugent, 2009a).

The COSO ERM Framework (2004), according to COSO is:

> ... *a process, effected by an entity's board of directors, management and other personnel, applied in strategy setting and across the enterprise, designed to identify potential events that may affect the entity, and manage risks to be within its risk appetite, to provide reasonable assurance regarding the achievement of entity objectives. (COSO, 2004, p. 2)*

The COSO ERM Framework (2004) aims to support value creation by enabling management to deal effectively with potential future events that create uncertainty and to mitigate the associated risks related to the downside outcomes of future events and to leverage on the favorable upside benefits of future events (COSO, 2004, pp. 1–2; Nugent, 2009a).

Thus, it seems quite clear that many financial institutions have failed dramatically to comply with the COSO ERM framework guidelines in the years that led to the financial crisis, and not just for badly designed risk models and processes or the use of unfit data (risk models development samples, stress testing, and scenario analyses assumptions), but rather for a major failure of compliance to corporate governance principles.

COSO (2004) indicates that enterprise objectives can be viewed in the context of four categories:

1. Strategic (governance, strategic objectives, business model, external forces, and so on).
2. Operations (business processes, upstream value chain, downstream value chain, financial, and so on).
3. Reporting (information technology, financial, internal, intellectual property, reputation, and so on).
4. Compliance (SEC, environment, legal, contractual, and so on) (COSO, 2004, pp. 2–3; Nugent, 2009a).

The COSO ERM Framework (2004) requires an *enterprise-wide approach* to risk management and also considers activities at all levels of the organization such as enterprise level (fundamental to the initial ERM framework), division level, business unit level, and subsidiary level (expanded ERM framework as needed over time) (COSO, 2009b, pp. 1–4; Nugent, 2009a).

The COSO ERM framework (2004) requires an entity to take a portfolio view of risk and the aim of the application of the framework is to determine how individual risks are interrelated at different levels (enterprise level, business level, and so on) (COSO, 2009b, pp. 8–9; Nugent, 2009a).

The COSO ERM Framework (2004) comprises the following eight components:

1. Internal environment: it encompasses the tone of an organization, and sets the basis for how risk is viewed and addressed by an entity's people.
2. Objective setting: objectives must exist before management can identify potential events affecting their achievement.
3. Event identification: internal and external events affecting achievement of an entity's objectives must be identified, distinguished between risk and opportunities.
4. Risk assessment: risks are analyzed, considering the likelihood and impact, as a basis for determining how they should be managed.
5. Risk response: management selects risk responses developing a set of actions to align risks with the entity's risk tolerance and its risk appetite.
6. Control activities: policies and procedures are established and implemented to help ensure the risk response are effectively carried out.
7. Information and communication: relevant information is identified, captured, and communicated throughout the organization in a form and timeframe that enables people to carry out their responsibilities.
8. Monitoring: the entirety of ERM is monitored and modifications made as necessary (COSO, 2004, pp. 3–4; Nugent, 2009a).

Amongst the goals of the application of the COSO ERM Framework (2004) there is an aim to establish the entity's risk culture since any action of the organization may affect its risk culture and thresholds. This framework should be used by management when formulating the enterprise corporate strategy, setting objectives, and the risk appetite that management and the board are willing to accept. Management and the board should also define the risk tolerance which represents the acceptable variation around objectives and its alignment with risk appetite (COSO, 2004, p. 6; Nugent, 2009a).

The COSO ERM Framework (2004) also involves identifying the incidents, occurring internally and externally, that might have a negative impact on the firm's strategy and achievement of its objectives. Furthermore, the Framework should allow management and the board to understand the extent to which potential events might impact objectives, assessing risk from two perspectives:

- likelihood (probability);
- impact.

The Framework (2004) also relies on a combination of both qualitative and quantitative risk assessments methodologies to assure a "sound" and rigorous resilience of this risk management philosophy. The Framework also relates the time horizons of risk to the objective horizons, assesses risk on both an inherent and a residual basis, and identifies and evaluates possible responses to risk. This approach allows evaluation of the most suitable options in relation to an enterprise's risk appetite, the cost/benefit of potential risk responses, and the degree to which the response will reduce impact and/or likelihood of a risk. The selection of risk response should be based on the evaluation on the portfolio of risks and responses (Ballou and Heitger, 2005, pp. 1–10; Nugent, 2009a).

In order to establish the COSO ERM Framework in an organization the following steps are required:

- determine a risk philosophy;
- survey risk culture;
- consider organizational integrity and ethical values;
- decide roles and responsibilities (Ballou and Heitger, 2005, pp. 1–10; Nugent, 2009a).

In order to implement the COSO ERM Framework (2004) an ad hoc organizational structure has to be established. An example is the following:

- vice president (VP) and chief risk officer (CRO);
- three reporting lines to the VP and CRO: ERM director, insurance risk manager, and corporate credit risk manager;
- ERM managers reporting to the ERM director;
- staff reporting to the insurance risk manager; staff reporting to the corporate credit risk manager; and staff reporting to the ERM managers;
- a FES commodity risk manager director with a dotted reporting line to the ERM director (The Institute of Internal Auditors, 2004a).

An example of a risk model based on the COSO ERM Framework (2004) is:

Environmental risks:
- capital availability;
- regulatory, political, and legal;
- financial markets and shareholder relation.

Process risks:
- operations risk;
- empowerment risk;
- information processing/technology risk;
- integrity risk;
- financial risk.

Information for decision making:
- operational risk;
- financial risk;
- strategic risk;
- hazard risk (The Institute of Internal Auditors, 2004a; Institute of Management Accountants (IMA), 2011).

In order to identify the proper risk responses according to the COSO ERM Framework (2004), management and the board have to quantify the risk exposure and identify the risk response options available in order to determine the residual risk and to assess the impact of these risks and their probability of occurrence. Thus, using a two-dimensional matrix (*Risk Map*) and (Color-coded Risk Map with Green Zone, Yellow Zone, and Red Zone) based on the probability of risk (high and low) and on the impact of risk (high and low), companies' management and board may select the following options:

- Accept Risk (Low Probability/Low Impact = Low Risk) => monitor.
- Avoid/Mitigate Risk (High Probability/High Impact = High Risk) => eliminate.
- Reduce/Control Risk (High Probability/Low Impact = Medium Risk) => control.
- Share Risk (Low Probability/High Impact = Medium Risk) => partner with someone (Ballou and Heitger, 2005, pp. 1–10; IMA, 2011).

In a recent COSO paper by Mark L. Frigo and Richard J. Anderson titled "Embracing Enterprise Risk Management: Practical Approaches For Getting Started" (Frigo and Anderson, 2011, pp. 6–8), the authors indicate examples of risk management templates that can help improve the assessment of all risk events related to an organization.
These templates include the following data:

- risk category (that is, operations, reputation, IT, strategic risk, and so on);
- description of risk;
- likelihood of risk – an estimate of the chance or probability of the risk event occurring (probability: high, medium, low);
- impact of risk – the significance of a risk to an organization (high, medium, low). It can be measured quantitatively or qualitatively;
- velocity (high, medium, low);
- readiness (red, yellow, and green readiness symbols);
- priority (1, 2, 3, 4, 5);
- risk owner(s);
- risk appetite metrics;
- residual risk – the level of risk that remains after management has taken action to mitigate the risk;
- monitoring;
- action plans;
- company oversight;
- board oversight.

Other key components of the COSO ERM Framework (2004) process include:

- communicating the results;
- monitoring management: oversight and periodic reviews (Ballou and Heitger, 2005, p. 8).

With regards to management oversight and periodic reviews, the COSO ERM Framework (2004) requires enterprises to apply the following practices:

- dashboard of risks and related responses (visual status of where key risks stand relative to risk tolerances);
- flowcharts of processes with key controls noted;
- narratives of business objectives linked to operational risks and responses;
- create a list of key risks to be monitored or used;
- management understanding of key business risk responsibility and communication of assignments;
- collect and display information;
- systematic evaluation of performance analyses;
- determine accountability for risks;
- ERM ownership;
- updates on changes in business objectives, systems and processes (COSO, 2004, pp. 6–7).

The highly publicized business failures, scandals, and frauds of 1999 to 2004 required a more rigorous implementation and enforcement of the laws, regulations, and application of the corporate governance principles and risk management practices that were reflected in the 2004 COSO ERM Framework.

As indicated by Ballou and Heitger (2005):

> *The responsibility of over-seeing risk management falls on the board of directors, while the ownership responsibility for enterprise risk management falls on the CEO and senior executives (Ballou and Heitger, 2005, p. 2).*

In September 2004, COSO issued the ERM – Integrated Framework, with the scope of establishing a standardized framework for approaching ERM (Ballou and Heitger, 2005, p. 2).

COSO includes representatives from several prestigious associations and institutions such as, "IMA (the Institute of Management Accountants), AICPA (American Institute of Certified Public Accountants), AAA (American Accounting Association), FEI (financial Executives International), and IIA (the Institute of Internal Auditors). PricewaterhouseCoopers" played a central role in the research and development activities that led to the 2004 COSO Framework, whereas the paper "Risk Assessment in Practice" (2012) has been developed by Deloitte and Touche LLP (Ballou and Heitger, 2005, p. 2; Curtis and Carey, 2012).

COSO's ERM Framework is defined as:

> *Enterprise Risk management is a process, effected by an entity's board, management, and other personnel, applied in a strategy setting and across the enterprise, designed to identify potential events that may affect the entity, and manage risks to be within its risk appetite, to provide reasonable assurance regarding the achievement of entity objectives. (Ballou and Heitger, 2005, p. 2)*

An appropriate implementation of the 2004 COSO ERM Framework requires organizations to adopt an *entity-wide portfolio approach* to risk management and to stimulate a cultural shift toward the potential benefits of its successful achievement. "Using the *building-block approach*, the entity-wide approach consists of implementing the ERM Framework on a limited basis across each of the eight interrelated components and with a focus on the entity-wide risks of all four categories (for example, strategic, operations, reporting, and compliance)." The ERM framework can then be expanded, cascading the framework to other levels of the organization and instilling a sense of ownership of risk management throughout the entire organization (Ballou and Heitger, 2005, pp. 2–5).

By reviewing, ex-post (after the 2007–2009 crisis and beyond), the recommended COSO steps for a practical, building-block approach to implementing the ERM – Integrated Framework, it is possible to identify a series of failures in the management of the ERM entity-wide portfolio approach of many leading institutions during the financial crisis and their poor corporate governance as well.

FAILURES RELATED TO THE INTERNAL ENVIRONMENT COMPONENT OF THE ERM FRAMEWORK

It is evident from the analysis of the events of the financial crisis that many institutions have failed to develop a proper risk management philosophy. In particular, they have failed to take the necessary steps to understand the risk appetite of key stakeholders' groups of the organization and to align the risk appetite of all stakeholder groups. Furthermore, just as clear is the massive failure of many institutions to create a risk management culture and in particular to establish integrity and ethical standards in every endeavor and proper incentives/compensation policies for employees and executives to support a risk culture and accountability. Even the role of risk committees and the degree of authority and independence of mind and spirit of the CRO did not prove to be very reliable or responsible in many organizations. In addition, the responsibility of all board members and senior executives on the entity-wide portfolio approach to risk management appears very weak and confused.

The failure in ERM is also particularly evident with regards to the Objective Setting component of the ERM Framework. As all qualified risk managers know very well, effective and proactive (preventive) risk management should start before the negative event occurs. In the consumer lending industry, for example, an effective risk management process starts before the credit origination process in the product design, product development, customer profiling, and business planning phases of the strategic planning process. Before lenders design, develop, and launch new products to the market, they have to establish clear and entity-wide level objectives, based on the risk appetite for the new products and for the entire entity-wide portfolio. This needs to take into account all potential risks related to the new initiative, the risk profile of the market segment they intend to target, and the reliability of the models they need to use to assess the risk of specific borrowers' profiles, product and collateral characteristics, and in particular markets (macroeconomic parameters). Thus a proactive involvement of risk management in the product and business planning stages is critical prior to launching a new product, initiatives, targeting new customers, or taking different approaches. Aligning stakeholders' risk appetites with those of the company's strategic objectives and strategies is also a critical aspect of a good business planning process, which in many instances during the crisis failed to be achieved. Evidence indicates that most risk managers were never invited to join the sales and marketing teams in the product design and development of new "exotic" subprime mortgage loans or to attend senior management meetings, thus limiting significantly the diffusion of the risk culture across the entire organization and at all levels (OECD, 2009, p. 31).

In the years leading up to the financial crisis, even the management of the Event Identification component of the ERM Framework seems to have failed to a certain extent. Many institutions, as reported in the previous chapters of this book, have apparently failed to identify risk events with appropriate early warning indicators in the early stage of the credit and housing market bubbles.

All institutions involved in the crisis seem to have failed to consider all the factors that have led to the crisis (with a holistic approach) and to proactively assess all risk categories and event interdependencies (based on scenario analyses, stress testing, property prices changes, delinquency and foreclosure rates, interest rates, liquidity issues, excessive leverage, high debt burden of borrowers, high concentrations of subprime loans, originate-to-distribute (OTD) securitization process, perverse executive compensation incentives, capital requirements, unregulated shadow banking, and so on) to determine the full impact of the systemic risk.

The failure that led to the crisis has consequently affected the Risk Assessment component of the ERM Framework, since many financial institutions and executives were so euphoric about the excitement, exuberance, and unprecedented short-term profitability, driven by the housing and credit bubbles and by the "too-big-to-fail" doctrine, that they have seriously underestimated or deliberately ignored all the evident warning signs of systemic risk. Even during the crisis, the poor disclosure and lack of transparency did not facilitate a correct assessment of the risk events (estimated probabilities/frequencies of risk events) or of the cost impact of these risk events (detective activities), through reliable and rigorous stress tests and realistic scenario analyses.

Needless to say, even the Risk Response component of the ERM Framework during the financial crisis did not prove to be very effective, since regulators, political leaders, policy makers, and corporate governance members of the financial institutions could easily have access to the same information reported in this work and even much more, but they did not always use it properly to implement timely and effective reforms or have not used it at all in some instances.

With regards to the Risk Response component of the ERM Framework, which suggests either to accept, avoid, share, or reduce the risk, many key players in the financial industry involved in the crisis have apparently chosen to reduce the risk of their positions related to the "toxic" collateralized debt obligations (CDOs) and mortgage-backed securities (MBS) by transferring it onto the unaware and trustful investors, through the OTD securitization process. So the Risk Response component of the ERM Framework was "effectively implemented" by many institutions "dumping" the risk on the investors and in the worst case scenario relying on the "too-big-too-fail" doctrine which is based on the principle of "privatizing the profits and socializing the losses."

Given the concepts reported in the previous paragraphs, it is quite evident that the remaining components of the ERM Framework resulted in a failure and were totally irrelevant given the euphoric environment of reckless risk-taking that led to the crisis. Financial firms and their senior executives most likely had no interest at all in effective risk control activities, information sharing, communication reporting (asymmetric information with investors was the key component of their perverse "gambling" business model), and monitoring.

In 2005 (the period preceding the financial crisis), Bowling and Rieger (2005) mentioned in their paper "Making Sense of COSO's New Framework for Enterprise Risk Management," that the interest of organizations in the ERM Framework has built slowly over the years, due also to the high perceived costs of implementation of the Public Accounting Reform and Investor Protection Act, better known as the SOX Act of 2002. As they stated: "ERM can provide a solid foundation upon which companies can enhance corporate governance and deliver greater shareholder value" (Bowling and Rieger, 2005, p. 29).

Bowling and Rieger (2005) also report in their paper that COSO's ERM Framework aims to take a broad portfolio view or risk of an entity and that, contrary to the past, risk management requires a top-down approach, rather than a traditional bottom-up and fragmented approach (abandon "risk-silo" mentality and embrace a holistic approach). This new approach, according to these authors, was driven also by the introduction of the "Section 404 of SOX, which requires public companies to have a stronger ownership of financial reporting controls by top management. Section 404 of SOX, in fact, mandated that companies use a suitable, recognized control framework for evaluating the effectiveness of internal controls" (Bowling and Rieger, 2005, pp. 29–30).

Regarding the ownership requirement of the ERM Framework, Bowling and Rieger (2005) also stated that CEOs and CFOs have to instill a sense of responsibility for risk management throughout the financial institutions and that key process owners are expected to extend the self-assessment applied in compliance with Section 404 of SOX to a larger number of business risks, not just the ones related to financial reporting. Following this guideline, it was quite evident that the objective of the authors was to overcome the limit of large banks having separate compliance activities for consumer, commercial, investment, and private banking divisions. A number of large banks often had several different silos of risk which were managed with a different set of risk tolerances for each. Evidently, as the financial crisis has demonstrated, the framework was not properly implemented to manage all risk categories in a holistic and integrated approach with a broad portfolio view. The aggregation of all risk management activities was meant to provide to the bank superior long-term value creation benefits thus avoiding the duplication of activities, costs, and efforts (Bowling and Rieger, 2005, pp. 32–34).

As Federal Reserve Governor Susan Schmidt Bies explained at the Risk Management Association and Consumer Bankers Association Retail Risk Conference in Chicago in July 2004:

> *Enterprise-wide risk management looks within and across business lines and activities of the organization as a whole – and the ERM advantage is to consider how one area of the firm may affect the risks of the other business lines and the enterprise as a whole. (Bowling and Rieger, 2005, pp. 32–33)*

Bowling and Rieger (2005) state that, "ERM is a vital engine for strengthening corporate governance since corporate governance is composed of the systems and processes an organization uses to protect the interests of diverse stakeholders." Thus, organizations need sound risk-taking in order to satisfy stakeholders' interests and to enable them to prosper over the years. The contribution to firms' value creation of a sound ERM Framework and corporate governance is also supported by a study undertaken by the University of Michigan Business School, and other publications which "assert that strong corporate governance programs lead to higher stock valuations and increased shareholder returns" (Bowling and Rieger, 2005, p. 34).

Frigo and Anderson (2011) of De Paul University report in their COSO ERM paper "Embracing Enterprise Risk Management: Practical Approaches for Getting Started," that after the 2007–2009 financial crisis, COSO's Enterprise Risk Management – Integrated Framework and other COSO thought papers have become a strong foundation for pursuing ERM benefits in any organization (Frigo and Anderson, 2011, pp. 1–8).

With the introduction in 2010 of the new Dodd–Frank Act in the US, according to these authors, boards of directors and senior management are today even more empowered with the responsibility of overseeing an organization's risk management activities, due to the growing awareness of its strategic importance to achieve the firms' objectives (Frigo and Anderson, 2011, pp. 1–8).

According to COSO's 2009 paper "Strengthening Enterprise Risk Management for Strategic Advantage," boards are increasingly engaged in overseeing management's monitoring processes to ensure that risk-taking is aligned with companies' objectives. Boards are also requesting of firms' management reports that can provide them with a robust and holistic top-down view of the key risks facing their organizations (COSO, 2009b, p. 4).

In other to strengthen ERM, COSO's 2009 paper also suggests that the board work more closely with management to provide appropriate risk oversight related to the firms' strategies and objectives through the following initiatives:

- discuss risk management philosophy and risk appetite;
- understand ERM practices;
- review portfolio of risks in relation to risk appetite;
- be apprised of the most significant risks and related responses (COSO, 2009b, pp. 4–5; Nugent, 2009a).

Based, however, on the major financial scandals, corporate governance, and risk management failures reported in the news in 2012 ("Liborgate," "London whale" and so on), almost a couple of years after the introduction of the Dodd–Frank Act (2010), it is quite evident that much still needs to be done to create a more resilient, diffused, and sustainable ERM culture in many financial institutions.

Frigo and Anderson (2011), in fact, realized that a successful implementation of the COSO ERM Integrated Framework is not an easy task, thus in their paper they suggest what they call the "Keys to Success" for organizations that want to start ERM initiatives, which consists of a set of guidelines that may significantly improve the chances of implementing the Framework (Frigo and Anderson, 2011, pp. 1–3).

These guidelines, according to Frigo and Anderson (2011), can be summarized in the following seven recommendations:

1. *support from the top is a necessity*. Top management has to perceive these initiatives of strategic importance for the companies' success and long-term sustainability. In the aftermath of the financial crisis of 2008, a number of companies have increased their attention to ERM as a critical part of new rules on corporate governance. For example, the corporate governance rules of the New York Stock Exchange require audit committees of listed corporations to oversee the risk assessment and risk management policies of their organizations. Even the US SEC expanded proxy disclosures pertaining to the extent of the board's role in risk oversight. Furthermore,

even credit agencies such as Standard and Poor's are also starting to seriously consider ERM practices as part of their credit rating assessment processes.

2. *build ERM using incremental steps.* According to the authors this is achievable through the following actions:
    – identify and implement key practices to achieve immediate, tangible results (in other words, to start with a short list of enterprise-wide risks and then to expand it to more detailed risk assessments);
    – provide an opportunity to change and further tailor ERM processes;
    – facilitate the identification and evaluation of benefits at each step (this could be done by reporting the list of incremental action steps with the related expected benefits received by these steps);
3. build focus initially on a small (and manageable) number of top risks;
4. leverage existing resources;
5. build on existing risk management activities (for example, internal audit, external audit, insurance, compliance, fraud prevention or detection measures, or certain credit or treasury reports);
6. embed ERM into the business fabric of the organization. Since COSO's ERM Integrated Framework is a company-wide process, ultimately owned by the CEO, the comprehensive nature of the ERM process and its pervasiveness across the organization and its people provides the basis for its effectiveness;
7. provide ongoing ERM updates and continuing education for directors and senior management (Frigo and Anderson, 2011, pp. 1–3).

With regards to the initial action steps and objectives, Frigo and Anderson (2011) suggest the following initiatives:

1. seek board and senior management leadership, involvement and oversight;
2. select a strong leader to drive the ERM initiative;
3. establish a management risk committee or working group;
4. conduct the initial enterprise-wide risk assessment and develop an action plan;
5. inventory the existing risk management practices (for example, as in the case of the risk management alignment guide in which the following data is reported in different columns: risk category, risk owner/s, risk appetite metrics, monitoring, action plans, company oversight, board oversight);
6. develop the Initial Risk Reporting (for example, reporting in various columns risk data according, for example, to the following criteria: type of risk, description of risk, likelihood of occurrence, impact, velocity, readiness, and priority) (Frigo and Anderson, 2011, pp. 3–7).

Furthermore, according to Frigo and Anderson (2011) the following activities are recommended to strengthen an organization's risk culture and practices:

*   a program of continuing ERM education for directors and executives;
*   ERM education and training for business-unit management;
*   policies and action plans to embed ERM processes into the organization's functional units such as procurement, IT, or supply chain units;

- continuing communication across the organization on risk and risk management processes and expectations;
- development and communication of a risk management philosophy for the organization;
- identification of targeted benefits to be achieved by the next step of ERM development;
- development of board and corporate policies and practices for ERM (Frigo and Anderson, 2011, pp. 7–8).

COSO's 2009 paper "Strengthening Enterprise Risk Management for Strategic Advantage" also points out the elements that companies have to consider to determine their risk appetite. These elements are:

- the existing risk profile (existing level and distribution of risk across risk categories, for example, financial risk, operational risk, reputation risk, and so on);
- the risk capacity (the maximum risk a firm may bear and remain solvent);
- the risk tolerance (the acceptable level of variation an entity is willing to accept around specific objectives);
- the desired level of risk (what is the desired risk/return level?) (COSO, 2009b, pp. 8–9).

Through a portfolio view of risks (Risk Portfolio in Relation to Risk Appetite), management and the board monitor key risk exposures and concentrations of risks affecting specific strategies or overlapping risk exposures for the enterprise in order to determine the priority of the risk exposures based on the assessment of risk probabilities and impact to the organization. Heat Maps are one type of tool used to have an effective visualization of the risks to help the board and management address the most critical ones based on the likelihood/frequency (high or low) and impact occurrences (high or low). As the financial crisis has demonstrated, the so-called tail-event or black swans have proved to be extremely useful as early warning signs of risks for the board members and management (COSO, 2009b, pp. 14–15).

By using these types of tools, management can increase their confidence that potential events are identified and managed more timely and effectively and in alignment with the organization's risk appetite, thus increasing the probability of achieving the company's objectives (COSO, 2009b, p. 15).

More recently, in 2010, COSO issued a new publication titled "Developing Key Risk Indicators To Strengthen Enterprise Risk Management," which aimed to create a sharper focus on emerging risks following the 2007–2009 financial crisis (Beasley, Branson, Hancock, 2010, p. 1).

The scope of this paper is to make boards' directors increasingly aware of their responsibilities related to effective oversight of management's execution of enterprise-wide risk management processes. Thus recently there has been a growing focus to strengthen the ERM Framework in order to provide a more robust and holistic enterprise-wide view of potential events that may affect the achievement of the organizations' strategies and objectives (Beasley, Branson, Hancock, 2010 pp. 1–5).

The scope of the paper is to raise attention not only to *key performance indicators (KPIs)*, which often shed insights about risk events that have already affected the organization, but also to *key risk indicators (KRIs)*, which aim to proactively identify potential impacts on the organizations' portfolio of risks.

Both the KPIs and KRIs provide boards and management with a high-level overview of the performance of the organization and its major operating units. However, according to COSO's paper (Beasley, Branson, Hancock, 2010, p. 1), the KPIs tend to focus almost exclusively on the historical performance (for example, monthly, quarterly, and year-to-date reports on the company's performance). The use of these new indicators is driven, instead, by the need to provide adequate *early warning indicators* of a developing risk to boards and management for a proactive strategic risk management approach. In other words, these indicators aim to provide timely leading-indicator information about internal or external events that signal emerging risks, such as macroeconomic shifts that affect the demand or issues in the internal operations and indicate the corrective or mitigating actions (strategic response) that need to be taken (Beasley, Branson, Hancock, COSO, 2010, p. 1).

In the COSO paper "Strengthening Enterprise Risk Management for Strategic Advantage" (2009b), special attention is given to the role of senior executives and boards of directors in risk oversight (COSO, 2009b, p. 16).

The paper indicates that since the recent financial crisis, a new focus has been given by senior management and board members to the risk management process and four specific areas are identified where senior management can work with its board to enhance the boards' risk oversight capabilities with an enterprise view of Risk Management – Integrated Framework (COSO, 2009b, pp. 10–17).

These areas are:

1. discuss risk management philosophy and risk appetite;
2. understand risk management practices;
3. review portfolio risks in relation to risk appetite based on some elements of risk appetite (that is, existing risk profile, risk capacity, risk tolerance, desired level of risk);
4. be apprised of the most significant risks and related responses.

Furthermore, according to this paper, senior management and board members should also use ERM in strategy settings to help them map strategies and top risk exposures, also using portfolio view models like Heat Maps to provide an effective visualization that can help focus discussions on those risk issues critical to the organization. The portfolio view of key risks' exposures should also help to proactively identify those low likelihood/frequency risk events, the so-called tail-events or black swans, that played a significant role in the financial crisis and which now, going forward, should deserve much closer attention from the board members (COSO, 2009b, p. 14).

To plan for more effective responses to significant risks, the paper also suggests that the organization's ERM system should function to bring to the board's attention the most significant risks affecting entity objectives and should allow the board to understand and evaluate how these risks may be correlated, thus providing to management useful insights on possible mitigation or response strategies (COSO, 2009b, p. 16).

The paper also encourages the widespread use of KRIs to provide relevant and timely information to both the board and senior management and to assure more effective risk oversight. According to the paper, the following are the elements of well-designed KRIs:

- they have to be based on established practices or benchmarks;
- they have to be developed consistently across the organization;
- they have to allow for measurable comparison across time and business units;

- they have to provide opportunities to assess the performance of risk owners on a timely basis;
- they have to consume resources efficiently (COSO, 2009b, pp. 17–18).

The IMA also suggests combining the balanced scorecard (BSC), a tool for communicating and cascading the company's strategy throughout the organization, with ERM to enhance performance management (IMA, 2011).

According to the IMA's paper titled "Enterprise Risk Management: Tools and Techniques For Effective Implementation" (2007), the risk management process consists of the following six steps:

1. set strategy/objectives;
2. identify risks;
3. assess risks;
4. treat risks;
5. control risks;
6. communicate risks (IMA, 2007, pp. 1–3).

According to the IMA, risk identification techniques include the following activities:

- brainstorming;
- event inventories and loss event data;
- interviews and self-assessment;
- facilitated workshops;
- strengths, weaknesses, opportunities, and threats (SWOT) analysis;
- risk questionnaires and risk surveys;
- scenario analysis;
- using technology (that is, intranet and ERM site);
- other techniques (that is, value chain analysis, system design review, process analysis, and benchmarking with other similar or dissimilar organizations) (IMA, 2007, pp. 4–27).

The risk analysis also includes activities such as the analysis of risk by drivers and the use of quantitative, qualitative, and combined quantitative and qualitative approaches to risk assessment (IMA, 2007, pp. 3–27).

To be more specific, the qualitative approaches include:

- risk identification;
- risk rankings;
- Risk Maps with impact and likelihood;
- risk mapped to objectives or division;
- identification of risk correlations (IMA, 2007, pp. 3–27; 2011).

The quantitative approaches include:

- probabilistic techniques;
- cash flow at risk (CFaR);

- earnings at risk (EaR) by risk factor;
- earnings distributions;
- earnings per share (EPS) distributions (IMA, 2007, pp. 11–27; 2011).

The combined quantitative/qualitative approaches include:

- validation of risk impact;
- validation of risk likelihood;
- validation of correlations;
- risk-corrected revenues;
- gain/loss curves;
- tornado charts;
- scenario analysis;
- benchmarking;
- net present value;
- traditional measures (IMA, 2007, pp. 12–27; 2011).

Furthermore, according to the IMA some common elements for the practical implementation of ERM include:

- CEO commitment (tone and messaging from the top);
- risk policies and/or mission statements, including adapting any company risk or audit committee charter to incorporate ERM;
- reporting to business units, executives, and the board;
- adoption or development of a risk framework;
- adoption or development of a common risk language;
- techniques for identifying risk;
- tools for assessing risks;
- tools for reporting and monitoring risk;
- incorporating risk into appropriate employees' job descriptions and responsibilities;
- incorporating risk into the budgeting function; and
- integrating risk identification and assessment into the strategy of the organization (IMA, 2007).

Kevin Davis of the University of Melbourne questions whether the failure of risk management in what are considered to be the most sophisticated financial institutions globally is due to faulty risk models or to failures in the overall governance and management of risk management practices and processes (Davis, 2011, pp. 15–21).

In his paper, Kevin Davis reported the findings of the Joint Forum (2010) which pointed out severe deficiencies identified in the risk models applied by many financial institutions and the growing but still limited use of more sophisticated techniques than Value-at-Risk (VaR). Among these methodologies are those used to measure the "extreme-tail" events and their outcomes as well as stress testing and scenario analysis. The issue under scrutiny also involves the potential gaps between risk modeling for specific activities and the firm-wide view of risk management (Davis, 2011, pp. 15–21).

Kashyap (2010) reports that the President's Working Group on Financial Regulation (2008), just before the Bear Stearns collapse, cited "risk management weaknesses at some large US and European financial institutions" as one of "the principal underlying causes of the turmoil in financial markets." That report faulted "regulatory policies, including capital and disclosure requirements that failed to mitigate risk management weaknesses" (Kashyap, 2010, pp. 15–18).

According to Dewatripont et al. (2010), the 2007–2009 financial crisis was not originated by the Basel II prudential regime, although it was true that some countries (including the US) did not implement the more advanced Basel framework when the crisis started, but mainly because the US investment banks were in any event entirely outside the Basel regime (since they did not finance their activity by taking deposits from the public). They also reported that these major investment banks had obtained from the Basel Committee a guarantee that the application of Basel II would not involve an increasing of average capital requirements for all banks, and that these major banks in some cases benefited a reduction of these requirements as an incentive to adopt the *Internal Ratings-based (IRB)* method. The result was that the 2007–2009 financial crisis generated a recourse to massive recapitalization of the international banking system due to the breakdown of the Basel prudential regime. There has been, in fact, an inability to measure the individual risk of a bank failure, the inability to anticipate systemic risk, and ultimately the inability to manage financial innovation. The Basel II Framework, according to Dewatripont et al. (2010) and to my 2008 paper, was inadequate for the following reasons: failing to take into account liquidity risk, model risk, and procyclicality, poor choice of regulatory criteria, a lack of balance between the three regulatory pillars, and the opacity of some financial instruments (shadow banking) (Dewatripont et al., 2010, pp. 86–87; Pezzuto, 2008).

An important element that has been adopted by policy makers for a more resilient financial system stability (Dodd–Frank Act) is the one suggested by Dewatripont et al. (2010) and myself (Pezzuto, 2008; 2010a), consisting in the requirement for issuing banks to retain a share of the securitized portfolio so that it might continue to have an incentive to monitor the quality of its borrowers after the securitization and sale of MBS (Dewatripont et al., 2010, pp. 91–92; Pezzuto, 2008; 2010a, p. 123).

This is clearly indicated in my article "Miraculous Financial Engineering of Legacy Assets?" in Robert Kolb's *Lessons from the Financial Crisis: Causes, Consequences, and Our Economic Future* in which I stated: "All banks and financial institutions should be held responsible for the securitization they create" (Pezzuto, 2010a, p. 123).

In 2008, I was among the first group of authors to propose in my papers and articles the concept of the "skin in the game" rule for originators/securitizers involved with securitizations processes.

Furthermore, I also, alternatively, recommended a stricter rule. I suggested that regulators require originators to retain a significant share (at least 5 percent of the securitizations they create at all times) of the securitized portfolio, or even to ban any type of non-recourse loans of the issuer and to make them all full recourse. The truth of the matter is that, with the OTD securitization process and the subsequent sales of these non-recourse mortgage loans as MBS and other derivatives to investors, financial institutions have lost the incentive to apply proper risk management (moral hazard). It is quite evident and even proved by many reports on the financial crisis (including the Financial Crisis Inquiry Commission – FCIC – final report) that financial firms' focus shifted, in the years preceding the crisis, from traditional and prudential risk management to making as much profit as possible (short-termism) and issuing as many mortgage loans as possible. The radical shift in the risk management culture and practice generated the credit bubble which contributed to boost the housing market bubble in conjunction with a booming shadow banking system, widespread asymmetric information, excess of liquidity at cheap ratess, and complacent rating agencies and regulators (Pezzuto, 2008; 2010a, pp. 119–123).

Furthermore, credit scoring and risk models for secured and unsecured lending products should factor in relevant macroeconomic and industry-wide data comparisons (benchmarks) in order to strengthen their risk assessment and to help make the financial system more resilient. The risk monitoring systems should more accurately assess key macroeconomic variables, and risk managers should develop more rigorous scenario analyses and stress tests based on appropriate data and reliable assumptions. Thus, leading global financial firms' risk management should enhance the overall reliability of early warning indicators of systemic risk with the support of global institutions such as the OECD, International Monetary Fund (IMF), World Bank, Financial Stability Board (FSB), Institute of International Finance, World Economic Forum, and so on.

According to Dewatripont et al., another risk management problem was related to the adoption of the criterion of VaR, which was solely concentrated on the probability of default and which did not take into account losses sustained subsequent to the moment of default. By adopting this criterion, regulators encouraged banks to focus on structurally complex financial instruments (such as CDOs) that shifted risk in the tail of the loss distribution (Dewatripont et al., 2010, p. 91).

They argued that, although the VaR criterion is suited to the shareholders of a commercial bank, who are protected by limited liability, it is certainly inappropriate for public authorities which have to compensate for losses, whatever their magnitude (Dewatripont et al., 2010, p. 91).

The Basel Committee has chosen a confidence level of 99 percent and a ten-day horizon to compute VaR, and the resulting VaR is multiplied by a factor of three to determine the minimum capital. The underlying assumption being that total risk capped by three times credit risk may work in normal times but not during systemic crises (tail-events) since the total risk can easily exceed the cap (Tian, 2010, p. 5).

One of the lessons learned from the 2007–2009 financial crisis is that, regardless of the huge investments in risk management tools and best practices that were in place for many years, apparently nothing seems to have been able to prevent the financial meltdown. With a forward-thinking approach, in order to create a more resilient corporate governance in the banking and other industries, it is necessary to develop a new mindset for strategic planning more focused on firm-wide risk assessment, scenario analyses, stress testing models, long-term and industry-wide perspectives, and enriched with macro-environmental indicators. Additional analyses would include: Financial Stress Index (FSI) introduced by IMF (Cardarelli et al., 2009), counterparty credit risk calculations, Credit Valuation Adjustment (CVA) measures, Monte-Carlo scenarios, advanced scenario generation simulations, Federal Reserve scenarios – (baseline, adverse, and severely adverse), audit checks for integrity, coherence and validity, asset and liability management (ALM) models, behavioral cash flows, fire-sale analyses, market depth, counter balancing capacity and dynamic strategies models.

Other analyses may include, funding liquidity risk, market liquidity risk, asset liquidity risk, concentration risk, going concern and contingency liquidity risk, LIBOR-OIS spreads, TED spread, ABX.HE indices, liquidity reserves, maturity transformation, leverage ratios, and also full liquidity transfer pricing capabilities, Sharpe ratio, Treynor ratio, Jensen's measure, KMV Model, Black–Scholes–Merton model, Shiller P/E Index, CAPM, RORAC, RAROC, RARORAC, NPV, DCF, EVA models, portfolio credit risk overview and stochastic models, Causal At-Risk models such as, Gross Margin at Risk (GMaR), CFaR, and EaR metrics, Fault Trees, Event Trees, and Bow-Tie Diagrams, Risk Maps and risk hierarchies, Combined Risk and Opportunity Maps, Heat Maps, MARCI charts (Mitigate, Assure, Redeploy, and Cumulative Impact), Basel III (Advanced Internal Ratings-Based – IRB – Approach), Dodd–Frank Act frameworks (that is, Dodd–Frank Act Stress Test – DFAST), Comprehensive Capital Analysis and Review (CCAR) data and reporting requirements, industry benchmarking, and others.

Firms need to integrate in their planning processes more advanced risk and opportunity management models and frameworks in order to better determine the firms' risk appetite, to prioritize and target best business opportunities, and to avoid the rise of new potential systemic and "tail-event" risks using early warning indicators. Business organizations, industries' regulators, and even countries' policy makers should not lose sight of the risk and opportunities of a highly interconnected and globalized world when making short-term decisions (Curtis and Carey, 2012).

An enhanced ERM framework starts with an increased commitment and involvement of senior management and board members in risk governance. An additional trigger of a more advanced enterprise-wide risk management culture may come from a regular involvement of senior risk professionals (CROs) in the cross-functional management committees and through the encouragement of cross-enterprise dialogue.

In compliance with the "Federal Reserve's newly announced enhanced prudential standards," systemically important financial institutions (SIFIs) and bank holding companies with more than $50 billion in assets (collectively, covered companies) and publicly traded bank holding companies with more than $10 billion in assets must establish a "risk committee of the board" (RC) that will be responsible for overseeing enterprise-wide risk management practices and follow certain procedural responsibilities. The Federal Reserve indicated that it expects all members of the RC to have an understanding of risk management principles and practices commensurate with the business and risk profile of the company (Deloitte Development LLC, 2011, p. 8).

Furthermore, the "CRO should have a high position within an organization to establish independence and also report directly to the RC and chief executive officer (CEO). The role of the CRO will be required to be clearly defined. At minimum, the CRO's role should include: implementing appropriate enterprise-wide risk management practices; directly overseeing the allocation of risk limits; monitoring compliance with risk limits; establishing policies and processes to identify, assess, monitor, address, and report both existing and emerging risks; managing and testing risk controls; and confirming that they are effectively resolved in a timely manner. The RC must be a free-standing committee, report directly to the board, that receives and reviews regular reporting from the CRO" (Deloitte Development LLC, 2011, p. 9).

Furthermore, the introduction of the ability-to-repay (ATR) and the qualified mortgage (QM) rule on January 10, 2013 by the US Consumer Financial Protection Bureau (CFPB), should improve the reliability of mortgages making sure that lenders offer mortgages that consumers can actually afford to pay back (Deloitte Development LL., 2013a, p. 1).

"The ATR rule requires lenders to consider, at a minimum, the following eight underwriting criteria in the lending decision: (1) income or assets; (2) employment status; (3) credit history; (4) monthly payment for the mortgage; (5) monthly payments on other loans associated with the property; (6) other mortgage-related obligations, such as property taxes; (7) other debt obligations; and (8) the borrower's debt-to-income ratio" (Deloitte Development LLC, 2013a, p. 2).

Regarding the bank capital requirements, on September 12, 2010 the Basel Committee (2010) announced enhanced capital requirements for banks with the introduction of the Basel III Framework. The goal of this new regulatory framework is to improve the banking sector's ability to absorb shocks arising from financial and economic stress (Basel Committee on Banking Supervision, 2010, pp. 1–4).

The Basel III publication of the Bank for International Settlements (BIS), dated December 2010, titled "Basel III: A Global Regulatory Framework for More Resilient Banks and Banking Systems," reports the following major new changes related to the Basel II Framework:

> The Basel III reforms aim to strengthen global capital and liquidity rules with the goal of promoting a more resilient banking sector. The objective of the reforms is to improve the banking sector's ability to absorb shocks arising from financial and economic stress, whatever the source, thus reducing the risk of spillover from financial sector to the real economy. The Basel III framework also aims to improve risk management and governance, strengthen banks' transparency and disclosures, and the resolution of systemically significant cross-border banks. (Basel Committee on Banking Supervision, 2010, p. 1)

The Basel Committee identified that:

> One of the main reasons that caused the economic and financial crisis to be so severe was that the banking sectors of many countries had built up excessive on- and off-balance sheet leverage. This was accompanied by a gradual erosion of the level and quality of the capital base. At the same time, many banks were holding insufficient liquidity buffers. The banking system therefore was not able to absorb the resulting systemic trading and credit losses and could not cope with the reintermediation of large off-balance sheet exposures that had built up in the shadow banking system. The crisis was further amplified by a procyclical deleveraging process and by the interconnectedness of systemic institutions through an array of complex transactions. During the most severe episode of the crisis, the market lost confidence in the solvency and liquidity of many banking institutions and the weaknesses of the banking sector were rapidly transmitted to the rest of the financial system and throughout the economy, resulting in a massive contraction of liquidity and credit availability. Ultimately, the public sector had to step in with unprecedented injections of liquidity, capital support, and guarantees, exposing taxpayers to large losses. (Basel Committee on Banking Supervision, 2010, pp. 1–2)

On October 7, 2008, almost two weeks after Lehman Brothers announced it would file for Chapter 11 bankruptcy protection, I wrote a paper in which I provided my interpretation of what I thought caused the financial crisis and I recommended the immediate development of a Basel III Framework to address liquidity issues, excessive leverage ratios, systemic risks, opaque off-balance-sheet vehicles, the procyclical limitation of the Basel II Framework, and other issues related to the highly unregulated and poorly controlled shadow banking system (Pezzuto, 2008).

To address the market failures revealed by the crisis, in 2010 the Basel Committee introduced a calendar for the roll out of the Basel III Framework with full implementation only indicated by 2019. The calendar cites a number of reforms to strengthen banking institutions or microprudential regulation which will help raise the resilience of individual banking institutions during periods of stress. The reforms also have a macroprudential focus, addressing system-wide risks that can build up across the banking sector, as well as the procyclical amplification of these risks over time. "The micro and macroprudential approaches to supervision are interrelated, as greater resilience at the individual bank level reduces the risk of system-wide shocks" (PwC, 2010, p. 18).

The Basel III Framework (2010) aims to enhance "the risk coverage of excessive leverage in the banking system and to provide an extra layer of protection against model risk and measurement error through the leverage ratio," which serves as a backstop to the risk-based capital measures. In order to enhance the quality and quantity of the regulatory capital base it also provides a narrower definition of regulatory capital. The Basel III Framework clarified that the predominant form of Tier 1 capital (Core Tier 1) must be represented by common share capital and retained earnings. Common equity will continue to qualify as core Tier 1 capital, but other hybrid capital instruments (upper Tier 1 and Tier 2) will be replaced by instruments that are more loss-absorbing and do not have incentives to redeem them.

Below is the list of Tier 1 capital components (Latham and Watkins, 2011, p. 29):

- components of Common Equity Tier 1 Capital (CET 1);
- common shares issued by bank;
- stock surplus (share premium);
- retained earnings (including interim profit or loss);
- accumulated other comprehensive income and other disclosed reserves;
- common shares issued by consolidated subsidiaries of the bank and held by third parties (that is, minority interest) that meet criteria for CET 1 (subject to additional conditions below);
- regulatory deductions;
- dividends removed from CET 1 in accordance with applicable accounting standards.

The major changes that Basel III introduces on the enhancement of the capital quality include: "the phase out of innovative hybrid capital instruments that have an incentive to redeem them through features such as step-up clauses, that were limited to 15 percent of Tier 1 capital base," the harmonization of Tier 2 capital instruments (distinctions between upper and lower "Tier 2 instruments will be abolished"), and the elimination of "Tier 3 capital instruments, which were only available to cover market risks. Finally, to improve market discipline, the transparency of the capital base is improved with all the elements of capital required to be disclosed along with a detailed reconciliation to the reported accounts." The list of Additional Tier 1 Capital components (Latham and Watkins, 2011, pp. 5–6; Basel Committee on Banking Supervision, 2010, p. 2) follows:

- instruments meeting criteria for inclusion as AT 1;
- stock surplus (share premium) resulting from instruments included in AT 1;
- instruments issued by consolidated subsidiaries of the bank and held by third parties (that is, minority interest) that meet criteria for AT 1 (subject to additional conditions below);
- regulatory deductions (Latham and Watkins, 2011, p. 30).

Below is the list of Tier 2 Capital components:

- instruments meeting criteria for inclusion as T 2;
- stock surplus (share premium) resulting from instruments included in T 2;
- instruments issued by consolidated subsidiaries of the bank and held by third parties (that is, minority interest) that meet criteria for T 2 (subject to additional conditions below);
- certain loan loss provisions or reserves;
- standardized banks: loan loss provisions or reserves held against future, presently unidentifiable losses that are freely available to meet losses, limited to 1.25 percent of risk weighed assets;
- IRB banks: excess (if any) of total eligible provisions (as provided in Basel II) over total expected loss amounts, limited to 0.60 percent of risk-weighted assets (RWA);
- regulatory deductions (Latham and Watkins, 2011, p. 30).

In response to "the failure to capture major on-and off-balance sheet risks, as well as derivative related exposures," which were destabilizing factors during the crisis, Basel III reforms have raised capital requirements for the trading book and complex securitization exposures. "The enhanced treatment introduces a stressed Value-at-Risk" (SVaR) "capital requirement based on a continuous 12-month period of significant financial stress. In addition, the Committee has introduced higher capital requirements for so-called re-securitizations" in both the *banking book* and *trading book*. Re-securitization exposures and certain liquidity commitments held in the banking book will require more capital. "In the trading book, commencing 31 December 2010, banks are subject to new 'stressed' Value-at-Risk models, increased counterparty risk charges, more restricted netting of offsetting positions, increased charges for exposures to other financial institutions, and increased charges for securitization exposures." The reforms also raise the standards of the Pillar 2 supervisory review process and strengthen Pillar 3 disclosures. There is also a new definition of "correlation trading portfolio" (Latham and Watkins, 2011, pp. 5–6, 49; PwC, 2010, pp. 19–32; Basel Committee on Banking Supervision, 2010, pp. 2–4).

The Basel Framework includes three pillars of regulation. Pillar I relates to regulatory capital charges. "The minimum capital requirements are based on market, credit and operational risk" to:

a) reduce risk of failure by cushioning against losses;
b) provide continuing access to financial markets to meet liquidity needs;
c) provide incentives for prudent risk management (Latham and Watkins, 2011, p. 12).

Pillar II relates to supervision. It regulates the "qualitative supervision by regulators of internal bank risk control and capital assessment process, including ability to require banks to hold more capital than required under Pillar I" (Latham and Watkins, 2011, p. 12).

Pillar III relates to the "market discipline. Public disclosure requirements compel improved bank risk management" (Latham and Watkins, 2011, p. 12).

The Basel III Framework also introduces measures to strengthen the capital requirements for counterparty credit exposures such as, default risk, CVAs' risk charge, and *asset value correlation (AVC) multiplier*, arising from a bank's derivatives, repos (sale and repurchase agreement), and securities financing activities. "These reforms raise the capital buffer backing these exposures, reduce procyclicality and provide additional incentives to move OTC derivatives contracts to central counterparties, thus helping reduce systemic risk across the financial system" (Basel Committee on Banking Supervision, 2010, p. 5; Latham and Watkins, 2011, p. 55).

Among the major scope of the Basel III Framework, the following goals can be identified:

- raising the quality, consistency, and transparency of the capital base;
- increased capital charges for banking book exposures and for trading book exposures;
- enhancing risk coverage;
- supplementing the risk-based capital requirements with a leverage ratio;
- reducing procyclicality and promoting countercyclical buffers with cyclicality of the minimum requirement, forward-looking provisioning, capital conservation, and creating broader macroprudential regulation for protecting the banking sector in periods of excess aggregate credit growth;
- addressing systemic risk and interconnectedness;
- strengthening the liquidity framework by developing two minimum standards for funding liquidity. These are the *Liquidity Coverage Ratio (LCR)* that aims to promote short-term resilience of a bank's liquidity risk profile by ensuring that it has significant high-quality liquid resources to survive an acute stress scenario lasting for one month and the *Net Stable Funding Ratio (NSFR)* which aims to promote resilience over a longer time horizon by creating additional incentives for a bank to fund its activities with more stable sources of funding on an ongoing structural basis. The NSFR has a time horizon of one year and has been developed to provide a sustainable maturity structure of assets and liabilities (PwC, 2010, pp. 13–35).

This is the formula of the LCR:

$$\frac{\text{Stock of high quality liquid assets}}{\text{Net cash outflows over a 30-day time period}} \geq 100\%$$

This is the formula of the NSFR:

$$\frac{\text{Available amount of stable funding}}{\text{Required amount of stable funding}} > 100\%$$

The LCR, according to the Basel Committee on Banking Supervision, "promotes the short-term resilience of a bank's liquidity risk profile. It does this by ensuring that a bank has an adequate stock of unencumbered high-quality liquid assets (HQLA) that can be converted into cash easily and immediately in private markets to meet its liquidity needs for a 30 calendar day liquidity stress scenario." Furthermore, "it will improve the banking sector's ability to absorb shocks arising from financial and economic stress, whatever the source, thus reducing the risk of spillover from the financial sector to the real economy." Although it is intended to provide resilience to potential liquidity disruptions over a 30-day horizon (short-term stress scenario), it does not consider a worst case scenario and assumes the following:

- a significant downgrade of the institution's public credit rating;
- a partial loss of deposits;
- a loss of unsecured wholesale funding;
- a significant increase in secured funding haircuts; and
- increases in derivatives' collateral calls and substantial calls on contractual and non-contractual off-balance-sheet exposures, including committed credit and liquidity facilities (PwC, 2010, p. 34; Basel Committee on Banking Supervision, 2010, p. 9; 2013).

The Net Stable Funding Ratio (NSFR) aims to limit over-reliance on short-term wholesale funding during times of buoyant market liquidity and encourage better assessment of liquidity risk across all on- and off-balance sheet items. (Basel Committee on Banking Supervision, 2010, p. 9)

The Basel Committee, with the Basel III Framework, has also considered the introduction of a Contingency Funding Plan for emergency funding needs during potentially adverse market conditions.

The monitoring tools of intraday liquidity risk include the following:

- contractual maturity mismatch;
- concentration of funding;
- available unencumbered assets;
- liquidity coverage ratio (LCR) by significant currency; and
- market-related monitoring tools (that is market-wide information; information on the financial sector; and bank-specific information) (PwC, 2010, pp. 9–12; Basel Committee on Banking Supervision, 2013, p. 40).

Basel III involves significant changes to capital requirements, as reported in the Table 4.1, and will be phased in over a 12-year period commencing January 1, 2011, with most changes becoming effective within the next six years.

Table 4.1   Basel III Capital Requirements

Category	Requirements
Minimum Capital Requirement	8% of RWA – unchanged
Capital Conservation Buffer	Additional common equity requirement (capital conservation buffer) of at least 2.5% of RWA with constraints on distributions dividends, bonuses will be introduced
Countercyclical Capital Buffer	A zero to 2.5% countercyclical capital buffer will be introduced
Minimum Tier 1 Capital Requirements	6% of RWA (up from 4%)
Tier 1 and Tier 2	The overall capital requirement (Tier 1 and Tier 2) will increase from 8% to 10.5% over the period 2013–2019
Common Equity Requirement	Between 2013 and 2019, the common equity component of capital (core Tier 1) will increase from 2% of a bank's RWA before certain regulatory deductions to 4.5% after such deductions. Thus, common equity will be at least 4.5% of RWA (plus conservation buffer)
Quality of Capital	Limits on acceptance of hybrid instruments for Tier 1 (subordination, discretionary, non-cumulative payments, no maturity), greater required deductions (of things like deferred tax assets, equity investments, goodwill, and so on) in calculating common equity. Tier 3 capital instruments eliminated
Leverage Ratio	A minimum 3% Tier 1 leverage ratio, measured against a bank's gross (and not risk-weighted) balance sheet, will be trialed until 2018 and adopted in 2019
Risk Weights	Increased weights for some activities such as securitization and trading based on stressed VaR test (for 12 months of stress)
Liquidity Coverage Ratio (LCR) NSFR	A "liquidity coverage ratio" requiring HQLA to equal or exceeding highly-stressed one-month cash outflows will be adopted from 2015. A "net stable funding ratio" requiring "available" stable funding to equal or exceed "required" stable funding over a one-year period will be adopted from 2018

Source: Adapted from Basel Committee on Banking Supervision (2010; 2013).

Basel III also requires the use of internal models with the following criteria:

- New Stressed VaR Requirement:
  - banks must calculate "stressed VaR" measures;
  - measure to replicate VaR calculations generated on bank's current portfolio if relevant market factors experiencing period of stress; based on 10-day, 99th percentile, one-tailed confidence interval VaR measure of the current portfolio, with model inputs calibrated to historical data from a continuous 12-month period of significant financial stress relevant to the bank's portfolio;
  - two major goals are: (1) evaluate capacity of bank's capital to absorb potential large losses, and (2) identify steps the bank can take to reduce risk and conserve capital;

- scenarios requiring simulation by banks include the 1987 equity crash, the ERM crises of 1992 and 1993, the fall in the bond markets in Q1 1994, the 1998 Russian financial crisis, the 2000 technology bubble burst, and the 2007/2008 subprime turbulence (last event new) (Latham and Watkins, 2011, p. 53).

- **Revised Capital Charge.** Each bank must meet, on daily basis, its capital requirements, expressed as the sum of:
  - higher of (1) previous day's VaR number (VaRt-1) and (2) average of daily VaR measures on each of preceding 60 business days (VaRavg), multiplied by multiplication factor (mc), plus;
  - higher of (1) latest available stressed-VaR number above (sVaRt-1) and (2) an average of stressed VaR numbers over the preceding 60 business days (sVaRavg), multiplied by multiplication of factor (ms);
  - multiplication factors mc and ms are set by the relevant supervisory authority on the basis of the assessment of quality of a bank's risk management system, subject to an absolute minimum of 3 for mc and absolute minimum of 3 for ms, plus an additional factor between 0 and 1 directly related to ex-post performance (backtesting) of the bank's model (based on VaR only and not stressed VaR) (Latham andWatkins, 2011, p. 53).

An important feature of the Basel III Framework is that it is improving the quality of regulatory capital and reducing the role for liabilities other than common equity. As Kevin Davis (2011) reports, "One lesson from the Global Financial Crisis was that the capital requirement distinction between "going-concern" capital and "gone-concern" capital (incorporating certain debt/hybrid instruments) was less relevant when Governments and regulators were unwilling to allow failure and losses to be imposed upon holders of those instruments" (Davis, 2011, p. 21).

One of the weak points of the Basel III Framework is the fact that its implementation is starting only in 2013 and its completion date is expected to be 2018 (Davis, 2011, p. 20).

The leverage ratio aims to limit bank leverage and act as a backstop to deal with the problems of model risk and measurement error in risk-weighted approaches. "Cross country compatibility requires comparable calculations including adjusting for differences in accounting standards, particularly because the denominator is a measure of exposure rather than assets, calculated using a mix of accounting rules and Basel approaches" (Davis, 2011, p. 21). Table 4.2 summarizes the main features of Basel III.

Under Basel II and Basel III, banks have a strong incentive to move to the Basel IRB status by improving risk management systems, thereby reducing required total regulatory capital (Latham and Watkins, 2011, p. 10).

The Foundation IRB measures credit risk using sophisticated formulas based on internally determined inputs of *Probability of Default (PD)* and inputs fixed by regulators of *Loss Given Default (LGD)*, *Exposure at Default (EAD)*, and *Maturity (M)*. This approach provides more risk-sensitive capital requirements than the standardized Basel Framework. It provides more differentiation in required capital between safer and riskier credits (Latham andWatkins, 2011, p. 10).

The Advanced IRB, instead, measures credit risk using sophisticated formulas and internally determined inputs of PD, LGD, EAD, and M. This approach provides the most risk-sensitive capital requirements. It also provides the most differentiation in

Table 4.2   Basel III Annex 4 Excerpt: Phase-in Arrangements

	2011	2012	2013	2014	2015	2016	2017	2018	As of January 1, 2019
Leverage Ratio	Supervisory monitoring		Parallel run 1 Jan 2013 – 1 Jan 2017 Disclosure starts 1 Jan 2015					Migration to Pillar 1	
Minimum Common Equity Capital Ratio			3.5%	4.0%	4.5%	4.5%	4.5%	4.5%	4.5%
Capital Conservation Buffer						0.625%	1.25%	1.875%	2.50%
Minimum common equity plus capital conservation buffer			3.5%	4.0%	4.5%	5.125%	5.75%	6.375%	7.0%
Phase-in of deductions from CET1 (including amounts exceeding the limit for DTAs, MSRs and financials)				20%	40%	60%	80%	100%	100%
Minimum Tier 1 Capital			4.5%	5.5%	6.0%	6.0%	6.0%	6.0%	6.0%
Minimum Total Capital			8.0%	8.0%	8.0%	8.0%	8.0%	8.0%	8.0%
Minimum Total Capital plus conservation buffer			8.0%	8.0%	8.0%	8.625%	9.25%	9.875%	10.5%
Capital instruments that no longer qualify as non-core Tier 1 capital or Tier 2 capital		Phased out over 10 year horizon beginning 2013							
Liquidity coverage ratio	Observation period begins				Introduce minimum standard				
Net stable funding ratio	Observation period begins							Introduce minimum standard	

Note: Shading indicates transition periods – all dates are as of January 1.

Source: Basel Committee publication: Basel III: A global regulatory framework for more resilient banks and banking systems, reproduced by permission of the Basel Committee on Banking Supervision. This table is available free of charge from the BIS website (www.bis.org).

required capital between safer and riskier credits. Transition to the Advanced IRB status is possible only with robust internal risk management systems and data (Latham and Watkins, 2011, p. 10).

As stated by Simon Johnson (2011d) the Basel III Framework is a step in the right direction to better regulate the banking industry and to reduce risk but unfortunately, due to its phased roll-out plan, it will take several years to achieve full implementation of the new regulatory capital requirements. Simon Johnson believes that it might however help reduce the risk associated with the so-called shadow banking issue. In fact he stated the following on Baseline Scenario concerning the importance of regulatory capital/equity:

> The "shadow banking" sector grew rapidly in large part because it was a popular way for very big banks to evade existing – and relatively low – capital requirements pre-2008. They created various kinds of off-balance sheet entities funded with little equity and a great deal of debt, and they convinced rating agencies and regulators that these were safe structures. Many of these funds collapsed in the face of losses on their housing-related assets, which turned out to be very risky – and there was not enough equity to absorb losses … The Basel III issues may be boring, but they are important. (Johnson, 2011d)

Simon Johnson (2010) in his article dated September 16, 2010, titled "Picking Up the Slack on Global Banking Rules," states that the Basel III Framework increases capital requirements only modestly and phases those increases in only gradually since apparently the regulators have concluded that moving to higher requirements quickly could reduce lending and damage growth. Thus, he argues that the new framework does not have adequate regulatory capital to make the financial system safer. In fact, he also states, taking the Hanson–Kashyap–Stein view: "… that banks should be required to hold enough capital at the peak of the cycle so that when they suffer losses … they still have enough capital so that the markets do not think they will fail" (Johnson, 2010).

Therefore, banks "have no need to dump assets in a desperate bid to survive. It's the forced asset sales of this nature that turn financial distress at particular institutions into broader asset price declines, which can lead to panics." Johnson argues that a more logical approach suggests at least a "15 percent Tier 1 capital base would be required in good times; the most forward-looking officials in G20 countries may aim for closer to 20 percent. Tier 1 is a good measure of loss-absorbing capital – what stands between the bank and insolvency." In his view, these are the capital requirements that would really help make banks much safer (Johnson, 2010).

Simon Johnson and James Kwak (2010a), authors of *13 Bankers: The Wall Street Takeover and the Next Financial Meltdown*, argue however, that:

> Capital requirements alone are not a reliable tool for preventing the collapse of systemically important financial institutions. Like other regulatory refinements, they depend on the ability and motivation of regulators to rein in financial institutions that have clear incentives to evade them at every opportunity. (Johnson and Kwak, 2010a, pp. 189–222; 2010b)

Johnson and Kwak are convinced instead that a "better solution is the 'dumber' one to avoid having banks that are too big (or too complex) to fail in the first place." In their book they have proposed "strict asset caps as a percent of GDP, that is, relative to the size of the overall economy on financial institutions that are adjusted for the types of assets and obligations held by those institutions – if they want to take more risk, they need to be smaller." The scope of their proposal is to make sure that in the case a bank will fail in the future, it does not have to be bailed out with taxpayer money (Johnson and Kwak, 2010a, pp. 189–222; 2010b).

On the topic of banks' capital requirements, Sheila Bair, Former Federal Deposit Insurance Corporation (FDIC) Chairman, said in May 2010 that European regulators need to force their banks to hold more capital to help stabilize financial markets and promote economic growth. In particular, regarding the Basel III Framework, she said that regulators around the world need to work together to make sure that the next round of capital standards for banks will meet "very aggressive" goals (Christie, 2010).

She also said that, "Congress needs to put some 'overarching constraints' on regulators to avoid a repeat of the 2008 financial crisis, which she said was exacerbated because of the 'absurdity' of policies that allowed big banks to reduce their capital holdings based on risk-modeling practices." She said the FDIC would work with Congress to keep the measure in the final bill (Christie, 2010).

Even Lord Adair Turner, former chairman of the Financial Services Authority (FSA) – the UK financial services industry regulator abolished in March 2013, said in March 2011 that the "best way to prevent another financial crisis is to force the largest banks to hold more equity capital against potential losses than required by the Basel III rules." Regulatory efforts to make it easier to wind down systemically important financial institutions, or SIFIs, and impose losses on their bondholders are positive, Lord Turner said (Masters and Braithwaite, 2011). He also added:

> If global regulators were benevolent dictators designing regulations for a banking system in a greenfield market economy, they would be wise to choose capital ratios far above even Basel III levels, something more like the 15 percent to 20 percent of RWA.

In mid-2012, the Council of the EU, through the Economic and Financial Affairs Council (ECOFIN) agreed on a package of measures that will implement Basel III throughout the EU, known as the Capital Requirements Directive IV (CRD IV). The outcome of this meeting was a single rule book that allows national supervisors to discretionally impose stricter prudential requirements and additional reporting where they deem necessary. One of the challenges is also represented by the fact that, as a consequence of the sovereign debt crisis in the Eurozone, the number of free-risk sovereign bonds in the period 2008–2012 has been constantly shrinking (Blair-Ford, 2012).

In my 2008 paper I warned of the risk of a potential systemic crisis in the peripheral European countries, as a consequence of the global financial crisis. Based on my assumption the impact of the crisis on these economies (severe and prolonged economic recession) combined with the existing structural problems and the lack of a European fiscal union would eventually spark a panic reaction in the financial markets due to the fear of the potential insolvency of sovereigns. The financial crisis certainly worsened the pre-crisis structural differences among the Eurozone countries, determining in 2012 for the weaker economies unsustainable sovereign debt funding costs, a worsened credit crunch for firms and households, and deeper recessionary trends (Pezzuto, 2008; Cohen, 2011; King, 2012).

Some banks have indeed interpreted quite lightly the Basel Framework on bank capital requirements before 2012 and they have underestimated systemic risks and or perhaps based their business model on regulators looking the other way. With Basel III things changed. Or, to put it more accurately, things are starting to change, due to the fact that many banks have to comply with new restrictive rules following a phased implementation plan that will take a few years for a full roll out. At the end of 2012, the US was under pressure to avoid penalizing the slowly improving economic growth following the 2007–2009 crisis, to push for more aggressive unconventional monetary and fiscal policies in order to boost economic growth and employment, and to avoid a potential credit crunch under the threat of the "Sequester, Fiscal Cliff, and Debt Ceiling." Thus, Ben Bernanke, Chairman of the Federal Reserve, accepted the postponement, for approximately six months (from January 1, 2013), of a significant part of the financial regulatory overhaul after banks said they would not be ready for the new Basel III rules.

At moment of writing this book (April 2013) my expectation is that the Fed will probably decide to adopt in the US the Basel III framework shortly (summer 2013) with a particular focus on the systemically important financial institutions (SIFIs). For these firms the Fed might even impose higher quantity and quality of capital requirements as a financial cushion to absorb losses of complex derivatives and structured products. The Fed will probably also pose a great attention on the financial firms' leverage ratio (which measures equity as a percentage of assets) since it is critical to mitigate potential SIFIs's failures and systemic risk. Furthermore, in January 2013 global central bank chiefs decided to give lenders four more years to meet the international liquidity requirements (LCR) of Basel III which was planned to take effect on January 1, 2015. This decision was made in order to avoid the impact of a worse credit crunch for businesses, households, and interbank lending during a difficult economic phase for many countries (in particular in Europe) still struggling with slower growth or recession, high unemployment rates, austerity programs, structural reforms, and high sovereign debt and budget deficits. Under the new rule, banks would only have to meet 60 percent of the LCR obligations by 2015, and the full rule would be phased in annually through 2019. In fact, the LCR will rise in equal annual steps of 10 percentage points to reach 100 percent on January 1, 2019 (minimum LCR requirement 60 percent in 2015; 70 percent in 2016; 80 percent in 2017; 90 percent in 2018; 100 percent in 2019). It seems, however, that the EU and US have been criticized by international regulators in early 2013 for misapplying parts of the capital rules, allowing lenders to count more of the sovereign debt they hold as risk free. In fact, under the 2010 plan, banks would have been allowed to use cash and government bonds to meet the LCR, subject to rules on the quality of the sovereign debt. Lenders could also have used highly-rated corporate debt or covered bonds to meet 40 percent of their LCR requirements. The new rule on LCR expands the range of corporate debt that banks can use (that is, broaden the class of liquid assets), allowing securities with a credit rating of as low as BBB- to be eligible. The 2010 version of the rule stipulated that such debt must have a rating of at least AA-. With the new LCR rule banks are also allowed to use highly-rated residential MBS and some equities. In fact, the revisions to the LCR incorporates amendments to the definition of HQLA and net cash outflows. With the new LCR rule, The Group of Central Bank Governors and Heads of Supervision (GHOS) agreed that, during periods of stress, it would be entirely appropriate for banks to use their stock of HQLA, thereby falling below the minimum. The additional securities will get bigger write-downs to their value than those that would have been eligible under the 2010 LCR, and they will not be allowed to count for more than 15 percent of a bank's LCR buffer. Central banks and regulators left the treatment of covered bonds in the LCR unchanged from 2010. Covered bonds are secured by assets such as mortgages or public-sector loans and are guaranteed by the issuer. They also expanded the range of risks on derivatives trades that will be taken into account (Basel Committee on Banking Supervision, 2013).

Mervyn King, Chairman of the GHOS and Governor of the Bank of England, said in January 2013: "The Liquidity Coverage Ratio is a key component of the Basel III framework. The agreement reached today is a very significant achievement. For the first time in regulatory history, we have a truly global minimum standard for bank liquidity. Importantly, introducing a phased timetable for the introduction of the LCR, and reaffirming that a bank's stock of liquid assets are usable in times of stress, will ensure that the new liquidity standard will in no way hinder the ability of the global banking system to finance a recovery" (Brunsden et al., 2013; Eavis, 2012; Basel Committee on Banking Supervision, 2013).

The Basel Committee has anticipated that it will also review the liquidity rule of Basel III, known as a Net-Stable Funding Ratio, which requires banks to back long-term lending with funding that won't dry up in a crisis (Brunsden et al., 2013; Eavis, 2012; Basel Committee on Banking Supervision, 2013).

In 2012 banks had to align their default/loss definition to the Basel rule and to adjust accordingly its banks' capital requirements on the basis of their RWA. In particular, regarding the main factors of differences in RWA densities across jurisdictions and banks, the Basel III Framework suggests taking into consideration the following elements: regulatory, supervisory, accounting, and legal framework, economic cycle, business model, lending, valuation and provisioning practices (external parameters), and also banks' internal parameters such as risk appetite and risk-bearing capacity, risk management and strategy, selected Basel Framework approaches (Advanced Internal Rating Based – AIRB, Foundation Internal Rating Based – FIRB, and so on), risk modeling capacity, availability of robust stress testing models, and so on (Le Leslé and Avramova, 2012).

The Basel III Framework should also somehow take into account the paradox and exceptional event generated by the prolonged financial crises of 2007–2009 and the subsequent Eurozone crisis that caused most sovereigns to be no longer risk-free securities/investments. Furthermore, as also correctly interpreted by the International Financial Reporting Standards (IFRS) 9 Financial Instruments: Impairment Rules for the Expected Loss Calculation of 12 Months and/or Lifetime Expected Losses, it is critical to develop a forward-looking approach which should incorporate multiple sources of data including delinquency, credit scores, financial results, macro-level economic indicators of expectations of future losses such as correlations with unemployment rates, national and local economic and business conditions, industry and geographical trends, and other forecasts (Ernst and Young, 2012).

Regarding the Basel III Framework, a 2010 *Economist* magazine article explained the potential weaknesses of the new capital requirement rule and the contribution of Basel II to the financial crisis. In fact in this article it states the following:

> *The most serious failure in Basel III is that it doesn't address the principal contribution of Basel II to the last financial crisis, namely, the calculation of risk-weights. One of the key components of Basel II was to increase the amount of capital banks had to hold against riskier assets. Extremely low-risk assets, meanwhile, could be held with very little or even no capital. Risk, moreover, was calculated primarily by reference to the rating assigned by one of the recognized ratings agencies. The consequence of this Basel II reform was to discourage banks*

from lending to risky enterprises, and to encourage the accumulation of apparently risk-free assets. This was a primary contributor to the structured finance craze, as securitisation was a way to "manufacture" apparently risk-free assets out of risky pools. What brought banks like Citigroup and Bank of America to their knees wasn't direct exposure to sub-prime loans, but exposure to triple-A-rated debt backed by pools of such loans, debt which turned out not to be risk-free at all. Since it did not change this risk-weighting, Basel III effectively doubles down on Basel II. Banks will need to hold more common equity than ever – against their risk-weighted assets. That massively increases the incentive to find low-risk-weight assets with some return, since these assets can be leveraged much more highly than risky assets. Unless I've missed something, lending to AA-rated sovereigns still carries a risk-weight of zero. So one result of Basel III could be to encourage banks to increase their lending to sovereigns at the margins of zero-risk-weight status. If that happens, anyone want to guess where the next crisis will crop up? (The Economist, 2010)

Felix Salmon (2010) reported on the Reuters web page that Basel III does not seem to completely address the problem related to tail-risk. In fact, he states Joe Nocera's explanation in the *Financial Times* (2010) who indicates that the whole VaR structure gives banks every incentive to push risk into the tails, and because tail-risk was mostly ignored before the 2007–2009 financial crisis, banks then went on to embrace other mechanisms – such as the Gaussian Copula Function – which essentially fattens the tails, stuffing them with ever more risk (Salmon, 2010).

As explained by Darrell Duffie, a Stanford University Finance Professor who served on Moody's Academic Advisory Research Committee, "The corporate CDO world relied almost exclusively on this Copula-Based Correlation Model." The Gaussian Copula soon became such a universally accepted part of the world's financial vocabulary and brokers started quoting prices for bond tranches based on their correlations. "Correlation trading has spread through the psyche of the financial markets like a highly infectious thought virus," wrote derivatives guru Janet Tavakoli in 2006 (Salmon, 2009).

Felix Salmon (2010) also reported another weakness in Basel III. The risk, according to him, is related to banks and the need to change the bankruptcy law. To be more specific he reports that, based on comments made by Paul Singer of Elliott Associates, "Lehman Brothers were not actually a function of any kind of monster hole in Lehman's balance sheet. Instead, after Lehman declared bankruptcy, its enormous derivatives book needed to be unwound very quickly, and it was that unwind which caused something between $50 billion and $75 billion of losses, precipitating the worst months of the crisis." He added that according to Singer, "The cause of Lehman's collapse was liquidity problems, and Basel III does a pretty good job tightening up the rules on bank liquidity (but for some analysts Basel Liquidity Rule have been watered down with the new Liquidity Coverage Ratio of January 2013). But if a bank with a big derivatives book does end up declaring bankruptcy, the effects can still be catastrophic. Again, that's not something that can readily be addressed in the Basel III architecture – it requires instead a lot of detailed tinkering with bankruptcy laws" (Salmon, 2010; Brunsden, 2012).

Joe Nocera wrote in his article on January 2, 2009 that:

One reason VaR became so popular is that it is the only commonly used risk measure that can be applied to just about any asset class. And it takes into account a head-spinning variety of variables, including diversification, leverage and volatility, that make up the kind of market risk that traders and firms face every day. Another reason VaR is so appealing is that it can measure both individual risks – the amount of risk contained in a single trader's portfolio, for instance – and firmwide risk, which it does by combining the VaRs of a given firm's trading desks and coming up with a net number. Top executives usually know their firm's daily VaR within minutes of the market's close. Risk managers use VaR to quantify their firm's risk positions to their board. In the late 1990s, as the use of derivatives was exploding, the Securities and Exchange Commission ruled that firms had to include a quantitative disclosure of market risks in their financial statements for the convenience of investors, and VaR became the main tool for doing so. Around the same time, an important international rule-making body, the Basel Committee on Banking Supervision, went even further to validate VaR by saying that firms and banks could rely on their own internal VaR calculations to set their capital requirements. So long as their VaR was reasonably low, the amount of money they had to set aside to cover risks that might go bad could also be low. (Nocera, 2009)

Joe Nocera (2009) in his article reports his interview with Nassim Nicholas Taleb, the best-selling author of *The Black Swan*. Taleb mentioned in the interview that, according to him, the crisis was predictable. Furthermore, Nocera reports that:

VaR uses this normal distribution curve … (a statistical measure that was first identified by Carl Friedrich Gauss in the early 1800s – hence the term "Gaussian") … to plot the riskiness of a portfolio. But it makes certain assumptions. VaR is often measured daily and rarely extends beyond a few weeks, and because it is a very short-term measure, it assumes that tomorrow will be more or less like today. Even what's called "historical VaR" – a variation of standard VaR that measures potential portfolio risk a year or two out, only uses the previous few years as its benchmark. As the risk consultant Marc Groz puts it, "The years 2005–2006," which were the culmination of the housing bubble, "aren't a very good universe for predicting what happened in 2007–2008." (Nocera, 2009)

Furthermore, Taleb reported to Joe Nocera (2009) that faulty historical data isn't his primary concern, what he cares about, with standard VaR, is not the number that falls within the 99 percent probability. He cares about what happens in the other 1 percent, at the extreme edge of the curve … or "something rare, something you've never considered a possibility." Taleb calls these events "fat tails" or "black swans," and he is convinced that they take place far more frequently than most human beings are willing to contemplate. Taleb also reports in the interview with Joe Nocera, "Ethan Berman, the chief executive of RiskMetrics (and no relation to Gregg Berman), told me that one of VaR's flaws, which only became obvious in this crisis, is that it didn't measure liquidity risk – and of course a liquidity crisis is exactly what we're in the middle of right now. One reason nobody seems to know how to deal with this kind of crisis is because nobody envisioned it." He also added: "VaR didn't see the risk because it generally relied on a two-year data history. Although it took into account the increased risk brought on by leverage, it failed to distinguish between leverage that came from long-term, fixed-rate debt – bonds and such that come due at a set date – and loans that can be called in at any time and can, as Brown put it 'blow you up in two minutes.' That is, the kind of leverage that disappeared the minute something bad arose" (Nocera, 2009).

Furthermore, Joe Nocera reports the following:

Guldimann, the great VaR proselytizer, sounded almost mournful when he talked about what he saw as another of VaR's shortcomings. To him, the big problem was that it turned out that VaR could be gamed. That is what happened when banks began reporting their VaRs. To motivate managers, the banks began to compensate them not just for making big profits but also for making profits with low risks. That sounds good in principle, but managers began to manipulate the VaR by loading up on what Guldimann calls "asymmetric risk positions." These are products or contracts that, in general, generate small gains and very rarely have losses. But when they do have losses, they are huge. These positions made a manager's VaR look good because VaR ignored the slim likelihood of giant losses, which could only come about in the event of a true catastrophe. A good example was a credit-default swap, which is essentially insurance that a company won't default. The gains made from selling credit-default swaps are small and steady – and the chance of ever having to pay off that insurance was assumed to be minuscule. It was outside the 99 percent probability, so it didn't show up in the VaR number. People didn't see the size of those hidden positions lurking in that 1 percent that VaR didn't measure. Even more critical, it did not properly account for leverage that was employed through the use of options. For example, said Groz, if an asset manager borrows money to buy shares of a company, the VaR would usually increase. But say he instead enters into a contract that gives someone the right to sell him those shares at a lower price at a later time – a put option. In that case, the VaR might remain unchanged. From the outside, he would look as if he were taking no risk, but in fact, he is. If the share price of the company falls steeply, he will have lost a great deal of money. Groz called this practice "stuffing risk into the tails." (Nocera, 2009)

Nocera (2009) also reported in the article the point of view of one former risk manager:

In the bubble, with easy profits being made and risk having been transformed into mathematical conceit, the real meaning of risk had been forgotten. Instead of scrutinizing VaR for signs of impending trouble, they took comfort in a number and doubled down, putting more money at risk in the expectation of bigger gains. It has to do with the human condition. (Nocera, 2009)

Furthermore, Nocera (2009) said in his article the following:

The damage was foreseeable and, in fact, foreseen. In 1998, before Li had even invented his copula function, Paul Wilmott wrote that "the correlations between financial quantities are notoriously unstable." Wilmott, a quantitative-finance consultant and lecturer, argued that no theory should be built on such unpredictable parameters. And he wasn't alone. During the boom years, everybody could reel off reasons why the Gaussian copula function wasn't perfect. Li's approach made no allowance for unpredictability: It assumed that correlation was a constant rather than something mercurial. Investment banks would regularly phone Stanford's Duffie and ask him to come in and talk to them about exactly what Li's copula was. Every time, he would warn them that it was not suitable for use in risk management or valuation.

In hindsight, ignoring those warnings looks foolhardy. But at the time, it was easy. Banks dismissed them, partly because the managers empowered to apply the brakes didn't understand the arguments between various arms of the quant universe. Besides, they were making too much money to stop. Li's Copula function was used to price hundreds of billions of dollars' worth of CDOs filled with mortgages. And because the Copula function used CDS prices to calculate correlation, it was forced to confine itself to looking at the period of time when those CDS had been in existence: less than a decade, a period when house prices soared. Naturally, default correlations were very low in those years. But when the mortgage boom ended abruptly and home values started falling across the country, correlations soared. Bankers securitizing mortgages knew that their models were highly sensitive to house-price appreciation. If it ever turned negative on a national scale, a lot of bonds that had been rated triple-A, or risk-free, by Copula-powered computer models would blow up. But no one was willing to stop the creation of CDOs, and the big investment banks happily kept on building more, drawing their correlation data from a period when real estate only went up. Assim Nicholas Taleb, a hedge fund manager and author of *The Black Swan*, is particularly harsh when it comes to the Copula. "People got very excited about the Gaussian Copula because of its mathematical elegance, but the thing never worked," he says. "Co-association between securities is not measurable using correlation," because past history can never prepare you for that one day when everything goes south. Anything that relies on correlation is charlatanism" (Nocera, 2009).

Going back to the weaknesses of the new Basel III rules, as reported by David Walker on the Banking Day website (2013), few believe Basel III alone will prevent future crises. As Bank of England Governor Mervyn King has put it: "It is no criticism of Basel III to say that it is not a "silver bullet" ... In the area of financial stability, it makes sense to have both belt and braces." He also added in this article on the Bank Day website: "Some prominent economists, including the University of Chicago's Eugene Fama and John Cochrane, the London School of Economics' Charles Goodhart and Princeton's Markus Brunnermeier, wrote in an open letter in late 2010 that the capital ratios should be much tougher" (Walker, 2013).

Walker (2013) in his article also lists Basel III's weaknesses, indicating that Basel III retains several flaws of the previous Basel II rules. In particular he states:

> Basel III relies heavily on an underlying mechanism – capital ratios – which spectacularly failed to prevent the global financial crisis. The crisis occurred even though most banks' capital ratios appeared strong. (Lehman Brothers reported 11 per cent Tier 1 capital just days before its collapse.) Banks responded to higher capital costs by pushing business of their balance sheets and into the "shadow banking system" where capital rules did not apply. (Walker, 2013)

Walker (2013) also reported in his article the following additional contributions on the matter:

> Bank of England Governor Mervyn King: "When sentiment changes only very high levels of capital would be sufficient to enable banks to obtain funding on anything like normal spreads to policy rates, as we can see at present ... That is what happened in 2007–08. Only very much higher levels of capital – levels that would be seen by the industry as wildly excessive most of the time – would prevent such a crisis." (Walker, 2013)

Economist Raghuram Rajan in the *Financial Times* reports: "The minimum hurdle that reforms should meet is whether they would have prevented the last crisis. Any feasible level of required capital would not cross this hurdle, so let us not rely too much on it to avert the next crisis." Basel III continues to rely too much on credit ratings. The IMF, among others, has argued in recent papers that "markets need to end their addiction to credit ratings" and remove "the mechanistic use of ratings in rules and regulations." Instead ratings should be used as one of several tools to manage risk.

Banks remain trusted to use their own internal models to measure risk, using models such as VaR which have been shown to have substantial flaws in many situations. Risk weightings still allow banks to create very high effective leverage. Under Basel III, banks need to hold equity against their RWA. This provides an incentive to find low-risk-weight assets which can then be leveraged. One attractive asset will be sovereign debt; AA-rated sovereign debt will still carry a zero risk weighting. Housing will continue to require less capital than business lending. Lending to most businesses, in contrast, will require capital of about 8 percent. The essence of the global financial crisis was risky assets – mostly US subprime mortgages – that had been carelessly assessed by the market and classified incorrectly as risk-free, then dispersed to all corners of the financial system. The risky assets were precisely those which were regarded as "safe" under Basel II – but which in fact were not. That is, the risky assets had low "official" risk but high real risk. (The risks were also correlated: many of them had a good chance of going bad at the same time, magnifying their likely economic impact.) Basel II gave market players enormous incentives to seek out such assets – in effect, to find the best regulatory arbitrage.

In a crisis where a large number of assets fall substantially in value, it matters little whether a bank's capital is 5, 10, or 15 percent. It will still be overwhelmed. To add to the problem, there is no asset so safe that it cannot be made unsafe by overbidding and overgearing. Nothing in Basel III prevents that problem from recurring. Beyond the issue of banks' safety is another issue which Basel III cannot address. The financial system inevitably breaks down if creditors are willing to lend to foolish investors. The bail-outs of creditors during the global financial crisis may have raised expectations that creditors will be rescued from future poor decisions. The most severe critics of the system believe Basel III does little to address underlying problems within the global financial system. Adrian Blundell-Wignall, the former Head of the Research Department at the Reserve Bank of Australia, then director of Equity Strategy Research of Citigroup (Australia, Ltd), who is now Deputy Director in the Directorate for Financial and Enterprise Affairs at the OECD, has gone further than most: his personal view is that the Basel II system proved so flawed that such frameworks might not be worth using. How effective will the new rules be?

These are easily the toughest global banking rules yet agreed. But there is no guarantee they will save the banks from their next episode of over-optimism. The 2008 crisis showed that when the web of global lending unravels, even well-capitalized institutions are at risk. Strong and sophisticated regulators will continue to be needed. And they will continue to have to make tough calls about the risks taken by individual institutions and overall risks within the financial system (Walker, 2013).

Furthermore, as reported by Don Alexander (2012) of RSD Solutions Inc., according to Paul Atkinson and Adrian Blundell-Wignall's work "Basel Regulation Needs to be rethought in the Age of Derivatives" (Blundell-Wignall and Atkinson, 2012a), Basel III regulations are overly complicated and desperately out of date. The proposals serve as a short-term patch for a fundamentally flawed system that is overly complex. They also indicate that the Basel proposals use a risk-weighting system for calculating capital charges that do not fully incorporate OTC derivative exposures that currently exceeds $600 trillion (end 2010). Banks have unlimited scope to arbitrage the system by reallocating portfolios away from assets with high risk weights to assets with low risk weights, thus saving on capital costs. The capital charges may actually encourage more risk-taking by systematically important institutions and may actually make the financial system more unstable and accident prone. They also stated that the CVA (marking unrealized losses to market) allows for the netting of gross exposures across counterparties, but may underestimate bank exposure and ignore positions for calculating the CVA charge due to highly concentrated derivative positions and bilateral netting. The CVA charge is additive across netted bilateral positions rewarding counterparty concentration. The result is a vast, poorly diversified, highly interconnected banking system with a small capital base that may under estimate potential risk exposure. Atkinson and Blundell-Wignall conclude by arguing that the Basel system should be replaced with one whose parameters cannot be arbitraged by portfolio reallocation and derivative activity. Despite Basel III, the current system remains vulnerable to systemic risks created by derivative exposures (Alexander, 2012).

In 2013, Andrew Bailey, the incoming Head of the UK – Prudential Regulation Authority (PRA), realized that a critical requirement for improving financial watchdogs' job is to enhance transparency on capital requirements. In fact, he proposed that "banks should be required to make their individualized capital requirements public so that investors can see which financial groups have attracted regulatory concerns about risk and why." This seems to be a great step forward in improving the safety and soundness of bank supervision that should be welcomed and harmonized across the international financial markets (Masters, 2013).

In the midst of the Eurozone debt crisis in 2011 (November 2011), IMF Managing Director, Christine Lagarde, was attacked by European officials when she called for a mandatory recapitalization of Europe's banks or, as IMF Financial Counsellor and Director of Monetary and Capital Markets Department, Jose Vinals, reported in the 2011 Global Financial Stability Report, "Risks are elevated and time is running out to tackle vulnerabilities that threaten the global financial system and the ongoing economic recovery," since "the damage could spread from Europe to banks in emerging market economies" (*The Telegraph*, 2011).

IMF Managing Director, Christine Lagarde, warned in June 2012 about world risks of falling incomes, environmental damage, and social unrest without a more sustainable approach to growth (Inman, 2012).

Christine Lagarde (Lagarde, 2012) at the end of 2012, in her article "The Future Global Economy" posted on Project-Syndicate, indicates the main policies and actions to undertake in order to turn the weak global economic recovery into a positive future. Among these she identifies the following:

1. "Accommodative monetary policy; fiscal adjustment in all advanced economies that includes concrete and realistic plans to reduce debt over the medium term, but does not undercut short-term growth; completing the banking-sector cleanup; and reforms to boost productivity and growth potential. All of this should be complemented by a rebalancing of global demand toward dynamic markets, including emerging economies.

2. The second milestone is a better global financial system. We need to move beyond the system that gave us the crisis – a financial sector which some, as the ancient Greeks might say, toyed with hubris and unleashed nemesis. Of course, there has been important progress, especially on the Basel III agenda to create more resilient capital and liquidity buffers. But momentum is flagging, both on implementing the agreed reforms and on progress in areas like derivatives and shadow banking. As a result, the system as a whole is not yet much safer than it was in September 2008, when Lehman

Brothers collapsed. It is still too complex; activities are still too concentrated in large institutions; and the specter of "too-big-to-fail" remains. Continuing excesses and repeated scandals show that the culture of finance has not really changed. Many in the financial-services industry are concerned about the costs of new regulations. A recent IMF study shows that better regulation would indeed nudge banks' lending rates up, but by relatively little. We also found that increasing capital buffers to appropriate levels helps, rather than hurts, economic growth. Reforming financial-sector taxation would also help to reduce excessive risk-taking and leverage. The bottom line is that the costs of reform are affordable. The costs of complacency are not.

3. The third milestone relates to the quality and inclusiveness of growth. While growth is essential for the future global economy, it must be a different kind of growth – inclusive and not simply the fallout of unfettered globalization. The policy implications of such a reorientation are profound. It requires a fiscal policy that focuses not only on efficiency, but also on equity – particularly on fairness in sharing the burden of adjustment, and on protecting the weak and vulnerable. It means expanding access to credit and financial services everywhere. And it means more transparency and better governance. Achieving these milestones presupposes greater global cooperation. A world that is bound closely together must be a world that works closely together if it is to prosper together. There is simply no other choice. We are multiple players, but we are engaged in a single game – a game that must be cooperative, not simply competitive. In such a world, multilateral institutions like the IMF play a vital role in boosting economic cooperation" (Lagarde, 2012).

As explained by Sober Look blog (2012), following the example in the US of the Dodd–Frank Act which created, among other things, an orderly liquidation authority (OLA) and rules that should end the too-big-to-fail doctrine even the Eurozone is progressing in the development of its new rules and governance related to banking (*banking union*). The building blocks of the banking union should include: (1) a single rule book for all banks in the UE; (2) a single supervisory mechanism (SSM); (3) a deposit guarantee scheme; and (4) a single crisis resolution scheme. (Sober Look, 2012).

The first pillar (Single Rule Book for Banks) consists of the CRD IV (Capital Requirements Directive IV)/Basel III Framework. These are the rules to be enforced by the single supervisory mechanism (SSM). Basel III phased implementation is scheduled from 2013 (January 1) to 2019.

The second pillar (a single supervisory mechanism – SSM) has been approved by EU members states in March 2013. The SSM is the first step toward an integrated "banking union." The European Central Bank (ECB) will have the responsibility for the supervision of the banks in the eurozone and will directly supervise banks having assets of more than 30 billion euros or constituting at least 20 percent of their home country's GDP, or which have requested or received direct public financial assistance from the European Financial Stability Facility or the European Stability Mechanism. For less significant banks the ECB will allow the supervision by national supervisors. The ECB may, however, at any moment decide to directly supervise one or more banks to ensure consistent application of high supervisory standards. The Single Supervisory Mechanism is for member states of the eurozone but is also open to other EU countries. The SSM is expected to enter into force in mid-2014.

The third pillar (a deposit guarantee scheme) is not yet in force (April 2013) since German banks have been opposed so far to a pan-European deposit guarantee scheme, however, since the first step towards a banking union has been accomplished in March 2013 (a single bank supervisor under the European Central Bank), and the second step will follow soon (the creation of a resolution agency), then it is quite likely to assume that the third step will follow as well. As I am writing this book (April 2013) the coverage of national Deposit Guarantee Schemes (DGS) in many EU countries is €100,000 per depositor, per institution. The objective of the third pillar of the banking union is to create a Common Deposit-Insurance Fund. The Cyprus banking crisis of March 2013 certainly raised significant attention to the need for a Europe-wide deposit guarantee fund and a single crisis resolution scheme. Furthermore, there is still a resistance (April 2013) from some member states to accept also the creation of a single bank recapitalization, restructuring, and liquidation mechanism (*crisis resolution fund*) due to their fear of a potential mutualization of risk. As stated above, however, this resistance will be overcome soon since the European banking union process is slowly but steadily progressing (Sober Look, 2012).

Some analysts have observed that it took European leaders a very long time to address the Greek crisis and the subsequent debt restructuring, and that the cost for European taxpayers has risen significantly over a period of several months due to slow, ineffective, and poor governance of the crisis resolution. On one side, one could argue that some European countries and the Troika have probably required proof of rigorous austerity plans' implementation from Greece and other weaker European economies prior to providing a comprehensive rescue plan/bail-out. According to a Bloomberg study, however, if Greece had defaulted in 2010 the cost would have been much lower but the losses (haircut) would have been mainly absorbed by banks. The Bloomberg study also estimated that when the intervention of the Troika in Greece is completed, approximately 70 percent of the debt and the related risk of default will be transferred from private banks to public institutions (that is, European taxpayers' money) (Onaran, 2012).

As explained earlier in this book, since 2008 the crisis has evolved: (1) from the subprime mortgage loans and mortgage-back securities crisis to the liquidity and confidence crisis; (2) from the credit crisis to the economic crisis, (3) from the economic crisis to the sovereign debt crisis; and then again (4) from the sovereign debt crisis to the banking crisis and confidence crisis in the Eurozone, and; (5) from the confidence crisis to the liquidity, credit, and economic crisis in the Eurozone, and so on.

Two common denominators of this crisis in both the US and Europe are the interconnectedness and the high social costs related to the various forms of crises (that is, higher unemployment rates, slow GDP growth or recessions, higher taxes, spending cuts and austerity programs, structural reforms and higher levels of volatility and uncertainty in the markets) although the root causes of the two crises are significantly different.

When the euro was physically introduced in Europe in 2002, a number of peripheral European countries began to benefit from lower interest rates, due to the common Eurozone currency with stronger economies, thus giving to the financial markets the perception of a reduced risk premium even though there was no formal banking, political, fiscal union, or a central bank with a lender of last resort mandate. This condition has generated a considerable flow of funds from banks of the more solid "core" European countries to the southern European states. Paul Krugman (2012) reports that in the years following the physical introduction of the euro, the capital inflows from other countries has generated a sort of bubble in some of the peripheral European markets (that is, real estate market in Spain or Ireland), average increases in salaries, and sovereign debts, while at the same time also contributing to current account imbalances and lower competitiveness of these countries (Krugman, 2012, pp. 197–200). Furthermore, it seems that a few EU countries with high debt-to-GDP ratios have restructured derivatives contracts before or after entering the euro in order to stagger payments owed to foreign banks over a longer period and to meet the deficit targets set by the EU for the member states of the Eurozone.

There is no doubt that the US financial crisis has had an impact on the European economies, contributing to the recessionary trends in the Eurozone and worsening the countries' imbalances that have been steadily growing since the introduction of the euro due to structural differences between countries. As Krugman (2012) states, in those years there were asymmetric financial shocks for the Eurozone due to the lack of fiscal integration. The 2008 financial crisis has badly hit the peripheral Eurozone countries causing a credit crunch, a sudden and dramatic reduction in GDP (and in particular of the industrial production), higher unemployment, reduced consumptions and investments – thus skyrocketing their deficits and debts as a result of the costs of bank bail-outs and nationalizations or the massive increase in unemployment benefits over a number of years. Since the beginning of the crisis, the high deficits and increased debts, the recession, and the downgrades and negative outlook of the credit rating agencies have brought some of these countries to the brink of collapse during 2011–2012 due to capital outflows from riskier economies, credit crunch, risk aversion of investors, and distrust amongst banks. The fear that the weaker economies (that is, Greece) would exit the single currency area and trigger a potential contagion among the Eurozone countries of the crisis has done the rest, causing panic (confidence crisis) in the financial markets (as proved by the higher sovereign bonds' yields and cost of CDS). At that point, the ECB, and in particular Mario Draghi, stepped in and, in coordination with the other Eurozone leaders, orchestrated the unconventional measures that have so far saved the euro and the Eurozone from the financial crisis (Krugman, pp. 166–187, 2012).

Before joining the euro, a single country could devaluate its currency (competitive devaluation) to boost exports and economic growth. However, once it joined the euro, the common centralized monetary policy under the responsibility of the ECB meant that this policy was no longer available. The ECB has notoriously always had the primary mission of assuring stability of the value of the currency and controlling the risks of higher inflation. Thus, during the period of prolonged crisis and recession (2008–2012) the single states could only count on the placement of government bonds but at a higher interest rate (before Mario Draghi's measures), and on the introduction of austerity programs and structural reforms.

In December 2011, Germany called for an EU treaty change to overcome the confidence crisis and to introduce new rules to save the euro and the Eurozone. This decision was triggered by the proposal of the newly appointed ECB president, Mario Draghi, to EU governments to agree a big "fiscal compact." The Fiscal Compact Treaty was signed in March 2012. The severe deterioration of fiscal conditions in the Eurozone since 2009 have meant that neither the Stability and Growth Pact, nor the Excessive Deficit Procedure (EDP) have proved to be effective in improving fiscal discipline in all countries in order to enforce structural reforms and revamp economic growth.

Thus, in 2013 a number of European countries began to express discomfort about the the strict terms of the existing agreement and the single currency mechanism, seeking new and more flexible solutions, or simply more time and resources, to overcome the heavy burden of high sovereign debts, recessionary trends, tough austerity programs and the rapidly changing turbulent dynamics of EU economies. Over the years a number of Eurozone countries, in spite of the adverse economic conditions (that is, recession) have implemented demanding and painful structural reforms on employment, labor market/ retirement, and fiscal policies and so on in order to achieve a challenging goal of fiscal consolidation and compliance to the planned timeline of sovereign debt and budget deficits reductions or balanced budgets.

In fact, since the start of the crisis in the Eurozone, austerity plans and structural reforms have been undertaken by countries to overcome problems with the debt and deficits and revamp economic growth and employment. Even the ECB has undertaken a series of both conventional and non-conventional monetary policies to handle short-and-medium term emergency phases of the Eurozone debt crisis and also to set the bases for a long-term enhanced monetary and fiscal integration. Regarding the process of enhancing the Eurozone banking and financial stability and economic growth, the following steps have been taken by regulators, policy makers, and governments so far (April 2013) (Europost, 2013):

- In 2011 and 2012 an aggressive monetary policy has been undertaken by the ECB in an attempt to arrest the financial and banking crisis, to facilitate banks' funding (liquidity), and to reduce the credit crunch for individuals and small businesses. The ECB has cut the refinance rate to 1 percent and has announced a string of liquidity measures, including a three-year LTRO and a relaxation of collateral requirements to achieve such goals. During 2010–2012 a confidence crisis about some Eurozone countries' potential insolvency (default) and the fear of contagion (triggered also by a series of credit agencies' downgrades in the Eurozone) has drastically increased CDS rates and sovereign bond yield spreads versus the more solid "core" European economies.

- A fiscal compact (Phillips, 2012) has been agreed by members states, consisting of a series of rules tightening budget surveillance and institutionalizing limits on public spending. Key to a "new legal framework" governing the fiscal compact is a "golden rule" enforcing balanced budgets that must be inscribed in domestic constitutions or at an "equivalent level." Governments will be deemed to have achieved balanced budgets so long as deficits do not exceed 0.5 percent of GDP and the rules will have to include automatic correction mechanisms. The European Court of Justice will be tasked with ensuring that this golden rule is transposed into national law. For those countries that breach existing EU rules forbidding deficits exceeding 3 percent of GDP, there would be automatic consequences unless a qualified majority of states decided otherwise. The Eurozone leaders also endorsed new rules proposed by the European Commission on November 23, 2011 that give the EU executive far-reaching new powers over domestic fiscal policy decision-making. Under the new rules, almost all fiscal policy-making are taken out of the hands of national assemblies and delivered up to European civil servants. Governments in member states that use the single currency are obliged to submit their budgets to both the commission and the Eurogroup of states for vetting – before they are submitted to their own national parliaments. If the commission does not like what it sees, it can demand changes to the budget, as well as other mid-term plans a government may have for its economy.

Those countries that have exceeded EU rules on the size of their debt and deficit are also subject to tighter monitoring by Brussels and are required to submit regular reports on how they are progressing in trying to correct the situation. The Commission can issue recommendations for how this should be done. All Eurozone states are forced to create independent fiscal councils – bodies of "experts" unaccountable to parliaments – who have to issue budgetary and economic forecasts. A country's budget has to be based on the reports of these fiscal councils. For countries in deeper troubles and facing serious financial difficulties, Brussels can send teams of inspectors – akin to the "Troika" monitors (European Commission, ECB, and IMF) sent to member states that have received bail-outs. The overseers can be sent to any state that the Commission decides, even if the country has not requested any international assistance. The Commission has the power to recommend to the Council of Ministers, representing the member states, that a country should take a bail-out.

- The European Stability Mechanism (ESM) was established in February 2012 as a permanent firewall for the Eurozone to provide immediate access to financial assistance programs for member states in financial difficulty. The ESM is an international organization located in Luxembourg. The ESM issues debt instruments in order to finance loans and other forms of financial assistance to euro area members states. ESM bail-outs are currently conditional on member states first signing a Memorandum of Understanding (MoU), which indicates the reforms or fiscal consolidation to be implemented in order to restore the financial stability. A second precondition for receiving an ESM bail-out is that the member state must have fully ratified the Fiscal Compact.

- There are still discussions (but at the moment no "green light") on the possibility of granting to the ESM a banking license. Romano Prodi (former President of the European Commission from 1999 to 2004) and Alberto Quadrio Curzio (Catholic University of Milan) have also recommended the use of Eurobonds and EuroUnionBonds to favor economic growth programs in the region but at the moment they have not been approved by the Eurozone state members (Prodi, 2012).

- As stated before, direct bank recapitalization by the ESM will be probably allowed soon (April 2013) now that the single supervisory mechanism (SSM) has been approved. In fact, as agreed by the EU summit in 2012, ESM direct bank recapitalisation is expected to be available soon after the approval of the European banking supervision unit although most likely based on stringent conditional clauses (that is a ceiling on the amount, state contributions, and a pecking order for bail-in and bail-out inspired by the criteria adopted in the Cyprus bank crisis resolution. A pecking order as the one just described, however, would result unable to break the vicious circle between sovereign debt and bank debt that overcomplicated the resolution of the Eurozone debt crisis in 2010–2012, thus it should be avoided.

- In 2012 the European Banking Authority (EBA) has required stress tests and increases in capital for banks with a significant capital shortfall.

- A Brookings Papers on Economic Activity of Spring 2012 (Shambaugh, 2012) issued in March 2012 reported that the euro was facing the following three interlocking crises challenging the viability of the currency union:
  - *a banking crisis* – due to undercapitalized banks that had also liquidity problems;
  - *a sovereign debt crisis* – due to a number of countries facing rising bond yields and challenges funding themselves;

- *a growth crisis* – with both a low overall level of growth in the euro area and an unequal distribution across countries (Shambaugh, 2012).

In the same study Shambaugh (2012) reports that bail-outs of banks have contributed to the sovereign debt problems, but banks are also at risk due to their holdings of sovereign bonds that may face default. Weak growth contributes to the potential insolvency of the sovereigns, but also, the austerity inspired by the debt crisis is constraining growth. Finally, a weakened banking sector holds back growth while a weak economy undermines the banks (Shambaugh, 2012).

In the same paper the authors have also provided the following recommendations for the crises resolution:

> It is possible that coordinated shifts in payroll and consumption taxes could aid the painful process of internal devaluation. The European Financial Stability Facility (EFSF) could be used to capitalize banks and to help break the sovereign/bank link. Fiscal support in core countries could help spur growth. Finally, the ECB could provide liquidity to sovereigns and increase nominal GDP growth as well as allow slightly faster inflation to facilitate deleveraging and relative price adjustments across regions. All these steps, especially if taken together in an attempt to treat the three crises holistically could substantially improve outcomes. At the same time, institutional reforms and fiscal consolidation programs may help move towards a true banking and fiscal union and to reduce the likelihood of new systemic risks in the future. Of course, politics, ideology, or additional economic shocks could all hinder improvement. The euro area is highly vulnerable and without deft policy may continue in crisis for a considerable amount of time. (Shambaugh, 2012)

- In the fall 2012, Mario Draghi announced the offer of the Outright Monetary Transactions (OMT) program to help restore regular flow of liquidity and affordable funding in the Eurozone (BBC News, 2012).
- The OECD (OECD, 2012) reported in their Economic Outlook OECD in November 2012 a capital shortage in the European banking system. Furthermore, in their *Economic Outlook Focus 10-02-2013: Strengthening Euro Area Banks* (OECD, 2013), they report the following analysis:

> Big changes are needed to strengthen the capital positions of euro area banks, according to OECD (November 2012). European banks remain at the heart of the euro area crisis. Despite actions to strengthen banks and build a banking union, confidence in the euro area banking system remains weak, and is likely to remain so until underlying concerns over low capitalization of some banks are addressed. Low bank capitalization persists in many countries despite an EU requirement that banks reach in 2012 a ratio of a minimum 9 percent of the best quality "Core Tier-1" capital to RWA, in excess of the current international requirements. Why has this new benchmark not been sufficient to boost confidence? In part, this is because it is based on risk-weighting of assets that likely understates risks, due to reliance on banks' own internal risk models and, for example, the zero risk-weight given to sovereign debt. The ratio of Core Tier-1 capital to unweighted assets of euro area banks currently falls well short of 5 percent in many cases. This standard has been identified as a benchmark for well-capitalized banks in a recent OECD paper and it is more demanding than the minimum Basel III leverage ratio that will apply from 2018. Increasing the capacity of European banks to absorb losses, by increasing

their capital relative to assets, needs to be addressed in the coming years. If the euro area's largest banks were to move to a 5 percent standard, the current capital shortage is estimated at around EUR 400 billion (4¼ percent of euro area GDP). This is not just a problem for banks in the "periphery" – there could be large capital needs in the major euro area countries. Future capital needs could be lessened if banks were required to separate commercial banking and market activities, reducing the total assets of the banking business.

- In early 2013 the EU Parliament introduced the new Basel III rules on liquidity ratios and The Group of Central Bank Governors and Heads of Supervision (GHOS) the Credit Rating agencies rules.
- Finally, in January 2013, IMF Managing Director, Christine Lagarde, speaking on France 2 TV once again warned about potential systemic risk in the banking sector. She mentioned that "banks have not yet learned the lessons from the financial crisis and that tighter rules for the banking industry are required to prevent new future crises. In fact, she stressed the point that large parts of the financial industry remain unsupervised" (Sucha, 2013).
- In February 2013, the EU approved a financial transaction tax for 11 Eurozone countries excluding, among others, the UK, Luxembourg, and the Czech Republic. Critics say that unless this tax is applied worldwide, or at least across Europe, it may not work effectively.
- Furthermore, the European Commission has introduced the "two pack" legislative package to strengthen the Commission surveillance of national budgetary of Eurozone nations. However, the proposal of a debt redemption fund (for countries that have debt in excess of 60 percent of GDP) has been strongly opposed by some member states.
- In 2013 the European Commission has passed the Capital Requirements Directive; "CRD IV" into law in order to introduce the regulatory standards on bank capital adequacy and liquidity of the Basel Committee on Banking Supervision into European law.

It is quite likely that with the "two pack" regulations European member states will be forced in the future, if they can pursue it, toward a more stringent regulation on fiscal consolidation and discipline which may also include a series of mandatory programs such as privatizations and dismissal of state-owned assets and shareholdings, issuance of covered bonds, more radical structural reforms, fiscal harmonization among in the European states, and so on. Political stability and financial, fiscal, monetary, and economic stability are highly interconnected, and nowadays always more globalized, thus the sustainability of the Eurozone area and of the global economy will depend significantly on the ability of political and economic leaders to achieve both well harmonized political and economic stability policies (with some degree of flexibility during recessionary trends), while also pursuing growth goals.

- In March 2013 the European Commission and Switzerland introduced a provisional agreement (EU) and a rule (Switzerland) aimed at imposing a stringent set of curbs on executive pay and giving more power on executive compensation to companies' shareholders. In particular, the EU agreement is aimed to limit bankers' pay (to cap bankers' bonuses).

- In March 2013, the EU and the IMF provided a €10 billion ($13.18 billion) bail-out package for Cyprus (the fourth Eurozone country to receive a full bail-out after Greece, Ireland, and Portugal, or the fifth if one counts the partial bail-out for Spain's banks) to keep Cyprus in the Eurozone and to avoid new tail-risk (contagion) to other bigger member states of the economic area. This resulted in Laiki Bank, the island's second largest bank, to be to wound down and imposed losses of up to 60 percent on uninsured bank deposits – over 100,000 euros – on a second, the Bank of Cyprus (Kambas, 2013).

1. The Cyprus bank crisis revealed a radical change of strategy of the Troika on bank crisis resolution and a clear intention to handle bank failures and bank crisis resolution primarily favoring a "bail-in" regime, thus lifting the burden of bank rescues from taxpayers and forcing losses primarily on bank shareholders and creditors but also to uninsured bank deposits. The lessons learned from the Eurozone crises reveal that: a single supervisory mechanism without a common resolution and safety net framework will do little to break the vicious circle between banks and sovereigns and reestablish a properly functioning monetary transmission mechanism.
2. Bank recapitalisation as well as resolution and deposit-insurance mechanisms would lack credibility without the assurance of fiscal backstops and burden-sharing arrangements.
3. Conversely, common safety nets and backstops without effective supervision and resolution would break sovereign-bank links, but risk distorting incentives, reinforcing tendencies for regulatory forbearance, and shifting losses to the Eurozone level. (Dell'Ariccia, Goyal, Koeva-Brooks, Tressel, 2013)

In spite of the relatively slow-moving implementation of the financial reforms over the years in Europe and in the US only about 38 percent of Dodd–Frank total required rulemakings have been finalized, now that some leading global banks, by and large, (1) have been rescued mainly with taxpayers' money, (2) have returned the funds they received from governments, (3) have agreed to pay settlements with regulators for wrongdoings or fraud charges, (4) have lobbied with billions of dollars to water down the new financial regulation, and (5) they continue to invest heavily in more profitable and risky OTC bets of derivatives (in the still largely unsupervised shadow banking system). Given the current economic situation (April 2013) in many countries around the world, it is even easier for banking lobbyies to oppose the new financial regulation arguing that it threatens economic recovery, and that it might create additional challenges in the current phase of painful recessionary trends or stagnant economic growth, high unemployment rates, credit crunch, and austerity programs in a number of countries.

In April 2013, in an attempt to constrain the riskiness of large lenders, US Fed officials considered a stricter cap on bank leverage higher than the 3 percent of assets level agreed internationally. In the US Congress there seems to be a bipartisan proposal to impose a 15 percent leverage ratio on the largest banks. Even Tom Hoenig, Vice Chairman of the Federal Deposit Insurance Corporation (FDIC), has reported that 10 percent would be a "reasonable" leverage ratio of tangible equity to tangible assets. A policy group, whose members, including Paul Volcker, former Fed chairman, and Sheila Bair, the previous head of the FDIC, instead have urged the Fed to set a leverage ratio of 8 percent. "The move is being considered amid growing skepticism about the Basel III capital accords, which impose higher capital requirements on banks around the world but allow them to vary the amount depending on the riskiness of individual assets. Officials are concerned that some banks are gaming the system" (Braithwaite and Nasiripour, 2013b). It is possible that in the Basel III will be implemented in the US in the summer 2013, as anticipated by the Fed, but with higher capital requirements for the SIFIs whereas more flexibility capital requirements will be applied to smaller banks. Furthermore, it is quite likely that the SIFIs will be subject to a minimum supplemental leverage ratio to incorporate certain off-balance sheet exposures. Basel III implementation in the US will probably also aim to improve risk mitigation of some of the weaknesses that contributed to cause the 2007–2009 financial crisis such as, the high leverage ratios, short-term funding and the consequent liquidity problems of financial firms.

Regarding the US clearing deadline, the so-called "Category Two" firms should be required to clear certain index CDS and interest-rate swaps starting June 10, 2013 but very few are expected to be ready by that date.

Meanwhile, however, the Globally Systemically Important Financial Institutions (G-SIFIs), in many circumstances, are also pursuing regulatory arbitrages, and relocating their investment banking and OTC operations to countries that offer "lighter" regulation and higher tax benefits. Furthermore, as a consequence of the 2007–2009 financial crisis, some of the leading global investment banks became even bigger than before the crisis in terms of total assets (M&A). This has generated an increase in industry concentration which is particularly evident in the derivatives and structured products market. It is a well-known fact that today (April 2013) just five banks (JPMorgan Chase, Citigroup, Bank of America, Morgan Stanley and Goldman Sachs) hold more than 90 percent of all derivatives contracts, and that many of these contracts are traded Over-the-Counter (OTD).

Furthermore, with regards to the threat that investors may be continuing to take risky bets in order to boost returns, in January 2013, Mark Carney, the Chairman of the G20's Financial Stability Board, former Governor of the Bank of Canada, and ex-Goldman Sachs banker, and soon to be Governor of the Bank of England, expressed his warning message to the financial markets saying: "Market participants and authorities need to be on guard against mispricing of risk in pricing of assets" (Shotter and Masters, 2013).

Following the message of US regulators (Fed and FDIC), who warned G-SIFIs not to rely too much on global regulatory reforms or resolution plans for potential future financial meltdowns since there is poor global coordination in different regions among regulators to achieve such goals, Mark Carney has stressed the point that "further progress is needed" in terms of drawing up "living wills" for cross-border resolution strategies of giant global banks' potential failures (Braithwaite et al., 2013; Shotter and Masters, 2013).

Analysts and Western rating agencies have raised some concerns since 2011 about emerging markets' financial stability (in particular in China), due to the drastic increase of the shadow banking industry in order to remove banks' funds from their balance sheets. The *Financial Times* reports a 600 percent increase in 2012 in shadow financing activities related to brokerage in China (Rabinovitch, 2013).

Regarding the ability of anticipating systemic crises, Dewatripont et al. (2010) indicate that prudential regulation must explicitly anticipate the various possible outcomes related to considerations that are both systematic and macroprudential. They also add that the Basel Framework of prudential regulation was entirely bereft of concrete arrangements directed to the prevention of such a systemic crisis. It was organized around the concept of VaR, estimated on the basis of historical data, thus the question: is the capital sufficient to limit the probability of collapse of an individual bank to some "acceptable" level set in advance by the regulators? Given the dramatic events of the 2007–2009 financial crisis, it is quite evident that the systemic risk was significantly underestimated by the Basel prudential regime. This was due primarily to the banks' lack of liquidity based on short-term financing. It is now known that in times of systemic crisis the interbank and money markets (short-term funding sources) stop working (Dewatripont et al., 2010, pp. 78–106).

Furthermore, systemic crises are supposed to be rare events and general statistical models use data from "normal" periods which are evidently inappropriate. The asset correlation and the institutions' interconnectedness are seriously affected by systemic crises. Still, the model used by regulators (that is, the Asymptotic Single Risk Factor – ASRF – model applied for credit risk) sometimes employs assumptions applicable to normal periods but are inappropriate relative to extreme "tail-events." As the tail-events are very rare, it is difficult to have enough data to assess such events (that is, use of 99.9 percent quartile). Last but not least, the Basel II Framework was only addressing the prevention and management of risk of an individual bank and not the stability of the entire financial system (Dewatripont et al., 2010, pp. 78–106).

Dewatripont et al. (2010) propose the following three types of reforms for the resolution of the Basel Regime:

- a much more powerful and independent banking supervision;
- much simpler and easy-to-apply prudential regulation;
- the installation of a prompt corrective action regime for the management of crises, including a special resolution regime for systematically important financial institutions (Dewatripont et al., 2010, pp. 78–106).

The corporate governance failure of the 2007–2009 financial crisis, however, does not only relate to credit, liquidity, market, operational risk management and to moral hazard. Rather other disciplines have been involved in the systemic failure that led to the financial meltdown. These are for example: fraud prevention and management, audit and internal controls. During the years leading up to the financial crisis there was certainly a failure of appropriate corporate governance (board oversight) and in particular by the audit and compensation committees of the board of directors (Kolb, 2010b, pp. 209–216; Posner, 2009, pp. 75–116).

As explained by Nugent (2009), corporate governance represents the relationship among shareholders, the board of directors, and top management, and their coordinated effort in determining direction and performance of a corporation. He also clarified that key board responsibilities include the following:

- set corporate strategy, direction, mission or vision;
- hire and fire the CEO and top management;
- control, monitor, and supervise top management;
- review and approve use/disposition of resources;
- care for shareholders' interests (Nugent, 2009a).

Wheelen and Hunger (2011) indicate that the role of the board in strategic management consists of:

- monitoring;
- evaluating and influencing;
- initiating and determining strategic directions (Wheelen and Hunger, 2011, p. 9).

One of the corporate governance failures of the 2007–2009 financial crisis is related to the agency problem and conflicts of interest among many of the stakeholders involved in the subprime, securitization, due diligence, and credit rating processes.

Wheelen and Hunger explain that the agency theory refers to the problems that arise in corporations because the agents (top management) are not willing to bear responsibility for their decisions unless they own substantial stock in the corporation (Wheelen and Hunger, 2011, p. 29).

What has occurred in this crisis is that in addition to substantial stock ownership, the structure of the compensation scheme has also seriously affected the *principal–agency relationship*.

Using Wheelen and Hunger's matrix of the styles of corporate governance it is possible to identify that during the years leading to the 2007–2009 financial crisis, in many financial institutions there has probably been a *chaos management* in corporate governance since, driven by excessive risk-taking and short-termism, neither board members nor top management has guaranteed effective oversight (Wheelen and Hunger, 2011, p. 34).

Based on the financial crisis key facts reported in this book, it is quite evident that there has been a major failure of at least one out of the three levels of *Kohlberg's moral development*, the so-called *principled level* or concern for universal values. The three levels are:

- Preconventional: concern for self.
- Conventional: concern for laws and norms.
- Principled: concern for universal values (Wheelen and Hunger, 2011, p. 42).

According to Nugent (2009), an important component of corporate governance is represented by the internal controls' discipline. Nugent indicates that internal controls are affected by the interaction between board of directors, management, and employees and their compliance to internal norms and laws and regulations (Nugent, 2009b).

According to J.H. Nugent (2009), COSO Integrated Framework's definition of Internal Control (IC) is the following:

> IC is broadly defined as a process, effected by an entity's board of directors, management and other personnel, designed to provide reasonable assurance regarding the achievement of objectives in the following three categories:
>
> 1. Effectiveness and Efficiency of Operations.
> 2. Reliability, Timeliness and Accuracy of Financial Reporting.
> 3. Compliance with Applicable Laws and Regulations (Nugent, 2009b).

Nugent (2009) states the COSO Integrated Framework consists of the following five components regarding IC:

- Control Environment – sets tone of organization – the best control is to have professionals of character and integrity leading the organization.
- Risk Assessment – process for identifying/responding to business risk.
- Control Activities – policies/procedures that ensure actions are taken to address risks.
- Information and Communication – infrastructure and dissemination of roles.
- Monitoring – assess quality of internal control over time (Nugent, 2009b).

In particular, according to Nugent, the components of the COSO Integrated Framework for internal controls include the following:

- Control Environment
  - integrity, ethical values, competence;
  - management philosophy and operating style;
  - the way management assigns authority and responsibility;
  - the way management organizes and develops people;
  - the attention and direction of the board of directors.
- Risk Assessment
  - process to identify, analyze, and manage related risks;
  - threats, vulnerabilities, and risks.
- Control Activities
  - assess risks;
  - develop controls, policies and procedures;
  - authorizations, verifications, reconciliations, reviews of performance, security of assets, segregation of duties;
  - control activities;
  - assess risks;
  - develop controls, policies and procedures;
  - authorizations, verifications, reconciliations, reviews of performance, security of assets, segregation of duties.
- Monitoring
  - a constant feedback process that identifies changes and the requirements for control updates as circumstances change (Nugent, 2009b).

Another important dimension of corporate governance which seems to have failed during the years leading up to the 2007–2009 crisis is the *fraud management process* of many financial institutions, as demonstrated by the fraud charges attributed to hedge funds and investment banks in the last few years.

Nugent (2009) quotes fraud as being defined as:

An intentional perversion of truth for the purpose of inducing another, in reliance upon it, to part with some valuable thing belonging to him or to surrender a legal right. A false representation of fact intended to deceive another.

Nugent (2009) goes on to state that, for an act to amount to fraud, four elements need to be present. These four elements are known as the *"KIDD" Principle*:

1. Knowledge
2. Intent
3. Damages and
4. Deceit

Unless these elements are present, it is likely the act will be deemed a mistake.

The business management literature indicates that in recent years there have been significant cases of companies' frauds being related to financial statements' frauds such as the famous Enron case.

Nugent (2009) quotes financial statement fraud as:

> *Intentionally improperly presenting and representing in a material manner either the entity's financial position or results of operations. (Nugent, 2009b)*

The Enron fraud and its subsequent collapse and the end of its auditing firm (Arthur Andersen) has mandated reforms of American Business Practices for Public Companies which are included in the well-known SOX Act of 2002. The scope of the introduction of these reforms was to enhance corporate responsibility, financial reporting, and disclosures, and to combat corporate and accounting fraud. The SOX Act established the creation of the Public Company Accounting Oversight Board (PCAOB). The SOX Act is applied to publicly held companies and their accounting/auditing firms (Nugent, 2009b).

The SOX Act restricts public accountants to their independent audit work (an attest function) and certain tax work for public companies. It requires management to assert that the financial reports are materially accurate, and disclosure controls and internal controls are properly designed and working; and if any material weaknesses or significant deficiencies exist in such controls, that they be reported upon. It requires that audit committees be composed entirely of independent board members (principally non-employee directors). It requires that audit committees must have a financial expert as a member and financial analysts to be independent and objective. It introduced the PCAOB to set standards for audits, attestations, and reviews of public companies and to register and regulate the auditors which audit public companies (Nugent, 2009b).

The SOX Act also requires that auditors report directly to the audit committee not to management; that audit committees must pre-approve all auditor services, and that auditors are precluded from offering some services for attest clients such as consulting services. The lead auditor has to be rotated after five years and must have a second partner review audit workpapers and the audit report. It also requires stricter employment standards – one year restriction on becoming employed by a client company if an auditor becomes the company CEO, CFO, Controller, and so on.

The PCAOB, based on Part B of the SOX Act, is overseen by the SEC which previously appointed the PCAOB Commissioners (although this is being amended because of a court challenge), must have five commissioners (two Certified Public Accounts (CPAs)/three non-CPAs), and it has to be funded by public companies through fees. It must regularly inspect accounting firms for potential violations of security laws. It is organized into six US regional offices.

The *Statement of Auditing Standards N° 99*: "Consideration of Fraud in a Financial Statement Audit" (*SAS 99*), which became effective on December 15, 2002, requires auditors to plan and introduce elements of unpredictability in the audit function such as:

- employ brainstorming;
- establish team communications;
- have domain knowledge;
- interview employees across all material processes;
- use analytical tools and methods;
- use random sampling;
- conduct surprise visits;
- change timing of audit functions (confirms, and so on);
- change technique – increase the sampling of transactions versus relying to a large degree on the perception of internal controls;
- evaluate low-profile accounts;
- look for bogus patterns – (Benford's Law);
- observe operations and walk material transactions through all material processes;
- review whistleblower files as well as lateral or downward transfers and firings;
- use audit software – CAATT Tools (ACL, IDEA, NLP, and so on);
- visualize some of the audit data;
- embed software monitors – requires client's permission in the client's systems (Nugent, 2009b).

Considering that SOX has been in existence since 2002 and that COSO's Frameworks were codified in a number of Statements on Auditing Standards (SASs) since 2004, it seems quite obvious the foregoing promulgations did not mitigate the failure in corporate governance, audit quality and adequacy, internal controls, and fraud management and risk management which occurred during the 2007–2009 financial crisis. An example of an alleged fraudulent behavior that occurred in the financial crisis is the one related to the *repo 105 repurchase agreements* in the Lehman Brothers case. A repo 105 was used by the investment bank Lehman Brothers three times according to a March 2010 report by the bankruptcy court examiner. The report stated that Lehman's auditors, Ernst and Young, were aware of this questionable classification. With the repurchase agreement, the investment bank created an accounting maneuver where a short-term loan is classified as a sale. The cash obtained through this "sale" is then used to pay down debt, allowing the company to appear to reduce its leverage by temporarily paying down liabilities – just long enough to reflect on the company's published balance sheet (end of period transaction that is shortly reversed via repurchase). After the company's financial reports are published, the company borrows cash and repurchases its original assets. The New York Attorney-General Andrew Cuomo filed charges against Ernst and Young in December 2010, alleging that the firm "substantially assisted ... a massive accounting fraud" by approving the accounting treatment. The *Wall Street Journal* drew attention to the increasing levels of fees that Ernst and Young had been paid by Lehman from 2001 to 2008 (Reed, 2010; Rappaport and Rappaport, 2010). It should be noted that no US law firm would write a favorable opinion on the Lehman use of repo 105s. Lehman had to go to the UK to find a law firm to draft such an opinion as the laws at the time in the

UK permitted such activity. Hence all Lehman repo 105 transactions were carried out through Lehman's London office (jurisdiction shopping) (Nugent, 2011).

External financial statements are prepared on the assumption that the firm is a *going concern*; that is, that it will continue to operate at least through the next annual accounting cycle and hopefully indefinitely thereafter. "Based on this assumption, assets are generally recorded at cost and depreciated over their expected useful lives. If the going concern assumption is no longer valid, the company's assets and liabilities should be reported at the amounts estimated to be collected or paid when they are liquidated. Going concern evaluations should be top-of-mind for the audit profession" (Putra, 2009). However, the financial crisis and the subsequent sovereign debt crisis in Europe have raised a number of doubts about going concern opinions and fair value accounting practices (mark-to-market accounting values of MBS and other derivatives backed by risky underlying assets) prior to the press-raising attention on the issue and regulatory bodies issuing clear statement and guidelines on the matter (Pezzuto, 2011b).

The Dodd–Frank Wall Street Reform and Consumer Protection Act

Following to the 2007–2009 financial crisis in the US, on July 21, 2010, President Barack Obama signed into law the Dodd–Frank Wall Street Reform and Consumer Protection Act. The law was initially proposed on December 2, 2009 in the House of Representatives by Barney Frank, and in the Senate Banking Committee by its Chairman, Senator Chris Dodd. The initial draft contained a proposal developed by Paul Volcker, the former US Fed Chairman, known as the *Volcker Rule* on January 2010. This rule aims to prohibit depository banks from proprietary trading (similar to the prohibition of combined investment and commercial banking in the Glass–Steagall Act) but the original version of the rule was approved in weakened form. Hence *Section 619* of the bill allows banks to invest up to 3 percent of their *Tier 1 capital* in private equity and hedge funds as well as trade for hedging purposes. The rule also imposes *countercyclical* capital requirements (Dodd–Frank Library online, 2011).

The Act is categorized into 16 titles and requires that regulators create 243 rules, conduct 67 studies, and issue 22 periodic reports. The stated aim of the legislation is:

> To promote the financial stability of the United States by improving accountability and transparency in the financial system, to end "too big to fail," to protect the American taxpayer by ending bail-outs, to protect consumers from abusive financial services practices, and for other purposes. (Polk, 2010, p. i)

The Act changes the existing regulatory structure, such as creating a host of new agencies (while merging and removing others) in an effort to streamline the regulatory process, increasing oversight of specific institutions regarded as a systemic risk, amending the Federal Reserve Act, promoting transparency, and additional changes. The Act purports to provide rigorous standards and supervision to protect the economy and American consumers, investors and businesses, purports to end taxpayer-funded bail-outs of financial institutions, claims to provide for an advanced warning system on the stability of the economy, creates rules on executive compensation and corporate governance, and eliminates some loopholes that led to the 2008 economic recession. The new agencies are either granted explicit power over a particular aspect of financial regulation, or that power is transferred from an existing agency. All of the new agencies, and some existing ones that are not currently required to do so, are also compelled to report to Congress on an annual (or biannual) basis, to present the results of current plans and to explain future goals. Important new agencies created include the Financial Stability Oversight Council, the Office of Financial Research, and the Bureau of Consumer Financial Protection (Polk, 2010, pp. 1–4; Senate Committee on Banking, Housing, and Urban Affairs, 2010, pp. 1–11).

As stated by Enrique E. Liberman (Liberman, 2010):

> *Perhaps the most significant result of the Dodd–Frank Act is the elimination of the "private adviser" exemption promulgated under the Advisers Act and defended in the important decision of the US Court of Appeals in Goldstein v. SEC in 2006. Under the prior regulatory regime, an investment adviser would be exempt from registration with the SEC if it was deemed a "private adviser" – namely that it advised fewer than 15 clients in any 12-month period, and did not advise registered investment companies or business development companies and did not hold itself out as an investment adviser. Many, if not most, investment advisers relied on the private adviser exemption in operating their businesses.*

The Dodd–Frank Act repeals such exemption, which means many investment advisers will now be required to register with the SEC, unless another exemption is available to an adviser. That being said, investment advisers can find some comfort in the fact that the Dodd–Frank Act did create a number of new exemptions for private fund advisers. Such exemptions from registration depend in part upon the amount of the adviser's assets under management (AUM), namely the various securities positions (and not art works) managed by such adviser. Some of these exemptions include:

- Mid-Sized Adviser Exemptions;
- Venture Capital Fund Adviser Exemptions;
- Small Business Investment Company Adviser Exemptions;
- Family Offices Exemptions;
- Foreign Private Adviser Exemptions.

The Dodd–Frank Act creates a change in America's financial markets since it impacts all Federal financial regulatory agencies, eliminating the Office of Thrift Supervision and creating the Financial Stability Oversight Council and the Office of Financial Research. It also allows the creation of several consumer protection agencies, including the Bureau of Consumer Financial Protection, however, few provisions of the Act became effective when the bill was signed. Only over the next months will the full impact and significance of the Act become known, as various regulatory agencies write rules that implement various sections of the Act (Polk, 2010, pp. 1–117).

The 16 titles of the ACT are:

Title I	Financial Stability
Title II	Orderly Liquidation Authority
Title III	Transfer of Powers to the Comptroller, the FDIC, and the Fed

Title IV   Regulation of Advisers to Hedge Funds and Others
Title V   Insurance
Title VI   Improvements to Regulation
Title VII   Wall Street Transparency and Accountability
Title VIII   Payment, Clearing and Settlement Supervision
Title IX   Investor Protections and Improvements to the Regulation of Securities
Title X   Bureau of Consumer Financial Protection
Title XI   Federal Reserve System Provisions
Title XII   Improving Access to Mainstream Financial Institutions
Title XIII   Pay It Back Act
Title XIV   Mortgage Reform and Anti-Predatory Lending Act
Title XV   Miscellaneous Provisions
Title XVI   Section 1256 Contracts
(Dodd–Frank info website, 2011).

Despite the fact the Dodd–Frank general framework introduced in 2011 is a more comprehensive, high-level framework than the subsequent detailed rules set by regulators, it is indeed a first step toward a sweeping overhaul of US banking rules enacted in response to the 2007–2009 financial crisis (Acharya et al., 2011, pp. 1–28).

The Dodd–Frank Wall Street Reform and Consumer Protection Act of 2010 aims to address in particular the following issues of the 2007–2009 financial crisis:

- identifying and regulating systemic risk (through the Systemic Risk Council);
- proposing an end to the too-big-too-fail doctrine;
- expanding the responsibility and authority of the Federal Reserve Bank (authority over all systemic institutions and responsibility for preserving financial stability);
- restricting discretionary regulatory interventions;
- reinstating a limited form of Glass–Steagall Act (the Volcker Rule);
- introducing more regulation and transparency of derivatives (Acharya et al., 2011, pp. 5–6).

In addition, according to Acharya et al. (2011) the Dodd–Frank Act introduces a range of reforms for mortgage lending practices, hedge fund disclosures, conflict resolution at rating agencies, requirements for securitization institutions to retain sufficient interest in the underlying assets, risk controls for money market funds, and shareholder say on pay and governance. Perhaps the most important reform, albeit secondary to the financial crisis according to Acharya et al., is the creation of the Bureau of Consumer Financial Protection (CCFP). In spite of the introduction of the Dodd–Frank Act, and more in particular of the Bureau of Consumer Finance Protection, however, these authors state that "in large part, that (the lending) bubble was the result of the intentional politically driven expansion of owner-occupied housing" and "the Dodd–Frank Act – notwithstanding the Bureau of Consumer Finance Protection … would have done little to prevent the enormous lending bubble specific to subprime mortgages in the United States. The Act does nothing to address the worst-performing shadow banks – Fannie Mae and Freddie Mac – which were at the center of the housing expansion and had to be taken into government conservatorship in the early fall of 2008, and have cost US taxpayers more than the total of all Wall Street institutions with no end in sight" (Acharya et al., 2011, pp. 1–23).

Among the features introduced by the Dodd–Frank Act is the creation of two new agencies which have the responsibility to monitor systemic risk and research the state of the economy. The Act also clarifies the comprehensive supervision of bank holding companies overseen by the Federal Reserve Bank. Title I creates the Financial Stability Oversight Council and the Office of Financial Research. The two new offices are attached to the Treasury Department, with the Treasury Secretary being Chair of the Council, and a Presidential appointment with Senate confirmation to serve as the Head of the Financial Research Office. The Financial Stability Oversight Council is charged with identifying threats to the financial stability of the United States, promoting market discipline, and responding to emerging risks to the stability of the United States financial system. At a minimum, it must meet quarterly. Specifically, there are three purposes assigned to the Council:

1. identify the risks to the financial stability of the US from both financial and non-financial organizations;
2. promote market discipline, by eliminating expectations that the Government will shield them from losses in the event of failure;
3. respond to emerging threats to the stability of the US financial system.

DUTIES

The Council has several duties related to:

1. enhance the integrity, efficiency, competitiveness, and stability of US financial markets;
2. promote market discipline; and
3. maintain investor confidence.

The Council must monitor the financial services industry, make general regulatory recommendations to agencies, and it may also compel the Federal Reserve to assume an oversight position of certain institutions considered to pose a systemic risk. It has to monitor domestic and international regulatory proposals and developments, and advise Congress in these areas. The Council and the associated Office of Financial Research are charged to facilitate information sharing and coordination among the member agencies and other Federal and State agencies regarding domestic financial services' policy development, rule-making, examinations, reporting requirements, and enforcement actions (Acharya et al., 2011, pp. 1–28).

According to Acharya et al. (2011), analyzing the Dodd–Frank Act from the economic theory of regulation perspective, it strives to give prudential regulators the authority and the tools to deal with the market failures related also to externalities (in the case of the 2007–2009 financial crisis these are related to the "enormous buildup of systemic risk in the financial system due to the large number of financial firms funded with short-term debt which failed all at once when a correction in the housing market took place"). The Volcker Rule, for example, seems to address, at least in part, a useful regulation to mitigate moral hazard (Acharya et al., 2011, pp. 6–7).

Acharya et al. (2011), however, identified some weaknesses in the Act related to the following aspects:

- the Act does not deal with the mispricing of pervasive government guarantees throughout the financial sector. This may allow many financial firms to finance their activities at below-market rates and take on excessive risk;
- systemically important firms may be made bear their own losses but not the costs they impose on others in the system;
- in several parts, the Act regulates a financial firm by its form (bank) rather than function (banking) thus preventing the Act from dealing well with the new organizational forms likely to emerge in the financial sector;
- the Act makes important omissions in reforming and regulating parts of the shadow banking system that are systemically important. It also fails to recognize that there are systemically important markets – collections of individual contracts and institutions – that also need orderly resolution when they experience freezes (Acharya et al., 2011, pp. 8–9).

According to Dodd–Frank (Acharya et al., 2011), the board of governors should be responsible for reducing the risk of the systemically most important firms based on the following policies:

- risk-based capital requirements;
- leverage limits;
- liquidity requirements;
- resolution plan and credit exposure report requirements;
- concentration limits;
- a contingent capital requirement;
- enhanced public disclosure;
- short-term debt limits;
- overall risk management requirements (Acharya et al. 2011, p. 92).

Regarding the *resolution authority* within the Dodd–Frank Act, Simon Johnson (Johnson, 2011c) argues that the resolution authority "approach to dealing with very big banks has, in effect, failed before it even started" because it applies only domestically and doesn't extend internationally to resolve big institutions with cross-border operations. He also warns that there is limited evidence the authority could be used preemptively, before losses threaten the system.

For the scope of measuring systemic risk, Acharya et al. (2011) recommend not to rely only on the classification-based criteria with specific thresholds, but to employ market-based measures that are more continuously variable. These measures are generally based on stock market data. One of these measures is called *Marginal Expected Shortfall (MES)* and estimates the loss that the equity of a given firm can expect if the broad market experiences a large fall. Thus they see "two valid approaches – relying on simple systemic risk criteria such as, size, leverage, and interconnectedness and relying on market-based estimates of systemic risk – as a complementary control" (Acharya et al., 2011, pp. 94–95).

According to Acharya et al. (2011b), the definition of capital in the Dodd–Frank Act and Basel III do not perfectly coincide. The proposed leverage ratio in Basel III is actually lower. The Dodd–Frank Act goes further by requiring that bank holding companies with a least $50 billion in assets or systemically important institutions maintain a debt-to-equity ratio of no more than 15 to 1 (or a leverage ratio of a least 6.5 percent) in case of grave threat to the financial stability (Acharya et al., 2011b, pp. 154–155).

Regarding the regulation of the OTC derivatives under the Dodd–Frank Act, Acharya et al. (2011) indicate that there are four key areas where the proposed OTC reforms will have the greatest global impact. These are:

1. consolidation within the US and across countries of clearinghouses and exchanges, and potentially also of large dealer banks;
2. emergence of global transparency platforms and services related to the processing of newly made available data on derivatives transactions and positions;
3. gradual transition of (some) end-user hedging demands to centralized platforms and exchanges;
4. separation of market making and proprietary trading/asset management positions in large financial institutions (Acharya et al., 2011c, pp. 367–405).

Altman et al. (2011) say:

> *The Dodd–Frank Act presents new rules for internal control and governance, independence, transparency and liability standards and establish an important supervisory responsibility in the Office of Credit Ratings at the SEC to "administer the rules of the Commission with respect to the practices of the Nationally Recognized Statistical Rating Organization (NRSRO) in determining ratings, for the protection of users of credit ratings; and in the public interest; to promote accuracy in credit ratings issued by NRSRO; and to ensure that such ratings are not unduly influenced by conflict of interest." (Altman et al., 2011, pp. 453–454)*

The Act, according to these authors, requires an internal control structure and an annual ratings review process, which gives the SEC the right to suspend or revoke the registration of an NRSRO with respect to a particular class or subclass of securities if the NRSRO has failed to comply over a sustained period of time. Furthermore the Act requires that the NRSRO should provide more disclosure on ratings information and more transparency in ratings performance and methodologies and procedures (Altman et al., 2011, pp. 453–454).

For these authors, the Act is a clear attempt to hold the rating agencies accountable, however, they also identified a major potential weakness. This is the fact that the success of the new legislation depends on the ability of the SEC to implement effective oversight (but in the past they have not been very successful on this matter). The authors' suggestion is to explore the creation of the equivalent of the PCAOB for rating agencies (Altman et al., 2011, pp. 453–454).

Regarding the conflicts of interest of rating agencies with their clients, the authors highlight that the Act prohibits "the sales and marketing considerations of an NRSRO from influencing the production of ratings by the NRSRO." The Act does not allow compliance officers to work on ratings or sales and installs a one-year look-back review when an employee of an NRSRO goes to work for an underwriter or a security firm that is subject to an NRSRO rating (Altman et al., 2011, p. 456).

Regarding the securitization reform, according to Richardson et al. (2011) Title IX, Subtitle D of the Dodd–Frank Act "largely misses the big picture" since the regulation requires a securitizer to retain "not less than 5 percent of the credit risk for any asset" that is "not a qualified residential mortgage" which seems to be a "one size fits all" type of solution (Richardson et al, 2011, pp. 477–481).

As stated earlier, regarding the compensation reform, the Dodd–Frank Act has introduced the most important reform in corporate governance since the 2002 SOX. The Act makes important recommendations about compensation with the following rules (Carpenter et al., 2011):

- say on pay;
- structure of compensation committee;
- disclosure of pay versus performance;
- claw-backs;
- hedging strategies;
- regulatory oversight of compensation in financial firms (Carpenter et al., 2011, pp. 497–499).

Critics of the current framework of the Dodd–Frank Wall Street Reform and Consumer Protection Act, such as Luigi Zingales (2011), have stated that apparently, as it stands today, few of the pages of the Act address any problem suspected to have caused the financial crisis (Zingales, 2011).

In particular, the criticism focuses on the lack of effective regulatory reforms regarding the role and responsibility of the credit rating agencies and their suspected conflicts of interest with powerful issuers of asset-backed securities (ABS), MBS, CDOs, and other complex derivatives. Even today, he says, bond investors tend to rely heavily on their risk assessment for their investments with the result that powerful issuers might benefit of laxer criteria (Zingales, 2011).

A second area of weakness identified by Zingales (2011) in the Dodd–Frank Act is the significant dependence of shadow banking on the official banking sector's liquidity and guarantees, and thus ultimately on the government. A third area of weakness concerns the limits on financial institutions' leverage. These, according to Zingales (2011), will only be changed in the next decade. Furthermore, even in the countries where the Basel III Framework will be implemented, the timeline for the full introduction of all the proposed changes will not be before 2019 (Zingales, 2011). I suggested (Pezzuto, 2008; 2010a, pp. 119–123), regarding the shadow banking industry, for example, that all financial instruments should be (mandatorily) traded only in regulated markets and that contracts should be, as much as possible, standardized and settled through clearinghouses, rather than being cleared directly between the contracting parties as they still are in the OTC market (Pezzuto, 2008, 2010a, pp. 119–123). Furthermore, I also suggested that all banks and financial institutions should be held responsible for the securitizations they create, thus the OTD model should not be used anymore, or at least it should be used only with mortgage loans with full recourse or "skin in the game" rule (on the issuer) from the investors and purchasers of MBS (Pezzuto, 2010a, pp. 119–123).

According to Zingales (2011), money-market funds' perverse incentives to take on excessive risk remain largely intact and, apparently, problems related to corporate governance (executive compensation policies), such as incentive pay, have been ignored by the Dodd–Frank Act. I made a recommendation on this same topic in 2010 when I suggested that regulators should develop more transparent corporate governance rules for financial institutions and compensation schemes for the management of these organizations to overcome the issue of excessive risk-taking (Pezzuto, 2010a, pp. 119–123). Zingales (2011) indicated also that the most highly touted change considered in the

Dodd–Frank Act is the one related to the separation between proprietary trading and commercial banking (also known as the Volcker rule, after former US Federal Reserve chairman Paul Volcker) seems to have nothing to do with what caused the crisis, and most likely, he states, was approved because it was ineffective (Zingales, 2011). Furthermore, The Dodd–Frank Act seems to provide a loophole for banks that claim to be *hedging* their bets. JPMorgan's recent big loss should encourage government officials to question the utility of the hedging exception (Kerin, 2012). In fact, in order to improve the safety of the financial system, the Dodd–Frank reform law aims to assure that most derivative deals would be executed on a *clearinghouse* that collects collateral from buyers and sellers to reduce the risk that one party's default would disrupt the broader market. Since, however, foreign-exchange swaps and forwards are short-term transactions and are already traded in a highly transparent, liquid and efficient market, the US Treasury has *exempted foreign-exchange swaps and forwards from Dodd–Frank Act rules*. Given the significant size ($648 trillion) of the global OTC derivatives market, some concerns exist on the resilience of the risk management system and new financial regulation to avoid to recurrence of another systemic crisis like the one of 2008.

Interviewed by Bloomberg, Stanford University's Business School Professor Darrell Duffie said that *foreign-exchange swaps* and the *forwards market* has taken voluntary steps to curb risks. He also added: "But the remaining amount of counter-party risk in the FX derivatives market is enormous. Does the logic of this exemption imply that *CDS* or *interest rate swaps* should also be exempted from regulation once practices improve in those markets? Surely that should not be the case" (Brush, 2012).

According to Craig Pirrong, Professor of Finance at the University of Houston, counterparty credit risk between OTC derivatives counterparties related to liquid standardized products can be partially mitigated through the use of clearinghouses since they require collateral (or margin) from their counterparties, through the netting of positions, and through other forms of credit enhancement. He also stated, however, that in order to avoid potential moral hazard and adverse section issues, even using clearinghouses, it is essential to have relatively high membership criteria and that the clearinghouses are subject to the same prudential oversight as that required for large SIFI (Pirrong, 2011).

Adrian Blundell-Wignall and Paul E. Atkinson of the OECD, however, argue that for G-SIFIs, "netting of derivatives provides no protection against market risk, and that the collateral and margin calls associated with the large movements in their balance sheets dominated by derivatives, are both pro-cyclical and dangerous." Thus the conclusion they come up with is to "separate retail banking from securities businesses and ensure the former are (particularly in Europe) well capitalized" (Blundell-Wignall and Atkinson, 2012b).

New York University Stern School of Business Professors Viral V. Acharya, Lasse H. Pedersen, Thomas Philippon, and Matthew Richardson (2010) propose that financial firms should be charged a sort of tax on systemic risk. In other words, these firms should "be required to purchase contingent capital insurance, that is, insurance against the losses they incur during systemic crises." They explain that "the cost of this insurance determines the firm's systemic risk tax" (Acharya et al., 2010).

Although it might be true that the main root cause of the financial crisis is probably not directly related to the unification of proprietary trading and commercial banking, it is well-known that the repeal of the Glass–Steagall Act in 1999 contributed to the so-called "too-big-to-fail" doctrine and the consequent moral hazard in conjunction with the opaque OTD securitization model of non-recourse lending products and a massive target of subprime borrowers subject to limited or no credit screening processes. The progressive and widespread deregulation of the financial markets and the non-regulated and monitored shadow banking system have certainly created the perverse conditions for the financial meltdown.

The limits of the Basel III Framework have already been stated, both in terms of phased implementation over the years and the inadequate capital requirements to manage banking system stability during periods of crises such as the one that started in 2008, and will not adequately mitigate future crises. Simon Johnson (2010) has clearly stated that capital requirements alone cannot save the banking system from systemic risks. Another important financial reform that is missing is the serious and unquestionable enforcement in the future of no bail-out policies for the banking sector. In the worst case scenario of an "inevitable" bail-out to avoid potential depression, the new financial regulations should have introduced a mandatory corporate governance change (forced "change management" policy with "no" golden parachutes or severance packages but just the guarantee of an investigation) (Johnson, 2010).

The financial reforms have to assure that the banking and financial sector have *ring-fencing rules* to avoid their systemic contagion and collapse. It makes no sense to introduce costly reforms such as the Dodd–Frank Act (the result of three years of study and research into the root causes of the financial crisis by the FCIC) and then have to bail-out the banking system over and over again.

John Taylor (2010), a Professor of Economics at Stanford, a Senior Fellow at the Hoover Institution, and author of *Getting Off Track: How Government Actions and Interventions Caused, Prolonged and Worsened the Financial Crisis* (Hoover Press, 2009) says the following about the Dodd–Frank Act: "The sheer complexity of the 2,319-page Dodd–Frank financial reform bill is certainly a threat to future economic growth. But if you sift through the many sections and subsections, you find much more than complexity to worry about" (Taylor, 2010).

"The main problem with the bill is that it is based on a misdiagnosis of the causes of the financial crisis, which is not surprising since the bill was rolled out before the congressionally mandated Financial Crisis Inquiry Commission finished its diagnosis" (Taylor, 2010).

The biggest misdiagnosis is the presumption that the Government did not have enough power to avoid the crisis. But the Federal Reserve had the power to avoid the monetary excesses that accelerated the housing boom that went bust in 2007. The New York Fed had the power to stop Citigroup's questionable lending and trading decisions and, with hundreds of regulators on the premises of such large banks, the Fed should have had the information to do so. The SEC could have insisted on reasonable liquidity rules to prevent investment banks from relying so much on short-term borrowing through repurchase agreements to fund long-term investments. And the Treasury working with the Fed had the power to intervene with troubled financial firms, and in fact used this power in a highly discretionary way to create an on-again off-again bail-out policy that spooked the markets and led to the panic in the fall of 2008 (Taylor, 2010).

Taylor also stated the following:

Instead of trying to make implementation of existing government regulations more effective, the bill vastly increases the power of government in ways that are unrelated to the recent crisis and may even encourage future crises (Taylor, 2010). The bill creates a new resolution, or orderly liquidation, authority in which the Federal Deposit Insurance Corporation (FDIC) can intervene between any complex financial institution and its creditors in any way it wants to. Effectively the bill institutionalizes the harmful bailout process by giving the government more discretionary power to intervene. The FDIC does not have the capability to take over large, complex financial institutions without causing disruption, so such firms and their creditors are likely to be bailed out again. The problem of "too big to fail" remains, and any cozy relationship between certain large financial institutions and the government that existed before the crisis will continue. (Taylor, 2010)

Another false remedy, according to Taylor, is a new *Bureau of Consumer Financial Protection* housed at, and financed by, the Fed. The new bureau will write rules for every type of financial service, most of which (such as payday loans) have no conceivable connection with the crisis. Yet another false remedy is a new Office of Financial Research at the Treasury that will look into systemic risk. The unrealistic hope here is that it will somehow do a better job than the Fed, which already had that responsibility leading up to the crisis (Taylor, 2010).

The bill does reduce the power of the Fed to intervene to bail-out the creditors of a single financial institution, as the Fed did in the case of Bear Stearns and AIG. But at the same time it authorizes bail-outs if the financial institution is a participant in any program or facility with broad-based eligibility that the Fed has established for emergency purposes, which is hardly a constraint on bail-outs in an interconnected financial system. It also gives complete discretion to the Fed and the Treasury to determine the policies and procedures governing emergency lending (Taylor, 2010).

Yet another false remedy, according to Taylor (2010), is a new regulation for non-financial firms that use financial instruments to reduce risks of interest-rate or exchange-rate volatility. The bill gives the *Commodity Futures Trading Corporation (CFTC)* authority to place margin requirements, which call for higher collateral on risk-reducing instruments, on such firms even though they had nothing to do with the crisis; their customers and employees will be penalized by the increased costs. And while the bill sensibly merges the *Office of Thrift Supervision* into the *Office of the Comptroller of the Currency*, it creates more regulatory ambiguity by assigning both the SEC and the CFTC the new job of regulating OTC derivatives with imprecise guidance on who does what (Taylor, 2010).

Other innocent bystanders hit by the legislation, according to Taylor (2010), are the stockholders of firms that had nothing to do with the crisis. The bill gives the SEC the explicit authority to impose "proxy access" provisions empowering shareholders to run their own candidates for boards. Research by David Larcker of Stanford Business School shows that stock prices react negatively to proxy access regulations (Taylor, 2010).

Some claim that corporate governance problems were a cause of the crisis because corporate boards of large complex banks did not prevent risky lending practices. But those who make this argument did not do so before the crisis, and they do not mention that hundreds of government regulators at these banks on a daily basis also failed to deal with the problem (Taylor, 2010).

By far the most significant error of omission in the bill is the failure to reform Fannie Mae and Freddie Mac, the Government-sponsored enterprises (GSE) that encouraged the origination of risky mortgages in the first place by purchasing them with the support of many in Congress. Some excuse this omission by saying that it can be handled later. But the purpose of "comprehensive reform" is to balance competing political interests and reach compromise; that will be much harder to do now that the Dodd–Frank bill became law. For example, many of the same activists who supported proxy-access provisions are those that also favor the Fannie and Freddie subsidies (Taylor, 2010).

Another serious error of omission is reform of the bankruptcy code to allow large complex financial firms to go through a predictable, rules-based Chapter 11 process without financial disruption and without bail-outs – a far better alternative than the highly discretionary resolution authority in the bill. Without this orderly bankruptcy alternative, the too-big-to-fail problem will not go away. At least Section 216 of the bill calls for a study of the matter, but this is obviously no substitute for action (Taylor, 2010).

The continuing debate over the Dodd–Frank bill in the days since it emerged from conference is good news. People may be waking up to the fact that the bill does not do what its supporters claim. It does not prevent future financial crises. Rather, it makes them more likely and in the meantime impedes economic growth (Taylor, 2010).

Yale economist Robert Shiller said that the Dodd–Frank financial reform law does not solve the problem of the too-big-to-fail issue which is the implicit government protection of large financial institutions. He also added that systemic risk, which prompted government bail-outs in 2008, is inherent in the modern financial machine. Dodd–Frank goes in the right direction, but he warned that it doesn't go far enough (Alden, 2010).

It is also critical to avoid excessive interference of the financial industry in the political system through new regulations that impose more transparency on political campaigns' financing by powerful financial institutions and the financial sector's lobbies. The same rules should also require more transparency on the independence of mind and spirit of mass media, academic, and industry experts' on analyses, publications, and reports related to the 2007–2009 financial crisis and other topics related to the financial industry. All opinion leaders (that is, political, academic, editorial, industry-related), when they express their opinions on the financial sector, should clearly report their affiliations with the financial institutions, and any grants or other financial benefits they receive from them, or any potential conflicts of interest they may have.

However, Rajan states that the failure of economists to spot the crisis is mainly due to specialization (economics has become highly compartmentalized), "the difficulty of forecasting," efficient markets ideology, "and the disengagement of much of the profession from the real world" (Rajan, 2011).

In summary, the Dodd–Frank Act – which is a sprawling piece of legislation, numbering over 2,300 pages in length and requiring federal regulators to embark on more than 400 rule-makings – according to former Secretary of the Treasury, Timothy Geithner, ended the era of too-big-to-fail institutions, strengthened capital requirements, stress tests, and enhanced transparency in the shadow banking market. The Dodd–Frank Act does not seem to effectively address yet the issue of reducing speculative bets on all financial derivatives. The use of clearinghouses for derivatives transactions seems to be a significant progress of this new regulation but at the moment, unfortunately, it is still not mandatory to trade transactions on electronic exchange platforms. "Section 941 of the Dodd–Frank Act requires securitizers to retain no less than 5 percent of the credit risk in assets they sell into a securitization. But Section 941 also provides that the risk retention requirements do not apply if the only assets in the pool collateralizing the ABS are 'qualified residential mortgages' (QRMs)." Furthermore, at the moment the Dodd–Frank Act still does not regulate the GSE (Fannie Mae, Freddie Mac, and Ginnie Mae) which account for the majority of MBS issuance in the US (Bachus and Hensarling, 2011).

An additional loophole in the Dodd–Frank Act has been identified by Matthew Richardson, an Economics Professor at New York University's Stern School of Business. He argue that the Volcker rule, drafted to prevent banks from taking on excessive risk, limits short-term investments made with firms' capital but it does not stop financial firms from making longer-term bets. In fact Matthew Richardson stated the following: "Bets that last months can go awry and belong outside federally backed banks" and also "from a systemic-risk perspective, it's really the longer-term holdings which are of issue" (Abelson, 2013).

Kimberly Krawiec, a Law Professor at Duke University in Durham, North Carolina, also added on the topic: "There were so many elements of the rule that in order to get it passed had to be softened quite a bit, and that may very well have been one" and "there's going to be more prop trading than what the general public and perhaps even some experts believe" (Abelson, 2013).

Thus, although some good norms have been introduced so far with the Dodd–Frank Act, there still seems to be a long way to go to assure fully comprehensive and effective financial regulation and to avoid other potential systemic crises.

In particular, regarding the OTC derivatives, the regulation both in the US and in the EU (Dodd–Frank, The Committee on Payment and Settlements Systems (CPSS)–International Organization of Securities Commissions (IOSCO), Basel III, and European Market Infrastructure Regulation – EMIR) has started to follow the proposals of the Pittsburgh G20 Summit of September 2009. These proposals endorsed the requirement that "all standardized OTC derivative contracts should be traded on exchanges or electronic trading platforms, where appropriate, and cleared through central counterparties by end-2012 at the latest. OTC derivative contracts should be reported to trade repositories. Non-centrally cleared contracts should be subject to higher capital requirements. We ask the FSB and its relevant members to assess regularly implementation and whether it is sufficient to improve transparency in the derivatives markets, mitigate systemic risk, and protect against market abuse" (Quarry et al., 2012, p. 4).

Thus, according to the G20 proposal *standardized OTC derivatives* (broadly defined class of OTC derivatives) should be cleared through *central counterparties (CCP)* and *OTC derivatives contracts* should be reported to *trade repositories* with commitments to a common approach to margin rules for uncleared derivatives transactions. The objective of the policy makers is to:

- improve transparency;
- reduce counterparty credit risk interconnections related to OTC contracts;
- keep safety and simplicity as first principles;
- ensure adequate incentives for central OTC derivatives clearing;
- seek more transatlantic consistency;
- strengthen clearinghouse risk management requirements (Quarry et al., 2012, pp. 2–3).

In fact, as reported by Alexander (2011), the failure of relatively few players (OTC counterparties) involved in very large numbers of OTC trades to price adequately the risk they were exposed to, caused a significant increase of systemic risk (Alexander, 2011).

The same author also stresses the point that "the obligation to clear OTC contracts under both the EU's proposed Market Infrastructure Regulation (EMIR) and the Dodd–Frank Act would result in increased collateralization of OTC and swap trades, reduced counterparty credit risk, and greater liquidity in the wholesale derivatives markets" (Alexander, 2011, p. 9).

He concludes his analysis by stating that CCP enhances the resilience of financial markets, creating a safer environment that embraces *mark-to-market valuation*, daily *collateralization and monitoring of all positions, multilateral netting, mutualization of risk, and a default fund* (Alexander, 2011, p. 9).

The 2010 Dodd–Frank Wall Street Reform and Consumer Protection Act (Dodd–Frank) aims to regulate the over-the-counter (OTC) derivatives market in order to achieve greater accountability and transparency, "Title VII of Dodd–Frank imposes higher capital and margin requirements, mandates electronic trading and central clearing, increases reporting and recordkeeping requirements, and introduces more rigorous business conduct standards" (Deloitte Development LLC, 2013b, p. 1).

The new regulation on OTC derivatives focus affects the following topics:

- "Electronic trading via swap execution facilities (SEFs) – require the creation of, and mandate to use, SEFs (platforms) for OTC derivative and the standardization of contracts" (Deloitte Development LLC, 2013b, pp. 1–6).
- "Clearing through central counterparties (CCPs) – mandatory clearing of certain swaps transactions through a designated clearing organization (DCO) requires an increase in capital requirements posed by CCPs. Contributions to the CCP guarantee fund and increased initial margin requirements both increase capital and funding needs" (Deloitte Development LLC, 2013b, pp. 1–6). However, the Financial Stability Oversight Council (FSOC) says in an annual report that industry concern of a collateral drought is unfounded" (Puaar, 2013). The US securities regulator (SEC) proposes that the rules governing OTC derivatives (security-based swaps) will apply to cross-border transactions (Lynch, 2013).
- "Reporting to swaps data repositories (SDRs) of all OTC derivatives for increased market transparency involves: (1) real-time reporting requirements; (2) swap data record-keeping and recording; (3) historical swaps reporting requirements" (Deloitte Development LLC, 2013b, pp. 1–6).
- "Adherence to business conduct standards." These standards include: "know your counterparty" (KYC) and are designed to prohibit certain abusive practices, mandate disclosures of material information to counterparties, and require SDs and MSPs also to undertake additional due diligence relating to dealings with counterparties" (Deloitte Development LLC, 2013b, pp. 1–6).

Furthermore, it is critical to improve the transparency of risk management practices of central counterparties. These clearers must be able to provide to banks sufficient data on their own risks in order to improve their transparency and to reduce potential systemic risks. Shifting for example over-the-counter trading to centralized clearing houses requires that the latter can assure banks that tough collateral and margin requirements are in place and that they can guarantee a crucial safety buffer.

Former FDIC chairman, Sheila Bair, in her 2012 book, *Bull By The Horns: Fighting to Save Main Street From Wall Street and Wall Street From Itself*, proposes to reform US financial regulation and, in particular, "careers in financial regulation (that is, examiners) as lifelong careers choices" – similar to the Foreign Service – rather than a revolving door to a better-paying job in the private sector. These regulators should also receive stronger training programs, ongoing educational support, and better pay. The federal regulatory staff might instead accept rotations to other agencies. She also added that there should be a lifetime ban on regulators working for financial institutions they have regulated (Bair, 2012; 2013).

Sheila Bair also proposed in her recommendations to reform the Senate Confirmation Process because to recruit "high-quality people of integrity to serve in government, we need to treat them with courtesy and respect, not as potential hostages in a high-stakes game of political cat and mouse. The Senate needs to reform the confirmation process. Otherwise, the only people left willing to take those jobs will be politically connected Washington lobbyists" (Bair, 2012; 2013).

In a telephone interview in March 2013 she also added that "US regulators lack the nerve to designate non-bank financial companies systemically important and aren't doing their job." Furthermore, she stated in the same interview that "what's frustrating is the ones that we said were systemic during the crisis, like AIG and GE Capital, they can't even say that they're systemic. We seem to be able to decide in a nanosecond if it involves shoveling taxpayer money out the door to keep these guys afloat" (Katz, 2013).

Sheila Bair chairs the Systemic Risk Council (SRC or Council), a group of prominent academics, financial experts, and former government officials such as Paul Volcker, Brooksley Born, Simon Johnson, John S. Reed, and others, created by The Pew Charitable Trusts and the CFA Institute to monitor the Dodd–Frank implementation and raise attention to policy makers, regulators, media, and general public if needed reforms go awry (systemicriskcouncil, 2013).

Another important consideration for an improved regulation of derivatives is the awareness that currently (April 2013) the US accounting rules allow banks to record a smaller portion of their derivatives than European peers. That underestimation of the risks financial firms face may affect how much capital they need. The US Financial Accounting Standards Board and the International Accounting Standards Board still do not converge in a common bookkeeping system. "Netting allows banks and trading partners to add up the positions they have with each other and show what would be owed if all contracts had to be settled suddenly." According to Anat Admati, a finance professor at Stanford University, "when a bank's solvency is in doubt, derivatives partners demand to be paid immediately, causing a run." "These liabilities do matter in times of distress," said Admati, author of the book *The Bankers' New Clothes*. She also added: "by netting, you are hiding fragilities" (Onaran, 2013).

Rating Agencies' Practices and New Rules for Improved Governance

Principle V.F. of the 2004 OECD Principles of Corporate Governance states that:

> *The corporate governance framework should be complemented by an effective approach that addresses and promotes the provision of analysis or advice by analysts, brokers, rating agencies and others that is relevant to decisions by investors, free from material conflict of interest that might compromise the integrity if their analysis or advice. (OECD, 2009, p. 48)*

Thus a key role in companies' and financial institutions' corporate governance processes is also played by the quality and reliability of the reports issued by credit rating agencies. The 2007–2009 financial crisis has demonstrated the critical failure of such analyses and reports.

The SEC in its report no. 446-A titled "SEC's Oversight of Bear Stearns and Related Entities" (2008a) and in their "Summary Report of Issues Identified in the Commission Staff's Examinations of Select Credit Rating Agencies" (2008b) for example confirmed that the credit rating agencies were under considerable commercial pressure in the years preceding the financial crisis to meet the needs of their clients and to undertake ratings quickly (SEC, 2008a, pp. 1–46.; SEC, 2008b, pp. 1–39).

Following the dramatic events of the financial crisis, the quality of the work performed by the credit rating agencies has been significantly questioned by the Financial Stability Forum (2008), as well as by the International Organization of Securities Commissions (IOSCO, 2008) and the SEC (2008b).

Even the FSA in the UK has reported such issues stating that: "Poor credit assessments by credit rating agencies have contributed both to the buildup to and the unfolding of recent events" (Kirkpatrick, 2009, pp. 24–25).

The UK FSA claimed that, "credit rating agencies assigned high ratings to complex structured subprime debt based on inadequate historical data and in some cases flawed models" thus causing a generalized loss of confidence in ratings by investors (Kirkpatrick, 2009, p. 25).

The SEC (2008) has issued "a highly critical report about the practices of credit rating agencies and has proposed a three-fold set of comprehensive reforms to regulate conflicts of interest, disclosures, internal policies and business practices" of credit rating agencies (Kirkpatrick, 2009, p. 25).

According to the proposed reforms by the SEC, credit rating agencies should not be involved in auditing their own work or to be more specific, they should not be rating an instrument that they had themselves advised on how to structure. This reform proposal is evidently based on the evidence that prior to the financial crisis credit rating agencies were significantly involved in advising clients on how to structure their instruments so as to obtain a desired rating. Thus, a clear conflict of interest emerged from this oversight analysis since the originators were paying not only for the ratings but also to obtain a specified rating (Kirkpatrick, 2009, p. 25).

Another serious weakness of the rating process related to the financial crisis was the way the ratings were used. "The Senior Supervisors Group (2008) reported that some banks relied entirely on the ratings and did not establish their own risk analysis of the instruments." It is quite evident that thanks to the OTD securitization model and the risk transfer of the instruments to the investors, banks were no longer committed to managing risk (moral hazard) and thus they concentrated only to place as many instruments as possible on the market at the lowest cost. They apparently only complied with the formal requirements of having a credit rating agency formally assessing their "toxic" instruments as low-risk assets, thus relying on the implicit guarantee that a good rating necessarily means a low-risk security (Kirkpatrick, 2009, pp. 7–8; Senior Supervisors Group, 2008, pp. 1–20).

Some market participants and regulators have proposed to eliminate references in regulations that establish the use of ratings and encouraging internal risk assessments and due diligence by investors, banks, and other players. I believe that credit rating agencies should be made financially accountable for the quality of the ratings they issue (Pezzuto, 2010a, pp. 119–123).

As reported by White (2009):

The rating agencies' overly optimistic ratings allowed the packagers of these securities to sell large "senior" slices as "safe" (low-interest bearing) investments and thus allowed substantial profits to be made on the packaging process, which in turn encouraged more subprime mortgages to be originated, etc. The rating agencies were also criticized for delays in downgrading these securities after other market participants had already recognized the problems (e.g. Lehman Brothers). These criticisms echoed others earlier in the decade, when Moody's and S&P had maintained "investment grade" ratings on Enron's debt until only five days before that company's bankruptcy filing in December 2001. (White, 2009)

Frank Partnoy (2009), Professor at the University of San Diego School of Law, wrote a white paper in 2009 commissioned by the Council of Institutional Investors to educate its members, policy makers, and the general public about proposals to regulate credit rating agencies and their potential impact on investors (although the views and opinions expressed in the paper are those of Professor Partnoy and do not necessarily represent views or opinions of Council members, board of directors, or staff). Partnoy states in the paper that "the global credit crisis has called into question this role of rating agencies as financial gatekeepers. The debacle was fueled in part by credit rating agencies 'licensing' complex, risky financial instruments with triple-A ratings they did not deserve. Both regulators and institutional investors relied on those ratings, to their peril" (Partnoy, 2009, p. 1).

Partnoy (2009) in his paper explores the pros and cons of several proposals for redesigning credit rating agency regulation. He focuses on two areas of primary importance – oversight and accountability – and offers specific recommendations in both areas.

Oversight: Congress should create a new *Credit Rating Agency Oversight Board (CRAOB)* with the power to regulate rating agency practices, including disclosure, conflicts of interest, and rating methodologies, as well as the ability to coordinate the reduction of reliance on ratings. Alternatively, he wrote, "Congress could enhance the authority of the SEC to grant it similar power to oversee the rating business."

Accountability: Congress should eliminate the effective exemption of rating agencies from liability and make rating agencies more accountable by treating them the same as banks, accountants, and lawyers (Partnoy, 2009, p. 1).

He also stated, "As financial gatekeepers with little incentive to 'get it right,' credit rating agencies pose a systemic risk. Creating a rating agency oversight board and strengthening the accountability of rating agencies is thus consistent with the broader push by US policy makers for greater systemic risk oversight. Over the long term, other measures for assessing credit risk may become more acceptable and accessible to regulators and investors. Meanwhile, a more powerful overseer and broader accountability would help reposition credit rating agencies as true information intermediaries" (Partnoy, 2009, p. 1).

David P. Cluchey (2011), Professor of Law at the University of Maine School of Law in his paper titled "The Financial Crisis and the Response of The United States: Will Dodd–Frank Protect Us From The Next Crisis?" indicates that the credit rating agencies' failure to identify and to respond to accounting improprieties at Enron and several other large corporations in the late 1990s led to a provision in the SOX requiring the SEC to study the role of the credit rating agencies and to report to Congress with recommendations for additional regulation. Congress enacted the Credit Rating Agency Reform Act of 2006 and the Act gave the SEC the authority to qualify NRSROs. According to Cluchey's paper, Congress found that credit rating agencies are of systemic importance to the US financial system and that their ratings on structured financial products were inaccurate and "contributed significantly to the mismanagement of risk by financial institutions and investors, which in turn adversely impacted the health of the economy in the United States and around the world" (Cluchey, 2011, pp. 216–219).

David P. Cluchey reports that, in Dodd–Frank, Congress approved a series of amendments to the Credit Rating Agency Reform Act of 2006, including a requirement that the agencies maintain an internal control structure, validated annually, to ensure that policies and methodologies for determining credit ratings are adhered to within the agency. The Dodd–Frank Act added to the sanctions available to the SEC in the event of a violation of the Act, allowing the Commission recourse against individuals as well as against the agency itself and providing that the Commission could revoke the registration of a rating agency as to a particular class or subclass of securities. The rating agency is required to keep sales and marketing from influencing credit ratings and to monitor conflicts of interest potentially generated by job offers from clients. Credit rating agency compliance officers are to be protected from conflicts of interest, including conflicts relating to compensation, and are given the responsibility to develop processes for receiving and handling complaints, including anonymous complaints. The SEC is required to establish an Office of Credit Ratings within the Commission. The office is required to conduct detailed annual examinations of each credit rating agency registered with the Commission and the Commission is required to make the essential findings of these examinations public. The Commission must enact rules providing for transparency on the ratings performance of the agencies and mandating substantial disclosure of each agency's rating methodology. Dodd–Frank imposes a series of corporate governance requirements for credit rating agencies, including the requirement that at least one half of the board of directors of the agency shall be independent (as defined by the statute), that the compensation of the independent directors not be linked to the business performance of the rating agency, that independent directors have a term on the board not exceeding five years, and that the board of directors has specific duties to oversee methodologies for determining credit ratings, conflicts of interest, the internal control system, and compensation and promotion policies (Cluchey, 2011, pp. 216–219).

In January 2013, the European Parliament approved new rules that should promote more competition, transparency, and accountability in the credit rating industry. Currently the global market of credit ratings is dominated (with cumulative market share of approximately 90 percent) by three firms (Fitch, Moody's, and Standard and Poor's). Furthermore, following the principles endorsed by the FSB in 2010, the new rules should also help reduce reliance on external credit ratings wherever possible, with suitable alternative standards of creditworthiness assessment (that is, internal credit risk assessments). Even the Basel Committee on Banking Supervision has proposed to reduce overreliance on credit rating agencies' ratings in the regulatory capital framework. The same orientation has been followed also in the US, with the Dodd–Frank Wall Street Reform and Consumer Protection Act, which has strengthened rules on credit rating agencies. In fact, in compliance with section 939A of the Dodd–Frank Act, the SEC is exploring ways to reduce regulatory reliance on external credit ratings and to replace them with alternative criteria (Europa, 2013a).

As reported in January 2013 by Michel Barnier, the European Commissioner for Internal Market and Services, in an interview: "2013 is a moment of truth for Europe." He also said: "We are still in the midst of a crisis, but the worst is behind us. The atmosphere has changed."

He has welcomed the agreement on new rules on credit rating agencies reached by the European Parliament. He also added: "This agreement will considerably improve the quality of ratings. Credit rating agencies will have to be more transparent when rating sovereign states and will have to follow stricter rules which will make them more accountable for mistakes in case of negligence or intent" (Europa, 2013b).

The new EU rules on credit rating agencies aim to achieve the following goals:

- to encourage more competition and the entrance of more players in the credit rating industry and to limit the high market concentration;
- to reduce investors' over-reliance on external ratings, requiring financial institutions to strengthen their own internal credit risk assessment;
- to mitigate the risk of conflicts of interest that threaten independence of credit rating agencies ("the new rules will require credit rating agencies to disclose publicly if a shareholder with 5 percent or more of the capital or voting rights of the credit rating agency holds 5 percent or more of a rated entity, and would prohibit a shareholder of a credit rating agency with 10 percent or more of the capital or voting rights from holding 10 percent or more of a rated entity");
- to prohibit ownership of 5 percent or more of the capital or the voting rights in more than one credit rating agency, unless the agencies concerned belong to the same group (cross-shareholding);
- to engage (the issuers) with at least two different credit rating agencies for the rating for structured finance instruments given the role these complex financial products have had in the financial crisis;
- to switch (the issuers) to a different agency every four years (mandatory rotation rule, not applicable to small credit rating agencies, or to issuers employing at least four credit rating agencies each rating more than 10 percent of the total number of outstanding rated structured finance instruments) for structured finance products with underlying re-securitized assets. Mandatory rotation would not be a requirement for the endorsement and equivalence assessment of third country credit rating agencies. In the original intentions of the European Commission, however, the mandatory rotation rule was not only meant for complex financial products;
- to increase disclosure and transparency on sovereign debt ratings and on the reasons underlying a rating decision;
- to empower investors to sue a credit rating agency which, intentionally or with gross negligence, infringes the obligations set out in the Credit Rating Agency Regulation, thereby causing damage to investors (Europa, 2013a).

The EU policy makers have deferred until the year 2020 the decision to explore the possibility of eliminating regulatory reliance (that is, the Basel Capital Requirement Framework) on external credit ratings and they have deferred until the year 2016 the possible creation of a European Agency to rate sovereign debt (Davenport, 2013).

To conclude, apparently it seems that the new regulations on the rating agencies should increase transparency and independence, and reliability of their ratings, since they potentially risk either revocation of the registration of an agency with the SEC or law suits, but according to a number of analysts and authors the rules approved are still too bureaucratic and complex to manage and to control, and do not represent a significant overhaul for the industry to avoid potential conflicts of interest or misjudgment of risk, which have greatly contributed to cause the 2007–2009 financial crisis. As stated in January 2013 by Sven Giegold, a German member of the European Parliament who played a key role in negotiating the law with EU countries, "This is no great breakthrough" (Cluchey, 2011, pp. 216–219; Davenport, 2013). Laurence Norman and Frances Robinson (2013) of the *Wall Street Journal* are even more critical of these new rules, stating in January 2013 the following: "The European Parliament approved new rules that will restrict credit-rating firms' freedom to change sovereign-debt ratings and will make the organizations more vulnerable to lawsuits" (Norman and Robinson, 2013).

Corporate Governance on Disclosure, and Accounting Standards and Regulatory Reform Needs

Another significant failure in banks and financial firms' corporate governance that contributed to the crisis is the one related to the disclosure of risk factors. In fact, Principle V.A. of the 2004 OECD Principles of Corporate Governance calls for the disclosure of material information on the "foreseeable risk factors" and Principle V.B. states that "information should be prepared and disclosed in accordance with high quality standards of accounting and financial and non-financial disclosure."

After the Enron scandal, the US accounting authorities – *Financial Accounting Standards Board (FASB)* tightened the potential to misuse off-balance-sheet entities (Special Purpose Vehicles or SPVs), yet the problem had once again appeared during the 2007–2009 financial crisis. Prudential standards encouraged banks to engage in regulatory arbitrage by taking mortgages and other assets off the balance sheet and to finance them separately in *Conduits, structured investment vehicles (SIV)*, or *Qualified Special Purpose Entities (QSPE)*. This has allowed these institutions to reduce their regulatory capital while booking fees from the transactions. Citibank, for example, created a CDO that carried a liquidity but that allowed any buyer who ran into financing problems to sell them back at original value to Citibank. This was not disclosed to shareholders and the bank (that is, the board) seemed unaware of the potential risk until November 2007 when $25 billion had to be brought back onto the balance sheet. Another issue which became important during the 2007–2009 financial crisis and beyond (European sovereign debt crisis) is the one of the accounting standards. This issue became evident when during the crisis concerns arose on the fair value or mark-to-market value of assets which were traded in unregulated markets (OTC). There has been a feeling in the markets that different banks used very different valuations for reporting on the same asset thus contributing to market opacity and reduced integrity (Pezzuto, 2011b; Kirkpatrick, 2009, pp. 25–27).

The FASB has called on the International Accounting Standards Board (IASB) to strengthen its standards to achieve better disclosure about valuations, methodologies, and uncertainty associated with valuations. The lessons learned from the financial crisis have also driven the International Auditing and Assurance Standards Board (IAASB) to consider the possibility of enhancing the guidance for audits of valuations of complex or illiquid financial products and related disclosures (Kirkpatrick, 2009, pp. 25–27; Pezzuto, 2010a, pp. 119–123).

According to Kevin Davis, "There were clearly substantial failings in disclosures leading up to the financial crisis. Banks did not disclose their off-balance sheet exposures to SIVs and Conduits. Investment banks underreported leverage through inappropriate accounting for transactions such as repurchase agreements" (Davis, 2011, p. 19).

IOSCO (2010) has addressed the issues arising from shadow banking, reporting potential "adverse impact on the price discovery process, information and liquidity searches and market integrity. The suggested regulatory principles focus on promoting pre- and post-trade transparency" (IOSCO, 2010, pp. 4–30).

In June 2010, even the FSB recommended a required review on disclosure to determine to what extent the recommendations of the Financial Stability Forum (2008) regarding disclosure have been implemented (FSB, 2010, pp. 1–50).

Caprio et al. suggest that in order to prevent future crises it is important to effectively reform lending practices, rating agencies, and the securitizations' processes. Most importantly, according to the authors, regulation and supervision should be strengthened further to avoid new crises (Caprio, 2008, pp. 34–45).

Hunter recommends several solutions to prevent future crises. Among these are to emphasize the "importance of transparency in the operation of an analysis by MBS insurers and bond rating agencies, and the development of a systematic way of evaluating counterparty risk within the financial system" (Hunter, 2008).

Kashyap reports that since the two major possible causes of the credit crisis that had led to the financial crisis were: (1) the interplay between the substantial amounts of MBS with exposure to subprime risk that were kept on the bank balance sheet even though the OTD securitization model was supposed to transfer risk to those institutions better able to bear it (but this is not what happened), and (2) the fact that banks financed these and other assets with short-term market borrowings (since it was cheaper), the natural regulatory reaction to prevent recurrences of these spillovers would be to mandate higher capital standards (Kashyap, 2010, pp. 1–2).

The narrow-focused vision however, Kayshap states, would probably not address some of the fundamental problems relating to corporate governance and internal management conflicts in banks – the so-called agency problems (Kashyap, 2010, p. 2).

The agency problems play an important role in shaping banks' capital structures. He argues that devising inappropriate incentive structures and internal controls for banks' management is the most critical pervasive issue for moral hazard and possible future crises. In particular, he underlines that "equity investors in a bank must constantly worry that bad decisions by management will dissipate the value of their shareholdings." By contrast, secured short-term creditors are better protected against the actions of wayward bank management. Thus the tendency for banks to finance themselves largely with short-term debt allowed their management to be subject to a lighter oversight of the shareholders. Imposing higher capital requirements reduces the risk of bank defaults even though it generates a trade-off due to the increase in capital ratios, thus banks' management have decided to use external vehicles (shadow banking) and financial engineering innovations to reduce capital requirements (Kashyap, 2010, pp. 2–9). The combination of short-term funding and massive recourse of off-balance-sheet shadow banking vehicles can create serious threats to the entire banking system. I have recommended (2010) reducing the risk of gambling that banks took in the last crisis that destabilized the system upon the wake of systemic crisis and throughout the whole period of high volatility and turbulence (Pezzuto, 2010a, pp. 119–123).

Kashyap (2010) confirmed in his paper that a preferred explanation for why bank balance sheets contained problematic assets is that there was a breakdown of incentives and risk control systems within banks. According to him short-term choice in funding was a major driver of this failure, since in the case of new products (and the exotic products which were massive in those days) it is hard to understand whether a financial manager is generating true excess returns adjusting for risk or a compensation for a risk that has not yet shown itself. *Tail-risks* should be fully controlled since they are by nature hard to quantify with precision before they occur. More reliable and robust statistical models, more risk culture, and better managerial approaches are necessary to effectively handle these "tail" risk events (Kashyap, 2010, pp. 5–11).

According to Richard Posner (2009) the financial crisis is a result of the following three prevention failures:

- excessive deregulation;
- neglect of warning signs;
- insouciance about the decline in the rate of personal savings and safety of such savings (Posner, 2009, p. 289).

Posner (2009) makes the following recommendations for solving such issues:

> Since "the existence of multiple federal financial regulatory bodies … has led to a fragmentation of regulatory authority, a lack of coordination, turf wars, yawning regulatory gaps with respect to hedge funds, bank substitutes, and novel financial instruments, and an inability to aggregate and analyze information about emerging problems in the financial markets", consolidation of the regulatory agencies would improve the government's ability to regulate crises in their incipience. He also adds that an international financial regulatory authority may be necessary to harmonize the countries' regulations, given the interdependence of the banking systems of the different nations. (Posner, 2009, pp. 289–290)

Furthermore, regarding the mitigation of risk of very low personal savings and heavy personal borrowings, which are both risk factors, he suggests considering the possibility of placing limits on credit cards, mortgage loans, and more generally, on easy credit to avoid overindebtedness, and removing the ability to easily eliminate debts by declaring bankruptcy. He also suggests regulatory changes that limit leverage, raise credit rating standards, and for changes in the compensation scheme of credit rating agencies. He also requires:

1. forbidding proprietary trading by banks;
2. adjusting reserve requirements to take more realistically into account the riskiness of bank's capital structure;
3. trading of CDS on exchanges and that they be fully collateralized;
4. resurrecting usury laws;
5. enforcing more disclosure by hedge funds and private equity funds; and
6. disclosing the full compensation of all senior executives which should be subject to public audit.

An additional fairly modest reform for Posner would be to require that a substantial share of the compensation of financial executives be backloaded and tied to the corporation's future performances. Finally, he suggests increasing the marginal income tax rate of persons who have very high incomes in order to reduce their excessive appetite to risk-taking (Posner, 2009, pp. 290–299).

With regards to the too-big-to-fail issue, the President of the Federal Reserve Bank of Dallas, Richard Fisher, recommended in January 2013 that TBTF banks (that is, the ones deemed too big to fail) must be broken apart to prevent the next financial crisis from happening. In fact, according to President Richard Fisher, implementing the Dodd–Frank Act is not enough to protect the country's financial system. He explained this concept with the following statements: "We recommend that TBTF financial institutions be restructured into multiple business entities. Only the resulting downsized commercial banking operations – and not shadow banking affiliates or the parent company – would benefit from the safety net of federal deposit insurance and access to the Federal Reserve's discount window." He also added: "We labor under the siren song of Dodd–Frank and the recent run-up in the pricing of TBTF bank stocks and credit, indulging in the illusion of hope that this complex legislation will end too big to fail and right the banking system." And he concluded with the following words: "Every customer, creditor and counterparty of shadow banking affiliates should also be required to sign a statement that acknowledges the fact that these entities are not protected by the federal government. The next financial crisis could cost more than two years of economic output, borne by millions of US taxpayers" (The Executive Gateway, 2013).

Toward the end of 2012, even Erkki Liikanen, Governor of Finland's central bank, has delivered proposals to the European Commission (*Liikanen committee's proposals*) for banking sector reform that include the following recommendations (Burgis, 2013):

1. **A *"ringfence"* around the traders.**
   "Proprietary trading and other significant trading activities should be assigned to a separate legal entity if the activities to be separated amount to a significant share of a bank's business ... As a consequence, deposits, and the explicit and implicit guarantee they carry, would no longer directly support risky trading activities." The proposal requires that if a bank's trading assets exceed €100 billion or 15–25 percent of its total assets, its trading activities should be hived off. The so-called "universal banking" model will remain, as the new entity that holds the trading activities will be part of the same overall banking group, but the trading division will have to hold its own capital, meaning that it stands or falls by its own activities and cannot, in theory at least, knock over the bread-and-butter retail banking operations. The idea is to get taxpayers off the hook by ensuring that governments do not have to step in to safeguard deposits if traders blow a hole in their balance sheet (Burgis, 2013).

2. **Disaster management.**
   "The resolution authority should request wider separation than considered mandatory above if this is deemed necessary to ensure resolvability and operational continuity of critical" (Burgis, 2013).
   Banks need to work out in advance how they could go under without pulling the rest of Europe's financial architecture down with them. If regulators considered that

a bank's trading operations were particularly risky, they should widen the ringfence to include more bits of the investment bank, to better shield deposits in the event of the investment bank failing (Burgis, 2013).

3. **Spreading the pain.**
"Banks should build up a sufficiently large layer of bail-inable debt that should be clearly defined, so that its position within the hierarchy of debt commitments in a bank's balance sheet is clear and investors understand the eventual treatment in case of resolution ... Bail-in instruments should also be used in remuneration schemes for top management so as best to align decision-making with longer-term performance in banks" (Burgis, 2013).

The report proposes new instruments that would ensure a bank's private creditors share some of the pain if that bank goes under. Liikanen is suggesting the European Commission adjust its existing proposal on bail-in, so that a specific category of debt is bailin-able. The Commission went for a wider definition, which effectively covers most unsecured bondholders. Top management, similarly, would be on the hook in the event of a bank failure, in theory ensuring that their decisions reflect the long-term interests of the institutions rather than immediate rewards (Burgis, 2013).

4. **The weighting game.**
"The Group proposes to apply more robust risk weights in the determination of minimum capital standards and more consistent treatment of risk in internal models ... Also, the treatment of real estate lending within the capital requirements framework should be reconsidered, and maximum loan-to-value (and/or loan-to-income) ratios included in the instruments available for micro- and macro-prudential supervision" (Burgis, 2013).

Liikanen wants the European Commission to assess whether the proposed amendments to capital requirements would be sufficient to keep both investment and retail banks safe and sound. After the disastrous role of reckless mortgages in prompting the financial crisis, it also wants regulators to keep a keener eye on banks' property lending (Burgis, 2013).

5. **Living dangerously.**
"The Group considers that it is necessary to augment existing corporate governance reforms by specific measures to (1) strengthen boards and management; (2) promote the risk management function; (3) rein in compensation for bank management and staff; (4) improve risk disclosure; and (5) strengthen sanctioning powers" (Burgis, 2013). The report diagnoses the failure of boards to rein in excessively risky behavior and notes that "the increase in size and the advent of banks that are too-big-to-fail have further reduced market participants' incentives to monitor banks effectively." In short, the report's authors worry that the people who run banks are either ill-equipped to control sprawling institutions or incentivized to run them dangerously. They want part of bankers' bonuses paid in debt, meaning they could be written down if short-term profits yield long-term troubles (Burgis, 2013).

Some doubts on the effectiveness of the new Dodd–Frank regulation to avoid new systemic financial crises have been raised by John Macey, Professor of Yale Law School in an interview (February 2012) with Tom Easton, US Finance Editor of the *Economist* magazine. In fact, during that interview the finance editor posed him a specific question asking whether the new regulation (Dodd–Frank Act) can be considered a success in terms of making another crisis significantly less likely. John Macey replied that he does not believe that the new regulation will achieve this goal. In particular, he stated the following: "[the new regulation] is a full employment bill for lawyers and regulators ... It is a massively complex [regulation] ... at its core it says, this is only an outline and what we are doing in each statute is just to require the creation of bureaucracy ... dozens of new bureaucracies created by Dodd–Frank ... We need to have a system, and this is a complete solution to financial crises ... in which instead of externalizing risk [risk socialized – TBTF policy] ... we need to make these guys internalize the costs associated with the risk-taking activities ... [when firms are] too systemically important or too politically important ... If we can't make a credible commitment as a Country to refrain from bailing out these institutions then we ought to break them up ... into parts that can be allowed to fail (Easton, 2012).

At the end of January 2013, Wolfgang Schauble, German finance minister, proposed a legislation on the separation of risky assets from depositors' cash in banks different from the one proposed by the Liikanen report (ring-fencing of proprietary trading). The Schauble proposal aims to confine the separation to bank's own account trading, whereas Liikanen's Commission proposal aims to separate all capital market activity, including market making. As reported by Markus Frühauf in the *Frankfurter Allgemeine* newspaper, however, Schauble's legislation does not seem to properly address the real issue of regulating the majority of trading activity by banks which remains ultimately insured by bank depositors (Eurointelligence, 2013).

Under the current agreement on the banking union in the Eurozone, the ECB will be the regulator of banks with assets of more than €30 billion, which means that it will supervise overall a few hundred banks (that is, 150 to 200) in the Eurozone out of a total of 6,000 banks.

There will be a separate supervisory body consisting of the ECB governing council as final arbiter, and a steering committee to solve disagreement. The SSM will become operational in March 2014. The EBA will continue to be in charge of harmonizing rules at EU-level. There will be probably no direct bank recapitalization (that is implementation) by the ESM until at least 2014. An important point related to the current banking union agreement is whether the threshold also includes off-balance-sheet vehicles (Eurointelligence, 2012).

In the UK, Sir John Vickers, Chairman of Britain's Independent Commission on Banking, proposed a plan (Vickers Rule) in order to ring-fence banks' retail divisions from their trading arms. Vickers' preferred option would be to maintain a buffer between investment banking and consumer funds. According to him, banks should not be restricted from proprietary trading in a way similar to the Volcker Rule because it would be too complicated to control, Furthermore, such a ban would eventually encourage moving proprietary trading to less regulated environments and locations. Also, Vickers said that banks' market making is indistinguishable from proprietary trading and such complexity would also affect regulatory oversight effectiveness. Volcker, on the contrary, believes that financial entities would eventually work to bridge any internal buffers in the long term.

There is no doubt, however, that in the absence of a global harmonization of regulatory framework on risk governance of banks and sovereign debts it will be very difficult to avoid regulatory arbitrages and to effectively reduce the likelihood of systemic risks.

Furthermore, according to Charles Wyplosz, despite the fact that the treaty includes a no-bail-out clause, Germany will probably have to accept ECB debt monetization in order to maintain a common Eurozone currency and to absorb a substantial amount of Euro Area public debts (Wyplosz, 2012).

Conclusion

A number of important steps have been taken by governments, central banks, and regulators since the beginning of the 2007–2009 financial crisis in the attempt to mitigate systemic risks, the *too-big-to-fail phenomenon*, and the limited transparency and accountability in the so-called shadow banking sector (that is, largely unregulated swaps and other derivatives market). Based on the findings reported in this chapter and in this book, it appears that the scope of creating a more resilient global financial system that could prevent the recurrence of future crises like the one of 2008 or worse, today remains a pure illusion. The new regulations that have been proposed to mitigate such risks will be somehow watered down or circumvented by the powerful global banking lobbies and will prove ineffective in making the financial system more resilient. Adding more complexity and bureaucracy to the regulation only gets things less manageable and effective and, ultimately, it increases the likelihood of new systemic risks since in many circumstances the new rules only aim to enhance ex-post control when the massive damage will have already occurred.

Some improvements have been made in the financial markets with the new financial regulation but a lot still needs to be done, and to be harmonized on a global scale, since banking and financial is a globalized and highly interconnected industry. The improvements consist of more forward-looking financial regulation and regulatory oversight, enhanced corporate governance, internal control, and ERM frameworks, and most of all, avoiding that the cost of future crises will be borne by taxpayers through effective *crisis resolution mechanisms*.

In fact, based on my personal opinion on the matter (April 2013), bank crisis losses and resolution costs should first and foremost be borne by the management, shareholders and subsequently by the creditors of the failing institution. The Single Resolution Authority (SRA) should enforce according to me the following pecking order for bank crisis resolutions (that is banks failures, restructuring, and recapitalizations): (1) losses and resolution costs should be borne by the financial firms' management team, board members, and shareholders, and even by bank employees at every level (in case of severe direct responsibility in the bank failure). Change management and corporate governance changes should be mandatory for failing banks due to severe negligence or wrongdoing of banks management and employees. The Single Resolution Authority should require claw-backs on bank managers' salaries, bonuses and other undeserved compensation incentives. No golden parachutes or severance packages should be granted to the management of failed banks; (2) bail-in of creditors – (a) subordinated debt holders; (b) senior bond holders; (c) covered bond holders granting higher protection to small individual bond holders versus institutional investors; then for the residual portion of the losses/resolution costs; (3) the bank crisis resolution fund. State funds should not be used for bailouts of failed banks to avoid the vicious circle between sovereign debt and bank debt that overcomplicated the resolution of the Eurozone debt crisis in 2010–2012; (4) only in unavoidable and exceptional circumstances and according to the following pecking order uninsured depositors, insured depositors, and taxpayers should be forced to bail-out bank crises. Furthermore, regulators and policy makers (lobbyists, politicians, external auditors, and so on) who have contributed with their intrusive behaviors or negligent supervision to the bank failure should also be held responsible of the failure and subject to investigation.

It is also critical to harmonize such rules on a global scale in order to avoid potential distortions in the handling of banking crises and to avoid regulatory arbitrages.

Thus, even the bankruptcy law should be changed so that when a bank files for Chapter 11 the ones to have the "skin in the game" according to my proposal of pecking order, should be the shareholders, board members, and employees, then the bank crisis resolution fund, and the banking system as a whole, and only exceptionally (and if it is really inevitable) and for the residual amount, the depositors and taxpayer who should be entitled to receive a tax credit for the amount they pay for the bail-out of the failed financial institutions.

This solution, even though it is quite drastic, however, might not completely stop systemically important financial firms from engaging in short-term oriented and excessive risk-taking strategies (*moral hazard* and *too-big-to-fail rule*). It is true that laying much of the burden of the financial institutions' potential bankruptcy on the shareholders, financial firms' management and employees, bondholders, and the banking system as a whole, might significantly mitigate the risk since they will all require a much tighter and effective oversight and corporate governance to avoid for themselves huge unexpected losses. The additional *stealth-level risk mitigation mechanism* would be represented by a professional association code of conduct to impose on managers and executives (CEO, and so on), service providers, and consultants, and auditors involved in financial frauds, money laundering, market-rigging, market abuse, or systemic risk activities to be (1) banned from all global banking and financial services firms' industry associations – that is, ABA, IIF, AICPA, GARP, IOSCO, and so on) for a minimum of five years up to a lifetime ban, and in addition, be subject to (2) claw-back policies, (3) no golden parachutes, and (4) individual criminal probes and charges.

Furthermore, the so-called "icing on the cake" in my proposal of new law on bank crisis resolution mechanism should be to prevent that individual wrongdoings and crimes can be charged only to the firms (instead of individuals) or that firms solve these charges only by paying settlements. New laws should foresee that firms will continue to pay settlements to settle charges but that these settlements will not free the dishonest executives and employees from their own individual criminal penalties for reckless conduct.

Last but not least, I would like to stress the idea that, in order to prevent the next financial crisis, the industry needs to implement more effective and simplified rules, but most of all, they need to make sure that financial firms' executives and bank regulators are more accountable. No more *complacency* and *conflicts of interest* should be tolerated from bankers, executives, and regulators and anybody else involved in the financial services industry (that is, securitizers, brokers, traders, auditors, rating agencies, and so on). Thus, the only way to achieve this is through the use of *industry-wide "blacklists"* and *"industry bans"* for those who fail to be accountable and contribute to generate or hide information (transparency) or transactions (individuals barred from banking for criminal convictions) that lead to *systemic risks, market abuses, frauds, money laundering,* and so on, for SIFIs. The "blacklists" and "industry bans" should be enforced by international professional associations and regulators for severe wrongdoings caused by any dishonest player involved in the banking and financial services industry (that is, any bank executive or employee, regulators, securitizers, brokers, traders, auditors, rating agencies, and so on).

Furthermore, it is important to assure more rigorous and harmonized transparency rules, credit standards, due diligence practices, and an harmonized definition of bad debts across different countries/ financial firms in order to avoid in the future the moral hazard, excessive risk taking, and excessive balance sheet expansion that have contributed to the 2008 financial crisis. Examples of such practices include: the exotic loans (that is NINJA loans), excessive loan-to-income ratios, loan-to-value ratios, loans exceeding the value of the house, no down payment, no or limited credit verifications, excessive concentration of subprime loans, manipulated and fraudulent loan applications, formal due diligence, generous credit ratings, and manipulations of trading positions (derivatives) to artificially inflate their values (short-term profit maximization) and to hide losses.

5 *The Need for Cultural Change in Organizations and Society*

Preventing New Systemic Crises through Reforms and a New Cultural Mindset

One of the lessons learned from this dramatic financial crisis is probably represented by the urgent need for cultural and mindset changes in the finance and banking industry, and more generally, in society as a whole. It is not, however, just the need for a nostalgic return to a non-globalized and less interconnected economy, or to a less aggressive and competitive free-market society since globalization and open-market economy have contributed to innovation, modernization, and wealth. This book and the majority of other articles, papers, and publications on the same topic over the last few years share at least one common theme; that moral hazard and perverse incentives, combined with psychological (over-confidence) and environmental aspects, are among the major triggering factors that generated the 2007–2009 financial crisis. The actual meltdown is probably related to the excessive leverage of financial firms, short-term funding, and the excessive risk-taking of their managements which generated the confidence and liquidity crisis. However, the underlying root causes of these triggering factors are certainly the deregulation, the non-regulated shadow banking sector and most of all the moral hazard, greed, and short-termism of many players in the industry. Furthermore, however, the numerous scandals that have been unveiled since 2010 show that the dramatic events and dishonest behaviors that led to the 2007–2009 financial crisis have not been triggered only by behavioral aspects (that is, overconfidence, market hype, irrational exuberance) and by lax regulation and oversight of those years, since they continued to occur even after the market crashed (Pezzuto, 2008; 2010a; 2012).

Nugent (2009) defines corporate cultures as a collection of common beliefs, expectations, behaviors, and values learned and shared by members of a group and transmitted from one generation of employees to another. Thus, based on the analysis of the basic facts about the crisis and my own first-hand observation of global bankers and financial services firms' management, it is not difficult to conclude that many firms over the years have developed a typical "clan" organizational culture (or perhaps "gang") of Darwinian orientation dominated by "self-interest, short-termism, reckless greed, cronyism, fear and intimidation" (Nugent, 2009a; Pezzuto, 2008).

For example, in 2012, the consulting firm Genesis Ventures issued a comprehensive independent written report for the senior management of Barclays in which they described that they have found in the Bank's US wealth management operations major cultural failings such as, a "revenue at all costs" strategy and "fear and intimidation" culture, according to the *Daily Mail*. Barclays's investment banking and retail banking operations have been hit by various scandals including the manipulation of the London Interbank Offered Rate (Libor) and mis-selling of payment protection insurance (Schäfer, 2013).

All over the world, during the past few years, consumers, producers, politicians, regulators, and ordinary citizens have shown increasing concern for environmental sustainability, reduction of pollution, the need for a green economy, the fight against the violation of human rights, the reduction of discrimination, inequality, corruption, fraud, criminality, bribery, and even perverse financial scandals (for example, Enron, Madoff, Parmalat, and others). In sum, there is a widespread desire for a return to integrity, sustainability, and a more just society where each person does the right thing for the right reason.

Thus, it seems as if many people around the world are becoming progressively more aware of the importance of preserving the world for themselves and for future generations, and limiting the severe damage humankind has so far caused to our planet, people, cultures, values, and lifestyles. Slowly, the frustration and challenges of the global financial, economic, debt, and social crises are pushing people to envision a new political and economic order toward a more sustainable future. Profit is still important to most, but its traditional dominance is starting to be balanced with other important priorities for people and companies. The numerous financial scandals unveiled since the beginning of the financial crisis, the disappointing economic and social aftermath that followed these scandals, and the illusionary wealth and happiness goals recklessly pursued by many, have proved to the entire world the limits of a crony capitalism without rules and values.

One example of the growing concern in society over the past 15 years for a broader and more balanced perspective of firms' growth, wealth, success, and sustainability is the widespread implementation in the business world of the famous Balanced Scorecard (BSC) methodology of Kaplan and Norton (1996), which aims to establish corporate long-term goals and strategies, and then to translate them into actions. The results of these strategies are measurable, simultaneously addressing multiple perspectives (financial, customer, processes, and learning goals) (Niven, 2006, pp. 11–24). In the past few years, a growing number of companies of all sizes have progressively paid more attention to other perspectives such as the environment, health, safety, sustainability, community impact, ethics, corporate governance, regulatory governance, corporate citizenship, and corporate social responsibility. Corporate strategies literature in recent years also focuses significantly more on the importance of balancing the firms' financial and portfolio strategies and goals with their organizational, environmental, and social strategies, in order to maximize benefits for all stakeholders and not just the short-term oriented goals of management and shareholders.

Despite the recent dramatic crises and the urge of companies and economies to return to the virtuous path of higher productivity and steady growth, people are starting to demand, as described in Figure 5.1, a more sustainable and rewarding lifestyle that would better compromise their wealth and career ambitions with good living standards despite the current growing concerns for recessionary trends.

Thus, it seems as if a large part of the Western world is aiming to maintain and boost growth, competitiveness, innovation, productivity, and wealth – but no longer at any cost. Wealth and success remain important goals for many individuals but when the benefits are progressively becoming the exclusive retreat of a restricted elite (that is, 1 percent)

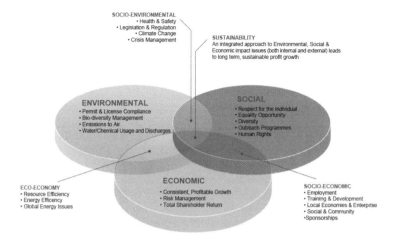

SOCIO-ENVIRONMENTAL
• Health & Safety
• Legislation & Regulation
• Climate Change
• Crisis Management

SUSTAINABILITY
An integrated approach to Environmental, Social &
Economic impact issues (both internal and external) leads
to long term, sustainable profit growth

ENVIRONMENTAL
• Permit & License Compliance
• Bio-diversity Management
• Emissions to Air
• Water/Chemical Usage and Discharges

SOCIAL
• Respect for the Individual
• Equality Opportunity
• Diversity
• Outreach Programmes
• Human Rights

ECO-ECONOMY
• Resource Efficiency
• Energy Efficency
• Global Energy Issues

ECONOMIC
• Consistent, Profitable Growth
• Risk Management
• Total Shareholder Return

SOCIO-ECONOMIC
• Employment
• Training & Development
• Local Economies & Enterprise
• Social & Community
•Sponsorships

Figure 5.1   Sustainability

Source: Seamus Mc Namara, Managing Director of Verify Technologies Ltd.

and most of the social costs and sacrifices are instead borne by the majority of citizens (that is, 99 percent), somehow, the "democratic" equation does not seem to work any longer. Recent research indicates that consumers today are much more concerned about the corporate social responsibility and citizenship of companies. More than 90 percent of US consumers say that issues dealing with the sustainability of the environment influence their day-to-day purchasing decisions. Furthermore, over 90 percent of them report to be willing to make a financial sacrifice to work for a socially responsible company (TNS, 2008).

In a world that is changing so significantly toward sustainability and a more balanced lifestyle, it is reasonable to expect that moving forward people may expect companies, even in the banking and financial sector, to change their culture and mindset in favor of a more sustainable orientation. This means, in other words, to avoid excessive risk-taking, short-term profitability, or outrageous executive compensation and incentives.

The trend is already spreading very fast across the world affecting all aspects of our society. Many universities today are focusing their programs on green economy, sustainability, balancing growth, wealth and the preservation of the environment, and people's quality of life. As the dramatic financial, debt, and economic crises have demonstrated, these big problems can cause significant disruptions in peoples' lives, ranging from prolonged periods of higher unemployment rates and higher volatility of the markets to economic recession and distressed families, and even to social unrest and health problems.

All this evidences that people are progressively starting to reconsider their priorities, their way of living, their values, goals, and their purchasing, investment and personal savings decisions. This might lead people to rethink their priorities in terms of what is really important in their lives. They might rethink how convenient or likely it is for themselves to move up the social ladder and to reach the higher levels on Maslow's Hierarchy of Needs Satisfaction model (Maslow, 2011, pp. 1–32) at least until they regain hope and trust in their leaders, in social justice, and fair opportunities. Of course, limited personal savings and/or excessive personal debt might still force some to struggle for survival even in a highly uncertain, ruthless, and unequal business world.

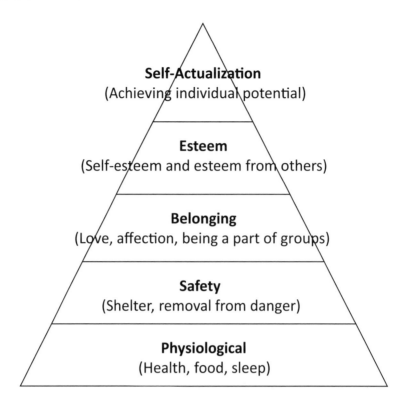

Figure 5.2   Maslow's Hierarchy of Needs (or Pyramid of Needs)

Source: Psychotherapy, Counselling and Life Coach Dr Tim Le Bon.

The basis of Maslow's theory of motivation, as described in Figure 5.2, is that human beings are motivated by unsatisfied needs, and that certain lower needs need to be satisfied before higher needs can be addressed. Per the teachings of Abraham Maslow (1943), there are general needs (physiological, survival, safety, hunger, thirst, love, and esteem) which have to be fulfilled before a person is able to act unselfishly. These needs were dubbed "deficiency needs." While a person is motivated to fulfill these basic needs, they continue to move toward growth, and eventually self-actualization. The satisfaction of these needs is quite healthy, while preventing their gratification makes people unsatisfied or frustrated (Maslow, 2011, pp. 1–32).

"As a result, for adequate workplace motivation, it is important that leaders understand which needs are active for individual employee motivation. In this regard, Abraham Maslow's model indicates that basic, low-level needs such as physiological requirements and safety must be satisfied" (that is, minimum and fair income, job security, a relatively stable and solid environment for personal development) "before higher-level needs such as self-fulfillment are pursued. As depicted in the hierarchical pyramid, when a need is satisfied it no longer motivates and the next higher need takes its place" (Maslow, 2011, pp. 1–32).

As hyper-competition, globalization, volatile markets, uncertainty, and continuous cost cutting and layoffs increase, making only the few very rich even richer (1 percent) and the majority of the people more distressed and less well off, people may start to think that it will not make much sense to move up toward the higher layers of the ladder of the Maslow Pyramid since the perceived chances to receive any fair benefit is very slim, compared with the high social costs and sacrifices required (hard work and more taxes) to get there, and to live every day in a very unstable, volatile, and uncertain environment. Such dissent has already begun to appear since 2009 in the US and other countries with sit-ins in major cities.

Probably the true and deeper roots of the global financial, economic, debt, and social crisis we are experiencing these days are due to the significant shift that has occurred over the last decades in the cultural and moral principles of most people in Western countries. This shift is related to "short-termism," greed, self-interest, and a progressive idealization of "easy money" and short-cuts to wealth and success, as the only pursuit in life. The crisis we have experienced since 2008 is not a failure of the free-enterprise system, free competition, and market capitalism, which still is and will remain the only sustainable democratic model of a modern society, but rather and more simply it is just the result of a drift toward a complete lack of ethical values and behaviors of many players in the economy and in particular of the elites, directly or indirectly, involved in the making of the crisis. As stated in my 2008 paper, the crisis was not the result of any economic ideology such as Libertarianism or Keynesianism, but rather just the consequence of the reckless pursuit of self-interest and greed at any cost and having no concern for what might happen to others. A sort of Machiavellian plot (Pezzuto, 2008; Rappaport and Bogle, 2011, pp. 19–61; Rappaport, 2005, pp. 65–76).

Furthermore, to worsen the situation, according to Nugent (2009), risk and the potential for fraudulent behavior increase as one is pushed down on Maslow's Scale of Needs' Satisfaction or fears to be left out of the game. That is, when one operates in an environment of ruthless pressure and intimidation, compulsive gambling ("revenue at all costs"), moral hazard, and when survival is the first priority, rational, logical behavior may take a back seat to acting ethically as now the hypothalamus and endocrine systems are controlling behavior. That is, ethics and morals may be somewhat relative to where one stands on Maslow's scale (Nugent, 2009).

Still according to the same author, the so-called Cressey fraud triangle that sits as a foundational element of SAS 99, explains the typical drivers of fraudulent behaviors. This triangle is represented by the combination of three key conditions that seem to lead to frauds: (1) incentives/pressures; (2) opportunities (weak internal controls); (3) rationalization/attitude (justification – being owed). Analyzing the 2007–2009 financial crisis, it appears quite evident that the combination of all these elements were present since in many instances senior executives were motivated by their moral hazard behaviors or fraudulent behaviors. The main triggers were: (1) perverse personal high short-term financial incentives and extreme competitive pressure to make the most profit during a booming market by whatever means (housing and lending markets' bubbles); (2) poor credit standards, poor risk management and weak internal controls, lax regulatory oversight, and an opaque shadow banking sector, all created the opportunity for both moral hazard and fraudulent behaviors; and (3) the belief that such bad behavior was justified as a common industry practice regardless of whether it was right or wrong (Nugent, 2009; Pezzuto, 2008).

As reported by Desmond (2002), a series of recent studies have been conducted by the European Values Study Group with the main aim to assess the changes in Western values. One of the major findings in the research is that the more economically strong countries become (emancipative orientations), the more the values of its people are moving toward individualism. In other words, this means that the increasing autonomy of individual people is shaping their own values and norms, moving away from traditional ones. The predominantly liberal way of life in Western countries, especially as far as religion, morality, and sexuality are concerned, makes personal choices take a central focus (Desmond, 2002 pp. 23–24).

However, Desmond (2002) talks about the rise of "post-materialism" in the most recent decade as the last stage reached in consumer behavior. It means that the focus is progressively stretching from someone's own well-being, materialism, and self-interest (individualism) to quality of life in general and environmental awareness (Desmond, 2002, p. 23).

Rappaport and Bogle (2011) argue that in today's business community, short-termism has gone from a simmer to a boil. Human nature has not changed, but the business environment has. Behaviors in this environment, they state, have pushed short-termism to the point where it constitutes a crisis that threatens to undermine economic growth, individual well-being, and possibly even the free-market system (Rappaport and Bogle, 2011, pp. 19–61).

Demirguc-Kunt and Serven reported that the 2007–2009 financial crisis was not a failure of the free markets but rather a reaction of market participants *to distorted incentives* (Demirguc-Kunt and Serven, 2009, pp. 117–118).

Mike Mayo, Managing Director of Credit Agricole Securities, in his book *Exile on Wall Street: One Analyst's Fight to Save the Big Banks from Themselves* reported on CNBC in 2007 a number of concerning issues regarding the mortgage loan market, such as declining loan quality and excess executive compensation and other evidences. He indicates that the only way to fix the banking sector is not to have a lot of rules that are not strictly enforced and that when things go wrong, the government steps in to protect banks from the market consequences of their own worst decisions. The more effective solution, he states, would come from letting market forces work, in conjunction with rules, and a better version of capitalism which consists of a reduction in the clout of big banks, and a sufficient true check and balance framework of oversight. Doing these things involves, however, a culture change to ensure that analysts can act with sufficient intellectual independence and integrity to critically analyze public companies that control a significant portion of the economy and perhaps make up a proportion of their firm's or their firm's clients' portfolios (Mayo, 2011, pp. 81–96).

The economic discipline has often addressed the concepts of rationality and self-interest, from the classical economists, such as Adam Smith (1776) and David Ricardo (1817), who indicated that rationality had the limited meaning of preferring more to less (capitalists choose to invest in the industry yielding the highest rate of return) to Kenneth Arrow (1986), who associates the concept of rationality to be concerned with the maximization of utility under a budget constraint. Herbert Simon (1957) makes the point that: "… economics sometimes uses the terms 'irrationality' rather broadly and the term 'rationality' correspondingly narrowly, so as to exclude from the domain many phenomena that psychology would include into it" (Kolb, 2010a, pp. 24–26).

Dobson and Reiner's (1996) definition of rationality moves from the realm of methods to that of ends. John Stuart Mill (1861) provides the classical statement of utilitarianism, whereas Milton Friedman (1963) argues that positive economics is in principle independent of any particular ethical position or normative judgments (Kolb, 2010a, pp. 24–26).

Paul Polman, CEO of Unilever, said in an interview:

People and companies are obsessed with short-termism. He added that the focus on delivering short-term shareholder value has led to widespread addiction to quick artificial highs – rather like a junkie hooked on heroin or a financial trader on cocaine. The ultimate cost of short-termism, he says, was the financial crisis of 2007–2009. Too many investors have become short-term gamblers: the more fluctuations in share price they can engineer, the better it is for them. It is not good for the companies or for society, but it is influencing the way firms are being run, all the same. (Saunders, 2011)

He prefers to satisfy customers over the investor, even if that means telling investors to accept some compromises to their profitability and payback period expectations.

To drag the world back to sanity, we need to know why we are here. The answer is: for consumers, not shareholders. If we are in synch with consumer needs and the environment in which we operate, and take responsibility for society as well as for our employees, then the shareholder will also be rewarded (Saunders, 2011).

It is not an easy pill for all to swallow – when Polman announced his intention to abandon earnings forecasts in 2010, Unilever's shares dropped 10 percent in one stroke. It's not surprising to learn he no longer makes financial presentations to hedge fund managers.

"I do not wish to be political, but my decisions are made in the long-term interests of the company. It would be easy for me to jack the share price up, collect a bonus and go sailing in the Bahamas, but in five or 10 years Unilever would not be in good shape" (Saunders, 2011).

Too many people think in terms of trade-offs, Polman says that:

If you do something which is good for you, then it must be bad for someone else. That's not right and it comes from old thinking about the way the world works and what business is for: Milton Friedman's optimization of short-term profits. We have to snap out of that old thinking and move to a new model. (Saunders, 2011)

Polman's new business model will decouple growth from environmental impact. It will double in size, but it will reduce the firm's overall effect on the environment. Consumers are asking for this new model of sustainability (growth and environment protection) – what is good for the firm does not have to be bad for people and society as whole – but governments are incapable of delivering it. It is needed for society and it energizes our people – it reduces costs and increases innovation (Saunders, 2011).

The cultural aspects of national cultures and short-termism should also be observed with attention since, as Hofstede (2001) and other highly reputable professionals such as Trompenaars and Hampden-Turner (1997) have indicated, national cultures have different orientations to risk avoidance, short-term versus long-term perspectives, individualism versus collectivism, and so on (Hofstede, 2001 p. 29; Trompenaars and Hampden-Turner, 1997, p. 129).

It often happens, particularly during prolonged periods of economic turbulence and social uncertainty (that is, recession, depression) that individuals from national and organizational cultures that score high on "uncertainty avoidance" and "individualism" (Hofstede's cultural dimensions, 2001) may have a higher tendency to believe that always "pleasing" the leaders and never upsetting the "establishment", no matter what the "clubby system" does, is the only way to keep their heads above water and to pursue their self-interests. A cultural mix such as this, based on self-interest, high uncertainty avoidance, and a sort of "feudal subservience" to a dominant and self-referential elite, does not encourage a shift towards a new cultural paradigm that allows a fair chance for everyone to achieve success and leadership based on merit, fair competition, and universalism. A combination of national cultures with high uncertainty avoidance, a clubby system of nepotism and crony capitalism, and countries with long-standing structural economic and social weaknesses, may indeed severely discourage people from questioning or even daring to change unequal, collusive, and sometimes even illegal and fraudulent practices up to the point in which the system is likely to collapse. Thus, the illusionary "safety" of being part of, or closely connected to, a powerful clan or lobby – even when the rules of these clubby systems might be wrong, unfair, and systematically risky – may even painfully delay the introduction of real structural reforms, effective regulations, and new cultural and business models that are critical for the long-term sustainability and prosperity of a true free-market democracy (that is, improved educational system, meritocracy, competitiveness, innovation and development, and social mobility) (Hofestede, 2001, p. 29; Pezzuto, 208; Sanderson 2013; Eurostat 2011b).

Regulators and policy makers have to pay significant attention to the fact that most of the leading Western countries' cultures these days are particularly centered on individualism and short-termism in order to maximize individuals' immediate benefits and success, often times even "cutting corners" in terms of the quality of their performances. Reckless self-interest and individualism are becoming, more and more, elements of a globalized cultural phenomenon. The puzzling evidence is that apparently people are becoming always more environmentally conscious, concerned about sustainability, and eager to work for socially responsible companies, but at the same time, as shareholders, they seem to pay limited attention to the numerous scandals experienced by banks and other financial firms (that is, mis-selling of payment protection insurance, manipulation of the Libor borrowing rate, money laundering and sanctions busting, and so on) when it comes to managing their own investments and personal wealth (regardless of the fact that some of them are institutional investors). In fact, as demonstrated by 2012 data, bank shares soared as lenders showed some signs of profitability recovering despite the continuing crisis and financial scandals. As reported by Patrick Jenkins in the *Financial Times* (2012): "In several cases 2012 share price performances were seemingly driven by some bizarre inverse correlation with lenders' misdeeds." Among the best performers were some of the leading banks involved in the most disastrous scandals (that is, Barclays, HSBC, Lloyds, JPMorgan Chase and Co., UBS). But as clearly explained by the *Financial Times* journalist, "With regulators in many jurisdictions now favoring pragmatism and a concern for economic growth over purist reforms, bank shareholders have very good reason to smile, in addition to the Basel Committee on Banking Supervision's decision to soften incoming regulatory liquidity rules" (TNS, 2008, Jenkins, 2013a).

It is important to introduce new corporate governance principles and criteria that encourage risk-taking, entrepreneurial spirit, innovation, and self-advancement (individualism) through norms that favor also transparency and regulatory oversight. The new rules should not discourage the natural propensity of such national and/or organizational cultures to continue to adapt to environmental changes and to pursue challenging achievements, progress, and sustainable results. It is critical to defend and to sustain with adequate policies and regulations the true symbol of every solid, well-balanced, and healthy democracy: the middle class.

Regulators and policy makers should have placed great attention on the enhancement of financial firms' ethics standards and the reduction of conflicts of interest. To achieve these goals financial institutions have to focus more resources and attention on these topics and to improve their corporate governance and internal processes and rules to effectively comply with this commitment. Thus, as suggested by Richard L. Daft (2009), a critical improvement may come from the ethics committees, and the introduction of a chief ethics officer, ethics hotlines, structured whistle-blowing mechanisms, code of ethics, value-based leadership styles, social audits, and more effective and independent ("of mind and spirit") internal control and board members (Daft, 2009, pp. 389–399) Furthermore a key contribution to improve financial firms' corporate governance may also come from activist investors and independent board members.

Fortunately, at least in the UK, it seems that something might be moving in the right direction in terms of setting ethical standards in the banking and financial services industry to restore some degree of trust. In fact, Anthony Browne, Chief Executive of the British Bankers' Association (BBA), called for the creation of an independent Banking Standards Review Council to oversee the industry. The BBA also called for the establishment of a code of conduct setting out ethical principles, which it said should apply to all bank employees. It suggested that a "blacklist" of employees could be developed to prevent those who fail to adhere to those standards from working in banking or financial services (Thompson et al., 2013).

These organizational changes are necessary in the financial firms in order to significantly reduce those "politically correct" but also bureaucratic behaviors that characterize many "clan" organizational cultures and inter-organizational lobbies (a restricted elite), leading them often to conflicts of interest and excessive risk-taking. In these types of organizations, based on powerful lobbies and oligarchies, managers at all levels do not have many alternatives. They either succumb to the "go with the flow" philosophy, even when there are plenty of red flags of the forthcoming disaster, or they get threatened, black-listed, and eventually sacked by firms' management and industry lobbies if they refuse to accept the clan culture of conflicts of interests, moral hazard, and "easy money" (short-termism perspective).

Freddie Mac's Chief Risk Officer, David Andrukonis, got fired in 2004 for warning Freddie Mac's management to immediately withdraw from the risky No Income/No Asset (NINA) borrowers' market (Jarsulic, 2010, pp. 106–107).

On this matter, Robert W. Kolb, mentioning Bebchuck and Fried (2004), says that "CEO and directors form a 'club' in which a mutual identification of interests and kind of mutual 'back-scratching' lead to excessive compensation," (Kolb, 2011, p. 248) and common strategies to sack whoever does not play their perverse games.

Often, the so-called regulated industries, even though they are still not fully regulated (that is, shadow banking), are characterized by systemic conflicts of interests that span from the banking lobbies, to the excessive complacency of policy makers and regulators. As stated in March 2011 by the Governor of the Bank of England, Mervyn King, "We allowed a [banking] system to build up which contained the seeds of its own destruction, and this has still not been remedied" (Moore, 2011; Blackwell, 2011).

As I wrote during the most acute phase of the financial crisis on October 7, 2008 (Pezzuto, 2008), according to the famous lessons of the Chicago School, there is no better and fair judge than the market to punish or reward "good" and "bad" players in the marketplace. The central issue in this very dramatic case is not whether one should prefer the theories of the Chicago School, (that is, Frank Knight, Friedrich von Hayek, Ronald Coase, George Stigler, Milton Friedman, Robert Fogel, Gary Becker, Richard Posner, Robert E. Lucas) associated with neoclassical price theory and libertarianism and with the view that regulation and other government intervention is always inefficient compared to free market, to the theories of Keynes about the need of governments' interventions to come out of a serious recessionary crisis or depression. The issue, as I wrote, is that the failure in this financial crisis is not due to economic ideologies (Libertarianism versus Keynesianism) but rather to the lack of ethical values and to the behaviors of many players involved in the subprime mortgage lending and securitization/collateralized debt obligation (CDO) trading processes (Pezzuto, 2008).

The Washington Post, *New York Times*, and *Chicago Tribune*, among other prominent newspapers, reported in May 2006 the report by the Office of Federal Housing Enterprise Oversight (OFHEO) which described "an epic culture of corruption" within the former top leadership of Fannie Mae, announcing that the company would be fined with a $400 million penalty. The same report also stated that Fannie Mae was managed with an "arrogant and unethical corporate culture" only driven by deceptive accounting practices to provide senior management steady increases in profits. The report indicated that Fannie Mae employees manipulated accounting from 1998 to 2004. James B. Lockhart, OFHEO's acting director, said in a statement as the report was released: "Our examination found an environment where the ends justified the means. Senior management manipulated accounting, reaped maximum, undeserved bonuses, and prevented the rest of the world from knowing" (Gordon, 2006; Manor, 2006; Peters, 2006).

There is no doubt that the 2007–2009 financial crisis and the numerous scandals that have followed in recent years have caused lasting damage to the reputation of the financial service industry. This conclusion has been reported by many surveys and also confirmed in a speech by Irene Dorner, the Chief Executive of HSBC US, to about 600 bankers, financial executives, lobbyists, and other industry members (Aspan, 2012).

She stated in that speech that such bad perception of bankers is based on "well-founded" criticism. She said that it will take a long time to rebuild the reputation and trust on the market. Dorner also encouraged banks to rethink their fundamental ways of doing business, and to foster meritocracy culture to make the organizations sustainable (Aspan, 2012).

It is going to take quite some time before the banks, and in particular the global systemically important financial institutions (SIFIs) that have been involved in the 2007–2009 financial crisis and several subsequent scandals in 2012, will be able to rebuild trust, admiration, respect, and good feelings, which are some of the building blocks of corporate reputation. Effective brand management requires that these banks will progressively improve their rankings on these building blocks over the years, thus restoring their reputation and perception in consumers' minds.

Furthermore, in a recent blog post, Sallie Krawcheck (2012), past President of Merrill Lynch, US Trust, Smith Barney, reported that "research shows that financial services is the least trusted US industry, with less than half of the public believing that banks will do the right thing." In the same post she make recommendations for what bankers can do to improve their reputation:

- "quit messing up;"
- "improve customer satisfaction, pay bank employees based on customer satisfaction and trust instead of based on shareholders, shareholders, shareholders;"
- "take responsibility when you're wrong and apologize. Really apologize;"
- "rethink product disclosures … and really rethink cost disclosures;"
- "appoint a consumer ombudsman who reports to the Board;"
- "change the community volunteer days from picking up trash in parks to providing financial planning to families who need it" (Krawcheck, 2012).

In an interview in the *Economist* magazine (2008), titled "A Personal View of the Crisis. Confessions of a Risk Manager," a risk manager of a large global bank confessed that there were evident warning signs of trouble in 2005. As he reported in the interview: "It was the hiccup in the structured-credit market in May 2005 which gave the strongest indication of what was to come." He indicated also that, "bonds were marked down by the rating agencies from investment grade to non-investment grade, or 'junk' and since they were widely held in structured-credit portfolios, the downgrades caused a big dislocation in the market." According to the risk manager there were evident warning signs of an initial liquidity crisis in 2005 and 2007 that have been partially overlooked by risk management due to the high pressures for earnings by traders and executives. He concludes that management did not pay attention to risk management and leaned toward giving the benefit of the doubt to the risk-takers, thus "collective common sense suffered as a result" (*Economist*, 2008).

In October 2012, Martin Wheatley, the head of the new UK Financial Conduct Authority, accused bankers of avoiding responsibility for misconduct by hiding behind committee management, and raised the proposal of prosecuting senior executives like in the US with the following statement: "In the future we want individuals held to account." He also recommended criminal prosecution for bankers who manipulated Libor and caused other serious market abuses in the financial-services industry and in other industries as well.

He added: "Part of the industry appears to feel that it can abuse customer relationships time and time again without taking any impact from it" (Moore, 2012).

On both sides of the Atlantic Ocean people are starting to feel strongly disappointed and frustrated with the lack of accountability of political, business, and economic leaders. As Moisés Naím (2011) reported in his article of October 26, 2011 in the *Financial Times* titled "Take Note America: The Public is Angry," the *Occupy Wall Street* protests and similar protests in other parts of the world are the signal that people are collectively experiencing rage at an elite that is doing obscenely well while many backslide. As he also stated in his article:

Americans' higher tolerance for inequality … is over; at least for now. The long, peaceful coexistence with income and wealth inequality is ending. Americans are now infuriated by the fact that chief executives at some of the nation's largest companies earned around 340 times more than a typical American worker. (Naím, 2011)

He also adds that there is research evidence that nothing makes people take to the streets in protest like public budget cuts and austerity measures. People are upset, and not only in the US, since there is "intolerance towards a hoarding by the 'few' of unfathomable wealth, and profiting even in the midst of the crisis. The rich are seen to be either benefiting from bail-outs and other stimulus measures, or to be immune to the fiscal austerity that governments in many countries have had to adopt to stabilize their economies" (Naím, 2011). In the US this phenomenon has been overcome within approximately a couple of years from the financial crisis as the country emerged from recession and unemployment progressively fell.

According to an Organisation for Economic Cooperation and Development (OECD) study (2011) titled "An Overview of Growing Income Inequalities in OECD Countries: Main Findings," the income inequality rose in 17 of its 22 countries surveyed between the mid-1980s and late-2000s (OECD, 2011, p. 22).

These inequality differences are mainly due to distribution of wages and salaries. The study also indicates that:

> Rising income inequality creates economic, social and political challenges ... since inequality ... breeds social resentment and generates political instability. It can also fuel populist, protectionist, and anti-globalization sentiments. People will no longer support open trade and free markets if they feel that they are losing out while a small group of winners is getting richer and richer. (OECD, 2011, p. 40)

Possible solutions to the problem proposed in the study are:

- more inclusive employment promotion facilitating access to employment for under-represented groups, such as youths, older workers, women, and migrants;
- more balanced policy measures between temporary and permanent employment contracts;
- more intensive human capital investment (that is, promoting the up-skilling of the workforce with job-related training and formal education over working life);
- tax reform and benefit policies for increasing redistributive effects (that is, based on government transfers and taxes) (OECD, 2011, pp. 40–41).

Brian Gloom of the *Financial Times* (2011) reported on October 27, 2011, in his article titled "Top Directors' Total Earnings Rise 49%," that FTSE 100 directors saw their total earnings rise by 49 percent in the past financial year, taking the average to just under £2.7 million, according to research by Incomes Data Services, the pay monitoring group. Steve Tatton, editor of the report, said: "Britain's economy may be struggling to return to pre-recession levels of output, but the same cannot be said of FTSE 100 directors' remuneration" (Groom, 2011).

Tatton also added: "At a time when employees are experiencing real wage cuts and risk losing their livelihoods, without further explanation it may be difficult for FTSE 100 companies to justify the significant increase in earnings awarded to their directors."

Brendan Barber, General Secretary of the Trades Union Congress, said: "These bumper settlements prove that chief executive officers' pay bears no resemblance to performance or economic reality" (Groom, 2011).

The answer to some of the most challenging contemporary crises may come from the wisdom of the past and from some of the most prominent, present, and past economists and thought leaders.

Financial reforms, rules, and regulations are fine but what really needs to be changed is the underlying culture of many people and organizations in the Western world with a "real" (not just the marketing on the corporate websites) return to integrity, to social responsibility, to accountability, to corporate citizenship, to community support, and to business ethics. Individuals and companies have to start thinking again about long-term sustainability, to the respect of others and of laws and regulations, and not just to their short-term benefits, how to take advantage of others, how to bypass rules and how to find short-cuts to immediately reach wealth and success regardless of what happens to others and to society as a whole.

Raghuram Rajan (2010) in his book *Fault Lines* stated: "The public has lost faith in the system where the rules of the game seem tilted in favor of a few" (Rajan, 2010, p. 154). He also adds:

> *If we do not mend the fault lines, we could well have another crisis, albeit different in its details from the current one. Another crisis will tax already stretched public and household finances, as well as the fraying political consensus behind the system, perhaps to breaking point. (Rajan, 2010, p. 155)*

Nouriel Roubini, in his article titled "The Instability of Inequality," regarding the current global wave of social and political turmoil and instability, states that while these protests have no unified theme, they express in different ways the serious concerns of the world's working and middle classes about their prospects in the face of a growing concentration of power among economic, financial, and political elites in advanced economies cutting jobs, generating inadequate final demand, excess capacity, and uncertain future demand. Consequently, cutting jobs weakens final demand because it reduces income and increases inequality. The result, according to Roubini, is that free markets don't generate enough final demand. He also states that the problem is not new since Karl Marx oversold socialism but was right in claiming that globalization, unfettered financial capitalism, and redistribution of income and wealth from labor to capital could lead capitalism to self-destruct. As he argued, unregulated capitalism can lead to bouts of over-capacity, under-consumption, and the recurrence of destructive financial crises, fueled by credit bubbles and asset-price booms and busts (Roubini, 2011a).

In his analysis, Roubini also adds that some of the lessons about the need for prudential regulation of the financial system were lost in the Reagan–Thatcher era, when the appetite for massive deregulation was created in part by the flaws in Europe's social–welfare model. Those flaws were reflected in yawning fiscal deficits, regulatory overkills, and a lack of economic dynamism that led to sclerotic growth then and the Eurozone's sovereign-debt crisis now (Roubini, 2011a). This creates a situation where economics would be defined as having unstable debt dynamics and/or multiple equilibriums (Stiglitz, 2011).

Roubini concludes that the laissez-faire Anglo–Saxon model has also now failed miserably. To stabilize market-oriented economies requires a return to the right balance between markets and provision of public goods. This means moving away from both the Anglo–Saxon model of unregulated markets and the continental European model of deficit-driven welfare states. Even an alternative "Asian" growth model – if there really is one – he states, has not prevented a rise in inequality in China, India, and elsewhere. An economic model that does not properly address gross inequality will eventually face a crisis of legitimacy (Roubini, 2011a).

Joseph E. Stiglitz in his article titled "To Cure The Economy" stated that the financial sector's inexcusable recklessness, given free rein by mindless deregulation, was the obvious precipitating factor of the crisis. He also states, however, that, based on his studies, the US economy was very sick even before the crisis and that the housing bubble merely papered over its weaknesses. Without bubble-supported consumption, there would have been a massive shortfall in aggregate demand. Fixing the financial sector was necessary for economic recovery, but not sufficient overall. To understand what needs to be done to prevent other crises in the future, in addition to the financial reforms leaders need to understand the economy's problems before the crises hit. He indicates on the matter three areas for improvement:

1. Rapid productivity increases in America and around the world in manufacturing has outpaced growth in demand, which means that manufacturing employment is decreasing and labor has shifted to services, which today represent over two-thirds of the gross domestic product (GDP) in developed economies.
2. Globalization is another factor contributing to growing inequality, shifting income from those who would spend it to those who won't which lowers aggregate demand and, by the same token, soaring energy prices shift purchasing power from the US and Europe to oil exporters who, recognizing the volatility of energy prices, rightly saved much of this income.
3. The emerging markets' massive buildup of foreign-exchange reserves (Stiglitz, 2011).

Stiglitz concludes that those countries that build up large reserves were able to weather the economic crisis better, so their incentive to accumulate reserves remained even stronger. Furthermore, while bankers have regained their huge bonuses, workers are seeing their wages eroded and their hours diminished, further widening the income gap. The solutions he proposes to solve the structural issues that existed in the US even before the financial crisis and to create a more sustainable economic environment are indicated below:

*   do not concentrate only on fiscal austerity (which is what both Europe and the US so far have chosen to solve their crises) but mainly on strong government expenditures;
*   facilitate restructuring to restore competitiveness through government-financed education and training;
*   promote energy conservation;
*   reduce inequality;
*   reform the global financial system to create an alternative to the buildup of reserves (Stiglitz, 2011).

Stiglitz, in his article titled "Inequality Is Holding Back the Recovery," argues that inequality is closely connected to slow recovery. According to him, the growing inequality of the last few years (after the financial crisis) does not contribute to a robust recovery and kills the "American dream." He also added that inequality represents a serious threat to America. He identifies among the major sources of inequality the following:

1. weak consumer spending due to economic conditions of the middle-class;
2. "the hollowing out of the middle class since the 1970s;"

3. "the weakness of the middle class is holding back tax receipts," thus, low tax receipts also means lower funds for the government to invest in infrastructure, education, research and development, and health;
4. it is more likely to have frequent and severe boom-and-bust cycles with inequality (Stiglitz, 2013).

He also stressed the concept that, by allowing inequality to grow, the country (US) is squandering its most valuable resource – its new generation – and also added: "Tocqueville, who in the 1830s found the egalitarian impulse to be the essence of the American character, is rolling in his grave" (Stiglitz, 2013).

Conclusion

The aftermath of the 2007–2009 financial crisis has certainly dramatically changed millions of people's lives, dreams, lifestyles, hopes, and expectations all over the world. For a few this crisis has meant huge profits (that is, some traders and investors), for many instead it has meant the loss of a job, of their home, of a career opportunity, of a company that went bankrupt, or an even heavier tax burden, lower salaries and bonuses, and reduced welfare benefits. But for all, certainly, one way or another, directly or indirectly, this crisis has meant coming to terms with the awareness that today we live in a complex, highly interconnected, and vulnerable globalized society and that large SIFIs can become a real threat for everyone if not properly regulated and controlled.

The triggering factors of this crisis bring back to my mind the economic theories of Hyman Minsky (Minsky, 1992) on the Financial Instability Hypothesis, but most of all the theory of The Modern Corporation and Private Property by Berle and Means (Berle et al, 1932) who warned about the concentration of economic power driven by the rise of the large corporations and the emergence of a powerful class of professional managers. As Mark S. Mizruchi (2004) said: "Berle and Means warned that the ascendance of management control and unchecked corporate power had potentially serious consequences for the democratic character of the United States." In fact for Berle et al. (1932) the separation of ownership from control actually led to an increased level of democratization in society but also to the ascendance of corporate power in American society. This theory has later on contributed to develop the foundation of our contemporary corporate governance theories such as the agency theory. The too-big-too-fail doctrine may also have its roots in what Berle et al. warned was the condition of excessive concentration of economic power in the hands of professional managers and large corporations. In an environment of euphoric growth, low interest rates and high liquidity, irrational exuberance, fragmented and lax regulatory oversight, and overconfidence in corporate power, among other things, the conditions were all set for a "perfect storm." Thus, there is no doubt that the 2007–2009 financial crisis was generated by triggering factors that were certainly economic but also and, perhaps mostly, conditioned by environmental (high pressure on unmatched results and euphoric expectations), cultural (corporate culture of aggressive collective megalomania), and psychological aspects (greed, self-interest, short-termism, masters of the world) (Berle et al., 1991; Mizruchi, 2004).

Then the question a reader might naturally raise, after reading this chapter is: *What can be done to help change the corporate culture that has led to these moral hazards and criminal behavior?*

There is probably no perfect answer to this difficult question and only time will tell whether the new rules, sanctions, charges, and educational programs undertaken will have a positive effect on the corporate cultural change and to reduce the incentives for wrongdoing.

My personal view on this question is that the goal could be achieved through a combination of things:

1. prove to the unethical corporate world that law enforcement will be timely and effectively executed, and that individual and corporate charges will be faced by dishonest "clans," regardless of their rich, influential, and powerful global lobbies;
2. good and positive behaviors and examples from political and industry leaders are often better and more effective ways to reshape corporate and industry cultures than thousands of words, rules, or sanctions.

These are some good examples that send a strong signal to the industry:

In October 2012 in an interview with the *Financial Times*, Morgan Stanley CEO James Gorman stated that Wall Street employees have been earning too much money and that now staff and remuneration have to be sacrificed as banks cope with lower profits (Alloway and Braithwaite, 2012). Furthermore, the same CEO announced in January 2013 his intention to take a pay cut for the second consecutive year to improve returns for shareholders (Alloway, 2013).

Another important signal to the corporate world of the need for an urgent and radical cultural and regulatory change in the financial industry came in January 2013 when President Obama appointed two former prosecutors as top financial regulators. Mary Jo White as chairman of the Securities and Exchange Commission (SEC), and Richard Cordray as First Director of the Consumer Financial Protection Bureau (Protess and Weiser, 2013).

It looks like finally something is starting to change in financial regulation. Yet, however, let's not be too optimistic about it. Only time (and hopefully the avoidance of new systemic crises) will tell if regulators are on the right track to create a more safe and resilient system. As everyone knows, as soon as a law has been passed, there is always someone who might have high incentives to circumvent it. Thus, a true overhaul of the governance in the financial services industry, I believe, will only be achievable with simple rules, tighter controls, individual criminal charges, scaling down of remuneration and incentives, reduced cronyism and conflicts among politics, regulators, and bankers, and most of all, with radical corporate cultural and values changes.

Now that finally the financial services industry has its hangover from the easy-money euphoric craze and that the world economy is almost out of the mess, it's time to mend the broken pieces and to restore hope and trust in the hearts and minds of the "Lost Generation" who probably just missed their "dream."

Lesson learned: "Don't mess up with your next generation to make 'big bucks' today. Even your children will be part of it. Think longer term as it will also take quite some time before you will rebuild your corporate reputation and self-respect. Money is a short-term reward, the well-being of your children and their future generation is a ticket for eternity."

6 Experts' Insights for Improved Governance

Thought Leaders' and Industry Experts' Perspective on the Financial Crisis and Their Recommendations on How to Create a More Sustainable Financial System

Aristotle's lesson on the pursuit of "wealth" seems to be a very contemporary concept and a sort of inspirational guideline to avoid in the future new financial, economic, debt and social crises like the ones we are experiencing these days (April 2013). It reminds us that the purpose of business is to create wealth in a way that makes the manager a better person and the world a better place. According to this concept it is possible to simultaneously create wealth, be ethical, and be happy (Brown and Ross, 2009, pp. 3–23).

My aim is to integrate in this book a comprehensive perspective on the topic based on: (1) a selective and relevant literature review; (2) my own extensive hands-on professional experience in the industry as a senior executive in risk management and management consultant (over 20 years); and (3) the precious contributions offered by leading experts on the topic of the financial crisis through personal interviews.

During the period January 2011 to June 2012 I undertook a set of interviews with some industry experts and scholars. The scope of these interviews was to integrate my extensive desk research work with valuable and original contributions that could provide additional insights and forward-looking perspectives on how to avoid similar future crises.

I decided to invite a restricted number of highly qualified professionals, prominent scholars, and thought leaders to be interviewed. They kindly accepted my invitation, despite the fact that I was unable to offer them any form of economic remuneration, They dedicated considerable time and attention to this initiative and have provided great original contributions to this book. In terms of selection criteria for the interviewed scholars and industry leaders, I have tried, as far as possible, to choose a well-balanced mix of diverse industry, professional, and seniority profiles (that is, professors, legendary and prominent scholars, banking officers, chief economists, regulators, financial analysts, journalists, and others). The diversity in the selection criteria aims to increase the holistic perspective on the topic of the interview and to reduce potential ideological biases or corporative conflicts of interest. Probably the main criterion I have used in the selection of the participants to my study (aside, of course, from their undeniable expertise on the topic of the research) was their declared commitment to give a truly unbiased and independent interview.

The interviews have been supported by a questionnaire, which has been validated prior to being used for the study.

The questionnaire consists of five closed-ended questions/statements (based on Likert scales) and five open-ended questions.

THOUGHT LEADERS AND INDUSTRY EXPERTS SELECTION CRITERIA

Academic Thought Leaders/Scholars:

- prominent publications on risk management, or finance, or corporate governance, or corporate social responsibility, and the 2007–2009 financial crisis;
- seasoned academic career as full professor and/or department chairs;
- top-ranking and/or award-winning professorship (voted "Professor of the Year") in their universities;
- willingness to openly express their opinion on the topics of the research, independence of mind and spirit, without the security of an anonymous interview;
- extensive industry advisory exposure and conferences lecturing.

Industry Experts/Thought Leaders:

- seasoned "hands-on" expertise in the field of finance, trading, investment banking, risk management, or board-level corporate governance of financial institutions;
- senior officer or executive (leadership) status or internationally recognized financial and economic analyst with leading global organizations;
- willingness to openly express their opinion on the topics of the research, independence of mind and spirit, without the security of an anonymous interview;
- speakers at international conferences on the topic of risk management, finance, corporate governance, corporate social responsibility, or corporate cultural change, and the 2007–2009 financial crisis;
- author or co-author of publications on the topics or contributor.

The following scholars, thought leaders, and industry experts (whose job title is the one they reported at the time of the interview) accepted my invitation to participate in this survey with their interviews:

Antonio Argandoña, Full Professor of Economics and holder of the "la Caixa" Chair of Corporate Social Responsibility and Corporate Governance at IESE Business School in Barcelona, Spain;

Alfonso Asaro, Director of Financial Services Analytical Applications Europe at Oracle Corporation and Expert of Enterprise Risk Management Programs, Austria;

Elio Borgonovi, Full Professor of Economics and Management of Public Administration at Bocconi University, Senior Professor of SDA Bocconi School of Management (Public Management and Policy Department) and Former Dean of SDA Bocconi School of Management from 1997 to 2002, Italy;

Antonio Castagna, Financial Modelling Expert at Iason Ltd., Financial Analyst, and Former Derivatives Trader, Italy;

Fabiano Colombini, Full Professor of Economics of Financial Institutions and Markets at the Faculty of Economics of Università di Pisa, Italy;

Aswarth Damodaran, the Kerschner Family Chair in Finance Education, Finance Department at New York University Stern School of Business, USA;

Gregorio De Felice, Head of Research and Chief Economist, Intesa Sanpaolo Bank, Italy;

Victor Di Giorgio, Vice President and Technology, Country Head Italy at Citi and Western Europe Corporate O&T Cultural Change Ambassador at Citi, Italy;

Darrell Duffie, Dean Witter Distinguished Professor of Finance at The Graduate School of Business, Stanford University, USA;

Charles Goodhart, Emeritus Professor at the London School of Economics and Director of the Financial Regulation Research Programme and former member of the Bank of England's Monetary Policy Committee (1997–2000), UK;

Etienne Koehler, Associate Professor of Financial Mathematics at La Sorbonne University of Paris and Expert of Credit Risk Analytics, France;

Alexander N. Kostyuk, Professor of Corporate Governance and Finance and Director of the International Center for Banking and Corporate Governance, Ukrainian Academy of Banking of the National Bank of Ukraine. Professor of Corporate Governance and Finance at the Hanken School of Economics (Finland). Editor-in-Chief, Corporate Ownership and Control journal; Editor-in-Chief, Corporate Board: Role, Duties and Composition journal; Editor-in-Chief, Risk Governance and Control: Financial Markets and Institutions journal; Editor-in-Chief, Journal of Governance and Regulation, Ukraine;

George Koukis, Founder and President of Temenos (one of the world's leading supplier of packaged banking software), Switzerland;

William W. Lang, Senior Vice President and Lending Officer Supervision, Regulation and Credit at the Federal Reserve Bank of Philadelphia and Fellow of the Wharton Financial Institutions Center, USA;

Fabio Mercurio, Head of Quant Business Managers at Bloomberg LP, New York and Director of the Research Committee of Iason Ltd. Previously, he was the Head of Financial Engineering at Banca IMI, USA;

Massimo Meterangelo, Head of Group Wide Portfolio Consolidation at Unicredit Group, Italy;

Wolfgang Munchau – President of Eurointelligence ASBL and Associate Editor of the *Financial Times*, UK/Belgium;

Fabrizio Pezzani, Full Professor of Business Administration, Accounting and Control and Director of the Bachelor Degree in Management of Public Administration and International Institutions (CLAPI) Bocconi University, and Senior Faculty member of the SDA Bocconi School of Management, Department of Policy Analysis and Public Management, Italy;

Richard A. Posner – Senior Lecturer in Law at University of Chicago Law School and Judge of the US Court of Appeals for the Seventh Circuit, USA;

Gabriele Sabato, Head of Portfolio Management – Retail Credit Risk at Ulster Bank/Royal Bank of Scotland, Ireland;

Giulio Sapelli, Full Professor of Economic History at the Università degli Studi di Milano, board member of Unicredit Banca-Impresa and President of Audit and Control Committee, scientific advisor of Organisation for Economic Cooperation and Development (OECD) for non-profit sector, Italy;

Giacomo Vaciago, Full Professor and Director of the Institute of Economics and Finance at Catholic University of Milan. Italy.

The following questions were submitted to these participants:

1. Was the 2007–2009 financial crisis predictable and avoidable?
2. What actionable economic/fiscal policies, reforms, or risk mitigation plans could have been immediately implemented to reduce the impact of the housing market and credit bubbles and the meltdown caused by the crisis?
3. Are the monetary and fiscal policies, the government bail-outs, (Troubled Asset Relief Program – TARP, Term Asset-Backed Securities Loan Facility – TALF, and so on), and the financial reforms introduced (for example, Dodd–Frank Act, of which the Volcker Rule is a central component, and so on) after 2008 valid long-term solutions to regulate and stabilize financial markets and to avoid the risk of new crises (double dip)?
4. What still needs to be changed in terms of financial regulation and regulatory oversight, corporate governance, managerial cultures, internal controls, (COSO) enterprise risk management (ERM) Framework, and Basel III Framework to prevent in the future other systemic crises?
5. What needs to be done to instill a new culture in the business world in order to improve corporate governance, executive accountability, fair compensation, and more generally, integrity and ethics in the financial markets?

Interview with **Antonio Argandoña** (personal communication, 2012), Full Professor of Economics and holder of the "la Caixa" Chair of Corporate Social Responsibility and Corporate Governance at IESE Business School in Barcelona, Spain.

Please use the following *Likert scale* to provide your answer:

1= Strongly Disagree; 2 = Disagree; 3 = Neither; 4 = Agree; 5 = Strongly Agree

1.1)	1	2	3	4	5
The 2007–2009 financial crisis was predictable and avoidable.				X	

1.2) Professor Argandoña was the 2007–2009 financial crisis predictable and avoidable?

The financial crisis was predictable because the existence of a bubble in the real estate sector was obvious in several countries, like the US, Ireland and Spain. In fact, as the bubble was growing, the possibility of a financial crash was more and more probable, and many economists and experts denounced it.

This does not mean that the date or the consequences of the financial crisis were predictable. The economic atmosphere was very optimistic in those countries, so that even in the summer of 2007 a short adjustment in the real estate market and a lower rate of gross domestic product (GDP) growth were forecasted, perhaps even a short recession, but not a big crisis. And the main reason was the expectation of a correct functioning of the global financial markets. The financing of the banks and other intermediaries was expected to continue without especial difficulties, just with somewhat higher interest rates and a few financial casualties. The possibility of a lack of financing for the financial institutions was not considered as real in the first months of 2007 and, of course, the experts and the authorities were confident that the market of sovereign debt would not suffer a big drawback.

All this changed in the months of June to August 2007. Then, the reality of a big global crisis was patent. The wholesale financial markets were closed, and almost all institutions had serious difficulties to refinance their operations. This was the direct consequence of the subprime crisis in the US: the evidence of the spread of toxic assets all over the world and the radical uncertainty that this created meant that the markets were not able to refinance banking operations, even at higher interest rates and tied to stricter conditions. I think that this was the differential aspect of the crisis that the experts were not able to predict.

Please use the following *Likert scale* to provide your answer:

1= Strongly Disagree; 2 = Disagree; 3 = Neither; 4 = Agree; 5 = Strongly Agree

2.1)	1	2	3	4	5
The economic/fiscal and monetary policies, financial reforms, and risk mitigation plans implemented by policy makers and regulators to reduce the impact of the housing market and credit bubbles were comprehensive and effective to reduce the financial meltdown.		X			

2.1) Professor Argandoña what actionable economic/fiscal policies, reforms, or risk mitigation plans could have been immediately implemented to reduce the impact of the housing market and credit bubbles and the meltdown caused by the crisis?

The answer to this question differs according to each country and moment. As explained in the first question, initially we expected a moderate recession, meant to be controlled through the traditional monetary and fiscal policies. Governments devoted their efforts to this, through fiscal help to disadvantaged families (unemployment benefits), expenditure incentives (for instance, to renew the fleet of cars) and infrastructure works. In the Spanish case, this was eased by the fact that the country had a surplus fiscal balance and a low level of public debt.

In turn, central banks immediately provided abundant liquidity to financial institutions. In this way, they replaced, in the short run, financial markets which were blocked at that time due to the subprime crisis. In Spain, these measures seemed to be sufficient, if we take into account the determined action undertaken by the Bank of Spain during the previous years, in order to cover for possible banking losses derived from excessive investment in housing. In fact, the international financial authorities repeatedly quoted Spain as a model of excellent management prior to the financial crisis.

What happened in the following months was the development of the successive stages of a crisis, whose hardness took a long time to arise. First, the fiscal measures were insufficient and badly approached. They took into account political interests to a higher extent than the real needs of the economy (this happened in Spain). Second, what started as a crisis caused by a housing bubble and exacerbated by the blocking of banks' financing, turned into a severe financial crisis which affected, first, some North American institutions and afterwards, other European banks, until it became apparent that it was not only a matter of liquidity but also of solvency. But, at that point, the solutions became very complex. In Spain, for instance, the authorities tried to hide the existence of a problem that affected many banks, because they were afraid of creating a systemic crisis, and they tried to keep it at a reduced and manageable level. This is evidenced by the repeated stress tests applied in Europe, which brought, in theory, satisfactory results, but which repeatedly proved to be insufficient. The situation caused by the bankruptcy of Lehman Brothers was the catalyst of the real extent of the crisis. From that moment, the measures were taken quickly, especially in the US, but at a lower pace in the European Union.

In Europe, all this was complicated further when – due to the acknowledgement made by the Greek Government that its public deficit was greater than the one announced – the risk premium rocketed: first the Greek one and then that of other countries (Portugal, Ireland, Italy, Spain …). The sovereign debt crisis has had specific features in each country: in Greece, it was mainly due to the lack of control and political will of both the government and the citizens; in Portugal, it was due to the difficulty to grow and a loose fiscal policy over the years; in Ireland, to having saved the banking system, in part because of imposition coming from the European Central Bank (ECB) and the European Union; in Spain, due to the fiscal stimulus measures and the lack of control of regional public spending. But the important thing, whichever the case, was the interaction between the different crises. As mentioned, the housing bubble translated into a recession that caused a financial crisis, and resorting to fiscal policies to solve all these problems turned the sovereign debt crisis into another stage of the financial crisis, provided that sovereign debt constitutes an important part of banks' assets.

Please use the following *Likert scale* to provide your answer:

1= Strongly Disagree; 2 = Disagree; 3 = Neither; 4 = Agree; 5 = Strongly Agree

3.1)	1	2	3	4	5
The monetary and fiscal policies, the government bail-outs, (TARP, TALF, and so on), and the financial reforms introduced (for example, Dodd–Frank Act, of which the Volcker Rule is a central component, and so on) after 2008 were valid long-term solutions to regulate and stabilize financial markets and to avoid the risk of new crises (double dip).			X		

3.2) Professor Argandoña are the monetary and fiscal policies, the government bail-outs, (TARP, TALF, and so on), and the financial reforms introduced (for example, Dodd–Frank Act, of which the Volcker Rule is a central component, and so on) after 2008 valid long-term solutions to regulate and stabilize financial markets and to avoid the risk of new crises (double dip)?

Again, each country has its own features. The expansionary monetary policy was necessary and it was clearly applied in some countries like the US, but more slowly and with less audacity in the European Zone. The liquidity supplied by the Central Banks stopped the first banking crises but it did not resolve the insolvency problems. The latter needed government bail-outs, which were undertook more vigorously in the US and Great Britain, also in some other European countries, but to a lower extent in others. In Spain, for instance, the measures to rescue banks were applied late and partially; the clarification of banking balances was slow and incomplete, and in spring 2012 the solution to the financial crisis is still not clearly defined.

Generally speaking, those solutions adopted quickly and generously have provided better outcomes. In countries like Spain, the difficult solution to the financial crisis has been complicated further by the sovereign debt crisis. Financial markets have punished governments not only because of their management of fiscal policies, but also because of the need and urgency to solve the banks' problems, provided that markets are not willing to lend to those institutions, but they fear as well that the implication of governments worsens the level of public debt and, in turn, the sovereign debt crisis. In this sense, the countries that implemented the adjustment prior to the sovereign debt crisis enjoyed a clear advantage, especially in the European Union. This was also true for other countries like the US with a broad access to international financing, subject to conditions which were not available to other countries, like the peripheral ones in the Euro Zone.

All in all, the measures suggested to solve the financial crisis are part of the available tools according to conventional economics: extraordinary supply of liquidity, at low interest rates, long terms, and softened collateral requisites, and the suppression of the stigma to entities that resort to them; the differences across countries are less important and adapted to their institutional and legal specificities, and the main difference lies on the speed and determination to undertake them.

The measures to confront the solvency problem are also well known: isolation of bank's toxic assets (bad banks, special funds, the governments and independent institutions' purchase of depreciated assets, and so on), capital provisions to confront the needs that stem from the crisis, new requisites for the provision of losses from depreciated assets, promotion of mergers (widely used in Spain, with poor results) and, mainly, recapitalization of the banking system through public or special funds, like the ones created by the European Union. Again, the speed in which losses were recognised and provisions were made was the key to the success of these measures.

In overall terms, I believe that the available tools were already known and that the pace and aggressiveness used differs from country to country, depending on their possibilities (be it legal, political or social, including the citizens' acceptance of reforms) and the wisdom of their politicians.

Please use the following *Likert scale* to provide your answer:

1= Strongly Disagree; 2 = Disagree; 3 = Neither; 4 = Agree; 5 = Strongly Agree

4.1)	1	2	3	4	5
There is a need for improved financial regulation, regulatory oversight, financial institutions' corporate governance (that is, COSO ERM, Internal Controls, Basel III, Dodd–Frank, Credit Ratings, and so on) and managerial cultures (that is, CSR, Ethics, and so on).					X

4.2) Professor Argandoña what still needs to be changed in terms of financial regulation and regulatory oversight, corporate governance, managerial cultures, internal controls, COSO ERM Framework, and Basel III Framework to avoid in the future other systemic crises?

Certainly, we need a deep review of the regulation, supervision and control tools. Here I will only state some of them.

It is important to make progress in the international homogenization of such mechanisms. It is logical that each country tried to maintain the highest possible autonomy, but we should take a step forward in the coordination mechanisms, especially in the case of banking crises that affect many countries, and also to prevent the spread of crises to other countries or to avoid that they affect other nation's institutions; this would create systemic crises which otherwise should not have happened.

In the Euro Zone we will need some type of bail-out mechanism for financial institutions, which should be common to the different countries. This should be part of the future reform of the ECB, and it is related to its task as a lender of last resort – not set out so far – as well as the existence of mechanisms of fiscal coordination, set out by the Euro Treaty. This will be a long but very necessary process, which will probably end up in important advances to elaborate a common fiscal policy and a shared European Treasury.

The regulation of rating agencies will always be a difficult problem. In my opinion, the problem does not lie in their tasks, but in the way the financial institutions, the governments and the regulators use those ratings. Applying automatically the ratings is very convenient for creditors but it reduces considerably the necessary flexibility to consider the debtors' situation and it transforms decisions which are meant to be easy, into deep crises.

Please use the following *Likert scale* to provide your answer:

1= Strongly Disagree; 2 = Disagree; 3 = Neither; 4 = Agree; 5 = Strongly Agree

5.1)	1	2	3	4	5
Among the root causes of the 2007–2009 financial crisis are there major failures in the financial firms' corporate governance, traders and executive's integrity, accountability, ethical behaviors, and their excessive compensation systems, in addition to industry deregulation and major failures in regulatory oversight?					X

5.2) Professor Argandoña what needs to be done to instill a new culture in the business world in order to improve corporate governance, executive accountability, fair compensation, and more in general, integrity and ethics in the financial markets?

The financial crisis was, to a great extent, an ethical crisis. In all crises, be them larger or smaller, the ethical dimension is always important, but I think that, in this case, not only individual ethical mistakes (greed, injustice, lies, lack of transparency, pride, arrogance, and so on) and organizational mistakes occurred, but also at least three relatively new issues arose.

One of them was the dismantling of protection mechanisms against immoral behaviors and governance mistakes. Many societies considered that those immoral behaviors were normal, acceptable, and with no risk, so they spread. Therefore, the preventive measures that should have avoided the detrimental consequences of those behaviors were reduced. That is, unwanted actions became often a general rule, and the mechanisms that should have avoided their impact were blocked.

The second novel factor was an increasing disconnection between, on one hand, ethics and the approaches taken by social sciences (economics, sociology political science, psychology …) and, on the other hand, the practices of those sciences. Somehow, during the recent years the separation thesis, which claims that social sciences outcomes are independent to ethics, has consolidated because these sciences are considered autonomous and self-sufficient, without any need for ethical control. In this way, we lost the chance of generating within those sciences mechanisms for identifying moral problems and, then, for creating correction mechanisms.

The third factor that I would like to mention is the change experienced by the Western society, at least to a higher extent than in the past. Our fellow citizens are more and more individualistic, emotiotivistic, utilitarian and materialistic, and this has changed the way of posing the ethical approach to the problems related to the crisis. The crisis affects the people's welfare, who consider themselves damaged by the crisis and they respond with a utilitarian reaction, asking for a quick solution to the problems, without caring about its cost. But this means, ultimately, that they insist on the same conception of ethics, or better called, the disconnection between ethics and the problems, that led to this crisis.

Alfonso Asaro, Director of Financial Services Analytical Applications Europe at Oracle Corporation and Expert of Enterprise Risk Management Programs, Austria.

Please use the following *Likert scale* to provide your answer:

1= Strongly Disagree; 2 = Disagree; 3 = Neither; 4 = Agree; 5 = Strongly Agree

1.1)	1	2	3	4	5
The 2007–2009 financial crisis was predictable and avoidable.				X	

1.2) Mr Asaro was the 2007–2009 financial crisis predictable and avoidable?

The crises – I would say more than one – did not happen unannounced; warning signs and credit deterioration were rather ignored or overlooked; however investigation on each and every financial scandal of the past has shown that while controls and governance were in place the reason for these events to happen was very much related to human factors in terms of negligence, incompetence and complacency. Business models have been designed and projected on the basis of a constant growth of real estate and financial market without taking into consideration the possibility of economic downturn or even the fact that growth cannot last indefinitely; financial institutions have reached an excessive degree of leverage and/or concentration, albeit not fully reflected by capital ratios due to massive utilization of derivative instruments and intergroup financial transactions. All relevant internal and external bodies responsible for risk management, governance and supervision (risk management, executive management, internal audit, external auditors, rating agencies, supervision) have not been able to identify or address the increasing risk profile.

Regulators were mostly focused on compliance rather than risk issues and their actions were determined and took place ex post, providing even more rigidity in the market and increasing liquidity constraints; furthermore, remedial actions have been taken after quite some time while a more timely action would have probably reduced the overall impact and severity.

Please use the following *Likert scale* to provide your answer:

1= Strongly Disagree; 2 = Disagree; 3 = Neither; 4 = Agree; 5 = Strongly Agree

2.1)	1	2	3	4	5
The economic/fiscal and monetary policies, financial reforms, and risk mitigation plans implemented by policy makers and regulators to reduce the impact of the housing market and credit bubbles were comprehensive and effective to reduce the financial meltdown.		X			

2.2) Mr Asaro what actionable economic/fiscal policies, reforms, or risk mitigation plans could have been immediately implemented to reduce the impact of the housing market and credit bubbles and the meltdown caused by the crisis?

There was a very slow response to the deterioration of the housing market which went into a free-fall, immediate support into debt renegotiation – for instance – would have reduced the amount and the impact of foreclosures and the overall costs for taxpayers.

Liquidity should have been injected into the market under close supervision from the regulator on a quid pro quo basis – that is on the basis of a presentation of a business plan – while a significant part of the injected liquidity has been used to repeat speculative behaviors without any real benefit for taxpayers or investors.

Regulatory actions have been taken on ex post basis on a rather emotional and erratic basis, on the assumption that an overregulated market would have prevented the repeating of the crisis; in reality the increasing regulatory pressure is simply draining skills and resources from financial institutions preventing them from addressing structural issues (capital compositions, capital allocation, risk management and accounting policies) in a more organized fashion.

Please use the following *Likert scale* to provide your answer:

1= Strongly Disagree; 2 = Disagree; 3 = Neither; 4 = Agree; 5 = Strongly Agree

3.1)	1	2	3	4	5
The monetary and fiscal policies, the government bail-outs, (TARP, TALF, and so on), and the financial reforms introduced (for example, Dodd–Frank Act, of which the Volcker Rule is a central component, and so on) after 2008 were valid long-term solutions to regulate and stabilize financial markets and to avoid the risk of new crises (double dip).		X			

3.2) Mr Asaro are the monetary and fiscal policies, the government bail-outs, (TARP, TALF, and so on), and the financial reforms introduced (for example, Dodd–Frank Act, of which the Volcker Rule is a central component, and so on) after 2008 valid long-term solutions to regulate and stabilize financial markets and to avoid the risk of new crises (double dip)?

No, as explained an overregulated market is not a stable or a safe market; administrative and reporting burdens – constantly changing or subject to different interpretations – will prevent banks from addressing structural issues in a more organized fashion.

Specifically:

- lending/liquidity injection should be released only upon presentation of a detailed business plan subject to monitoring;
- applications of concepts like countercyclical approach are very difficult to implement, eventually should see the involvement of state agencies;
- some of the rules presented are probably in contradiction;
- there is still limited attention to human factor;
- stress testing exercises are requiring significant resources without much benefits.

Please use the following *Likert scale* to provide your answer:

1= Strongly Disagree; 2 = Disagree; 3 = Neither; 4 = Agree; 5 = Strongly Agree

4.1)	1	2	3	4	5
There is a need for improved financial regulation, regulatory oversight, financial institutions' corporate governance (that is, COSO ERM, Internal Controls, Basel III, Dodd–Frank, Credit Ratings, and so on) and managerial cultures (that is, CSR, Ethics, and so on).				X	

4.2) Mr Asaro what still needs to be changed in terms of financial regulation and regulatory oversight, corporate governance, managerial cultures, internal controls, COSO ERM Framework, and Basel III Framework to avoid in the future other systemic crises?

The ongoing trend is definitively leaning towards an overregulated financial market. However the delays that all major regulations (Basel III, International Accounting Standards (IAS)) are encountering in the final approval process are showing that some regulatory actions have been taken with excessive haste or with unrealistic expectations about its impact and implications.

Some of the major points of concern refer to the following:

- Basel III would create an overregulated market giving too much power to regulators to steer banks' decisions;
- increased capital requirements would force the bank to look for additional funds in a time where going to market is quite expensive, thus forcing also to look for external shareholders and modify existing governance model and making banks less intrinsically stable;
- risk is not managed through increased capital requirements, particularly liquidity risks;
- application of concepts like countercyclical approach are very difficult to apply in practice;
- the introduction of SIFI concept – systemically important financial institution – is altering what is supposed to be a level playing field;
- American regulation is mostly addressing compliance issues but not enough operational issues.

The incoming regulation however is having a positive impact in many areas, such as:

- increased involvement of management into risk and governance decisions, particularly of chief finance officers (CFO);
- awareness of the business implications of a prolonged liquidity shortage or economic downturn;
- importance of an efficient and complete management information system;
- better understanding of how risks are generated and should be managed;
- centrality of a good Corporate Governance model in place to ensure long-term stability.

All in all, apart from some pure technical issues such as liquidity risk management, the incoming regulation will be effective as long as it will address the human factor, bearing in mind the differences in the cultural and business environment.

Please use the following *Likert scale* to provide your answer:

1= Strongly Disagree; 2 = Disagree; 3 = Neither; 4 = Agree; 5 = Strongly Agree

5.1)	1	2	3	4	5
Among the root causes of the 2007–2009 financial crisis, are there major failures in the financial firms' corporate governance, traders and executive's integrity, accountability, ethical behaviors, and their excessive compensation systems, in addition to industry deregulation and major failures in regulatory oversight?					X

5.2) Mr Asaro what needs to be done to instill a new culture in the business world in order to improve corporate governance, executive accountability, fair compensation, and more in general, integrity and ethics in the financial markets?

A detailed analysis of existing regulation in place would probably show that if properly applied it would be more than sufficient to address human behaviors, while there are some technical flaws and inconsistencies which have still to be addressed.

Addressing the human factor is always by far the most complex and articulated issue, considering each organization is a living entity and as such human interactions are relatively unpredictable.

In this respect, actions should be taken to address:

- closer and more detailed scrutiny during the approval process of bank's management;
- review of compensation scheme, linking it to longer-term goals;
- encourage executive job rotation as a measure to reduce complacency and the risk of fraudulent behaviors;
- review external auditors' rules of engagement and standards.

Interview with **Elio Borgonovi** (personal communication, 2012), Full Professor of Economics and Management of Public Administration at Bocconi University, Senior Professor of SDA Bocconi School of Management (Public Management and Policy Department) and Former Dean of SDA Bocconi School of Management from 1997 to 2002, Italy.

Please use the following *Likert scale* to provide your answer:

1= Strongly Disagree; 2 = Disagree; 3 = Neither; 4 = Agree; 5 = Strongly Agree

1.1)	1	2	3	4	5
The 2007–2009 financial crisis was predictable and avoidable.				X	

1.2) Professor Borgonovi was the 2007–2009 financial crisis predictable and avoidable?

The financial crisis was not predictable and avoidable if we consider the consolidated mainstream of the economic theories, based on the idea that the economic growth could be continuous and mainly related to productivity. Also the idea of economic growth driven by consumption and by the traditional industries, like automotive and real estate, in some way did not enable most of the analysts to understand that the financial bubble was actually different from the previous ones, that characterized the last years of the last century and the first years of the new decades. Also the delocalization of many productions and the financial value created by boosting paper economy gave the illusion of an increasing wealth that was not based on the real economy indicators.

Nevertheless, there were clear signals of high-risk growth. The subprime loans mean to abandon any risk evaluation criteria. The distribution of the risk through the derivatives is irrational because it is based on a wrong concept of risk sharing. Actually you have risk sharing when different autonomous economic entities accept to take part in a high risky business, or when a company can create a diversification of its activity. On the contrary, even if there are financial lenders specialized and focused on subprime or banks that have a large part of their investment in real estate companies (as it happened in Spain and in some other countries), the distribution all around the world of derivatives has a pandemic effect. When the pillars fall down, the whole paper castle falls down too, because of the sudden reduction of trust among banks, institutional investors and individual savers.

Moreover, the diffusion of other financial products, as hedge funds and credit default swaps (CDS), based on the philosophy of high risk, high financial performance in a very short time and investment criteria based on the payback period encouraged and consolidated the short-term economic evaluation against long-term evaluation criteria. This perspective again was strengthened by the remuneration scheme or path of top and senior managers in financial institutions, who pursued short-term financial results in order to get high bonuses or stock options.

Please use the following *Likert scale* to provide your answer:

1= Strongly Disagree; 2 = Disagree; 3 = Neither; 4 = Agree; 5 = Strongly Agree

2.1)	1	2	3	4	5
The economic/fiscal and monetary policies, financial reforms, and risk mitigation plans implemented by policy makers and regulators to reduce the impact of the housing market and credit bubbles were comprehensive and effective to reduce the financial meltdown.		X			

2.2) Professor Borgonovi what actionable economic/fiscal policies, reforms, or risk mitigation plans could have been immediately implemented to reduce the impact of the housing market and credit bubbles and the meltdown caused by the crisis?

In my view, the policies have been characterized by the objective of dealing with the short-term effects. At the beginning many governments decided policies to avoid bankruptcy of banks and financial institutions, but this was not enough to restore trust in the financial market. A second step was aimed to reduce public deficit in many cases through increase of taxation that reduced consumption. The difficulties of public finance in many countries reduced the capacity to invest in new public infrastructure, in order to increase the aggregate demand. These policies had a depressive effect on the economy, except in fast growing countries, in particular the BRICS (Brazil, Russia, India, China, South Africa). The US tried to support economic growth through an increase of liquidity and this had some recovery effects, while Europe wasn't able to do the same because of the institutional limitation of the ECB, and because Germany stood on the financial rigor rather than accepting a coordinated policy for economic growth at the European level. From their hand, many US, European and western countries banks went close to bankruptcy and tried to reduce the risk, reducing loans to families and enterprises. The credit crunch became something similar to poison for many companies that went to bankruptcy, increasing unemployment all around the world.

In this situation, when the crisis exploded, governments should have adopted clear and coordinated policies to deleverage the financial market to support middle classes, instead of leaving them alone to deal with the crisis and to introduce new rules on remuneration schemes and paths for top and senior managers and to introduce new rules for transparency in the financial transactions. Moreover, Western countries should have launched new deal programs involving private and public actors in the perspective of purchasing power parity (PPP).

Please use the following *Likert scale* to provide your answer:

1= Strongly Disagree; 2 = Disagree; 3 = Neither; 4 = Agree; 5 = Strongly Agree

3.1)	1	2	3	4	5
The monetary and fiscal policies, the government bail-outs, (TARP, TALF, and so on), and the financial reforms introduced (for example, Dodd–Frank Act, of which the Volcker Rule is a central component, and so on) after 2008 were valid long-term solutions to regulate and stabilize financial markets and to avoid the risk of new crises (double dip).	X				

3.2) Professor Borgonovi are the monetary and fiscal policies, the government bail-outs, (TARP, TALF, and so on), and the financial reforms introduced (for example, Dodd–Frank Act, of which the Volcker Rule is a central component, and so on) after 2008 valid long-term solutions to regulate and stabilize financial markets and to avoid the risk of new crises (double dip)?

As I answered in question 2, the policies have three main weaknesses:

1. they tried to face short-term effect;
2. they are not coordinated (as you can see from the failure of many financial summit, G8, Euro Group, G20, and so on);
3. none of them, or very few of them, are oriented to change the economic model that was the cause of the crisis.

What is missing is the understanding that the crisis can't be overcome only using economic policies. In order to overcome the crisis, changes are needed in the culture and in new ways of involving people. The consequence of the crisis is to squeeze the middle class and to reduce actual democracy. My view is that the positive effects of globalization and an actual recovery will be obtained only by creating new democracy models, to motivate, involve and empower as many people as possible, because the strongest and renewable energy is people. No fair market will be sustainable without more democracy, either in Western developed countries or in fast developing countries.

Please use the following *Likert scale* to provide your answer:

1= Strongly Disagree; 2 = Disagree; 3 = Neither; 4 = Agree; 5 = Strongly Agree

4.1)	1	2	3	4	5
There is a need for improved financial regulation, regulatory oversight, financial institutions' corporate governance (that is, COSO ERM, Internal Controls, Basel III, Dodd–Frank, Credit Ratings, and so on) and managerial cultures (that is, CSR, Ethics, and so on).					X

4.2) Professor Borgonovi what still needs to be changed in terms of financial regulation and regulatory oversight, corporate governance, managerial cultures, internal controls, COSO ERM Framework, and Basel III Framework to avoid in the future other systemic crises?

In terms of managerial culture there is a need to go back to the basics. This means to recover an approach more oriented to the long-term perspective and more able to create a better balance between strategic thinking and strategic objectives from one hand and return on investment (ROI), payback, internal rate of return (IRR) financial criteria. In term of public policies there's a need to strengthen the feasibility evaluation in terms of impact evaluation. Nowadays policy evaluations are mainly based on economic or financial models that do not consider qualitative and behavior aspects.

In terms of economic culture, the rational choice approach must be balanced by a more systemic approach in which political, institutional, social, cultural aspects have a relevant role. The "systemic crisis" can be overcome only through a "systemic way of thinking," able to deal with complex issues that cannot be reduced to simplify solutions.

Finally, I'm convinced that nowadays there's too much focus on the capacity of a country to attract financial capitals and investors, when the real need is to focus on knowledge, competencies, skills, attitudes of millions and hundred millions of people. The crisis was determined by the trust that became a modern non-religious faith in technology, scientific progress, innovation, financial innovation, consumption as a driver of production and growth. Only by putting the welfare and wellbeing of people and societies first will it be possible to overcome the crisis in a sustainable perspective. After being a "guru" of the hyper-competition, Michael Porter changed his approach since six to seven years ago, sustaining the CSV approach that means Corporate Shared Value. Involving people and communities in the production process and distributing the economic value and qualitative benefits among different stake holders are the basis of a sustainable and economic growth and societal development, in which human rights, health and other services related to the person are respected.

Please use the following *Likert scale* to provide your answer:

1= Strongly Disagree; 2 = Disagree; 3 = Neither; 4 = Agree; 5 = Strongly Agree

5.1)	1	2	3	4	5
Among the root causes of the 2007–2009 financial crisis are there major failures in the financial firms' corporate governance, traders and executive's integrity, accountability, ethical behaviors, and their excessive compensation systems, in addition to industry deregulation and major failures in regulatory oversight?					X

5.2) Professor Borgonovi what needs to be done to instill a new culture in the business world in order to improve corporate governance, executive accountability, fair compensation, and more in general, integrity and ethics in the financial markets?

Despite the fact that in the US and many other countries' business schools there are courses on ethics, business ethics, and corporate social responsibility, the dominant culture remained to put profit as the main or unique goal of a business and GDP as the main or unique measure of growth and development. Five years ago I had the chance to read the result of a survey on more than 2,000 high level managers trained in the most prestigious business schools: more than 80 percent (if I remember well, 83 percent) ranked profit as the first objective of their company, only 13 percent ranked consumer satisfaction as a priority and the remaining 4–5 percent ranked other objectives as priorities. I'm also convinced that globalization was confused with standardization that meant to replicate the same business model in different countries and environments, without considering the need to adapt to differences. At the beginning this approach was successful, because many countries followed the dominant culture, but later on this approach showed its weaknesses.

Interview with **Antonio Castagna** (personal communication, 2012), Financial Modelling Expert at Iason Ltd., Financial Analyst, and Former Derivatives Trader, Italy.

Please use the following *Likert scale* to provide your answer:

1= Strongly Disagree; 2 = Disagree; 3 = Neither; 4 = Agree; 5 = Strongly Agree

1.1)	1	2	3	4	5
The 2007–2009 financial crisis was predictable and avoidable.			X		

1.2) Mr Castagna was the 2007–2009 financial crisis predictable and avoidable?

Anything happening in the universe is the effect of one or more causes. Human behavior is one of the causes, maybe the main one, when we observe economic phenomena. The difference between a physical and economic system is that we are infinitely less able to isolate it from the rest of the universe and study only the relevant causes for the effects we are interested in.

Economists think Economics is a (social) science: it is so in the sense that it is possible to describe how some causes operated on some effects, also with sophisticated quantitative models mimicking the ones adopted by physicists in natural sciences, but unfortunately most of times and for the most important effects, the explanatory power of these models can be measured only ex post, since ex ante either the model is not able to take into account all the relevant factors, or input values are simply missing.

The subprime crisis is somehow emblematical: in the end the explanations to what happened are more or less all reasonable (apart from the moral judgment against the banking system that often underlies them, and that has to do with the political ideas of the economists or of the public officers).

Our idea is that the origin of the crises is the abundant liquidity that the US Federal Reserve injected in the market after September 2001 to prevent a recession. The fear of a healthy cyclical underperformance of the economic system and the will to control the social macroeconomic system as if it were a physical system, led the US Monetary Authorities to lower interest rates and keep them at depressed levels for a long time. The recession was avoided but, as Karl Popper warned in his works, the heterogenesis of the ends is always the major threat to the success of social experiments.

It was quite predictable that the monetary easing would produce some relief as far as the GDP was concerned, but there were also some other less easy to detect consequences: banks started to lend money to less creditworthy clients, since they were hungry for yields in a low-yield economy with a lot of liquidity to invest. Is it a fault of the banking system to lend liquidity in excess also to less creditworthy customers after having lent money to prime clients? We strongly doubt so, as we strongly doubt that the crisis is a proof of market's irrationality.

In fact, also the financial engineering was a rational economic decision to fairly allocate the risks to different economic agents with different risk appetite. The problem is rather the perception of the risks, but everything is bright when the world goes round well, and everything is bleak when things turn to bad outcomes. It is just in human nature.

The unintended consequences of the public authorities and regulators make their actions highly dangerous. Then, when a crises bursts out, they make even more mistakes trying to remedy the damages that were mainly originated by their decisions. As an example, the attempt to avoid the default of some banks (with Lehman Brothers the only notable exception) has been the biggest of all mistakes, since now the banking system is heading toward a sort of old style socialist regime of regulation and in some cases of ownership.

To sum up, negative consequences can be always predicted in general terms because we are not able (luckily, we daresay) to completely command the evolution of the economic system, so crises will always happen and in our opinion they could only be worsened by the greater and greater public intervention to direct the private economic system, which typically produces big distortions to the ordinary economic working. In specific terms negative consequences will never be predicted because it is quite impossible to take into account the infinite numbers of factors contributing to the final outcome of the economic, and more generally of the social, systems.

Please use the following *Likert scale* to provide your answer:

1= Strongly Disagree; 2 = Disagree; 3 = Neither; 4 = Agree; 5 = Strongly Agree

2.1)	1	2	3	4	5
The economic/fiscal and monetary policies, financial reforms, and risk mitigation plans implemented by policy makers and regulators to reduce the impact of the housing market and credit bubbles were comprehensive and effective to reduce the financial meltdown.	X				

2.2) Mr Castagna what actionable economic/fiscal policies, reforms, or risk mitigation plans could have been immediately implemented to reduce the impact of the housing market and credit bubbles and the meltdown caused by the crisis?

Mainly policies were of three types:

1. Public bail-out of banks (in US): in our opinion it would have been better to use tax-payers money to protect small customers and savings, letting banks go bust. Punishment is the only way to learn on Earth: default is healthy, provides the good attitude to evaluate investment projects, and it is fair. Public intervention in the rescue of banks will pose many problems that we are starting seeing: external decision on how much managers should be paid, which activities the bank should or should not do and so on. We have already tested where all this leads in the socialist system of last centuries.
2. Ample liquidity (worldwide): major economies are buying time by printing money (in Europe in a disguised way). We are afraid that in the end the bill must be paid anyway, so there will be a wealth loss shared by the vast majority of people, and in the end this is the only possible way to solve the problems. Nothing is created from nothing.
3. New regulation of financial markets: this is probably the most disconcerting part of the public policies. On one hand public authorities try to create a safer system, but on the other hand this means that basically banks cannot do their work anymore. They should be the most risk averse economic agents of the economy and still they have a primary role in the modern monetary economy which is not compatible with such restrictions. In the US the Volcker rule and the Dodd–Frank Act will make the investment bank activity quite unattractive; in the rest of the world the Basel III rules are very conservative and penalizing the trading book.

What is difficult to understand is why a financial crisis (we refer only to the subprime one), that is basically due to credit problems, has produced such a restrictive regulation of the trading activity. Banks in the US suffered from defaults on assets in the banking book, not in the trading book. Nevertheless, public opinion has been led to believe that the shame was on the greedy bankers trading in the markets: a very effective communication strategy that shunned the blame from the public authorities and the effects of their past policies (see point 1.1).

We are quite sure that the effects of the policies implemented will produce heavy negative effects in the future.

Please use the following *Likert scale* to provide your answer:

1= Strongly Disagree; 2 = Disagree; 3 = Neither; 4 = Agree; 5 = Strongly Agree

3.1)	1	2	3	4	5
The monetary and fiscal policies, the government bail-outs, (TARP, TALF, and so on), and the financial reforms introduced (for example, Dodd–Frank Act, of which the Volcker Rule is a central component, and so on.) after 2008 were valid long-term solutions to regulate and stabilize financial markets and to avoid the risk of new crises (double dip).	X				

3.2) Mr Castagna are the monetary and fiscal policies, the government bail-outs, (TARP, TALF, and so on), and the financial reforms introduced (for example, Dodd–Frank Act, of which the Volcker Rule is a central component, and so on) after 2008 valid long-term solutions to regulate and stabilize financial markets and to avoid the risk of new crises (double dip)?

The TARP, TALF in the US, and similar policies like the Long Term Refinancing Operation (LTRO) in Europe, are a way to buy time, but they cannot be seen as a long-term solution. The new regulation for the financial markets proposed in the US (Dodd–Frank act, Volcker rule) are punishing the trading activity of the banks, although the crisis originated from the banking book activity (in the end, the subprime crisis was produced by loans to bad debtors). We can hardly see how these can be considered solutions to future crises, since in our opinion they are acting on the wrong side.

More generally we always doubt the effectiveness of the public policies since usually they produce unintended consequences that are only partially predictable.

In Europe, the crisis spurred a harshening of the Basel regulation, mainly on the interbank counterparty risk measurement and on the liquidity risk monitoring. Also in this case, the regulation has been irrationally punitive for the trading activities and very little was done for the banking activity (the credit risk has not been overhauled, and only the treatment for the securitizations changed). The higher requirements of capital for banks put them under pressure in the market: probably at the moment banking is the most unattractive business in the market. Moreover, banks have been used in the last year to give an indirect support to government bonds, through the LTRO program, whose funds collected by banks (especially Italian and Spanish) have been invested in domestic Treasuries. The perverse effect is that now banks are fully loaded with sovereign bonds whose spreads is increasing (April 2012) and thus it is increasing the market pressure on them (that is, higher bank risk = higher funding costs).

We doubt there are sensible long-term policies to be implemented. There is too much debt around in the world, private in the US, public in Europe. The wealth economies are able to create is meagre thus it (the wealth) is no more capable to repay this debt. The only solution is a repudiation (in the US this basically happened), with a dramatic redistribution of the residual wealth. We should be looking at the past examples of Russia and Argentina to get a grasp on what may happen sooner or later (so we are not saying that we can find effective public policies in these past local crises).

Please use the following *Likert scale* to provide your answer:

1= Strongly Disagree; 2 = Disagree; 3 = Neither; 4 = Agree; 5 = Strongly Agree

4.1)	1	2	3	4	5
There is a need for improved financial regulation, regulatory oversight, financial institutions' corporate governance (that is, COSO ERM, Internal Controls, Basel III, Dodd–Frank, Credit Ratings, and so on) and managerial cultures (that is, CSR, Ethics, and so on).				X	

4.2) Mr Castagna what still needs to be changed in terms of financial regulation and regulatory oversight, corporate governance, managerial cultures, internal controls, COSO ERM Framework, and Basel III Framework to avoid in the future other systemic crises?

Internal risk management policies should be improved. Banking has been poorly managed as a business, especially if one compares the management of the production process of industrial companies to the management of the production process of financial institutions. This may appear a strong statement, but if one looks behind the apparently robust quantitative tools employed and prescribed also by regulations to monitor the banking activity, one can see that they are actually weak given the complex nature of financial intermediation. A relative soundness of risk management practices could (and still can) be found only in the trading activity, whereas the banking activity was (and still is) much behind the curve, notwithstanding the traumatic changes of the financial environment.

In any case, we believe that the improvement of risk management practices, and of the monitoring of the production process of financial intermediation, should be a bottom-up action springing from the banks' awareness of the complexity of their business, and not pushed by regulation.

Ethics, corporate social responsibility (CSR), managerial culture are in our opinion just a smokescreen, either to hide the real causes of some events (public authorities are using them to shun the blame of many aspects of the crisis), or because people still need to believe that human actions can actually have a strong influence on the future, fearing to recognize that eventually we are all at the mercy of the general randomness of the universe.

Please use the following *Likert scale* to provide your answer:

1= Strongly Disagree; 2 = Disagree; 3 = Neither; 4 = Agree; 5 = Strongly Agree

5.1)	1	2	3	4	5
Among the root causes of the 2007–2009 financial crisis are there major failures in the financial firms' corporate governance, traders and executive's integrity, accountability, ethical behaviors, and their excessive compensation systems, in addition to industry deregulation and major failures in regulatory oversight?	X				

5.2) Mr Castagna what needs to be done to instill a new culture in the business world in order to improve corporate governance, executive accountability, fair compensation, and more in general, integrity and ethics in the financial markets?

Economy does not have anything to do with Ethics, just as a modern democratic state does not have anything to do with an ethical state.

There exists a general principle whereby if actions of an economic agent cause damages to someone else, then the latter should be compensated (and in that case the first agent fined). Actions should not be judged under an ethical perspective, which should remain something related to the private sphere of individuals. We are frightened by the idea that there are Ethical rules prescribing what we should or should not do.

Similarly, we are skeptical about compensations' limits and similar things. If a manager does a good job (he/she makes profits without causing damage to other people) why should he/she not be paid incredibly high bonuses? It is a stockholders' decision to use their money as they wish.

In the end, economic agents aim at making profits, and this is what they also did before and during the crisis. If they breach the law, they should be punished; if they did not, then they cannot be blamed for the crisis, which in our opinion was mainly due to unintended consequences of the early 2000s monetary policies, rather than to the irrational, unethical, greedy market operators.

Besides, one should consider if it was unethical or greedy lending money to unworthy people before the crisis. We remember public speeches by politicians (for example Brown in the UK), boasting the percentage of houses owned by private people as an achievement. We realized after the crisis that many of those people were not creditworthy enough to get a mortgage and buy a house. We could not remember any warning to the banking system for reckless operations they were conducting. If bankers were greedy and unethical, their behavior allowed some people to enjoy for a short time having a house that they should never have had.

Interview with **Fabiano Colombini** (personal communication, 2012), Full Professor of Economics of Financial Institutions and Markets at the Faculty of Economics of Università di Pisa.

Please use the following *Likert scale* to provide your answer:

1= Strongly Disagree; 2 = Disagree; 3 = Neither; 4 = Agree; 5 = Strongly Agree

1.1)	1	2	3	4	5
The 2007–2009 financial crisis was predictable and avoidable.					X

1.2) Professor Colombini was the 2007–2009 financial crisis predictable and avoidable?

The financial crisis, as indicated by the Financial Crisis Inquiry Committee (FCIC) final report of January 2011, was both predictable and avoidable.

There were evident signs of a growing housing bubble in the years preceding the crisis that were further inflated by the rapidly growing subprime mortgage lending market. The latter has also been significantly fueled by the rapid expansion of the securitization and derivatives markets. The massive recourse of financial institutions to securitization and derivatives was aimed to transfer credit risk to financial markets. This practice was based on the illusionary assumption of house prices increasing indefinitely and therefore banks, investment banks, insurance companies and financial firms would not face major losses in case of troubles (borrowers' defaults), since they could always sell the borrowers' houses to solve any potential loan repayment issue. When the downturn in house prices actually occurred, many homeowners had the value of their outstanding mortgages exceeding the value of their homes and therefore, with little or no savings, they could not afford their mortgage repayments.

The financial crisis was predictable since on the basis of standard credit screening and monitoring practices of modern banks, these institutions were certainly aware of the riskier profile of the subprime borrowers and of their potential inability to repay the mortgage loans. They did not monitor credit risk with the necessary diligence since they were transferring that risk to others (that is, financial markets) using derivatives and rising levels of leverage.

The financial crisis was predictable since based on standard practices of experienced investment banks, these institutions were deliberately carrying out also high risky trading activities and speculations on the mortgage-backed securities (MBS) using high levels of leverage.

The financial crisis was predictable, since the financial institutions developed a massive shadow banking sector over the years, through credit intermediation, leveraging on entities and activities outside the regular banking system which drastically increased the chances of systemic risks and regulatory arbitrages.

The financial crisis was also predictable since evident conflicts of interest and transparency issues jeopardized the rating activity of credit rating agencies (CRAs) but were not timely detected and addressed by regulators.

The financial crisis was also predictable, as demonstrated by the unusual growth of the securitization and derivatives activities and techniques, since many institutions have deliberately spread the high credit risk of subprime mortgages to investors through financial markets and financial intermediaries with a myopic approach. Supervisory authorities could have timely stopped these perverse practices imposing tighter oversight on financial intermediaries and financial markets but it did not happen.

It is important to stress two main points: the bad supervisory task and, at the same time, the time lags in the public intervention. The financial crisis became global due to the fact that many toxic securities were allowed to grow rapidly over the years, while many early warning signs were systematically ignored, thus ultimately leading the financial system to the brink of collapse.

Government interventions to bail-out banks, insurance companies, and financial firms generated a massive increase of sovereign debt and of the Debt/GDP ratio, therefore generating fears in the financial markets on the solvency of some Eurozone countries, and thus adding the sovereign debt crisis to the previous financial crisis.

The subprime mortgage financial crisis, which started in the United States of America in 2007 and then spread almost all over the world, and the sovereign debt crisis, which started in Europe in 2009 and then spread in several Eurozone states, reveals some common features: losses in the financial instruments portfolios and the loans portfolios; related write-downs in the firms' financial statements; reductions in the capital ratios, liquidity problems or solvency issues; and several failures of financial intermediaries.

The subprime mortgage crisis could have been prevented essentially by adopting a more aggressive and strict supervisory activity at the right time with effective interventions by the supervisory authorities in order to stop the irrational financial practices undertaken by financial intermediaries and financial markets. These practices, instead, have significantly increased, with little attention to their potential aftermath and systemic risks for the entire economy, thus setting the stage for a reckless multiplication and spreading of risks.

Please use the following *Likert scale* to provide your answer:

1= Strongly Disagree; 2 = Disagree; 3 = Neither; 4 = Agree; 5 = Strongly Agree

2.1)	1	2	3	4	5
The economic/fiscal and monetary policies, financial reforms, and risk mitigation plans implemented by policy makers and regulators to reduce the impact of the housing market and credit bubbles were comprehensive and effective to reduce the financial meltdown.			X		

2.2) Professor Colombini what actionable economic/fiscal policies, reforms, or risk mitigation plans could have been immediately implemented to reduce the impact of the housing market and credit bubbles and the meltdown caused by the crisis?

The economic/fiscal and monetary policies, financial reforms, and risk mitigation plans introduced during the crisis have contributed to restore confidence in the financial intermediaries and financial markets. Almost all governments decided interventions to stabilise the financial system and the economy through the provision of liquidity to the banking system and the recapitalisation of financial intermediaries, thus reestablishing the confidence and the regularity of transactions among financial institutions. The result was the resolution of liquidity and funding problems in financial industries.

Central banks have used conventional and unconventional instruments to rescue financial institutions increasing volumes of their balance sheet and money supply in the financial and economic system. The monetary interventions by central banks could have been more effective through a more strict coordination among central banks. Moreover, central bank interventions stressed two main consequences: an enormous creation of liquidity and the expansion of the volumes and values of central banks' balance sheets indicating a sort of bad banking activity and, at the same time, an increase of risks.

The Federal Reserve (Fed) response to the financial crisis was very aggressive. It has used a variety of unconventional instruments with the aim of easing financial conditions of banks and improving liquidity of financial institutions. Therefore the Fed's balance sheet changed significantly.

The ECB response to the financial crisis was effective, at least in the short term, through the use of the LTRO as an unconventional instrument to inject massive liquidity to banks and indirectly to give support to the placement of public debt. Therefore the ECB's balance sheet changed.

The Fed has a wider range of unconventional instruments and policies, in comparison with ECB, to restore confidence and to provide liquidity to the financial markets and financial intermediaries. With its policies the Fed can help recreating better conditions in the markets. In the medium and long term the differences between the monetary policies and instruments used by the Fed and ECB can generate a gap for Europe in comparison with the US.

It took quite some time for the economic and fiscal instruments, financial reforms, and risk mitigation plans to be implemented and therefore the financial impact of the housing and credit bubbles was reduced only after much time. It is important to stress that time lags have played a major role in the severity of the financial crisis. Even more so the time lags required to execute proper interventions to address the financial and economic dislocations generated by troubled subprime mortgage borrowers and financial intermediaries, shocked financial markets, high volatility and so on.

During the financial crisis a major priority for policy makers was to determine the actual size of the problem. In other words, the amount of toxic assets in the financial firms' balance sheets in order to identify the real dimension of the crisis for the financial systems before taking any decision on the appropriate solutions and plans to undertake.

Please use the following *Likert scale* to provide your answer:

1= Strongly Disagree; 2 = Disagree; 3 = Neither; 4 = Agree; 5 = Strongly Agree

3.1)	1	2	3	4	5
The monetary and fiscal policies, the government bail-outs, (TARP, TALF, and so on), and the financial reforms introduced (for example, Dodd–Frank Act, of which the Volcker Rule is a central component, and so on) after 2008 were valid long-term solutions to regulate and stabilize financial markets and to avoid the risk of new crises (double dip).		X			

3.2) Professor Colombini are the monetary and fiscal policies, the government bail-outs, (TARP, TALF, and so on), and the financial reforms introduced (for example, Dodd–Frank Act, of which the Volcker Rule is a central component, and so on.) after 2008 valid long-term solutions to regulate and stabilize financial markets and to avoid the risk of new crises (double dip)?

The monetary and fiscal policies, the government bail-outs and financial reforms (Dodd–Frank Act, Volcker Rule) were quite useful to stabilise financial markets. These interventions helped creating better conditions in financial markets. In the US the monetary expansion policies by the Fed improved the liquidity, the government bail-outs removed toxic assets from the balance sheets of banks, and the financial reforms created better conditions to prevent future crises.

The monetary expansion policy contributed to improve liquidity in the interbank markets and money markets and, at the same time, in the activity of financial intermediaries.

The government bail-outs brought new liquidity to banks and financial intermediaries and helped removing from the financial firms' balance sheets instruments that became illiquid. These bail-outs have been created for large financial intermediaries which were considered "too big to fail." In financial industries, a number of banks and financial intermediaries failed and there was a process of concentration which, in accordance with predictions, will continue in the years to come due to the aftermath of the financial crisis and its duration.

In the US the Dodd–Frank Act defines new rules for the financial system taking into account some relevant factors: derivatives, proprietary trading, systemic risks, big sizes, consumers' protection, shareholders' protection, investors' protection. This financial reform introduces changes in rules, supervision, supervisory authorities, derivatives markets and banking business. Moreover, this financial reform introduces supervisory authorities for the protection of customers, shareholders and investors, regulation for the over-the-counter (OTC) derivatives market through the clearinghouses and standard contracts, and rules for banks trading without own funds (naked short-selling). The financial reform tends to reduce the excessive speculation carried out by banks and therefore the positive or negative impact on profits. The creation of the Financial Service Oversight Council has the task to introduce an early warning system for the early identification of systemic risks. The public bail-out of financial institutions "too big to fail" is neglected and the public money will not be used. Some principles established by the financial reform represent improvements. As the final architecture has to be built, it is very difficult to predict the real impact on financial intermediaries and financial markets.

These measures should improve the stability of the financial system but it is very difficult to avoid financial crises in the future. It is important to stress time lags in the interventions of the public authorities as it involves an increasing spreading of bad assets and negative consequences of the crisis all over the world. These measures, however, cannot be considered a long-term solution to prevent and to avoid financial crises in the future. The past failed experience suggests the importance of regulation and the critical role of supervision and supervisory authorities and, at the same time, stresses the importance of changes in the practices of the financial systems. The introduction of new techniques and new management approaches which cannot be included in a formal regulation and supervision framework but that, at the same time, are critical for the successful implementation of sustainability risk–reward strategies and to avoid incurring in the future in new financial crises in some part of the world spreading the risk on a global scale through contagion.

Please use the following *Likert scale* to provide your answer:

1= Strongly Disagree; 2 = Disagree; 3 = Neither; 4 = Agree; 5 = Strongly Agree

4.1)	1	2	3	4	5
There is a need for improved financial regulation, regulatory oversight, financial institutions' corporate governance (that is, COSO ERM, Internal Controls, Basel III, Dodd–Frank, Credit Ratings, and so on) and managerial cultures (that is, CSR, Ethics, and so on).				X	

4.2) Professor Colombini what still needs to be changed in terms of financial regulation and regulatory oversight, corporate governance, managerial cultures, internal controls, COSO ERM Framework, and Basel III Framework to avoid in the future other systemic crises?

There is a need to improve financial regulation, regulatory oversight, financial institutions' corporate governance and managerial cultures. All these initiatives can go in the direction of preventing future financial crises even though there are no certain solutions of how to avoid other crises.

The financial regulation can be improved taking into account the experience of financial intermediaries and financial markets during the past financial crises. The Dodd–Frank Act has been issued in order to prevent the major failures learned from the financial crises and their impact on financial intermediaries.

Improving financial regulation means leveling off the playing field on an international scale.

It is particularly important to improve ERM as an integrated approach to identify, measure, and manage all risks involved in the company's operation. Risk transfer, and in particular credit risk transfer, can be a valuable early warning sign of growing systemic risk in the financial system. Improving ERM requires also improving internal controls by non-executives to guarantee a more resilient and effective risk management monitoring for financial intermediaries.

There is a need for change in financial regulation, but most of all, there is an even more urgent need for change in regulatory oversight and corporate governance. The intensity and the spreading of financial crises essentially are concerned with methods, time lags, and ways of conducting oversight activities in the context of financial intermediaries and financial markets. Time lags have negatively affected the spreading of credit risks to a wide range of securities.

The introduction of Basel III can certainly contribute to improve the quality and quantity of capital required by banks strengthening the capacity to absorb write-downs. Basel III leaves unregulated the so-called shadow banking system.

Sovereign debt is usually a proportion of the financial instruments portfolios of banks and the sovereign debt crisis in Europe stresses the importance of capital requirements. The capital adequacy is calculated by the risk-weighted assets (RWA) in the single banking systems, thus there is an overlap and conflict between the risk-weighting approach of Basel III as prudential regulation and the rating-weighting approach of European Banking Authority (EBA) guidelines as discretionary regulation. It implies readjustments in the capital adequacy by increasing capital of the single banks in the states where the rating of securities held in portfolios is lower.

It is necessary to develop managerial cultures and compensation schemes in financial industries that focus on long-term goals. Furthermore, these objectives should be correlated to risk and long-term value creation indicators such as the RAPM (risk adjusted performance measurement). It is important to verify that the goals and objectives do not lead to excessive risk taking.

Please use the following *Likert scale* to provide your answer:

1= Strongly Disagree; 2 = Disagree; 3 = Neither; 4 = Agree; 5 = Strongly Agree

5.1)	1	2	3	4	5
Among the root causes of the 2007–2009 financial crisis are there major failures in the financial firms' corporate governance, traders and executive's integrity, accountability, ethical behaviors, and their excessive compensation systems, in addition to industry deregulation and major failures in regulatory oversight?					X

5.2) Professor Colombini what needs to be done to instill a new culture in the business world in order to improve corporate governance, executive accountability, fair compensation, and more in general, integrity and ethics in the financial markets?

There is certainly a need for a new culture in the business world to improve financial firms' corporate governance, traders and executive's integrity, ethics, and fair compensation.

One way it can start is with basic principles of behavior with rational selection, measurement, and management of risks at different points of the economic and financial system: corporate sector, financial sector, public sector. All these sectors should be able to manage several kinds of risks and therefore to take into account the rise of any risk considering the importance and the impact, in particular, of the credit risk and a rational use of credit risk transfer techniques. It means that each sector has to take the credit risk at the level for which internal instruments can manage it or, alternatively, to take the credit risk and to transfer it to financial markets spreading the credit risk through at levels for which financial markets will be able to manage it.

Risk management is important also for the public sector which has to issue and place financial instruments on the financial markets taking into account volumes, maturities, interest rates and their spreads and their rational combination.

The key point is to apply a proper risk management framework at different levels of the economic and financial system which involves the use of rational instruments.

New principles and new culture have to be taught also at the universities focusing more on the negative consequences of financial crises.

A key learning point should be a better understanding of the losses in economic development and in GDP growth related to financial crises. These consequences include: financial distress and periods of time for which value shocks, market volatility, and bad circumstances represent critical factors that institutions, investors, and ordinary people need to cope with. It is very difficult to determine and to predict the origins of financial crises but it is still more difficult to estimate the period of time necessary to restore confidence in the markets and to recreate standard conditions of financial stability for financial intermediaries and other market players. Even more important is the difficulty to determine the required time to return to normal credit granting to the real economy.

Interview with **Aswarth Damodaran** (personal communication, 2012), the Kerschner Family Chair in Finance Education, Finance Department at New York University Stern School of Business, USA.

Please use the following *Likert scale* to provide your answer:

1= Strongly Disagree; 2 = Disagree; 3 = Neither; 4 = Agree; 5 = Strongly Agree

1.1)	1	2	3	4	5
The 2007–2009 financial crisis was predictable and avoidable.				X	

1.2) Professor Damodaran was the 2007–2009 financial crisis predictable and avoidable?

Everything is avoidable in hindsight.

Please use the following *Likert scale* to provide your answer:

1= Strongly Disagree; 2 = Disagree; 3 = Neither; 4 = Agree; 5 = Strongly Agree

2.1)	1	2	3	4	5
The economic/fiscal and monetary policies, financial reforms, and risk mitigation plans implemented by policy makers and regulators to reduce the impact of the housing market and credit bubbles were comprehensive and effective to reduce the financial meltdown.			X		

2.2) Professor Damodaran what actionable economic/fiscal policies, reforms, or risk mitigation plans could have been immediately implemented to reduce the impact of the housing market and credit bubbles and the meltdown caused by the crisis?

Since the crisis had its roots in bad risk taking incentives that rewarded risk takers for taking upside risk while protecting them on the downside, any policies that can reduce this asymmetry in risk taking will have a positive effect. Thus, I think that commercial banking (where the government does provide a backstop with deposit insurance) has to be separated from proprietary trading and investing.

Please use the following *Likert scale* to provide your answer:

1= Strongly Disagree; 2 = Disagree; 3 = Neither; 4 = Agree; 5 = Strongly Agree

3.1)	1	2	3	4	5
The monetary and fiscal policies, the government bail-outs, (TARP, TALF, and so on), and the financial reforms introduced (for example, Dodd–Frank Act, of which Volcker Rule is a central component, and so on) after 2008 were valid long-term solutions to regulate and stabilize financial markets and to avoid the risk of new crises (double dip).			X		

3.2) Professor Damodaran are the monetary and fiscal policies, the government bail-outs, (TARP, TALF, and so on), and the financial reforms introduced (for example, Dodd–Frank Act, of which Volcker Rule is a central component, and so on) after 2008 valid long-term solutions to regulate and stabilize financial markets and to avoid the risk of new crises (double dip)?

No. In fact, no plan will stop the next crisis. We are very good at fighting the last war but the next one will be very different.

Please use the following *Likert scale* to provide your answer:

1= Strongly Disagree; 2 = Disagree; 3 = Neither; 4 = Agree; 5 = Strongly Agree

4.1)	1	2	3	4	5
There is a need for improved financial regulation, regulatory oversight, financial institutions' corporate governance (that is, COSO ERM, Internal Controls, Basel III, Dodd–Frank, Credit Ratings, and so on) and managerial cultures (that is, CSR, Ethics, and so on).			X		

4.2) Professor Damodaran what still needs to be changed in terms of financial regulation and regulatory oversight, corporate governance, managerial cultures, internal controls, COSO ERM Framework, and Basel III Framework to avoid in the future other systemic crises?

Follow two rules. Keep it simple (take out complexity) and less is more (don't keep adding to the rule book ... it is not working).

Please use the following *Likert scale* to provide your answer:

1= Strongly Disagree; 2 = Disagree; 3 = Neither; 4 = Agree; 5 = Strongly Agree

5.1)	1	2	3	4	5
Among the root causes of the 2007–2009 financial crisis are there major failures in the financial firms' corporate governance, traders and executive's integrity, accountability, ethical behaviors, and their excessive compensation systems, in addition to industry deregulation and major failures in regulatory oversight?			X		

5.2) Professor Damodaran what needs to be done to instill a new culture in the business world in order to improve corporate governance, executive accountability, fair compensation, and more in general, integrity and ethics in the financial markets?

Forget about it. This is nonsense. Human beings act in their self-interest. Ask the organized religions whether you can change basic human nature. So, stop with the "do-goodism," accept the fact that human beings will over react and cause crises and build in systems that can handle these crises.

Interview with **Gregorio De Felice** (personal communication, 2012), Head of Research and Chief Economist, Intesa Sanpaolo Bank, Italy. From 1994 to 1999, lecturer in Monetary Economics at Bocconi University. From 2007 to 2010, Chairman of AIAF, the Italian Association of Financial Analysts. He holds offices at the Italian Bankers' Association (ABI), the European Banking Federation (EBF) and the European Securities Markets Authority (ESMA). He is a member of the Board of Directors of Prometeia, Istituto per gli Studi di Politica Internazionale (ISPI), Fondazione Partnership per Bocconi, Associazione per gli Studi di Banca e Borsa, Associazione Studi e Ricerche per il Mezzogiorno (SRM), Gruppo Economisti di Impresa (GEI), Associazione Italiana Politiche Industriali (AIP), Fondazione Banca Sicula, Fondazione Bruno Visentini, Fondazione Ricerca e Imprenditorialità and some pension funds of the Intesa Sanpaolo Group. He is a member of the Scientific Committee of a number of economic associations, including the Associazione Nazionale per l'Enciclopedia della Banca e della Borsa and the Rosselli Foundation. He is the Italian representative to the ICBE (International Club of Bank Economists) and the ICCBE (International Conference of Commercial Bank Economists). He is the author of many publications in the fields of monetary policy and financial markets, banking and the management of public debt.

Please use the following *Likert scale* to provide your answer:

1= Strongly Disagree; 2 = Disagree; 3 = Neither; 4 = Agree; 5 = Strongly Agree

1.1)	1	2	3	4	5
The 2007–2009 financial crisis was predictable and avoidable.			X		

1.2) Professor De Felice was the 2007–2009 financial crisis predictable and avoidable?

The financial turmoil came at a time when the overall situation in the world economy looked extremely favorable. However, several elements indicated that disequilibria were increasing: the rapid growth in monetary and credit aggregates; an extended period of low real interest rates; the unusually high price of many assets, both real and financial.

As a matter of fact, when concerns began to mount about the valuation of complex products, liquidity risk and counterparty risk, and led to the collapse of the market for structured products based on mortgages, the violence and the speed of the impact took virtually everyone by surprise: it is instructive that, throughout the summer of 2007, both Ben Bernanke and Treasury Secretary Henry Paulson offered public assurances that the turmoil would have been contained. Also unpredictable were the dimensions and the length of the crisis, which extended from the US real estate market to the sovereign bond market and the real economy as a whole – and is still not over.

Was the crisis avoidable? It is not an easy question. Asset bubbles may be hard to recognize; moreover, monetary policy – working through interest rates – may be ineffective in dis-inflating a bubble, even in the case it is identified.

The Federal Reserve has basically two targets: macroeconomic stability (which can be achieved through interest rates) and financial stability (which requires a variety of instruments: regulation, supervisory oversight, and the lender-of-last-resort function).

The problem is that it did not use the right tools – that is, supervision and regulation – to handle the huge increase in credit growth. Like most other central banks, it adopted a pro-deregulation view, ignoring market failures and the systemic effects of credit market supervision. As the Fed itself explicitly recognized, "… the market discipline that 'sophisticated investors' are supposed to provide was lacking … [it] took too long to ramp up some supervisory policies in the face of mounting risks" (Yellen and May, 2008).

Failures in regulation, supervision, corporate governance and the management of risk were undoubtedly among the major causes of the crisis. The lack of focus on long-term sustainability encouraged short-termism and moral hazard, leading to excessive risk-taking; financial innovation provided new means to hide exposures and increase leverage.

As the Italian case demonstrates, a more prudent approach to financial regulation would probably have reduced the impact of the shock. However, contagion was a very peculiar feature of the crisis: due to interconnections among financial institutions, disturbances in the American real estate market impacted on the stability of institutions and markets all around the world, and produced serious negative consequences for the economy at large.

More than four years have passed since the start of the crisis, and the identification of systemic risk can still be considered a nascent field. Consensus has grown around the idea that having a system-wide perspective is a fundamental attribute of a well-specified prudential set-up, but no common paradigm exists yet. Further fundamental and applied research is needed, and new analytical tools have to be developed in order to identify and measure systemic risk in a forward-looking way.

Please use the following *Likert scale* to provide your answer:

1= Strongly Disagree; 2 = Disagree; 3 = Neither; 4 = Agree; 5 = Strongly Agree

2.1)	1	2	3	4	5
The economic/fiscal and monetary policies, financial reforms, and risk mitigation plans implemented by policy makers and regulators to reduce the impact of the housing market and credit bubbles were comprehensive and effective to reduce the financial meltdown.		X			

2.2) Professor De Felice what actionable economic/fiscal policies, reforms, or risk mitigation plans could have been immediately implemented to reduce the impact of the housing market and credit bubbles and the meltdown caused by the crisis?

A wide range of measures has been introduced by monetary, fiscal and regulatory authorities to reduce the impact of the US real estate crisis. Almost from the first day of the turmoil, central banks have been injecting liquidity in the market, to ensure that overnight rates stayed at levels consistent with policy goals. Direct State support has been provided for a number of institutions. Regulators encouraged their banks to seek private sector recapitalization. Recommendations were made concerning how lending criteria and the use of derivatives and structured products might be improved in the future. Notwithstanding these efforts, the crisis rapidly extended from the US subprime market to the global economy.

Probably, the crucial issue is not *what else* the authorities should have done *immediately after* the explosion of the crisis – it is what should have they done *before*. The analytical and political mistake at the turn of the millennium was to believe that the financial system was fundamentally self-correcting: the crisis made clear that this assumption was wrong, and some level of regulation in the financial system was required.

A second question is *when* the reforms that have been introduced following the outbreak of the crisis will definitely be finalized and will come into force. Take the United States. The nearly 300 pages which have been put forward by five federal agencies with the aim to enact the so-called Volcker Rule have been defined "unintelligible" by the financial community. Moreover, the Dodd–Frank Act has hardly touched Fannie Mae and Freddie Mac – a remarkable omission, indeed, considering the role played by the real estate sector in igniting the crisis.

Please use the following *Likert scale* to provide your answer:

1= Strongly Disagree; 2 = Disagree; 3 = Neither; 4 = Agree; 5 = Strongly Agree

3.1)	1	2	3	4	5
The monetary and fiscal policies, the government bail-outs, (TARP, TALF, and so on), and the financial reforms introduced (for example, Dodd–Frank Act, of which the Volcker Rule is a central component, and so on) after 2008 were valid long-term solutions to regulate and stabilize financial markets and to avoid the risk of new crises (double dip).			X		

3.2) Professor De Felice are the monetary and fiscal policies, the government bail-outs, (TARP, TALF, and so on), and the financial reforms introduced (for example, Dodd–Frank Act, of which the Volcker Rule is a central component, and so on) after 2008 valid long-term solutions to regulate and stabilize financial markets and to avoid the risk of new crises (double dip)?

The Dodd–Frank Act embodied extremely ambitious targets: create suitable conditions for resumption of growth and employment, protect consumers, increase control over the stock market and compensation policies, put an end to bail-outs, eliminate moral hazard connected with excessively large banks, and prevent the outbreak of a new financial crisis. As a matter of fact, it was little more than a skeleton in its initial version, giving regulators ample room for discretion in implementing even the most important aspects of the new regulatory framework.

More than one year and a half after the Act was signed, only 100 of the total 393 rulemaking requirements have been met with finalized rules – and additional rules have been proposed that would meet 155 more requirements.[1] Though primary regulation looks extensive and reasonably well-defined, the path towards reshaping the US regulatory and supervisory framework in order to achieve financial stability is still long, and subject to substantial political uncertainty.

Moreover – even admitting that reforms are brought to a rapid conclusion in the US – a consistent approach to regulation is needed on the two sides of the Atlantic. The financial system is global, and global rules are required in order to prevent regulatory arbitrage and contrast adverse spill-over effects.

This is a critical issue. The regulatory dialogue, which had been effective at the G20 level at the peak of the crisis, has been declining during the last couple of years; progress towards shared commitments, though not irrelevant, has been uneven.

In the European Union, comprehensive legislation has been approved in the direction of implementing the G20 financial agenda. Three new supervisory authorities have been created; regulation has been introduced for hedge funds, private equity funds, and credit rating agencies; an agreement has been reached on central clearing and reporting of OTC derivatives trades; Basel III standards have been incorporated into the updated Capital Requirements Directive.

On the contrary, regulators in the United States mainly concentrated on SIFIs and crisis resolution, leaving Basel issues aside. Basel II has never been implemented for commercial banks; issues related to Basel 2.5 remain undecided; a proposal has still to be released on how to introduce Basel III in the American regulatory framework.

Finally, further deviations from the G20 agenda have been suggested in the United Kingdom by the Vickers Report – released in September last year – on the two fronts of capital requirements and the separation between domestic retail services and global wholesale and investment banking operations (ring-fencing).

It is crucial that regulators and supervisors on the two sides of the Atlantic search for common ground to keep global cooperation on track: rules that could cause serious spillover effects – of which the Volcker Rule could be a good example[2] – should not be introduced without proper international coordination.

Please use the following *Likert scale* to provide your answer:

---

1   Data as of April 2, 2012 – drawn from Davis Polk, "*Dodd–Frank Progress Report,*" April 2012.

2   A major concern about the Volcker Rule relates, for example, to the treatment of foreign government securities. Critics suggest that the proposed regulations should provide an exemption for trading in foreign government securities comparable to the exemption for US Government securities, to avoid unintended adverse effects on foreign government bond markets.

1= Strongly Disagree; 2 = Disagree; 3 = Neither; 4 = Agree; 5 = Strongly Agree

4.1)	1	2	3	4	5
There is a need for improved financial regulation, regulatory oversight, financial institutions' corporate governance (that is, COSO ERM, Internal Controls, Basel III, Dodd–Frank, Credit Ratings, and so on) and managerial cultures (that is, CSR, Ethics, and so on).					X

4.2) Professor De Felice what still needs to be changed in terms of financial regulation and regulatory oversight, corporate governance, managerial cultures, internal controls, COSO ERM Framework, and Basel III Framework to avoid in the future other systemic crises?

First, regulatory efforts should be extended in scope. Notwithstanding valuable preliminary work by the Financial Stability Board (FSB) and, more recently, by the European Commission, non-bank intermediaries – which are also an important source of systemic risk – still remain virtually un-regulated. Further measures on banks (if any) should be adopted only at a global level, in order to prevent competitive distortions. In this respect, the EBA proposal to establish a temporary and exceptional capital buffer could imply a strong disadvantage for European banks, compared to players in other jurisdictions: translating into a general deleveraging, it could affect economic growth in a negative way. Similarly, a tax on financial transactions (so-called FTT) could lead to a migration of transactions outside the EU, if implemented only at the European level.

Greater attention has also to be paid to the significance of capital ratios, which are a key indicator of banks' resilience and solvency within the Basel Framework. The question is: are capital ratios really comparable among banks and among jurisdictions?

Although regulation has changed significantly over time, the Basel capital Framework remains heavily dependent on RWAs. Only in 2013 a new solvency measure will be introduced – the leverage ratio – defined as Tier 1 capital over total un-weighted on-and-off-balance sheet assets; migration to Pillar 1 measures is expected to take place in January 2018, after appropriate review and calibration.

A recent report by the International Monetary Fund[3] highlights that, while greater convergence will be fostered by Basel III in the definition and composition of capital (that is: the numerator of capital ratios), RWAs (the denominator) still remain the outcome of a mix of approaches: Basel I, Basel II (in its standardized, simplified, foundation or advanced version), Basel 2.5 for market risk weighting, and so on. Taking a sample of 50 banks in Europe, North America and Asia-Pacific, who all reported a Core Tier 1 of 9 percent in June 2011, the paper demonstrates that corresponding leverage ratios and RWA densities[4] vary significantly, both across and within regions. The conclusion is that the same 9 percent Core Tier 1 ratio can mask strong differences across banks in the level of risk it supports.

Risk-modeling choices of banks are influenced by a number of institutional, accounting, regulatory, and bank-specific factors. Discrepancies in RWAs are probably unavoidable, reflecting differences in banks' business models and different views on risk among regulators. However, higher consistency in methodologies and transparency in the outputs

---

3   Vanessa Le Leslé and Sofiya Avramova, "Revisiting Risk Weighted Assets: Why do RWAs Differ Across Countries and What Can be Done About It?," IMF Working Paper (WP/12/90).

4   RWA density is measured as the percentage of RWAs on total assets.

should be pursued, in order to avoid that divergences in the application of Basel standards call into question the credibility and effectiveness of the whole capital framework.

Please use the following *Likert scale* to provide your answer:

1= Strongly Disagree; 2 = Disagree; 3 = Neither; 4 = Agree; 5 = Strongly Agree

5.1)	1	2	3	4	5
Among the root causes of the 2007–2009 financial crisis are there major failures in the financial firms' corporate governance, traders and executive's integrity, accountability, ethical behaviors, and their excessive compensation systems, in addition to industry deregulation and major failures in regulatory oversight?				X	

5.2) Professor De Felice what needs to be done to instill a new culture in the business world in order to improve corporate governance, executive accountability, fair compensation, and more in general, integrity and ethics in the financial markets?

Excessive compensation certainly contributed to the global crisis. The misalignment of reward and risk, the emphasis on short-termism, and the imbalance between executive pay and firms' existing capital levels contributed to the recession. As the downturn became more severe, public anger increased around the world: excessive salaries appeared unjustifiable in a time of recession, especially when companies had received public money.

The crisis gave a boost to regulatory activity in the field of compensation, both at the national and the international level. Just to give an example, in March 2008 the Bank of Italy issued a regulation on banks' organization and corporate governance, with the aim of establishing a framework that combines the search for profit with sound and prudent management. With reference to compensation, the central bank recommends that the shareholders' meeting is involved in setting remuneration policies and establishing equity-based compensation plans. As regards the variable component of managers' pay, the idea is that risk-weighting methods are adopted along with mechanisms to ensure that compensation is linked to both short and long-term results. In addition, specific rules are laid down for control bodies, non-executive directors, and managers in charge of internal control functions.

In 2009, the FSB developed its Principles for Sound Compensation Practices and the related Implementation Standards, with the aim of aligning compensation with prudent risk-taking, particularly at relevant financial institutions. Though a number of gaps remain, progress has been made by national authorities of the G20 countries in implementing the FSB guidelines.

Recent rejection by Citigroup investors of the CEO pay award can be taken as a sign that the "say on pay" legislation is beginning to have an effect. The rule has been introduced by the Dodd–Frank Act, following Principle 9 of the FSB, and forces companies to submit remuneration policies to the shareholders' meeting: Citi became the first big US bank to lose such a ballot, and the 12th among Standard and Poor's companies.

Since the opinion of shareholders is non-binding, it is probably too soon to declare that firms' attitudes on executive pay will be radically altered as a consequence of negative votes. However, in order to avoid reputation damage, companies could be solicited to consult shareholders on remuneration packages in advance, and listen to their concerns.

As a matter of fact, if the first part of the solution to governance problems lies in setting proper rules of the game, the second part lies in revitalizing values and attitudes which encourage economic actors to behave according to these rules.

Interview with **Victor Di Giorgio** (personal communication, 2012), Vice President and Technology Country Head Italy at Citi and Western Europe Corporate O&T Cultural Change Ambassador at Citi. Disclaimer: The opinions expressed on this interview represent only my personal view, acting solely in my individual private capacity. Any information presented, and any opinions given, do not represent in any form the views of any of the Citi legal entities and/or businesses. Views and opinions should not be ascribed to Citi or to any other named firm or entity.

Please use the following *Likert scale* to provide your answer:

1= Strongly Disagree; 2 = Disagree; 3 = Neither; 4 = Agree; 5 = Strongly Agree

1.1)	1	2	3	4	5
The 2007–2009 financial crisis was predictable and avoidable.				X	

1.2) Mr Di Giorgio was the 2007–2009 financial crisis predictable and avoidable?

It is my personal opinion that the financial and economic crisis was avoidable, at least theoretically. As described in the FCIC final report, there were many indicators and most of them were, consciously or unconsciously, ignored. These are now called warning signs or red flags but at the time the crisis sparked off the financial institutions were not prepared nor had the right skills to interpret them. The reason for this misinterpretation was probably due to lack of precedents and history as well as weaknesses in controls, ineffective supervision from financial regulators and obviously insufficient accountability and ethics. Nevertheless none of the indicators alone, or all in different combination, could easily let anybody reach to such a dramatic conclusion.

Please use the following *Likert scale* to provide your answer:

1= Strongly Disagree; 2 = Disagree; 3 = Neither; 4 = Agree; 5 = Strongly Agree

2.1)	1	2	3	4	5
The economic/fiscal and monetary policies, financial reforms, and risk mitigation plans implemented by policy makers and regulators to reduce the impact of the housing market and credit bubbles were comprehensive and effective to reduce the financial meltdown.			X		

2.2) Mr Di Giorgio what actionable economic/fiscal policies, reforms, or risk mitigation plans could have been immediately implemented to reduce the impact of the housing market and credit bubbles and the meltdown caused by the crisis?

My point of view is that all the above actions were a necessary but not sufficient condition. The US Government housing policy created the environment for the subprime market to grow to non-expectable levels but the 2008 crisis could have occurred, maybe to different extents, also without the housing bubble. The progress made in the financial markets – which have become increasingly globalized – and the current technology which has transformed the efficiency, speed, and complexity of financial transactions have transformed too rapidly the business models of various financial institutions which focused their activities increasingly on risky trading activities with short-term profits. Further and equally important actions had to be taken in increasing the standards of accountability and ethics at all level in the financial industry. A strong corporate culture and "risk awareness" attitude should be a habitual part of how people operate professionally. Corporations should foster an environment where people are encouraged to act with urgency courage and conviction around risk.

Please use the following *Likert scale* to provide your answer:

1= Strongly Disagree; 2 = Disagree; 3 = Neither; 4 = Agree; 5 = Strongly Agree

3.1)	1	2	3	4	5
The monetary and fiscal policies, the government bail-outs, (TARP, TALF, and so on), and the financial reforms introduced (for example, Dodd–Frank Act, of which Volcker Rule is a central component, and so on) after 2008 were valid long-term solutions to regulate and stabilize financial markets and to avoid the risk of new crises (double dip).				X	

3.2) Mr Di Giorgio are the monetary and fiscal policies, the government bail-outs, (TARP, TALF, and so on), and the financial reforms introduced (for example, Dodd–Frank Act, of which the Volcker Rule is a central component, and so on) after 2008 valid long-term solutions to regulate and stabilize financial markets and to avoid the risk of new crises (double dip)?

Similarly to what was stated in answer 2 both the bail-outs and the reforms were "*conditio sine qua non*" to reestablish credibility on the financial industry and stabilize the markets.
These have already started to change the business model and the organization of some financial institutions by increasing the transparency and strengthening the corporate governance. At the same time the financial regulatory authorities have to wield the power to regulate the financial systems. Once more the values of a strong culture should result in independent and objective reviews even if that would mean to critically challenge the institutions and the entire system if needed.

Please use the following *Likert scale* to provide your answer:

1= Strongly Disagree; 2 = Disagree; 3 = Neither; 4 = Agree; 5 = Strongly Agree

4.1)	1	2	3	4	5
There is a need for improved financial regulation, regulatory oversight, financial institutions' corporate governance (that is, COSO ERM, Internal Controls, Basel III, Dodd–Frank, Credit Ratings, and so on) and managerial cultures (that is, CSR, Ethics, and so on).			X		

4.2) Mr Di Giorgio what still needs to be changed in terms of financial regulation and regulatory oversight, corporate governance, managerial cultures, internal controls, COSO ERM Framework, and Basel III Framework to avoid in the future other systemic crises?

We need to distinguish the need for additional or improved laws and regulations from an inadequate Corporate Social Responsibility and poor culture.

While the new overall framework is, in my opinion, almost there, it is important to emphasize that rules and regulations need to be, first of all, strictly applied. In the recent crisis in some cases the regulators could have intervened by simply enforcing the existing laws but this didn't happened. Needless to add that in the current fast-changing arena – where all institutions have to compete – the rules have to be constantly aligned and therefore there may be a need for a more frequent review and amendments.

Strong competiveness, market globalization and new technologies lead to exacerbation in creation of new kind of investment products that often auditors are not able, or lack the appropriate tools, to assess in terms of risk.

The authorities not only need be truly independent and empowered but also need to work in parallel with companies in order to maintain a strong corporate governance inspired by soundproof ethics and principles.

The banking world is undergoing a dramatic change and the pace of change will likely continue to accelerate. Financial institutions face a challenging economic environment, and will have to operate in an increasingly complex political and regulatory world. The collective impact to the operating environment insists that institutions continue to modify their behaviors, their business models, and their mind set.

Please use the following *Likert scale* to provide your answer:

1= Strongly Disagree; 2 = Disagree; 3 = Neither; 4 = Agree; 5 = Strongly Agree

5.1)	1	2	3	4	5
Among the root causes of the 2007–2009 financial crisis are there major failures in the financial firms' corporate governance, traders and executive's integrity, accountability, ethical behaviors, and their excessive compensation systems, in addition to industry deregulation and major failures in regulatory oversight?				X	

5.2) Mr Di Giorgio what needs to be done to instill a new culture in the business world in order to improve corporate governance, executive accountability, fair compensation, and more in general, integrity and ethics in the financial markets?

As previously stated a combination of actions need to be pursued in order to regain trust and credibility. The crisis, which was initially limited to the financial sector has then become an economic crisis and in some cases has turned out into a political crisis and therefore needs to be addressed by these components together. Governments, regulators, national central banks, and financial institutions need to work together to set clear criteria and principles in order to reach the common purpose of "Responsible Finance." Rules need to be clear, not subject to interpretation and factual. Regulators need to be independent, pragmatic and watchful and so on.

There's no simple answer to this question; recent events have demonstrated how rules like the Volcker Rule – which is not yet in effect and has already showed some gaps – alone are not enough if there is not a strong culture behind. A thorough program with the scope of creating, or building where needed, a new culture based on firm principles can be the starting point for a more ethical approach to the crisis. Fair compensation, accountability, acting with courage, and conviction are all different aspects of the same topic.

It is not a matter of how many rules you put in the game but maybe of how much is your willingness of playing by them and not trying to avoid them or bend them to your needs.

Interview with **Darrell Duffie** (personal communication, 2012), Dean Witter Distinguished Professor of Finance at The Graduate School of Business, Stanford University, USA.

Please use the following *Likert scale* to provide your answer:

1= Strongly Disagree; 2 = Disagree; 3 = Neither; 4 = Agree; 5 = Strongly Agree

1.1)	1	2	3	4	5
The 2007–2009 financial crisis was predictable and avoidable.			X		

1.2) Professor Duffie was the 2007–2009 financial crisis predictable and avoidable?

The easy answer is "No," because we know that, by and large, it was not predicted, despite many chances by many "experts" to do so. There are some exceptions. Professors Shiller, Rajan, and Roubini had predicted some of the key elements. But most regulators whose responsibility was to predict and head off the crisis did not do so. Few academic and business economists did so. So, I conclude that it was very hard to predict, in anything like its full breadth.

Please use the following *Likert scale* to provide your answer:

1= Strongly Disagree; 2 = Disagree; 3 = Neither; 4 = Agree; 5 = Strongly Agree

2.1)	1	2	3	4	5
The economic/fiscal and monetary policies, financial reforms, and risk mitigation plans implemented by policy makers and regulators to reduce the impact of the housing market and credit bubbles were comprehensive and effective to reduce the financial meltdown.				X	

2.2) Professor Duffie what actionable economic/fiscal policies, reforms, or risk mitigation plans could have been immediately implemented to reduce the impact of the housing market and credit bubbles and the meltdown caused by the crisis?

The United States, despite some mistakes, acted quite quickly and robustly once the crisis was in full force. The measures of the Fed included massive quantitative easing and support for fixed income markets (including mortgage markets) and banks, as well as liquidity, including swap lines in concert with other central banks. The Congress enacted TARP relatively quickly (after an initial delay). The Treasury absorbed Fannie Mae and Freddie Mac immediately. American International Group (AIG) was quickly bailed out (inefficiently, but nonetheless rapidly and fully). These all served the purpose stated in your question. It probably would have been wise to immediately eliminate a large fraction of the principal due on all residential mortgage debt currently in default (and only the mortgages already in default). The government or banks would have paid a massive amount to do this, but it would have helped. It would have also been wise to re-write the mortgage servicing agreement so as to better encourage the restructuring of mortgages yet to default. See Geanakoplos et al. (2012); Geanakoplos and Fostel (2012a, 2011b), Geanakoplos (2011; 2010a; 2010b) on the last two points.

Please use the following *Likert scale* to provide your answer:

1= Strongly Disagree; 2 = Disagree; 3 = Neither; 4 = Agree; 5 = Strongly Agree

3.1)	1	2	3	4	5
The monetary and fiscal policies, the government bail-outs, (TARP, TALF, and so on), and the financial reforms introduced (for example, Dodd–Frank Act, of which Volcker Rule is a central component, and so on) after 2008 were valid long-term solutions to regulate and stabilize financial markets and to avoid the risk of new crises (double dip).				X	

3.2) Professor Duffie are the monetary and fiscal policies, the government bail-outs, (TARP, TALF, and so on), and the financial reforms introduced (for example, Dodd–Frank Act, of which the Volcker Rule is a central component, and so on) after 2008 valid long-term solutions to regulate and stabilize financial markets and to avoid the risk of new crises (double dip)?

This question would take ten pages to begin to answer. Sorry. I will merely say that some of these are more valid than others. The Dodd–Frank and Volcker Rule are extremely complex. They have many costs and benefits, and include many weaknesses and strengths. TARP, the Primary Dealer Credit Facility (PDCF), TALF, and similar liquidity programs were simpler, in relative terms, and were good ideas.

Please use the following *Likert scale* to provide your answer:

1= Strongly Disagree; 2 = Disagree; 3 = Neither; 4 = Agree; 5 = Strongly Agree

4.1)	1	2	3	4	5
There is a need for improved financial regulation, regulatory oversight, financial institutions' corporate governance (that is, COSO ERM, Internal Controls, Basel III, Dodd–Frank, Credit Ratings, and so on) and managerial cultures (that is, CSR, Ethics, and so on).					X

4.2) Professor Duffie what still needs to be changed in terms of financial regulation and regulatory oversight, corporate governance, managerial cultures, internal controls, COSO ERM Framework, and Basel III Framework to avoid in the future other systemic crises?

This is another question that would take too long for me to answer. Significant works remain in all of these areas. We are just getting started. Key areas: more robust market infrastructure, higher bank capital and liquidity requirements, much better systemic risk monitoring, better boards of directors, more funding for better regulatory supervision, more independent internal lines of reporting for risk management.

Please use the following *Likert scale* to provide your answer:

1= Strongly Disagree; 2 = Disagree; 3 = Neither; 4 = Agree; 5 = Strongly Agree

5.1)	1	2	3	4	5
Among the root causes of the 2007–2009 financial crisis are there major failures in the financial firms' corporate governance, traders and executive's integrity, accountability, ethical behaviors, and their excessive compensation systems, in addition to industry deregulation and major failures in regulatory oversight?				X	

5.2) Professor Duffie what needs to be done to instill a new culture in the business world in order to improve corporate governance, executive accountability, fair compensation, and more in general, integrity and ethics in the financial markets?

Education is key. I teach at a University. This is what we do. So, I have a conflict of interest in suggesting more and better education. Better investigative journalism and higher transparency standards would also help. Better regulatory supervision would help here as well. Other sources: *How Big Banks Fail – And What to Do About It* (Princeton University Press, 2010); *The Squam Lake Report – Fixing the Financial System* (I am a co-author, one of 15) (Princeton University Press, 2010).

Interview with **Charles Goodhart** (personal communication, 2012), Emeritus Professor at the London School of Economics and Director of the Financial Regulation Research Programme and former member of the Bank of England's Monetary Policy Committee (1997–2000), UK.

Please use the following *Likert scale* to provide your answer:

1= Strongly Disagree; 2 = Disagree; 3 = Neither; 4 = Agree; 5 = Strongly Agree

1.1)	1	2	3	4	5
The 2007–2009 financial crisis was predictable and avoidable.			X		

1.2) Professor Goodhart was the 2007–2009 financial crisis predictable and avoidable?

The financial crisis obviously was not predicted. There were a few people who could see some dangers, but I don't think anyone predicted the exact course the crisis was going to take. I think that I would disagree that the crisis was predictable. I would not strongly disagree that some people saw that there were dangers. Regarding this point it is also important to determine when it was actually predicted. Michael Lewis (2010), for example in the book *The Big Short: Inside the Doomsday Machine* mentions that by the end of 2006 certain people were predicting that the housing market in the US would have a downturn. I don't think anyone went far enough to predict that no doubt the housing market crisis would lead to a full-fledged banking crisis. There was not a systemic industry-wide perspective.

Please use the following *Likert scale* to provide your answer:

1= Strongly Disagree; 2 = Disagree; 3 = Neither; 4 = Agree; 5 = Strongly Agree

2.1)	1	2	3	4	5
The economic/fiscal and monetary policies, financial reforms, and risk mitigation plans implemented by policy makers and regulators to reduce the impact of the housing market and credit bubbles were comprehensive and effective to reduce the financial meltdown				X	

2.2) Professor Goodhart what actionable economic/fiscal policies, reforms, or risk mitigation plans could have been immediately implemented to reduce the impact of the housing market and credit bubbles and the meltdown caused by the crisis?

I think that regulators initially underestimated the extent of the crisis, because the subprime market was a relatively small part of the overall system. They did not see how it was going to become a full-fledged crisis. Certainly initially there was too much concern about moral hazard, that is if they stepped in at an early stage it would have encouraged people to take more and more risk in the future. The ECB acted fast; the Fed acted next since it cut interest rates by the autumn; the Bank of England rather took the rear at this stage, and the Bank of Japan was in any case in a different state.

The problem with Taylor's function is that what really matters is the future, the expectations, because interest rates changes do not have an effect on output and inflation until later on in the future. It is not clear, if one takes into account expectations, where the economy is going. It was not so much an issue related to too low interest rates but it was rather that the authorities were focusing on a particular set of goods and services prices rather than worrying about assets prices. If one looks at what was happening to asset prices it is quite clear that monetary policies were more expansionary than the authorities thought.

Please use the following *Likert scale* to provide your answer:

1= Strongly Disagree; 2 = Disagree; 3 = Neither; 4 = Agree; 5 = Strongly Agree

3.1)	1	2	3	4	5
The monetary and fiscal policies, the government bail-outs, (TARP, TALF, and so on), and the financial reforms introduced (for example, Dodd–Frank Act, the Volcker Rule, and so on.) after 2008 were valid long-term solutions to regulate and stabilize financial markets and to avoid the risk of new crises (double dip).		X			

3.2) Professor Goodhart are the monetary and fiscal policies, the government bail-outs, (TARP, TALF, and so on), and the financial reforms introduced (for example, Dodd–Frank Act, of which the Volcker Rule is a central component, and so on) after 2008 valid long-term solutions to regulate and stabilize financial markets and to avoid the risk of new crises (double dip)?

The risk of new crises will never be completely avoided. The policies that were undertaken in the autumn of 2008 prevented a very severe panic, developing into a second round of great depression, as in 1929–1933. The problem is that some of the regulatory measures that have been introduced since then are actually enhancing the credit crunch being very procyclical, making in the short run the economic situation worse rather than better. An excess of regulations and reforms will create more problems than benefits. I think that the end position that the authorities want to get to is correct but the problem is that to get to the end position they have to make banks tighten up. This happens, though, just at a moment that banks are tightening in any case and thus they are reducing credit expansion even further than it would otherwise occur.

Regarding the Volcker Rule, I think that the main problem was the boom and burst in the property market which had nothing at all to do with the repeal of the Glass–Steagall Act and the "Too-Big-To-Fail" doctrine. The difficulty with the Volcker Rule is that it is very hard to distinguish between when a financial intermediary is speculating with its own money and when it is taking reasonable steps to protect its position as a market maker. The Vickers approach is simply a mechanism, among several others, to try to limit the contingent liability of the taxpayers to have to finance a further crisis. I am not sure if it is the best way of limiting the liability of the British taxpayers but I can see why they want to do it.

I believe that the financial activities tax is a far better mechanism for taxing the banks than the financial transaction tax or Tobin tax. The problem with the Tobin tax is that the tax is paid in the market where the institution wants to take the transaction, and such a market can be very mobile, one can set up the market wherever one likes it, and what this will mean is that the market for financial transactions will move outside the tax area.

Regarding the recent statements of Bank of England's Governor, Mervyn King, on regulatory and oversight failures that have led to the financial crisis and the need for radical reforms of financial institutions, I believe that it is always wise to try and learn from past errors. But I am not sure that recognizing these errors will necessarily mean that the regulations the Bank of England is trying to introduce are best designed.

Please use the following *Likert scale* to provide your answer:

1= Strongly Disagree; 2 = Disagree; 3 = Neither; 4 = Agree; 5 = Strongly Agree

4.1)	1	2	3	4	5
There is a need for improved financial regulation, regulatory oversight, financial institutions' corporate governance (that is, COSO ERM, Internal Controls, Basel III, Dodd–Frank, Credit Ratings, and so on) and managerial cultures (that is, CSR, Ethics, and so on).					X

4.2) Professor Goodhart what still needs to be changed in terms of financial regulation and regulatory oversight, corporate governance, managerial cultures, internal controls, COSO ERM Framework, and Basel III Framework to avoid in the future other systemic crises?

I think that the whole basis for managerial remuneration in banking needs reconsideration.
    Furthermore, the way the whole regulation (Basel III) tends to be hitched onto a single capital ratio or a single liquidity ratio is less than desirable. Therefore I believe there is a need for financial regulation, regulatory oversight, and improvement to financial institutions' corporate and managerial cultures.

Please use the following *Likert scale* to provide your answer:

1= Strongly Disagree; 2 = Disagree; 3 = Neither; 4 = Agree; 5 = Strongly Agree

5.1)	1	2	3	4	5
Among the root causes of the 2007–2009 financial crisis are there major failures in the financial firms' corporate governance, traders and executive's integrity, accountability, ethical behaviors, and their excessive compensation systems, in addition to industry deregulation and major failures in regulatory oversight?					X

5.2) Professor Goodhart what needs to be done to instill a new culture in the business world in order to improve corporate governance, executive accountability, fair compensation, and more in general, integrity and ethics in the financial markets?

I believe that an effective way to address these issues is to have an improved mechanism for handling remuneration of senior bank officials. Thus, I agree that among the root causes of the 2007–2009 financial crisis there are major failures in corporate governance, executive compensation, and regulatory governance too. I would like to see the remuneration of regulators also conditional to how the system is working. Remuneration is indeed a major incentive for a lot of people. We need to avoid rewarding failures.

Interview with **Etienne Koehler** (personal communication, 2012), Associate Professor of Financial Mathematics at La Sorbonne University of Paris and Expert of Credit Risk Analytics, France.

Please use the following *Likert scale* to provide your answer:

1= Strongly Disagree; 2 = Disagree; 3 = Neither; 4 = Agree; 5 = Strongly Agree

1.1)	1	2	3	4	5
The 2007–2009 financial crisis was predictable and avoidable		X		X	

1.2) Professor Koehler was the 2007–2009 financial crisis predictable and avoidable?

Two different questions: was it predictable (1) and was it avoidable (2).

1. Predictability: some banks (for example, Goldman Sachs) had published six months before the crisis in financial magazines that this was getting dangerous. Some other banks also refused to continue this business. Given the time that it takes to write an article, get it reviewed and printed means that some banks were aware of the danger some time before the crisis. However the analysis of the risk of the products was far from enough. Namely the impact of downgrading on these transactions (for example on the overcollateralization ratio) was really understated.
2. Possibility to avoid: given the regulation at this time it does not seem to be avoidable. Someone (in trading or risk department) saying to her/his hierarchy for example, in 2005: "I refuse these products because I think that they are dangerous" would probably have lost her/his job based on the reason that the competition was making good profit on these trades: a marketable feature of these transactions was the fact that the equity IRR was very high.

Also: the market was rather one way but there was no possibility of detecting it.

Please use the following *Likert scale* to provide your answer:

1= Strongly Disagree; 2 = Disagree; 3 = Neither; 4 = Agree; 5 = Strongly Agree

2.1)	1	2	3	4	5
The economic/fiscal and monetary policies, financial reforms, and risk mitigation plans implemented by policy makers and regulators to reduce the impact of the housing market and credit bubbles were comprehensive and effective to reduce the financial meltdown.	X				

2.2) Professor Koehler what actionable economic/fiscal policies, reforms, or risk mitigation plans could have been immediately implemented to reduce the impact of the housing market and credit bubbles and the meltdown caused by the crisis?

The possibility to have credit even with no income and no asset for guarantee, except the house purchased and the belief that it will be possible later to sell this house with a profit due to an expected price increase, was clearly extremely risky but in an economy where "everything" is based on credit how could restriction measures have been politically acceptable?

Also products such as some tranches of collateralized debt obligations (CDOs) on asset-backed securities (ABS) were considered as riskless (or with a good credit quality)

because they were backed up by AAA monolines. These monolines were AAA because they did not need to post collateral. They did not need to post collateral because they were insuring riskless products and were AAA ...

Please use the following *Likert scale* to provide your answer:

1= Strongly Disagree; 2 = Disagree; 3 = Neither; 4 = Agree; 5 = Strongly Agree

3.1)	1	2	3	4	5
The monetary and fiscal policies, the government bail-outs, (TARP, TALF, and so on), and the financial reforms introduced (for example, Dodd–Frank Act, of which Volcker Rule is a central component, and so on) after 2008 were valid long-term solutions to regulate and stabilize financial markets and to avoid the risk of new crises (double dip).		X			

3.2) Professor Koehler are the monetary and fiscal policies, the government bail-outs, (TARP, TALF, and so on), and the financial reforms introduced (for example, Dodd–Frank Act, of which the Volcker Rule is a central component, and so on) after 2008 valid long-term solutions to regulate and stabilize financial markets and to avoid the risk of new crises (double dip)?

As long as there are big chunks of the financial activity which cannot be seen by the regulator (is the market only one way, if yes, there will be a snowball effect when the market decides that it is time to close these positions? What is the total amount of products of a given type, including size, direction, and counterparties?), it will be difficult to avoid the risk of new crises.

Some products are also profitable when crises arise as such condition may lead to the temptation to spread rumors meant to make people think that the situation is dangerous which in turns actually increases the probability of a crisis.

Please use the following *Likert scale* to provide your answer:

1= Strongly Disagree; 2 = Disagree; 3 = Neither; 4 = Agree; 5 = Strongly Agree

4.1)	1	2	3	4	5
There is a need for improved financial regulation, regulatory oversight, financial institutions' corporate governance (that is, COSO ERM, Internal Controls, Basel III, Dodd–Frank, Credit Ratings, and so on) and managerial cultures (that is, CSR, Ethics, and so on).					X

4.2) Professor Koehler what still needs to be changed in terms of financial regulation and regulatory oversight, corporate governance, managerial cultures, internal controls, COSO ERM Framework, and Basel III Framework to avoid in the future other systemic crises?

At least a view by the regulator of total notional amount of products of a given type, including size, direction and counterparties. This is useless though if the regulator does not have a way to treat big flows of information.

Please use the following *Likert scale* to provide your answer:

1= Strongly Disagree; 2 = Disagree; 3 = Neither; 4 = Agree; 5 = Strongly Agree

5.1)	1	2	3	4	5
Among the root causes of the 2007–2009 financial crisis are there major failures in the financial firms' corporate governance, traders and executive's integrity, accountability, ethical behaviors, and their excessive compensation systems, in addition to industry deregulation and major failures in regulatory oversight?					X

5.2) Professor Koehler what needs to be done to instill a new culture in the business world in order to improve corporate governance, executive accountability, fair compensation, and more in general, integrity and ethics in the financial markets?

More effective power to risk departments, that is more direct access of the risk department to the board in order to present an analysis of the risks seen in the financial institution. Bonuses paid over several years. Profit estimation under different scenarios including downgrading of big institutions. Contra cyclical regulation measures (this is not the case with Basel III).

Interview with **Alexander N. Kostyuk** (personal communication, 2012), Professor of Corporate Governance and Finance and Director of the International Center for Banking and Corporate Governance, Ukrainian Academy of Banking of the National Bank of Ukraine. Professor of Corporate Governance and Finance at the Hanken School of Economics (Finland); Editor-in-Chief, *Corporate Ownership and Control* journal; Editor-in-Chief, *Corporate Board: Role, Duties and Composition* journal; Editor-in-Chief, *Risk Governance and Control: Financial Markets and Institutions* journal; Editor-in-Chief, *Journal of Governance and Regulation*.

Please use the following *Likert scale* to provide your answer:

1= Strongly Disagree; 2 = Disagree; 3 = Neither; 4 = Agree; 5 = Strongly Agree

1.1)	1	2	3	4	5
The 2007–2009 financial crisis was predictable and avoidable.				X	

1.2) Professor Kostyuk was the 2007–2009 financial crisis predictable and avoidable?

The financial crisis was predictable thanks to several reasons. First, there was a very sharp growth in the US mortgage market accelerated by bullish housing market. Second, an increased imbalance of borrowing by US banks including investment at their European counterparts. Third, a weak progress in development of internal corporate control mechanisms in the US. Fourth, weak shareholder activism in mitigating the excessive power of CEOs.

Please use the following *Likert scale* to provide your answer:

1= Strongly Disagree; 2 = Disagree; 3 = Neither; 4 = Agree; 5 = Strongly Agree

2.1)	1	2	3	4	5
The economic/fiscal and monetary policies, financial reforms, and risk mitigation plans implemented by policy makers and regulators to reduce the impact of the housing market and credit bubbles were comprehensive and effective to reduce the financial meltdown.		X			

2.2) Professor Kostyuk what actionable economic/fiscal policies, reforms, or risk mitigation plans could have been immediately implemented to reduce the impact of the housing market and credit bubbles and the meltdown caused by the crisis?

International harmonization of financial regulation was very ineffective. Many countries in Europe were not ready to adopt common rules and standards for corporate governance and regulation in financial companies. The FSB has been linked to the problems of financial crisis too late although its recommendation would be very useful at the early stage for emerging countries. Corporate governance reforms were not made in synchronic manner by European countries and some disparity in efforts to reform corporate governance has been detected in France, UK, Germany and other developed countries. Risk management issues related to financial institutions have not been put in the agenda of the state programs.

Please use the following *Likert scale* to provide your answer:

1= Strongly Disagree; 2 = Disagree; 3 = Neither; 4 = Agree; 5 = Strongly Agree

3.1)	1	2	3	4	5
The monetary and fiscal policies, the government bail-outs, (TARP, TALF, and so on), and the financial reforms introduced (for example, Dodd–Frank Act, of which Volcker Rule is a central component, and so on) after 2008 were valid long-term solutions to regulate and stabilize financial markets and to avoid the risk of new crises (double dip).			X		

3.2) Professor Kostyuk are the monetary and fiscal policies, the government bail-outs, (TARP, TALF, and so on), and the financial reforms introduced (for example, Dodd–Frank Act, of which the Volcker Rule is a central component, and so on) after 2008 valid long-term solutions to regulate and stabilize financial markets and to avoid the risk of new crises (double dip)?

The effect of the state support and bail-out plans was very weak. The first reason was that these programs and plans have been undertaken by many countries too late to be effective. As a result, these programs were mainly focused on solving the problems of large financial institutions (bailout) through massive injection of state funds instead of predicting the main root causes of the incumbent crisis. The second reason was linked to the lack of consensus among the developed countries on how to mitigate systemic risks spreading during the crisis. It is obvious that the Financial Stability Board (FSB) should have immediately received from the central banks and the Bank of International Settlements (BIS) a list of the systemically important financial institutions in order to provide to them very brief and wise instructions and guidelines on how to avoid systemic risks and handle more effectively the emergency phase of the crisis.

Please use the following *Likert scale* to provide your answer:

1= Strongly Disagree; 2 = Disagree; 3 = Neither; 4 = Agree; 5 = Strongly Agree

4.1)	1	2	3	4	5
There is a need for improved financial regulation, regulatory oversight, financial institutions' corporate governance (that is, COSO ERM, Internal Controls, Basel III, Dodd–Frank, Credit Ratings, and so on) and managerial cultures (that is, CSR, Ethics, and so on).					X

4.2) Professor Kostyuk what still needs to be changed in terms of financial regulation and regulatory oversight, corporate governance, managerial cultures, internal controls, COSO ERM Framework, and Basel III Framework to avoid in the future other systemic crises?

There is primarily a need to improve corporate governance in financial institutions. The Basel III Framework is still missing many important issues of corporate governance (as of May 2012) like the role of CEO, internal control and the role of independent directors, remuneration of independent directors, the role of CFO, gender diversity, and so on. The most important issue is that Basel III almost completely ignores contrasting features in Anglo–Saxon and German models of corporate governance. Basel III does not give any distinctions how to utilize the most important features of corporate governance models. Unification or specification of corporate governance reforms is still a disputable issue in many countries of the world that generates increased uncertainty in the market.

Please use the following *Likert scale* to provide your answer:

1= Strongly Disagree; 2 = Disagree; 3 = Neither; 4 = Agree; 5 = Strongly Agree

5.1)	1	2	3	4	5
Among the root causes of the 2007–2009 financial crisis are there major failures in the financial firms' corporate governance, traders and executive's integrity, accountability, ethical behaviors, and their excessive compensation systems, in addition to industry deregulation and major failures in regulatory oversight?					X

5.2) Professor Kostyuk what needs to be done to instill a new culture in the business world in order to improve corporate governance, executive accountability, fair compensation, and more in general, integrity and ethics in the financial markets?

The first thing financial institutions should do to improve corporate governance is to ignite shareholders' activism. The say-on-pay principle should be made popular worldwide. Stock exchanges should improve their listing rules, including more detailed requirements for financial firms to protect shareholders' interests and activism. At least large financial institutions should be forced to apply deferred compensation schemes and the malus principle in order to minimize systemic risks. The role of stock exchange as a rule-making institution should be remarkably strengthened.

Interview with **George Koukis** (personal communication, 2012) – Founder and President of TEMENOS (one of the world's leading supplier of packaged banking software), Switzerland.

Please use the following *Likert scale* to provide your answer:

1= Strongly Disagree; 2 = Disagree; 3 = Neither; 4 = Agree; 5 = Strongly Agree

1.1)	1	2	3	4	5
The 2007–2009 financial crisis was predictable and avoidable.					X

1.2) Mr Koukis was the 2007–2009 financial crisis predictable and avoidable?

The Clinical answer is YES. Not because of the FCIC's report but because we live in the twenty-first century, we have sophisticated tools, experience, education. The signs were all there but the smart top lines managers of institutions predominantly dominated by the Government (Federal Reserve, Investment Bankers and top companies) decided to use it to their advantage.

Please use the following *Likert scale* to provide your answer:

1= Strongly Disagree; 2 = Disagree; 3 = Neither; 4 = Agree; 5 = Strongly Agree

2.1)	1	2	3	4	5
The economic/fiscal and monetary policies, financial reforms, and risk mitigation plans implemented by policy makers and regulators to reduce the impact of the housing market and credit bubbles were comprehensive and effective to reduce the financial meltdown.		X			

2.2) Mr Koukis what actionable economic/fiscal policies, reforms, or risk mitigation plans could have been immediately implemented to reduce the impact of the housing market and credit bubbles and the meltdown caused by the crisis?

In order to protect the public and honest investors then greater control on leverage, risk management, and credit control should be the first priority.

At an operational level, more transparency so decisions are based on factual data, especially for complex and exotic products.

The risks were known to the Federal bank years before the meltdown. One can only speculate as to what were the objectives and benefits accruing to the policy makers at the expense of the public they are supposed to protect. Therefore their actions were consistent with the original objectives and as such inadequate to deal with the crisis.

Please use the following *Likert scale* to provide your answer:

1= Strongly Disagree; 2 = Disagree; 3 = Neither; 4 = Agree; 5 = Strongly Agree

3.1)	1	2	3	4	5
The monetary and fiscal policies, the government bail-outs, (TARP, TALF, and so on), and the financial reforms introduced (for example, Dodd–Frank Act, of which the Volcker Rule is a central component, and so on) after 2008 were valid long-term solutions to regulate and stabilize financial markets and to avoid the risk of new crises (double dip).		X			

3.2) Mr Koukis are the monetary and fiscal policies, the government bail-outs, (TARP, TALF, and so on), and the financial reforms introduced (for example, Dodd–Frank Act, of which the Volcker Rule is a central component, and so on) after 2008 valid long-term solutions to regulate and stabilize financial markets and to avoid the risk of new crises (double dip)?

All measures taken so far, are supposed to address the problem as defined and understood by the governments of the day. But are these measures to fix the fundamental problem or are we just appeasing the public until the next election?

For instance I am against any interference of any government in the way the free markets should operate. If a conglomerate fails let someone else, a stronger/better managed conglomerate, take it over and run it efficiently. Was the AIG or RBS bail-out necessary? Are the banks managed properly or in order to achieve unrealistic growth rates and equally unrealistic personal remuneration? Do they take criminal risks to maximize profits knowing very well that if they get into real trouble then the government will bail them out? This is criminal intent yet I believe that this is more their thinking rather than prudent management.

The Fed had data on the imminent crisis, economists knew it, banks knew it, rating agencies who officially gave AAA ratings knew it, official banking sector was valued at $11 trillion and unofficial (shadow) banking was $13 trillion (according to the FCIC final report) in other words, off-balance sheet, the shady, risky, deals were larger than the official banking business.

If the above measures were ignored by people of the same mentality then it is "a window dressing" process and as the FCIC points out, it may happen again. When the FSA in the UK gets a bonus for selling banks to Iceland and for not seeing the mess at RBS, then our systems (social responsibility systems) are in question because we basically reward failure.

Please use the following *Likert scale* to provide your answer:

1= Strongly Disagree; 2 = Disagree; 3 = Neither; 4 = Agree; 5 = Strongly Agree

4.1)	1	2	3	4	5
There is a need for improved financial regulation, regulatory oversight, financial institutions' corporate governance (that is, COSO ERM, Internal Controls, Basel III, Dodd–Frank, Credit Ratings, and so on) and managerial cultures (that is, CSR, Ethics, and so on).					X

4.2) Mr Koukis what still needs to be changed in terms of financial regulation and regulatory oversight, corporate governance, managerial cultures, internal controls, COSO ERM Framework, and Basel III Framework to avoid in the future other systemic crises?

There are a lot of suggestions and guidelines that are going some way to address these issues like the Basel Frameworks, now Basel III and possibly we will see many more recommendations. Most of the frameworks like Internal Control, ERM, and risk management have been available for a long time, it does not need sophisticated tools to know that lending money to an unemployed person that has no chance of ever repaying it will invevitably lead to a failure of the financial institution. The same nonsense generated innovation of exotic derivative products designed to produce immense profits but without creating any new factory (real economy value).; The same nonsense is related to pretending to ignore that people will lose their jobs in a few months (due to the crisis) but you continue to speculate anyway due to personal reckless greed. This is more difficult to regulate and mitigate, unless we re-write the rules and agree the basic framework of exhibiting social responsibility in our daily actions.

Please use the following *Likert scale* to provide your answer:

1= Strongly Disagree; 2 = Disagree; 3 = Neither; 4 = Agree; 5 = Strongly Agree

5.1)	1	2	3	4	5
Among the root causes of the 2007–2009 financial crisis are there major failures in the financial firms' corporate governance, traders and executive's integrity, accountability, ethical behaviors, and their excessive compensation systems, in addition to industry deregulation and major failures in regulatory oversight?					X

5.2) Mr Koukis what needs to be done to instill a new culture in the business world in order to improve corporate governance, executive accountability, fair compensation, and more in general, integrity and ethics in the financial markets?

The financial crisis was not a sudden event, people in certain top positions not only knew it was about to happen, but it was engineered. In the same way that if G.W. Bush did not change legislation then Enron would not be able to consummate such a monumental fraud, the largest corporate collapse in history. And many other companies like Worldcom, Parmalat, and the .com companies' fraud that generated the 2000 panic and other firms that I would put in the same category.

The underlying issue is greed. I do not believe that suddenly in 2008 or in any given year someone said "let's concoct a scheme of how to get rich," it has happened gradually over the last 50–60 years. Extreme consumerism, growth rates, and population explosion has forced us to think short term; and by definition we have lost our values. The future of our children and grandchildren is based on debt simply to protect our today, a lifestyle characterized by what we have today. Coupled with this we have politicians who only make decisions for the next election; business people react to quarterly results and annual bonuses while they fire people (create unemployment to prop up stock prices). Investment bankers demand double digit returns. We do not care anymore for anything, our environment is polluted, our resources depleted, we kill people in the name of our individual gods, or support despots under the guise of democracy, while the geopolitical problems increase in numbers with time, a sad reflection on humanity to use war and strife as a growth stimulator.

My remedy for correcting this situation, in broad terms:

- Smallest possible government.
- Government spending to be tied to GDP.
- Any major decisions regarding public spending to be approved by voters with a majority of 80 percent.
- Flat tax rate of 10–15 percent.
- Regulate finance to be transparent; if public money is used then we need legislation so that banking goes back to what it was supposed to be.
- Educate young people from the first day at school respect for the world around them, teach them responsibility, accountability and ethics.
- Educate people that double digit ROI is not sustainable and leads to major havoc in any society.

There is no ethical leadership in anything that affects our life today. It is very difficult to fix this problem because of the complexity of the society that we live in. Teaching people about ethics, in the world where investment bankers, hedge funds and rating agencies pursue money and power, will take at least a generation. The magnitude of the current financial crisis is such, the problems are so deep rooted, that fixing them will require the consent of many nations, agreeing on many sensitive issues.

Interview with **William W. Lang** (personal communication, 2012), Senior Vice President and Lending Officer Supervision, Regulation and Credit at the Federal Reserve Bank of Philadelphia and Fellow of the Wharton Financial Institutions Center, USA.

Please use the following *Likert scale* to provide your answer:

1= Strongly Disagree; 2 = Disagree; 3 = Neither; 4 = Agree; 5 = Strongly Agree

1.1)	1	2	3	4	5
The 2007–2009 financial crisis was predictable and avoidable.					X

1.2) Dr Lang was the 2007–2009 financial crisis predictable and avoidable?

My answer depends in part on how one defines the financial crisis as well as how one defines predictable.

I would define the beginning of the financial crisis as the events occurring in the summer of 2007 with the downgrades of structured finance products (principally asset-backed CDOs), the subsequent collapse of the asset-backed commercial paper (ABCP) market and the resulting extraordinary actions by the Federal Reserve to maintain market liquidity. As I will explain below, I believe those events were largely predictable and avoidable.

I don't believe that the shape or magnitude of the subsequent liquidity crises that eventually followed the initial shocks of 2007, particularly the events following Lehman, were predictable. The magnitude and character of liquidity crises are inherently difficult to predict. However, the potential risk of serious financial disruption should have been understood. Since I have already claimed that the beginnings of the financial crisis were avoidable, then the subsequent liquidity crises were avoidable.

Why were the events leading up to the crisis in the summer of 2007 predictable and avoidable? It was certainly predictable that a flattening of house prices would cause large-scale defaults in residential mortgages. There is considerable evidence that this relationship was fairly widely understood among mortgage experts. Analysts differed as to the probability of a flattening of housing prices, but almost all gave some reasonable probability to such an outcome given the very rapid run up in prices and most models predicted large numbers of defaults if this occurred. In other words, while there was over optimism about continued rises in house prices, there was recognition of the risk to that forecast and there was, among mortgage experts, a general understanding that lots of defaults would occur in that event.

It was also predictable that some of the structured securities (Asset-backed, CDOs) were vulnerable in this situation. While this was less widely understood than the potential for large-scale defaults, the evidence indicates that a number of important market participants understood that a flattening or modest decline in housing prices would mean losses in the CDO market.

It was less predictable that a poor housing market could threaten the financial health of giant financial firms. In most cases, the true exposure of those firms to CDOs was not well understood even by the CEOs of those companies. Regulators and other market participants also did not understand the extent of concentrated exposures in large financial organizations. Thus, given the information that people had at their disposal, they could not predict the potential vulnerability of large financial firms to the housing market. However, it was certainly possible for this information to be obtained. The clearest evidence that it was possible to understand that exposure was excessive can be seen by the counter-example of Goldman Sachs. Senior management at Goldman understood their exposures and drastically reduced it in early 2007. Thus, the crisis was not predictable given the information that senior management and regulators were acting upon. However, the information was "knowable" and I would therefore say these events were predictable.

Since the financial crisis would have been avoided if very large financial firms did not build up such large concentrations of exposures, particularly to CDOs, the crisis was avoidable.

Please use the following *Likert scale* to provide your answer:

1= Strongly Disagree; 2 = Disagree; 3 = Neither; 4 = Agree; 5 = Strongly Agree

2.1)	1	2	3	4	5
The economic/fiscal and monetary policies, financial reforms, and risk mitigation plans implemented by policy makers and regulators to reduce the impact of the housing market and credit bubbles were comprehensive and effective to reduce the financial meltdown.				X	

2.2) Dr Lang what actionable economic/fiscal policies, reforms, or risk mitigation plans could have been immediately implemented to reduce the impact of the housing market and credit bubbles and the meltdown caused by the crisis?

Post-crisis, US monetary authorities moved rapidly to lower interest rates and engage in quantitative easing. These policies were effective policies that mitigated the potential for more disastrous financial and macroeconomic collapse. Moreover, given the buildup of problems up to the initial crisis of the summer of 2007, substantial financial dislocation and recession were inevitable. Monetary policy was effective in limiting the damage.

Fiscal policy was also expansionary, although a bigger short-run stimulus was necessary given the magnitude of the financial shock. Ideally, a larger short-run fiscal stimulus should have been combined with some real reforms to reduce long-term structural imbalances. Nevertheless, overall US fiscal policy did provide some important and needed stimulus.

While overall policy was effective, there have been areas that were less effective. This generally relates to policies that have delayed the return of price discovery and market clearing. In particular, housing and foreclosure prevention policies did not decisively address underlying issues. There needed to be some combination of more drastic modifications, including more principal relief for some households, while simultaneously speeding up the disposition of properties for those cases not amenable to mortgage modifications through short sales or foreclosures.

Similarly, "toxic assets" should have been thoroughly removed from bank's balance sheets. Such actions would have been a strong complement to the capital injections and the capital stress tests. In addition, for smaller banks, capital injections were too small and too many troubled banks have been allowed to linger for too long.

For the most part, financial reforms have not been important in preventing a financial meltdown as most of these reforms were designed to prevent or mitigate future crises. They have had little impact on the course of the current crisis. The one exception was the introduction of the stress tests which have helped with market confidence, transparency, and strengthening capital.

Please use the following *Likert scale* to provide your answer:

1= Strongly Disagree; 2 = Disagree; 3 = Neither; 4 = Agree; 5 = Strongly Agree

3.1)	1	2	3	4	5
The monetary and fiscal policies, the government bail-outs, (TARP, TALF, and so on), and the financial reforms introduced (for example, Dodd–Frank Act, of which the Volcker Rule is a central component, and so on) after 2008 were valid long-term solutions to regulate and stabilize financial markets and to avoid the risk of new crises (double dip).			X		

3.2) Dr Lang are the monetary and fiscal policies, the government bail-outs, (TARP, TALF, and so on), and the financial reforms introduced (for example, Dodd–Frank Act, of which the Volcker Rule is a central component, and so on) after 2008 valid long-term solutions to regulate and stabilize financial markets and to avoid the risk of new crises (double dip)?

The fiscal stimulus policies as well as expansionary monetary policies to enhance liquidity are valid long-term tools to stabilize markets during a financial crisis or potential financial crisis. These policies were effective and would likely be effective in the future. They are important policies in reducing the risk of a double dip recession.

Capital injection programs are appropriate tools if the failure of one or a few institutions threatens the financial system, however, policy should be designed to greater lessen the need for this approach.

The regulatory reforms are not sufficient steps to avoid the risks of new crises, although many of the reforms are positive improvements. Enhanced prudential standards for systemically important firms as well as improved resolution mechanisms are helpful policies. It is unlikely that the Volcker Rule will have any significant impact in stemming systemic risk.

While regulatory reforms do contain positive elements, I am skeptical that they are sufficient steps in addressing systemic crises and they may have some important unintended consequences. Regulatory reform in the US has started from a premise that problems in the financial system often arose from problems in sectors that were not subject to "bank-like" safety and soundness regulation. The response to that premise is that bank-like regulation must be broadened to cover all significant players in the financial market.

This vast expansion of regulatory oversight has significant drawbacks. If we continue to have an innovative and competitive financial sector in the US, it will not be possible for regulators to prevent some firms from taking serious missteps. Despite attempts to improve resolution, a failure of a SIFI will still raise the threat of a liquidity crisis. Serious financial problems at a SIFI generate the threat of large and wide-scale losses for the SIFI's creditors and therefore, counterparties to those creditors may refuse to continue providing funding. This can create a cascading downward spiral that leads to a financial crisis as potential lenders hoard their funds waiting until the dust settles. Enhanced capital standards will not eliminate the potential for excessive risk taking and even a strong resolution structure will not eliminate the financial damage caused when a large number of counterparties are expected to suffer losses due to a failure of one or a few firms.

An alternative approach would be to have a very concentrated and tightly controlled financial sector that acts much like a public utility. This can create a more stable financial system but stifles financial innovation and growth.

My preferred alternative is to treat the ability of a firm to create systemic risk in the same way we treat monopoly power. That is, the creation of systemic risk is a significant market externality and should not be allowed. This would require a break-up and/or restructuring of SIFIs to reduce their systemic impact. This should also be combined with a less intrusive regulatory structure for overseeing the financial system.

Please use the following *Likert scale* to provide your answer:

1= Strongly Disagree; 2 = Disagree; 3 = Neither; 4 = Agree; 5 = Strongly Agree

4.1)	1	2	3	4	5
There is a need for improved financial regulation, regulatory oversight, financial institutions' corporate governance (that is, COSO ERM, Internal Controls, Basel III, Dodd–Frank, Credit Ratings, and so on) and managerial cultures (that is, CSR, Ethics, and so on).					X

4.2) Dr Lang what still needs to be changed in terms of financial regulation and regulatory oversight, corporate governance, managerial cultures, internal controls, COSO ERM Framework, and Basel III Framework to avoid in the future other systemic crises?

My previous answer discussed improvements in financial regulation through a system that prohibits financial institutions from becoming systemically important and requires breaking up firms that have become systemically important.

While such a system is desirable, there will always be the potential that a firm will be systemically important but that this will not be understood by regulators. There is no foolproof regulatory design to prevent crises. Strengthening the financial system requires multiple defenses that include careful design of regulations as well as strong corporate governance and supervisory oversight. These are layered defenses that can work together to build a more stable financial system. Thus, improvements in regulatory oversight and corporate governance are important elements in creating a more stable financial sector regardless of the change in regulations.

In the areas of corporate governance and supervisory oversight, developing structural approaches to combating complacency and group think are necessary. In terms of corporate governance, positive steps have been taken to ensure greater independence and expertise by members of corporate boards. Greater emphasis needs to be placed on creation of internal/external challenges to senior management views within a company. This goes well beyond traditional audits which focus on process rather than strategic direction of a company. Company boards and senior management should receive ratings on the effectiveness of that challenge process as well as requirements to provide external reports on the effectiveness of this process. Similarly, regulators should have better internal and external challenge mechanisms to avoid complacency and group think. The increase in multi-disciplinary approaches to supervision and improved quality of horizontal data analytics (for example, stress tests) are steps in the right direction but more will be needed.

Improvements in compensation structures that discourage excessive risk taking and to promote transparency, within a firm and to the public, are very important steps to avoid the behaviors that led to the financial crisis. Misaligned incentives were a significant factor in generating the crisis.

Integrity and business ethics are very important, however, business ethics cannot be separated from the overall ethics in a society. That is, advancing business ethics primarily involves promotion of better ethics throughout the educational, political, and social systems. I don't think programs primarily aimed at corporate boards will be effective without a broader societal effort on ethics, values, and integrity.

Please use the following *Likert scale* to provide your answer:

1= Strongly Disagree; 2 = Disagree; 3 = Neither; 4 = Agree; 5 = Strongly Agree

5.1)	1	2	3	4	5
Among the root causes of the 2007–2009 financial crisis are there major failures in the financial firms' corporate governance, traders and executive's integrity, accountability, ethical behaviors, and their excessive compensation systems, in addition to industry deregulation and major failures in regulatory oversight?					X

5.2) Dr Lang what needs to be done to instill a new culture in the business world in order to improve corporate governance, executive accountability, fair compensation, and more in general, integrity and ethics in the financial markets?

Failures in corporate governance and poor incentive structures were a major cause of the financial crisis. Large financial companies had large, concentrated exposures to the mortgage market through asset-backed CDOs. The evidence indicates that the highest levels of management and the board of directors at some of the largest and most sophisticated financial firms did not understand their true exposure to the mortgage market. This lack of understanding was possible because the exposure was hidden in complicated ways through complex financial structures. At many large financial firms, the corporate governance process was not sufficiently strong to uncover the relevant information about this risk exposure. The fact that there are counter-examples where firms understood their exposure and acted on this knowledge suggests that weak corporate governance processes were a root cause of the crisis.

Poor incentive structures were also a central factor. Corporate managers that were making huge compensation from mortgage-related positions had the incentives to grow that business without regard to the potential harm to the long-term franchise value of the firm. Moreover, these managers had an incentive to build up the volume of asset-backed CDOs since the complex nature of these instruments meant the buildup of risk exposure was not transparent to senior management and the board of directors. This is just a particular manifestation of the standard corporate governance problem. Unfortunately, the failure of those governance processes had particularly disastrous consequences.

Stronger business ethics and accountability would be positive contributors to financial stability. However, a financial system should be sufficiently strong to protect against catastrophic crisis even where business ethics are weak. This is critical since even if there was a broad improvement in business ethics, there will always be some individuals with poor business ethics. In addition, as I mentioned previously, improvement in business ethics would likely be a result in improvements in ethics more broadly within a society. I am skeptical of the efficacy of improving ethical behavior through targeted programs aimed at business ethics.

Interview with **Fabio Mercurio** (personal communication, 2012), Head of Quant Business Managers at Bloomberg LP, New York and Director of the Research Committee of Iason Ltd. Previously, he was the Head of Financial Engineering at Banca IMI, USA.

Please use the following *Likert scale* to provide your answer:

1= Strongly Disagree; 2 = Disagree; 3 = Neither; 4 = Agree; 5 = Strongly Agree

1.1)	1	2	3	4	5
The 2007–2009 financial crisis was predictable and avoidable.				X	

1.2) Dr Mercurio was the 2007–2009 financial crisis predictable and avoidable?

In the early 2000s the housing market soared along with the practice of lending money to borrowers with a low credit score. A relatively easy access to credit created an increasing demand for real estate, which raised house prices. New potential buyers could be discouraged by the increasing price of homes. To attract them, banks relaxed their lending criteria even more, offering the so-called NINJA mortgages to people with no job, no income, no asset and low credit score. Banks also structured loans by offering artificially low rates for the first few years of the loan, which were compensated by potentially higher rates later on. All these elements contributed to the real estate bubble. It was not too hard to realize that home prices were artificially inflated and wouldn't grow indefinitely, and that many home owners would soon be unable to fulfill their payment obligations on their mortgages, as it actually happened.

Mortgage securitization also played a fundamental role. Subprime mortgages have been repackaged into CDOs and sold to the market. Banks made additional profits, which in turn created an additional incentive for offering more loans. Erroneously, subprime loans were still seen as an opportunity rather than an excessive risk to take on. Rating agencies have their share of responsibility too. The high rating assigned by them to potentially very risky CDO tranches revealed their lack of adequate modeling tools. This lack of sophistication was well known by practitioners and academics, and it was not hard to predict it could lead to a disaster.

A common practice among financial institutions was to value CDOs with a Gaussian copula. Despite its obvious advantage, this approach was clearly too simplistic to properly assess the risk of these structures. The shortcomings of Gaussian copulas were well known to academics and quants. For some reason, their warnings went unheeded.

Please use the following *Likert scale* to provide your answer:

1= Strongly Disagree; 2 = Disagree; 3 = Neither; 4 = Agree; 5 = Strongly Agree

2.1)	1	2	3	4	5
The economic/fiscal and monetary policies, financial reforms, and risk mitigation plans implemented by policy makers and regulators to reduce the impact of the housing market and credit bubbles were comprehensive and effective to reduce the financial meltdown.		X			

2.2) Dr Mercurio what actionable economic/fiscal policies, reforms, or risk mitigation plans could have been immediately implemented to reduce the impact of the housing market and credit bubbles and the meltdown caused by the crisis?

I disagree that the economic/fiscal and monetary policies, financial reforms, and risk mitigation plans implemented by policy makers and regulators to reduce the impact of the housing market and credit bubbles were comprehensive and effective to reduce the financial meltdown.

Please use the following *Likert scale* to provide your answer:

1= Strongly Disagree; 2 = Disagree; 3 = Neither; 4 = Agree; 5 = Strongly Agree

3.1)	1	2	3	4	5
The monetary and fiscal policies, the government bail-outs, (TARP, TALF, and so on), and the financial reforms introduced (for example, Dodd–Frank Act, of which the Volcker Rule is a central component, and so on) after 2008 were valid long-term solutions to regulate and stabilize financial markets and to avoid the risk of new crises (double dip).			X		

3.2) Dr Mercurio are the monetary and fiscal policies, the government bail-outs, (TARP, TALF, and so on), and the financial reforms introduced (for example, Dodd–Frank Act, of which the Volcker Rule is a central component, and so on) after 2008 valid long-term solutions to regulate and stabilize financial markets and to avoid the risk of new crises (double dip)?

The Dodd–Franks goes in the right direction. As far as derivatives are concerned, however, it will be hard to have them all cleared or traded in exchanges. In fact, many deals are bespoke to satisfy specific needs of clients. Payoff structures can be rather complicated and involve different asset classes. These deals are highly customized, and hence illiquid by definition. Their pricing and risk management is model dependent, and heavily dependent on illiquid or even unknown market data and the model calibration to it. The discrepancy between different models can be huge, and an agreement on the pricing procedure to use is almost impossible to achieve.

Please use the following *Likert scale* to provide your answer:

1= Strongly Disagree; 2 = Disagree; 3 = Neither; 4 = Agree; 5 = Strongly Agree

4.1)	1	2	3	4	5
There is a need for improved financial regulation, regulatory oversight, financial institutions' corporate governance (that is, COSO ERM, Internal Controls, Basel III, Dodd–Frank, Credit Ratings, and so on) and managerial cultures (that is, CSR, Ethics, and so on).					X

4.2) Dr Mercurio what still needs to be changed in terms of financial regulation and regulatory oversight, corporate governance, managerial cultures, internal controls, COSO ERM Framework, and Basel III Framework to avoid in the future other systemic crises?

A recent article (2012) in Bloomberg News says that, "The largest global banks would have needed an extra 485.6 billion euros ($639.5 billion) in their core reserves to meet Basel capital rules had the standards been enforced last June." The same article also says that, "Basel III will more than triple the core capital that lenders must hold to at least 7 percent of their assets, weighted for risk." Banks will need to carefully choose the businesses they are in, and in particular the product they will be selling.

Risk management in banks is becoming stronger and stronger. Risk managers now tend to impose extremely conservative reserve levels at trade inception, creating a disincentive for the bank to trade fancy exotic products and take on excessive risks. Exotic deals, which are no longer appealing to customers, are thus becoming not appealing to sell-side traders as well.

This is good news. Many exotic structures turned out to be toxic to customers, but many others created big losses to banks too. Structuring fancy deals with the purpose of maximizing the bank's initial revenue can be lethal if model risk is not properly accounted for and if the structured deals are hard to hedge.

A lot is being done in terms of regulations, but more should be done. For instance, we should have more and better rules and controls on the financial data used to calculate the mark-to-market value of derivatives portfolios. In particular, clear procedures should be set for the cases where the underlying market is very illiquid or even non-existing. We should also have better stressed tests procedure and independent valuation of deals. In this respect, regulators should hire competent and experienced people from the banking industry. Too often, regulators do not have the necessary quantitative skills to properly address the above issues.

Please use the following *Likert scale* to provide your answer:

1= Strongly Disagree; 2 = Disagree; 3 = Neither; 4 = Agree; 5 = Strongly Agree

5.1)	1	2	3	4	5
Among the root causes of the 2007–2009 financial crisis are there major failures in the financial firms' corporate governance, traders and executive's integrity, accountability, ethical behaviors, and their excessive compensation systems, in addition to industry deregulation and major failures in regulatory oversight?					X

5.2) Dr Mercurio what needs to be done to instill a new culture in the business world in order to improve corporate governance, executive accountability, fair compensation, and more in general, integrity and ethics in the financial markets?

Integrity and ethics in the financial markets have been an issue and definitely a major cause of the recent financial crisis.

Fancy financial products have been structured so as to maximize the initial profit for the bank. Then they have been sold to clients who had no idea of the risks involved, and often times even no specific need of buying them.

The compensation plan for traders mostly offered incentives for moral hazard. Structurers, sales people, and traders had no downside risk. If the market didn't do anything crazy until the next bonus payment time, the chance of reporting big gains, and hence getting big bonuses, was huge. In the unlikely event that a major disaster happened in the market, they knew that being fired is the worst that could happen to them, but likely only after having cashed enough big money.

At the same time, risk management was not so strong on average. Many risk managers were aware that some risks were not properly measured, and saw the danger of some practices. But the trading floor had the power. They were generating revenues, and risk management was a cost center. In some case, risk managers have been kindly asked to stop creating unnecessary alarmism.

Interview with **Massimo Meterangelo** (personal communication, 2012), Head of Group Wide Portfolio Consolidation at Unicredit Group, Italy.

Please use the following *Likert scale* to provide your answer:

1= Strongly Disagree; 2 = Disagree; 3 = Neither; 4 = Agree; 5 = Strongly Agree

1.1)	1	2	3	4	5
The 2007–2009 financial crisis was predictable and avoidable.				X	

1.2) Mr Meterangelo was the 2007–2009 financial crisis predictable and avoidable?

I think the crisis would have been avoidable considering:

1. Reliability of rating agencies ratings: I think the certification process of many financial operations/instruments should have been reviewed, and banks sometimes used in a perverted way the rating agencies and accounting firms certifications.
2. Banks should have used in a more sensible way their capital, I mean, is it necessary to have a supranational institution (such as BIS) to suggest to use in a proper, fair, and clever way your own capital? If a bank was not confident about its capital soundness, it could and should have used a countercyclical buffer without a top-down suggestion or requirement.
3. Property assessments: was it not clear that over assessing the property value was a bad practice? I think so, but everyone didn't stop from doing this, even if in my opinion this would have led to a bubble that at a certain point would have exploded as it really happened.
4. It was clear that instruments such as CDS and other derivatives are potentially dangerous because are not traded on an exchange and there is no required reporting of transactions to a government agency. Besides the dimension of this market is huge and could mine the economy.

Please use the following *Likert scale* to provide your answer:

1= Strongly Disagree; 2 = Disagree; 3 = Neither; 4 = Agree; 5 = Strongly Agree

2.1)	1	2	3	4	5
The economic/fiscal and monetary policies, financial reforms, and risk mitigation plans implemented by policy makers and regulators to reduce the impact of the housing market and credit bubbles were comprehensive and effective to reduce the financial meltdown.			X		

2.2) Mr Meterangelo what actionable economic/fiscal policies, reforms, or risk mitigation plans could have been immediately implemented to reduce the impact of the housing market and credit bubbles and the meltdown caused by the crisis?

My answer is that it didn't do enough, because I think that policy makers and regulators did something to reduce the impact of the housing market but something more could have been done, a lot in terms of best practice and cultural environment.

In relation to the Italian context, the crisis didn't have the impact (2012) as in other countries because the financial system still is developing and it is not complex as in the US (for example).

I have the general feeling that banks suffer from short-sightedness, because they are used to generate profits (or at least try to) in the short term without thinking of the consequences in the medium-long term. I'm referring to the political class and the top management of many financial institutions.

I think that it is not so clear for banks that they have an important role for the economic, social, and financial environment and I think that they should not just pursue the profit. Obviously I'm not stating that banks should be state-run, but that an unwise management should be sanctioned in some way. I disagree with leaving everything to the market rules, for this reason I still don't agree with the US decision to let Lehman Brothers fail.

Please use the following *Likert scale* to provide your answer:

1= Strongly Disagree; 2 = Disagree; 3 = Neither; 4 = Agree; 5 = Strongly Agree

3.1)	1	2	3	4	5
The monetary and fiscal policies, the government bail-outs, (TARP, TALF, and so on), and the financial reforms introduced (for example, Dodd–Frank Act, of which the Volcker Rule is a central component, and so on) after 2008 were valid long-term solutions to regulate and stabilize financial markets and to avoid the risk of new crises (double dip).		X			

3.2) Mr Meterangelo are the monetary and fiscal policies, the government bail-outs, (TARP, TALF, and so on), and the financial reforms introduced (for example, Dodd–Frank Act, of which the Volcker Rule is a central component, and so on) after 2008 valid long-term solutions to regulate and stabilize financial markets and to avoid the risk of new crises (double dip)?

Let's focus on the Volcker Rule (so named because of former United States Federal Reserve Chairman Paul Volcker): for the second time in less than 80 years, the US commercial banks are being told to stick to their main goal (deposits) after the Glass–Steagall Act issued in the 1933.

I think the decision to keep commercial and investment banks split is very wise and necessary, so I'm for the Volcker rule because it is aimed to avoid a bank becoming too big to fail: on the point I'd say three things:

1. In Italy the credit process had a similar path, I mean, in 1936 with a new bank regulation the short-term activity and medium-long term activities were split (something similar to the Glass–Steagall Act) and this regulation lasted until 1990 with the decision to come back to an universal bank and no term separation mainly in order to answer to some European Union (EU) directives aimed to increase the competition.

2. In the US in 1999 the Glass–Steagall Act was amended by the Gramm–Leach–Bliley Act removing barriers in the market among banking companies, securities companies, and insurance companies that prohibited any one institution from acting as any combination of an investment bank, a commercial bank, and an insurance company. But why? I mean: is there a regulation better, more effective, and more solid than one other? Is the separation between commercial banks and investment banks the solution? Or maybe both of them are working if bankers can be punished if they don't stick to a fair and ethical interpretation of their role?

3. I have a concern about Volcker Rule from an international point of view: this because there is the risk that not all the countries would like to follow this path, not to penalize their own financial institution with new separation rules. We could expect the use of many financial resources from the banks in order to affect the political decisions and to slow down this proposal.

Please use the following *Likert scale* to provide your answer:

1= Strongly Disagree; 2 = Disagree; 3 = Neither; 4 = Agree; 5 = Strongly Agree

4.1)	1	2	3	4	5
There is a need for improved financial regulation, regulatory oversight, financial institutions' corporate governance (that is, COSO ERM, Internal Controls, Basel III, Dodd–Frank, Credit Ratings, and so on) and managerial cultures (that is, CSR, Ethics, and so on).					X

4.2) Mr Meterangelo what still needs to be changed in terms of financial regulation and regulatory oversight, corporate governance, managerial cultures, internal controls, COSO ERM Framework, and Basel III Framework to avoid in the future other systemic crises?

I think that from an organizational point of view the risk management culture should be a pillar of every financial institution aimed to lead and support every bank strategy: because of this ERM should be supported from the top management of every bank.

In terms of credit ratings something should be changed: the goal should be really to decide if rating agencies and their assessment have to be taken in account because sound, but if the decision is this one the agencies should be considered accountable. In this moment they are not so I think the regulators have to clarify this point.

Please use the following *Likert scale* to provide your answer:

1= Strongly Disagree; 2 = Disagree; 3 = Neither; 4 = Agree; 5 = Strongly Agree

5.1)	1	2	3	4	5
Among the root causes of the 2007–2009 financial crisis are there major failures in the financial firms' corporate governance, traders and executive's integrity, accountability, ethical behaviors, and their excessive compensation systems, in addition to industry deregulation and major failures in regulatory oversight?					X

5.2) Mr Meterangelo what needs to be done to instill a new culture in the business world in order to improve corporate governance, executive accountability, fair compensation, and more in general, integrity and ethics in the financial markets?

I think, again, that the main point here is related to the fact that a bank is a company looking for gains and that has a huge impact of its activity on the economic and social environment.

Probably it is difficult, but it is mandatory to combine somehow short-term strategies (the necessity of top management to be measured by the shareholders on the basis of the quarterly outcomes) with medium to long-term strategies (sometimes the market needs more time to respond to some bank decision-strategy).

Another thing we should avoid is to sell every product without well informing the customers of the risk profile of the investment, just pursuing the bonus, without understanding that a customer acquiring something not good according to his risk profile will default and having defaulting customers it is not really the goal of a bank.

Interview with **Wolfgang Munchau** (personal communication, 2011), President of Eurointelligence ASBL and Associate Editor of the *Financial Times*, UK.

Please use the following *Likert scale* to provide your answer:

1= Strongly Disagree; 2 = Disagree; 3 = Neither; 4 = Agree; 5 = Strongly Agree

1.1)	1	2	3	4	5
The 2007–2009 financial crisis was predictable and avoidable.				X	

1.2) Mr Munchau was the 2007–2009 financial crisis predictable and avoidable?

Some economists foresaw the crisis, which means that it was foreseeable. The crisis challenged prevailing economic and financial dogma, but it has not yet brought us new robust models to interpret a world with a dominant financial sector. I have nothing new or original to say on the causes of the crisis.

Please use the following *Likert scale* to provide your answer:

1= Strongly Disagree; 2 = Disagree; 3 = Neither; 4 = Agree; 5 = Strongly Agree

2.1)	1	2	3	4	5
The economic/fiscal and monetary policies, financial reforms, and risk mitigation plans implemented by policy makers and regulators to reduce the impact of the housing market and credit bubbles were comprehensive and effective to reduce the financial meltdown.		X			

2.1) Mr Munchau what actionable economic/fiscal policies, reforms, or risk mitigation plans could have been immediately implemented to reduce the impact of the housing market and credit bubbles and the meltdown caused by the crisis?

The housing bubble was mostly ignored by policy makers, as bubbles so often are. There were no effective countercyclical policies in place in Spain and Ireland. In Spain, the Bank of Spain limited the banks' exposure to MBS and CDOs but not to the real economy bubble. Both countries should have tax policies as a counter-cyclical device.

Please use the following *Likert scale* to provide your answer:

1= Strongly Disagree; 2 = Disagree; 3 = Neither; 4 = Agree; 5 = Strongly Agree

3.1)	1	2	3	4	5
The monetary and fiscal policies, the government bail-outs, (TARP, TALF, and so on), and the financial reforms introduced (for example, Dodd–Frank Act, of which the Volcker Rule is a central component, and so on) after 2008 were valid long-term solutions to regulate and stabilize financial markets and to avoid the risk of new crises (double dip).		X			

3.1) Mr Munchau are the monetary and fiscal policies, the government bail-outs, (TARP, TALF, and so on), and the financial reforms introduced (for example, Dodd–Frank Act, of which the Volcker Rule is a central component, and so on) after 2008 valid long-term solutions to regulate and stabilize financial markets and to avoid the risk of new crises (double dip)?

The actions taken so far are not long-term solutions, though I think Basel III constitutes some progress. We still have to construct effective bank resolution regimes, and global lender of last resort systems.

Please use the following *Likert scale* to provide your answer:

1= Strongly Disagree; 2 = Disagree; 3 = Neither; 4 = Agree; 5 = Strongly Agree

4.1)	1	2	3	4	5
There is a need for improved financial regulation, regulatory oversight, financial institutions' corporate governance (that is, COSO ERM, Internal Controls, Basel III, Dodd–Frank, Credit Ratings, and so on) and managerial cultures (that is, CSR, Ethics, and so on).					X

4.2) Mr Munchau what still needs to be changed in terms of financial regulation and regulatory oversight, corporate governance, managerial cultures, internal controls, COSO ERM Framework, and Basel III Framework to avoid in the future other systemic crises?

As to policy action now, my recommendation is to use the tools of economic policy to prevent a slump (i/r, QE, stimulus), while simultaneously fixing the imbalances in China, structural deficiencies in Europe, and so on. I would size down and consolidate the banking system.

Please use the following *Likert scale* to provide your answer:

1= Strongly Disagree; 2 = Disagree; 3 = Neither; 4 = Agree; 5 = Strongly Agree

5.1)	1	2	3	4	5
Among the root causes of the 2007–2009 financial crisis are there major failures in the financial firms' corporate governance, traders and executive's integrity, accountability, ethical behaviors, and their excessive compensation systems, in addition to industry deregulation and major failures in regulatory oversight?					X

5.2) Mr Munchau what needs to be done to instill a new culture in the business world in order to improve corporate governance, executive accountability, fair compensation, and more in general, integrity and ethics in the financial markets?

Bubbles will come again. They always have. No ethical systems can prevent an outbreak of occasional insanity.

Interview with **Fabrizio Pezzani** (personal communication, 2012), Full Professor of Business Administration, Accounting and Control and Director of the Bachelor Degree in Management of Public Administration and International Institutions (CLAPI) Bocconi University, and Senior Faculty member of the SDA Bocconi School of Management, Department of Policy Analysis and Public Management, Italy.

Please use the following *Likert scale* to provide your answer:

1= Strongly Disagree; 2 = Disagree; 3 = Neither; 4 = Agree; 5 = Strongly Agree

1.1)	1	2	3	4	5
The 2007–2009 financial crisis was predictable and avoidable.					X

1.2) Professor Pezzani was the 2007–2009 financial crisis predictable and avoidable?

The financial crisis has not been predicted with a reliable degree of accuracy but rather it was more simply envisioned as a likely scenario by a number of analysts and practitioners, and much less by the academic world and scholars. The lack of full predictability of the crisis was not due to technical limitations and poor risk management, forecasting, or stress testing modeling, since given the data available to most economists, risk managers, and financial analysts, it could have been certainly predictable. There were many undisputable early warning signs to prove that it was predictable. Instead, it was not timely and accurately predicted due mainly to cultural and ideological reasons. In the years preceding the financial crisis, there was an excessive ideological overconfidence in the financial industry's "rational ability" to maximize profits and shareholders' value creation without taking excessive risks.

There was also the idea that markets were self-correcting and that large financial institutions were well equipped to handle huge risks without the threat of facing potential implosion. What they were probably missing was that they did not consider "irrational behavior" a likely option for the explosive growth of the housing market, the uncontrolled financial innovation, and the shadow banking sector. They did not consider that people's

324 Predictable and Avoidable

destiny is primarily driven by human behaviors, their expectations, emotions, self-interests, and weaknesses, and not by rigidly designed mathematical or economic models, and business practices supported by illusionary and "rational" self-regulating ideology.

As it is well known, the decisions to purchase or sell securities are based on expectations and not so much on rigid and "rational" mathematical models, but evidently this basic concept has been completely ignored in those years. From this point of view the financial crisis represents a major failure of a cultural model that has led to an uncontrollable growth of financialization of the economy. This economic model that has led to the financial crisis is the result of a cultural ideology that has advocated profit maximization as the sole purpose of the financial sector.

As the famous Greek philosopher, Aristotle (384 BC–322 BC) explained there is a close link between "action" and "purpose," therefore, if the goal is profit maximization, the action will always be oriented to achieve such objective. Thus, this purpose has been achieved through a strong deregulation of the financial sector followed by a reckless and uncontrolled use of financial innovation in opaque markets as a process accelerator for the achievement of the goal. The aftermath of all this profit-maximization philosophy is the financial crisis and the reduced role of the real economy, which became ancillary to the financial industry. The choice to expand the financial sector much more than the real economy has shifted our society in a sort of virtual reality in which finance poses more emphasis and amplifies the weaknesses of human nature.

Please use the following *Likert scale* to provide your answer:

1= Strongly Disagree; 2 = Disagree; 3 = Neither; 4 = Agree; 5 = Strongly Agree

2.1)	1	2	3	4	5
The economic/fiscal and monetary policies, financial reforms, and risk mitigation plans implemented by policy makers and regulators to reduce the impact of the housing market and credit bubbles were comprehensive and effective to reduce the financial meltdown.	X				

2.2) Professor Pezzani what actionable economic/fiscal policies, reforms, or risk mitigation plans could have been immediately implemented to reduce the impact of the housing market and credit bubbles and the meltdown caused by the crisis?

The cultural model of the people who have managed the risk mitigation and rescue plans of the financial crisis is the same one of those who have created it. Going back to what I have mentioned in the first question, changing the regulation and introducing banking and financial markets reforms, that is, the "action," without changing the "purpose" is just an expensive and useless exercise. This is quite simple since the "action" or the new rules and reforms will always be bypassed by the "purpose." This assumption can be easily proved with an example. After the scandals of 2001, new and more stringent rules have been introduced, like the Sarbanes-Oxley (SOX) Act, so in the end the result was still the same, as demonstrated by the global financial crisis, since the problems showed up again, and this time with even more devastating consequences. So today, we are back to square one and those who have caused the financial crisis are still in charge to impose new rules and regulations that will never solve the real issues.

Please use the following *Likert scale* to provide your answer:

1= Strongly Disagree; 2 = Disagree; 3 = Neither; 4 = Agree; 5 = Strongly Agree

3.1)	1	2	3	4	5
The monetary and fiscal policies, the government bail-outs, (TARP, TALF, and so on), and the financial reforms introduced (for example, Dodd–Frank Act, of which the Volcker Rule is a central component, and so on) after 2008 were valid long-term solutions to regulate and stabilize financial markets and to avoid the risk of new crises (double dip).	X				

3.2) Professor Pezzani are the monetary and fiscal policies, the government bail-outs, (TARP, TALF, and so on), and the financial reforms introduced (for example, Dodd–Frank Act, of which the Volcker Rule is a central component, and so on) after 2008 valid long-term solutions to regulate and stabilize financial markets and to avoid the risk of new crises (double dip)?

The answer is still the same. Absolutely not! Any policy makers' initiative to propose new rules and regulations in the public interest that foster economic democracy and reduce inequality is opposed to the purpose of profit maximization of bankers and financial institutions and thus it becomes antagonistic to its purpose. The purpose of reducing inequality and increasing democracy is antagonistic to the one of profit maximization and the two are mutually exclusive. The critical issue is to redefine our socio-cultural model and not simply to change rules and regulations.

Evidences show that what we have today is a model incapable of responding to society's problems. In fact, the more economists interfere with the economy the worse it gets; the more sociologists and psychologists are involved with family issues the worse they get; the more scholars of government and political sciences are involved with these topics the worse the political system becomes; and the greater is the number of university graduates, the more it decreases the cultural level.

In summary, we need to ask ourselves whether it is a "strong" economy, a necessary condition for a good society, or the other way around.

Please use the following *Likert scale* to provide your answer:

1= Strongly Disagree; 2 = Disagree; 3 = Neither; 4 = Agree; 5 = Strongly Agree

4.1)	1	2	3	4	5
There is a need for improved financial regulation, regulatory oversight, financial institutions' corporate governance (that is, COSO ERM, Internal Controls, Basel III, Dodd–Frank, Credit Ratings, and so on) and managerial cultures (that is, CSR, Ethics, and so on).			X		

4.2) Professor Pezzani what still needs to be changed in terms of financial regulation and regulatory oversight, corporate governance, managerial cultures, internal controls, COSO ERM Framework, and Basel III Framework to avoid in the future other systemic crises?

If we believe that the financial crisis was simply generated by bad regulation, then it would be sufficient to enforce more stringent and mechanistic rules to avoid in the future similar crises in our society. If we assume, instead, that the root causes of the financial crisis are related to cultural and value-problems, then the issue to address regards how to reorient social models and values.

The failure of this kind of capitalism is quite evident in the country were the financial crisis started, the US, where the debt has reached a remarkable level – 140 percent of GDP – but at the same time there is a very high degree of concentration of wealth in the hands of a few. The two combined factors might even disintegrate American society, which is already on the brink of social collapse before it may reach the economic one.

In summary, it is an issue of rules and purpose. It is a cultural problem, not just a technical one. It is necessary to look at the big picture and to broaden the analytical framework.

Please use the following *Likert scale* to provide your answer:

1= Strongly Disagree; 2 = Disagree; 3 = Neither; 4 = Agree; 5 = Strongly Agree

5.1)	1	2	3	4	5
Among the root causes of the 2007–2009 financial crisis are there major failures in the financial firms' corporate governance, traders and executive's integrity, accountability, ethical behaviors, and their excessive compensation systems, in addition to industry deregulation and major failures in regulatory oversight?					X

5.2) Professor Pezzani what needs to be done to instill a new culture in the business world in order to improve corporate governance, executive accountability, fair compensation, and more in general, integrity and ethics in the financial markets?

Either we change the "purpose" or we will have to start all over again after every failure and new crisis. Ethics in the ancient Greek sense of the term indicates the place where happiness and human safety are generated. But the meaning of ethics actually changes from time to time, thus when the meaning of happiness coincides with short-term wealth accumulation the consequent risk is that people may start to believe that moral hazard is just "business as usual" and that even fraudulent behaviors might be perceived as "the risk of the game." In an extreme sense then Mr Madoff could be almost considered a person with an ethical "purpose." Then the only difference between him and many others that have done similar things is that he got caught and arrested.

As I have reported at a conference in Venice (Italy) on January 25, 2012 by the title "The Fate of The Euro. A Socio-Cultural 'Armageddon'", the socio-cultural model that has prevailed in the last decades, is a form of dominant sensate materialism which indicates that in our society people identify as truth only what they see, touch, and measure, hence the science that explains "the truth," is the one of rational technical knowledge. This has become the unquestionable order of moral knowledge. Thus the prevailing culture has become extremely pragmatic. This approach, defined as the illusion of rationality, finds its origins in the study of natural science but extends to social sciences, such as economics and finance, based on the assumption that these self-referential disciplines are independent, as in natural sciences, from the contextual environment, thus neglecting to recognize the inherent emotionality of mankind that is always a variable that influences the decision-making process.

What people think is an integral part of the reality in which they live, thus they perceive no separation in the decision-making process between their own ideas and values and their contextual environment. Ultimately, they will always be influenced by their emotional expectations, and euphoric or depressive moods.

This is exactly what happens when people purchase or sell securities. It's not just about expectations and knowledge. Economics and finance take this "imprinting" and become a self-referential discipline that imposes the acceptable behaviors for companies and people showing them the path to the "truth." Economics and finance become the gateway to a good society and their rules cannot be questioned or challenged. The rules are the independent variable and the companies and the people the dependent ones. This way our society becomes a community evaluated primarily on quantitative criteria, which exacerbates social conflicts and ultimately lead to increased forms of individualism aimed at achieving in the short-term maximization of results. These behaviors tend to justify misconduct for the achievement of people's goals, thus paving the way for ancestral human greed.

The cultural model is one that has pursued the privatization and maximization of profits and socialization of losses. The rapid growth of financial activities has created an extraordinarily oversized financial economy compared to the real economy – the amount of CDS is 12 times the world GDP – and its control is highly concentrated in the hands of very few institutions whose power today is able to determine stability of individual states. Finance becomes an instrument of global hegemony to assert the interests of small groups, and the context in which it operates is in fact an oligopoly dominated by restricted global lobbies.

Regarding the current economic scenario, the sharing of more stringent policies is fundamental to restore budget discipline. Thus in this sense fiscal policy must accompany the current process since it is necessary to find the cure that can address the root causes of the problems. Over time, instead, it is necessary as a society and economy to become less dependent on global finance and the values it embodies.

Interview with **Richard A. Posner** (personal communication, 2011), Senior Lecturer in Law at University of Chicago Law School and Judge of the US Court of Appeals for the Seventh Circuit, USA.

Please use the following *Likert scale* to provide your answer:

1= Strongly Disagree; 2 = Disagree; 3 = Neither; 4 = Agree; 5 = Strongly Agree

1.1)	1	2	3	4	5
The 2007–2009 financial crisis was predictable and avoidable.				X	

1.2) Professor Posner was the 2007–2009 financial crisis predictable and avoidable?

It was predictable in the sense that a number of financial journalists, economists, and traders predicted that the housing bubble would collapse and if so could precipitate a financial crisis. But there was considerable uncertainty and most journalists, economists, and traders believed there would be no crisis, including the world's governments and their central banks, such as our Federal Reserve. It was eminently avoidable, by sensible monetary and fiscal policy and more intelligent regulation of banks and other financial institutions.

Please use the following *Likert scale* to provide your answer:

1= Strongly Disagree; 2 = Disagree; 3 = Neither; 4 = Agree; 5 = Strongly Agree

2.1)	1	2	3	4	5
The economic/fiscal and monetary policies, financial reforms, and risk mitigation plans implemented by policy makers and regulators to reduce the impact of the housing market and credit bubbles were comprehensive and effective to reduce the financial meltdown.			X		

2.2) Professor Posner what actionable economic/fiscal policies, reforms, or risk mitigation plans could have been immediately implemented to reduce the impact of the housing market and credit bubbles and the meltdown caused by the crisis?

The immediate response to the crisis – flooding the economy and particularly the banking system with money – was correct, except for the disastrous decision to allow Lehman Brothers to collapse. As soon as it became evident (probably by November 2008) that the financial crisis had precipitated a downward spiral in the economy comparable to that of the Great Depression of the 1930s, a large stimulus (deficit-spending) program of public works and assistance to states (in excess of $1 trillion) should have been instituted immediately, with insistence on prompt expenditure.

Please use the following *Likert scale* to provide your answer:

1= Strongly Disagree; 2 = Disagree; 3 = Neither; 4 = Agree; 5 = Strongly Agree

3.1)	1	2	3	4	5
The monetary and fiscal policies, the government bail-outs, (TARP, TALF, and so on), and the financial reforms introduced (for example, Dodd–Frank Act, of which the Volcker Rule is a central component, and so on) after 2008 were valid long-term solutions to regulate and stabilize financial markets and to avoid the risk of new crises (double dip).			X		

3.2) Professor Posner are the monetary and fiscal policies, the government bail-outs, (TARP, TALF, and so on), and the financial reforms introduced (for example, Dodd–Frank Act, of which the Volcker Rule is a central component, and so on) after 2008 valid long-term solutions to regulate and stabilize financial markets and to avoid the risk of new crises (double dip)?

The monetary and fiscal policies adopted in the wake of the crisis, including the bail-outs, are strictly short-term solutions; the nation cannot afford them other than as temporary measures. The financial reforms can't yet be evaluated, because the precise form they will take depends on decisions by the financial regulatory agencies that have not been made yet. I am pessimistic that the reforms will be effective; the financial industry is too powerful and the industry too complex to be fully understood by government agencies.

Please use the following *Likert scale* to provide your answer:

1= Strongly Disagree; 2 = Disagree; 3 = Neither; 4 = Agree; 5 = Strongly Agree

4.1)	1	2	3	4	5
There is a need for improved financial regulation, regulatory oversight, financial institutions' corporate governance (that is, COSO ERM, Internal Controls, Basel III, Dodd–Frank, Credit Ratings, and so on) and managerial cultures (that is, CSR, Ethics, and so on).				X	

4.2) Professor Posner what still needs to be changed in terms of financial regulation and regulatory oversight, corporate governance, managerial cultures, internal controls, COSO ERM Framework, and Basel III Framework to avoid in the future other systemic crises?

Managerial cultures cannot be changed from the outside. Corporate governance will not reduce risk taking by financial corporations because the governors – the members of the corporation's board of directors – do not have strong incentives for monitoring the corporation's behavior, nor have they any incentive to reduce the corporation's profitability; and risk and expected return are of course positively correlated. Compensation limits are promising in principle: when financial managers can obtain huge compensation in the short run, their incentives to reduce long-run risks evaporate. But regulation of compensation is almost impossible, not only because there are so many ways to evade them, but also because limits on compensation are inherently arbitrary and likely to cause a "brain drain" to companies or countries not subject to the limits. The financial industry is thoroughly globalized, so international controls are desirable, but unlikely to be effective because of resistance by individual nations. Of particular concern is widespread dishonesty in collection and reporting of financial conditions; Greece is not alone in cooking its books in an effort to stave off default.

Please use the following *Likert scale* to provide your answer:

1= Strongly Disagree; 2 = Disagree; 3 – Neither; 4 – Agree; 5 = Strongly Agree

5.1)	1	2	3	4	5
Among the root causes of the 2007–2009 financial crisis are there major failures in the financial firms' corporate governance, traders and executive's integrity, accountability, ethical behaviors, and their excessive compensation systems, in addition to industry deregulation and major failures in regulatory oversight?				X	

5.2) Professor Posner what needs to be done to instill a new culture in the business world in order to improve corporate governance, executive accountability, fair compensation, and more in general, integrity and ethics in the financial markets?

As I said earlier, I don't think managerial cultures can be changed from the outside. Competition is Darwinian and forces financial firms and their employees to take a high level of risk and engage in any profitable practice that is not forbidden by effectively enforced law. Fairness, integrity, transparency, and other virtues will have no sway on firms and their employees unless backed by law.

Interview with **Gabriele Sabato** (personal communication, 2012), Head of Portfolio Management – Retail Credit Risk at Ulster Bank. PhD in Banking and Finance, and Credit Risk Management. Ireland.

Please use the following *Likert scale* to provide your answer:

1= Strongly Disagree; 2 = Disagree; 3 = Neither; 4 = Agree; 5 = Strongly Agree

1.1)	1	2	3	4	5
The 2007–2009 financial crisis was predictable and avoidable.				X	

1.2) Dr Sabato was the 2007–2009 financial crisis predictable and avoidable?

When examining the causes for the financial crisis, most people start directly with the real estate market focusing on the subprime mortgages and unscrupulous lenders and casting the blame on the unsustainable real estate bubble which began to collapse in 2006. Whereas this is true, it is not the whole story. A poor regulatory framework based on the belief that banks could be trusted to regulate themselves is, in my opinion, among the main sources of the crisis. It is quite obvious that regulators across the world have not efficiently monitored the risk management functions of most banks. At the same time, risk management at most banking institutions has failed to enforce the basic rules for a safe business: that is, avoid strong concentrations and minimize volatility of returns.

Please use the following *Likert scale* to provide your answer:

1= Strongly Disagree; 2 = Disagree; 3 = Neither; 4 = Agree; 5 = Strongly Agree

2.1)	1	2	3	4	5
The economic/fiscal and monetary policies, financial reforms, and risk mitigation plans implemented by policy makers and regulators to reduce the impact of the housing market and credit bubbles were comprehensive and effective to reduce the financial meltdown.		X			

2.2) Dr Sabato what actionable economic/fiscal policies, reforms, or risk mitigation plans could have been immediately implemented to reduce the impact of the housing market and credit bubbles and the meltdown caused by the crisis?

In my opinion, governments, central banks, and policymakers were unprepared to face such a crisis and hired all sort of different consultants that provided them with mixed theories most of which are weak or unfit to solve the problem. One of the first measures that I remember was taken at the beginning of the crisis was to force banks to increase the number of non-executive directors in their board. Several studies (for example, Beltratti and Stulz, 2011; Schmid et al., 2011) have now proved that this measure is totally useless to improve risk management in financial institutions. This is just an example, but I could mention many others too often also in conflict with other geographies (for example, Europe vs. US). Alignment between policy makers across the world is paramount in my opinion to ensure common rules. Moreover, the monitoring of those rules needs to be strong and effective in each country.

Please use the following *Likert scale* to provide your answer:

1= Strongly Disagree; 2 = Disagree; 3 = Neither; 4 = Agree; 5 = Strongly Agree

3.1)	1	2	3	4	5
The monetary and fiscal policies, the government bail-outs, (TARP, TALF, and so on), and the financial reforms introduced (for example, Dodd–Frank Act, of which the Volcker Rule is a central component, and so on) after 2008 were valid long-term solutions to regulate and stabilize financial markets and to avoid the risk of new crises (double dip).	X				

3.2) Dr Sabato are the monetary and fiscal policies, the government bail-outs, (TARP, TALF, and so on), and the financial reforms introduced (for example, Dodd–Frank Act, of which the Volcker Rule is a central component, and so on) after 2008 valid long-term solutions to regulate and stabilize financial markets and to avoid the risk of new crises (double dip)?

Government bail-outs and financial reforms introduced after 2008 and the double dip which we are entering now are not correlated, in my opinion. The reasons for this follow up of the first crisis are completely different from the first and are a consequence of the markets that have still not recovered in full from the first crisis. The measures taken after the 2008 crisis were effective in the short term to save the situation from a complete Armageddon, but as it is evident, they were not effective in the long run.

Please use the following *Likert scale* to provide your answer:

1= Strongly Disagree; 2 = Disagree; 3 = Neither; 4 = Agree; 5 = Strongly Agree

4.1)	1	2	3	4	5
There is a need for improved financial regulation, regulatory oversight, financial institutions' corporate governance (that is, COSO ERM, Internal Controls, Basel III, Dodd–Frank, Credit Ratings, and so on) and managerial cultures (that is, CSR, Ethics, and so on).					X

4.2) Dr Sabato what still needs to be changed in terms of financial regulation and regulatory oversight, corporate governance, managerial cultures, internal controls, COSO ERM Framework, and Basel III Framework to avoid in the future other systemic crises?

I have often indicated three main points that banks and regulators need to improve: (1) lack of a defined capital allocation strategy; (2) disaggregated vision of risks; and (3) inappropriate risk governance structure.

1. Most banks used to grow their lending portfolios driven by market demand without a clear capital allocation strategy. Regulatory pressures, such as Basel III and a greater focus on corporate governance, can be a stimulus for many changes in the industry. One of these has been the recognition of the need to articulate risk appetite more clearly. Risk appetite translates risk metrics and methods into business decisions, reporting, and day-to-day business discussions. It sets the boundaries which form a dynamic link between strategy, target setting, and risk management. Articulating risk appetite is a complex task which requires the balancing of many views. Some elements can be quantified, but ultimately it is a question of judgment. A bank with a well-defined risk appetite framework will provide internal senior management and external stakeholders with a clear picture of where it currently stands and how it wants to grow in terms of concentration and expected returns of its assets.

2. Although many institutions, particularly the large national and international financial institutions, have already adopted ERM approaches, others are still using reactive rather than proactive methods of risk monitoring and detection. Typically, these methods are the traditional silo approaches to risk management and are rapidly becoming insufficient in preventing increasingly diversified risks (especially credit, market, and operational risks). Silo-based approaches are reactive and their functions segregated; each silo has its own tools and applications to assist with specific management and reporting requirements. Problems arise because these independent systems do not communicate with one another and across business lines (see Sabato, 2010). A silo-view of risks is still a common practice at most banks and this does not allow senior management to have a full picture of risk concentrations and correlations. Similar assets, or assets with a high correlation between them, can seat in different books (for example, credit and trading book) or off-balance and their risk may never be aggregated causing a significant understatement of the capital needed. I will expand on this subject in the next paragraph, providing a view of what should be the minimum level of risk aggregation that would ensure avoiding "hidden correlations."

3. Last, the current risk governance structure often in place at most banks is not efficient and effective. This topic is extremely correlated with the previous ones. Only a clear, well-organized risk structure will be able to provide enterprise-wide risk measures and aggregate risks appropriately before reporting them to the CRO and ultimately to the board (see Aebi et al, 2011).

Please use the following *Likert scale* to provide your answer:

1= Strongly Disagree; 2 = Disagree; 3 = Neither; 4 = Agree; 5 = Strongly Agree

5.1)	1	2	3	4	5
Among the root causes of the 2007–2009 financial crisis are there major failures in the financial firms' corporate governance, traders and executive's integrity, accountability, ethical behaviors, and their excessive compensation systems, in addition to industry deregulation and major failures in regulatory oversight?					X

5.2) Dr Sabato what needs to be done to instill a new culture in the business world in order to improve corporate governance, executive accountability, fair compensation, and more in general, integrity and ethics in the financial markets?

I have two main suggestions in this regard:

Debt-based incentives and CRO and CEO both on the same reporting line to the board. Those two elements can significantly help the stability and sustainability of banks' returns.

Interview with **Giulio Sapelli** (personal communication, 2012), Full Professor of Economic History at the Università degli Studi di Milano, board member of Unicredit Banca-Impresa and President of Audit and Control Committee, scientific advisor of OECD for non-profit sector, Italy;

Please use the following *Likert scale* to provide your answer:

1= Strongly Disagree; 2 = Disagree; 3 = Neither; 4 = Agree; 5 = Strongly Agree

1.1)	1	2	3	4	5
The 2007–2009 financial crisis was predictable and avoidable.					X

1.2) Professor Sapelli was the 2007–2009 financial crisis predictable and avoidable?

A crisis of such unprecedented dimension, complexity, interconnection, and explosive global contagion, somehow unfortunately, came as no surprise to those who have studied the American economist Hyman Philip Minsky and his *instability hypothesis*. According to *Minsky's theory* even a small event can change the qualitative characteristic of a system thus leading, over time, to a devastating and systemic crisis. Just like it happened during the years preceding the 2007–2009 financial crisis a number of concurrent factors have set the stage for the dramatic financial meltdown and its dramatic economic and social consequences. There were very aggressive monetary policies flooding the market with liquidity; housing market and lending bubbles; booming innovative and complex financial engineering products; high correlations and interconnections among products and institutions, and high-risk lending practices, naked short-selling and speculations, carry trade, and incorrect assets pricing. Most of all, there was poor corporate governance, badly designed short-term remuneration incentives for executives, and major failures in regulatory oversight. Adding them all up, it's no surprise that the whole *house of cards* ultimately collapsed with its devastating consequences that are just before our eyes today.

Please use the following *Likert scale* to provide your answer:

1= Strongly Disagree; 2 = Disagree; 3 = Neither; 4 = Agree; 5 = Strongly Agree

2.1)	1	2	3	4	5
The economic/fiscal and monetary policies, financial reforms, and risk mitigation plans implemented by policy makers and regulators to reduce the impact of the housing market and credit bubbles were comprehensive and effective to reduce the financial meltdown.	X				

2.2) Professor Sapelli what actionable economic/fiscal policies, reforms, or risk mitigation plans could have been immediately implemented to reduce the impact of the housing market and credit bubbles and the meltdown caused by the crisis?

There is no doubt that the policies, interventions, and poor regulatory oversight undertaken, or not timely taken in the years preceding the crisis, by the authorities have significantly contributed to the financial meltdown and to the worsening of the systemic contagion across different industries and markets.

Please use the following *Likert scale* to provide your answer:

1= Strongly Disagree; 2 = Disagree; 3 = Neither; 4 = Agree; 5 = Strongly Agree

3.1)	1	2	3	4	5
The monetary and fiscal policies, the government bail-outs, (TARP, TALF, and so on), and the financial reforms introduced (for example, Dodd–Frank Act, of which the Volcker Rule is a central component, and so on) after 2008 were valid long-term solutions to regulate and stabilize financial markets and to avoid the risk of new crises (double dip).		X			

3.2) Professor Sapelli are the monetary and fiscal policies, the government bail-outs, (TARP, TALF, and so on), and the financial reforms introduced (for example, Dodd–Frank Act, of which the Volcker Rule is a central component, and so on) after 2008 valid long-term solutions to regulate and stabilize financial markets and to avoid the risk of new crises (double dip)?

The problem according to me is not to reform and regulate the financial industry but rather to break it up. In other words, to go back to the Glass–Steagall Act (separation of the commercial banks and full-service brokerage firms or investment banking activities).

Another issue is to eliminate the so-called shadow banking and, in particular, all OTC activities, which should be traded only in clearinghouses.

The main triggering factors that combined fueled the financial crisis are the industry over-deregulation, the excess of power attributed to top managers, their perverse remuneration incentives, and their wide asymmetric information, but also the conflicts of interest between management and shareholders (*agency problem*). The theory of aligning management and shareholders' interests through stock options, shareholders' value, or *management-by-objectives (MBO) schemes* does not really solve the problems of conflicts of interest. As the evidence has demonstrated, these approaches only end up encouraging management to adopt more opportunistic behaviors, taking advantage of their *bargaining power* and *asymmetric information*. As indicted by Michael Jensen, executives have often adopted a dysfunctional and short-term orientated shareholder value maximization approach instead of a more sustainable "long-run value" creation one.

Even the use of independent board members, who should have independence of mind and spirit, is often a purely illusionary approach, since what really counts is not that board members have no parental or personal relationships with management, but rather that they follow Aristotle's *theory of time*.

According to this theory: "The meaningful time is not the past or the present but just the future." Thus, this means that a board member is really independent only if he or she does not expect to receive future benefits from his or her current corporate involvement. In other words, he or she does not have the intention to seek in the future benefits from the people he or she is controlling (that is, management), in exchange for a lighter oversight such as the sale of consulting services or other professional opportunities.

It has been reported that after the financial meltdown many analysts, who were working for credit rating agencies, left these companies to go to work for their former client companies (the financial firms that received their "generous" ratings).

Personally, I prefer the American-style approach in the selection of board members where it is less frequent to find relatives and friends of the management in the role of independent board members, but as previously stated, the issue of true independence of mind and spirit is not necessarily related to parental relationships, although it is obviously more common.

I have some experience about it since I have spent many years as a board member of various large Italian companies such as ENI, Unicredit, Ferrovie dello Stato (Italian State Railways).

Please use the following *Likert scale* to provide your answer:

1= Strongly Disagree; 2 = Disagree; 3 = Neither; 4 = Agree; 5 = Strongly Agree

4.1)	1	2	3	4	5
There is a need for improved financial regulation, regulatory oversight, financial institutions' corporate governance (that is, COSO ERM, Internal Controls, Basel III, Dodd–Frank, Credit Ratings, and so on) and managerial cultures (that is, CSR, Ethics, and so on).					X

4.2) Professor Sapelli what still needs to be changed in terms of financial regulation and regulatory oversight, corporate governance, managerial cultures, internal controls, COSO ERM Framework, and Basel III Framework to avoid in the future other systemic crises?

There is certainly a need for a radical change in regulatory oversight but any reforms in financial regulation has no sense unless it is fully supported by real cultural changes.

The financial crisis was primarily driven by moral and cultural failures. The moral hazard, conflicts of interest, and the failure of a cultural model are based primarily on short-term profit maximization. Thus, new rules and regulations (if possible) must address these cultural issues and the issue of perverse incentives, otherwise there will be no real solution for similar crises.

This issue of the need for cultural change was already identified in 1976 by David Riesman of Harvard University when he raised the attention on the leadership qualities to be taught at Harvard Business School. Today very often Business Ethics and Corporate Social Responsibility are just used as rhetorical slogans. Today in the financial industry, quite often, there is a real separation between moral values and business purposes. This is the dramatic aftermath and regression of the marginalist economic principles that have spread, over the years, their dogmas to large corporations and business schools, shaping ultimately the minds and souls of *anomic* business executives and leaders to the exclusive pursuit of short-term profit-maximization goals.

Please use the following *Likert scale* to provide your answer:

1= Strongly Disagree; 2 = Disagree; 3 = Neither; 4 = Agree; 5 = Strongly Agree

5.1)	1	2	3	4	5
Among the root causes of the 2007–2009 financial crisis are there major failures in the financial firms' corporate governance, traders and executive's integrity, accountability, ethical behaviors, and their excessive compensation systems, in addition to industry deregulation and major failures in regulatory oversight?					X

5.2) Professor Sapelli what needs to be done to instill a new culture in the business world in order to improve corporate governance, executive accountability, fair compensation, and more in general, integrity and ethics in the financial markets?

There is not solution to such crises, to the *agency theory*, and to potential conflicts of interest at all levels in the organizations, and among organizations unless the compensation schemes are changed. One way to achieve this cultural change might be to eliminate perverse remuneration schemes. I would suggest to start by eliminating the MBO as a goal-setting incentives scheme. The new compensation schemes should have fixed and no longer variable components or equity-based remuneration schemes. We need to go back to the "old-fashioned" model of salaries and fixed bonuses based on discretional criteria. We need to strengthen the corporate governance's principle of balance of power without over-regulation. We need to enhance the role of auditors and independent directors. More education and training should be provided by financial institutions on corporate governance, corporate social responsibility, accountability, and business ethics. But as usual in life, the best and most effective corporate training is represented by good examples of moral behaviors by the organizational leaders, rigorous audit, effective due diligence and oversight activities, and by the adoption of fair and more transparent remuneration schemes.

Interview with **Giacomo Vaciago** (personal communication, 2012), Full Professor and Director of the Institute of Economics and Finance at Catholic University of Milan. Italy. Please use the following *Likert scale* to provide your answer:

1= Strongly Disagree; 2 = Disagree; 3 = Neither; 4 = Agree; 5 = Strongly Agree

1.1)	1	2	3	4	5
The 2007–2009 financial crisis was predictable and avoidable.				X	

1.2) Professor Vaciago was the 2007–2009 financial crisis predictable and avoidable?

The financial crisis was in fact predicted (see for instance: Borio and Lowe, 2002b) by those who noticed that an excessively expansive macroeconomic policy had been causing speculative bubbles which if not cured early would have led sooner or later to a major crisis.

Please use the following *Likert scale* to provide your answer:

1= Strongly Disagree; 2 = Disagree; 3 = Neither; 4 = Agree; 5 = Strongly Agree

2.1)	1	2	3	4	5
The economic/fiscal and monetary policies, financial reforms, and risk mitigation plans implemented by policy makers and regulators to reduce the impact of the housing market and credit bubbles were comprehensive and effective to reduce the financial meltdown.		X			

2.2) Professor Vaciago what actionable economic/fiscal policies, reforms, or risk mitigation plans could have been immediately implemented to reduce the impact of the housing market and credit bubbles and the meltdown caused by the crisis?

The gravity of the crisis – which started in the interbank market as a "liquidity problem" – was not immediately perceived. Now we know more about "systemic risk" and "contagion" effects and we have learnt the importance of "firewalls;" these were precisely the alternative solutions that should have been adopted right at the beginning.

Please use the following *Likert scale* to provide your answer:

1= Strongly Disagree; 2 = Disagree; 3 = Neither; 4 = Agree; 5 = Strongly Agree

3.1)	1	2	3	4	5
The monetary and fiscal policies, the government bail-outs, (TARP, TALF, and so on), and the financial reforms introduced (for example, Dodd–Frank Act, of which the Volcker Rule is a central component, and so on) after 2008 were valid long-term solutions to regulate and stabilize financial markets and to avoid the risk of new crises (double dip).				X	

3.2) Professor Vaciago are the monetary and fiscal policies, the government bail-outs, (TARP, TALF, and so on), and the financial reforms introduced (for example, Dodd–Frank Act, of which the Volcker Rule is a central component, and so on) after 2008 valid long-term solutions to regulate and stabilize financial markets and to avoid the risk of new crises (double dip)?

Unfortunately most of the reforms are not yet in place: they are still being discussed or in need of being implemented. This is why the situation is still very fragile and this implies that the expectations of economic agents are still dominated by uncertainty. A big effort to rebuild an economy after a war has a very positive psychological effect, but the situation today is very different from that of a war scenario.

Please use the following *Likert scale* to provide your answer:

1= Strongly Disagree; 2 = Disagree; 3 = Neither; 4 = Agree; 5 = Strongly Agree

4.1)	1	2	3	4	5
There is a need for improved financial regulation, regulatory oversight, financial institutions' corporate governance (that is, COSO ERM, Internal Controls, Basel III, Dodd–Frank, Credit Ratings, and so on) and managerial cultures (that is, CSR, Ethics, and so on).				X	

4.2) Professor Vaciago what still needs to be changed in terms of financial regulation and regulatory oversight, corporate governance, managerial cultures, internal controls, COSO ERM Framework, and Basel III Framework to avoid in the future other systemic crises?

Appetite for risk (which caused the crisis) has to be greatly reduced by regulatory reforms (à la Glass–Steagall), which take us back to a world in which finance is the servant and not the master.

Please use the following *Likert scale* to provide your answer:

1= Strongly Disagree; 2 = Disagree; 3 = Neither; 4 = Agree; 5 = Strongly Agree

5.1)	1	2	3	4	5
Among the root causes of the 2007–2009 financial crisis are there major failures in the financial firms' corporate governance, traders and executive's integrity, accountability, ethical behaviors, and their excessive compensation systems, in addition to industry deregulation and major failures in regulatory oversight?				X	

5.2) Professor Vaciago what needs to be done to instill a new culture in the business world in order to improve corporate governance, executive accountability, fair compensation, and more in general, integrity and ethics in the financial markets?

In emerging countries the major policies are quite rightly consistent with long-run targets. The same approach should be rediscovered in our own countries where unfortunately short-termism has prevailed in recent years. You make money if you are right tomorrow: but in a year's time?

Organization	Thought Leader	Q1	Q2	Q3	Q4	Q5
IESE	Antonio Argandoña	4	2	3	5	5
ORACLE	Alfonso Asaro	4	2	2	4	5
Bocconi University	Elio Borgonovi	4	2	1	5	5
Iason Ltd.	Antonio Castagna	3	1	1	4	1
University of Pisa	Fabiano Colombini	5	3	2	4	5
NYU Stern	Aswarth Damodaran	4	3	3	3	3
Intesa Sanpaolo Bank	Gregorio De Felice	3	2	3	5	4
Citi	Victor Di Giorgio	4	3	4	3	4
Stanford University	Darrell Duffie	3	4	4	5	4
LSE	Charles Goodhart	3	4	2	5	5
Sorbonne University	Etienne Koehler	2/4	1	2	5	5
Ukrainian Academy of Banking	Alexander N. Kostyuk	4	2	3	5	5
Temenos	George Koukis	5	2	2	5	5
F.R.B.	William W. Lang	5	4	3	5	5
Bloomberg LP	Fabio Mercurio	4	2	3	5	5
Unicredit	Massimo Meterangelo	4	3	2	5	5
Eurointelligence ASBL and FT	Wolfgang Munchau	4	2	2	5	5
Bocconi University	Fabrizio Pezzani	5	1	1	3	5
University of Chicago	Richard A. Posner	4	3	3	4	4
Ulster Bank	Gabriele Sabato	4	2	1	5	5
University of Milan	Giulio Sapelli	5	1	2	5	5
Catholic University of Milan.	Giacomo Vaciago	4	2	4	4	4
Average Score		4,0	2,3	2,4	4,5	4,5
Std. Deviation		0,7	0,9	1,0	0,7	1,0

Figure 6.1   Thought Leaders' Responses to the Interviews

Source: Prof. Ivo Pezzuto's *Thought Leaders Survey on Corporate Governance in the Financial Industry in the Post-Crisis Period* (2012).

Summary of the Research Findings from the Thought Leaders' Interviews

Given the limited number of participants to the survey (small panel), of course, I did not have the objective to come up with generalizable research findings that could prove the specific research questions or hypotheses. Because this "Thought Leaders' Research Survey" is of a qualitative nature, the scope of the analysis and of its findings is to be able to provide to the reader of this book some original and valuable insights on the topics of research from highly qualified experts and opinion leaders that, combined with the very detailed analyses I have undertaken on secondary data sources, and my own expertise in the topics, could allow the reader to come to his/her conclusion on the root causes of the financial crisis, on the likelihood that it could have been predicted and avoided, and on the financial reforms that have been so far introduced, or that could be improved to create a more resilient financial system.

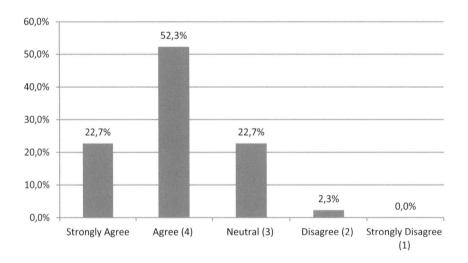

Figure 6.2   Responses to Statement 1

Source: Prof. Ivo Pezzuto's *Thought Leaders Survey on Corporate Governance in the Financial Industry in the Post-Crisis Period* (2012).

Research finding: as indicated in Figure 6.2, for 75 percent of the interviewed thought leaders the 2007–2009 financial crisis was predictable and avoidable.

Research finding in Figure 6.3: For approximately 70 percent of the interviewed thought leaders policy makers and regulators' interventions to mitigate the impact of the financial crisis were not adequate enough or timely executed.

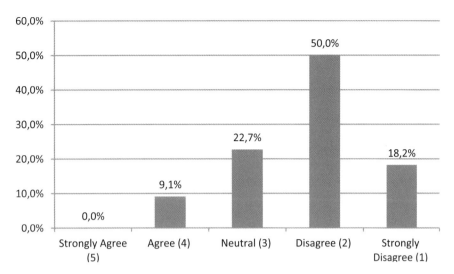

Figure 6.3   Responses to Statement 2

Source: Prof. Ivo Pezzuto's *Thought Leaders Survey on Corporate Governance in the Financial Industry in the Post-Crisis Period* (2012).

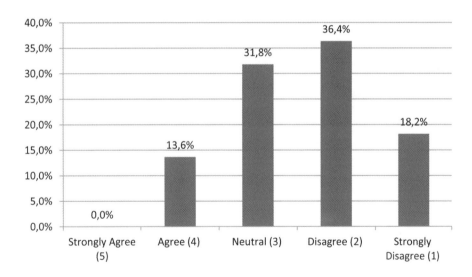

Figure 6.4   Responses to Statement 3

Source: Prof. Ivo Pezzuto's *Thought Leaders Survey on Corporate Governance in the Financial Industry in the Post-Crisis Period* (2012).

Research finding: For more than half (55 percent) of the interviewed thought leaders the financial reforms introduced after 2008 are not valid long-term solutions. According to 31.8 percent of the participants it is too early (mid-2012) to determine whether the financial reforms will be effective to avoid the risk of new crises in the future.

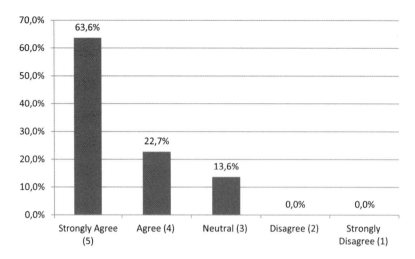

Figure 6.5   Responses to Statement 4

Source: Prof. Ivo Pezzuto's *Thought Leaders Survey on Corporate Governance in the Financial Industry in the Post-Crisis Period* (2012).

Research finding: For 86.3 percent of the interviewed thought leaders there is a need for improved financial regulation, regulatory oversight, and financial institutions' corporate governance, and most of them (63.6 percent) indicate that there is a strong need for change.

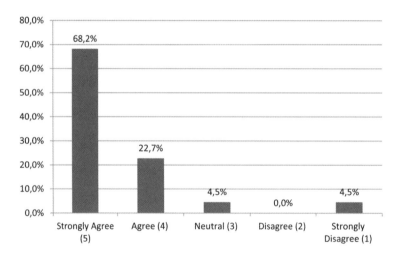

Figure 6.6   Responses to Statement 5

Source: Prof. Ivo Pezzuto's *Thought Leaders Survey on Corporate Governance in the Financial Industry in the Post-Crisis Period* (2012).

Research finding: For 91 percent of the interviewed thought leaders among the root causes of the financial crisis there are major failures in the financial firms' corporate governance, traders and executive's integrity, accountability, ethical behaviors, and their excessive compensation systems, in addition to industry deregulation and major failures in regulatory oversight.

CHAPTER 7

Conclusion

The fact-based evidences and analyses reported in this book, in addition to the industry experts' and thought leaders' contributions seem to prove the following findings:

- the 2007–2009 financial crisis had multiple triggering factors that evolved over the years;
- the crisis was predictable and avoidable (Rushe, 2011b);
- the crisis is a result of major failure in regulation, corporate governance, perverse short-term financial/economic incentives, and accountability at all levels in and out of the industry that combined with other factors and externalities have led over the years to the build-up of a systemic tail risk;
- ethics, corporate responsibility, corporate citizenship, corporate culture changes still have a long way to go in financial institutions and markets;
- effective and forward-looking financial regulation is necessary but it will have a challenging time to be harmonized and implemented on a global scale, especially during periods of economy recession, high debt and budget deficits, slow gross domestic product (GDP) growth and high levels of unemployment;
- in many countries the financial reforms seem to be mostly focused on compliance rule and they marginally address structural issues (Asaro, 2012).

The main triggering factors of the financial crisis are:

- lack of "common sense" in addressing systemic risk with an enterprise-wide and industry-wide perspective and the overreliance on inadequate risk models, data, and assumptions;
- most probably greed, conflicts of interest, moral hazard, and perverse short-term financial incentives at all levels in and out of the industry;
- a home ownership society, which in principle is good, but combined with the housing market and lending bubbles, reckless "creative" financial engineering and risk-taking, and lax regulatory oversight, turned into what Warren Buffett defined as "financial weapons of mass destruction";
- inadequate monetary policy of the US Federal Reserve in the early 2000s in relation to global imbalances and the rapid expansion of shadow banking;
- inadequate regulation and regulatory oversight of "banking" and "shadow banking;"

- the Fed's failure to notice the housing bubble, despite warnings, and to timely deflate the housing and the credit bubbles;
- excessive level of leverage in the financial sector and shadow banking (structured investment vehicles – SIVs, special purpose vehicles – SPVs, Conduits);
- unrealistic expectations on the constantly rising asset prices (housing market) which have led to the mispricing of mortgage-backed securities' (MBS) collateral;
- poor risk assessment of MBS by credit rating agencies and due diligence by securitizers;
- self-regulating ideology assumption of large financial institutions and overconfidence in the risk management models ("narrow-focused" view of risk management), which were based on historical data from low volatility periods;
- lax underwriting standards for the subprime mortgage loans;
- massive growth of "exotic" mortgage products and of "creative" and complex structured finance products with significant asset correlation and target market concentration;
- massive adverse selection of poorly screened subprime borrowers and fraud/manipulated mortgage loans applications;
- failure of regulators to consider the high level of interconnection among financial institutions due to the complexity of the innovative financial engineering products (collateralized debt obligation – CDOs), the globalization of the markets, and a poorly regulated and controlled shadow banking sector;
- excessive confidence (or moral hazard) in the risk distribution process (risk transfer) through the originate-to-distribute (OTD) securitization process and "pseudo-credit insurance protection" with the credit default swaps (CDS);
- wrong assumptions and bad forecasting, scenario analysis, and stress testing with a systemic industry-wide perspective (extreme tail-events);
- major failure of financial institutions' corporate governance, compliance, risk management, audit, internal controls, due diligence, information disclosure, application of Basel capital adequacy framework;
- inability to properly integrate in the risk models/bureau scores macroeconomic indicators and industry-wide indicators for a broader and more holistic perspective;
- inability of many financial institutions to develop a real corporate social responsibility, business ethics, and sustainability culture;
- failure to consider the potential systemic risk of an industry-wide exponential growth of complex (and mispriced) innovative financial engineering products traded by undercapitalized and overleveraged financial institutions in opaque markets.

In summary, given all these combined factors, it seems quite unlikely that the 2007–2009 financial crisis was just the result of a so-called "black swan" but rather a sort of *time bomb!*

All in all, to conclude, it seems as if in addition to a new and more simplified but effective financial regulation, all thought leaders involved in the survey undertaken for this book have expressed a strong desire, similar to that of many ordinary people in all countries, for more civic education, respect of others and of legal and moral norms, and a return to integrity. In other words, by and large, they hope for a return to a more patient and pragmatic approach to life and sustainability which could be termed "long-termism." Most of all, it seems as if these thought leaders, just like the majority of ordinary people, today are looking for credible, enlightened, and accountable political, economic, moral leaders to trust. Leaders just like Blessed Mother Teresa of Calcutta, Blessed Pope John Paul II, Abraham Lincoln, John F. Kennedy, Dr Martin Luther King, Mahatma Gandhi, Nelson Mandela, Yitzhak Rabin, and many others that can make the difference with their lives and acts and that may show the way for others to follow for a better and more sustainable future comprised of peace, justice, prosperity, freedom, and democracy all around the world

I believe that in order to create a more stable and resilient financial system that might prevent future financial crises, the following recommendations should be considered:

1. A new cultural paradigm. "Long-termism" or *responsible capitalism* should become the "mantra" of every leader (political and business). They should change their mindset toward long-term vision and value creation objectives instead of focusing only on short-term profit maximization and opportunistic behaviors that often lead only to moral hazard, new bubbles, and window-dressing techniques designed to pump up stock prices, personal reputation, and short-term compensation. Responsible capitalism has to become a value in our society. John Maynard Keynes used to say "in the long run we are all dead" but as it is well known it takes a long-term perspective to envision, plan and execute a sound industrial policy for the sustainable growth of a country and the full implementation of structural reforms. After all, even Keynes wasn't at all unconcerned with the long run as fully displayed in his famous essay, "Economic Possibilities for our Grandchildren" (*The Economist*, 2013).

2. Tighter but simplified regulatory reforms, and most of all, more effective oversight.

3. Change in financial firms' corporate governance framework in order to discourage excessive short-term risk-taking (risk appetite) and to reward mainly superior long-term performances, corporate social responsibility, and sustainability.

4. Overhauling of executive remuneration incentives. More transparency and disclosure on financial firms' executive remuneration and incentives. Compensation should be made more transparent and simplified and it should be based on risk-adjusted performances of the banks. Remuneration payments should be held back until the full consequences of a strategy plays out, and claw-backs should be introduced to reduce as much as possible an excessive short-term results orientation. Dividends and bonuses to executives should be paid only after having verified the capital requirement adequacy of the financial firms. Shareholders should enforce a *say-on-pay* policy for their executive remuneration based on risk-adjusted parameters and long-term profit and value creation performances. Stricter policies should be enforced on "golden parachutes" and severance packages. Salaries in the financial sector should be more harmonized and aligned by shareholders (*say-on-pay*) with salaries of other sectors (real economy). Banking and finance has to return to being a complementary and support function to the development of the real economy. There should be less disproportion between banks' and financial firms' executive compensation and their firms' Return on Equity (ROE), value creation (EVA), dividend pay-outs, and average employees' salaries. There should be also less disproportion between average employees' taxation rates and their firms' taxation rates.

5. Introduction of a *systemic risk tax* (that requires financial firms "to purchase a contingent capital insurance against the losses they incur during systemic crises") to get the financial sector to internalize systemic risk (with risk-based insurance premiums based the systemic riskiness of the activities) and the cross-border

resolution of potential future banking crises (Acharya et al., 2010). Furthermore, banks' management and shareholders, and the bank crisis resolution fund should be held primarily accountable for banks bail-ins of their failed banks and, only for the residual portion and in exceptional circumstances, other stakeholders (depositors, taxpayers) should be liable for the rescue plans.

6. More direct board member involvement and accountability in risk oversight.

7. Forward-looking capital requirements (and a great focus on leverage ratios) should be introduced addressing realistic risk assumptions, stress testing, worst case scenarios, and adverse business cycles or bubbles. No more undercapitalized banks using off-balance sheet vehicles to artificially reduce their capital requirements.

8. No more shadow-banking, all derivatives should be traded in regulated and controlled markets (central clearinghouses) and traded using only electronic platforms and devices. Even non-standard derivatives such as the so-called over-the-counter (OTC) derivatives (that is, swaps), should be backed, as much as possible, by collateral and subject to full transparency and disclosure.

9. New regulations on a global scale should hold credit rating agencies more responsible for the reliability of the ratings and their outlooks (within the timeframe of their outlook, and taking into account also a pre-determined volatility band). Alternatively, as already prescribed by the Dodd–Frank Act, the use and over-reliance on nationally recognized statistical rating organization (NRSRO) ratings should be significantly reduced (or even better eliminated) by many statutory and regulatory requirements (as it can no longer assure that high ratings correspond with low volatility and high liquidity). It should instead encourage investors to conduct their own analysis. Furthermore, in addition to the attribution of an "expert liability" to the rating agencies and the prohibition for their compliance officers to work on ratings, methodologies, or sales, the requirement for NRSROs to conduct a one-year look-back review when an NRSRO employee goes to work for an obligor or underwriter of a security or money market instrument subject to a rating by that NRSRO should be substituted with a rule that forbids employees of an NRSRO rating agency to work for a former client for a minimum period of five years (US Government, 2010).

10. Regulations on a global scale should significantly reduce credit rating agencies' potential conflicts of interest with their clients, imposing a separation of business units for the offer of credit ratings and consulting/advisory services with limitations for three years in the assignment of credit ratings to clients that also purchase advisory/consulting services and vice versa.

11. The same regulation should be extended also to other institutions in order to limit other potential conflicts of interests. For example, in the US and in other countries, regulators and supervisory authorities' officers (that is, Fed, the Securities and Exchange Commission (SEC), the Federal Deposit Insurance Corporation (FDIC), the European Central Bank (ECB), the International Monetary Fund (IMF), and so on) should not be allowed to join (to be hired by) the financial firms or their boards if they have reviewed/audited them within the past five years. After the financial crisis there have been many evidences in the US and in Europe of changing seats practices with former senior regulators taking the job of compliance chief at companies they used to supervise (that is, Mr Hector Sants of the Financial Services Authority (UK) hired by Barclays as head of compliance and government and regulatory relations, and many others) (Wilson, 2012b).

12. OTD securitizations and the sale of products like MBS, as reported in the Dodd–Frank Act, should be liable for the "skin in the game" policy, but for a higher percentage than the one prescribed by the Dodd–Frank Act of at least 5 percent of the credit risk.

13. Chief Risk Officers (CROs), Compliance Officers and Internal Audit Directors of systemically important financial institutions (SIFI) should be hired (and eventually "fired" if required) by boards (and not by management) and should have a dotted reporting line (matrix organization) to boards and a regular, close, and direct interaction with regulatory oversight authorities. CROs should not report to the Chief Finance Officer (CFO) but directly to the CEOs and should regularly participate in all management committees, and assure timely and effective corrective actions of any major risk identified by the committees (or reported to the committees) in close coordination with all the firms' functions and should constantly communicate status reports of the actions plans to the CEO, management team, and to the board.

14. Group CROs and CEOs should be held accountable for their firm-wide risk management framework and in case of severe wrongdoing that generates systemic risk, they should be held liable for individual criminal charges; compliance officers and CEOs should face a similar individual liability for anti-money laundering (AML), frauds, regulatory rules' violations (including also regulatory reporting officers), and market abuse charges (that is, rates rigging) and deliberately boosting systemic risks for their own short-term speculative purposes. There should be no asymmetric rules globally on these roles to avoid arbitrages.

15. More transparency and disclosure on the risk management practices on derivatives trading in order to avoid in the future cases such as JPMorgan Chase ("London Whale").

16. Separation of commercial and proprietary trading. Limiting the risks of the too-big-to-fail threat by introducing tougher anti-trust rules on industry concentration, giant banks, and global lobbies that limit the principles of free market and fair competition (Johnson, 2012, January 12). The Dodd–Frank Act should make it more difficult for proprietary trading activities to be classified as portfolio "hedging" in order to bypass regulation while instead they are still bets and not risk mitigation operations. The current Dodd–Frank Act rule on the matter (Volcker Rule) does not seem to be aggressive enough for the scope ("skin in the game" by the investment advisor – up to 3 percent of Tier 1 capital in the aggregate) (US Government, 2010). Hedging activities are designed not to reward proprietary risk-taking. For clearinghouses, the need to clearly define contract standardization, collateralization, netting, insolvency, and central clearing counterparty membership criteria.

17. Systemically risky financial speculations should be significantly discouraged in order to avoid severe financial instability. This objective, however, as demonstrated by reputable research findings, should not be achieved through bans of these financial instruments (naked short-selling) and trading facilities. In fact, in early 2013, the IMF has criticized the ban of speculative bets on countries' creditworthiness since it could distort financial markets and increase the cost of raising debt (Atkins, 2013b). Regulatory supervisors should be able to monitor and to stop (if necessary), with the support of online and real-time early warning alerts, any activity related to complex and potentially systemically risky trading operations (including also *high frequency trading* – HFT), in addition to reviewing ex-post reporting of all derivatives transactions of the financial institutions.

18. A harmonized global regulation of no more bail-outs for defaulting financial firms and more integrated cross-border resolution strategies for bank failures that may assure bank recapitalizations, emergency rescue plans, bail-outs, rules for take-overs by other financial institutions in order to avoid potential systemic risks and bank runs.

19. Creation in the EU of a single federal deposit guarantee organization covering all banks in the union to avoid potential bank runs. There should also be a common oversight authority (banking union) and a common fund that would deal with bail-outs needed for the cross-border banks that are major players in the European banking system (bank crisis resolution fund). In addition, there should be a single EU authority (to guarantee full transparency and disclosure on banks solvency) with ultimate decision-making powers for the major banks, and a common set of banking rules (that is, European Banking Authority (EBA)/ECB, and so on) (Isidore, 2012).

20. Bank crisis resolution mechanisms should operate based on the following pecking order: (1) losses and resolution costs should be borne first and foremost by the financial firms' management team, board members, and financial firms' shareholders, and even by bank employees at every level (in case of severe direct responsibility in the bank failure). Change management and corporate governance changes should be mandatory for failing banks due to severe negligence or wrongdoing of banks management and employees. The Single Resolution Authority should require claw-backs on bank managers' salaries, bonuses and other undeserved compensation incentives. No golden parachutes or severance packages should be granted to the management of failed banks; (2) bail-in of creditors – (a) subordinated debt holders; (b) senior bond holders; (c) covered bond holders granting higher protection to small individual bond holders versus institutional investors; (3) the bank crisis resolution fund. State funds should not be used for bailouts of failed banks to avoid the vicious circle between sovereign debt and bank debt that overcomplicated the resolution of the Eurozone debt crisis in 2010–2012; (4) only in unavoidable and exceptional circumstances other stakeholders according to the following pecking order (that is, uninsured depositors, insured depositors, and taxpayers) should be forced to bail-out bank crises. Furthermore, regulators and policy makers (lobbyists, politicians, external auditors, and so on) who have contributed with their intrusive behaviors or negligent supervision to the bank failure should also be held responsible of the failure and subject to investigation. It is also critical to harmonize such rules on a global scale in order to avoid potential distortions in the handling of banking crises and to avoid regulatory arbitrages. In Europe a future banking union, as a part of its bank resolution mechanism for bank failures and for bank restructuring, should also contemplate the use of a *European Bad Bank*, and a forced wind down plan for insolvent banks in case of systemic risk and contagion threats when either bail-in or a bail-out plans cannot be implemented.

21. Banking supervision in the Eurozone countries should be centralized by the ECB for all banks and financial institutions and not just for a few systemically important financial institutions (SIFI). Furthermore, the definition of SIFIs in Europe and in the US should be reconsidered since a number of the financial and non-financial institutions that failed during the 2007–2009 financial crisis and the Eurozone crisis and that were bailed-out with taxpayers' money would not be included in the current definition of SIFI.

22. The Eurozone banks should have to pay their taxes at a European level (EU), thus increasing their independence from the local states' political and fiscal control. These taxes might also be used (within a certain limit and under certain conditions)

to strengthen the Eurozone bail-out fund (bank crisis resolution mechanisms) thus significantly limiting the social cost of potential future banking crises. A fiscal regulation should be centralized and harmonized in the Eurozone in order to reduce asymmetric conditions (rates) that may favor the economic development and competitiveness of some countries while penalizing others, of course, after a rigorous process of fiscal consolidation, tax evasion reduction, and sustainable return to structural GDP growth.

23. Radical reforms should be introduced by bank shareholders to reward real performance of banks' executives. Bonuses and dividends should be paid considering also risk-adjusted performances, claw-backs, and long-term orientation. Reduction of inefficiencies, improved productivity, and enhanced competitiveness should be pursued in banks and financial firms through organizational restructuring and new business models that might involve employees' redundancies, branch closures, mergers, and clearinghouses for all derivatives. Less nepotism, cronyism, bureaucracy, and political clan culture (clubby system) in corporate environments and more equal opportunity, productivity, and merit-based careers for talented individuals. Less *sliding doors* between financial institutions and politics. Companies should attract more high caliber candidates with independence of mind and spirit and fewer "Yes Men."

24. A fiscal union should also be pursued in the Eurozone with joint and several liability for newly issued debt, after the more urgent implementation of the banking union. European leaders should put an end to the excessive asymmetric adjustments resulting from the national austerity programs.

25. More press and media independence to guarantee a more transparent and fair economic and political analysis. Independent media and press should be the watchdogs of a responsible democracy based on rigorous governance. No government subsidies should be granted to press and media to reduce the political influence on these organizations. Full disclosure should also be enforced on private fund raising granted to these organizations, on the corporate governance and shareholders' control over these firms, and on the potential conflicts of interest between press and media organizations and political and economic lobbies. The same policies in terms of transparency and disclosure should also be applied to all government subsidies granted to any sector.

26. Following the banking, fiscal, treasury, and financial union and the centralized banking oversight in the Eurozone, the ECB will also have to become, in the near future, a lender of last resort, like the Fed in the US, in order to help sustain long-term coordinated pan-European economic growth, price stability, and financial markets' stability plans with both conventional and non-conventional policies. Quantitative easing should be allowed.

27. Harmonize the Dodd–Frank Act and the Basel III Framework on a global scale and aim to reduce regulatory arbitrages and regulatory loopholes, systemic risks, and the highly concentrated and unregulated shadow banking sector with its high leverage ratios. Regulators should prevent excessive risk-taking by financial institutions, requiring stricter rules for undercapitalized and overleveraged firms with limited liquidity and short-term funding. They should impose higher (equity) capital requirements, lower leverage ratios, and less risky funding strategies. In particular, they should drastically limit financial firms' use of complex and opaque financial engineering and structured products to reduce their capital requirements (Pezzuto, 2008; 2010a, pp. 119–123; Wolf, 2013).

28. Central banks should review their *collateral rule* to make the financial system more solid and resilient.
29. Extend also, under the Dodd–Frank and Basel III rules, the government-sponsored enterprises (GSEs) (Fannie Mae, Freddie Mac, Ginnie Mae). Basel III should also properly and fully regulate the so-called shadow banking system.
30. Aggressive economic reforms to reduce long-term structural current account imbalances in combination with fiscal stimuli.
31. Even in the US the Government should take action in order to reduce its high level of sovereign debt, despite the current economic recovery, to offset the impact of rising interest rates (Fed's tapering).
32. In the Eurozone a more aggressive coordinated economic growth policy should be introduced along with a number of effective fiscal incentives to encourage a more harmonized pan-European program toward innovation, productivity, performance-based compensation, and to limit as much as possible nepotism, bribes, corruption, and cartels/oligopolies. Some of the less competitive peripheral European countries require an urgent implementation of structural reforms to revamp their social and economic development. Innovation and economic growth has been mainly hampered by the collapse of industrial production, a sharp increase in firms' bankruptcies and lay-offs; reduced firm's creditworthiness and ratings; reduced consumer spending; a long recession, credit crunch, anemic inflows of foreign capitals; excessive sovereign debt; high taxation, high corruption, and tax evasion; a sizeable underground economy; high cost of politics; bureaucracy and inefficiencies; limited internal competition, low productivity; lack of job market flexibility and small business elites and lobbies, with strong political connections, mainly focused on defending their "status quo." These countries need to unleash new ideas, talents, and economic models based on a global vision. They also need a cultural change towards improved accountability, transparency, respect of rules, and social responsibility. Furthermore, it is very important that they promote superior quality of education and more investments in human capital development (by companies, individuals, and institutions) in order to foster innovation, research excellence, creativity, knowledge, and competitiveness. Last but not least, enhanced links and specially designed programs between firms and universities/technical schools should be encouraged in these countries in order to improve the match between demand for labor and supply of skills in the job market but also a more decisive role of political leaders in fostering the development of important international trade agreements for domestic firms.
33. Business ethics and corporate social responsibility should become central in the business education curricula – not just profit maximization and GDP growth. Ethical codes accreditations should become prerequisites for all careers in managerial professions and certifications, as well as for academic, regulatory bodies, and corporate economists. Individuals who fail to match ethical codes standards should be barred by their industry for a number of years or for life in the case of severe criminal charges for wrongdoing.
34. Break-up and/or restructuring of SIFIs should be encouraged to reduce their systemic impact. This should also be combined with a less intrusive regulatory structure for overseeing the financial system (Lang, 2012).
35. Reduce inequality and income distribution to improve consumptions/economic growth.

36. Use of euro project bonds for investments in infrastructures in the Eurozone and of the euro bonds and other potential bonds to support long-term stability in the Eurozone (that is, EuroUnionBond, rescue bonds, and so on) (Quadro Curzio, 2011).

37. Provide incentives for the best professional talents to pursue careers in the real economy rather than in the more profitable finance and investment banking sector.

38. Simplify and make the Dodd–Frank Act more effective to overcome the real causes that generated the 2007–2009 financial crisis with a forward-thinking orientation. Furthermore, new tougher rules and much more expensive fines should be introduced to make it less convenient (cost effective) for financial institutions and greedy executives to pursue wrongdoings, otherwise the payment of fines and settlements will not effectively discourage their misconduct (that is, severe fines for companies, but also for their executives, including executives' conviction and potential bans from the industry for years or for life). Regulators and policy makers should request more than just settlements for wrongdoing. For serious frauds, market abuse behaviors, and other very serious and systemically risky policy violations, they should impose tougher rules such as mandatory change management, criminal conviction of individual executives, claw-backs of their financial compensations/bonus/dividends based on wrongdoing, no golden parachutes, and in some cases, also ban executives from working in the industry for a number for years or for their lifetime. Furthermore, financial institutions and executives should be banned from distributing dividends to investors to force them to comply with tighter corporate governance in case of excessive risk taking. Furthermore, policy makers and shareholders should also ban executives and managers from receiving bonuses worth more than their pay. It is also time to make regulators and supervisory authorities more accountable for their regulatory and supervisory activities. New rules should also apply mandatory change management policies for regulators and regulatory oversight authorities that fail to properly do their job. In worst case scenarios, regulators should also contemplate cancelling banking licenses for serious violations.

39. Donations to parties and political leaders for political campaigns should be fully transparent to reduce "secret" lobbyist pressures on political leaders. More transparency should be ensured for any kind of "gift-granting" or "special condition" (that is, cheap rates mortgage loans, and so on) offered to policy makers, regulators, supervisory authorities, or opinion leaders for lobbyist purposes. New tougher rules on bribery, tax evasion, corruption, and money laundering, should be introduced and offshore tax havens should be strongly discouraged. The London Interbank Offered Rate (Libor) rate-setting process should be completely redesigned to allow for more transparency, objectivity, and reliability.

40. Introduce norms in Europe and in the US that may improve social cohesion and breed a new generation of socially responsible business and political leaders who can pursue their goals and ambitions of successful careers and personal lives in the best interest of the whole society and not only to satisfy their greed, selfishness, and short-term speculative goals (Pezzuto, 2008). With approximately 7 billion people living on the Earth and a rapidly growing and ageing population, an unprecedented struggle among several developed and emerging markets is taking place for growth, scarce resources allocation, access to superior higher education, innovation, increased productivity, and global competitiveness. This globalization phenomenon is becoming a great opportunity (that is new markets with huge growth potential

to serve but also low cost countries where to place firms' production process or international supply-chains networks) but also a real challenge for many nations, communities, households, and individuals, as it imposes sustained growth rates to absorb the needs of a fast-growing global population and higher expected per capita consumption rates. These global forces are seriously challenging the global economic and environmental sustainability and the social cohesion among more and less developed and competitive countries in the global battlefield. Increased debt (public or private) alone and the use of massive unconventional monetary and fiscal policies to solve liquidity and solvency crises cannot be the only sustainable cure for an overcrowded world with different consumption, interest, productivity, and growth rates that often continues to consume more resources that it can afford to. New regional or global economic frameworks and paradigms will probably be necessary to improve global economic sustainability and to rethink the current global competitiveness of a number of mature Western economic regions.

The proposed 40 recommendations for improved regulatory and corporate governance might not be a fully comprehensive set of solutions designed to reduce the current high level of political, economic, and financial uncertainty, and the social unrest in a number of countries. The current (April 2013) high levels of uncertainty and volatility in the markets associated also with stagnation of some mature economies, and "QE (Quantitative Easing) wars", will probably continue to persist for a while in our mature economies until economic recovery will be reached and hopefully not undermined by liquidity traps and lack of liquidity to the real economy. In the US, the mortgage lending market is still largely "subsidized" through Fannie and Freddy and the level of debt and leverage is still very high, thus it is still difficult to determine today what will be the real impact on the huge levels of outstanding debt (and high leverage) when the exit strategy of the Fed will actually start (high interest rates) as well as reduced Government subsidies. Nevertheless, I like to believe that the structural adjustments currently being introduced in Europe, US, and elsewhere, as well as the reforms of corporate governance, financial regulation, labor market, taxation, and welfare, might just represent the painful but necessary steps in the right direction toward a new equilibrium of prosperity, innovation, sustainability, and global competitiveness.

It seems that in the last two decades banking and finance have grown exponentially, taking advantage of globalization, free trade agreements, state-of-the-art online and real-time technological innovations, industry deregulation, political support, and product innovation (financial engineering). This exponential global growth has also led in many cases to the primacy of powerful banking and finance lobbies over politics, real economy, and society as a whole. The too-big-to-fail doctrine is a direct consequence of this change in society. Since the financial crisis is also the consequence of this drift toward excessive growth of deregulated globalized banking and financial markets, the logical solution to prevent such systemic risks in the future necessarily requires limits on the unregulated and uncontrolled growth and primacy of the banking and financial markets over all other stakeholders in our society.

I mentioned in my 2008 working paper on the financial crisis the following:

The complex issue today is also related to how can our society, political and legal systems, business schools, universities, educators, religious entities, communities change the greedy, individualistic, and short-term orientation of some key players of the financial markets' industry (hedge funds, mutual funds, private equity funds, investment banks and others) to become more socially responsible and committed to the long-term sustainability of their organizations, employees, stakeholders, communities, nations, and to the world peace and sustainable development. (Pezzuto, 2008)

Our moral responsibility as a society is to live, share, develop, enrich and hand-over the world we have received from our parents and ancestors to the next generations. Hopefully it will be a better world than the one we have inherited. Our responsibility is to breed a new generation of business and political leaders who can pursue their goals and ambitions of successful careers and personal lives in the best interest of the whole society and not only to satisfy their greed, selfishness, and short-term speculative goals.

If our legislators and our regulatory authorities believe that just by assuring billions of dollars to avoid global economic collapse or by imposing new and stricter laws, policies, sanctions and controls on these ruthless and unethical senior executives will be sufficient to assure a new era of socially responsible leaders, then they are just heading for a very big disappointment or other speculative disasters to come. (Pezzuto, 2008)

Banks, investment funds, and financial institutions in general base their mission, reputation, corporate image and identity on their professional behaviors, transparency, reliability, solidity, competence, and integrity. "Trust" is the single word that should theoretically symbolize and summarize what a bank really means to customers, other financial institutions, and society as a whole (Pezzuto, 2008).

The solution to similar dramatic economic and social crises and the best prevention of new ones can be only assured by: (1) a true cultural and mindset change; (2) a new political and economic order; (3) a new approach to sustainability; (4) a return to integrity; (5) a real inspirational leadership; (6) "long-termism;" and (7) decisions based more on common sense, accountability, expertise, social responsibility, and prudential approaches. The laissez-faire Anglo–Saxon model of economic freedom with excessive liberalization of unregulated financial markets, lack of transparency and disclosure, excessive risk-taking, and high perverse incentives to top earners is seriously challenged these days.

One example of a serious lack in transparency in the financial markets has been reported by Bloomberg's article titled "Secret Fed Loans Gave Banks Undisclosed $13B" (Ivry et al., 2011).

This article stated the following:

The Fed didn't tell anyone which banks were in trouble so deep they required a combined $1.2 trillion on Dec. 5, 2008, their single neediest day. Bankers didn't mention that they took tens of billions of dollars in emergency loans at the same time they were assuring investors their firms were healthy. And no one calculated until now that banks reaped an estimated $13 billion of income by taking advantage of the Fed's below-market rates, Bloomberg Markets magazine reports in its January issue.

Saved by the bail-out, bankers lobbied against government regulations, a job made easier by the Fed, which never disclosed the details of the rescue to lawmakers even as Congress doled out more money and debated new rules aimed at preventing the next collapse.

A fresh narrative of the financial crisis of 2007 to 2009 emerges from 29,000 pages of Fed documents obtained under the Freedom of Information Act and central bank records of more than 21,000 transactions. While Fed officials say that almost all of the loans were repaid and there have been no losses, details suggest taxpayers paid a price beyond dollars as the secret funding helped preserve a broken status quo and enabled the biggest banks to grow even bigger.

Only if the G20 political leaders jointly reform what went wrong in the last decades will there again be a more resilient and sustainable open-market, properly regulated, served by a disciplined business environment for long-term prosperity. Otherwise, in the years to come, there will be more bubble-burst events and the leaders will continue to state that it is just the result of natural and unpredictable economic cycles.

The Answer to the First Main Question of this Book:
What are the Combined Factors That Have Contributed to Generate the 2007–2009 Financial Crisis?

The numerous evidences and analyses provided in this book seem to prove that there were many combined factors, not only related to chance or an unfortunate coincidence, which have contributed to generate the 2007–2009 financial crisis.

The Answer to Second Main Question of this Book:
Was the Financial Crisis Predictable and/or Avoidable?

The detailed analyses, figures, graphs, tables, and answers of most of the thought leaders lead to the conclusion that the 2007–2009 financial crisis was both predictable and predicted. For many it was also avoidable with proactive contingency plans and actions, or at least more controllable by sensible monetary and fiscal policy and more intelligent and proactive regulation of banks and other financial institutions. Thus, it can be concluded with reasonable accuracy that the hypothesis underlying the second main question has been proven.

The Answer to the Third Main Question of this Book:
What Changes Would be Necessary in Terms of Financial Reforms, Corporate Governance Models, Managerial Cultures, and Internal Controls and Enterprise Risk Management (ERM) Framework to Prevent other Systemic Crises in the Future?

There seems to be a general consensus on this third research question among the thought leaders' responses and leading scholars that the following initiatives might reduce the risks of future systemic crises:

- strengthening financial markets' infrastructures infrastructures and introducing an improved Glass-Steagall Act;
- increasing bank capital and liquidity requirements (Basel III) and limiting leverage ratios;

- developing much better systemic risk monitoring;
- employing more independent and accountable boards of directors;
- providing more funding for better regulatory supervision and more independent internal lines of reporting for risk management;
- developing effective transparency, disclosure, corporate social responsibility, and corporate citizenship in all financial firms;
- using the tools of economic policy to prevent a slump, fixing imbalances and structural deficiencies, and even downsizing or consolidating the banking system;
- making financial reforms and corporate governance practices simpler and more effective;
- investing more in business ethics education and socially responsible leadership.

Findings Related to Assumption 1

The findings of this book seem to prove assumption 1, which states:

a) The 2007–2009 credit crisis was predictable and proactively controllable given the available data, good "old" common sense, best practices, and solid credit and risk management practices, education, expertise, and an industry-wide perspective.

Dean Baker (Baker, 2002), Co-Director of the Center for Economic and Policy Research (CEPR), reported the existence of a housing bubble since August 2002, and stated that the housing bubble, the credit bubble, and the lax underwriting criteria of financial institutions were all correlated to one another and related to a potential serious financial disruption. He stated that, in the period 1953–1995, housing prices mirrored the inflation rate and that there was also no obvious explanation for the increase in home purchase prices relative to rental prices. He also indicated that after 1995 housing prices increased at a rate well above the inflation differential, thus demonstrating the existence of a housing bubble (Baker, 2002). In fact, in the period 1997–2006 there was a 124 percent increase in house values. He also reported that since 1995 home sales prices have increased nearly 30 percent more than the overall rate of inflation – the average ratio of equity to home values was near record lows and that the end of the housing bubble would lead to serious financial disruptions, since many families were already heavily indebted (Baker, 2002, p. 18). In fact, the household debt-to-income ratio (US household liabilities as a share of disposable income) reached a peak in 2007 at 138 percent. The analysis of Robert Shiller (2005, pp. 31–56) confirmed the same conclusion about the housing bubble and the consequent financial crisis.

Combining all these evidences with the simultaneous existence of a credit bubble, triggered by record low interest rates, massive capital inflow from surplus foreign countries, and aggressive predatory lending practices, along with a significantly higher lending concentration on the more profitable and risky lower-end segment of the market – the subprime borrowers (23.5 percent of the total US mortgage market in 2006), the probability of a potential financial meltdown in the coming years was not a just "tail-risk" event or a so-called "black swan," but rather just a very predictable analysis based on standard financial institutions' data and risk management expertise, common sense, risk management expertise, an industry-wide perspective, and some basic macroeconomic data.

Given these conditions, the only doubt for a number of scholars and industry experts who predicted the financial crisis before 2007 (such as Richard Posner, Simon Johnson, Joseph Stiglitz, Paul Krugman, Dean Baker, Nouriel Roubini, Robert Shiller, Raghuram Rajan, and others) was related to when the boom–burst scenario would actually happen, rather than whether it would occur.

According to these authors, all the complex and highly interrelated root causes and the early warnings of the financial crisis were on everybody's radar during the years leading up to the crisis, but unfortunately, they were systematically ignored by policy makers and regulators.

By combining all the elements together, it become very clear that the stated assumption is sound and that the financial crisis was both predictable and actually predicted by a number of authors before 2007. The only thing, as stated, that could not be fully determined was when the meltdown would actually occur. The denial of regulators and policy makers of the bubbles (housing and lending) only made things worse since they did not take serious and immediate action to effectively mitigate the systemic risk until the dramatic collapse of Lehman Brothers and its aftermath.

The findings reported in this book related to the stated assumption are based on an extensive literature review, on the personal insights and seasoned professional experience of the author of this book in the field of lending and risk management, and on the highly insightful contributions of the thought leaders who participated in the survey created for this research work.

Combining all the elements from these three sources, it becomes quite evident and undisputable that the financial crisis was predictable, predicted, and avoidable.

Among these findings, the following ones, combined together, provide a good set of early warning signals that might have helped to predict the financial crisis:

- the existence of a housing market bubble;
- the unrealistic expectations over the constant rising housing market value and the excessive borrowers' recourse to refinancing;
- the existence of a credit bubble;
- the significant increase of mortgage lending to the subprime market (high-risk areas/borrowers' profiles);
- deteriorating underwriting criteria (for example, decrease in collateral requirements, higher combined loan-to-value (CLTV) ratios, low or no downpayment, decrease in fraction loans with full documentation and verifications);
- the mispricing of risk of subprime mortgage loans – in fact, the spread between prime and subprime mortgages decreased in the years preceding the crisis, even though these loans originated to riskier borrowers' profiles, with lax screening criteria and limited documentation;
- the impressive increase in the household debt service ratio since 2002, also defined as "the ratio of debt payments to disposable personal income";
- the rapid increase in delinquency, default, and foreclosure rates (vintage analyses);
- the fast growth of non-recourse mortgage loans subject to OTD securitization (moral hazard) which, combined with the perverse and unprecedented executive and traders' compensation incentives, and limited or no regulatory oversight, created underlying conditions for the too-big-to-fail doctrine;

- the total compensation for major US banks and investment firms in 2007 was estimated at \$137 billion, driven by the massive use of stock options, which motivated financial firms to take on more risk and leverage;
- the rating agencies Standard and Poor's and Moody's earned as much as three times more for grading the most complex unregulated investment pools known as CDOs as they did from corporate bonds;
- the subprime loan securitization rate grew from less than 30 percent in 1995 to over 80 percent in 2006;
- portfolios that were more likely to be securitized had higher default rates than portfolios not subject to securitization. In fact, evidence has been found that increasing recourse to loan sale and asset securitization changed lender behavior and lending standards;
- staggering growth rate of the private-label residential mortgage-backed securities (RMBS) market in the period 2003–2007;
- in the three year period 2004–2006, the growth rate of CDO issuance was 656 percent in the US market and more than 5,700 percent in the European market. There was also a huge increase in loan syndications, and proprietary trading and investing;
- securitizers were to some extent aware of it, but a high house price appreciation in 2003–2005 masked the true riskiness of subprime mortgages (moral hazard);
- inadequate risk models (with development samples' data based on previous periods of rising house prices) and frequent manipulation of borrowers' data by predatory lenders;
- a sharp relative increase in mortgage debt-to-income ratios from 2001 to 2005;
- homeowners have been borrowing against equity in their homes at unprecedented rates;
- very low to negative borrowers' savings rates;
- the proliferation of many new and non-conventional mortgage products such as NINJA loans, interest-only loans, negative amortization loans, and so on;
- excessive reliance for securitization only on Fair Isaac and Company (FICO) scores;
- overstated and inflated incomes and collateral value appraisals;
- inconsistency between increasing average scores and riskier borrowers' profiles;
- in the period 2001–2006 the number of loans more than quadrupled, while the average loan size almost doubled, debt-to-income ratio and CLTV ratio increased, loan documentation decreased, borrowers' profiles worsened, but surprisingly in the same period, the average borrower's score increased;
- in the period 2001–2006, the quality of loans dramatically deteriorated as the underwriting criteria loosened;
- the Fed funds rate increase to 5.25 percent (2006) from 1 percent, given the high percentage of adjustable-mortgage rate (AMR) subprime mortgage loans, would easily represent a predictable early warning sign of worsening delinquency and foreclosure rates for a large number of subprime loans across the country;
- since 2006, the negative correlation between home price decline and delinquency rates and foreclosure rates increases;
- the early warning signs (initial quarters) of the vintage delinquent rates deterioration years after year since 2003;
- borrowers having negative equity in their houses had an incentive to default during adverse market conditions;

- the high loan-to-value (LTV) borrowers in 2006 are much riskier than those of 2001;
- the value of the Financial Obligation Ratio (FOR) has increased significantly since 2000, from 9.07 percent for 2000Q1 to 11.55 percent for 2008 due to mortgage debt payments, whereas the FOR of renters has declined over the same period of time;
- subprime mortgages are more sensitive to changes in house prices and to initial LTV ratio. The decline in house prices in 2005 was a trigger of the credit crisis;
- poor corporate governance and regulatory oversight, and large deregulation of financial markets;
- underestimation of the "tail-risk" events such as the national decline in house prices;
- Loeffler (2008) has demonstrated in his study that if banks had used a simple autoregressive model of housing prices (using the Office of Federal Housing Enterprise Oversight (OFHEO) index, which dates back to 1975), they would have been able to forecast housing price declines which ultimately would have alerted banks to the systemic risk in the housing market – the bubble–burst scenario (Loeffler, 2008, pp. 11–12);
- a clear sign of the incumbent credit crisis was evident in the initial three quarters of 2007 when the syndicated bank loan volume sharply declined by 20.53 percent;
- the shadow banking system, consisting of non-depository banks and other financial entities, grew dramatically after the year 2000 and played a critical role in the financial crisis;
- the massive increase of the derivatives market was an early warning sign since, in addition to expanding the highly volatile and unregulated shadow banking system with a high level of leverage, it was also hiding the advantage sought by many financial institutions to reduce the amount of the capital requirement needing to be held for their trading activities, through hedging with derivatives;
- as identified by the SEC, not enough disclosure was provided to investors to make their investment decisions;
- in 2007 Bear Stearns's leverage reached a ratio of 33 to one, meaning that if its assets fell by 3 percent the bank would be insolvent;
- investment banks and the so-called shadow banking sector were mainly outside of the Basel regime at the time of the crisis;
- a McClatchy investigation found that, even as the housing market was about to crumble, Moody's was forcing out executives who questioned the agency's high ratings of structured products and keeping in its compliance department people who supported their "generous" rating policy;
- an early warning sign of the crisis was also the apparent lack of correlation between the exponential growth of risky subprime MBS with rapidly rising delinquency rates and the relatively stable or declining CDO spreads before 2007;
- another early warning sign was represented by the spread between the Libor rate (interbank rates) and the overnight rates;
- another apparent lack of correlation was between the rapid growth of subprime mortgage loan delinquency rates and the relatively stable bank CDS rates/spreads before 2007;
- last but not least, the billions of dollars of law suits' expenses and fines paid by the leading financial institutions in the US and Europe since 2008 indicate that they certainly must have had some responsibility in the making of the 2007–2009 financial crisis.

As confirmed by Richard Posner (personal communication, 2012) in an interview with the author of this book, the financial crisis "was eminently avoidable, by sensible monetary and fiscal policy and more intelligent regulation of banks and other financial institutions."

The Financial Crisis Inquiry Commission (FCIC) in their final report (2011, p. xvii), after three years of investigation, stated the following which confirms the assumptions of hypothesis 1:

> We conclude this financial crisis was avoidable. This crisis was the result of human action and inaction, not of Mother Nature or computer models gone haywire. The captains of finance and the public stewards of our financial system ignored warnings and failed to question, understand, and manage evolving risks within a system essential to the well-being of the American public … Despite the expressed view of many on Wall Street and in Washington that the crisis could not have been foreseen or avoided, there were warning signs. The tragedy was that they were ignored or discounted.

The FCIC report (FCIC, 2011, xvii) also adds the following list of early warning signs that were ignored:

> There was an explosion in risky subprime lending and securitization, an unsustainable rise in housing prices, widespread reports of egregious and predatory lending practices, dramatic increases in household mortgage debt, and exponential growth in financial firms' trading activities, unregulated derivatives, and short-term "repo" lending markets, among many other red flags. Yet there was pervasive permissiveness; little meaningful action was taken to quell the threats in a timely manner.

L. Randall Wray (2010), Professor of Economics at the University of Missouri-Kansas City and Senior Scholar at the Levy Economics Institute of Bard College, said that the explanation for the financial and economic crisis that has gripped the world economy has shifted sharply from deregulation and lack of governmental oversight of financial institutions to fraud and criminal activity. According to him, the US Federal Bureau of Investigation began to warn of an "epidemic" of mortgage fraud back in 2004, and his colleague Bill Black has been pointing to the role played by fraud since the crisis began. He has stated that there was ample fraud in the "pump-and-dump" schemes during the dot-com bubble at the end of the 1990s, which was closely followed by the commodities market speculative boom and bust. And before those episodes we had in quick succession the developing country debt crisis of the early 1980s, the US Saving and Loan fiasco of the mid 1980s (with bank crises in many other nations), the Japanese meltdown and the Asian crisis, the Mexican peso crisis, Long Term Capital Management and Russian default, and the Enron affair (Randall Wray, 2010).

He also stated the following:

> The age of what Minsky called "money manager capitalism" had arrived – a form that put finance first. And, importantly, this new capitalism took a global form – a new globalization of finance developed. Again for complex reasons, the interests of money managers did not coincide with those of Big Corporations and Big Unions – the "leveraged buy-out" was used to strip firms of assets, load them with debt, and bust their unions. Wages stopped growing; consumers relied

on debt to maintain living standards. Globalized finance also helped to globalize production – with low wage workers in developing nations helping to depress incomes in developed nations. Thus, "financialization" of the economies concurrently meant both "globalization" as well as rising inequality. (Randall Wray, 2010)

The weight of finance moved away from institutions – that were guided by a culture of developing relations with customers – toward "markets" (the OTD model of securitizing pools of mortgages is a good example). This virtually eliminated underwriting (assessing credit worthiness of customers) and also favored the "short view" (immediate profits) of traders (you are only as good as your last trade) over the long view of financial institutions that hold loans. In addition, the philosophy of "maximization of total shareholder returns" as well as the transition away from partnerships in investment banking toward public holdings promoted pump and dump schemes to increase the value of stock options that rewarded CEOs and traders. A "trader mentality" triumphed that encouraged practices based on the "zero sum" approach: in every trade there is a winner and a loser. As practiced, the bank would be the winner and the customer would be duped (Randall Wray, 2010).

This transformation helps to explain why fraud became rampant as normal business practice. Competition among traders and top management to beat average returns led to ever-lower underwriting standards to increase the volume of trades – with fees booked on each one – and with strong incentives to "cook the books" (record false accounting profits). Once accounting fraud is underway, there is a strong incentive to engage in ever more audacious fraud to cover the previous crimes. In the end, the US financial system (and perhaps many others) became nothing but a massive criminal conspiracy to defraud borrowers (through such instruments as "liar's loans," NINJAS – no income, no job, no assets, no problem! – and "no-doc" loans) as well as investors in securitized products (MBS, CDOs that were securities of the worst MBS, and on to CDOs squared and cubed). All of this led to layering and leveraging of debt on debt and debt on income. At the peak, US indebtedness was five times its national income – meaning each dollar of income was pre-committed to service five dollars of debt! This was, of course, impossible. The pyramid of debt collapsed like a house of cards (Randall Wray, 2010).

Findings Related to Assumption 2

The findings of this book seem to prove assumption 2, which states:

> *b) The 2007–2009 credit crisis was a major systemic failure of banks' risk management units and corporate governance, credit rating agencies, investment firms, and banking and financial markets' oversight bodies, and regulatory authorities.*

Multiple evidences reported in this book unquestionably prove a major failure in proper and timely risk assessment and oversight of many financial institutions' risk management, internal control, and corporate governance bodies, as well as external organizations such as risk model vendors, securitizers, rating agencies, independent auditing firms, and regulatory bodies, directly or indirectly involved in the 2007–2009 financial crisis.

The entire book provides plenty of evidences supporting the hypothesis of a major failure of the risk management departments of many financial institutions as a significant driver of the subprime mortgage loans crisis. Given the current available information, however, it is difficult to determine today whether such failure was result of:

a) simply poor risk management performance due to lack of know-how, inadequate risk models, or bad assumptions in their scenario analyses;
b) the consequence of high pressures of financial firms' corporate governance on risk management to drastically lax underwriting and risk control criteria;
c) a combination of the previous two situations;
d) a deliberate choice to relax credit criteria of both risk management and top management to pursue short-term profitability and unprecedented compensation and incentives rewards regardless of excessive risk-taking.

Given the available data today, it is not possible to provide a definite answer to this question; however, it is certainly proved by the analyses reported in this book that a major failure did occur in financial firms' risk management, audit, internal controls, and corporate governance which has led to the financial crisis.

In spite of the fact that today it cannot be proved with absolute certainly if one or more of these players were actually responsible for this dramatic failure, the extensive and fact-based evidences reported in this work provide a sufficient number of observations that may lead to reasonable deductive conclusions. These conclusions are:

If condition (a) is correct then the notion must be accepted that many financial firms' risk management departments in the US and in a number of other countries simultaneously failed in their practices for a number of years, even though they were supposed to have different policies, procedures, risk appetite preferences, corporate strategies, mission, vision, corporate cultures, internal controls, due diligence processes, and risk management expertise. Even people who do not have experience in banking and finance imagine this being practically impossible, given the level of expertise in the industry, the available state-of-the-art technologies, and shared best practices on a global scale industry-wide. Furthermore, as reported by many top bankers involved in the crisis to the FCIC, many key players in the industry were mirroring each other's strategy and reckless approaches taking excessive risk, with excessive leverage, with perverse financial incentives and poor controls. Any risk manager would easily predict that if all players are "gambling with risk" simultaneously and there is limited to no real regulatory oversight, the systemic risk or "tail-risk" event or "black swan" is not a remote probability but rather a self-fulfilling prophecy. Mirroring each other's strategy means that these players actually knew what the other was doing and thus they could easily suspect the high probability of a systemic failure in the industry. This explains the too-big-to-fail (TBTF) doctrine assumption.

The conditions (b and d) reported above are both reliable potential explanations of the financial crisis, based on the fact-based analyses reported in this book, which prove that there was a major failure in risk management, audit, internal control, and corporate governance of many financial institutions and of the poor regulatory oversight.

The condition (c), although possible, seems to be unlikely since it is based on the assumption that many if not all risk managers in the industry had inadequate know-how and strategic insight to understand what was really happening in the market which prevented them from raising warning signs (directly or indirectly) to management or regulatory authorities, unless of course they knew that regulatory authorities were fully aware of the issue but would not stop "the game."

The fact-based elements that prove the stated assumption (that is, there were early warning signs and that the financial crisis was both predictable and avoidable) also proves, as a result of cause and effect relationship, the underlying second assumption, in the sense that there was a major failure not to identify and report these risks by financial institutions' risk management, audit and internal control, corporate governance, credit rating agencies, and regulatory oversight.

The FCIC in their final report (2011), after three years of investigation, stated the following which confirms the second assumption:

> *We conclude dramatic failures of corporate governance and risk management at many systemically financial institutions were a key cause of this crisis. There was a view that instincts for self-preservation inside major financial firms would shield them from fatal risk-taking without the need for a steady regulatory hand, which, the firms argued, would stifle innovation. Too many of these institutions acted recklessly, taking on too much risk, with too little capital, and with too much dependence on short-term funding ... Financial institutions and credit rating agencies embraced mathematical models as reliable predictors of risk, replacing judgment in too many instances. Too often, risk management became risk justification. (FCIC, 2011, pp. xviii–xix)*

The FCIC (2011) has also stated the following:

> *We conclude that the failures of credit rating agencies were essential cogs in the wheel of financial destruction. The three rating agencies were key enablers of the financial meltdown. The mortgage-related securities at the heart of the crisis could not have been marked and sold without their seal of approval. Investors relied on them, often blindly. In some cases, they were obliged to use them, or regulatory capital standards were hinged on them. This crisis could not have happened without the rating agencies. Their ratings helped the market soar and their down-grades through 2007 and 2008 wreaked havoc across markets and firms ... The result was disastrous: 83 percent of the mortgage securities rated triple-A that year ultimately were downgraded. (FCIC, 2011, p. xxv)*

Findings Related to Assumption 3

The findings of this book seem to prove assumption 3, which states:

> *c) Time and resources available to policy makers and regulators have not always been used in the most effective way to solve the problems generated by the financial crisis and in some cases (Dodd–Frank in the home lending arena and the repeal of the Glass–Steagall Act) may well have precipitated and prolonged the crisis.*

Multiple evidences reported in this book indicate that the impact of progressive deregulation and/or no-regulation of the financial firms' industry since the 1980s in the US and in other countries has significantly contributed to create the opaque market conditions that favored the financial crisis.

For example, a number of laws and reforms in the US since the 1980s contributed to create a less regulated and controlled banking environment such as the Depository Institutions Deregulation and Monetary Control Act (DIDMCA) of 1980, the Alternative Mortgage Transaction Parity Act (AMTPA) in 1982, the Tax Reform of 1986, the 1991 Federal Deposit Insurance Corporate Improvement Act (FDICIA), the "New Bankruptcy Law" or The Bankruptcy Abuse Prevention and Consumer Protection Act of 2005 (BAPCPA), and in particular the repeal in 1999 of the Glass–Steagall Act, which has fostered the role of the banks in the development of the subprime mortgage market.

Numerous evidences reported in this book prove that time and resources available to policy makers and regulators have not always been used in the most effective way to solve the problems generated by the financial crisis and they might have prolonged the crisis.

On this topic, the FCIC (2011) indicated in their final report the following:

> We conclude the government was ill prepared for the crisis, and its inconsistent response added to the uncertainty and panic in the financial markets … Key policy makers – the Treasury Department, the Federal Reserve Board, and the Federal Reserve Bank of New York – who were best positioned to watch over our markets were ill prepared for the events of 2007 and 2008 … They thought risk had been diversified when, in fact, it had been concentrated … From the spring of 2007 on, policy makers and regulators were caught off guard as the contagion spread, responding on an ad hoc basis with specific programs to put fingers in the dike. There was not comprehensive and strategic plan for containment, because they lacked a full understanding of the risks and interconnections in the financial markets. Some regulators have conceded this error. We had allowed the system to race ahead of our ability to protect it. When Bear Stearns's hedge funds, which were heavily invested in mortgage-related securities, imploded in June 2007, the Federal Reserve discussed the implications of the collapse. Despite the fact that so many other funds were exposed to the same risks as those hedge funds, the Bear Stearns funds were thought to be "relatively unique." Days before the collapse of Bear Stearns in March 2008, SEC Chairman Christopher Cox expressed "comfort about the capital cushion" at the big investment banks. It was not until August 2008, just weeks before the government takeover of Fannie Mae and Freddie Mac, that the Treasury Department understood the measure of the dire financial conditions of those two institutions. And just a month before Lehman's collapse, the Federal Reserve Bank of New York was still seeking information on the exposures created by Lehman's more than 900,000 derivatives contracts. In addition, the government's inconsistent handling of major financial institutions during the crisis – the decision to rescue Bear Stearns and then to place Fannie Mae and Freddie Mac into conservatorship, followed by its decision not to save Lehman Brothers and then to save AIG – increased uncertainty and panic in the market. The FCIC also indicated that the prime example of pivotal failure is the Federal Reserve since it could have immediately set more prudent mortgage-lending standards. The FCIC stated that their record of examination is replete with evidence of failures. According to these records, financial institutions made, bought, and sold mortgage securities they never examined, did not care to examine, or knew to be defective. (FCIC, 2011, pp. xxi–xxiii)

As stated by Richard Posner (personal communication, 2011) in an interview with myself:

> The disastrous decision was to allow Lehman Brothers to collapse. As soon as it became evident (probably by November 2008) that the financial crisis had precipitated a downward spiral in the economy comparable to that of the Great Depression of the 1930s, a large stimulus (deficit-

spending) program of public works and assistance to states (in excess of $1 trillion) should have been instituted immediately, with insistence on prompt expenditure.

Darrel Duffie (personal communication, 2012) said that it probably would have been wise to immediately eliminate a large fraction of the principal due on all residential mortgage debt currently in default (and only the mortgages already in default). The government or banks would have paid a massive amount to do this, but it would have helped. It would have also been wise to re-write the mortgage servicing agreement so as to better encourage the restructuring of mortgages yet to default.

Even regarding the banking reform (Dodd–Frank Act), introduced after the financial crisis, a large number of reputable authors and scholars and many of the thought leaders who participated in my survey reported that these new rules came too late, are too complicated, are not detailed or specific enough, and do not address all the relevant problems that caused the financial crisis, thus do not effectively prevent new crises from happening again. Improvements, such as the ones recommended in this book on corporate governance, should be made to these regulations and to their effective implementation to assure a more resilient solid and financial stability environment.

For example Johnson and Kwak, (2010a) and Aswarth Damodaran (personal communication, 2012), have recommended to separate commercial banking (where the government does provide a backstop with deposit insurance) from proprietary trading and investing to avoid the too-big-to fail doctrine. According to them the Volcker Rule (included in the Dodd–Frank Act) does not fully and comprehensively address this issue (Johnson and Kwak, 2010a, pp. 205–213). Thus, it has been proved that these rules have not been implemented as fast and effectively as was necessary. Furthermore, as demonstrated by many evidences in this book and by the economic news of the last three years, many of the systemic risks related to the highly unregulated and uncontrolled shadow banking and OTC derivatives markets are still a potential threat to the markets since they have not been properly addressed by policy makers and regulators.

Findings Related to Assumption 4

The findings of this book seem to prove assumption 4, which states:

d) Greed and conflicts of interest of many stakeholders have significantly contributed to generate the crisis and to avoid, after the bail-out, the introduction of adequate structural reforms for the industry.

The first evidence in this matter comes directly from the US Government. In the final report based on their three-year investigation activity, the so-called FCIC (FCIC, 2011, pp. xxii–xxiii), clearly stated the following:

We conclude there was a systemic breakdown in accountability and ethics … Unfortunately – as has been the case in past speculative booms and bursts – we have witnessed an erosion of standards of responsibility and ethics that exacerbated the financial crisis. This was not universal, but these breaches stretched from the ground level to the corporate suites. They resulted not only in significant financial consequences but also in damage to the trust of investors, businesses, and the public in the financial system.

The report catalogues the rising incidence of mortgage fraud, which flourished in an environment of collapsing lending standards and lax regulation. The number of suspicious activity reports – reports of possible financial crime filed by depository banks and their affiliates – related to mortgage fraud grew 20-fold between 1996 and 2005 and then more than doubled again between 2005 and 2009. One study places the losses resulting from fraud on mortgage loans made between 2005 and 2007 at $112 billion. (FCIC, 2011, p. xxii)

Lenders made loans that they knew borrowers could not afford and that could cause massive losses to investors in mortgage securities. The Commission's review of many prospectuses provided to investors found that it was not disclosed to them significant information on the poor underwriting standards applied by mortgage originators ... These conclusion must be viewed in the context of human nature and individual and societal responsibility. First, we need to pin this crisis on mortal flaws like greed hubris ... Second, we clearly believe this crisis was a result of human mistakes, misjudgments, and misdeeds that resulted in systemic failures for which our nation has paid dearly. As you read this report, you will see that specific firms and individuals acted irresponsibly. Yet a crisis of this magnitude cannot be the work of a few bad actors, and such was not the case here. At the same time, the breadth of this crisis does not mean that "everyone is at fault;" many firms and individuals did not participate in the excesses that spawned disaster. (FCIC, 2011, pp. xxii–xxiii)

As reported by Robert Kolb (2010) and others, many industry players had perverse short-term incentives to neglect the existence of a housing market bubble and lending bubble and the risk of a potential systemic crisis. Among these there were many mortgage brokers, mortgage originators, banks, risk managements, auditors, credit rating agencies, securitizers, members of banks and hedge funds corporate governance, due diligence reviewers, regulatory authorities and examiners (Kolb, 2010, pp. 209–215).

Numerous authors reported the assumption that greed and conflicts of interest of many stakeholders involved in the subprime MBS process have significantly contributed to generate the 2007–2009 financial crisis. Some of the most important contributions on this hypothesis are present in the book and publications of Nobel Laureate, Joseph E. Stiglitz, Nobel Laureate Paul Krugman, MIT economist Simon Johnson, Judge and University of Chicago Law School Professor Richard Posner and many others, including also some of the thought leaders who participated in this book's survey.

Concluding a two-year bipartisan investigation, Senator Carl Levin, D-Mich. and Senator Tom Coburn M.D., R-Okla., Chairman and Ranking Republican on the Senate Permanent Subcommittee on Investigations, released on April 13, 2011 a 635-page final report on their inquiry into the key causes of the financial crisis. The report catalogs conflicts of interest, heedless risk-taking, and failures of federal oversight that helped push the country into the deepest recession since the Great Depression (Levin, 2011a).

Using emails, memos, and other internal documents, this report tells the inside story of an economic assault that cost millions of Americans their jobs and homes, while wiping out investors, good businesses, and markets. High-risk lending, regulatory failures, inflated credit ratings, and Wall Street firms engaging in massive conflicts of interest contaminated the US financial system with toxic mortgages and undermined public trust in US markets. Using their own words in documents subpoenaed by the Subcommittee, the report discloses how financial firms deliberately took advantage of their clients and investors, how credit rating agencies assigned AAA ratings to high-risk securities, and how regulators sat on their hands instead of reining in the unsafe and unsound practices all around them. Rampant conflicts of interest are the threads that run through every chapter of this sordid story (Levin, 2011a).

"The free market has helped make America great, but it only functions when people deal with each other honestly and transparently. At the heart of the financial crisis were unresolved, and often undisclosed, conflicts of interest," said Dr Coburn. "Blame for this mess lies everywhere from federal regulators who cast a blind eye, Wall Street bankers who let greed run wild, and members of Congress who failed to provide oversight" (Levin, 2011a).

The Levin–Coburn report expands on evidence gathered at four Subcommittee hearings in April 2010, examining four aspects of the crisis through detailed case studies: high-risk mortgage lending, using the case of Washington Mutual Bank, a $300 billion thrift that became the largest bank failure in US history; regulatory inaction, focusing on the Office of Thrift Supervision's failed oversight of Washington Mutual; inflated credit ratings that misled investors, examining the actions of the nation's two largest credit rating agencies, Moody's and Standard and Poor's; and the role played by investment banks, focusing primarily on Goldman Sachs, creating and selling structured finance products that foisted billions of dollars of losses on investors, while the bank itself profited from betting against the mortgage market (Levin, 2011a).

New Evidence: Today's report presents new facts, new findings, and recommendations, with more than 700 new documents totaling over 5,800 pages. It recounts how Washington Mutual aggressively issued and sold high-risk mortgages to Wall Street, Fannie Mae, and Freddie Mac, even as its executives predicted a housing bubble that would burst, and offers new detail about how its regulator deferred to the bank's management. New documents show how Goldman used net short positions to benefit from the downturn in the mortgage market, and designed, marketed, and sold CDOs in ways that created conflicts of interest with the firm's clients and at times led to the bank's profiting from the same products that caused substantial losses for its clients. Other new information provides additional detail about how credit rating agencies rushed to rate new MBS and collect lucrative rating fees before issuing mass ratings downgrades that shocked the financial markets and triggered a collapse in the value of mortgage-related securities. Over 120 new documents provide insights into how Deutsche Bank contributed to the mortgage mess (Levin, 2011a).

"Our investigation found a financial snake pit rife with greed, conflicts of interest, and wrongdoing," said Levin (Levin, 2011a).

Among the report's highlights are the following:

- High-risk Lending. With an eye on short-term profits, Washington Mutual (WaMu) launched a strategy of high-risk mortgage lending in early 2005, even as the bank's own top executives stated that the condition of the housing market "signifies a bubble" with risks that "will come back to haunt us." Executives forged ahead despite repeated warnings from inside and outside the bank that the risks were excessive, its lending standards and risk management systems were deficient, and many of its loans were tainted by fraud or prone to early default. WaMu's chief credit officer complained at one point that "any attempts to enforce a more disciplined underwriting approach were continuously thwarted by an aggressive, and often times abusive group of sales employees within the organization." From 2003 to 2006, WaMu shifted its loan originations from low-risk, fixed-rate mortgages, which fell from 64 percent to 25 percent of its loan originations, to high-risk loans, which jumped from 19 percent to 55 percent of its originations. WaMu and its subprime lender, Long Beach Mortgage, securitized hundreds of billions of dollars in high-risk, poor quality, sometimes fraudulent mortgages, at times without full disclosure to investors, weakening US financial markets. New analysis shows how WaMu sold some of its high-risk loans to Fannie Mae and Freddie Mac, and played one off the other to make more money.

- Regulatory Failures. The Office of Thrift Supervision (OTS), WaMu's primary regulator, repeatedly failed to correct WaMu's unsafe and unsound lending practices, despite logging nearly 500 serious deficiencies at the bank over five years, from 2003 to 2008. New information details the regulator's deference to bank management and how it used the bank's short-term profits to excuse high-risk activities. Although WaMu recorded increasing problems from its high-risk loans, including delinquencies that doubled year after year in its risky option ARM portfolio, OTS examiners failed to clamp down on WaMu's high-risk lending. OTS did not even consider bringing an enforcement action against the bank until it began losing substantial sums in 2008. OTS also failed, until 2008, to lower the bank's overall high rating or the rating awarded to WaMu's management, despite the bank's ongoing failure to correct serious deficiencies. When the FDIC advocated taking tougher action, OTS officials not only refused, but impeded FDIC oversight of the bank. When the New York State Attorney-General sued two appraisal firms for colluding with WaMu to inflate property values, OTS took nearly a year to conduct its own investigation and finally recommended taking action – a week after the bank had failed. The OTS Director treated WaMu, which was its largest thrift and supplied 15 percent of the agency's budget, as a "constituent" and struck an apologetic tone when informing WaMu's CEO of its decision to take an enforcement action. When diligent oversight conflicted with OTS officials' desire to protect their "constituent" and the agency's own turf, they ignored their oversight responsibilities.
- On December 13, 2011 the *Financial Times* reported that three former WaMU executives (Kerry Killinger, ex-Chief Executive of WaMu, Stephen Rotella, former Chief Operating Officer, and David Schneider, the ex-Home Loans PPresident) agreed to a $64m settlement with the FDIC over their role in the biggest bank collapse in US history (Braithwaite, 2011).
- The $64 million includes cash, payments from the directors' liability insurance and surrender of bankruptcy claims for "golden parachutes," bonuses, and retirement plans. One person familiar with the terms of the agreement said the executives would end up paying a relatively small amount as their insurance pay-out would cover the "bulk" of the "inflated" headline sum (Braithwaite, 2011).
- Carl Levin, a Democratic senator, said the deal showed "again how bank executives can beat the system." He said the WaMu trio "got bonus upon bonus when the bank did well, but when they led the bank to collapse, insurance and indemnity clauses shielded them from paying any penalty for their wrongdoing" (Braithwaite, 2011).
- Inflated Credit Ratings. The Report concludes that the most immediate cause of the financial crisis was the July 2007 mass ratings downgrades by Moody's and Standard and Poor's that exposed the risky nature of mortgage-related investments that, just months before, the same firms had deemed to be as safe as Treasury bills. The result was a collapse in the value of mortgage-related securities that devastated investors.

Internal emails show that credit rating agency personnel knew their ratings would not "hold" and delayed imposing tougher ratings criteria to "massage the ... numbers to preserve market share." Even after they finally adjusted their risk models to reflect the higher-risk mortgages being issued, the firms often failed to apply the revised models to existing securities, and helped investment banks rush risky investments to market before tougher rating criteria took effect. They also continued to pull in lucrative fees of up to $135,000 to rate a MBS and up to $750,000 to rate a CDO – fees that might have been lost if they angered issuers by providing lower ratings. The mass rating downgrades they finally initiated were not an effort to come clean, but were necessitated by skyrocketing mortgage delinquencies and securities plummeting in value. In the end, over 90 percent of the AAA ratings given to MBS in 2006 and 2007 were downgraded to junk status, including 75 out of 75 AAA-rated Long Beach securities issued in 2006. When sound credit ratings conflicted with collecting profitable fees, credit rating agencies chose the fees (Levin, 2011a).

- Investment Banks and Structured Finance. Investment banks reviewed by the Subcommittee assembled and sold billions of dollars in mortgage-related investments that flooded financial markets with high-risk assets. They charged $1 to $8 million in fees to construct, underwrite, and market a MBS, and $5 to $10 million per CDO. New documents detail how Deutsche Bank helped assembled a $1.1 billion CDO known as Gemstone 7, stood by as it was filled it with low-quality assets that its top CDO trader referred to as "crap" and "pigs," and rushed to sell it "before the market falls off a cliff." Deutsche Bank lost $4.5 billion when the mortgage market collapsed, but would have lost even more if it had not cut its losses by selling CDOs like Gemstone. When Goldman Sachs realized the mortgage market was in decline, it took actions to profit from that decline at the expense of its clients. New documents detail how, in 2007, Goldman's Structured Products Group twice amassed and profited from large net short positions in mortgage-related securities. At the same time the firm was betting against the mortgage market as a whole, Goldman assembled and aggressively marketed to its clients poor quality CDOs that it actively bet against by taking large short positions in those transactions. New documents and information detail how Goldman recommended four CDOs, Hudson, Anderson, Timberwolf, and Abacus, to its clients without fully disclosing key information about those products, Goldman's own market views, or its adverse economic interests. For example, in Hudson, Goldman told investors that its interests were "aligned" with theirs when, in fact, Goldman held 100 percent of the short side of the CDO and had adverse interests to the investors, and described Hudson's assets as "sourced from the Street," when in fact, Goldman had selected and priced the assets without any third-party involvement. New documents also reveal that, at one point in May 2007, Goldman Sachs unsuccessfully tried to execute a "short squeeze" in the mortgage market so that Goldman could scoop up short positions at artificially depressed prices and profit as the mortgage market declined (Levin, 2011a).
- Recommendations. The Report offers 19 recommendations to address the conflicts of interest and abuses it exposed. The recommendations advocate, for example, strong implementation of the new restrictions on proprietary trading and conflicts of interest; and action by the SEC to rank credit rating agencies according to the accuracy of their ratings. Other recommendations seek to advance low-risk mortgages, greater transparency in the marketplace, and more protective capital, liquidity, and loss reserves (Levin, 2011a).

Luigi Zingales, Robert C. McCormack Professor of Entrepreneurship and Finance of the University of Chicago Booth School of Business, in his paper titled "Capitalism After the Crisis" (2009), reports that:

> The enormous profitability allowed the (financial) industry to spend disproportionate amounts of money lobbying the political system. In the last 20 years, the financial industry has made $2.2 billion in political contributions, more than any other industry tracked by the Center for Responsive Politics. And over the last ten years, the financial industry topped the lobbying-expenses list, spending $3.5 billion. (Zingales, 2009)

He also added:

> The explosion of wages and profits in finance also naturally attracted the best talents – with implications that extended beyond the financial sector, and deep into government. Thirty years ago, the brightest undergraduates were going into science, technology, law, and business; for the last 20 years, they have gone to finance. Having devoted themselves to this sector, these talented individuals inevitably end up working to advance its interests: A person specialized in derivative trading is likely to be terribly impressed with the importance and value of derivatives, just as a nuclear engineer is likely to think nuclear power can solve all the world's problems. (Zingales, 2009)

Thus, according to Zingales (2009) and to Arjoon (2010), combining the brightest talents in finance, with disproportionate greed, ambition, narcissistic behavior, short-termism, and lax regulation, resulted in the explosive impact of the 2007–2009 financial crisis (Zingales, 2009; Arjoon, 2010, pp. 59–82).

The hypothesis of Greed, Moral Meltdown and Public Policy Disasters as the root cause of the 2007–2009 financial crisis and the need for good regulation have also been confirmed by Wargo et al. (2009, pp. 1–22).

Almost five years after the 2007 – 2009 financial crisis even in Europe, real reforms of the financial sector (aside from the European Market Infrastructure Regulation – EMIR, Capital Requirements Directive IV/Basel III Framework, and the Single Supervisory Mechanism of the European banking system) struggle to be implemented due also to the lobbying pressure of the financial industry which has warned (in particular in the UK) regulators and policy makers that in case of tougher rules they will relocate their operations to other countries or they will reduce lending to SMEs. For example, in March 2011, Britain's biggest bank HSBC revealed it relocated its headquarters from London to Hong Kong due to the increase in financial regulations (Armitstead, 2011).

In the UK and other European countries, banks have firmly opposed the introduction of more regulation and the Tobin tax on financial transactions since they argue it could stifle growth and damage the financial centers (in the UK it would cost £25.5 billion, job losses, and it would wipe out the City's derivative markets) (Treanor, 2011; Hobson, 2011). The Tobin tax needs to be harmonized globally in the financial markets otherwise it will encourage regulatory arbitrages (financial firms capitalize on loopholes in regulatory systems in order to circumvent unfavorable regulation). Furthermore, if the Tobin tax remains implemented only in a few countries will result ineffective and thus ultimately it will be watered down by banking lobbies.

The Tobin tax should not be applied on all financial transactions but only on risky ones to avoid speculation (transactions for "real" hedging purposes should not be penalized by the Tobin tax).

Another example is the strong opposition of European banks to new banking regulation that occurred toward the end of 2011. Banks opposed the introduction of the Basel III capital requirements framework and the EBA's recommendations on bank's capital increase to prevent new banking crises, new potential risks related to the sovereign debt crisis, and its potential contagion aftermath.

In December 2011, the UK Financial Services Authority (FSA) reported to have undertaken an investigation to prevent banks from deliberately understating the risks on their balance sheets to boost their capital position. Most big lenders use internal models to calculate risk-weighted assets (RWA) and to calculate the core tier one capital ratio, which is the key measure of bank safety. Banks with fewer RWAs have higher ratios and have to hold less capital. Bankers expect to have to hold more capital against their real estate portfolios. As the Basel III framework will probably require banks to hold more capital over the next five years (since 2013) to comply with the forthcoming regulations on capital and leverage ratios, banks are likely to respond to this challenge by either generating additional credit crunch and deleveraging (that is charging more for loans and/or cutting back lending to small and medium size enterprises) or they might be tempted to deliberately make internal risk models less robust in order to avoid recapitalizations, or even they might put a "tremendous pressure" on politicians, senior officials, and regulators to reduce the burden for smaller banks requesting to "soften" the Basel III rules for these banks. Since according to a number of analysts there are still a lot of bad loans in the banks' balance sheets (and probably even some "zombie" banks around which should be shut down in an orderly manner) and not enough capital to write down those loans, Eurozone banks will either request to soften the regulatory frameworks due to the still uncertain economic environment, or they will further shrink their balance sheets, or alternatively they may need to lobby more aggressively in order to receive governments' support or the support of the European banking union – Eurozone bank resolution mechanism (when available), or both, in order to clean-up their balance sheets (toxic assets) and to be recapitalized. The FSA has told some banks to make their models for commercial property more robust by ensuring they include recent losses, or switch to the more standardized higher-risk weights (Masters and Hammond, 2011).

To conclude on the confirmation of the bankers' greed and moral hazard hypothesis, it is worthwhile to report the findings of the FSA report on the failure of the Royal Bank of Scotland (RBS) during the 2007–2009 financial crisis (Jenkins et al., 2011).

The findings of this near 500-page report clearly indicate the bank's management and regulatory failings that brought about RBS's collapse following its takeover of Dutch rival ABN Amro. The failure of RBS in 2008 precipitated a £45bn Government rescue. FSA Chairman Lord Turner said that the bank had a weak capital position, an over-reliance on short-term funding, and "underlying deficiencies in RBS management, governance and culture which made it prone to make poor decisions" (Jenkins et al., 2011).

The Report condemns the FSA's "flawed supervisory approach which failed adequately to challenge the judgment and risk assessments of the management of RBS" (Jenkins et al., 2011).

Lord Turner said that the law should be changed to allow the directors of failed banks to be automatically banned, fined, and stripped of their remuneration (Jenkins et al., 2011).

Findings Related to Assumption 5

The findings of this book seem to prove assumption 5, which states:

e) Unregulated shadow banking practices and complex innovative OTC financial engineering transactions still continue to threaten the global financial markets for new potential risky arbitrages, bubbles, and crises.

The book provides many examples and contributions that prove and confirm the hypothesis that, although a number of improvements have been introduced with the Dodd–Frank Act, a lot still remains to be done in order to prevent and avoid future financial crises due to the unregulated shadow banking practices and complex innovative OTC financial engineering transactions.

Zingales (2011), among many other authors, has clearly stated that much of the shadow banking industry has not yet been regulated by the Dodd–Frank Act, thus allowing for the buildup of new systemic risky conditions that may lead to similar or even worse crises in the future (Zingales, 2011).

As reported by all the contributors of this book, the bulk of the root causes of the 2007–2009 financial crisis (the shadow banking sector) have not yet been really addressed by the new financial reforms as a result of the powerful and influential global banking and investment funds lobbies.

This remains a key open issue in need of a prompt political solution otherwise the new complex and over-articulated financial reforms recently introduced will only address the less critical symptoms of the 2007–2009 financial crisis, while the the real and most severe underlying causes remain unaddressed.

According to Randall Wray (2010), the new financial reforms' austerity policies to reduce spending and where possible to raise taxes adopted by governments in most nations are unlikely to prove effective and might ultimately even increase the probability of another crash or of even deeper downturns (Randall Wray, 2010).

Findings Related to Assumption 6

The findings of this book seem to prove assumption 6, which states:

f) New corporate governance frameworks, new effective reforms, and new sets of values and accountability principles need to be introduced in the financial industry in order to drastically turn the raiders' culture that has led the dramatic crisis into a new socially responsible and sustainable culture in the financial markets.

In addition to the evidences reported by the extensive literature review that confirm this hypothesis, and to the responses of the thought leaders' survey, one recent and additional confirmation on this hypothesis came in April 2011 from the US Senate Permanent Subcommittee on Investigation Chairman, Carl Levin, who said that the crisis could have been averted if Dodd–Frank had been enacted earlier. The US Senate Permanent Subcommittee on Investigation found four overall causes of the crisis – high–risk lending, regulatory failures, inflated credit ratings, and investment bank abuses – and listed 19 bipartisan recommendations for averting future meltdowns (Knutson, 2011).

Thus, this demonstrates that the last assumption is correct in the sense that new reforms, new rules, and new corporate governance models are necessary to prevent new crises in the future.

The US Senate Permanent Subcommittee on Investigation has confirmed the last assumption recommending the following regulatory improvements to avoid new crises in the future (Levin, 2011b, pp. 12–14):

- ensure that "qualified mortgages" are low risk (federal regulators should use their regulatory authority to ensure that all mortgages deemed to be "qualified residential mortgages" have a low risk of delinquency or default);
- require meaningful risk retention (federal regulators should issue a strong risk retention requirement under Section 941 by requiring the retention of not less than a 5 percent credit risk in each, or a representative sample of, an asset-backed securitization's tranches, and by barring a hedging offset for a reasonable but limited period of time);
- safeguard against high-risk products (federal banking regulators should safeguard taxpayer dollars by requiring banks with high-risk structured finance products, including complex products with little or no reliable performance data, to meet conservative loss reserve, liquidity, and capital requirements);
- require greater reserves for negative amortization loans (federal banking regulators should use their regulatory authority to require banks issuing negatively amortizing loans, that allow borrowers to defer payments of interest and principal, to maintain more conservative loss, liquidity, and capital reserves);
- safeguard bank investment portfolios (federal banking regulators should use the Section 620 banking activities study to identify high-risk structured finance products and impose a reasonable limit on the amount of such high-risk products that can be included in a bank's investment portfolio);
- complete OTS dismantling (the Office of the Comptroller of the Currency (OCC) should complete the dismantling of the OTS, despite attempts by some OTS officials to preserve the agency's identity and influence within the OCC);
- strengthen enforcement (federal banking regulators should conduct a review of their major financial institutions to identify those with ongoing, serious deficiencies, and review their enforcement approach to those institutions to eliminate any policy of deference to bank management, inflated capital adequacy, asset quality, management, earnings, liquidity, and sensitivity to market risk (CAMELS) ratings, or use of short-term profits to excuse high-risk activities);
- strengthen CAMELS Ratings (federal banking regulators should undertake a comprehensive review of the CAMELS ratings system to produce ratings that signal whether an institution is expected to operate in a safe and sound manner over a specified period of time, asset quality ratings that reflect embedded risks rather than short-term profits, management ratings that reflect any ongoing failure to correct identified deficiencies, and composite ratings that discourage systemic risks);
- evaluate impacts of high-risk lending (the Financial Stability Oversight Council should undertake a study to identify high-risk lending practices at financial institutions, and evaluate the nature and significance of the impacts that these practices may have on US financial systems as a whole);

- rank credit rating agencies by accuracy (the SEC should use its regulatory authority to rank the NRSRO in terms of performance, in particular the accuracy of their ratings);
- help investors hold credit rating agencies accountable (the SEC should use its regulatory authority to facilitate the ability of investors to hold credit rating agencies accountable in civil lawsuits for inflated credit ratings, when a credit rating agency knowingly or recklessly fails to conduct a reasonable investigation of the rated security);
- strengthen credit rating agency operations (the SEC should use its inspection, examination, and regulatory authority to ensure credit rating agencies institute internal controls, credit rating methodologies, and employee conflict of interest safeguards that advance rating accuracy);
- Ensure credit rating agencies recognize risk (the SEC should use its inspection, examination, and regulatory authority to ensure credit rating agencies assign higher risk to financial instruments whose performance cannot be reliably predicted due to their novelty or complexity, or that rely on assets from parties with a record for issuing poor quality assets);
- strengthen disclosure (the SEC should exercise its authority under the new Section 78o-7(s) of Title 15 to ensure that the credit rating agencies complete the required new ratings forms by the end of the year and that the new forms provide comprehensible, consistent, and useful ratings information to investors, including by testing the proposed forms with actual investors);
- reduce ratings reliance (federal regulators should reduce the federal government's reliance on privately issued credit ratings);
- review structured finance transactions (federal regulators should review the RMBS, CDO, CDS, and asset-backed securities index (ABX) activities described in this Report to identify any violations of law and to examine ways to strengthen existing regulatory prohibitions against abusive practices involving structured finance products);
- narrow proprietary trading exceptions (to ensure a meaningful ban on proprietary trading under Section 619, any exceptions to that ban, such as for market-making or risk-mitigating hedging activities, should be strictly limited in the implementing regulations to activities that serve clients or reduce risk);
- design strong conflict of interest prohibitions (regulators implementing the conflict of interest prohibitions in Sections 619 and 621 should consider the types of conflicts of interest in the Goldman Sachs case study, as identified in Chapter VI(C)(6) of this Report);
- study bank use of structured finance (regulators conducting the banking activities study under Section 620 should consider the role of federally insured banks in designing, marketing, and investing in structured finance products with risks that cannot be reliably measured and naked CDS or synthetic financial instruments).

Regarding the opportunity for a cultural change in the industry to create more socially responsible and sustainable financial markets, the evidences of this book and the contributions of the thought leaders have proved the last assumption, which indicates that a significant change seems to be required.

In order to achieve this objective, based on the evidences of this book the focus should be placed on more generalized education on social responsibility topics in our programs and levels; on a more proactive role of the press and new agencies to disclose the risk and social costs of poor social responsibility and on the more effective impact of investigative journalism; finally, it is important to have more transparency and disclosure on the financial institutions and political institutions with more transparent disclosure of their risk-weighted performances, their compensation schemes, their corporate social responsibility initiatives, and their risk-taking strategies on their websites for the investors and all other stakeholders to analyze. This way there could be a better oversight on these organizations and corporate leaders based on social control and pressure from the media and public opinion leaders through the mass media and the social networks.

One of the lessons learned from the 2007–2009 financial crisis according to Richard Posner (personal communication, 2012), as he reported to me in his interview, is the following:

> The financial industry is too powerful and the industry too complex to be fully understood by government agencies ... Competition is Darwinian and forces financial firms and their employees to take a high level of risk and engage in any profitable practice that is not forbidden by effectively enforced law. Fairness, integrity, transparency, and other virtues will have no sway on firms and their employees unless backed by law.

As reported by *The Atlantic* (2011), "For the country's biggest financial institutions, it's still worth it to break the law, because the government has no way to make the banks pay for acting illegally" (*The Atlantic*, 2011).

The Atlantic's article (2011) titled "Too Big to Stop: Why Big Banks Keep Getting Away With Breaking the Law," reports the following statements on the matter:

> Occasionally, a news event brings the need for financial reform momentarily into the partial spotlight, like last week when Judge Jed Rakoff rejected a proposed settlement between the SEC and Citigroup over a complex security called a CDO (actually, a CDO-squared) that the bank manufactured and pushed onto investor clients solely so it could bet against it. In April 2010, when the SEC sued Goldman over similar behavior, that was big-time news for weeks. But Citigroup's behavior in "Class V Funding III" was far worse. (The Atlantic, 2011)

The issue in the Goldman case was whether the bank properly disclosed that John Paulson, a hedge fund manager, was involved in the selection of securities for the deal, because he wanted to bet against them. This time, Citigroup's own proprietary "trading desk" asked its CDO "structuring desk" to create a debt instrument that it could bet against. The trading desk came up with a list of securities to include in the new CDO and passed it on to the structuring desk, which in turn sent it to a supposedly independent third party that would manage the CDO itself, called Credit Suisse Alternative Capital, LLC (CSAC).

The SEC and Citi negotiated a settlement in which the bank would pay $285 million ($190 million for its profits plus a $95 million penalty) but neither admitted nor denied the allegations. Judge Rakoff (who previously gave the SEC a hard time over a settlement with Bank of America over the closing of the Merrill Lynch acquisition) refused to approve the settlement, saying that it offered no factual basis on which to even decide whether it was fair, adequate, reasonable, and in the public interest.

For Citi, the settlement boiled down to two things: a $95 million penalty and a promise not to break the law in the future. Anyone who can do basic arithmetic can see that it's worth it to break the law under those terms so long as you have a two-thirds chance of getting away with it.

The best interpretation of the SEC's position is that it's right: it doesn't have a strong enough case to win in court, so this meager settlement is the best it can do. But even so, that isn't the end of the story. In that case, we either need a stronger SEC or we need stronger laws, which are up to Congress. If banks really can get away with their alleged wrongdoings through the controversial practice of "neither admitting nor denying culpability" and they may continue to avoid individual criminal charges for their employees just paying settlements, thus wrongdoings, market abuses, frauds (and perhaps even conspiracies) will continue to be "cost-effective" practices for these institutions with limited impact on their reputation and brand equity. If these misconducts are indeed not effectively discouraged other severe systemic crisis are likely to occur in the future and the banks' accountability issue will remain unsolved.

Conclusion

So apparently one of the lessons learned from the evidences of the financial and sovereign debt crisis is that leading global financial institutions and their lobbies are just too powerful, influential, and "untouchable" to be effectively regulated and controlled. They are just too rich and highly interconnected with politics, the corporate world (that is, lending, investments, treasury, venture capital, shareholdings, and so on) and many other stakeholders to effectively challenge their super-power.

Over the years, before and after the 2007–2009 crisis, these financial firms becoming always bigger, more globalized and powerful, have inspired over-confidence in their top management and traders, and the feeling that they could get away with almost any wrongdoing without any major external threat, since in the worst case scenario the wrongdoing would be either completely bailed out by governments or paid with the settlement of a fine at the corporate level.

Only when the laws will enforce incredibly expensive charges for their firms, immediate and mandatory change management and corporate governance actions, no millionaire severance packages and golden parachutes' policies, or claw-backs of what has been improperly rewarded, things might start to change. But all these recommendations for improved corporate, regulatory, banking, monetary, and fiscal governance require true visionary, inspiring, and independent leaders to be effectively executed. Only the future events will confirm whether the authorities in the US and in the Eurozone have had the necessary courage, shared vision, social responsibility commitment, and inspiring leadership to make the difference, to save the world from severe economic recessions, and to reform the banking and financial services industry on a global scale. Banking and finance is certainly globalized these days whereas politics is still mostly local and often short-term oriented (that is, focused on the next elections). Thus, only time will tell whether leaders will have the necessary credibility and determination to repair economic dislocation of the past years and to prevent the recurrence of other crises in the future. It is not a simple task, but for sure a necessary and urgent one. If this task will be achieved it will be possible to generate in the coming years a *Creative Destruction* moment (Schumpeter, 1942) that would trigger a *new renaissance* for the overall Eurozone area, otherwise the Western economies could end up still trapped by a stagnant and painful deep recession for a while. This would be the inevitable outcome if governments continue to buy themselves some time, with tactical short-term political maneuvers that will only defer the problems to a later stage, thus worsening the future economic and social scenario of their countries. Should that be the case, there will be a gloomy scenario for the future economic recovery of the Western economies in the years to come, but I want to end this book on a positive and optimist note.

The 2007–2009 financial crisis and its aftermath, which I call since October 2008 (Pezzuto, 2008) the crisis of "common sense," lack of accountability, and moral hazard (that is, civic duty and moral courage) will certainly have a lasting impact on people lives, emotions, and memories. Crises, after all, are not necessarily only negative events as long as they help people learn from what went wrong and make better and wiser decisions in the future.

Hopefully a positive outcome of this devastating experience could be the high level of awareness of the dramatic economic and social consequences that this long-lasting crisis has produced. Another positive thing to remember is that reckless selfish and opportunistic behaviors of a few are not necessarily in the best interest of the entire society, thus a radical overhaul of cultural values is encouraged to reject short-termism, greed, short-cuts to wealth and success, and the absence of ethics and emphatic feelings. A greater attention to leaders' integrity and accountability should be set as a primary requirement for all private and public organizations. One more hopefully positive outcome that may arise from this crisis is the progressive introduction of a set of limited but effective internationally harmonized reforms on governance and oversight for the banking and financial services industry that might create a more stable and resilient system and prevent the recurrence of other systemic crises. Many authors, industry experts, and scholars, argue that prosecuting Wall Street executives will never be possible since their organizations are Too-Big-To-Fail and their executives Too-Big-To-Jail. Like many other people, and not for the mere desire of fierce criticism, I like to believe instead that no one is "Too-Big-To-Fail" or "Too-Big-To-Jail" if this is in the best interest of our society and free market economy. Thus, regarding the "too-big-to-fail" doctrine I recommend the Wall Street executives (with exceptions of course) to read here below a few lines of a very popular "old book" that may remind them what I believe is the true concept of "too-big-to-fail" and perhaps, hopefully, might even enlighten their minds and spirits, and the ones of those who have the power and responsibility over financial regulation and governance, for the development of a more resilient and stable financial system and a more responsible capitalism.

But Mary stood weeping outside the tomb … Jesus (Yehoshua) said to her, "Mary." She turned and said to him in Aramaic, "Rabboni!" (Rabbi!). Jesus said to her, "Do not hold me, for I have not yet ascended to the Father; but go to my brethren and say to them, I am ascending to my Father and your Father, to my God and your God." Mary Magdalene went and said to the disciples, "I have seen the Lord;" and she told them that he had said these things to her.

(St. John's Gospel: 20:11–18)

References

Abelson, M. (2013). *Secret Goldman Team Sidesteps Volcker After Blankfein Vow*. Bloomberg.com. Retrieved from http://tinyurl.com/bk8x6ka (accessed on January 8, 2013).

ACFE (2010). *2010 Report To The Nation On Occupational Fraud and Abuse*. Association of Certified Fraud Examiners. Retrieved from http://www.acfe.com/rttn.aspx (accessed on October 18, 2011).

Acharya, V., Franks, J. (2009). *Capital Budgeting at Banks: The Role Of Government Guarantees*. Agenda: Advancing Economics in Business. Oxera. Retrieved from http://tinyurl.com/7dytk99 (accessed on May 20, 2011).

Acharya, V., Schnabl, P. (2009). *Securitization Without Risk Transfer*. Working Paper, NYU Stern School of Business. Retrieved from http://tinyurl.com/742de9n (accessed on May 20, 2011).

Acharya, V.V., Kulkarni, N., Richardson, M. (2011). Capital, Contingent Capital, and Liquidity Requirements (Chapter 6) *in Regulating Wall Street: The Dodd–Frank Act and the New Architecture of Global Finance*. Publisher: Wiley; 1st edition.

Acharya, V.V., Shachar, O., Subrahmanyam, M. (2011). Regulating OTC Derivatives (Chapter 13) *in Regulating Wall Street: The Dodd–Frank Act and the New Architecture of Global Finance*. Publisher: Wiley; 1st edition.

Acharya, V.V., Pedersen, L.H., Philippon, T., Richardson, M. (2010). A Tax on Systemic Risk. NYU Stern School of Business Paper. Retrieved from http://tinyurl.com/agngvoj (accessed on December 23, 2012).

Acharya, V.V., Brownlees, C., Engle, R., Farazmand, F., Richardson, M. (2011). Measuring Systemic Risk (Chapter 4) *in Regulating Wall Street: The Dodd–Frank Act and the New Architecture of Global Finance*. Publisher: Wiley; 1st edition.

Acharya, V.V., Cooley, T., Richardson, M., Walter, I., Scholes, M. (2011). The Dodd–Frank Wall Street Reform and Consumer Protection Act (Prologue) in *Regulating Wall Street: The Dodd–Frank Act and the New Architecture of Global Finance*. Publisher: Wiley; 1st edition.

Adams, R., Hermali, B.E., Weisbach, M.S. (2008). *The Role of Boards of Directors In Corporate Governance: A Conceptual Framework and Survey*. NBER Working Paper, 14486. Retrieved from http://www.nber.org/papers/w14486.pdf (accessed on March 14, 2011).

Akerlof, G.A., Shiller, R.J. (2009). *Animal Spirits: How Human Psychology Drives the Economy, and Why It Matters for Global Capitalism*. Princeton University Press.

Alden, W. (2010, October 26). Shiller: Dodd–Frank Does Not Solve Too Big To Fail. Article posted on *The Huffington Post Business*. Retrieved from http://tinyurl.com/7qrs7mj (accessed on October 10, 2011).

Alexander, A. (2012, March 8). *Rethinking Basel III and the Regulation of Derivatives*. Article posted on RSD Solutions – Blogs [Web log message]. Retrieved from http://tinyurl.com/bggnost (accessed on November 5, 2012).

Alexander, K. (2011). *Solutions to Regulatory Differences between the US Dodd–Frank Act and the European Commission's Proposal, in Particular in Ensuring Equal Conditions for Market Access for EU and Third Country Central Counterparties (CCPS)*. In European Parliament's Committee on Economic and Monetary Affairs (ed.): Derivatives, central counterparties and trade repositories: compilation of briefing notes. Brussels: European Parliament, pp. 6–23 Retrieved from http://tinyurl.com/bcwam8c (accessed on December 7, 2012).

Alloway, T. (2013, January 24). Morgan Stanley Chief to Take Pay Cut. *Financial Times*. Retrieved from http://tinyurl.com/alasco2 (accessed on January 25, 2013).

Alloway, T., Braithwaite, T. (2012, October 4). M Stanley Chief Warns on Wall St Pay. *Financial Times*. Retrieved from http://tinyurl.com/a8xxcmn (accessed on December 2, 2012).

Altman, E.I., Öncü, S., Richardson, M., Schmeits, A., White, L.J. (2011). Regulation of Rating Agencies (Chapter 15) *in Regulating Wall Street: The Dodd–Frank Act and the New Architecture of Global Finance*. Publisher: Wiley; 1st edition.

Anderson, J., Dash, E. (2008, August 28). *For Lehman, More Cuts and Anxiety*. The New York Times. com. Retrieved from http://tinyurl.com/brqvzge (accessed on October 14, 2009)

Angelides, P. (2012, August 20). *The Unrepentant and Unreformed Bankers*. Article posted on *The Huffington Post Business*. [Web log message]. Retrieved from http://tinyurl.com/9atmqx9 (accessed on August 23, 2012).

Ard, L., Berg, A. (2010, March). Bank Governance: Lessons from the Financial Crisis. *World Bank Public Policy Journal*. Retrieved from http://tinyurl.com/6mcnufc (accessed on June 5, 2011).

Argandoña, A. (personal communication, April 17, 2012). *Interview with Prof. Dr. Antonio Argandoña, Professor of Economics and holder of the "la Caixa" Chair of Corporate Social Responsibility and Corporate Governance at IESE Business School in Barcelona*, on the topics of Prof. Ivo Pezzuto's Thought Leaders' Survey.

Argandoña, A. (2012). *Three Ethical Dimensions of the Financial Crisis*. IESE Business School Working Paper No. 944. Retrieved from SSRN: http://ssrn.com/abstract=2079578 (accessed on March 23, 2012).

Arjoon, S. (2010). Narcissistic Behavior and the Economy: The Role of Virtues. *Journal of Markets and Morality*, 13(1) (Spring 2010), 59–82. Retrieved from http://tinyurl.com/7fzastt (accessed on October 14, 2011).

Armitstead, L. (2011, March 5). HSBC Reveals Plans to Quit London for Hong Kong. *The Telegraph*. Retrieved from http://tinyurl.com/7f4p5np (accessed on June 5, 2011).

Asaro, A. (personal communication, April 29, 2012). *Interview with Mr. Alfonso Asaro, Director of Financial Services Analytical Applications Europe at Oracle Corporation (Austria) and Expert of Enterprise Risk Management Programs*, on the topics of Prof. Ivo Pezzuto's Thought Leaders' Survey.

Aspan, M. (2012). *Banks Must Do "A Lot More" to Repair Image*: HSBC's Dorner. American Banker website. Retrieved from http://tinyurl.com/a6x8hek (accessed on January 2, 2013).

Associated Press (2012, April 18). Citigroup Investors Give Thumbs Down To Executive Pay. *Los Angeles Times* Business. Retrieved from http://tinyurl.com/8yd6ews (accessed on May 2, 2012).

Association of Certified Fraud Examiners (ACFE) (2010). *2010 Report to the Nation On Occupational Fraud and Abuse*. Association of Certified Fraud Examiners. Retrieved from http://www.acfe.com/rttn.aspx (accessed on October 18, 2011).

Associazione per lo Sviluppo degli Studi di Banca e Borsa (ASSB) (2011, November). Workshop Paper of the Monetary Analysis Conference titled *Osservatorio Monetario n° 3/2011*. [Monetary Overview n° 3/2011] presented by ASSB (Associazione per lo Sviluppo degli Studi di Banca e Borsa) at Università Cattolica del Sacro Cuore (Milan).

Atkins, R. (2013a, March 31). Blow For ECB as Wider Loan Rates Hit South. *Financial Times Limited*. Retrieved from http://tinyurl.com/d6o2emu (accessed on April 5, 2013).

Atkins, R. (2013b, April 11). IMF Warns Europe Over Naked CDS Ban. *Financial Times Limited*. Retrieved from http://tinyurl.com/d3nuygp (accessed on April 11, 2013).

Bachus, S., Hensarling, J. (2011). *One Year Later: The Consequences of the Dodd–Frank Act*. The US Financial Services Committee. Retrieved from http://tinyurl.com/7xe6egl (accessed on June 4, 2012).

Baily, M.N., Litan, R.E., Johnson, M.S. (2010). The Origins of the Financial Crisis (Chapter 11). In Kolb, R.W. *Lessons from the Financial Crisis. Causes, Consequences, and Our Economic Future*. John Wiley and Sons, Inc.

Baily, M.N., Lund, S., Atkins, C. (2009). *Will US Consumer Debt Reduction Cripple the Recovery?* McKinsey Global Institute. Retrieved from http://tinyurl.com/clwml84 (accessed March 5, 2011).

Bainbridge, S.M. (2010). *The Corporate Governance Provisions of Dodd–Frank*. UCLA School of Law, Law-Econ Research Paper No. 10–14. Retrieved from http://tinyurl.com/amckp6k (accessed February 15, 2011).

Bair, S. (2012). *Bull By The Horns: Fighting To Save Main Street From Wall Street And Wall Street From Itself*. Free Press; 1st edition.

Bair, S. (2013, March 22). *Three Ways to Tame Wall Street*. Moyers and Company. Retrieved from http://tinyurl.com/c96f3w2 (accessed April 15, 2013).

Baker, D. (2002). *The Run-Up in Home Prices: Is it Real or is it Another Bubble?* Center for Economic and Policy Research. Retrieved from http://tinyurl.com/d9375cn (accessed on March 14, 2011).

Ballou, B., Heitger, D. (2005). A Building-Block Approach for Implementing COSO's Enterprise Risk Management – Integrated Framework. *Management Accounting Quarterly*, 6(2). Retrieved from http://tinyurl.com/dxvabjk (accessed on July 6, 2011).

Barber, L., Steen, M. (2012, December 13). FT Person of The Year: Mario Draghi. *Financial Times'* FT.com. Retrieved from http://tinyurl.com/ckgxwzh (accessed on December 13, 2012).

Barth, J.R., Li, T., Wenling, L., Phumiwasana, T., Yago, G. (2009). *The Rise and Fall of the U.S. Mortgage and Credit Markets. A Comprehensive Analysis of the Meltdown*. Milken Institute. Retrieved from http://tinyurl.com/bxdhd6 (accessed on December 10, 2012).

Barth, J.R., Li, T., Wenling, L., Yago, G. (2010). The Financial Crisis: How did we get here and where do we go next? New Evidence on How the Crisis Spread Among Financial Institutions (Chapter 13). In Kolb, R.W. *Lessons from the Financial Crisis. Causes, Consequences, and Our Economic Future*. John Wiley and Sons, Inc.

Basel Committee on Banking Supervision (2010). *Basel III: A Global Regulatory Framework For More Resilient Banks And Banking Systems*. Bank for International Settlements. Retrieved from http://www.bis.org/publ/bcbs189.pdf (accessed on September 7, 2011).

Basel Committee on Banking Supervision (2011a). *Global Systemically Important Banks: Assessment Methodology and the Additional Loss Absorption Requirements*. Retrieved from http://www.bis.org/publ/joint26.pdf (accessed on September 7, 2011).

Basel Committee on Banking Supervision (2011b). *Range of Methodologies for Risk and Performance Alignment of Remuneration*. Retrieved from http://www.bis.org/publ/bcbs194.pdf (accessed on September 7, 2011).

Basel Committee on Banking Supervision (2011c). *Report on Asset Securitization Incentives*. Retrieved from http://www.bis.org/publ/joint26.pdf (accessed on September 7, 2011).

Basel Committee on Banking Supervision (2013). *Basel III: The Liquidity Coverage Ratio and Liquidity Risk Monitoring Tools*. Retrieved from http://www.bis.org/publ/bcbs238.htm (accessed on September 14, 2013).

Baskin, J.B., Miranti, P.J. (1997). *A History of Corporate Finance*. Cambridge University Press.

BBC News Europe, (2012, September 6). *ECB's Mario Draghi Unveils Bond-Buying Euro Debt Plan*. BBC New Business. Retrieved from http://tinyurl.com/brvokog (accessed on October 12, 2012).

BBC News Europe (2013). *Pope's New Year Address Deplores Rampant Capitalism*. BBC News Europe. Retrieved from http://tinyurl.com/aav6zk4 (accessed on January 1, 2013).

Beasley, M.S., Branson, B.C., Hancock, B.V. (2010a). *Developing Key Risk Indicators to Strengthen Enterprise Risk Management – How Key Risk Indicators can Sharpen Focus on Emerging Risks*. Committee of Sponsoring Organizations of the Treadway Commission. Retrieved from http://tinyurl.com/c8mo5na (accessed on July 27, 2011).

Beasley, M.S., Branson, B.C., Hancock, B.V. (2010b). *COSO's 2010 Report on ERM – Current State of Enterprise Risk Oversight and Market Perceptions of COSO's ERM Framework*. Committee of Sponsoring Organizations of the Treadway Commission, Retrieved from http://tinyurl.com/bmgvkr9 (accessed on July 20, 2011).

Bebchuk, L.A., Cohen, A., Spamann, H. (2010). *The Wages of Failure: Executive Compensation at Bear Stearns and Lehman 2000–2008*. John M. Olin Center's Program on Corporate Governance and a working paper (No. 287) of the European Corporate Governance Institute. Retrieved from http://tinyurl.com/browebh (accessed on July 20, 2011).

Bebchuk, L.A., Cohen, A., Wang, C.C.Y. (2012). *Golden Parachutes and The Wealth of Shareholders*. Discussion Paper No. 683. 12/2010, Revised 10/2012. Harvard Law School. Retrieved from http://tinyurl.com/browebh (accessed on November 1, 2012).

Bebchuk, L.A., Fried, J.M. (2004a). *The Pay Without Performance: The Unfulfilled Promise of Executive Compensation*. Harvard University Press, 2004; UC Berkeley Public Law Research Paper No. 537783., Retrieved from http://tinyurl.com/ceqj4um (accessed on July 20, 2011).

Bebchuk, L.A., Fried, J.M. (2004b). *Stealth Compensation via Retirement Benefits*. Harvard Law School and European Corporate Governance Institute (ECGI). Retrieved from http://tinyurl.com/bmh43c3 (accessed on July 20, 2011).

Bebchuk, L.A., Fried, J.M. (2010). *Paying for Long-Term Performance*. Harvard Law School, National Bureau of Economic Research (NBER), and European Corporate Governance Institute (ECGI). Retrieved from http://tinyurl.com/crq5acn (accessed on September 5, 2010).

Bebchuk, L.A., Fried, J.M., Walker, D.I. (2002). *Managerial Power and Rent Extraction in the Design of Executive Compensation*. The University of Chicago Law Review, 69, pp. 751–846. Retrieved from http://tinyurl.com/boaa746 (accessed on July 20, 2011).

Beltratti, A., Stulz, R.M. (2011). *The Credit Crisis Around the Globe: Why Did Some Banks Perform Better?* Charles A. Dice Center Working Paper No. 2010-5; Fisher College of Business Working Paper No. 2010-03-005. Retrieved from http://tinyurl.com/btf3spw (accessed on February 1, 2012).

Bender, M. (2007). *Subprime Lending: An Update of the Issues and Approaches*. LexisNexis.

Berle, A., Means, G.C., Weidenbaum, M.L., Jensen, M. (1991). *The Modern Corporation and Private Property*. Transaction Publishers, Reprint edition.

Berle, A.A., Means, G.C. (1932). *The Modern Corporation and Private Property*. New York: Macmillan.

Berndt, A., Gupta, A. (2010). The Pitfalls of Originate-to-Distribute in Bank Lending (Chapter 34). In Kolb, R.W. *Lessons from the Financial Crisis. Causes, Consequences, and Our Economic Future*. John Wiley and Sons, Inc.

Binham, C. (2012, August 30). Barclays at Risk of US Scrutiny in Qatar Probe. *Financial Times'* FT.com. Retrieved from http://tinyurl.com/9c9342z (accessed on September 2, 2012).

Binham, C. (2013, February 6) RBS Pays £390m To Settle Libor Probe. *Financial Times'* FT.com. Retrieved from http://tinyurl.com/a7ay6re (accessed on February 6, 2013).

Blackwell, R. (2011, February 28). Should Big-Bank Execs Go to Jail for the Financial Crisis? *American Banker*. Retrieved from http://tinyurl.com/c45t9ol (accessed on April 20, 2011).

Blair-Ford, S. (2012, May 30). Regulation Blog 2012 – ECOFIN's Agreement on CRD IV. Posted on Gtnew.com. [Web log message]. Retrieved from http://tinyurl.com/cft4aog (accessed on June 4, 2012).

Blair-Smith, E. (2012, December 21). American Dream Fades for Generation Y Professionals. Bloomberg.com. Retrieved from http://tinyurl.com/cmb8wsz (accessed on December 27, 2012).

Blanchard, O.J., Amighini, A., Giavazzi, F. (2011). *Macroeconomia* [Macroeconomics]. Il Mulino.

Blundell-Wignall, A., Atkinson, P.E. (2012a, February 28). *Basel Regulation Needs To Be Rethought In The Age Of Derivatives, Part I*. Voxeu.org. Retrieved from http://tinyurl.com/ad82oz8 (accessed on October 27, 2012).

Blundell-Wignall, A., Atkinson, P.E. (2012b). Deleveraging, Traditional versus Capital Markets Banking and the Urgent Need to Separate and Recapitalise G-SIFI Bank. *OECD Journal: Financial Market Trends*. Volume 2012(1). Retrieved from http://tinyurl.com/a82egpw (accessed on December 23, 2012).

Borgonovi, E. (personal communication, April 21, 2012). *Interview with Prof. Elio Borgonovi, Full Professor of Economics and Management of Public Administration at Bocconi University, Senior Professor of SDA Bocconi (Public Management and Policy Department)*, on the topics of Prof. Ivo Pezzuto's Thought Leaders' Survey.

Borio, E.V., Lowe, P.W. (2002a). *Asset Prices, Financial and Monetary Stability: Exploring the Nexus*. Bank for International Settlements Paper No. 114. Retrieved from http://tinyurl.com/77mfnzs (accessed on January 11, 2011).

Borio, E.V., Lowe, P.W. (2002b). Assessing the Risk of Banking Crises. Bank for International Settlements Paper, *BIS Quarterly Review*, pp. 43–52. Retrieved from http://tinyurl.com/7slmjxn (accessed on January 11, 2011).

Bowling, D., Rieger, L. (2005). *Making Sense of COSO's New Framework for Enterprise Risk Management*. Bank Accounting and Finance, Aspen Publishers Inc. Retrieved from http://tinyurl.com/6ncg98u (accessed on July 26, 2011).

Braithwaite, T. (2011, December 13). Former WaMu Executives in $64m Settlement. *Financial Times*. Retrieved from http://tinyurl.com/7ahzobh (accessed on December 14, 2011).

Braithwaite, T. (2012a, May 2). Goldman and M Stanley Attack Fed Proposal. *Financial Times'* FT.com. Retrieved from http://tinyurl.com/89tl9wq (accessed on May 2, 2012).

Braithwaite, T. (2012b, May 2). US in $1bn Suit Against BofA Over Home Loans. *Financial Times*.

Braithwaite, T., Jenkins, P., Nasiripour, S. (2013, January 28). Fed Warns On Lack of Unity by Regulators. *Financial Times*.

Braithwaite, T., McCrum, D. (2012, April 18). Chill Winds to Blow After Citi Pay Vote. *Financial Times Limited*. Retrieved from http://tinyurl.com/cs4myyb (accessed on April 20, 2012).

Braithwaite, T., Nasiripour, S. (2013a, January 7). US Banks Pay $20bn Mortgage Crisis Bill. *Financial Times*. Retrieved from http://tinyurl.com/bhytxts (accessed on January 8, 2013).

Braithwaite, T., Nasiripour, S. (2013b, April 30). Fed Weighs Tighter Cap On Bank Leverage. *Financial Times Limited*. Retrieved from http://tinyurl.com/cy7wokv (accessed on April 30, 2013).

Braithwaite, T., Scannell, K. (2012, August 29). Citigroup In $590m Lawsuit Settlement. *Financial Times*. Retrieved from http://tinyurl.com/9j2j66s (accessed on September 2, 2012).

Braithwaite, T., Scannell, K., Bryant, C. (2013, April 3). Bundesbank Launches Deutsche Probe. *Financial Times Limited*. Retrieved from http://tinyurl.com/cs9z4fy (accessed on April 3, 2013).

Braithwaite, T., Scannell, K., McCrum, D. (2011, September 3). Banks Sued Over Mortgage Deals. *Financial Times*. Retrieved from http://tinyurl.com/7jvxxd2 (accessed on September 3, 2011).

Braithwaite, T., Scannell, K., McCrum, D. (2013, April 24). Citigroup Sees Off Shareholder Revolt on Executive Pays. *Financial Times Limited*. Retrieved from http://tinyurl.com/bpkznkq (accessed on April 25, 2013).

Brandeis Raushenbush, P. (2011, October 25). Religion, Morality and the Financial Industry: An Interview With Chief Rabbi Lord Sacks. *Huffington Post*. Retrieved from http://tinyurl.com/7obtsfk (accessed on February 9, 2012).

Brittan, S. (2012, July 5). The Fight Against Crony Capitalism. *Financial Times*. Retrieved from http://tinyurl.com/atum58b (accessed on December 7, 2012).

Brown, L., Ross, D. (2009). *Nicomachean Ethics (Oxford World's Classics)*. Oxford University Press.

Brown, P., (2000). *Augustine of Hippo: A Biography*. University of California Press; Revised edition.

Brunsden, J. (2012, December 10). *Basel Liquidity Rule May Be Watered Down Amid Crisis*. Bloomberg. Retrieved from http://tinyurl.com/aomq3kk (accessed on January 10, 2012).

Brunsden, J., Broom, G., Moshinsky, B. (2013, January 7). *Banks Win 4-Year Delay as Basel Liquidity Rule Loosened*. Bloomberg. Retrieved from http://tinyurl.com/b9aey8u (accessed on January 9, 2013).

Brush, S. (2012, November 16). *U.S. Treasury Exempts Foreign Exchange Swaps From Dodd–Frank*. Bloomberg. Retrieved from http://tinyurl.com/coo3thx (accessed on December 19, 2012).

Brush, S., Mattingly, P. (2012, December 20). *UBS $1.5 Billion Libor Settlement Signals More to Come*. Bloomberg. Retrieved from http://tinyurl.com/d4njh6h (accessed on December 20, 2012).

Buckberg, E., Dunbar, F.C., Egan, M., Schopflocher, T., Sen, A., Vogel, C. (2010). *Subprime and Synthetic CDOs: Structure, Risk, and Valuation*. Nera Economic Consulting. Retrieved from http://tinyurl.com/7h245fz (accessed on March 15, 2011).

Burgis, T. (2013, October 2). The Liikanen Report Decoded. *Financial Times*. Retrieved from http://tinyurl.com/ae9hqx7 (accessed on December 5, 2012).

Campbell, D., Kopecki, D. (2013, January 9). Dimon Says JPMorgan Executives "Acted Like Children" on Loss. Bloomberg Retrieved from http://tinyurl.com/an7njhg (accessed on January 10, 2013).

Caprio, G. Jr., Demirg-Kunt, A., Kane, E.J. (2008). *The 2007 Meltdown in Structured Securitization: Searching for Lessons not Scapegoats*. Working paper. Retrieved from http://tinyurl.com/8xd8lg2 (accessed on September 2, 2011).

Cardarelli, R., Elekdag, S., Lall, S. (2009). *Financial Stress, Downturns and Recovery*, Working Paper, 09/100. Retrieved from http://tinyurl.com/cogfem8 (accessed on April 15, 2010).

Carpenter, J., Cooley, T., Walter, I. (2011). Reforming Compensation and Corporate Governance (Chapter 17) in *Regulating Wall Street: The Dodd–Frank Act and the New Architecture of Global Finance*. Publisher: Wiley; 1st edition.

Case, K.E., Shiller, R.J. (2003). *Is There a Bubble in the Housing Market?* Brookings Papers on Economic Activity, 2:2003. Retrieved from http://www.econ.yale.edu/~shiller/pubs/p1089.pdf (accessed on May 15, 2011).

Castagna, A. (personal communication, April 14, 2012). *Interview with Mr. Antonio Castagna, Financial Modelling Expert at Iason Ltd., Financial Analyst, and Former Derivatives Trader*, on the topics of Prof. Ivo Pezzuto's Thought Leaders' Survey.

Cave, E. (2010, July 7). Milton Friedman Got It Wrong On Profit Being The Only Aim, HSBC Chief Green Argues. *The Telegraph*. Retrieved from http://tinyurl.com/7oubykb (accessed on May 15, 2011).

Censky, E. (2012, April 13). *Bernanke: Lack of Oversight Worsened Crisis*. CNN Money. Retrieved from http://tinyurl.com/7azrbrm (accessed on April 17, 2012).

Chomsisengphet, S., Pennington-Cross, A. (2006). *The Evolution of the Subprime Mortgage Market*. Federal Reserve Bank of St. Louis Review, Jan–Feb issue.

Christie, R. (2010, May 24). *FDIC's Bair Says Europe Should Make Banks Hold More Capital*. Article posted on Bloomberg Business Week. Retrieved from http://www.webcitation.org/5pylqZc12 (accessed on July 18, 2011).

Clairmont, F.F. (2008, October 27). *Alan Greenspan's Mea Culpa: The Torments of Contritionues*. Posted on Global Research. Retrieved from http://tinyurl.com/6vkwow3 (accessed on May 15, 2011).

Cluchey, D.P. (2011). *The Financial Crisis and the Response of the United States: Will Dodd–Frank Protect Us from the Next Crisis?* Paper of the University of Maine School of Law. Retrieved from http://tinyurl.com/au3x69p (accessed on November 16, 2012).

Cohen, J.P., Coughlin, C.C., Lopez, D.A. (2012). *The Boom and Bust of U.S. Housing Prices from Various Geographic Perspectives*. Federal Reserve Bank of St. Louis Review, September/October 2012, 94(5), pp. 341–67. Retrieved from http://tinyurl.com/c237fmz (accessed on December 28, 2012).

Cohen, N. (2011, November 28). OECD Warns of Eurozone Contagion Risk. *Financial Times*. Retrieved from http://tinyurl.com/cmyshwo (accessed on November 28, 2011).

Colombini, F. (personal communication, May 10, 2012). *Interview with Prof. Fabiano Colombini, Full Professor of Economics of Financial Institutions and Markets at the Faculty of Economics of Università di Pisa*, on the topics of Prof. Ivo Pezzuto's Thought Leaders' Survey.

Colombini, F., Calabrò, A. (2011). *Crisi Finanziarie: Banche e Stati. L'insostenibilità del Rischio di Credito* [Financial Crises: Banks and Sovereign Debts. The Unsustainable Credit Risk].Utet Giuridica.

Committee of Sponsoring Organizations of the Treadway Commission (COSO) (2004). *Enterprise Risk Management – Integrated Framework Executive Summary*. Retrieved from http://tinyurl.com/4pp2pov (accessed on July 18, 2011).

Committee of Sponsoring Organizations of the Treadway Commission (COSO) (2008). *Internal Control – Integrated Framework – Guidance on Monitoring Internal Control Systems, Volume 2 – Guidance*. Retrieved from http://tinyurl.com/cuenyk4 (accessed on July 19, 2011).

Committee of Sponsoring Organizations of the Treadway Commission (COSO) (2009a). *Guidance on Monitoring Internal Control Systems*. Retrieved from http://tinyurl.com/c7k2m54 (accessed on July 19, 2011).

Committee of Sponsoring Organizations of the Treadway Commission (COSO) (2009b). *Strengthening Enterprise Risk Management for Strategic Advantage*. Retrieved from http://tinyurl.com/7nmnzzp (accessed on July 19, 2011).

Congleton, R.D. (2010). The Political Economy of the Financial Crisis Cures of 2008 (Chapter 4). In Kolb, R.W. *Lessons from the Financial Crisis. Causes, Consequences, and Our Economic Future*. John Wiley and Sons, Inc.

Cooper, R. (2012, June 28). *Barclays Must Repair "Systematic Dishonesty", Says Former Boss Martin Taylor*. The Telegraph.co.uk. Retrieved from http://tinyurl.com/7lshv7f (accessed on June 28, 2012).

Core, J.E., Guay, W.R. (2010). *Is There a Case for Regulating Executive Pay in the Financial Services Industry?* Retrieved from http://tinyurl.com/86lfla7 (accessed on March 21, 2011).

Croucher, S. (2012, December 6). Deutsche Bank Ex-Staff Claim $12bn Loss Hidden to Avoid Government Bailout. *International Business Times*. Retrieved from http://tinyurl.com/bfysad5 (accessed on December 7, 2012).

Curtis, P., Carey, M. (2012). *Risk Assessment in Practice*. Research Commissioned by COSO to Deloitte and Touche LLP. Retrieved from http://tinyurl.com/bgm4n34 (accessed on December 23, 2012).

Daft, R.L. (2009). *Organization Theory and Design*. South-Western College Pub. 10th edition.

Damodaran, A. (personal communication June 1, 2012). *Interview with Dr Aswath Damodaran, Kerschner Family Chair in Finance Education Finance Department at New York University Stern School of Business*, on the topic of Prof. Ivo Pezzuto's Thought Leaders' Survey.

Davenport, C. (2013, January 16). *EU Lawmakers Approve Limited Rules for Rating Agencies*. Reuters. Retrieved from http://tinyurl.com/a4ecbp7(accessed on March 5, 2013).

Davis, K. (2011). *Regulatory Reform Post the Global Financial Crisis: An Overview*. University of Melbourne. Retrieved from http://tinyurl.com/75nb9xh (accessed on July 19, 2011).

Davis, Polk, and Wardwell LLP (2011). *Compensation Clawback Under Dodd–Frank: Impact on Foreign Issuers*. Davis, Polk, and Wardwell LLP. Retrieved from http://tinyurl.com/aw7cxj3 (accessed on July 19, 2011).

De Felice, G. (personal communication April 23, 2012). *Interview with Prof. Gregorio De Felice, Head of Research and Chief Economist, Intesa Sanpaolo Bank*, on the topic of Prof. Ivo Pezzuto's Thought Leaders' Survey.

Dell'Ariccia, G., Igan, D., Laeven, L. (2008). *Credit Booms and Lending Standards: Evidence from the Subprime Mortgage Market*. Working Paper, IMF. Retrieved from http://tinyurl.com/7oszbzu (accessed on March 14, 2011).

Dell'Ariccia, G., Goyal, R., Koeva-Brooks, P., Tressel, T. (2013). *A Banking Union For The Eurozone*. Article published on Vox. EU.org. Retrieved from http://tinyurl.com/lylnoqs (accessed on April 7, 2013).

Deloitte Development LLC. (2011). *First Look. A Practical Guide To The Federal Reserve's Newly Announced Enhanced Prudential*. Retrieved from http://tinyurl.com/cd2j935 (accessed on december 15, 2012).

Deloitte Development LLC. (2013a). *First Look. Implications of the Ability-to-Repay Rule and The Qualified Mortgage Definition*. Retrieved from http://tinyurl.com/ccnwpbc (accessed on December 15, 2012).

Deloitte Development LLC. (2013b). *OTC Derivatives Reform: This is Just the Beginning*. Retrieved from http://tinyurl.com/d9rg3yq (accessed on April 20, 2013).

Demirguc-Kunt, A., Serven, L. (2009). *Are All the Sacred Cows Dead? Implications of the Financial Crisis for Macro and Financial Policies*. Working Paper 4807, World Bank.

Demyanyk, Y., Hasan, I. (2009). *Financial Crises and Bank Failures: A Review of Prediction Methods*. Federal Reserve Bank of Cleveland and Lally School of Management. Bank of Finland. Retrieved from http://tinyurl.com/cv9gzlt (accessed on March 15, 2011).

Demyanyk, Y., Van Hemert, O. (2007). *Understanding the Subprime Mortgage Crisis*. Federal Reserve Bank of St. Louis and NYU Stern Department of Finance. Retrieved from http://papers.ssrn.com/sol3/papers.cfm?abstract_id=1020396 (accessed on March 15, 2011).

Demyanyk, Y., Van Hemert, O. (2011). Understanding the Subprime Mortgage Crisis. Federal Reserve Bank of Cleveland and NYU Stern Department of Finance. *Review of Financial Studies*, 24(6), pp. 1848–1880. Reprint by permission of Oxford University Press on behalf of The Society of Financial Studies.

de Servigny, A., Renault, O. (2004). *The Standard and Poor's Guide to Measuring and Managing Credit Risk*. McGraw-Hill, 1st edition.

Desmond, J. (2002). *Consuming Behaviour*. Palgrave Macmillan, p. 23.

Deutsche Telekom Website (2005). *The Risk and Opportunity Management System*. Retrieved from http://tinyurl.com/chvr8mj (accessed on June 15, 2009).

Dewatripont, M., Rochet, J.C., Tirole, J. (2010). *Balancing the Banks: Global lessons from the Financial Crisis*. Princeton University Press.

Di Giorgio, V. (personal communication May 8, 2012). *Interview with Mr Victor Di Giorgio, Vice President and Technology Country Head Italy at Citi and Head of the European Corporate Cultural Change Program at Citi*, on the topic of Prof. Ivo Pezzuto's Thought Leaders' Survey.

Dodd–Frank Library (2011, November). *The Dodd–Frank Wall Street Reform and Consumer Protection Act*. Online library of the October Research publication. Retrieved from http://tinyurl.com/6oajq4b (accessed on November 17, 2011).

Doms, M., Furlong, F., Krainer, J. (2007, June 8). *House Prices and Subprime Mortgage Delinquencies*. FRBSF Economic Letter. Number 2007–14. Retrieved from http://tinyurl.com/73z8rs9 (accessed on March 8, 2011).

Dough Roller (2011, January 11). *157 Banks Taken Over by the FDIC in 2010*. Retrieved from http://tinyurl.com/bqh7fm6 (accessed on March 8, 2011).

Duffie, D. (personal communication, May 28, 2012). *Interview with Darrell Duffie, Dean Witter Distinguished Professor of Finance at The Graduate School of Business, Stanford University*, on the topic of Prof. Ivo Pezzuto's Thought Leaders' Survey.

Duffie, D., Zhu, H. (2011). *Does a Central Clearing Counterparty Reduce Counterparty Risk?* Graduate School of Business Stanford University Paper. Retrieved from http://tinyurl.com/6wcfphm (accessed on January 2, 2012).

Eagleham, J. (2013). Bank Made Huge Bet, and Profit, on Libor. *The Wall Street Journal*. Retrieved from http://tinyurl.com/apcq6gk (accessed on January 9, 2013).

Easton, J. (2012). Too Big Not To Fail. Video Interview with John Macey, Professor of Yale Law School. *Economist Magazine* website. Retrieved from http://tinyurl.com/7vuqqw4 (accessed on January 9, 2013).

Eavis, P. (2012, November 9). *Regulators Postpone Some Basel Rules*. The New York Times Deal Book. Retrieved from http://tinyurl.com/ajf7hw9 (accessed on January 10, 2013).

Economist (2008, August 7). *A Personal View of the Crisis. Confessions of a Risk Manager. The Economist* magazine. Retrieved from http://tinyurl.com/5syd4ru (accessed on October 9, 2010).

Economist (2010, September 15). *The Biggest Weakness of Basel III*. Publisher: *The Economist* magazine. Retrieved from http://tinyurl.com/248zw8m (accessed on May 18, 2011).

Elliott, L. (2012, June 29). *Bank of England Governor Refuses to Back Bob Diamond*. The guardian.co.uk. Retrieved from http://tinyurl.com/6ps5fye (accessed on June 29, 2012).

Epstein, G., Carrick-Hagenbarth, J. (2010). *Financial Economists, Financial Interests and Dark Corners of the Meltdown: It's Time to set Ethical Standards for the Economics Profession*. PERI (Political Economy Research Institute), University of Massachusetts Amerst, working paper series n° 239. Retrieved from http://tinyurl.com/74nwfov (accessed on January 5, 2011).

Ericson, M., He, E., Schoenfeld, A. (2009, April). Tracking the $700 Billion Bailout. *New York Times*. Retrieved from http://tinyurl.com/6wvst28 (accessed on March 7, 2011).

Ernst and Young (2012, March). *IFRS Practical Matters. Impairment – Assessing The Impact Of The New Proposal*. Published by EYGM Limited. Retrieved from http://tinyurl.com/8crnxjw (accessed on August 7, 2012).

Eurointelligence (2011, November 28). *Moody's Warns of Multiple Defaults in the Eurozone*. Eurointelligence Daily Briefing. Retrieved from http://tinyurl.com/7mo9pc5 (accessed on November 28, 2011).

Eurointelligence (2012, December 13). *A Banking Union for 150 Out of 6000 Banks*. Eurointelligence Daily Briefing. Retrieved from http://tinyurl.com/ape2tut (accessed on January 10, 2013).

Eurointelligence (2013, January 31). *El Pais Has Found Documentary Evidence Showing That Mariano Rajoy Took Money*. Eurointelligence Daily Briefing. Retrieved from http://tinyurl.com/bytdsm3 (accessed on January 31, 2013).

Europa (2013a). *New Rules on Credit Rating Agencies (CRAs) – Frequently Asked Questions.* Retrieved from Europa – European Union website http://tinyurl.com/bzduas5, last updated January 16, 2013 (accessed on January 17, 2013).

Europa (2013b). *Commissioner Barnier Web Page.* Information retrieved from Europa – European Union website http://tinyurl.com/7pl66pq, last updated January 17, 2013 (accessed on January 17, 2013).

European Commission (2012). *What are the main features of the "six-pack" and the Treaty on Stability, Coordination and Governance (TSCG)?* Economic and Financial Affairs of the European Commission. Retrieved from http://tinyurl.com/7kwwpu8 (accessed on October 13, 2012).

Europost (2013, January 13). *Next is Bank Crisis Resolution.* Europost website. Retrieved from http://tinyurl.com/aj63cru (accessed on January 27, 2013).

Fahlenbrach, R., Stulz, R.M., (2010). *Bank CEO Incentives and the Credit Crisis.* Fisher College of Business Working Paper Series. Retrieved from http://tinyurl.com/mcz979 (accessed on March 20, 2011).

Federal Deposit Insurance Corporation (FDIC) (2011, March 8). *Failed Banks List.* Retrieved from FDIC website http://tinyurl.com/226vl3, last updated July 3, 2011 (accessed on March 8, 2011).

Financial Stability Board (2010). *Thematic Review on Compensation. Peer Review Report.* Retrieved from http://tinyurl.com/6qswyoj (accessed on October 16, 2011).

Financial Stability Board (2012). *Global Shadow Banking Monitoring Report 2012.* Retrieved from http://tinyurl.com/cbbugg3 (accessed on December 20, 2012).

Financial Stability Forum (2008). *Report of the Financial Stability Forum on Enhancing Market and Institutional Resilience.* Basel. Retrieved from http://tinyurl.com/6sg8nqt (accessed on July 15, 2011).

Fitz-Gerald, K. (2011, October 16). *Four US Banks Hold a Staggering 95.9% of U.S. Derivatives: The $600 Trillion Time Bomb That's Set to Explode.* True Democracy Party.net. Retrieved from http://tinyurl.com/7y9hao4 (accessed on October 16, 2011).

Flanders, S. (2012, September 6). *ECB's Mario Draghi Unveils Bond-Buying Euro Debt Plan.* BBC New Business. Retrieved from http://tinyurl.com/brvokog (accessed on October 12, 2012).

Fostel, A., Geneakoplos, J. (2008). Leverage Cycles and the Anxious Economy. *American Economic Review*, 98, pp. 1211–1244. Retrieved from http://tinyurl.com/6qwdqfz (accessed on July 15, 2011).

Frank, N., González-Hermosillo, B., Hesse, H. (2008). *Transmission of Liquidity Shocks: Evidence from the 2007 Subprime Crisis.* IMF Working Paper. Retrieved from http://tinyurl.com/ltqjtz (accessed on March 8, 2011).

Franke, G., Krahnen, J.P. (2005). *Default Risk Sharing Between Banks and Markets: The Contribution of Collateralized Debt Obligations.* Center for Financial Studies, Frankfurt, Working Paper Series No. 2005/06. Retrieved from http://tinyurl.com/7a497xy (accessed on December 9, 2011).

Freeland, C. (2009, October 24). U.S. Banks' Big Profits Are "Gifts" From State, Says Soros. *Financial Times.* Retrieved from http://tinyurl.com/89v5ep8 (accessed on April 12, 2011).

Fried, J.M., Shilon, N. (2011a). Excess-Pay Clawbacks. *Journal of Corporation Law*, 36, pp. 722–751. Retrieved from http://tinyurl.com/a7nap44 (accessed on December 16, 2011).

Fried, J.M., Shilon, N. (2011b). Excess Pay and the Dodd–Frank Clawback. On the Conference Board Director Notes based on "Excess-Pay Clawbacks," by J. Fried and N. Shilon, *Journal of Corporation Law*, 36, pp. 722–751. No. DN-V3N20, October 2011.

Friedman, H.H., Friedman, L.W. (2010). The Global Financial Crisis of 2008: What Went Wrong? (Chapter 5). In Kolb, R.W. *Lessons from the Financial Crisis. Causes, Consequences, and Our Economic Future.* John Wiley and Sons, Inc.

Friedman, J., Posner, R.A. (2011). *What Caused the Financial Crisis.* University of Pennsylvania Press.

Frigo, M.L., Anderson, R.J. (2011). *Embracing Enterprise Risk Management – Practical Approaches For Getting Started*. Committee of Sponsoring Organizations of the Treadway Commission. Retrieved from http://tinyurl.com/7w89egz (accessed on July 19, 2011).

Gabriel, S., Rosenthal., S. (2007). *Secondary Markets, Risk, and Access to Credit: Evidence from the Mortgage Market*. Working Paper, Syracuse University and UCLA. Retrieved from http://papers.ssrn.com/sol3/papers.cfm?abstract_id=1087114 (accessed on March 14, 2011).

Geanakoplos, J. (2010a). *The Leverage Cycle*, in D. Acemoglu, K. Rogoff and M. Woodford, eds., NBER Macroeconomic Annual 2009, vol. 24: 1–65, University of Chicago Press, 2010 [plus erratum] [CFP 1304].

Geanakoplos, J. (2010b). *Solving the Present Crisis and Managing the Leverage Cycle*. Federal Reserve Bank of New York Economic Policy Review, August 2010, pp. 101–131 [CFP 1305].

Geanakoplos, J. (2011). *What's Missing from Macroeconomics: Endogenous Leverage and Default*, in Marek Jarocinski, Frank Smets, and Christian Thimann (eds.), Approaches to Monetary Policy Revisited – Lesson from the Crisis, Sixth ECB Central Banking Conference 18–19 November 2010, European Central Bank, 2011, pp. 220–238 [CFP 1332].

Geanakoplos, J., Fostel, A. (2012a). Tranching, CDS, and Asset Prices: How Financial Innovation Can Cause Bubbles and Crashes. *American Economic Journal: Macroeconomics* (January 2012), 4(1): 190–225 [CFP 1353].

Geanakoplos, J., Fostel, A. (2012b). Why Does Bad News Increase Volatility and Decrease Leverage? (with A. Fostel), *Journal of Economic Theory* (March 2012), 147(2): 501–525 [CFP 1354].

Geanakoplos, J. et al. (2012). *Getting at Systemic Risk via an Agent-Based Model of the Housing Market*. American Economic Review: Papers and Proceedings (May 2012), 102(3): 53–58 [CFP 1358].

Gerardi, K.S., Shapiro, A.H., Willen, P.S. (2009). *Subprime Outcome: Risky Mortgages, Homeownership Experience, and Foreclosure*. Federal Reserve Bank of Boston/Atlanta and Bureau of Economic Analysis. Retrieved from http://finance.wharton.upenn.edu/~rlwctr/Willen2.pdf (accessed on March 12, 2011).

Gerding, E. (2010). The Outsourcing of Financial Regulation to Risk Models (Chapter 37). In Kolb, R.W. *Lessons from the Financial Crisis. Causes, Consequences, and Our Economic Future*. John Wiley and Sons, Inc.

Gibson, M. (2004). *Understanding the Risk of Synthetic CDOs*. Federal Reserve Board. Retrieved from http://tinyurl.com/czo2tce (accessed on June 14, 2011).

Gjerstad, S., Smith, V.L. (2009). Monetary Policy, Credit Extension, and Housing Bubbles: 2008 And 1929. *Critical Review: A Journal of Politics and Society*, 21(2–3). Retrieved from http://tinyurl.com/7pjw9qu (accessed on June 14, 2011).

Goff, S., Alloway., T. (2012, August 15). StanChart Sought Swift End To NY Dispute. *Financial Times*. Retrieved from http://tinyurl.com/9prmfat (accessed on August 15, 2012).

Goff, S., Smith, A. (2011, November 3). Barclays Chief Rediscovers Remorse. *Financial Times*. Retrieved from http://tinyurl.com/7psnunw (accessed on November 4, 2011).

Goodhart, C. (personal communication, May 8, 2012). *Interview with Prof. Dr. Charles Goodhart, Emeritus Professor at the London School of Economics and Director of the Financial Regulation Research Programme and former member of the Bank of England's Monetary Policy Committee (1997–2000), on the topic of Prof. Ivo Pezzuto's Thought Leaders' Survey*.

Goodman, L., Ashworth, R., Landy, B., Yang, L. (2012). *The Coming Crisis in Credit Availability*. Amherst Mortgage Insight of the Amherst Securities Group LP. Retrieved from http://tinyurl.com/ac27t5z (accessed on November 20, 2012).

Goodman, P. (2008, April 13). A Fresh Look at the Apostle of Free Markets. *The New York Times*. Retrieved from http://tinyurl.com/7qo2fyt (accessed on January 3, 2011).

Gordon, G. (2006, May 24). *Fannie Mae Fined $400M for Bad Accounting*. Washington Post.com. Retrieved from http://tinyurl.com/atb7jdz (accessed on January 19, 2011).

Gordon, M. (2013, January 17). *Big Banks Get Tax Break On Foreclosure Abuse Deal*. Huffington Post. com. Retrieved from http://tinyurl.com/ab3w78c (accessed on January 18, 2013).

Gorton, G. (2008). *The Panic of 2007*. Working Paper, Yale School of Management and NBER. Presented at the Jackson Hole Conference. Retrieved from http://tinyurl.com/pfkmlt (accessed on March 14, 2011).

Gorton, G. (2009). *Slapped in the Face by the Invisible Hand: Banking and the Panic of 2007*. Federal Reserve Bank of Atlanta's 2009 Financial Markets Conference. Retrieved from http://tinyurl. com/6to6j4g (accessed on January 3, 2011).

Gorton, G., Metrick, A. (2009). *Securitized Banking and The Run on Repo*. Working Paper 15223 National Bureau of Economic Research. Retrieved from http://www.nber.org/papers/w15223.pdf (accessed on October 5, 2011).

Gramlich, E. (2007). *Subprime Mortgages: America's Latest Boom and Bust*. Urban Institute Press.

Greely, M.L, Greene, P. (2008, September 19). "Say On Pay" Has Its Day? *The Deal Magazine*. Retrieved from http://tinyurl.com/6lkqu9o (accessed on July 19, 2011).

Greenlaw, D., Hatzius, J., Kashyap, A.K., Shin, H.S. (2008). *Leveraged Losses: Lessons from the Mortgage Market Meltdown*. Paper for the US Monetary Policy Forum Conference. Retrieved from http:// tinyurl.com/7bfc83e (accessed on January 7, 2012).

Griffin, D., Harper, C. (2012, July 26). *Former Citigroup CEO Weill Says Banks Should Be Broken Up*. Bloomberg.com. Retrieved from http://tinyurl.com/bvaeqw5 (accessed on July 26, 2012).

Groom, B. (2011, October 27). Top Directors' Total Earnings Rise 49%. *Financial Times*. Retrieved from http://tinyurl.com/7amwyr5 (accessed on October 27, 2011).

Grossman, S.J., Hart, O.D. (1983). An Analysis of the Principal-Agent Problem. *Econometrica*, 51(1), pp. 7–45.

Harjani, A. (2012). *Roubini: My "Perfect Storm" Scenario Is Unfolding Now*. CNBC.com Retrieved from http://tinyurl.com/cx24eej (accessed on July 9, 2012).

Harris, A. (2012, August 22). *FDIC Sues Goldman, JPMorgan over Mortgage-Backed Securities*. Bloomberg. com. Retrieved from http://tinyurl.com/8zalud5 (accessed on August 22, 2012).

Hill, C.W.L. (2012). *International Business: Competing in the Global Marketplace*. McGraw-Hill/Irwin, 9th global edition.

Hinton, P., Cohen-Cole, E. (2011). *Is Mortgage Underwriting to Blame for Subprime Losses? Disentangling the Effects of Poor Underwriting From the Economic Downturn*. NERA (National Economic Research Associates, Inc.) Economic Consulting. Retrieved from http://tinyurl.com/6a47vyc (accessed on March 12, 2011).

Hobson, R. (2011, November 4). *Tobin Tax Would Cost £25.5bn and Cause Job Losses Says Think-Tank*. Posted on London Loves Business. Retrieved from http://tinyurl.com/c7tg6mc (accessed on November 4, 2011).

Hofstede, G. (2001). *Culture's Consequences, Comparing Values, Behaviors, Institutions, and Organizations Across Nations*. Sage Publications.

Hojnacki, S. (2008). The Subprime Mortgage Lending Collapse – Should We Have Seen It Coming? *Journal of Business and Economics Research*, December, Volume 6, Number 12.

Holmstrom, B. (1979). Moral Hazard and Observability. *The Bell Journal of Economics*, 10(1), pp. 74–91.

Holt, N. (2012, November 26). *FSA Fines UBS £29.7m over Rogue Trader*. Money Marketing.co.uk. Retrieved from http://tinyurl.com/cfafe6l (accessed on November 28, 2012).

Hughlett, M. (1997). Subprime Loan Risk Bring Rewards to Norwest. *Knight Ridder/Tribune Business News*.

Hunter, G. (2008). *Anatomy of the 2008 Financial Crisis: An Economic Analysis Postmortem*. Working paper. Retrieved from http://tinyurl.com/7p3cfm4 (accessed on March 14, 2011).

Iacoviello, M., Minetti, R. (2005). International Business Cycles with Domestic and Foreign Lenders. Elsevier B.V.: Journal of Monetary Economics 53 (2006) 2267–2282 Retrieved from http://tinyurl.com/cg6ylks (accessed on March 15, 2011).

ICGN (International Corporate Governance Network) (2006). *ICGN Remuneration Guidelines*. London.

Inman, P. (2012, June 12). IMF Chief Christine Lagarde Warns World Risks Triple Crisis. *The Guardian*. Retrieved from http://tinyurl.com/ccy5k8k (accessed on August 13, 2012).

Inman, P. (2013, January 31). High Streets Banks Hit By Fresh Mis-Selling Scandal. *The Guardian*. Retrieved from http://tinyurl.com/badnl7m (accessed on February 6, 2013).

Inside Mortgage Finance (2008). *Mortgage Originations Statistics*. Inside Mortgage Finance. Retrieved from http://tinyurl.com/bt4v8wl (accessed on January 11, 2011).

Institute of International Finance (2008). *Final Report of the IIF Committee on Market Best Practices: Principles of Conduct and Best Practice Recommendations*. IFF, Washington, DC. Retrieved from http://www.iif.com/press/press+75.php (accessed on July 15, 2011).

Institute of Management Accountants (IMA) (2007). *Enterprise Risk Management: Tools and Techniques for Effective Implementation*. Retrieved from http://tinyurl.com/anqboto (accessed on October 6, 2010).

Institute of Management Accountants (IMA) (2011). *Enterprise Risk Management: Framework, Elements, and Integration*. Retrieved from http://tinyurl.com/addqv9d (accessed on December 12, 2012).

International Business Times Staff Reporter (2010, October 11), *Foreclosure Scandal: Double Whammy for US Homeowners*. Retrieved from http://tinyurl.com/bwg5wx8 (accessed on June 7, 2011).

Investing Answers (2011). *The TED Spread*. Retrieved from http://tinyurl.com/cr5pafa (accessed on July 22, 2011).

Investors' Working Group (IWG) (2009). *U.S. Financial Regulatory Reform: The Investors' Perspective*. An Independent Taskforce Sponsored by CFA Institute Centre for Financial Market Integrity and Council of Institutional Investors. Retrieved from http://tinyurl.com/c78dbxx (accessed on July 22, 2011).

IOSCO (The International Organization of Securities Commissions) (2008). *Report on the Sub-prime Crisis*. Retrieved from http://tinyurl.com/ccresud (accessed on July 15, 2011).

IOSCO (The International Organization of Securities Commissions) (2010). *Issues Raised by Dark Liquidity Consultation Report*. Retrieved from http://tinyurl.com/c8rqw6p (accessed on August 3, 2011).

Isidore, C. (2012, June 6). *Europe Unveils Bank-Bailout Plan*. CNN Money.com. Retrieved from http://tinyurl.com/75lx89s (accessed on June 6, 2012).

Ivry, B., Keoun, B., Kuntz, P. (2011, November 28). *Secret Fed Loans Gave Banks Undisclosed $13B*. Bloomberg.com. Retrieved from http://tinyurl.com/7qtcwgm (accessed on November 28, 2011).

Jacobs, B.I. (2010). Tumbling Tower of Babel. Subprime Securitization and the Credit Crisis (Chapter 29). In Kolb, R.W. *Lessons from the Financial Crisis. Causes, Consequences, and Our Economic Future*. John Wiley and Sons, Inc.

Jaffe, D.M. (2008). *The U.S. Subprime Mortgage Crisis: Issues Raised and Lessons Learned*. Working Paper No. 28, Commission on Growth and Development. Retrieved from http://tinyurl.com/bo9slkn (accessed on March 14, 2011).

Jarsulic, M. (2010). *Anatomy of a Financial Crisis: A Real Estate Bubble, Runaway Credit Markets, and Regulatory Failure*. Palgrave Macmillan.

Jenkins, P. (2012, December 8). JPMorgan Nears £500 Million Bonus Tax Deal. *Financial Times*. Retrieved from http://tinyurl.com/agg5tgn (accessed on December 8, 2012).

Jenkins, P. (2013a, January 7). Bank Shares Buoyed On a Sea of Scandal. *Financial Times*. Retrieved from http://tinyurl.com/af62jla (accessed on January 7, 2013).

Jenkins, P. (2013b, April 3). Salz Attacks Warped Top Pay At Barclays. *Financial Times*. Retrieved from http://tinyurl.com/dxhrhnm (accessed on April 3, 2013).

Jenkins, P., Goff, S., Murphy, M., Masters, B. (2011, December 12). Damning RBS Report Urges Law Change *Financial Times*. Retrieved from http://tinyurl.com/d934xnk (accessed on December 12, 2011).

Jenkins, P., Masters, B. (2013, January 10). UBS Chief Seeks a New Moral Path. *Financial Times*. Retrieved from http://tinyurl.com/aztr2ch (accessed on January 10, 2013).

Jensen, M.C. (2001). *Value Maximization, Stakeholder Theory, and the Corporate Objective Function*. Amos Tuck School of Business at Dartmouth College Working Paper No. 01–09. Negotiation, Organization and Markets Unit Harvard Business School Working Paper No. 01–01. Retrieved http://tinyurl.com/c9hoabc from (accessed on July 14, 2011).

Johnson, M. (2011, July 5). Bankia Executives Face Fraud Probe. *Financial Times*.

Johnson, S. (2010, September 16). *Picking Up the Slack on Global Banking Rules*. The New York Times.com's Econmix blog [Web log message]. Retrieved from http://tinyurl.com/37g5fks (accessed on September 16, 2010).

Johnson, S. (2011a, January 12). *Could Huntsman and the Democrats Ally on Bank Reform?* The New York Times.com's Econmix blog [Web log message]. Retrieved from http://tinyurl.com/7zdlacj (accessed on January 13, 2012).

Johnson, S. (2011b, March 10). *Battle of the Banking Policy Heavyweights*. The New York Times.com's Econmix blog [Web log message]. Retrieved from http://tinyurl.com/4atjwex (accessed on March 10, 2011).

Johnson, S. (2011c, March 31). *The Myth of Resolution Authority*. The New York Times.com's Econmix blog [Web log message]. Retrieved from http://tinyurl.com/anybj47 (accessed on May 7, 2011).

Johnson, S. (2011d, June 15). *The Big Banks Fight On*. The New York Times.com's Econmix blog [Web log message]. Retrieved from http://tinyurl.com/44rlnrn (accessed on June 15, 2011).

Johnson, S., Kwak, J. (2010a). *13 Bankers. The Wall Street Takeover and the Next Financial Meltdown*. Pantheon Books Inc.

Johnson, S., Kwak, J. (2010b, April 1). *Capital Requirements Are Not Enough*. New York Times.com's Econmix blog [Web log message]. Retrieved from http://tinyurl.com/csqrp99 (accessed on April 1, 2010).

Jones, S. (2012, January 11). *Credit Suisse Offers Trades for Eurozone Shorting*. Financial Times.com. Retrieved from http://tinyurl.com/7pe2w2z (accessed on August 11, 2012).

Kambas, M. (2013). *Cyprus Bailout Scrapes Through Island's Parliament*. Reuters. Retrieved from http://tinyurl.com/ccnnp6q (accessed on April 30, 2013).

Kaplan, S.N. (2012). *Executive Compensation and Corporate Governance in the U.S.: Perceptions, Facts and Challenges*. Chicago Booth Research Paper No. 12–42, Fama-Miller Working Paper. Retrieved from http://tinyurl.com/azk4lzo (accessed on December 13, 2012).

Kashyap, A.K. (2010). *Lessons from the Financial Crisis for Risk Management*. Paper prepared for the Financial Crisis Inquiry Commission. Retrieved from http://tinyurl.com/ck2jkzd (accessed on May 25, 2011).

Katz, I. (2013, March 1). *Bair Says Regulators Lack Spine to Name Systemic Firms*. Publisher: Bloomberg. com. Retrieved from http://tinyurl.com/cb72yth (accessed on April 15, 2013).

Kaufman, T. (2012). *U.S. Needs Shareholders' Rights. Huffington Post Business*. Retrieved from http://tinyurl.com/773zdmw (accessed on May 1, 2012).

Keith, A., Mueller, C. (2009). *The Subprime Mortgage Crisis. PowerPoint presentation posted online*. Retrieved from http://tinyurl.com/c3tesoa (accessed on January 10, 2011).

Kerin, J. (2012, October 26). *Loopholes In The Dodd–Frank Act*. Investopedia.com. Retrieved from http://tinyurl.com/8syuzu2 (accessed on December 5, 2012).

Keynes, J.M. (1936). *The General Theory of Employment, Interest and Money*. Macmillan Cambridge University Press, for Royal Economic Society in 1936.

Keys, B.J., Mukherjee, T., Seru, A., Vig, V. (2010). Did Securitization Lead to Lax Screening? Evidence from Subprime Loans (Chapter 28). In Kolb, R.W. *Lessons from the Financial Crisis. Causes, Consequences, and Our Economic Future*. John Wiley and Sons, Inc.

Kiff, J.J., Mills, P. (2007). *Money for Nothing and Checks for Free: Recent Developments in U.S. Subprime Mortgage Markets*. IMF Working Paper 07–188. Retrieved from http://tinyurl.com/c4hhwk2 (accessed on March 13, 2011).

King, S. (2012, January 16). *The Eurozone's Three Deadly Sins*. The A-List Financial Times Blog [Web log message]. Retrieved from http://tinyurl.com/7teadwr (accessed on January 16, 2012).

Kirchhoff, S., Hagenbaugh, B. (2004, February 24). Greenspan Says ARMs Might be Better Deal. *USA Today*. Retrieved from http://tinyurl.com/566em (accessed on January 10, 2011).

Kirkpatrick, G. (2009). *The Corporate Governance Lessons from the Financial Crisis*. OECD 2009 Financial Markets Trends. Retrieved from http://tinyurl.com/2ekq8fd (accessed on January 10, 2011).

Kirkup, J. (2011, December 5). Nick Clegg: "We Will Tackle Executive Pay". *The Telegraph*. Retrieved from http://tinyurl.com/7hs4s8k (accessed on December 5, 2011).

Kirman, A. (2010, November). The Economic Crisis is a Crisis for Economic Theory. Paper presented at the CESifo Economic Studies Conference on "What's wrong with modern macroeconomics?" Munich. *CEsifo Economic Studies*, 56(4), pp. 498–535. Retrieved from http://tinyurl.com/bp7sp62 (accessed on August 5, 2011).

Knutson, T. (2011, April 14). *All Were To Blame, Senate Panel Reports*. Thomson Reuters Accelus. Retrieved from http://tinyurl.com/73wnvea (accessed on April 15, 2011).

Koehler, E. (personal communication, April 25, 2012). *Interview with Prof. Etienne Koehler, Associate Professor of Financial Mathematics at La Sorbonne University of Paris and Expert of Credit Risk Analytics*, on the topic of Prof. Ivo Pezzuto's Thought Leaders' Survey.

Kolb, R.W. (2010a). *Finance Ethics. Critical Issues in Theory and Practice*. John Wiley and Sons, Inc.

Kolb, R.W. (2010b). Incentives in the Originate-to-Distribute Model of Mortgage Production (Chapter 27). In Kolb, R.W. *Lessons from the Financial Crisis. Causes, Consequences, and Our Economic Future*. John Wiley and Sons, Inc.

Kolb, R.W. (2011). *The Financial Crisis of Our Time*. Oxford University Press, Inc.

Kopecki, D., Moore, M.J. (2012, May 10). *JPMorgan Loses $2 Billion in Chief Investment Office*. Bloomberg.com. Retrieved from http://tinyurl.com/7ozdeqw (accessed on June 3, 2012).

Kostyuk, A.N. (personal communication, May 29, 2012). *Interview with Prof. Dr. Alexander N. Kostyuk, Professor of Corporate Governance and Finance and Director of the International Center for Banking and Corporate Governance, Ukrainian Academy of Banking of the National bank of Ukraine*, on the topic of Prof. Ivo Pezzuto's Thought Leaders' Survey.

Kotler, P., Kartajaya, H., Setiawan, I. (2010). *Marketing 3.0: From Products to Customers to the Human Spirit*. Wiley, 1st edition.

Koukis, G. (personal communication, May 7, 2012). *Interview with Mr George Koukis*, Founder and President of TEMENOS, on the topics of Prof. Ivo Pezzuto's Thought Leaders' Survey.

Krahnen, J.P., Wilde, C. (2008). *Risk Transfer with CDOs*. Working Paper Series: Finance and Accounting. Goethe University Frankfurt am Main. Retrieved from http://tinyurl.com/6mnfkgx (accessed on January 20, 2012).

Krawcheck, S. (2013, January 14). *How Banks Can Regain Trust*. Blog post on Linkedin website of Sallie Krawcheck, Past President of Merrill Lynch, US Trust, Smith Barney. Retrieved from http://tinyurl.com/aggnvmt (accessed on January 20, 2012).

Krugman, P. (2009). *The Return of Depression Economics and the Crisis of 2008*. W.W. Norton and Company.

Krugman, P. (2012). *End This Depression Now!* W.W. Norton and Company.

Kulikowski, L. (2008, August 22). *Lehman Brothers Amputates Mortgage Arm*. The Street.com. Retrieved from http://tinyurl.com/bl4uwss (accessed on May 9, 2009).

Kwak, J. (2010, April 12). *The Cover-Up*. Baseline Scenario [Web log message]. Retrieved from http://tinyurl.com/c9vspfg (accessed on January 10, 2011).

Laeven, L., Valencia, V. (2012). *Resolution of Banking Crises: The Good, the Bad, and the Ugly*. Working Paper, IMF. Retrieved from http://tinyurl.com/bkeynas (accessed on December 20, 2012).

Lagarde, C. (2012, December 31). *The Future Global Economy*. Article posted on Project Syndicate. Retrieved from http://tinyurl.com/ar7hgzk (accessed on January 5, 2013).

Lahart, J. (2009, January 2). Mr. Rajan Was Unpopular (But Prescient) at Greenspan Party. *The Wall Street Journal*. Retrieved from http://tinyurl.com/axj7a2 (accessed on January 7, 2011).

Lang, W.W. (personal communication, March 29, 2012). *Interview with Dr William W. Lang, Senior Vice President and Lending Officer Supervision, Regulation and Credit at the Federal Reserve Bank of Philadelphia and Fellow of the Wharton Financial Institutions Center*, on the topics of Prof. Ivo Pezzuto's Thought Leaders' Survey.

Lang, W.W., Jagtiani, J. (2010). *The Mortgage and Financial Crises: The Role of Credit Risk Management and Corporate Governance*. Federal Reserve Bank of Philadelphia. Retrieved from http://tinyurl.com/73ko6kk (accessed on January 15, 2011).

Latham and Watkins LLP (2011, March). *Regulatory Capital Reform Under Basel III*. PowerPoint Presentation. Posted online. Retrieved from http://tinyurl.com/7ypyx8q (accessed on June 5, 2011).

Lawrence, D., Solomon, A. (2002). *Managing a Consumer Lending Business*. Solomon Lawrence.

Lea, M. (2008). *Lessons Learned From The U.S. Mortgage Market Crisis*. Wharton University of Pennsylvania (PowerPoint Presentation). Retrieved from http://tinyurl.com/cdz3ehr (accessed on March 14, 2011).

Le Leslé, V., Avramova, S. (2012). *Revisiting Risk-Weighted Assets. "Why Do RWAs Differ Across Countries and What Can Be Done About It?"* IMF Working Paper 12/90. Retrieved from http://tinyurl.com/9rxbetv (accessed on August 20, 2012).

Levin, C. (2011a, April 13). *U.S. Senate Investigations Subcommittee Releases Levin-Coburn Report On the Financial Crisis*. Carl Levin U.S. Senator of Michigan Website. Retrieved from http://tinyurl.com/cfkh3bq (accessed on October 15, 2011).

Levin, C. (2011b). *Wall Street and the Financial Crisis: Anatomy of a Financial Collapse*. U.S. Senate Permanent Subcommittee on Investigations. Retrieved from http://tinyurl.com/42jumcl (accessed on October 15, 2011).

Lewis, M. (2009, August). *The Man Who Crashed the World*. Vanity Fair Politics. Retrieved from http://tinyurl.com/7kpzp6f (accessed on March 10, 2011).

Lewis, M. (2010). *The Big Short: Inside the Doomsday Machine*. Publisher: W.W. Norton and Company; 1st edition.

Liberman, E.E. (2010, August 25). *Impact of Dodd–Frank Act on Investment Advisers to Private Art Funds*. Posted online on the Art Fund Association LLC. Retrieved from http://tinyurl.com/6sb79zl (accessed on October 15, 2011).

Liebowitz, S. (2009, July 3). New Evidence on the Foreclosure Crisis. *The Wall Street Journal*. Retrieved from http://tinyurl.com/mvr6mz (accessed on May 15, 2011).

Lizza, R. (2009, October 12). Inside the Crisis: Larry Summers and the White House Economic Team. *The New Yorker*. Retrieved from http://tinyurl.com/ycbz5o9 (accessed on June 12, 2011).

Löeffler, G. (2008). *Caught In The Housing Crash*: *Model Failure or Management Failure?* Working Paper, University of Ulm.

Löeffler, G., Posch, P.N. (2011). *Credit Risk Modeling Using Excel and VBA* (The Wiley Finance Series). Wiley, 2nd edition.

Lynch, S.N. (2013, April 26). *US SEC To Propose Cross-Border Rules for Security-Based Swaps*. Reuters. Retrieved from http://tinyurl.com/c7mpt5r (accessed on April 29, 2013).

Malaysia Finance Blog (2010, February 26). *Robert Shiller – Dr. Doom of 2000s*. Retrieved from http://tinyurl.com/6rdsjym [Web log message] (accessed on January 25, 2011).

Manor, R. (2006, May 24). "Arrogant and Unethical". Fannie Mae to Pay $400 Million Penalty. *Chicago Tribune*. Retrieved from http://tinyurl.com/b2rov39 (accessed on June 9, 2011).

Margasak, L. (2012, July 5). *Countrywide Used Loan Discounts to Buy Congress, Fannie Mae Execs, Other Government Officials*: *Report. Huffington Post*. Retrieved from http://tinyurl.com/bl7uqvx (accessed on July 7, 2012).

Martenson, C. (2007, January 23). Connect the Dots. *Atlantic Free Press*. Retrieved from http://tinyurl.com/ywpkhl (accessed on January 10, 2011).

Martinuzzi, E. (2012, December 20). *Deutsche Bank, UBS Convicted by Milan Judge for Fraud Role*. Bloomberg.com. Retrieved from http://tinyurl.com/bunwt9t (accessed on December 20, 2012).

Martinuzzi, E., Dunbar, N. (2013, January 17). *Deutsche Bank Derivative Helped Monte Paschi Mask Losses*. Bloomberg.com. Retrieved from http://tinyurl.com/bhq5jhc (accessed on December 17, 2013).

Maslow, A.H. (2011). *Hierarchy of Needs*: *A Theory of Human Motivation*. Retrieved from http://tinyurl.com/6whn67t (accessed on January 17, 2011).

Masters, B. (2012, December 5). UK Regulator Unveils New Libor Rules. *Financial Times*. Retrieved from http://tinyurl.com/awbrs7o (accessed on December 6, 2012).

Masters, B. (2013, March 1). Bailey Calls For Bank Capital Transparency. *Financial Times*. Retrieved from http://tinyurl.com/bqm4ewa (accessed on April 1, 2013).

Masters, B., Binham, C., Scannell, K. (2012, June 27). Barclays Pays $450m to End Libor Probe. *Financial Times*. Retrieved from http://tinyurl.com/6veo937 (accessed on June 28, 2012).

Masters, B., Braithwaite, T. (2011, March 16). Basel III Capital Rules Too Low, Says Turner. *Financial Times*. Retrieved from http://tinyurl.com/cx6dd7l (accessed on June 14, 2011).

Masters, B., Hammond, E. (2011, December 11). FSA Crackdown on Understated Property Risks. *Financial Times*. Retrieved from http://tinyurl.com/bl8t9j7 (accessed on December 12, 2011).

Masters, B., Jenkins, P. (2012, July 1). Concerns Over Libor Rate Raised in 2007. *Financial Times*. Retrieved from http://tinyurl.com/7f3j4a4 (accessed on July 2, 2012).

Maynardkeynes.org (2011). *Keynes the Speculator*. Retrieved from http://tinyurl.com/clyglf2 (accessed on October 13, 2011).

Maynardkeynes.org (2011). *Keynes The Speculator*. Retrieved from http://tinyurl.com/clyglf2 (accessed on October 13, 2011).

Mayo, M. (2011). *Exile on Wall Street: One Analyst's Fight to Save the Big Banks from Themselves*. Wiley, 1st edition.

Mengle, D. (2007). *Credit Derivatives. An Overview*. Paper presented at the Atlanta Fed's 2007 Financial Markets Conference, "Credit Derivatives: Where's the Risk?" held May 14–16. Retrieved from http://tinyurl.com/n2k8px (accessed on April 5, 2011).

Mercurio, F. (personal communication, April 2, 2012). *Interview with Dr Fabio Mercurio, Head of Quant Business Managers at Bloomberg LP, New York and director of the research committee of Iason Ltd.*, on the topics of Prof. Ivo Pezzuto's Thought Leaders' Survey.

Merriam-Webster's Online Dictionary (2009). *Definition of the Term Risk*. Retrieved from http://www.merriam-webster.com/dictionary/risk (accessed on June 14, 2009).

Merrouche, N. (2010). *What Caused the Global Financial Crisis? – Evidence on the drivers of Financial Imbalances 1999–2007*. WP/10/265 Working Paper, IMF. Retrieved from http://tinyurl.com/adw6y94 (accessed on September 13, 2011).

Meterangelo, M. (personal communication, March 26, 2012). *Interview with Mr Massimo Meterangelo., Head of Group Wide Portfolio Consolidation at Unicredit Group*, on the topics of Prof. Ivo Pezzuto's Thought Leaders' Survey.

Mian, A., Sufi., A. (2008). *The Consequences of Mortgage Credit Expansion: Evidence from the 2007 Mortgage Default Crisis*. Working Paper, UC Berkeley and University of Chicago. SSRN portal. Retrieved from http://tinyurl.com/d8fxlc3 (accessed on March 14, 2011).

Minsky, H.P. (1982). *Can "It" Happen Again?: Essays on Instability and Finance*. M.E. Sharpe.

Minsky, H.P. (1992). *The Financial Instability Hypothesis*. Working Paper No. 74. The Jerome Levy Economics Institute of Bard College. Prepared for *Handbook of Radical Political Economy*, edited by Arestis, P. and Sawyer, M. Edward Elgar.

Mizruchi, M.S. (2004). *Berle and Means Revisited: The Governance and Power of Large U.S. Corporations. April 2004*. Forthcoming in Theory and Society. University of Michigan. Retrieved from http://tinyurl.com/an355tw (accessed on November 15, 2012).

Monks, A.G., Minow, N. (2011). *Corporate Governance*. Wiley, 5th edition.

Moore, C. (2011, March 4). Mervyn King Interview: We Prevented a Great Depression ... but People Have the Right to be Angry. *The Telegraph*. Retrieved from http://tinyurl.com/62zpoho (accessed on March 5, 2011).

Moore, J. (2012, October 1). Bad Bankers Warned: Repent or Go to Jail. *The Independent*. Retrieved from http://tinyurl.com/8z7cy7g (accessed on December 12, 2012).

Moore, M. (2009). *Capitalism: A Love Story*. [American Documentary Film]. Produced by Paramount Vantage and Overture Films.

Morse, A., Nanda, V., Seru, A. (2009). Are Incentive Contracts Rigged By Powerful CEOs? *Journal of Finance*, 66(5), pp. 1779–1821.

Mortgage Bankers Association website (2011). *Mortgage Bankers Association National Delinquency Survey*. Retrieved from http://tinyurl.com/cgbxcc9 (accessed on January 11, 2011).

Münchau, W. (personal communication, May 28, 2012). *Interview with Mr Wolfgang Munchau, President of Eurointelligence ASBL and Associate Editor of the Financial Times*, on the topics of Prof. Ivo Pezzuto's Thought Leaders' Survey.

Murphy, K.J. (1999). *Executive Compensation*. University of Southern California, Marshall School of Business; University of Southern California – Department of Economics; USC Gould School of Law. Retrieved from http://tinyurl.com/c35whq9 (accessed on July 21, 2011).

Murphy, K.J., Sandino, T. (2009). *Executive Pay and "Independent" Compensation Consultants*. Marshall School of Business Working Paper No. FBE 10–09. Retrieved from SSRN: http://ssrn.com/abstract=1148991 (accessed on October 5, 2011).

Nagourney, A. (2012, November 27). California Finds Economic Gloom Starting to Lift. *The New York Times*. Retrieved from http://tinyurl.com/b6aw7op (accessed on December 10, 2012).

Naím, M. (2011, October 26). *Take Note America: The Public Is Angry*. The A-List. *Financial Times'* FT.com blog [Web log message]. Retrieved from http://tinyurl.com/d9km98n (accessed on October 26, 2011).

Nasiripour, S. (2011a, November 15). D Bank and Citi Settle Mortgage Bond Claims. *Financial Times*. Retrieved from http://tinyurl.com/blw6lxd (accessed on November 15, 2011).

Nasiripour, S. (2011b, December 2). Massachusetts Sues Top Five Lenders. *Financial Times*. Retrieved from http://tinyurl.com/buv7d48 (accessed on November 15, 2011).

Nasiripour, S. (2011c, December 13). Morgan Stanley Books $1.8bn Loss. *Financial Times*. Retrieved from http://tinyurl.com/7q7pdqx (accessed on December 13, 2011).

Nasiripour, S. (2011d, December 21). BofA to Pay $335m Over Discrimination Claims. *Financial Times*. Retrieved from http://tinyurl.com/cnf84rf (accessed on December 21, 2011).

Nasiripour, S. (2012, January 25). Obama to Form Mortgage Fraud Task Force. *Financial Times*. Retrieved from http://tinyurl.com/7kyc2gz (accessed on January 25, 2012).

Nasiripour, S., Alloway, T. (2012, August 15). Seven Banks in New York Libor Probe. *Financial Times*. Retrieved from http://tinyurl.com/d2m3s23 (accessed on August 16, 2012).

Nasiripour, S., Scannell, K. (2011, December 16). SEC Charges Ex-Fannie and Freddie Chiefs. *Financial Times*. Retrieved from http://tinyurl.com/84a59r9 (accessed on December 17, 2011).

Nelson, E. (2011). *Friedman's Monetary Economics in Practice*. Finance and Economics Discussion Series Divisions of Research and Statistics and Monetary Affairs Federal Reserve Board, Washington, DC. Retrieved from http://tinyurl.com/6s2dcgr (accessed on October 15, 2011).

Nestor Advisors. 2009. *Governance in Crisis: A Comparative Case Study of Six US Investment Banks*. NeAD Research Note 0109. London.

Nielsen, R.P. (2010). High-Leverage Finance Capitalism, the Economic Crisis, Structurally Related Ethics Issues, and Potential Reforms. *Business Ethics Quarterly*, Volume: 2, Issue: April, Pages: 299–330. Retrieved from http://tinyurl.com/6mv6ddd (accessed on July 8, 2011).

Niven, P.R. (2006). *Balanced Scorecard Step-by-Step: Maximizing Performance and Maintaining Results*. Wiley, 2nd edition.

NNDB.com (2012). *Robert E. Rubin*. Retrieved from http://tinyurl.com/cr9kfdf (accessed on January 3, 2013).

Nocera, J. (2009, January 2). Risk Management. *The New York Times*. Retrieved from http://tinyurl.com/bb78pn6 (accessed on January 2, 2009).

Nocera, J. (2010, April 16). A Wall Street Invention Let the Crisis Mutate. *The New York Times*. Retrieved from http://tinyurl.com/bsvy9fg (accessed on October 13, 2010).

Norman, L., Robinson, F. (2013). EU Tightens Rules on Credit Rating Firms. *The Wall Street Journal*. Retrieved from http://tinyurl.com/agwrk37 (accessed on January 16, 2013).

Nugent, J.H. (2009a). *Corporate Finance and Governance* (PowerPoint Presentation). Graduate School of Management at the University of Dallas, Irving, TX.

Nugent, J.H. (2009b). *Internal Controls: Essentials for Business* (PowerPoint Presentation). Graduate School of Management at the University of Dallas, Irving, TX.

Nugent, J.H. (2011). *Contributions on the Topics of Prof. Ivo Pezzuto's Thought Leaders Survey Provided by John Nugent*. Professor of the Graduate School of Management at the University of Dallas, Irving, TX.

NUS Think Business Staff (2012, November 22). *Giving Capitalism Its Groove Backs*. Published in the National University of Singapore (NUS) Business School Think Business website. Retrieved from http://tinyurl.com/bsae9xr (accessed on December 27, 2012).

Obstfeld, M., Rogoff, K. (2009). *Global Imbalances and the Financial Crisis: Products of Common Causes*. University of California, Berkeley, and Harvard University Paper prepared for the Federal Reserve Bank of San Francisco Asia Economic Policy Conference, Santa Barbara, CA, October 18–20.

Onaran, Y. (2007, August 22). *Lehman Brothers Shuts Down Subprime Unit, Fires 1,200 (Update4)*. Bloomberg.com. Retrieved from http://tinyurl.com/cahf979 (accessed on January 19, 2009).

Onaran, Y. (2012, March 15). *Greek Restructuring Delay Helps Banks as Risks Shift*. Bloomberg.com. Retrieved from http://tinyurl.com/7cn96eb (accessed on March 16, 2012).

Onaran, Y. (2013, February 20). *U.S. Banks Bigger Than GDP as Accounting Rift Masks Risk*. Bloomberg. com. Retrieved from http://tinyurl.com/a3b64ru (accessed on April 7, 2013).

Organisation for Economic Co-operation and Development (OECD) (2004). *OECD Principles of Corporate Governance*. Retrieved from http://tinyurl.com/884tqk9 (accessed on June 21, 2011).

Organisation for Economic Co-operation and Development OECD (2009). *Corporate Governance and the Financial Crisis: Key Findings and Main Messages*. Retrieved from http://www.oecd.org/dataoecd/3/10/43056196.pdf (accessed on June 20, 2011).

Organisation for Economic Co-operation and Development (OECD) (2011). *An Overview of Growing Income Inequalities in OECD Countries: Main Findings*. Retrieved from http://www.oecd.org/dataoecd/40/12/49170449.pdf (accessed on December 6, 2011).

Organisation for Economic Co-operation and Development (OECD) (2012). *OECD Economic Outlook November 2012*. Retrieved from http://tinyurl.com/cd6dcy4 (accessed on December 20, 2012).

Organisation for Economic Co-operation and Development (OECD) (2013). *OECD Economic Outlook. Focus: Strengthening Euro Area Banks, 10–01–2013*. Retrieved from http://tinyurl.com/a2a3kmg (accessed on January 20, 2013).

O'Toole, J. (2012, March 11). *Big Banks at Center of Interest Rate Probe*. CCN Money. Retrieved from http://tinyurl.com/6qumf96 (accessed on March 15, 2012).

Owen, A. (2008). *Risk and Opportunity Management Framework*. Thurrock Council. Retrieved from http://tinyurl.com/84p9db2 (accessed on June 20, 2009).

Pagano, M., Volpin, P. (2009). *Credit Ratings Failures and Policy Options*. Centre for Studies in Economics and Finance. Retrieved from http://tinyurl.com/cgp56p6 (accessed on March 15, 2011).

Partnoy, F. (2009). *Rethinking Regulation of Credit Rating Agencies: An Institutional Investor Perspective*. White paper commissioned by the Council of Institutional Investors. Retrieved from http://tinyurl.com/apeh2b4 (accessed on October 5, 2012).

Partnoy, F., Eisinger, J. (2013, January 2). *What's Inside America's Banks?* The Atlantic.com Retrieved from http://tinyurl.com/aohxqg6 (accessed on March 12, 2013).

Peters, J.W. (2006, May 23). Fannie Mae to Pay $400 Million in Fines. *New York Times*. Retrieved from http://tinyurl.com/a9h6sar (accessed on October 15, 2011).

Pezzani, F. (personal communication, May 7, 2012). *Interview with Prof. Fabrizio Pezzani, Full Professor of Business Administration, Accounting and Control and Director of the Bachelor Degree in Management of Public Administration and International Institutions (CLAPI) Bocconi University and Senior Faculty member of the SDA Bocconi Graduate School of Management*, on the topics of Prof. Ivo Pezzuto's Thought Leaders' Survey.

Pezzuto, I. (2008). *Miraculous Financial Engineering or Toxic Finance? The Genesis of the U.S. Subprime Mortgage Loans Crisis and its Consequences on the Global Financial Markets and Real Economy*. SMC University Working Paper Series 2008. Retrieved from http://tinyurl.com/7nwjwg7 (accessed on January 10, 2011).

Pezzuto, I. (2009, March 11). *Sob Pressão, Reunião Do G-20 Corre Risco De Desapontar Expectativas* [Under Pressure, The G-20 Meeting is At Risk of Expectations Disappointment]. Agência Estado.

Pezzuto, I. (2010). Miraculous Financial Engineering or Legacy Assets (Chapter 16) in Kolb, R.W. *Lessons from the Financial Crisis. Causes, Consequences, and Our Economic Future*. John Wiley and Sons, Inc.

Pezzuto, I. (2011, September 22). *Bancos Europeus Precisarão De Resgate Como Nos EUA, Dizem Analistas* [European Banks Will Need a Bailout as in the USA, Analysts Say]. Agência Estado.

Pezzuto, I. (2012, May 26–25). SMC University Power Point Presentation titled *Miraculous Financial Engineering or Toxic Finance? The Genesis of the U.S. Subprime Mortgage Loans Crisis and its Consequences on the Global Financial Markets and Real Economy*. Work presented at the International Conference on International Competition in Banking: Theory and Practice organized by the Ukrainian Academy of Banking of the National Bank of Ukraine (Sumy, May 25–26).

Phillips, L. (2012, December 9). *EU Leaders Embrace "Fiscal Compact" Demanded by Central Bank*. Article posted on EU Observer.com. Retrieved from http://euobserver.com/19/114561 (accessed on December 10, 2011).

Pirrong, C. (2011). *The Economics of Central Clearing: Theory and Practice*. International Swaps and Derivatives Association, Inc. (ISDA) Discussion Papers Series Number One – May 2011. Retrieved from http://tinyurl.com/bdsrmu8 (accessed on March 5, 2012).

Plotz, D. (2001, June 29). Larry Summers: How the Great Brain Learned to Grin and Bear It. *Slate Magazine*. Retrieved from http://www.slate.com/id/111151/ (accessed on May 16, 2011).

Polk, D. (2010). *Summary of the Dodd–Frank Wall Street Reform and Consumer Protection Act, Enacted into Law on July 21, 2010*. Davis Polk and Wardwell LLP. Retrieved from http://tinyurl.com/2v96ghh (accessed on March 8, 2011).

Pope Emeritus Benedict XVI (2009). *Encyclical Letter Caritas in Veritate* [Charity in Truth] Vatican website. Retrieved from http://tinyurl.com/7obg266 (accessed on March 8, 2011).

Posner, R.A. (2009). *A Failure of Capitalism*. Harvard University Press.

Posner, R.A. (personal communication, May 6, 2012). *Interview with Judge Richard A. Posner, Senior Lecturer in Law of the University of Chicago Law School and judge of the U.S. Court of Appeals for the Seventh Circuit*, on the topics of Prof. Ivo Pezzuto's Thought Leaders' Survey.

Pratley, N. (2012, July 17). *HSBC Money-Laundering Scandal Almost Puts Barclays in Shade*. The Guardian Nils Patley on Finance [Web log message]. Retrieved from http://tinyurl.com/btx8zs3 (accessed on August 23, 2012).

President's Working Group on Financial Markets (2008). Policy Statement of Financial Market Development, US Treasury. Retrieved from http://tinyurl.com/6nhk9tw (accessed on June 6, 2011).

PricewaterhouseCoopers (2010). *The New Basel III Framework: Navigating Changes in Bank Capital Management*, A PowerPoint publication of PwC's Financial Services Institute (FSI). Retrieved from http://tinyurl.com/7zsc39r (accessed on June 15, 2011).

Protess, B., Weiser, B. (2013, January 24). A Signal to Wall Street In Obama's Pick For Regulators. *New York Times Deal Book*. Retrieved from http://tinyurl.com/ahh3axz (accessed on January 24, 2013).

Prodi, R. (2012, August 23). *Euro Union Bond: I Perché di un Rilancio*. [Euro Union Bond: The Driver of a Recovery]. *Il Sole 24 Ore*, posted on Romano Prodi web page. Retrieved from http://tinyurl.com/ah5vclb (accessed on January 10, 2012).

Puaar, A. (2013, April 29). *FSOC Downplays Collateral Shortfall Fears*. eFinancial News. Retrieved from http://tinyurl.com/c8dpqbx (accessed on April 29, 2013).

Putra, L.D. (2009, October 23). *Concerning "Going Concern" Qualification*. Accounting, Financial and Tax.com. Retrieved from http://tinyurl.com/7e4heoo (accessed on October 19, 2011).

Quadro Curzio, A. (2011). On the Different Types of Eurobonds. Essay published in the *Economia Politica/a. XXVIII, n. 3, December 2011* Journal of Catholic University of Milan. Retrieved from http://tinyurl.com/9oj8p6e (accessed on January 11, 2012).

Quarry, J.,Wilkinson, B., Pittaway, T., Cheah, J. (2012). *OTC Derivatives Clearing. Perspectives On The Regulatory Landscape and Considerations For Policymakers.* Oliver Wyman Financial Services. Retrieved from http://tinyurl.com/b5b49cn (accessed on December 20, 2012).

Rabinovitch, S. (2011, November 15). IMF Warns On Chinese Financial System. *Financial Times.* Retrieved from http://tinyurl.com/d6o8t9f (accessed on November 15, 2011).

Rabinovitch, S. (2013, Janaury 27). China's Brokerages Turn Shadow Banks. *Financial Times.* Retrieved from http://tinyurl.com/a6v4kpb (accessed on January 29, 2013).

Rajan, R. (2005). *Has Financial Development Made The World Riskier?* Proceedings, Federal Reserve Bank of Kansas City, Issue August, pp. 313–369. Retrieved from http://tinyurl.com/7otlcj4 (accessed on February 5, 2011).

Rajan, R. (2008, January 9). *Bankers' Pay is Deeply Flawed.* Published on T.com Financial Times. Retrieved from http://tinyurl.com/7nbz6nw (accessed on January 10, 2011).

Rajan, R. (2010). *Fault Lines: How Hidden Fractures Still Threaten the World Economy.* Princeton University Press, Reprint edition.

Rajan, R. (2011, February 5). *Why Did Economists Not Foresee The Crisis?* From Fault Lines Official Blog [Web log message]. Retrieved from http://tinyurl.com/6v93vwk (accessed on June 6, 2011).

Randall, M.J. (2011, January 28). Warning Signs Preceded Crisis. *The Wall Street Journal.*

Randall Wray, L. (2010, November 5). *A Minskian Explanation of the Causes of the Current Crisis.* Levy Economics Institute Blog [Web log message]. Retrieved from http://www.multiplier-effect.org/?p=778 (accessed on November 10, 2011).

Rappaport, A. (2005, May/June 2005). The Economics of Short-Term Performance Obsession. *Financial Analysts Journal,* 61(3), pp. 65–76.

Rappaport, A., Bogle, J.C. (2011). *Saving Capitalism From Short-Termism: How to Build Long-Term Value and Take Back Our Financial Future Crisis?* McGraw-Hill, 1st edition.

Rappaport, L. Rappaport, M. (2010, December 21). Ernst Accused of Lehman Whitewash. *The Wall Street Journal Law.* Retrieved from http://tinyurl.com/c9cbxdf (accessed on January 7, 2011).

Reed, K. (2010, December 21). E&Y Sued Over Lehman's Audit. *Accountancy Age.* Retrieved from http://tinyurl.com/blrpdlz (accessed on January 7, 2011).

Reinhart, C.M., Rogoff, K. (2009). *This Time Is Different: Eight Centuries of Financial Folly.* Princeton University Press.

Reuters (2011, October 17). *Schaeuble Says Tobin Tax Opposition is "Parochial."* Reuters website. Retrieved from http://tinyurl.com/d7x6snr (accessed on October 17, 2011).

Richardson. M., Ronen, J., Subrahmanyam, M. (2011). Securitization Reform (Chapter 16) *in Regulating Wall Street: The Dodd–Frank Act and the New Architecture of Global Finance.* Publisher: Wiley; 1 edition.

Robledo, S.J. (2006, September 24). *The Descent. One Extreme View of How Long This Market Will Last.* New York Magazine website. Retrieved from http://nymag.com/realestate/features/21675/ (accessed on March 18, 2011).

Roubini, N. (2006). *Why Central Banks Should Burst Bubbles.* International Finance 9:1, 2006: pp. 87–107. Retrieved from http://tinyurl.com/c2ojajz (accessed on April 17, 2011).

Roubini, N. (2010). *Crisis Economics: A Crash Course in the Future of Finance.* Penguin.

Roubini, N. (2011a, October 13). *The Instability of Inequality.* Project Syndicate. Retrieved from http://tinyurl.com/5uogqpp (accessed on October 20, 2011).

Roubini, N. (2012, April 13). *Eurozone Needs a Growth Strategy, Not More Austerity*. Retrieved from http://tinyurl.com/dy6k4md (accessed on January 10, 2013).

Rushe, D. (2008, October 26). Nouriel Roubini: I Fear The Worst is Yet to Come. *The Sunday Times*. Retrieved from http://tinyurl.com/bwga66n (accessed on April 17, 2011).

Rushe, D. (2011a, June 21). *JP Morgan Pays SEC $153m To Settle Charges Over Mortgage Securities*. Guardian.uk.com. Retrieved from http://tinyurl.com/3sesnlc (accessed on June 23, 2011).

Rushe, D. (2011b, June 27). *The Financial Crisis Was "Avoidable", Concludes US Government Inquiry*. Guardian.uk.com. Retrieved from http://tinyurl.com/5w9nt3j (accessed on January 28, 2011).

Sabato, G. (2010). *Credit Risk Scoring Models*. Retrieved from http://tinyurl.com/btxjxum (accessed on May 18, 2012).

Sabato, G. (personal communication, April 28, 2012). *Interview with Dr Gabriele Sabato, Head of Portfolio Management – Retail Credit Risk at Ulster Bank (Ireland). PhD in Banking and Finance, Credit Risk Management*, on the topics of Prof. Ivo Pezzuto's Thought Leaders' Survey.

Sabry, F., Okongwu, C. (2009, February 19). "How Did We Get Here? The Story of the Credit Crisis". NERA (National Economic Research Associates, Inc.) Economic Consulting. Retrieved from http://tinyurl.com/c5rkedd (accessed on March 12, 2011).

Salmon, F. (2009, February 23). *Recipe for Disaster: The Formula That Killed Wall Street*. Wired.com. Retrieved from http://tinyurl.com/chaqm5 (accessed on October 10, 2012).

Salmon, F. (2010, September 15). *The Biggest Weakness of Basel III*. Reuters blog. Retrieved from http://tinyurl.com/ak3twlx (accessed on October 10, 2012).

Salmon, J., Duncan, H. (2012). *Serious Fraud Office Investigating Barclays Over Payments Made to Qatari Bank at Height of Financial Crisis*. Dailymail.co.uk., MailOnline News. Retrieved from http://tinyurl.com/8pc7upe (accessed on September 2, 2012).

Sanderson, R. (2013). Inside Business: Italy's Clubby System Needs Fresh Blood. *Financial Times*. Retrieved from http://tinyurl.com/c2a6ahm (accessed on April 26, 2013).

Sapelli, G. (personal communication, May 7, 2012). *Interview with Prof. Giulio Sapelli, Full Professor of Economic History at the Università degli Studi di Milano, board member of UNICREDIT BANCA – IMPRESA and President of Audit and Control Committee, scientific advisor of OECD for non-profit sector*, on the topics of Prof. Ivo Pezzuto's Thought Leaders' Survey.

Saunders, A. (2011, March 1). *The MT Interview: Paul Polman of Unilever*. MT – Management Today. co.uk. Retrieved from http://tinyurl.com/chnn4cd (accessed on October 1, 2011).

Saunders, A., Allen, L. (2010). *Credit Risk Management In and Out of the Financial Crisis: New Approaches to Value at Risk and Other Paradigms*. Wiley, 3rd edition.

Scannell, K. (2009, April 3). FASB Eases Mark-to-Market Rule. *The Wall Street Journal* http://tinyurl.com/d75wsc (accessed on April 20, 2010).

Scannell, K. (2011a, June 21). JP Morgan Pays $154m to End Fraud Case. *Financial Times*. Retrieved from http://tinyurl.com/d7jze3u (accessed on June 21, 2011).

Scannell, K. (2011b, October 20). Citi Pays $285m to Settle SEC Case. *Financial Times*. Retrieved from http://tinyurl.com/cmaryyv (accessed on October 20, 2011).

Scannell, K. (2011c, November 28). Citigroup's SEC Settlement Rejected. *Financial Times*. Retrieved from http://tinyurl.com/blp8nsk (accessed on November 28, 2011).

Scannell, K., Masters, B., Binham, C., Burgis, T., Shotter, J. (2012, December 19). UBS Pays Price for "Epic" Libor Scandal. *Financial Times*. Retrieved from http://tinyurl.com/bhtq52p (accessed on December 20, 2012).

Scannell, K., Nasiripour, (2013, Febrary 5). US DoJ Accuses S&P of $5bn Fraud. *Financial Times*. Retrieved from http://tinyurl.com/aogxuvs (accessed on February 5, 2013).

Schäfer, D. (2012a, May 1). UBS Shareholders Set To Rebel Over Pay. *Financial Times*. Retrieved from http://tinyurl.com/cobnst7 (accessed on May 1, 2012).

Schäfer, D. (2012b, November 16). Bad Year Ahead for Bankers' Bonuses. *Financial Times*. Retrieved from http://tinyurl.com/adtysmc (accessed on December 2, 2012).

Schäfer, D. (2013, January 22). US Unit Culture Report Adds to Barclays' Woes. *Financial Times*. Retrieved from http://tinyurl.com/ayx3kkl (accessed on January 23, 2013).

Schäfer, D., Nasiripour, S. (2012, August 21). Fed Probes RBS Over Dealings with Iran. *Financial Times*. Retrieved from http://tinyurl.com/c8wg34u (accessed on August 23, 2012).

Schiff, P. (2006, December 16). *Peter Schiff Warned About The Future of the Economy on Fox News Bulls and Bears*. Retrieved from http://tinyurl.com/3s6rlk (accessed on April 5, 2011).

Schiff, P.D., Downes, J. (2007). *Crash Proof: How to Profit From the Coming Economic Collapse*. Wiley.

Schmid, M.M., Sabato, G., Aebi, V. (2011). *Risk Management, Corporate Governance, and Bank Performance in the Financial Crisis*. Retrieved from http://tinyurl.com/cym5hly (accessed on April 12, 2012).

Schumpeter, J.A. (1942). *Capitalism, Socialism, and Democracy*. Harper and Row.

Security and Exchange Commission (SEC) (2008a). *SEC's Oversight of Bear Stearns and Related Entities: Broker-Dealer Risk Assessment Program*. Washington. Retrieved from http://tinyurl.com/7ea3u8s (accessed on September 10, 2011).

Security and Exchange Commission (SEC) (2008b), *Summary Report of Issues Identified in the Commission Staff's Examinations of Selected Credit Rating Agencies*. Washington. Retrieved from http://tinyurl.com/5cc96m (accessed on September 10, 2011).

Senate Committee on Banking, Housing, and Urban Affairs (2010). *Summary: Restoring American Financial Stability*. Retrieved from http://tinyurl.com/2euk8jj (accessed on September 10, 2011).

Senior Supervisors Group (2008). *Observations on Risk Management Practices during the Recent Market Turbulence*. Retrieved from http://tinyurl.com/bqd2wkx (accessed on May 12, 2011).

Shambaugh, J.C. (2012). *The Euro's Three Crises*. Brookings Papers on Economic Activity Spring 2012. McDonough School of Business, Georgetown University and NBER. Retrieved from http://tinyurl.com/aldgwbc (accessed on June 23, 2012).

Sharpe, W.F. (1964). Capital Asset Prices: a Theory of Market Equilibrium Under Conditions of Risk. *Journal of Finance* 19(3), pp. 425–442.

Shiller, R.J. (2003a). *The New Financial Order: Risk in the 21st Century*. Princeton University Press.

Shiller, R.J. (2003b). From Efficient Market Theory to Behavioral Finance. Cowles Foundation Paper N°. 1055. *Journal of Economic Perspectives*, Volume 17, n°1 – Winter 2003, pp. 83–104.

Shiller, R.J. (2005). *Irrational Exuberance*. Crown Business, 2nd edition.

Shiller, R.J. (2006). Tools for Financial Innovation: The Neoclassical Versus Behavioral Finance. Cowles Foundation Paper N°. 1180. *The Financial Review*, 41, pp. 1–8.

Shiller, R.J. (2008). *The Subprime Solution: How Today's Global Financial Crisis Happened, and What to Do about It*. Princeton University Press, 1st edition.

Shin, H.S. (2009). Reflections on Northern Rock: The Bank Run That Heralded the Global Financial Crisis. *Journal of Economic Perspectives*, 23(1), pp. 101–119.

Shotter, J., Masters, B. (2013, January 28). Carney Cautious On Failing Banks. *Financial Times*. Retrieved from http://tinyurl.com/b4g7sy8 (accessed on January 29, 2013).

Siddiqi, N. (2005). *Credit Risk Scorecards: Developing and Implementing Intelligent Credit Scoring* (Wiley and SAS Business Series). Wiley.

Silver-Greenberg, J., Eavis, P. (2012, May 10). JPMorgan Discloses $2 Billion in Trading Losses. *The New York Times Deal Book*. Retrieved from http://tinyurl.com/7bkp9q4 (accessed on October 15, 2012).

Simpson, V.L. (2011, October 24). Vatican Calls For Radical Economic Reform Of World's Financial Systems. *Huffington Post*. Retrieved from http://tinyurl.com/3zxeuug (accessed on October 24, 2011).

Singh, T. (2008, December 8). *The Dalai Lama Blames "Greed" For Financial Crisis*. New Europe website. Retrieved from http://tinyurl.com/btml24f (accessed on March 8, 2011).

Smith, A. (1776). *An Inquiry into the Nature and Causes of the Wealth of Nations*. W. Strahan and T. Cadell, London.

Smith, A. (2011, January 3). *Bank of America in $3 Billion Mortgage Settlement*. CNN Money.com. Retrieved from http://tinyurl.com/29o72v4 (accessed on March 8, 2011).

Smith, E.B. (2008, September 25). *"Race to Bottom" at Moody's, S&P Secured Subprime's Boom, Bust*. Bloomberg.com. Retrieved from http://tinyurl.com/53fn4j (accessed on April 10, 2011).

Sober Look (2012, September 28). *Why Basel III Won't Work*. Article posted on the Sober Look.com website. [Web log message]. Retrieved from http://tinyurl.com/9wzt7yj (accessed on October 13, 2012).

SOMO (2011, April 6). *Reforming the Banks: Still a Long Way to Go*. Posted on SOMO Website. Center for Research On Multinational Corporations. Retrieved from http://tinyurl.com/748f5dx (accessed on March 3, 2011).

Sornette, D. (2003). *Why Stock Markets Crash (Critical Events in Complex Financial Systems)*. Princeton University Press.

Stacey, K., Thompson, J., Saigol, L. (2013, April 10). Pressure Mounts On Former HBOS Leaders. *Financial Times*. Retrieved from http://tinyurl.com/cu8jjvx (accessed on April 12, 2013).

Standard and Poors (2008). *S&P Case-Shiller Home Price Index*. Retrieved from http://tinyurl.com/ydrbsa2 (accessed on January 12, 2011).

Stathis, M. (2006). *America's Financial Apocalypse: How to Profit from the Next Great Depression*. Publisher: AVA Publishing (November 14, 2006)

Stathis, M. (2008). *America's Financial Apocalypse: How to Profit from the Next Great Depression*. AVA Publishing.

Stathis, M. (2007). *Cashing in on the Real Estate Bubble*. AVA Publishing, 1st edition.

Stempel, J. (2012). *U.S. Sues Bank of America over "Hustle" Mortgage Fraud*. Reuters.com. Retrieved from http://tinyurl.com/8ryhoeq (accessed on October 24, 2012).

Stern, A. (2008, October 14). *Financial Crisis Haunts Milton Friedman's Legacy*. Reuters.com. Retrieved from http://tinyurl.com/cxtlld8 (accessed on October 22, 2011).

Stern, J.M., Shiely, J.S., Ross, I. (2001). *The EVA Challenge: Implementing Value Added Change in an Organization*. Wiley, 1st edition.

Stevenson, D.C. (1994–2009). The Internet Classics Archive: *Nicomachean Ethics* by By Aristotle. Written 350 B.C.E. Translated by W.D. Ross. Book I. Retrieved from http://tinyurl.com/2yz6zf (accessed on August 6, 2010).

Stewart, H. (2009, July 26). This is How We Let the Credit Crunch Happen, Ma'am … *The Guardian*. Retrieved from http://tinyurl.com/kvhk3a (accessed on October 9, 2009).

Stiglitz, J.E. (2003). *The Roaring Nineties: A New History of the World's Most Prosperous Decade*. W.W. Norton and Company.

Stiglitz, J.E. (2010). *Freefall. America, Free Markets, and the Sinking of the World Economy*. W.W. Norton and Company.

Stiglitz, J.E. (2011, October 3). *To Cure The Economy*. Project Syndicate. Retrieved from http://tinyurl.com/5w3rnuf (accessed on October 20, 2011).

Stiglitz, J.E. (2013, January 19). *Inequality Is Holding Back the Recovery*. The New York Times Opinionator website. [Web log message]. http://tinyurl.com/aqxj9ro (accessed on January 20, 2013).

Sucha, Z. (2013). *Lagarde: Banking Regulation, Coordinated Deficit Cuts Needed*. World Business Press Online. http://tinyurl.com/bhqsp9n (accessed on January 27, 2013).

Sullivan, J.D. (2009). *The Moral Compass of Companies: Business Ethics and Corporate Governance as Anti-Corruption Tools, International Finance Corporation*. Retrieved from http://tinyurl.com/c99wzl3 (accessed on May 5, 2011).

Swan, P.L. (2010). The Global Crisis and Its Origins (Chapter 8). In Kolb, R.W. *Lessons from the Financial Crisis. Causes, Consequences, and Our Economic Future*. John Wiley and Sons, Inc.

Systemicriskcouncil (2013). *The Systemic Risk Council web page*. Retrieved from http://www.systemicriskcouncil.org/ (accessed on April 15, 2013).

Taleb, N.N. (2007). *The Black Swan: The Impact of the Highly Improbable*. Random House, 1st edition.

Taleb, N.N. (2010). *Why Did The Crisis of 2008 Happen?*. 3rd version. Retrieved from http://tinyurl.com/28bjylw (accessed on October 5, 2012).

Task, A. (2013, February 22). Nouriel Roubini Is Bullish … For Now: "The Mother of All Bubbles" Has Begun. *The Daily Ticker*. Retrieved from http://tinyurl.com/a4dwyhe (accessed on April 25, 2013).

Taylor, J.B. (2009). *The Financial Crisis and The Policy Responses: An Empirical Analysis of What Went Wrong*. National Bureau of Economic Research Working Paper 14631. Retrieved from http://tinyurl.com/cgx8fpe (accessed on March 15, 2011).

Taylor, J.B. (2010, July 1). The Dodd–Frank Financial Fiasco. *The Wall Street Journal*. Retrieved from http://tinyurl.com/2fl9e78 (accessed on October 11, 2011).

The Atlantic (2011, December 14). *Too Big to Stop: Why Big Banks Keep Getting Away With Breaking the Law*. Retrieved from http://tinyurl.com/cg3fdve (accessed on December 15, 2011).

The Economist (2008, August 7). A Personal View of the Crisis. Confessions of a Risk Manager. *The Economist* magazine. Retrieved from http://tinyurl.com/5syd4ru (accessed on October 9, 2010).

The Economist (2010, September 15). *The Biggest Weakness of Basel III*. *The Economist* magazine. Retrieved from http://tinyurl.com/248zw8m (accessed on May 18, 2011).

The Economist (2012, July). Banksters. How Britain's Rate-Fixing Scandal Might Spread – and What To Do About It. *The Economist*.

The Economist (2013, May 10). Keynes. In The Long Run, We'll Live To 300 and Work. *The Economist*. Retrieved from http://tinyurl.com/cn4a752 (accessed on April 4, 2012).

The Executive Gateway (2013, January 16). *Fed's Fisher Says Too-Big-To-Fail Banks Need Restructure*. Executive Gateway website. [Web log message]. http://tinyurl.com/bj36nxl (accessed on January 20, 2013).

The Financial Crisis Inquiry Commission (FCI) (2011). *The Financial Crisis Inquiry Report*. The US Government Printing Office. Retrieved from http://fcic.gov/report (accessed on January 15th, 2011).

The Institute of Internal Auditors (2004a). *Applying COSO's Enterprise Risk Management – Integrated Framework*.

The Institute of Internal Auditors (2004b). *A Framework for Control. COSO's Five Components of Internal Control*.

The New York Times (1999, November 13). Clinton Signs Legislation Overhauling Banking Laws. *NYT Business Day*. Retrieved from http://tinyurl.com/2g5sosn (accessed on January 11, 2011).

The New York Times (2010, August 12). Robert E. Rubin. *The New York Times Topics*. Retrieved from http://tinyurl.com/cwq4vfg (accessed on April 19, 2011).

The Telegraph (2010, September 9). Goldman Sachs Fined £17.5m by FSA Over Failure to Report US Fraud Inquiry. *The Telegraph*. Retrieved from http://tinyurl.com/c85z9um (accessed on March 8, 2011).

The Telegraph (2011, September 21). IMF: Banks Need More Cash To Hedge Against Euro Crisis. *The Wall Street Job Report*. Retrieved from http://tinyurl.com/8b7plvz (accessed on January 10, 2013).

Thompson, J., Jenkins, P., Schäfer, D. (2013, January 14). Top UK Banks Back New Watchdog. *Financial Times*. Retrieved from http://tinyurl.com/9wzjwdg (accessed on January 15, 2013).

Tian, J. (2010). *Shadow Banking System, Derivatives and Liquidity Risks*, SUNY at Albany – Department of Economics Working paper. Retrieved from http://tinyurl.com/bwuwvgg (accessed on April 26, 2011).

TNS, a Kantar Group Company (2008, April 30). *TNS Global Study "The Green Life" Reveals Spectrum of Environmental Attitudes Across United States and the World*. TNS Global website. Retrieved from http://tinyurl.com/dyks75u (accessed on June 9, 2011).

Touryalai, H. (2012a, August 14). Standard Chartered Coughs Up $340M To Settle Money Laundering Charges. *Forbes*. Retrieved from http://tinyurl.com/d22tcye (accessed on November 9, 2012).

Touryalai, H. (2012b, September 28). Will New Libor Rules Prevent Rate-Rigging? *Forbes*. Retrieved from http://tinyurl.com/d79fckp (accessed on October 10, 2012).

Treanor, J. (2011, September 28). Osborne Expected to Oppose EU's Proposal for Tobin Tax on Banks. *The Guardian*. Retrieved from http://tinyurl.com/5w37ggo (accessed on November 1, 2011).

Trompenaars, F., Hampden-Turner, C. (1997). *Riding the Waves of Culture: Understanding Diversity in Global Business*. McGraw-Hill, 2nd edition.

Tully, S. (2007, September 3). Risk Returns with a Vengeance. *Fortune*. Retrieved from http://tinyurl.com/yofqyb (accessed on April 5, 2011).

UBS (2008). *Shareholder Report on UBS's Write-Downs*. UBS Company website. Retrieved from http://tinyurl.com/6px5cfp (accessed on March 8, 2011).

Uppal, S. (2011, May). *Corporate Governance: Reforms Post Global Financial Crisis*. StraitsBridge Advisors presentation at the Robert Walter Executive Dialog Series in Singapore. Retrieved from http://tinyurl.com/chwtzhb (accessed on July 9, 2011).

US Bankruptcy Court Southern District of New York – *Examiner's report (2010). Lehman Brothers Holdings Inc. Chapter 11 Case No 08 13555 (JMP)*. Report of Anton R. Valukas Examiner. Volume 2 of 9. Retrieved from http://tinyurl.com/cf2f9dd (accessed on August 15, 2011).

US Government (2010). *Brief Summary of the Dodd–Frank Wall Streeet Reform and Consumer Protection Act*. Retrieved from http://tinyurl.com/clgpalm (accessed on May 23, 2012).

Utt, R.D. (2010). The Subprime Mortgage Problem. Causes and Likely Cures (Chapter 18). In Kolb, R.W. *Lessons from the Financial Crisis. Causes, Consequences, and Our Economic Future*. John Wiley and Sons, Inc., 133.

Vaciago, G. (personal communication, May 4, 2012). *Interview with Economist Prof. Giacomo Vaciago, Full Professor of Università Cattolica del Sacro Cuore of Milan*, on the topics of Prof. Ivo Pezzuto's Thought Leaders' Survey.

Viswanatha, A. (2013, January 16). *UPDATE 3-Goldman, Morgan Stanley Cut $557 Mln Foreclosure Deal*. Reuters.com. Retrieved from http://tinyurl.com/avvv84x (accessed on January, 16 2013).

von Hayek, F.A. (1935). *Prices and Production*. Published in the USA by Augustus M. Kelly, Publishers New York

von Hayek, F.A. (1949). *Individualism and Economic Order*. London. Routledge and Kegan.

Walker, D. (2013). *Banking Day Backgrounder: Basel III*. Banking Day.com Retrieved from http://tinyurl.com/beeelgp (accessed on January 17, 2013).

Wargo, D.T., Baglini, N., Nelson, K. (2009). *The Global Financial Crisis – caused by Greed, Moral Meltdown and Public Policy Disasters*. Temple University. Retrieved from http://tinyurl.com/856tgzm (accessed on June 8, 2009).

Warnock, F., Warnock, V. (2006). *International Capital Flows and U.S. Interest Rates*. International Finance Discussion Paper No. 860, International Finance Division, Board of Governors of the Federal Reserve System (September).

Welsh, I. (2009, February 19). *Warning: The Financial Crisis Is NOT a Black Swan Event*. Firedoglake.com. Retrieved from http://tinyurl.com/7dsgfwp (accessed on March 7, 2011).

Wheelen, T.L., Hunger, D.J. (2011). *Strategic Management and Business Policy: Toward Global Sustainability*. Prentice Hall, 13th edition.

Wheelhouse Advisors (2009, March 31). *Implementing Compensation Reforms*, The ERM Current™, Current Trends in Enterprise Risk Management. Retrieved from http://tinyurl.com/8yerego (accessed on August 3, 2011).

White, L.J. (2009, January 24). Agency Problems – and Their Solution. *The Online Magazine of the American Enterprise Institute*. Retrieved from http://tinyurl.com/ybhy2y2 (accessed on January 5, 2011).

Williams, R. (2011, November 1). Time for Us to Challenge The Idols of High Finance. *Financial Times*. Retrieved from http://tinyurl.com/7ec8vkc (accessed on November 1, 2011).

Wilson, H. (2012, November 8). Dexia Rescued for The Third Time in Four Years. *The Telegraph*. Retrieved from http://tinyurl.com/abudeo7 (accessed on November 10, 2012).

Wolf, M. (2013, March 17). Why Bankers are Intellectually Naked. *Financial Times*. Retrieved from http://tinyurl.com/d6hfx22 (accessed on March 17, 2013).

Wyplosz, C. (2012). *Germany May Face Bankruptcy Unless It Accepts ECB Debt Monetization*. Eurointelliegence.com. Retrieved from http://tinyurl.com/ba98jqo (accessed on December 21, 2012).

Yellen, J.L. (2008). *President's Speech to the Chartered Financial Analyst Institute, Annual Conference Vancouver, British Columbia on May 13, 2008*. Janet L. Yellen, President and CEO, Federal Reserve Bank of San Francisco. Retrieved from http://tinyurl.com/c679sls (accessed on April 3, 2012).

Zingales, L. (2009). *Capitalism After the Crisis*, on Issue n°1 – Fall 2009 of National Affairs. Retrieved from http://tinyurl.com/mb4paf (accessed on June 7, 2011).

Zingales, L. (2010). A Market-Based Regulatory Policy to Avoid Financial Crises. *Cato Journal*, Vol. 30, No. 3 (Fall 2010). pp. 535–540. Retrieved from http://tinyurl.com/2vx9322 (accessed on June 7, 2011).

Zingales, L. (2011, September 22). *The Unexamined Crisis*, Project Syndicate. Retrieved from http://tinyurl.com/3lhgce8 (accessed on October 20, 2011).

Zingales, L. (2012). *A Capitalism for the People: Recapturing the Lost Genius of American Prosperity*. Basic Books.

Zumbrun, J. (2010, April 19). *Clinton Says Rubin, Summers Gave "Wrong" Derivatives Advice*. Bloomberg.com. Retrieved from http://tinyurl.com/28m4jsb (accessed on January 5, 2011).

Index